W9-CBH-803

Communicating an Experience
Reviewing a Movie
Thinking About Slang
Analyzing Language Uses
Analyzing Euphemisms
Analyzing Emotive Language
Forming New Concepts Through
    Experience
Diagramming the Structure of Concepts
Forming New Concepts Through
    Generalizing and Interpreting
Analyzing the Concept of Responsibility
The Concepts of Information and
    Ownership
Creating and Applying Mind Maps
Creating a Narrative Description
Analyzing Process Relationships
Creating a Process Description
Analyzing Comparative Relationships
Analyzing Analogical Relationships
Creating Analogies to Capture Life
Creating a Causal Chain
Creating a Scenario of Contributory
    Causes
Analyzing Causal Relationships
Identifying Reports, Inferences, and
    Judgments
Evaluating Factual Information
"Real" and Manipulated Images in Film
Analyzing an Incorrect Inference
Analyzing Judgments
Analyzing Moral Dilemmas
Nurturing Your Moral Growth
Identifying Arguments with Cue Words
Evaluating the Truth of Reasons
Evaluating Arguments
Freedom of Speech on the Internet
Composing an Extended Argument

Evaluating Inductive Arguments
Designing a Poll
Applying the Scientific Method
Evaluating Experimental Results
Designing a Scientific Experiment
Identifying Fallacies
Applying the "Guide to Reasoning"
Thinking About Your Career Plans
Describing Your Dream Job
Improving Your Relationships
Creating Analogies to Capture Life
Creating a Causal Chain
Creating a Scenario of Contributory
    Causes
Analyzing Causal Relationships
Identifying Reports, Inferences, and
    Judgments
Evaluating Factual Information
"Real" and Manipulated Images in Film
Analyzing an Incorrect Inference
Analyzing Judgments
Analyzing Moral Dilemmas
Nurturing Your Moral Growth
Identifying Arguments with Cue Words
Evaluating the Truth of Reasons
Evaluating Arguments
Freedom of Speech on the Internet
Composing an Extended Argument
Evaluating Inductive Arguments
Designing a Poll
Applying the Scientific Method
Evaluating Experimental Results
Designing a Scientific Experiment
Identifying Fallacies
Applying the "Guide to Reasoning"
Thinking About Your Career Plans
Describing Your Dream Job
Improving Your Relationships

Thinking Critically

Eighth Edition

John Chaffee, Ph.D.

*Director, Center for Critical
Thinking and Language Learning,
LaGuardia College,
City University of New York*

HOUGHTON MIFFLIN COMPANY   BOSTON   NEW YORK

For Jessie and Joshua

Senior sponsoring editor: Suzanne Phelps Weir
Development manager: Sarah Helyar Smith
Development editor: Meg Botteon
Senior project editor: Carol Newman
Editorial assistant: Robert Woo
Manufacturing coordinator: Carrie Wagner
Marketing manager: Cindy Graff Cohen

(Photo credits continue on page 542.)

Copyright © 2006 by John Chaffee. All rights reserved.

No part of this work may be reproduced or transmitted in any form or by any means, electronic or mechanical, including photocopying and recording, or by any information storage or retrieval system without the prior written permission of the copyright owner unless such copying is expressly permitted by federal copyright law. With the exception of non-profit transcription in Braille, Houghton Mifflin is not authorized to grant permission for further uses of copyrighted selections reprinted in this text without the permission of their owners. Permission must be obtained from the individual copyright owners as identified herein. Address requests for permission to make copies of Houghton Mifflin Company material to College Permissions, Houghton Mifflin Company, 222 Berkeley Street, Boston, MA 02116-3764.

Printed in the U.S.A.

Library of Congress Catalog Card Number: 2004114279
ISBN: 0-618-53648-5

123456789-CW-08 07 06 05 04

CONTENTS

Chapter 12 Thinking Critically, Living Creatively   486

READINGS

PREFACE

Critical thinking is the cornerstone of higher education, the hallmark of an educated person, and teaching a course in critical thinking is one of the most inspiring and rewarding experiences that a teacher can have. Because the thinking process is such an integral part of who we are as people, the prospect of expanding students' thinking implies expanding who they are as human beings — the perspective from which they view the world, the concepts and values they use to guide their choices, and the impact they have on the world as a result of those choices. Teaching students to become critical thinkers does not mean simply equipping them with certain intellectual tools; it involves their personal transformation and its commensurate impact on the quality of their lives and those around them. This is truly education at its most inspiring!

Thinking Critically, Eighth Edition, is a comprehensive introduction to the cognitive process and helps students develop the higher-order thinking abilities needed for academic study and career success. Based on a nationally recognized interdisciplinary program in Critical Thinking established in 1979 at LaGuardia College (The City University of New York) and involving more than eighteen hundred students annually, *Thinking Critically* integrates various perspectives on the thinking process drawn from a variety of disciplines such as philosophy, cognitive psychology, linguistics, and the language arts (English, reading, and oral communication).

Thinking Critically addresses a crucial need in higher education by introducing students to critical thinking and fostering sophisticated intellectual and language abilities. Students apply their evolving thinking abilities to a variety of subjects drawn from academic disciplines, contemporary issues, and their life experiences. *Thinking Critically* is based on the assumption, supported by research, that learning to think more effectively is a synthesizing process, knitting critical thinking abilities together with academic content and the fabric of students' experiences. Thinking learned in this way becomes a constitutive part of who students are.

Features

This book has a number of distinctive characteristics that make it an effective tool for both instructors and students. *Thinking Critically*

- **teaches the fundamental thinking, reasoning, and language abilities that students need for academic success.** By focusing on the major thinking and language abilities needed in all disciplines, and by including a

wide variety of readings, the text helps students perform more successfully in other courses.

- **stimulates and guides students to think clearly about complex, contro-versial issues.** The many diverse readings provide in-depth perspectives on significant social issues. More important, the text helps students develop the thinking and language abilities necessary to understand and discuss intelligently these complex issues.

- **presents foundational thinking, reasoning, and language abilities in a developmentally sequenced way**. The text begins with basic abilities and then carefully progresses to more sophisticated thinking and reasoning skills. Cognitive maps open each chapter to help students understand the thinking process as well as the interrelationship of ideas in that chapter.

- **engages students in the active process of thinking.** Exercises, discussion topics, readings, and writing assignments encourage active participation, stimulating students to critically examine their own and others' thinking and to sharpen and improve their abilities. *Thinking Critically* provides structured opportunities for students to develop their thinking processes in a progressive, reflective way.

- **provides context by continually relating critical thinking abilities to students' daily lives.** Once students learn to apply critical thinking skills to situations in their own experiences, they then apply these skills to more abstract, academic contexts. Additionally, by asking students to think critically about themselves and their experiences, the text fosters their personal development as mature, responsible critical thinkers.

- **integrates the development of thinking abilities with the four language skills so crucial to success in college and careers: reading, writing, speaking, and listening.** The abundant writing assignments (short answer, paragraph, and essay), challenging readings, and discussion exercises serve to improve students' language skills.

- **is accompanied by a provocative critical thinking videotape.** A one-hour critical thinking videotape developed by the author, entitled *Thinking Towards Decisions*, is designed to work in conjunction with Chapter 2, "Thinking Critically." The tape uses a creative interweaving of a dramatic scenario, expert testimony, and a seminar group to develop students' critical thinking abilities.

- **includes a critical thinking test.** "Tom Randall's Halloween Party," or the Test of Critical Thinking Abilities, developed by the author, is in-cluded in the Instructor Resource Manual (in a form that can be taken out and reproduced) and in interactive form on the web site and provides for a comprehensive evaluation of student thinking and language abilities. Using a court case format arising from a fatal student drinking incident, the test challenges students to gather and weigh evidence, ask relevant questions, construct informed beliefs, evaluate expert testimony and summation arguments, reach a verdict, and then view the entire case from a problem-solving perspective.

- **uses illustrations and photographs to stimulate thinking.** Photographs and illustrations, many created specifically for this book by the artist Warren Gebert, provoke thoughtful responses, present key concepts, and visually engage the reader.

- **includes substantive treatment of creative thinking.** A revised Chapter 1 links critical thinking to creative thinking. The chapter analyzes the creative process and develops creative thinking abilities, creating a template for approaching issues and problems both critically and creatively throughout the text. Chapter 12, "Thinking Critically, Living Creatively," reinforces these connections and encourages students to create a life philosophy through moral choices.

- **includes a section on "Constructing Extended Arguments"** that presents a clear model for researching and writing argumentative essays.

New to the Eighth Edition

Overall Changes

Thoughtful Exploration of Recent Events in the United States and Beyond
The enduring themes surrounding the events of September 11, 2001 have been infused throughout the text, encouraging students' (and faculty's) critical reflection and analysis. I urge students to consider not just the World Trade Center attack but larger themes and dilemmas such as patriotism, individual freedom versus national security, and journalists' need to balance security issues against their mission to report breaking news and investigate pressing issues. The text presents a global view by providing news articles and speeches from other countries, allowing students to compare these views with U.S. perspectives. The catastrophe of 9/11 and its political, social, and economic aftermath has altered each of our lives in profound and lasting ways, and it continues to inform *Thinking Critically*. The Eighth Edition further develops issues and themes related to this event that demand our critical reflection and analysis.

Two Portfolios of Color Images   The ability of students to think critically about visual information has been greatly enhanced with the addition of two four-color sections, "Thinking Critically About Images: Truth and Reality in Popular Culture" and "Thinking Critically About Images: Truth and Reality in the Media." From advertising to current events to web sites, these sections provoke careful and creative analysis of the ways our values, beliefs, and perceptions are influenced (and, occasionally, manipulated) by visual information.

Thorough Integration of Internet Activities   Many activities now begin in the print text and move to the book's companion web site (at <http://college. hmco.com/english>). These activities, indicated by a distinctive icon in the text, encourage students to move seamlessly from the classroom to the world beyond, offering additional links and web-based activities to enhance their critical and creative engagement with the exercises.

More and Newer Readings   Forty in-text readings and dozens more on the companion web site reflect the latest thinking on cross-disciplinary topics such as human cloning, globalization, the environment, and challenges to civil liberty, giving instructors more choice and currency while retaining those readings most popular with users. Three more reflective readings by Annie Dillard, Carlo Rotella, and Alan Lightman in Chapter 12 describe the pleasures and challenges of living creatively and thoughtfully. Additional short excerpts within Thinking Activities draw from current thinking in fields such as structural engineering, medicine, and marketing.

Glossary   A new glossary helps students remember and review not only critical thinking terms but Internet terms as well, supporting less computer-savvy students in the Internet activities.

Changes by Chapter

Chapter 1 Thinking

- The theme of "Living Creatively," in response to reviewer suggestions, has been revised and moved to this first chapter to enhance the relationship between thinking critically, thinking creatively, and applying these skills to your life outside the classroom.
- New reading: Malcolm X, from *The Autobiography of Malcolm X*, relates his determination to become literate despite overwhelming obstacles.

Chapter 2 Thinking Critically

- New section on identifying the qualities of a critical thinker enables students to create a detailed portrait of a critical thinker, a model for them to emulate; Socrates is highlighted.
- In response to reviewer suggestions and feedback on how *Thinking Critically* is used to plan a syllabus, "Analyzing Issues" and the "Mary Barnett" case are now included in Chapter 2. Students now move from exploring strategies for discussing ideas in an organized way to putting those strategies to work as they analyze the Mary Barnett case.

Chapter 3 Solving Problems

- The casebook of readings on individual freedoms and national security is now featured in this chapter. A new reading, "Construction of an Enemy" by Eleanor Stein, examines the internment of Muslim Arabs and persons of Muslim faith by the Bush administration.
- A poem by W. H. Auden, "The Unknown Citizen (To JS/07/M/378 This Marble Monument Is Erected By the State)," included in the Questions for Analysis following the casebook, enables further exploration of the themes of bureaucracy, privacy, and identity.

Chapter 4 Perceiving

- Additional online resources complement the Thinking Activities on analyzing different accounts of the murder of Malcolm X and the World Trade Center and Pentagon attacks.
- New Thinking Passages on the theme of "Perception and Global Conflict": Amartya Sen, "A World Not Neatly Divided"; Ian Buruma, "The Origins of Occidentalism"; and Thomas Friedman, "War of Ideas, Part 6."

Chapter 5 Believing and Knowing

- Enhanced online Thinking Activity, "Analyzing Different Accounts of the Confrontation at Tiananmen Square," brings in audio and video accounts and a diversity of witness perspectives.

Chapter 6 Language and Thought

- New Thinking Activity: Robin Tolmach Lakoff, "From Ancient Greece to Iraq, the Power of Words in Wartime."

- Online audio and video archive of political speeches to complement Thinking Passage: "with Political Speeches."

Chapter 7 Forming and Applying Concepts

- Enhanced discussion of mind maps on the companion web site.

Chapter 8 Relating and Organizing

- New readings on environmental issues provide opportunities to examine complex causal relationships and their impact on a significant current issue: Bill McKibbin, "Worried? Us?"; and Alan Thein Dorning, "The Conundrum of Consumption."

Chapter 9 Reporting, Inferring, and Judging

- Enhanced Internet Activity: "Looking Critically @ 'Real' and Manipulated Images in Film" with many more online examples and resources.

Chapter 10 Constructing Arguments

- Section "Composing an Argumentative Paper" revised and retitled to "Constructing Extended Arguments." Includes updated section on research and evaluating sources.
- A new reading on cloning, "Even If It Worked, Cloning Wouldn't Bring Her Back" by Thomas H. Murray.

Chapter 11 Reasoning Critically

- New reading: World Health Organization/UNAIDS, "'3x5' Progress Report."
- New reading on Critical Thinking and Obedience to Authority: Anahad O'Connor, "Pressure to Go Along with Abuse Is Strong, but Some Soldiers Find Strength to Refuse."

Chapter 12 Thinking Critically, Living Creatively

- In response to reviewer suggestions, the section on "Deciding on a Career" is now presented here as a capstone to the course. Three additional readings describe creative, engaging, joyful, and perilous choices that others have made as they integrate their life philosophies with their careers: Annie Dillard, "The Stunt Pilot"; Carlo Rotella, "Cut Time"; and

Alan Lightman, "Spellbound by the Eternal Riddle, Scientists Revel in Their Captivity."

Supplements for Instructor and Student

Instructor Resource Manual

Major work has produced an enhanced Instructor Resource Manual designed to help instructors tailor this book to their own courses.

- **Critical thinking courses:** Part 1, "Using *Thinking Critically*," written by John Chaffee, contains an overview of the field of critical thinking as well as suggestions and exercises of interest to instructors using this text. Also included is the Test of Critical Thinking Abilities.

- **Reading and writing courses:** Parts 2 and 3 — "Thinking Critically and Reading" and "Thinking Critically and Writing" — present assignments, useful suggestions, and syllabi for instructors using *Thinking Critically* in reading and writing courses. Part 2, "Reading," has been significantly revised by Professor Dawn Graziani of Santa Fe Community College. New activities and consideration of recent scholarship in language acquisition and the teaching of college reading skills in a diverse community, as well as new sample syllabi, enhance the use of Critical Thinking in courses with an emphasis on critical reading skills.

- **First-Year Studies courses and seminars:** Part 4, "Thinking Critically and Freshman Studies," written and revised by Fred Janzow of Southeast Missouri State University, details how to use the text in courses and seminars explicitly devoted to first-year students. This section includes a sample syllabus, specific suggestions, and activities designed for the special needs of first-year students.

- The manual concludes with both a comprehensive bibliography of critical and creative thinking resources and a bibliography that contains suggested fiction and nonfiction readings and films relating to the themes of the text.

Companion Web Site

The greatly expanded web site to accompany *Thinking Critically* includes a wealth of content to supplement both students' and instructors' needs. Both sites can be accessed from <http://college.hmco.com/english>.

The **student site** contains critical thinking and Internet terms, in searchable form; a fun, creative test of critical thinking abilities that puts the student on a jury for a complex case; links to sites offering additional information or activities on each topic addressed in *Thinking Critically;* valuable resources to supplement the book's critical examinations of Internet activities; checklists, lists, and worksheets to help students think through and solve problems; more practice with the critical thinking skills for each chapter; Thinking Activities continued from the book and supplemented with additional readings; and information about essay writers whose works are or have been particularly influential.

The **instructor site** contains evaluation and performance criteria for the Test of Critical Thinking Abilities; detailed discussions of the video segments; sample exam questions grouped by the thinking ability being evaluated; information and handouts from Part 1 of the IRM; sample syllabi and reading or writing activities for Parts 2, 3, and 4 of the IRM; and a quiz to help students identify arguments from Part 4 of the IRM.

Acknowledgments

Many persons from a variety of disciplines have contributed to this book at various stages of its development over the past editions, and I thank my colleagues for their thorough scrutiny of the manuscript and their incisive and creative comments. In addition, I offer my deepest gratitude to the faculty members at LaGuardia who have participated with such dedication and enthusiasm in the Critical Thinking program, and to the countless students whose commitment to learning is the soul of this text.

The following reviewers also provided evaluations that were of great help in preparing the eighth edition:

Patricia Baldwin, Pitt Community College

James Fulcher, Lincoln College

Ann Shanks Glauser, University of Georgia

Dawn M. Graziani, Santa Fe Community College

Peggy Jolly, University of Alabama at Birmingham

Allen Ketcham, Texas A&M University, Kingsville

Christy McDaniel, ECPI College of Technology

W. Terry McNeill, Alamance Community College

A. Fiona Pearson, DeVry University

Nancy Ramirez, Pima College, Downtown Campus

Steven J. Rayshick, Quinsigamond Community College

Victoria F. Sarkisian, Marist College

Nancy A. Stanlick, University of Central Florida

I have been privileged to work with a stellar team of people at Houghton Mifflin Company who are exemplary professionals and also valued friends. The incomparable Suzanne Phelps Weir is *Thinking Critically*'s sterling champion, providing the kind of wise and imaginative attention that every author hopes for, while displaying an unerring talent for shaping the present to meet the future. Sarah Helyar Smith orchestrated this revision with the same commitment to excellence that she brings to every project, integrating an incisive intelligence, a conscientious attention to detail, and a delightfully unique personal spirit. Meg Botteon once again displayed her superior talents as an editor in every phase of the process: conceptualizing new themes and reorganization, researching powerful and timely readings, and assuming major responsibility for the extraordinary color inserts. Additionally, Meg brought her singular expertise to enhancing the book's web site and editing the IRM.

Carol Newman is always a special pleasure to work with: passionately exacting, an uncompromising commitment to excellence, and with an authentically unique perspective that demands you to expect the unexpected. Anne Leung has been an invaluable resource, gently but consistently shepherding the book through every stage of its revision with clarity and grace. And Cindy Graff Cohen continues to display extraordinary gifts in devising innovative marketing strategies and implementing them with aplomb, while displaying uncommon courage in the face of adversity.

This book also benefited from the talented contributions of Connie Gardner, who displayed her typical excellence in researching photographs, and Warren Gebert, whose genius has enriched the text through his one-of-a-kind illustrations that both provoke thought and engender delight. Special thanks also to Dawn M. Graziani for her superb contributions to the IRM.

Finally, I thank my wife, Heide, and my children, Jessie and Joshua, for their complete and ongoing love, support, and inspiration. It is these closest relationships that make life most worth living. And I wish to remember my parents, Charlotte Hess and Hubert Chaffee, who taught me lasting lessons about the most important things in life. They will always be with me.

Although this is a published book, it continues to be a work in progress. In this spirit, I invite you to share your experiences with the text by sending me your comments. I hope that this book serves as an effective vehicle for your own critical thinking explorations in living an examined life. You can contact me on line at JCthink@aol.com, and visit my web site at <www.thinking-world.com>. My mailing address is LaGuardia College, City University of New York, Humanities Department, Long Island City, NY 11101.

John Chaffee

Thinking Critically

Thinking

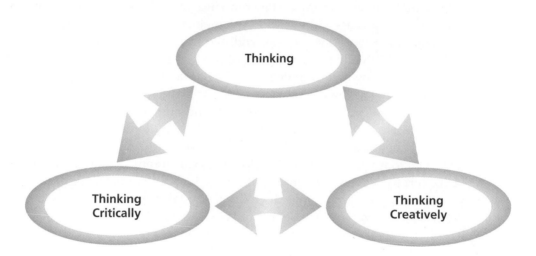

Thinking can be developed and improved by becoming aware of, carefully examining, and practicing the thinking process.

Thinking is the extraordinary process we use every waking moment to make sense of our world and our lives. Successful thinking enables us to solve the problems we are continually confronted with, to make intelligent decisions, and to achieve the goals that give our lives purpose and fulfillment. It is an activity that is crucial for living in a meaningful way.

This book is designed to help you understand the complex, incredible process of thinking. You might think of this text as a map to guide you in exploring the way your mind operates. This book is also founded on the conviction that you can improve your thinking abilities by carefully examining your thinking process and working systematically through challenging activities. Thinking is an active process, and you learn to do it better by becoming aware of and actually using the thought process, not simply by reading about it. By participating in the thinking activities contained in the text and applying these ideas to your own experiences, you will find that your thinking — and language — abilities are becoming sharper and more powerful.

College provides you with a unique opportunity to develop your mind in the fullest sense. Entering college initiates you into a community of people dedicated to learning, and each discipline, or subject area, represents an organized effort to understand some significant dimension of human experience. As you are introduced to various disciplines, you learn new ways to understand the world, and you elevate your consciousness as a result. This book, in conjunction with the other courses in your college experience, will help you become an "educated thinker," expanding your mind and developing your sensibilities.

Becoming an educated thinker will also help you achieve your career goals. In this rapidly evolving world, it is impossible to predict with precision your exact career (or careers) or the knowledge and skills that this career will require. But as an educated thinker you will possess the essential knowledge and abilities that will enable you to adapt to whatever your career situation demands. In addition, becoming an educated thinker will elevate your understanding of the world in which you live and help you develop insight into your "self" and that of others, qualities that are essential to high achievement in most careers.

Achieving the goal of becoming an educated thinker involves two core processes that are the mainsprings of our thoughts and actions: **Thinking critically** and **thinking creatively.** The process of *thinking critically* involves thinking for ourselves by carefully examining the way that we make sense of the world. Taking this approach to living is one of the most satisfying aspects of being a mature human being.

VISUAL THINKING

The Mystery of the Mind

● Why is thinking a difficult process to understand? Why does improving our thinking involve sharing ideas with other people? Why does each person think in unique ways?

thinking critically *Carefully exploring the thinking process to clarify our understanding and make more intelligent decisions*

We are able to think critically because of our natural human ability to *reflect* — to think back on what we are thinking, doing, or feeling. By carefully thinking back on our thinking, we are able to figure out the way that our thinking operates and thus learn to do it more effectively. In this book we will be systematically exploring the many dimensions of the way our minds work, providing the opportunity to deepen our understanding of the thinking process and stimulating us to become more effective thinkers.

Of course, carefully examining the ideas produced by the thinking process assumes that there are ideas that are worth examining. We produce such ideas by thinking creatively, an activity we can define as follows:

thinking creatively *Using our thinking process to develop ideas that are unique, useful, and worthy of further elaboration*

In this chapter we will examine three areas of our lives in which we can use our critical thinking and creative thinking abilities to understand our world and make informed decisions.

- Working toward goals
- Making decisions
- Living creatively

Living an "Examined" Life

You are an artist, creating your life portrait, and your paints and brush strokes are the choices you make each day of your life. This metaphor provides you with a way to think about your personal development and underscores your responsibility for making the most intelligent decisions possible.

Every day you encounter a series of choices, forks in your life path that have the cumulative effect of defining you as a person. In thinking about these choices, you may discover that there are habitual patterns in your life that rarely change. If you find that your life is composed of a collection of similar activities and routines, don't despair; this is typical, not unusual. However, it

VISUAL THINKING

You Are the Artist of Your Life

● In what ways does this metaphor help you understand your personal development? In what ways does it highlight the role of personal responsibility in your life? What choices will you have to make in order to reach your full potential as a person?

may be an indication that you are not living your life in the most thoughtful fashion possible, that your choices have become automatic, and that your experiences are fixed in certain "ruts." If this is the case, it may be time to reflect on your life, reevaluate the choices you are making, and consider living your life in a more reflective and creative fashion.

Our world has become a complex and challenging place in which to live. The accelerated pace at which many people live often makes them feel as though they are rushing from deadline to deadline, skating on the surface of life instead of exploring its deeper meanings. What is the purpose of your life? Who are you, and who do you want to become? These are essential questions that form the core of life, and yet the velocity of our lives discourages us from even posing these questions, much less trying to answer them.

Your efforts to become thoughtful and reflective, to explore the nature of your self and the meaning of your life, is made even more difficult by the unthinking world in which we live. Consider all of the foolish opinions, thoughtless decisions, confused communication, destructive behavior, and self-absorbed, thoughtless people whom you have to deal with each day. Reflect on the number of times you have scratched your head and wondered, "What was that person thinking?" And how many times have you asked yourself, "What was I thinking?" The disturbing truth is that many people don't think very well; they are not making use of their potential to think clearly and effectively.

Over 2,500 years ago the Greek philosopher Socrates cautioned, "The unexamined life is not worth living," underscoring the insight that when we don't make use of our distinctive human capacity to think deeply and act intelligently, our lives have diminished meaning. You have the capacity to create a richly fulfilling life, but you must develop and make full use of your thinking potential to do so. By becoming a true educated thinker, you will have the tools to unlock the mysteries of your self and meet the challenges of the world.

Working Toward Goals

> "Ah, but a man's reach should exceed his grasp, / Or what's a heaven for?"
>
> — *Robert Browning*

My future career goal is to become a professional photographer, working for <u>National Geographic Magazine</u> and traveling around the world. I originally had different dreams, but gradually drifted away from them and lost interest. Then I enrolled in a photography course and loved it. I couldn't wait until the weekend was over to attend class on Monday or to begin my next class project — reactions that were really quite unusual for me! Not everyone is certain at my age about what they would like to become, and I think it is important to discover a career you will enjoy because you are going to spend the rest of your life doing it. I have many doubts, as I think everyone does. Am I good enough? The main thing I fear is rejection, people not liking my work, a possibility that is unavoidable in life. There is so much competition in this world that sometimes when you see someone better at what you do, you can feel inadequate. These problems and obstacles that interfere with my goals will have to be overcome. Rejection will have to be accepted and looked at as a learning experience, and competition will have to be used as an incentive for me to work at my highest level. But through it all, if you don't have any fears, then what do you have? Lacking competition and the possibility of rejection, there is no challenge to life.

As revealed in this student passage, goals play extremely important functions in your life by organizing your thinking and giving your life order and direction. Whether you are preparing food, preparing for an exam, or preparing for a career, goals suggest courses of action and influence your decisions. By performing these functions, goals contribute meaning to your life. They give you something to aim for and lead to a sense of accomplishment when you reach them, like the satisfaction you may have received when you graduated from high school or entered college. It is your thinking abilities that enable you first to identify what your goals are and then to plan how to reach these goals.

Most of your behavior has a purpose or purposes, a goal or goals, that you are trying to reach. You can begin to discover the goals of your actions by asking the question "why?" of what you are doing or thinking. For example, answer the following question as specifically as you can:

Why did you come to class today?

This question may have stimulated any number of responses:

- Because I want to pass this course.
- Because I was curious about the topics to be discussed.
- Because I woke up early and couldn't get back to sleep.

Whatever your response, it reveals at least one of your goals in attending class.

Using your response to the question "Why did you come to class today?" as a starting point, try to discover part of your goal patterns by asking a series of why questions. After each response, ask "why?" again. (For example: Why did you come to class today? Because I want to pass this course. Why do you want to pass this course? Because . . .) Try to give thoughtful and specific answers.

As you may have found in completing the activity, this "child's game" of repeatedly asking "why?" begins to reveal the network of goals that structure your experience and leads you to progressively more profound questions regarding your basic goals in life, such as "Why do I want to be successful?" or "Why do I want a happy and fulfilling life?" These are complex issues that require thorough and ongoing exploration. A first step in this direction is to examine the way your mind works to achieve your goals, which is the "goal" of this section. If you can understand the way your mind functions when you think effectively, then you can use this knowledge to improve your thinking abilities. This in turn will enable you to deal more effectively with new situations you encounter. To begin this process, think about an important goal you have achieved in your life, and then complete Thinking Activity 1.1. Thinking Activities are designed to stimulate your thinking process and provide the opportunity to express your ideas about important topics. By sharing these ideas with your teacher and other members of the class, you are not only expanding your own thinking; you are also expanding theirs. Each student in the class has a wealth of experiences and insights to offer to the class community.

THINKING ACTIVITY 1.1

Analyzing a Goal That You Achieved

1. Describe an important goal that you recently achieved
2. Identify the steps you had to take to achieve this goal in the order in which they were taken, and estimate the amount of time each step took.
3. Describe how you felt when you achieved your goal.

Achieving Short-Term Goals

By examining your response to Thinking Activity 1.1, you can see that thinking effectively plays a crucial role in helping you to achieve your goals by enabling you to perform two distinct, interrelated activities:

1. Identifying the appropriate goals
2. Devising effective plans and strategies to achieve your goals

You are involved in this goal-seeking process in every aspect of your daily life. Some of the goals you seek to achieve are more immediate ("short-term") than others, such as planning your activities for the day or organizing your activities for an upcoming test.

Although achieving these short-term goals seems like it ought to be a manageable process, the truth is your efforts probably meet with varying degrees of success. You may not always achieve your goals for the day, and you might occasionally find yourself inadequately prepared for a test. By improving your mastery of the goal-seeking process, you should be able to improve the quality of every area of your life. Let's explore how to do this.

Identify five short-term goals you would like to achieve in the next week. Now rank these goals in order of importance, ranging from the goals that are most essential for you to achieve to those that are less significant.

Once this process of identifying and ranking your goals is complete, you can then focus on devising effective plans and strategies to achieve your goals. In order to complete this stage of the goal-seeking process, select the goal that you ranked 1 or 2, and then *list all of the steps* in the order in which they need to be taken to achieve your goal successfully. After completing this list, estimate how much time each step will take and plan the step in your daily/weekly schedule. For example, if your goal is to prepare for a quiz in biology, your steps might include:

Goal: Prepare for biology quiz in 2 days

STEPS TO BE TAKEN	TIME INVOLVED	SCHEDULE
1. Photocopy the notes for the class I missed last week	20 minutes	after next class
2. Review reading assignments and class notes	2 hours	tonight
3. Make a summary review sheet	1 hour	tomorrow night
4. Study the review sheet	30 minutes	right before quiz

Although this method may seem a little mechanical the first few times you use it, it will soon become integrated into your thinking processes and become a natural and automatic approach to achieving the goals in your daily life. Much of our failure to achieve our short-term goals is due to the fact that we skip one or more of the steps in this process. Common thinking errors in seeking our goals include the following:

- We neglect to explicitly identify important goals.

- We concentrate on less important goals first, leaving insufficient time to work on more important goals.

Method for Achieving Short-Term Goals

Step 1: Identify the goals.
Identify the short-term goals.
Rank the goals in order of importance.
Select the most important goal(s) to focus on.

Step 2: Devise effective plans to achieve your goals.
List all of the steps in the order in which they should be taken.
Estimate how much time each step will take.
Plan the steps in your daily/weekly schedule.

- We don't identify all of the steps required to achieve our goals, or we approach them in the wrong order.

- We underestimate the time each step will take and/or fail to plan the steps in our schedule.

Achieving Long-Term Goals

Identifying immediate or "short-term" goals tends to be a fairly simple procedure. Identifying the appropriate "long-term" goals is a much more complex and challenging process: career aims, plans for marriage, paying for children's college, goals for personal development. Think, for example, about the people you know who have full-time jobs. How many of these people get up in the morning excited and looking forward to going to work that day? The unfortunate fact is that many people have not been successful in identifying the most appropriate career goals for themselves, goals that reflect their true interests and talents.

How do you identify the most appropriate long-term goals for yourself? To begin with, you need to develop an in-depth understanding of yourself: your talents, your interests, the things that stimulate you and bring you satisfaction. You also need to discover what your possibilities are, either through research or actual experience. Of course, your goals do not necessarily remain the same throughout your life. It is unlikely that the goals you had as an eight-year-old are the ones you have now. As you grow, change, and mature, it is natural for your goals to change and evolve as well. The key point is that you should keep examining your goals to make sure that they reflect your own thinking and current interests.

Research studies have shown that high-achieving people are able to envision a detailed, three-dimensional picture of their future in which their goals and aspirations are clearly inscribed. In addition, they are able to construct a mental plan that includes the sequence of steps they will have to take, the amount of time each step will involve, and strategies for overcoming the obstacles they are likely to encounter. Such realistic and compelling concepts of the future enable these people to make sacrifices in the present to achieve their long-term goals. Of course, they may modify these goals as circumstances change and they acquire more information, but they retain a well-defined flexible plan that charts their life course.

Research also reveals that people who are low achievers tend to live in the present and the past. Their concepts of the future are vague and ill defined: "I want to be happy," or "I want a high-paying job." This unclear concept of the future makes it difficult for them to identify the most appropriate goals for themselves, to devise effective strategies for achieving these goals, and to make the necessary sacrifices in the present that will ensure that the future becomes a reality. For example, imagine that you are faced with the choice of studying for an exam or participating in a social activity. What would you do? If you are focusing mainly on the present rather than the future, then the temptation to go out with your friends may be too strong. But if you see this exam as connected to a future that is real and extremely important to you, then you are better equipped to sacrifice a momentary pleasant time for your future happiness.

THINKING ACTIVITY 1.2

Analyzing an Important Future Goal

Apply some of the insights we have been examining about working toward goals to a situation in your own life.

1. Describe as specifically as possible an important longer-term goal that you want to achieve in your life. Your goal can be academic, professional, or personal.
2. Explain the reasons that led you to select the goal that you did and why you believe that your goal makes sense.
3. Identify both the major and minor steps you will have to take to achieve your goal. List your steps in the order in which they need to be taken and indicate how much time you think each step will take. Make your responses as specific and precise as possible.
4. Identify some of the sacrifices that you may have to make in the present in order to achieve your future goal.

Born as Malcolm Little in Omaha, Nebraska, the son of an activist Baptist preacher, Malcolm X saw racial injustice and violence from a very young age. His father, Earl Little, was outspoken in his support for Black Nationalist leader Marcus Garvey; as a result, the family was the target of harassment and was forced to move frequently. In 1931, Earl Little's body was found on the town's trolley tracks. Although the local police dismissed it as an accident, Earl Little's death was believed to have been a murder committed by white supremacists. Malcolm dropped out of high school after a teacher's contemptuous discouragement of his ambitions to become a lawyer. For the next several years, he moved between Boston and New York, becoming profitably involved in various criminal activities. After a conviction for burglary in Boston, he was sentenced to prison. There he began writing letters to former friends as well as to various government officials. His frustration in trying to express his ideas led him to a course of self-education, described in the following excerpt from *The Autobiography of Malcolm X*. After his release from prison, Malcolm converted to Islam and rose to prominence in the Nation of Islam. A pilgrimage that he made to Saudi Arabia led him to begin working toward healing and reconciliation for all Americans of all races. Unfortunately, the enemies he had made and the fears he had provoked did not leave Malcolm X much time to share this message. Three assassins gunned him down as he spoke at the Audubon Ballroom in Harlem on February 15, 1965.

THINKING PASSAGE

FROM *THE AUTOBIOGRAPHY OF MALCOLM X* ### by Malcolm X with Alex Haley

I became increasingly frustrated at not being able to express what I wanted to convey in letters that I wrote, especially those to Mr. Elijah Muhammad. In the street, I had been the most articulate hustler out there—I had commanded attention when I said something. But now, trying to write simple English, I not only wasn't articulate, I wasn't even functional. How would I

Source: Excerpt from *The Autobiography of Malcolm X* by Malcolm X and Alex Haley. Copyright © 1964 by Alex Haley and Malcolm X and copyright © 1965 by Alex Haley and Betty Shabazz. Reprinted by permission of Random House, Inc.

sound writing in slang, the way I would *say* it, something such as, "Look, daddy, let me pull your coat about a cat, Elijah Muhammad—"

Many who today hear me somewhere in person, or on television, or those who read something I've said, will think I went to school far beyond the eighth grade. This impression is due entirely to my prison studies.

It had really begun back in the Charlestown Prison, when Bimbi first made me feel envy of his stock of knowledge. Bimbi had always taken charge of any conversation he was in, and I had tried to emulate him. But every book I picked up had few sentences which didn't contain anywhere from one to nearly all of the words that might as well have been in Chinese. When I just skipped those words, of course, I really ended up with little idea of what the book said. So I had come to the Norfolk Prison Colony still going through only book-reading motions. Pretty soon, I would have quit even these motions, unless I had received the motivation that I did.

I saw that the best thing I could do was get hold of a dictionary—to study, to learn some words. I was lucky enough to reason also that I should try to improve my penmanship. It was sad. I couldn't even write in a straight line. It was both ideas together that moved me to request a dictionary along with some tablets and pencils from the Norfolk Prison Colony school.

I spent two days just riffling uncertainly through the dictionary's pages. I'd never realized so many words existed! I didn't know *which* words I needed to learn. Finally, just to start some kind of action, I began copying. In my slow, painstaking, ragged handwriting, I copied into my tablet everything printed on that first page, down to the punctuation marks. I believe it took me a day. Then, aloud, I read back, to myself, everything I'd written on the tablet. Over and over, aloud, to myself, I read my own handwriting.

I woke up the next morning, thinking about those words—immensely proud to realize that not only had I written so much at one time, but I'd written words that I never knew were in the world. Moreover, with a little effort, I also could remember what many of these words meant. I reviewed the words whose meanings I didn't remember. Funny thing, from the dictionary's first page right now, that "aardvark" springs to my mind. The dictionary had a picture of it, a long-tailed, long-eared, burrowing African mammal, which lives off termites caught by sticking out its tongue as an anteater does for ants.

I was so fascinated that I went on—I copied the dictionary's next page. And the same experience came when I studied that. With every succeeding page, I also learned of people and places and events from history. Actually the dictionary is like a miniature encyclopedia. Finally the dictionary's A section had filled a whole tablet—and I went on into the B's. That was the

VISUAL THINKING

Opening Your Mind to New Possibilities

● How can rigid thinking and a lack of imagination prevent you from achieving your goals? How can you open your mind and free your imagination in order to understand all of your future possibilities?

way I started copying what eventually became the entire dictionary. It went a lot faster after so much practice helped me to pick up handwriting speed. Between what I wrote in my tablet, and writing letters, during the rest of my time in prison I would guess I wrote a million words.

I suppose it was inevitable that as my word-base broadened, I could for the first time pick up a book and read and now begin to understand what the book was saying. Anyone who has read a great deal can imagine the new world that opened. Let me tell you something: from then until I left that prison, in every free moment I had, if I was not reading in the library, I was reading on my bunk. You couldn't have gotten me out of books with a wedge. Between Mr. Muhammad's teachings, my correspondence, my visitors—usually Ella and Reginald—and my reading of books, months passed without my even thinking about being imprisoned. In fact, up to then, I never had been so truly free in my life.

Questions for Analysis

In describing how he worked toward the goals of becoming literate and knowledgeable, Malcolm X touches on a variety of important issues related to developing thinking and language abilities. We can analyze some of the issues raised by answering the following questions:

1. Malcolm X states that, although he was an articulate "street hustler," this ability was of little help in expressing his ideas in writing. Explain the differences between expressing your ideas orally and in writing, including the advantages and disadvantages of each form of language expression.

2. Malcolm X envied one of the other inmates, Bimbi, because his stock of knowledge enabled him to take charge of any conversation he was in. Explain why knowledge—and our ability to use it—leads to power in our dealings with others. Describe a situation from your own experience in which having expert knowledge about a subject enabled you to influence the thinking of other people.

3. Malcolm X states about pursuing his studies in prison that "up to then, I never had been so truly free in my life." Explain what you think he means by this statement.

Many of our poor decisions involve relatively minor issues — for example, selecting an unappealing dish in a restaurant, agreeing to go out on a blind date, taking a course that does not meet our expectations. Although these decisions may result in unpleasant consequences, the discomfort is neither life-threatening nor long lasting (although a disappointing course may seem to last forever!). However, there are many more significant decisions in our lives in which poor choices can result in considerably more damaging and far-reaching consequences. For example, one reason that the current divorce rate in the United States stands at 50 percent is the poor decisions people make before or after the vows "till death do us part." Similarly, the fact that many employed adults wake up in the morning unhappy about going to their jobs, anxiously waiting for the end of the day and the conclusion of the week (TGIF!) so they are free to do what they really want to do, suggests that somewhere along the line they made poor career decisions, or they felt trapped by circumstances they couldn't control. Our jobs should be much more than a way to earn a pay-check — they should be vehicles for using our professional skills, opportunities for expressing our creative talents, stimulants to our personal growth and intellectual development, and experiences that provide us with feelings of fulfillment and self-esteem. In the final analysis, our careers are central elements of our lives and important dimensions of our life-portraits. Our career decision is one that we better try to get right!

An important part of becoming an educated thinker is learning to make effective decisions. Let's explore the process of making effective decisions and then apply your knowledge to the challenge of deciding on the most appropriate career for yourself.

THINKING ACTIVITY 1.3

Analyzing a Previous Decision

1. Think back on an important decision that you made that turned out well and describe the experience as specifically as possible.

2. Reconstruct the reasoning process that you used to make your decision. Did you:

   • Clearly define the decision to be made and the related issues?

   • Consider various choices and anticipate the consequences of these various choices?

   • Gather additional information to help in your analysis?

   • Evaluate the various pros and cons of different courses of action?

   • Use a chart or diagram to aid in your deliberations?

   • Create a specific plan of action to implement your ideas?

   • Periodically review your decision to make necessary adjustments?

An Organized Approach to Making Decisions

As you reflected on the successful decision you were writing about in Thinking Activity 1.3, you probably noticed your mind working in a more or less systematic way as you thought your way through the decision situation. Of course, we often make important decisions with less thoughtful analysis by acting impulsively or relying on our "intuition." Sometimes these decisions work out well, but often they don't, and we are forced to live with the consequences of these mistaken choices. People who approach decision situations thoughtfully and analytically tend to be more successful decision-makers than people who don't. Naturally, there are no guarantees that a careful analysis will lead to a successful result — there are often too many unknown elements and factors beyond our control. But we can certainly improve our success rate as well as our speed by becoming more knowledgeable about the decision-making process. Expert decision-makers can typically make quick, accurate decisions based on intuitions that are informed, not merely impulsive. However, as with most complex abilities in life, we need to learn to "walk" before we can "run," so let's explore a versatile and effective approach for making decisions.

The decision-making approach we will be using consists of five steps. As you gradually master these steps, they will become integrated into your way of thinking, and you will be able to apply them in a natural and flexible way.

Step 1: Define the Decision Clearly. This seems like an obvious step, but a lot of decision-making goes wrong at the starting point. For example, imagine that you decide that you want to have a "more active social life." The problem with this characterization of your decision is it defines the situation too generally and therefore doesn't give any clear direction for your analysis. Do you want to develop an intimate, romantic relationship? Do you want to cultivate more close friendships? Do you want to engage in more social activities? Do you want to meet new people? In short, there are many ways to define more clearly the decision to have a "more active social life." The more specific your definition of the decision to be made, the clearer will be your analysis and the greater the likelihood of success.

Strategy: *Write a one-page analysis that articulates your decision-making situation as clearly and specifically as possible.*

Step 2: Consider All the Possible Choices. Successful decision-makers explore all of the possible choices in their situation, not simply the obvious ones. In fact, the less obvious choices often turn out to be the most effective ones. For example, a student in a recent class of mine couldn't decide whether he should major in accounting or business management. In discussing his situation with other members of the class, he revealed that his real interest was in the area of graphic design and illustration. Although he was very talented, he considered this area to be only a hobby, not a possible career choice. Class members pointed out to him that this might turn out to be his best career choice, but he needed first to see it as a possibility.

Strategy: List as many possible choices for your situation as you can, both obvious and not obvious. Ask other people for additional suggestions, and don't censor or prejudge any ideas.

Step 3: Gather All Relevant Information and Evaluate the Pros and Cons of Each Possible Choice. In many cases you may lack sufficient information to make an informed choice regarding a challenging, complex decision. Unfortunately, this doesn't prevent people from plunging ahead anyway, making a decision that is often more a gamble than an informed choice. Instead of this questionable approach, it makes a lot more sense to seek out the information you need in order to determine which of the choices you identified has the best chance for success. For example, in the case of the student mentioned in Step 2, there is important information he would need to secure in order to determine whether he should consider a career in graphic design and illustration, including asking: What are the specific careers within this general field? What sort of academic preparation and experience are required for the various careers? What are the prospects for employment in these areas, and how well do they pay?

Strategy: For each possible choice that you identified, create questions regarding information you need to find out, and then locate that information.

In addition to locating all relevant information, each of the possible choices you identified has certain advantages and disadvantages, and it is essential that you analyze these pros and cons in an organized fashion. For example, in the case of the student described earlier, the choice of pursuing a career in accounting may have advantages like ready employment opportunities, the flexibility of working in many different situations and geographical locations, moderate-to-high income expectations, and job security. On the other hand, disadvantages might include the fact that accounting may not reflect a deep and abiding interest of the student, he might lose interest over time, or the career might not result in the personal challenge and fulfillment that he seeks.

Strategy: Using a format similar to that outlined in the following worksheet, analyze the pros and cons of each of your possible choices.

Define the decision:

Possible choices	Information needed	Pros	Cons
1.			
2.			
(etc.)			

Step 4: Select the Choice That Seems to Best Meet the Needs of the Situation. The first four steps of this approach are designed to help you analyze your decision situation: to clearly define the decision, generate possible choices, gather relevant information, and evaluate the pros and cons of the choices you identified. In the final step, you must attempt to synthesize all that you have learned, weaving together all of the various threads into a conclusion that you believe to be your "best" choice. How do you do this? There is no one simple way to identify your "best" choice, but there are some useful strategies for guiding your deliberations.

Strategy: Identify and prioritize the goal(s) of your decision situation and determine which of your choices best meets these goals. This process will probably involve reviewing and perhaps refining your definition of the decision situation. For example, in the case of the student whom we have been considering, some goals might include choosing a career that will

(a) provide financial security
(b) provide personal fulfillment
(c) make use of special talents
(d) offer plentiful opportunities and job security

Once identified, the goals can be ranked in order of their priority, which will then suggest what the "best" choice will be. For example, if the student ranks goals (a) and (d) at the top of the list, then a choice of accounting or business administration might make sense. On the other hand, if the student ranks goals (b) and (c) at the top, then pursuing a career in graphic design and illustration might be the best selection.

Strategy: Anticipate the consequences of each choice by "preliving" the choices. Another helpful strategy for deciding on the best choice is to project yourself into the future, imagining as realistically as you can the consequences of each possible choice. As with previous strategies, this process is aided by writing your thoughts down and discussing them with others.

Step 5: Implement a Plan of Action and Then Monitor the Results, Making Necessary Adjustments. Once you have selected what you consider your best choice, you need to develop and implement a specific, concrete plan of action. As was noted in the section on short-term goals, the more specific and concrete your plan of action, the greater the likelihood of success. For example, if the student in the case we have been considering decides to pursue a career in graphic design and illustration, his plan should include reviewing the major that best meets his needs, discussing his situation with students and faculty in

Method for Making Decisions

Step 1: Define the decision clearly.

Step 2: Consider all the possible choices.

Step 3: Gather all relevant information and evaluate the pros and cons of each possible choice.

Step 4: Select the choice that seems to best meet the needs of the situation.

Step 5: Implement a plan of action and then monitor the results, making necessary adjustments.

that department, planning the courses he will be taking, and perhaps speaking to people in the field.

> *Strategy: Create a schedule that details the steps you will be taking to implement your decision and a timeline for taking these steps.*

Of course, your plan is merely a starting point for implementing your decision. As you actually begin taking the steps in your plan, you will likely discover that changes and adjustments need to be made. In some cases, you may find that, based on new information, the choice you selected appears to be the wrong one. For example, as the student we have been discussing takes courses in graphic design and illustration, he may find that his interest in the field is not as serious as he thought and that although he likes this area as a hobby, he does not want it to be his life work. In this case, he should return to considering his other choices and perhaps adding additional choices that he did not consider before.

> *Strategy: After implementing your choice, evaluate its success by identifying what's working and what isn't, and make the necessary adjustments to improve the situation.*

THINKING ACTIVITY 1.4

Analyzing a Future Decision

1. Describe an important decision in your academic or personal life that you will have to make in the near future.

VISUAL THINKING

Weighing Your Decision Carefully

● Why do many people tend to make quick decisions rather than approaching their decisions thoughtfully and analytically? Describe a decision you made that was based on thoughtful analysis. How did it turn out?

2. Using the five-step decision-making approach we just described, analyze your decision and conclude with your "best" choice.

Share your analysis with other members of the class and listen carefully to the feedback they give you.

⊚ Discovering "Who" You Are

Each of us possesses an original combination of interests, abilities, and values that characterizes our personality. Discovering the appropriate goals for yourself involves becoming familiar with your unique qualities: the activities that interest you, the special abilities and potentials you have, and the values that define the things you consider to be most important. Once you have a reasonably clear sense of "who" you are and what you are capable of, you can then begin exploring those goals, from career paths to personal relationships, that are a good match for you. However, developing a clear sense of "who" you are is a challenging project and is one of the key goals of this text. Many people are still in the early stages of self-understanding, and this situation makes identifying the appropriate career particularly difficult.

What Are Your Interests?

In order to live a life that will be stimulating and rewarding to you over the course of many years, you must choose a path that involves activities that you have a deep and abiding interest in performing. If you want to be a teacher, you should find helping people learn to be an inspiring and fulfilling activity. If you want to be an architect, you should find the process of creating designs, working with others, and solving construction problems to be personally challenging activities. When people achieve a close match between their natural interests and the activities that constitute a career, they are assured of living a life that will bring them joy and satisfaction.

Although there is not necessarily a direct connection between interests and eventual career, carefully examining your interests should nevertheless provide you with valuable clues in discovering a major and a career that will bring lifelong satisfaction. In addition, thinking critically about your interests will help you to seek relationships that support and complement your goals and to select course work and a major that you will genuinely enjoy.

THINKING ACTIVITY 1.5

Identifying Your Interests

1. Create a listing of the interests in your life, describing each one as specifically as possible. Begin with the present and work backward as far as you can remember, covering your areas of employment, education, and general activities. Make the listing as comprehensive as you can, includ-

ing as many interests as you can think of. (Don't worry about duplication.) Ask people who know you how they would describe your interests.

2. Once you have created your list, classify the items into groups based on similarity. Don't worry if the same interest fits into more than one group.

3. For each group you have created, identify possible careers that might be related to the interests described in the group.

A student example follows:

Interest Group #1

- I enjoy helping people solve their problems.
- I am interested in subjects like hypnotism and mental therapy.
- I have always been interested in the behavior of people.
- I enjoy reading books on psychology.

Possible Majors and Careers: clinical psychologist, occupational therapist, social worker, gerontologist, behavioral scientist, community mental health worker, industrial psychologist

Interest Group #2

- I am interested in the sciences, especially chemistry and anatomy.
- I like going to hospitals and observing doctors and nurses at work.
- When I was in high school, I always enjoyed biology and anatomy labs.
- I am interested in hearing about people's illnesses and injuries.

Possible Majors and Careers: doctor, nurse, physical therapist, paramedic, biomedical worker, chemical technician, mortician, medical laboratory technician

Interest Group #3

- I enjoy going to museums and theaters.
- I enjoy painting and drawing in my free time.
- I enjoy listening to music: classical, jazz, and romantic.
- I enjoy reading magazines like *Vogue*, *Vanity Fair*, and *Vanidades*.

Possible Majors and Careers: actor, publicist, advertising executive, interior designer, fashion designer

What Are Your Abilities?

In general, the activities that you have a sustained interest in over a period of time are activities that you are good at. This is another key question for you to address as you pursue your career explorations: "What are the special abilities and talents that I possess?" Each of us has a unique combination of special talents, and it is to our advantage to select majors and careers that utilize these natural abilities. Otherwise, we will find ourselves competing against people who do have natural abilities in that particular area. For example, think of those courses you have taken that seemed extremely difficult to you despite your strenuous efforts while other students were successful with apparently much less effort (or, conversely, those courses that seemed easily manageable to you while other students were struggling). There is a great deal of competition for desirable careers, and if we are to be successful, we need to be able to use our natural strengths.

How do you go about identifying your natural abilities? One productive approach to begin identifying your abilities is to examine important accomplishments in your life, a strategy described in Thinking Activity 1.6. In addition, there are career counselors, books, and computer software programs that can help you zero in on your areas of interest and strength. However, we sometimes possess unknown abilities that we simply haven't had the opportunity to discover and use. With this in mind, it makes sense for you to explore unfamiliar areas of experience to become aware of your full range of potentials.

THINKING ACTIVITY 1.6

Identifying Your Abilities

1. Identify the ten most important accomplishments in your life. From this list of ten, select three accomplishments of which you are most proud. Typically, these will be experiences in which you faced a difficult challenge or a complex problem that you were able to overcome with commitment and talent.
2. Compose a specific and detailed description (one to two pages) of each of these three accomplishments, paying particular attention to the skills and strategies you used to meet the challenge or solve the problem.
3. After completing the descriptions, identify the abilities that you displayed in achieving your accomplishments. Then place them into groups, based on their similarity to one another. Here is how one student completed this activity:

Accomplishments:

1. Graduating from high school
2. Getting my real estate license
3. Succeeding at college
4. Owning a dog
5. Winning a swim team championship
6. Moving into my own apartment
7. Finding a job
8. Getting my driver's license
9. Buying a car
10. Learning to speak another language

Accomplishment #1: Graduating from High School

The first accomplishment I would like to describe was graduating from high school. I never thought I would do it. In the eleventh grade I became a truant. I only attended classes in my major, after which I would go home or hang out with friends. I was having a lot of problems with my parents and the guy I was dating, and I fell into a deep depression in the middle of the term. I decided to commit suicide by taking pills. I confided this to a friend, who went and told the principal. I was called out of class to the principal's office. He said he wanted to talk to me, and it seemed like we talked for hours. Suddenly my parents walked in with my guidance counselor, and they joined the discussion. We came to the conclusion that I would live with my aunt for two weeks, and I would also speak with the counselor once a day. If I didn't follow these rules they would place me in a group home. During those two weeks I did a lot of thinking. I didn't talk to anyone from my neighborhood. Through counseling I learned that no problems are worth taking your life. I joined a peer group in my school, which helped me a lot as well. I learned to express my feelings. It was very difficult to get back into my schedule in school, but my teachers' help made it easier. I committed myself to school and did very well, graduating the following year.

Abilities/Skills from Accomplishment #1:

- I learned how to analyze and solve difficult problems in my life.

- I learned how to understand and express my feelings.

- I learned how to work with other people in order to help solve each other's problems.

- I learned how to focus my attention and work with determination toward a goal.

- I learned how to deal with feelings of depression and think positively about myself and my future.

⊚ Living Creatively

Sometimes students become discouraged about their lives, concluding that their destinies are shaped by forces beyond their control. Although difficult circumstances *do* hamper our striving for success, this fatalistic sentiment can also reflect a passivity that is the opposite of thinking critically. As a critical thinker, you should be confident that you can shape the person that you want to become through insightful understanding and intelligent choices.

In working with this book, you will develop the abilities and attitudes needed to become an educated thinker and a successful person. You will also integrate these goals into a larger context, exploring how to live a life that is creative, professionally successful, and personally fulfilling. By using both your creative and your critical thinking abilities, you can develop informed beliefs and an enlightened life philosophy. In the final analysis, the person who looks back at you in the mirror is the person you have created.

THINKING ACTIVITY 1.7

Describing Your Current and Future Self

1. Describe a portrait of yourself as a person. What sort of person are you? What are your strengths and weaknesses? In what areas do you feel you are creative?
2. Describe some of the ways you would like to change yourself.

"Can I Be Creative?"

The first day of my course Creative Thinking: Theory and Practice, I always ask the students in the class if they think they are creative. Typically fewer than half of the class members raise their hands. One reason for this is that people often confuse being "creative" with being "artistic" — skilled at art, music, poetry, creative writing, drama, dance. Although artistic people are certainly creative, there are an infinite number of ways to be creative that are *not* artistic. This is a mental trap that I fell into growing up. In school I always dreaded art class because I was so inept. My pathetic drawings and art projects were always good for a laugh for my friends, and I felt no overwhelming urges to write poetry, paint, or compose music. I was certain that I had simply been born "uncreative" and accepted this "fact" as my destiny. It wasn't until I graduated from college that I began to change this view of myself. I was working as a custom woodworker to support myself, designing and creating specialized furniture for people, when it suddenly struck me: I was being creative! I then began to see other areas of my life in which I was creative: playing sports, decorating my apartment, even writing research papers. I finally understood that being creative was a state of mind and a way of life. As writer Eric Gill expresses it, "The artist is not a different kind of person, but each one of us is a different kind of artist."

Are you creative? Yes! Think of all of the activities that you enjoy doing: cooking, creating a wardrobe, raising children, playing sports, cutting or braiding hair, dancing, playing music. Whenever you are investing your own personal ideas, putting on your own personal stamp, you are being creative. For example, imagine that you are cooking your favorite dish. To the extent that you are expressing your unique ideas developed through inspiration and experimentation, you are being creative. Of course, if you are simply following someone else's recipe without significant modification, your dish may be tasty — but it is not creative. Similarly, if your moves on the dance floor or the basketball court express your distinctive personality, you are being creative, as you are when you stimulate the original thinking of your children or make your friends laugh with your unique brand of humor.

Living your life creatively means bringing your unique perspective and creative talents to all of the dimensions of your life. The following passages are written by students about creative areas in their lives. After reading the passages, complete Thinking Activity 1.8, which gives you the opportunity to describe a creative area from your own life.

One of the most creative aspects of my life is my diet. I have been a vegetarian for the past five years, while the rest of my family has continued to eat meat. I had to overcome many obstacles to make this lifestyle work for me, including family dissension. The solution was simple: I had to learn how to cook creatively. I have come to realize that my diet is an ongoing learning process. The more I learn about and experiment with different foods, the healthier and happier I become. I feel like an explorer setting out on my own to discover new things about food and nutrition. I slowly evolved from a person who could cook food only if it came from a can into someone who could make bread from scratch and grow yogurt cultures. I find learning new things about nutrition and cooking healthful foods very relaxing and rewarding. I like being alone in my house baking bread; there is something very comforting about the aroma. Most of all I like to experiment with different ways to prepare foods, because the ideas are my own. Even when an effort is less than successful, I find pleasure in the knowledge that I gained from the experience. I discovered recently, for example, that eggplant is terrible in soup! Making mistakes seems to be a natural way to increase creativity, and I now firmly believe that people who say that they do not like vegetables simply have not been properly introduced to them!

As any parent knows, children have an abundance of energy to spend, and toys or television do not always meet their needs. In response, I create activities to stimulate their creativity and preserve my sanity. For example, I involve them in the process of cooking, giving them the skin from peeled vegetables and a pot so they make their own "soup." Using catalogs, we cut out pictures of furniture, rugs, and curtains, and they paste them onto cartons to create their own interior decors: vibrant living rooms, plush bedrooms, colorful family rooms. I make beautiful boats from aluminum foil, and my children spend hours in the bathtub playing with them. We "go bowling" with empty soda cans and a ball, and they star in "track meets" by running an obstacle course we set up. When it comes to raising children, creativity is a way of survival!

After quitting the government agency I was working at because of too much bureaucracy, I was hired as a carpenter at a construction site, although I had little knowledge of this profession. I learned to handle a hammer and other tools by watching other co-workers, and within a matter of weeks I was skilled enough to organize my own group of workers for projects. Most of my fellow workers used the old-fashioned method of construction carpentry, building panels with inefficient and poorly made bracings. I redesigned the panels in order to save construction time and materials. My supervisor and site engineer were thrilled with my creative ideas, and I was assigned progressively more challenging projects, including the construction of an office building that was completed in record time.

THINKING ACTIVITY 1.8

Describing a Creative Area

1. Describe a creative area of your life in which you are able to express your unique personality and talents. Be specific and give examples.
2. Analyze your creative area by answering the following questions:
   - Why do you feel that this activity is creative? Give examples.
   - How would you describe the experience of being engaged in this activity? Where do your creative ideas come from? How do they develop?
   - What strategies do you use to increase your creativity? What obstacles block your creative efforts? How do you try to overcome these blocks?

Becoming More Creative

Although we each have nearly limitless potential to live creatively, most people use only a small percentage of their creative gifts. In fact, there is research to suggest that people typically achieve their highest creative point as young children, after which there is a long, steady decline into uncreativity. Why? Well, to begin with, young children are immersed in the excitement of exploration and discovery. They are eager to try out new things, act on their impulses, and make unusual connections between disparate ideas. They are not afraid to take risks in trying out untested solutions, and they are not compelled to identify the socially acceptable "correct answer." Children are willing to play with ideas, creating improbable scenarios and imaginative ways of thinking without fear of being ridiculed.

All of this tends to change as we get older. The weight of "reality" begins to smother our imagination, and we increasingly focus our attention on the nuts and bolts of living rather than on playing with possibilities. The social pressure to conform to group expectations increases dramatically. Whether the group is our friends, classmates, or fellow employees, there are clearly defined "rules" for dressing, behaving, speaking, and thinking. When we deviate from these rules, we risk social disapproval, rejection, or ridicule. Most groups have little tolerance for individuals who want to think independently and creatively. As we become older, we also become more reluctant to pursue untested courses of action because we become increasingly afraid of failure. Pursuing creativity inevitably involves failure, because we are trying to break out of established ruts and go beyond traditional methods. For example, going beyond the safety of a proven recipe to create an innovative dish may involve some disasters, but it's the only way to create something genuinely unique. The history of creative discoveries is littered with failures, a fact we tend to forget when we are debating whether we should risk an untested idea. Those people who are courageous enough to risk failure while expressing their creative impulses are rewarded with unique achievements and an enriched life.

THINKING ACTIVITY 1.9

Identifying Creative Blocks

Reflect on your own creative development, and describe some of the fears and pressures that inhibit your own creativity. For example, have you ever been penalized for trying out a new idea that didn't work out? Have you ever suffered the wrath of the group for daring to be different and violating the group's unspoken rules? Do you feel that your life is so filled with responsibilities and the demands of reality that you don't have time to be creative?

Although the forces that discourage us from being creative are powerful, they can nevertheless be overcome with the right approaches. We are going to explore four productive strategies:

- Understand and trust the creative process.
- Eliminate the "Voice of Criticism."
- Establish a creative environment.
- Make creativity a priority.

Understand and Trust the Creative Process   Discovering your creative talents requires that you understand how the creative process operates and then have confidence in the results it produces. There are no fixed procedures or formulas for generating creative ideas because creative ideas *by definition* go beyond established ways of thinking to the unknown and the innovative. As the ancient Greek philosopher Heraclitus once said, "You must expect the unexpected, because it cannot be found by search or trail."

Although there is no fixed path to creative ideas, there are activities you can pursue that make the birth of creative ideas possible. In this respect, generating creative ideas is similar to gardening. You need to prepare the soil; plant the seeds; ensure proper water, light, and food; and then be patient until the ideas begin to sprout. Here are some steps for cultivating your creative garden:

- *Absorb yourself in the task:* Creative ideas don't occur in a vacuum. They emerge after a great deal of work, study, and practice. For example, if you want to come up with creative ideas in the kitchen, you need to become knowledgeable about the art of cooking. The more knowledgeable you are, the better prepared you are to create valuable and innovative dishes. Similarly, if you are trying to develop a creative perspective for a research paper in college, you need to immerse yourself in the subject, developing an in-depth understanding of the central concepts and issues. Absorbing yourself in the task "prepares the soil" for your creative ideas.

- *Allow time for ideas to incubate:* After absorbing yourself in the task or problem, the next stage in the creative process is to *stop* working on the task or problem. Even when your conscious mind has stopped actively working on the task, the unconscious dimension of your mind continues working — processing, organizing, and ultimately generating innovative ideas and solutions. This process is known as *incubation* because it mirrors the process in which baby chicks gradually evolve inside the egg until the moment comes when they break out through the shell. In the same way, your creative mind is at work while you are going about your business until the moment of *illumination,* when the incubating idea finally erupts to the surface of your conscious mind. People report that these illuminating moments — when their mental light bulbs go on — often occur when they are engaged in activities completely unrelated to the task. One of the most famous cases was that of the Greek thinker Archimedes, whose moment of illumination came while he was taking a bath, causing him to run naked through the streets of Athens shouting, "Eureka" ("I have found it").

- *Seize on the ideas when they emerge and follow them through:* Generating creative ideas is of little use unless you recognize them when they appear and then act on them. Too often people don't pay much attention to these ideas when they occur, or they dismiss them as too impractical. You must have confidence in the ideas you create, even if they seem wacky or far-out. Many of the most valuable inventions in our history started as improbable ideas, ridiculed by the popular wisdom. For example, the idea of Velcro started with burrs covering the pants of the inventor as he walked through a field, and Post-it Notes resulted from the accidental invention of an adhesive that was weaker than normal. In other words, thinking effectively means thinking creatively *and* thinking critically. After you use your creative thinking abilities to generate innovative ideas, you then must employ your critical thinking abilities to evaluate and refine the ideas and design a practical plan for implementing them.

Eliminate the "Voice of Criticism"   The biggest threat to our creativity lies within ourselves, the negative "Voice of Criticism" (VOC). This VOC can undermine your confidence in every area of your life, including your creative activities, with statements like:

This is a stupid idea and no one will like it.

Even if I could pull this idea off, it probably won't amount to much.

Although I was successful the last time I tried something like this, I was lucky and I won't be able to do it again.

These statements, and countless others like them, have the ongoing effect of making us doubt ourselves and the quality of our creative thinking. As we lose confidence, we become more timid, more reluctant to follow through on ideas and present them to others. After a while our cumulative insecurity discourages us from even generating ideas in the first place, and we end up simply conforming to established ways of thinking and the expectations of others. And in so doing we surrender an important part of ourselves, the vital and dynamic creative core of our personality that defines our unique perspective on the world.

Where do these negative voices come from? Often they originate in the negative judgments we experienced while growing up, destructive criticisms that become internalized as a part of ourselves. In the same way that praising children helps make them feel confident and secure, consistently criticizing them does the opposite. Although parents, teachers, and acquaintances often don't intend these negative consequences with their critical judgments and lack of positive praise, the unfortunate result is still the same: a Voice of Criticism that keeps hammering away at the value of ourselves, our ideas, and our creations. As a teacher, I see this VOC evident when students present their creative projects to the class with apologies like "This isn't very good, and it probably doesn't make sense."

How do we eliminate this unwelcome and destructive voice within ourselves? There are a number of effective strategies you can use, although you should be aware that the fight, while worth the effort, will not be easy.

- *Become aware of the VOC:* You have probably been listening to the negative messages of the VOC for so long that you may not even be consciously aware of it. To conquer the VOC, you need to first recognize when it speaks. In addition, it is helpful to analyze the negative messages, try to figure out how and why they developed, and then create strategies to overcome them. A good strategy is to keep a VOC journal, described in Thinking Activity 1.10.

- *Restate the judgment in a more accurate or constructive way:* Sometimes there is an element of truth in our self-judgments, but we have blown the reality out of proportion. For example, if you fail a test, your VOC may translate this as "I'm a failure." Or if you ask someone for a date and get turned down, your VOC may conclude: "I'm a social misfit with emotional bad breath!" In these instances, you need to translate the reality accurately: "I failed this test — I wonder what went wrong and how I can improve my performance in the future," and "This person turned me down for a date — I guess I'm not his or her type, or maybe he or she just doesn't know me well enough."

- *Get tough with the VOC:* You can't be a wimp if you hope to overcome the VOC. Instead, you have to be strong and determined, telling yourself as soon as the VOC appears, "I'm throwing you out and not letting you back in!" This attack might feel peculiar at first, but it will soon become an automatic response when those negative judgments appear. Don't give in to the judgments, even a little bit, by saying, "Well, maybe I'm just a little bit of a jerk." Get rid of the VOC entirely, and good riddance to it!

- *Create positive voices and visualizations:* The best way to destroy the VOC for good is to replace it with positive encouragements. As soon as you have stomped on the judgment "I'm a jerk," you should replace it with "I'm an intelligent, valuable person with many positive qualities and talents." Similarly, you should make extensive use of positive visualization, as you "see" yourself performing well on your examinations, being entertaining and insightful with other people, and succeeding gloriously in the sport or dramatic production in which you are involved. If you make the effort to create these positive voices and images, they will eventually become a natural part of your thinking. And since positive thinking leads to positive results, your efforts will become self-fulfilling prophecies.

- *Use other people for independent confirmation:* The negative judgments coming from the VOC are usually irrational, but until they are dragged out into the light of day for examination, they can be very powerful. Sharing our VOC with others we trust is an effective strategy because they can provide an objective perspective that reveals to us the irrationality and destructiveness of these negative judgments. This sort of "reality testing" strips the judgments of their power, a process that is enhanced by the positive support of concerned friends with whom we have developed relationships over a period of time.

THINKING ACTIVITY 1.10

Combatting the "Voice of Criticism"

1. Take a small notebook or pad with you one day, and record every self-defeating criticism that you make about yourself. At the end of the day classify your self-criticisms by category. For example: negative self-criticism about your physical appearance, your popularity with others, your academic ability.
2. Analyze the self-criticisms in each of the categories and try to determine where they came from and how they developed.
3. Use the strategies described in this section, and others of your own creation, to start fighting these self-criticisms when they occur.

Establish a Creative Environment   An important part of eliminating the negative voices in our minds is to establish environments in which our creative resources can flourish. This means finding or developing physical environments conducive to creative expression as well as supportive social environments. Sometimes working with other people is stimulating and energizing to our creative juices; at other times we require a private place where we can work without distraction. For example, I have a specific location in which I do much of my writing: sitting at my desk, with a calm, pleasing view, music on the stereo, a cold drink, and a supply of Tootsie Roll Pops. I'm ready for creativity to strike me, although I sometimes have to wait for some time! Different environments work for different people: You have to find the environment(s) best suited to your own creative process and then make a special effort to do your work there.

The people in our lives who form our social environment play an even more influential role in encouraging or inhibiting our creative process. When we are surrounded by people who are positive and supportive, this increases our confidence and encourages us to take the risk to express our creative vision. They can stimulate our creativity by providing us with fresh ideas and new perspectives. By engaging in *brainstorming* (described on page 102), they can work with us to generate ideas and then later help us figure out how to refine and implement the most valuable ones.

However, when the people around us tend to be negative, critical, or belittling, then the opposite happens: We lose confidence and are reluctant to express ourselves creatively. Eventually, we begin to internalize these negative criticisms, incorporating them into our own VOC. When this occurs, we have the choice of telling people that we will not tolerate this sort of destructive behavior or, if they can't improve their behavior, moving them out of our lives. Of course, sometimes this is difficult because we work with them or they are related to us. In this case we have to work at diminishing their negative influence and spending more time with those who support us.

Make Creativity a Priority   Having diminished the voice of negative judgment in your mind, established a creative environment, and committed yourself to trusting your creative gifts, you are now in a position to live more creatively. How do you actually do this? Start small. Identify some habitual patterns in your life and break out of them. Choose new experiences whenever possible — for example, ordering unfamiliar items on a menu or getting to know people outside your circle of friends — and strive to develop fresh perspectives on things in your life. Resist falling back into the ruts you were previously in by remembering that living things are supposed to be continually growing, changing, and evolving, not acting in repetitive patterns like machines.

THINKING ACTIVITY 1.11

Becoming More Creative

Select an area of your life in which you would like to be more creative. It can be in school, on your job, an activity you enjoy, or in your relationship with someone. Make a special effort to inject a fresh perspective and new ideas into this area, and keep a journal recording your efforts and their result. Be sure to allow yourself sufficient time to break out of your ruts and establish new patterns of thinking, feeling, and behaving. Focus on your creative antennae as you "expect the unexpected," and pounce on new ideas when they emerge from the depths of your creative resource.

THINKING PASSAGE

Original Spin

The process of creating yourself through your choices is a lifelong one that involves all the creative and critical thinking abilities that we have been exploring in this book. The processes of creative thinking and critical thinking are related to one another in complex, interactive ways. We use the creative thinking process to develop ideas that are unique, useful, and worthy of further elaboration, and we use the critical thinking process to analyze,

VISUAL THINKING

"Expect the Unexpected" — Heraclitus

● Can you think of a time in which a creative inspiration enabled you to
see a solution to a problem that no one else could see? What can we do
to increase these creative breakthroughs in our lives? What strategies
can we use to "expect the unexpected"?

evaluate, and refine these ideas. Creative thinking and critical thinking work as partners, enabling us to lead fulfilling lives. The following article, "Original Spin" by Lesley Dormen and Peter Edidin, provides a useful introduction to creative thinking and suggests strategies for increasing your creative abilities. After reading the article and reflecting on its ideas, answer the questions that follow.

ORIGINAL SPIN
by Lesley Dormen and Peter Edidin

Creativity, somebody once wrote, is the search for the elusive "Aha," that moment of insight when one sees the world, or a problem, or an idea, in a new way. Traditionally, whether the discovery results in a cubist painting or an improved carburetor, we have viewed the creative instant as serendipitous and rare — the product of genius, the property of the elect.

Unfortunately, this attitude has had a number of adverse consequences. It encourages us to accept the myth that the creative energy society requires to address its own problems will never be present in sufficient supply. Beyond that, we have come to believe that "ordinary" people like ourselves can never be truly creative. As John Briggs, author of *Fire in the Crucible: The Alchemy of Creative Genius*, said, "The way we talk about creativity tends to reinforce the notion that it is some kind of arbitrary gift. It's amazing the way 'not having it' becomes wedded to people's self-image. They invariably work up a whole series of rationalizations about why they 'aren't creative,' as if they were damaged goods of some kind." Today, however, researchers are looking at creativity, not as an advantage of the human elite, but as a basic human endowment. As Ruth Richards, a psychiatrist and creativity researcher at McLean Hospital in Belmont, MA, says, "You were being creative when you learned how to walk. And if you are looking for something in the fridge, you're being creative because you have to figure out for yourself where it is." Creativity, in Richards' view, is simply fundamental to getting about in the world. It is "our ability to adapt to change. It is the very essence of human survival."

In an age of rampant social and technological change, such an adaptive capability becomes yet more crucial to the individual's effort to maintain balance in a constantly shifting environment. "People need to recognize that what Alvin Toffler called future shock is our daily reality," says Ellen

Source: "Original Spin" by Lesley Dormen and Peter Edidin, *Psychology Today,* July/August 1989. Reprinted with permission from Psychology Today Magazine. Copyright © 1989 (Sussex Publishers, Inc.).

McGrath, a clinical psychologist who teaches creativity courses at New York University. "Instability is an intrinsic part of our lives, and to deal with it every one of us will need to find new, creative solutions to the challenges of everyday life." . . .

But can you really become more creative? If the word *creative* smacks too much of Picasso at his canvas, then rephrase the question in a less intimidating way: Do you believe you could deal with the challenges of life in a more effective, inventive and fulfilling manner? If the answer is yes, then the question becomes, "What's stopping you?"

Defining Yourself as a Creative Person

People often hesitate to recognize the breakthroughs in their own lives as creative. But who has not felt the elation and surprise that come with the sudden, seemingly inexplicable discovery of a solution to a stubborn problem? In that instant, in "going beyond the information given," as psychologist Jerome Bruner has said, to a solution that was the product of your own mind, you were expressing your creativity.

This impulse to "go beyond" to a new idea is not the preserve of genius, stresses David Henry Feldman, a developmental psychologist at Tufts University and the author of *Nature's Gambit*, a study of child prodigies. "Not everybody can be Beethoven," he says, "but it is true that all humans, by virtue of being dreamers and fantasizers, have a tendency to take liberties with the world as it exists. Humans are always transforming their inner and outer worlds. It's what I call the 'transformational imperative.'"

The desire to play with reality, however, is highly responsive to social control, and many of us are taught early on to repress the impulse. As Mark Runco, associate professor of psychology at California State University at Fullerton and the founder of the new *Creativity Research Journal*, says, "We put children in groups and make them sit in desks and raise their hands before they talk. We put all the emphasis on conformity and order, then we wonder why they aren't being spontaneous and creative."

Adults too are expected to conform in any number of ways and in a variety of settings. Conformity, after all, creates a sense of order and offers the reassurance of the familiar. But to free one's natural creative impulses, it is necessary, to some extent, to resist the pressure to march in step with the world. Begin small, suggests Richards. "Virtually nothing you do can't be done in a slightly different, slightly better way. This has nothing to do with so-called creative pursuits but simply with breaking with your own mind-sets and trying an original way of doing some habitual task. Simply defer judgment on yourself for a little while and try something new. Remember,

VISUAL THINKING

"Express Yourself!"

● Our creative talents can be expressed in virtually every area of our lives. How is the woman in the photo expressing herself creatively? What are some of your favorite activities in which you are able to express your unique personality in innovative ways?

the essence of life is not getting things right, but taking risks, making mistakes, getting things *wrong*."

But it also must be recognized that the creative life is to some degree, and on some occasions, a solitary one. Psycholinguist Vera John-Steiner, author of *Notebooks of the Mind: Explorations of Thinking*, is one of many creativity researchers who believe that a prerequisite for creative success is "intensity of preoccupation, being pulled into your activity to such an extent that you forget it's dinnertime." Such concentration, John-Steiner believes, is part of our "natural creative bent," but we learn to ignore it because of a fear that it will isolate us from others. To John-Steiner, however, this fear is misplaced. Creative thought, she has written, is a "search for meaning," a way to connect our inner sense of being with some aspect of the world that preoccupies us. And she believes that only by linking these two aspects of reality — the inner and the outer — can we gain "some sense of being in control of life."

Avoiding the Myths

David Perkins, co-director of Project Zero at the Harvard Graduate School of Education, asks in *The Mind's Best Work*, "When you have it — creativity, that is — what do you have?" The very impalpability of the subject means that often creativity can be known only by its products. Indeed, the most common way the researchers define creativity is by saying it is whatever produces something that is: a. original; b. adaptive (i.e., useful); c. meaningful to others. But because we don't understand its genesis, we're often blocked or intimidated by the myths that surround and distort this mercurial subject.

One of these myths is, in Perkins's words, that creativity is "a kind of 'stuff' that the creative person has and uses to do creative things, never mind other factors." This bit of folk wisdom, that creativity is a sort of intangible psychic organ — happily present in some and absent in others — so annoys Perkins that he would like to abolish the word itself.

Another prevalent myth about creativity is that it is restricted to those who are "geniuses" — that is, people with inordinately high IQs. Ironically, this has been discredited by a study begun by Stanford psychologist Lewis Terman, the man who adapted the original French IQ test for America. In the early 1920s, Terman had California schoolteachers choose 1,528 "genius" schoolchildren (those with an IQ above 135), whose lives were then tracked year after year. After six decades, researchers found that the putative geniuses, by and large, did well in life. They entered the professions in large numbers and led stable, prosperous lives. But very few made notable creative contributions to society, and none did extraordinary creative work.

According to Dean Simonton, professor of psychology at the University of California at Davis and the author of *Genius, Creativity and Leadership* and *Scientific Genius*, "There just isn't any correlation between creativity and IQ. The average college graduate has an IQ of about 120, and this is high enough to write novels, do scientific research, or any other kind of creative work."

A third myth, voiced eons ago by Socrates, lifts creativity out of our own lives altogether into a mystical realm that makes it all but unapproachable. In this view, the creative individual is a kind of oracle, the passive conduit or channel chosen by God, or the tribal ancestors, or the muse, to communicate sacred knowledge.

Although there *are* extraordinary examples of creativity, for which the only explanation seems to be supernatural intervention (Mozart, the story goes, wrote the overture to *Don Giovanni* in only a few hours, after a virtually sleepless night and without revision), by and large, creativity begins with a long and intensive apprenticeship.

Psychologist Howard Gruber believes that it takes at least 10 years of immersion in a given domain before an eminent creator is likely to be able to make a distinctive mark. Einstein, for example, who is popularly thought to have doodled out the theory of relativity at age 26 in his spare time, was in fact compulsively engaged in thinking about the problem at least from the age of 16.

Finally, many who despair of ever being creative do so because they tried once and failed, as though the truly creative always succeed. In fact, just the opposite is true, says Dean Simonton. He sees genius, in a sense, as inseparable from failure. "Great geniuses make tons of mistakes," he says. "They generate lots of ideas and they accept being wrong. They have a kind of internal fortress that allows them to fail and just keep going. Look at Edison. He held over 1,000 patents, but most of them are not only forgotten, they weren't worth much to begin with."

Mindlessness Versus Mindfulness

"Each of us desires to share with others our vision of the world, only most of us have been taught that it's wrong to do things differently or look at things differently," says John Briggs. "We lose confidence in ourselves and begin to look at reality only in terms of the categories by which society orders it."

This is the state of routinized conformity and passive learning that Harvard professor of psychology Ellen Langer calls, appropriately enough, mindlessness. For it is the state of denying the perceptions and promptings of our own minds, our individual selves. Langer and her colleagues' extensive research over the past 15 years has shown that when we act mindlessly, we behave automatically and limit our capacity for creative response. Mired down in a numbing daily routine, we may virtually relinquish our capacity for independent thought and action.

By contrast, Langer refers to a life in which we use our affective, responsive, perceptive faculties as "mindful." When we are mindful, her research has shown, we avoid rigid, reflexive behavior in favor of a more improvisational and intuitive response to life. We notice and feel the world around us and then act in accordance with our feelings. "Many, if not all, of the qualities that make up a mindful attitude are characteristic of creative people," Langer writes in her new book, *Mindfulness*. "Those who can free themselves of mindsets, open themselves to new information and surprise, play with perspective and context, and focus on process rather than outcome are likely to be creative, whether they are scientists, artists, or cooks."

Much of Langer's research has demonstrated the vital relationship between creativity and uncertainty, or conditionality. For instance, in one experiment, Langer and Alison Piper introduced a collection of objects to one group of people by saying, "This is a hair dryer," and "This is a dog's chew toy," and so on. Another group was told "This *could be* a hair dryer," and "This *could be* a dog's chew toy." Later, the experimenters for both groups invented a need for an eraser, but only those people who had been conditionally introduced to the objects thought to use the dog's toy in this new way.

The intuitive understanding that a single thing is, or could be, many things, depending on how you look at it, is at the heart of the attitude Langer calls mindfulness. But can such an amorphous state be cultivated? Langer believes that it can, by consciously discarding the idea that any given moment of your day is fixed in its form. "I teach people to 'componentize' their lives into smaller pieces," she says. "In the morning, instead of mindlessly downing your orange juice, *taste it*. Is it what you want? Try something else if it isn't. When you walk to work, turn left instead of right. You'll notice the street you're on, the buildings and the weather. Mindfulness, like creativity, is nothing more than a return to who you are. By minding your responses to the world, you will come to know yourself again. How you feel. What you want. What you want to do."

Creating the Right Atmosphere

Understanding the genesis of creativity, going beyond the myths to understand your creative potential, and recognizing your ability to break free of old ways of thinking are the three initial steps to a more creative life. The fourth is finding ways to work that encourage personal commitment and expressiveness.

Letting employees learn what they want to do has never been a very high priority in the workplace. There, the dominant regulation has always been, "Do what you are told."

Today, however, economic realities are providing a new impetus for change. The pressure on American businesses to become more productive and innovative has made creative thinking a hot commodity in the business community. But innovation, business is now learning, is likely to be found wherever bright and eager people *think* they can find it. And some people are looking in curious places.

Financier Wayne Silby, for example, founded the Calvert Group of funds, which today manages billions of dollars in assets. Silby, whose business card at one point read Chief Daydreamer, occasionally retreats for inspiration to a sensory deprivation tank, where he floats in warm water sealed off from light and sound. "I went into the tank during a time when the government was changing money-market deposit regulations, and I needed to think how to compete with banks. Floating in the tank I got the idea of joining them instead. We wound up creating an $800-million program. Often we already have answers to our problems, but we don't quiet ourselves enough to see the solutions bubbling just below the surface." Those solutions will stay submerged, he says, "unless you create a culture that encourages creative approaches, where it's OK to have bad ideas."

Toward this goal, many companies have turned to creativity consultants, like Synectics, Inc., in Cambridge, MA. Half the battle, according to Synectics facilitator Jeff Mauzy, is to get the clients to relax and accept that they are in a safe place where the cutthroat rules of the workplace don't apply, so they can allow themselves to exercise their creative potential in group idea sessions.

Pamela Webb Moore, director of naming services (she helps companies figure out good names for their products) at Synectics, agrees. One technique she uses to limber up the minds of tightly focused corporate managers is "sleight of head." While working on a particular problem, she'll ask clients to pretend to work on something else. In one real-life example, a Synectics-trained facilitator took a group of product-development and marketing managers from the Etonic shoe corporation on an "excursion," a conscious walk away from the problem — in this case, to come up with a new kind of tennis shoe.

The facilitator asked the Etonic people to imagine they were at their favorite vacation spot. "One guy," Moore says, "was on a tropical island, walking on the beach in his bare feet. He described how wonderful the water and sand felt on his feet, and he said, 'I wish we could play tennis barefoot.' The whole thing would have stopped right there if somebody had complained that while his colleague was wandering around barefoot, they were supposed to come up with a *shoe*. Instead, one of the marketing people there was intrigued, and the whole group decided to go off to play tennis barefoot on a rented court at 10 at night."

While the Etonic people played tennis, the facilitator listed everything they said about how it felt. The next morning, the group looked at her assembled list of comments, and they realized that what they liked about playing barefoot was the lightness of being without shoes, and the ability to pivot easily on both the ball of the foot and the heel. Nine months later, the company produced an extremely light shoe called the Catalyst, which featured an innovative two-piece sole that made it easier for players to pivot.

The Payoff

In *The Courage to Create*, Rollo May wrote that for much of [the twentieth] century, researchers had avoided the subject of creativity because they perceived it as "unscientific, mysterious, disturbing and too corruptive of the scientific training of graduate students." But today researchers are coming to see that creativity, at once fugitive and ubiquitous, is the mark of human nature itself.

Whether in business or the arts, politics or personal relationships, creativity involves "going beyond the information given" to create or reveal something new in the world. And almost invariably, when the mind exercises its creative muscle, it also generates a sense of pleasure. The feeling may be powerfully mystical, as it is for New York artist Rhonda Zwillinger, whose embellished artwork appeared in the film *Slaves of New York*. Zwillinger reports, "There are times when I'm working and it is almost as though I'm a vessel and there is a force operating through me. It is the closest I come to having a religious experience." The creative experience may also be quiet and full of wonder, as it was for Isaac Newton, who compared his lifetime of creative effort to "a boy playing on the seashore and diverting himself and then finding a smoother pebble or prettier shell than ordinary, while the greater ocean of truth lay all undiscovered before me."

But whatever the specific sensation, creativity always carries with it a powerful sense of the mind working at the peak of its ability. Creativity truly is, as David Perkins calls it, the mind's best work, its finest effort. We may never know exactly how the brain does it, but we can feel that it is exactly what the brain was meant to do.

Aha!

Questions for Analysis

1. According to the authors, "Creativity . . . is the search for the elusive 'Aha,' that moment of insight when one sees the world, or a problem, or an idea, in a new way." Describe an "aha" moment that you have had recently, detailing the origin of your innovative idea and how you implemented it.

2. Identify some of the influences in your life that have inhibited your creative development, including the "myths" about creativity that are described in the article.

3. Using the ideas contained in this chapter and in this article, identify some of the strategies that you intend to use in order to become more creative in your life: for example, becoming more "mindful," destroying the "voice of criticism," and creating an atmosphere more conducive to creativity.

Final Thoughts

The first line of this chapter stated, "Thinking is the extraordinary process we use every waking moment to make sense of our world and our lives." Throughout this chapter we have explored the different ways our thinking enables us to make sense of the world by working toward goals, making decisions, and living creatively. Of course, our thinking helps us make sense of the world in other ways as well. When we attend a concert, listen to a lecture, or try to understand someone's behavior, it is our thinking that enables us to figure out what is happening. In fact, these attempts to make sense of what is happening are going on all the time in our lives, and they represent the heart of the thinking process.

If we review the different ways of thinking we have explored in this chapter, we can reach several conclusions about thinking:

- Thinking is directed toward a purpose. When we think, it is usually for a purpose — to reach a goal, make a decision, or analyze an issue.

- Thinking is an organized process. When we think effectively, there is usually an order or organization to our thinking. For each of the thinking activities we explored, we saw that there are certain steps or approaches to take that help us reach goals, make decisions, and live creatively.

We can put together these conclusions about thinking to form a working definition of the term.

> **thinking** *A purposeful, organized cognitive process that we use to understand the world and make informed decisions.*

Thinking develops with use over a lifetime, and we can improve our thinking in an organized and systematic way by following these steps:

- Carefully examining our thinking process and the thinking process of others. In this chapter we have explored various ways in which our thinking works. By focusing our attention on these (and other) thinking approaches and strategies, we can learn to think more effectively.
- Practicing our thinking abilities. To improve our thinking, we actually have to think for ourselves, to explore and make sense of thinking situations by using our thinking abilities. Although it is important to read about thinking and learn how other people think, there is no substitute for actually doing it ourselves.

Examining critical thinking and creative thinking is a rich and complex enterprise. These two dimensions of the thinking process are so tightly interwoven that both must be addressed together in order to understand them individually. For example, you can use your creative thinking abilities to visualize your ideal future. With this idea as a starting point, you can then use your critical thinking abilities to refine your idea and research existing opportunities. Once a clear goal is established, you can use your creative thinking abilities to generate possible ideas for achieving this goal while your critical thinking abilities will help you evaluate your various options and devise a practical, organized plan.

It is apparent that creative thinking and critical thinking work as partners to produce productive and effective thinking, enabling us to make informed decisions and lead successful lives. As this text unfolds, you will be given the opportunity to become familiar with both of these powerful forms of thought as you develop your abilities to think both critically and creatively.

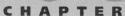

CHAPTER 2 Thinking Critically

Carefully Exploring Situations with Questions

Thinking Independently

Viewing Situations from Different Perspectives

Supporting Diverse Perspectives with Reasons and Evidence

Thinking Critically

Carefully exploring the thinking process to clarify our understanding and make more intelligent decisions.

Thinking Actively

Analyzing Issues

Discussing Ideas in an Organized Way

Becoming a Critical Thinker

47

In ancient Greece, most advanced students studied philosophy in order to achieve "wisdom." (The term *philosophy* in Greek means "lover of wisdom.") In today's world, many college students are hoping through their studies to become the modern-day equivalent: informed, *critical thinkers*. A critical thinker is someone who has developed a knowledgeable understanding of our complex world, a thoughtful perspective on important ideas and timely issues, the capacity for penetrating insight and intelligent judgment, and sophisticated thinking and language abilities.

The word *critical* comes from the Greek word for "critic" (*kritikos*), which means "to question, to make sense of, to be able to analyze." It is by questioning, making sense of situations, and analyzing issues that we examine our thinking and the thinking of others. These critical activities aid us in reaching the best possible conclusions and decisions. The word *critical* is also related to the word *criticize,* which means "to question and evaluate." Unfortunately, the ability to criticize is often only used destructively, to tear down someone else's thinking. Criticism, however, can also be *constructive* — analyzing for the purpose of developing a better understanding of what is going on. We will engage in constructive criticism as we develop our ability to think critically.

Thinking is the way you make sense of the world; thinking critically is thinking about your thinking so that you can clarify and improve it. In this chapter you will explore ways to examine your thinking so that you can develop it to the fullest extent possible. That is, you will discover how to *think critically.*

thinking critically *Carefully exploring the thinking process to clarify our understanding and make more intelligent decisions.*

Becoming a critical thinker transforms you in positive ways by enabling you to become an expert learner, view the world clearly, and make productive choices as you shape your life. Critical thinking is not simply one way of thinking; it is a total approach to understanding how you make sense of a world that includes many parts.

The best way to develop a clear and concrete idea of the critical thinker you want to become is to think about people you have known who can serve as critical thinking models. They appear throughout humanity. The Greek philosopher Socrates was in many ways the original critical thinker for whom we have a historical record, and the depth and clarity of his thinking is immortalized in the *Dialogues* recorded by Plato, his student. As a renowned teacher in his native city of Athens, Socrates had created his own school and spent decades teaching young people how to analyze important issues through dialectical questioning — an approach that became known as the Socratic Method. At the age of seventy, he was deemed a dangerous troublemaker by the ruling politicians. Based on his teachings, students were asking embarrassing questions; in particular, they were questioning the politicians' authority and threatening their political careers. The politicians gave Socrates an ultimatum: Either leave the city where he had spent his entire life, never to return, or be put to death. Rather than leave his beloved Athens and the life he had created, Socrates chose death. Surrounded by his family and friends, he calmly drank a cup of hemlock-laced tea. He reasoned that leaving Athens would violate the intellectual integrity upon which he had built his life and had taught his students to uphold. Instead of sacrificing his beliefs, he ended his life, concluding with the words: *"Now it is time for us to part, I to die and you to live. Whether life or death is better is known to God, and to God only."*

Today especially, we all need to become philosophers, to develop a philosophical framework. Critical thinking is a modern reworking of a philosophical perspective.

Who would *you* identify as expert critical thinkers? To qualify, the people you identify should have lively, energetic minds. Specifically, they should be:

- *Open-minded:* In discussions they listen carefully to every viewpoint, evaluating each perspective carefully and fairly.

- *Knowledgeable:* When they offer an opinion, it's always based on facts or evidence. On the other hand, if they lack knowledge of the subject, they acknowledge this.

- *Mentally active:* They take initiative and actively use their intelligence to confront problems and meet challenges instead of simply responding passively to events.

- *Curious:* They explore situations with probing questions that penetrate beneath the surface of issues instead of being satisfied with superficial explanations.

- *Independent thinkers:* They are not afraid to disagree with the group opinion. They develop well-supported beliefs through thoughtful analysis instead of uncritically "borrowing" the beliefs of others or simply going along with the crowd.

VISUAL THINKING

"Now It Is Time for Us to Part, I to Die and You to Live . . ."

● What can you tell about Socrates' reaction to his impending death based on this painting by Jean Louis David? What is the reaction of his family and friends? If you were a close friend of Socrates, what would be your reaction? Why?

- *Skilled discussants:* They are able to discuss ideas in an organized and intelligent way. Even when the issues are controversial, they listen carefully to opposing viewpoints and respond thoughtfully.
- *Insightful:* They are able to get to the heart of the issue or problem. While others may be distracted by details, they are able to zero in on the essence, seeing the "forest" as well as the "trees."
- *Self-aware:* They are aware of their own biases and are quick to point them out and take them into consideration when analyzing a situation.
- *Creative:* They can break out of established patterns of thinking and approach situations from innovative directions.
- *Passionate:* They have a passion for understanding and are always striving to see issues and problems with more clarity.

THINKING ACTIVITY 2.1

WHO IS A CRITICAL THINKER?

Think about people you know whom you admire as expert thinkers and list some of the qualities these people exhibit that you believe qualify them as "critical thinkers." For each critical thinking quality, write down a brief example involving the person. Identifying such people will help you visualize the kind of people you'd like to emulate. As you think your way through this book, you will be creating a *portrait* of the kind of critical thinker you are striving to become, a *blueprint* you can use to direct your development and chart your progress.

This chapter explores some of the cognitive abilities and attitudes that characterize critical thinkers, including the following:

- Thinking actively
- Carefully exploring situations with questions
- Thinking independently
- Viewing situations from different perspectives
- Supporting diverse perspectives with reasons and evidence
- Discussing ideas in an organized way

The remaining chapters in the book examine additional thinking abilities that you will need to develop in order to become a fully mature critical thinker.

Thinking Actively

When you think critically, you are actively using your intelligence, knowledge, and abilities to deal effectively with life's situations. When you think actively, you are

- Getting involved in potentially useful projects and activities instead of remaining disengaged
- Taking initiative in making decisions on your own instead of waiting passively to be told what to think or do
- Following through on your commitments instead of giving up when you encounter difficulties
- Taking responsibility for the consequences of your decisions rather than unjustifiably blaming others or events "beyond your control"

When you think actively, you are not just waiting for something to happen. You are engaged in the process of achieving goals, making decisions, and solving problems. When you react passively, you let events control you or permit others to do your thinking for you. Thinking critically requires that you think actively — not react passively — to deal effectively with life's situations.

Influences on Your Thinking

As our minds grow and develop, we are exposed to influences that encourage us to think actively. We also, however, have many experiences that encourage us to think passively. For example, some analysts believe that when people, especially children, spend much of their time watching television, they are being influenced to think passively, thus inhibiting their intellectual growth. Listed here are some of the influences we experience in our lives along with space for you to add your own influences. As you read through the list, place an *A* next to those items you believe in general influence you to think *actively* and a *P* next to those you consider to be generally *passive* influences.

Activities:

Reading books
Writing
Watching television
Dancing
Drawing/painting
Playing video games
Playing sports
Listening to music

People:

Family members
Friends
Employers
Advertisers
School/college teachers
Police officers
Religious leaders
Politicians

THINKING ACTIVITY 2.2

Influences on Our Thinking

All of us are subject to powerful influences on our thinking, influences that we are often unaware of. For example, advertisers spend billions of dollars to manipulate our thinking in ways that are complex and subtle. For this exercise, choose one of the following tasks:

1. Watch some commercials, with several other class members if possible, and discuss the techniques each advertiser is using to shape your thinking. Analyze with the other viewers how each of the elements in a commercial — images, language, music — affects an audience. Pay particular

attention to the symbolic associations of various images and words, and identify the powerful emotions that these associations elicit. Why are the commercials effective? What influential roles do commercials play in our culture as a whole?

2. Select a commercial web site and do an in-depth analysis of it. Explain how each of the site's elements — design, content, use of music or video, and links — works to influence our thinking.

Of course, in many cases people and activities can act as both active and passive influences, depending on the specifics of situations and our individual responses. For example, consider employers. If we are performing a routine, repetitive job, work tends to encourage passive, uncreative thinking. We are also influenced to think passively if our employer gives us detailed instructions for performing every task, instructions that permit no exception or deviation. On the other hand, when our employer gives us general areas of responsibility within which we are expected to make thoughtful and creative decisions, then we are being stimulated to think actively and independently.

Becoming an Active Learner

Active thinking is one of the keys to effective learning. Each of us has our own knowledge framework that we use to make sense of the world, a framework that incorporates all that we have learned in our lives. When we learn something new, we have to find ways to integrate this new information or skill into our existing knowledge framework. For example, if one of your professors is presenting material on Sigmund Freud's concept of the unconscious or the role of Heisenberg's uncertainty principle in the theory of quantum mechanics, you need to find ways to relate these new ideas to things you already know in order to make this new information "your own." How do you do this? By actively using your mind to integrate new information into your existing knowledge framework, thereby expanding the framework to include this new information.

For example, when your professor provides a detailed analysis of Freud's concept of the unconscious, you use your mind to call up what you know about Freud's theory of personality and what you know of the concept of the unconscious. You then try to connect this new information to what you already know, integrating it into your expanding knowledge framework. In a way, learning is analogous to the activity of eating: You ingest food (*information*) in one form, actively transform it through digestion (*mental processing*), and then integrate the result into the ongoing functioning of your body.

Carefully Exploring Situations with Questions

Thinking critically involves actively using your thinking abilities to attack problems, meet challenges, and analyze issues. An important dimension of thinking actively is the ability to ask appropriate and penetrating questions. Active learners explore the learning situations they are involved in with questions that enable them to understand the material or task at hand and then integrate this new understanding into their knowledge framework. In contrast, passive learners rarely ask questions. Instead, they try to absorb information like sponges, memorizing what is expected and then regurgitating what they memorized on tests and quizzes.

Questions can be classified in terms of the ways that people organize and interpret information. We can identify six such categories of questions, a schema that was first suggested by the educator Benjamin Bloom:

1. Fact   **4.** Synthesis

2. Interpretation   **5.** Evaluation

3. Analysis   **6.** Application

Active learners are able to ask appropriate questions from all of these categories. These various types of questions are closely interrelated, and an effective thinker is able to use them in a productive relation to one another. Also, these categories of questions are very general and at times overlap with one another. This means that a given question may fall into more than one of the six categories of questions. Following is a summary of the six categories of questions. Sample forms of questions from each category can be found on the companion web site.

1. *Questions of Fact:* Questions of fact seek to determine the basic information of a situation: who, what, when, where, how. These questions seek information that is relatively straightforward and objective.

2. *Questions of Interpretation:* Questions of interpretation seek to select and organize facts and ideas, discovering the relationships between them. Examples of such relationships include the following:
   - *Chronological relationships:* relating things in time sequence
   - *Process relationships:* relating aspects of growth, development, or change
   - *Comparison/contrast relationships:* relating things in terms of their similar/different features
   - *Causal relationships:* relating events in terms of the way some events are responsible for bringing about other events

3. *Questions of Analysis:* Questions of analysis seek to separate an entire process or situation into its component parts and to understand the relation of these parts to the whole. These questions attempt to classify various elements, outline component structures, articulate various possibilities, and clarify the reasoning being presented.

4. *Questions of Synthesis:* Questions of synthesis have as their goal combining ideas to form a new whole or come to a conclusion, making inferences about future events, creating solutions, and designing plans of action.

5. *Questions of Evaluation:* The aim of evaluation questions is to help us make informed judgments and decisions by determining the relative value, truth, or reliability of things. The process of evaluation involves identifying the criteria or standards we are using and then determining to what extent the things in common meet those standards.

6. *Questions of Application:* The aim of application questions is to help us take the knowledge or concepts we have gained in one situation and apply them to other situations.

Mastering these forms of questions and using them appropriately will serve as powerful tools in your learning process.

Becoming an expert questioner is an ongoing project. When you are talking to people about even everyday topics, get in the habit of asking questions from all of the different categories. Similarly, when you are attending class, taking notes, or reading assignments, make a practice of asking — and trying to answer — appropriate questions.

As children, we were natural questioners, but this questioning attitude was often discouraged when we entered the school system. Often we were given the message, in subtle and not so subtle ways, that "schools have the questions; your job is to learn the answers." The educator Neil Postman has said: "Children enter schools as question marks and they leave as periods." In order for us to become critical thinkers and effective learners, we have to become question marks again.

THINKING ACTIVITY 2.3

Analyzing a Complex Issue

Review the following decision-making situation (based on an incident that happened in Springfield, Missouri), and then critically examine it by posing questions from each of the six categories we have considered in this section:

1. Fact
2. Interpretation
3. Analysis

4. Synthesis
5. Evaluation
6. Application

Imagine that you are a member of a student group at your college that has decided to stage the controversial play *The Normal Heart* by Larry Kramer. The play is based on the lives of real people and dramatizes their experiences in the early stages of the AIDS epidemic. It focuses on their efforts to publicize the horrific nature of this disease and to secure funding from a reluctant federal government to find a cure. The play is considered controversial because of its exclusive focus on the subject of AIDS, its explicit homosexual themes, and the large amount of profanity contained in the script. After lengthy discussion, however, your student group has decided that the educational and moral benefits of the play render it a valuable contribution to the life of the college.

While the play is in rehearsal, a local politician seizes upon it as an issue and mounts a political and public relations campaign against it. She distributes selected excerpts of the play to newspapers, religious groups, and civic organizations. She also introduces a bill in the state legislature to withdraw state funding for the college if the play is performed. The play creates a firestorm of controversy, replete with local and national news reports, editorials, and impassioned speeches for and against it. Everyone associated with the play is subjected to verbal harassment, threats, crank phone calls, and hate mail. The firestorm explodes when the house of one of the key spokespersons for the play is burned to the ground. The director and actors go into hiding for their safety, rehearsing in secret and moving from hotel to hotel.

Your student group has just convened to decide what course of action to take. Analyze the situation using the six types of questions listed previously and then conclude with your decision and the reasons that support your decision.

◎ Thinking Independently

Answer the following questions with *yes, no,* or *not sure,* based on what you believe to be true.

1. Is the earth flat?
2. Is there a God?
3. Is abortion wrong?

4. Have alien life forms visited the earth?
5. Should men be the breadwinners and women the homemakers?

Your responses to these questions reveal aspects of the way your mind works. How did you arrive at these conclusions? Your views on these and many other issues probably had their beginnings with your family. As we grow up, we learn how to think, feel, and behave in various situations. In addition to our parents, our "teachers" include our brothers and sisters, friends, religious leaders, schoolteachers, books, and television. Most of what we learn we absorb without even being aware of the process. Many of your ideas about the issues raised in the preceding questions were most likely shaped by the experiences you had growing up.

As a result of our ongoing experiences, however, our minds — and our thinking — continue to mature. Instead of simply accepting the views of others, we use this standard to make our decisions: Are there good reasons or evidence that support this thinking? If there are good reasons, we can actively decide to adopt these ideas. If they do not make sense, we can modify or reject them.

How do you know when you have examined and adopted ideas yourself instead of simply borrowing them from others? One indication of having thought through your ideas is being able to explain *why* you believe them, explaining the reasons that led you to these conclusions.

For each of the views you expressed at the beginning of this section, explain how you arrived at it and give the reasons and evidence that you believe support it.

Example: Is the earth flat?

Explanation: I was taught by my parents and in school that the earth was round.

Reasons/Evidence:

a. *Authorities:* My parents and teachers taught me this.

b. *References:* I read about this in science textbooks.

c. *Factual evidence:* I have seen a sequence of photographs taken from outer space that show the earth as a globe.

d. *Personal experience:* When I flew across the country, I could see the horizon line changing.

Of course, not all reasons and evidence are equally strong or accurate. For example, before the fifteenth century the common belief that the earth was flat was supported by the following reasons and evidence:

- *Authorities:* Educational and religious authorities taught people the earth was flat.

- *References:* The written opinions of scientific experts supported belief in a flat earth.
- *Factual evidence:* No person had ever circumnavigated the earth.
- *Personal experience:* From a normal vantage point, the earth looks flat.

Many considerations go into evaluating the strengths and accuracy of reasons and evidence. Let's examine some basic questions that critical thinkers automatically consider when evaluating reasons and evidence by completing Thinking Activity 2.4.

THINKING ACTIVITY 2.4

Evaluating Your Beliefs

Evaluate the strengths and accuracy of the reasons and evidence you identified to support your beliefs on the five issues by addressing questions such as the following:

- *Authorities:* Are the authorities knowledgeable in this area? Are they reliable? Have they ever given inaccurate information? Do other authorities disagree with them?
- *References:* What are the credentials of the authors? Are there other authors who disagree with their opinions? On what reasons and evidence do the authors base their opinions?
- *Factual evidence:* What are the source and foundation of the evidence? Can the evidence be interpreted differently? Does the evidence support the conclusion?
- *Personal experience:* What were the circumstances under which the experiences took place? Were distortions or mistakes in perception possible? Have other people had either similar or conflicting experiences? Are there other explanations for the experience?

In critically evaluating beliefs, it makes sense to accept traditional beliefs insofar as they enrich and sharpen our thinking. If they don't stand up to critical scrutiny, then we need to have the courage to think for ourselves, even if it means rejecting "conventional wisdom."

Analogously, thinking for yourself doesn't always mean doing exactly what you want to; it may mean becoming aware of the social guidelines and expectations of a given situation and then making an informed decision about what is in your best interests. Thinking for yourself often involves balancing your view of things against those of others, integrating yourself into social structures without sacrificing your independence or personal autonomy.

Viewing Situations from Different Perspectives

Although it is important to think for yourself, others may have good ideas from which you can learn and benefit. A critical thinker is willing to listen to and examine carefully other views and new ideas.

As children we understand the world from only our own point of view. As we grow, we come into contact with people who have different viewpoints and begin to realize that our viewpoint is often inadequate, we are frequently mistaken, and our perspective is only one of many. If we are going to learn and develop, we must try to understand and appreciate the viewpoints of others. For example, consider the following situation:

> Imagine that you have been employed at a new job for the past six months. Although you enjoy the challenge of your responsibilities and you are performing well, you find that you simply cannot complete all your work during office hours. To keep up, you have to work late, take work home, and even occasionally work on weekends. When you explain this to your employer, she says that although she is sorry that the job interferes with your personal life, it has to be done. She suggests that you view these sacrifices as an investment in your future and that you should try to work more efficiently. She reminds you that there are many people who would be happy to have your position.

1. Describe this situation from your employer's standpoint, identifying reasons that might support her views.
2. Describe some different approaches that you and your employer might take to help resolve this situation.

For most of the important issues and problems in your life, one viewpoint is simply not adequate to provide a full and satisfactory understanding. To increase and deepen your knowledge, you must seek *other perspectives* on the situations you are trying to understand. You can sometimes accomplish this by using your imagination to visualize other viewpoints. Usually, however, you need to seek actively (and *listen* to) the viewpoints of others. It is often very difficult for people to see things from points of view other than their own, and if you are not careful, you can make the mistake of thinking that the way you see

VISUAL THINKING

Thinking Independently

● What are the reasons that people too often get locked into passive, dependent ways of thinking? What strategies can we use to overcome these forces and think independently? Describe a time when you took an independent, and unpopular, stand on an issue. What was the experience like?

things is the way things really are. In addition to identifying with perspectives other than your own, you also have to work to understand the *reasons* that support these alternate viewpoints. This approach deepens your understanding of the issues and also stimulates you to evaluate critically your beliefs.

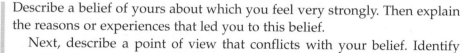

THINKING ACTIVITY 2.5

Analyzing a Belief from Different Perspectives

Describe a belief of yours about which you feel very strongly. Then explain the reasons or experiences that led you to this belief.

Next, describe a point of view that conflicts with your belief. Identify some of the reasons why someone might hold this belief. A sample student response to this activity can be found on the companion web site.

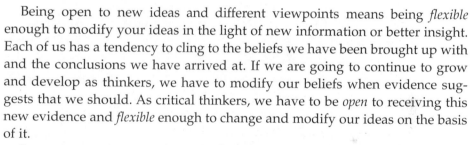

Being open to new ideas and different viewpoints means being *flexible* enough to modify your ideas in the light of new information or better insight. Each of us has a tendency to cling to the beliefs we have been brought up with and the conclusions we have arrived at. If we are going to continue to grow and develop as thinkers, we have to modify our beliefs when evidence suggests that we should. As critical thinkers, we have to be *open* to receiving this new evidence and *flexible* enough to change and modify our ideas on the basis of it.

In contrast to open and flexible thinking, *un*critical thinking tends to be one-sided and close-minded. People who think this way are convinced that they alone see things as they really are and that everyone who disagrees with them is wrong. The words we use to describe this type of person include "dogmatic," "subjective," and "egocentric." It is very difficult for such people to step outside their own viewpoints in order to see things from other people's perspectives.

THINKING ACTIVITY 2.6

Writing from Interactive Perspectives

Think of a well-known person, either historical (e.g., Socrates) or contemporary (e.g., Oprah Winfrey), and identify different perspectives from which that person can be viewed. For example, consider viewing Oprah Winfrey as

- pop culture icon
- a black activist
- a wealthy celebrity
- a self-help guru
- an actress

Next, select two perspectives from the ones you identified and, using research, provide an explanatory background for each perspective. Then, through investigative analysis, describe the interactive relationship between the two perspectives, the basis on which they interact, and the ways in which each supports the other. Finally, in a summary conclusion to your findings, assess the significance of the two perspectives for contemporary thought.*

Supporting Diverse Perspectives with Reasons and Evidence

When you are thinking critically, you can give good reasons to back up your ideas. It is not enough simply to take a position on an issue or make a claim; we have to *back up our views* with other information that we feel supports our position. There is an important distinction as well as relationship between *what* you believe and *why* you believe it.

If someone questions why you see an issue the way you do, you probably respond by giving reasons or arguments you feel support your belief. For example, consider the issue of whether using a cell phone while driving should be prohibited. As you try to make sense of this issue, you should attempt to identify not just the reasons that support your view but also the reasons that support other views. The following are reasons that support each view of this issue.

---

*This activity was developed by Frank Juszcyk.

"You Leave — I Was Here First!"

● Critical thinkers actively try to view issues from different perspectives. Why would someone take the position "Let's get rid of illegal immigrants in America?" How would native Americans view the person making that statement? What is your perspective on illegal immigrants in this country? Why?

Issue:

Cell phone use while driving should be prohibited.

SUPPORTING REASONS:

1. Studies show that using cell phones while driving increases accidents.

Cell phone use while driving should be permitted.

SUPPORTING REASONS:

1. Many people feel that cell phones are no more distracting than other common activities in cars.

Now see if you can identify additional supporting reasons for each of these views on cell phone use while driving.

SUPPORTING REASONS: SUPPORTING REASONS:

2.   **2.**

3.   **3.**

4.   **4.**

Seeing all sides of an issue combines two critical thinking abilities:

- Viewing issues from different perspectives
- Supporting diverse viewpoints with reasons and evidence

Combining these two abilities enables you not only to understand other sides of an issue but also to understand *why* these views are held.

THINKING ACTIVITY 2.7

Analyzing Different Sides of an Issue

For each of the following issues, identify reasons that support each side of the issue.

Issue:

1. Multiple-choice and true/false exams should be given in college-level courses.

Multiple-choice and true/false exams should not be given in college-level courses.

Issue:

2. Immigration quotas should be reduced.

Immigration quotas should be increased.

Issue:

3. The best way to deal with crime is to give long prison sentences.

Long prison sentences will not reduce crime.

Issue:

4. When a couple divorces, the children should choose the parent with whom they wish to live.

When a couple divorces, the court should decide all custody issues regarding the children.

THINKING ACTIVITY 2.8

Analyzing Different Perspectives

Working to see different perspectives is crucial in helping you get a more complete understanding of the ideas being expressed in the passages you are reading. Read each of the following passages and then do the following:

1. Identify the main idea of the passage.

2. List the reasons that support the main idea.

3. Develop another view of the main issue.

4. List the reasons that support the other view.

Additional passages for analysis can be found on the companion web site.

- In a letter that has stunned many leading fertility specialists, the acting head of their professional society's ethics committee says it is sometimes acceptable for couples to choose the sex of their children by selecting either male or female embryos and discarding the rest. The group, the American Society of Reproductive Medicine, establishes positions on ethical issues, and most clinics say they abide by them. One fertility specialist, Dr. Norbet Gleicher, whose group has nine centers and who had asked for the opinion, was quick to act on it. "We will offer it immediately," Dr. Gleicher said of the sex-selection method. "Frankly, we have a list of patients who asked for it." Couples would have to undergo *in vitro* fertilization, and then their embryos would be examined in the first few days when they consisted of just eight cells. Leading fertility specialists said they were taken aback by the new letter and could hardly believe its message. "What's the next step?" asked Dr. William Schoolcraft. "As we learn more about genetics, do we reject kids who do not have superior intelligence or who don't have the right color hair or eyes?" (*New York Times*, September 28, 2001).

- When Dr. Hassan Abbass, a Veterans Affairs Department surgeon, and his wife arrived at the airport to leave for vacation last May 24, they were pulled aside and forced to submit to a careful search before boarding the plane. They became one of thousands of Americans of Middle Eastern heritage who have complained that a secretive and side-scale "profiling" system sponsored by the government and aimed at preventing air terrorism has caused them to be unfairly selected for extra scrutiny at airports. "Profiling" of this type is being used more frequently in many areas of law-enforcement, raising fundamental questions of how a free society balances security fears with civil liberties and the desire to avoid offensive stereotyping (*New York Times,* August 11, 1997).

Discussing Ideas in an Organized Way

Thinking critically often takes place in a social context. Although every person has his or her own perspective on the world, no single viewpoint is adequate for making sense of complex issues, situations, or even people. As we will see in the chapters ahead, we each have our own "lenses" through which we view the world — filters that shape, influence, and often distort the way we see things. The best way to expand our thinking and compensate for the bias that we all have is to be open to the viewpoints of others and willing to listen and to exchange ideas with them. This process of give-and-take, of advancing our views and considering those of others, is known as discussion. When we participate in a *discussion,* we are not simply talking; we are exchanging and exploring our ideas in an organized way.

Unfortunately, our conversations with other people about important topics are too often not productive exchanges. They often degenerate into name calling, shouting matches, or worse. Consider the following dialogue:

PERSON A: A friend of mine sent a humorous e-mail in which he wrote about "killing the president." He wasn't serious, of course, but two days later the FBI showed up on his doorstep! This is no longer a free society — it's a fascist regime!

PERSON B: Your friend's an idiot and unpatriotic as well. You don't kid about killing the president. Your friend is lucky he didn't wind up in jail, where he deserves to be!

PERSON A: Since when is kidding around treason? With the way our freedoms are being stolen, we might as well be living in a dictatorship!

PERSON B: You're friend isn't the only idiot — you're an idiot, too! You don't deserve to live in America. It's attitudes like yours that make terrorist attacks possible, like those against the World Trade Center and the Pentagon.

PERSON A: You're calling me a terrorist? I can't talk to a fascist like you!

PERSON B: And I can't talk to an unpatriotic traitor like you. America: Love it or leave it! Good-bye and good riddance!

If we examine the dynamics of this dialogue, we can see that the two people here are not really

- Listening to each other
- Supporting their views with reasons and evidence
- Responding to the points being made
- Asking — and trying to answer — important questions
- Trying to increase their understanding rather than simply winning the argument

In short, the people in this exchange are not *discussing* their views; they are simply *expressing* them, and each is trying to influence the other person into agreeing. Contrast this first dialogue with the following one. Although it begins the same way, it quickly takes a much different direction.

PERSON A: A friend of mine sent a humorous e-mail in which he wrote about "killing the president." He wasn't serious, of course, but two days later the FBI showed up on his doorstep! This is no longer a free society — it's a fascist regime!

PERSON B: Your friend's an idiot and unpatriotic as well. You don't kid about killing the president. Your friend is lucky he didn't wind up in jail, where he deserves to be!

PERSON A: Since when is kidding around treason? With the way our freedoms are being stolen, we're living in a repressive dictatorship!

PERSON B: Don't you think it's inappropriate to be talking about killing the president, even if you are kidding? And why do you think we're living in a repressive dictatorship?

PERSON A: Well, you're probably right that e-mailing a message like this isn't very intelligent, particularly considering the leaders who have been assassinated — John F. Kennedy and Martin Luther King, for example — and the terrorist attacks that we have suffered. But the only way FBI agents could have known about the e-mail is if they are monitoring our private e-mails on an ongoing basis. Doesn't that concern you? It's like "Big Brother" is watching our every move and pouncing when we do something they think is wrong.

PERSON B: You're making a good point. It is a little unnerving to realize that our private conversations on the Internet may be monitored by the government. But doesn't it have to take measures like this in order to ensure we're safe? After all, remember the catastrophic attacks that destroyed the World Trade towers and part of the Pentagon, and the Oklahoma City bombing. If the government has to play the role of "Big Brother" to make sure we're safe, I think it's worth it.

PERSON A: I see what you're saying. But I think that the government has a tendency to go overboard if it's not held in check. Just consider the gigantic file the FBI compiled on Martin Luther King and other peaceful leaders, based on illegal wiretaps and covert surveillance.

PERSON B: I certainly don't agree with those types of activities against peaceful citizens. But what about people who are genuine threats? Don't we have to let the government do whatever's necessary to identify and arrest them? After all, threatening to kill the president is like telling airport personnel that you have a bomb in your suitcase — it's not funny, even if you're not serious.

PERSON A: You're right: It's important for the government to do what's necessary to make sure we're as safe as possible from terrorist threats. But we can't give it a blank check to read our e-mail, tap our phones, and infringe on our personal freedoms in other ways. After all, it's those freedoms that make America what it is.

PERSON B: Yes, I guess the goal is to strike the right balance between security and personal freedoms. How do we do that?

PERSON A: That's a very complicated question. Let's keep talking about it. Right now, though, I better get to class before my professor sends Big Brother to look for me!

How would you contrast the level of communication taking place in this dialogue with that in the first dialogue? What are the reasons for your conclusion?

Naturally, discussions are not always quite this organized and direct. Nevertheless, this second dialogue does provide a good model for what can take place in our everyday lives when we carefully explore an issue or a situation with someone else. Let us take a closer look at this discussion process.

Listening Carefully

Review the second dialogue and notice how each person in the discussion listens carefully to what the other person is saying and then tries to comment directly on what has just been said. When you are working hard at listening to others, you are trying to understand the point they are making and the reasons for it. This enables you to imagine yourself in their position and see things as they see them. Listening in this way often brings new ideas and different ways of viewing the situation to your attention that might never have occurred to you. An effective dialogue in this sense is like a game of tennis — you hit the ball to me, I return the ball to you, you return my return, and so on. The "ball" the discussants keep hitting back and forth is the subject they are gradually analyzing and exploring.

Supporting Views with Reasons and Evidence

Critical thinkers support their points of view with evidence and reasons and also develop an in-depth understanding of the evidence and reasons that support other viewpoints. Review the second dialogue and identify some of the reasons used by the participants to support their points of view. For example, Person B expresses the view that the government may have to be proactive in terms of identifying terrorists and ensuring our security, citing as a reason the horrific consequences of terrorist attacks. Person A responds with the concern that the government sometimes goes overboard in situations like this, citing as a reason the FBI's extensive surveillance of Martin Luther King.

Responding to the Points Being Made

When people engage in effective dialogue, they listen carefully to the people speaking and then respond directly to the points being made instead of simply trying to make their own points. In the second dialogue, Person B responds to Person A's concern that "'Big Brother' is watching our every move" with the acknowledgment that "It is a little unnerving to realize that our private conversations on the Internet may be monitored by the government" and also with the question "But doesn't it have to take measures like this in order to ensure we're safe?" When you respond directly to other people's views, and they to yours, you extend and deepen the explorations into the issues being discussed. Although people involved in the discussion may not ultimately agree, they should develop a more insightful understanding of the important issues and a greater appreciation of other viewpoints. Examine the second sample dialogue and notice how each person keeps responding to what the other is saying, creating an ongoing, interactive discussion.

Asking Questions

Asking questions is one of the driving forces in your discussions with others. You can explore a subject first by raising important questions and then by trying to answer them together. This questioning process gradually reveals the various reasons and evidence that support each of the different viewpoints involved. For example, although the two dialogues begin the same way, the second dialogue moves in a completely different direction from that of the first when Person A poses the question "Since when is kidding around treason?" Asking this question directs the discussion toward a mutual exploration of the issues and away from angry confrontation. Identify some of the other key questions that are posed in the dialogue.

A guide to the various types of questions that can be posed in exploring issues and situations begins on page 54 of this chapter.

Increasing Understanding

When we discuss subjects with others, we often begin by disagreeing. In an effective discussion, however, our main purpose should be to develop our understanding — not to prove ourselves right at any cost. If we are determined to prove that we are right, then we are likely not to be open to the ideas of others and to viewpoints that differ from our own.

Imagine that instead of ending, the second dialogue had continued for a while. Create responses that expand the exploration of the ideas being examined, and be sure to keep the guidelines for effective discussions in mind as you continue the dialogue.

PERSON B: Yes, I guess the goal is to strike the right balance between security and personal freedoms. But how do we do that? (etc.)

THINKING ACTIVITY 2.9

Creating a Dialogue

Select an important social issue and write a dialogue that analyzes the issue from two different perspectives. As you write your dialogue, keep in mind the qualities of effective discussion: listening carefully to the other person and trying to comment directly on what has been said, asking and trying to answer important questions about the subject, and trying to develop a fuller understanding of the subject instead of simply trying to prove yourself right.

After completing your dialogue, read it to the class (with a classmate as a partner). Analyze the class's dialogues by using the criteria for effective discussions that we have examined. Sample student dialogues can be found on the companion web site.

Becoming a Critical Thinker

In this chapter we have discovered that critical thinking is a total approach to the way we make sense of the world that involves an integrated set of thinking abilities and attitudes:

- *Thinking actively* by using our intelligence, knowledge, and skills to question, explore, and deal effectively with ourselves, others, and life's situations
- *Carefully exploring situations* by asking — and trying to answer — relevant questions
- *Thinking independently* by carefully examining various ideas and arriving at our own thoughtful conclusions
- *Viewing situations from different perspectives* to develop an in-depth, comprehensive understanding and *supporting viewpoints with reasons and evidence* to arrive at thoughtful, well-substantiated conclusions
- *Discussing ideas in an organized way* in order to exchange and explore ideas with others

These critical thinking qualities are a combination of cognitive abilities, basic attitudes, and thinking strategies that enable you to clarify and improve your understanding of the world. Becoming a critical thinker is a lifelong process. Developing the thinking abilities needed to understand the complex world you live in and to make informed decisions requires ongoing analysis, reflection, and practice. Critical thinkers are better equipped to deal with the difficult challenges that life poses: to solve problems, to establish and achieve goals, and to make sense of complex issues.

Creating a Thinking World

Fulfilling your potential as a critical thinker and living a meaningful life means developing productive relationships with others. Critical thinkers are people who consistently make the effort to view situations from others' perspectives, to think — and feel — empathetically within their own point of view. This empathetic understanding is the basis for developing healthy relationships and an in-depth understanding of the world. Let's imagine a world in which everyone was committed to the critical thinking ideals of thoughtful reflection and empathetic understanding. What would such a world be like?

It would be a world in which people would not act rashly or speak foolishly without thinking. They would be reflective, carefully considering different points of view and thinking deeply about important issues. People would listen to what you had to say and would treat your views with respect, and if they disagreed with your point of view, they would explain why by providing intelligent reasons. At work, your boss would provide you with personal support and opportunities to take initiative, guiding you when you made mistakes, encouraging you to excel, and awarding you full credit for your accomplishments. Your relationships with family members would always be loving and honest as you worked together harmoniously for common purposes. Your relationship with your romantic partner would be intimate and supportive, expressing deep commitment and emotional honesty. Parents would nurture their children with unconditional love and raise them to respect the needs of others. People of all ages would display enlightened values, empathizing with the needs of others and trying to help those less fortunate. Lying, cheating, stealing, personal violence: None of these would exist; instead, they would be replaced by kindness, generosity, consideration, and goodwill. This would be a world filled with open-minded people who would welcome diverse ideas, customs, and personal differences. Racism, sexism, ageism, and all other forms of discrimination would be things of the past as all people would be treated with tolerance and consideration.

On a social level, all people would see themselves as members of the same community, with a responsibility for the well-being of all members, not just themselves. Everyone would work together to create a better life for all. Wise and principled political leaders would be elected by a thoughtful citizenry, and they would govern with insight, honesty, and compassion. Children would be educated in a system that encouraged their individual talents and respected their unique value. Television shows would be designed to stimulate thinking and expand understanding as well as to entertain. People on talk shows would express thoughtful, articulate opinions, never stooping to superficial analyses or personal insults. On the road, people would drive with safety and consideration, never letting their anger or desire to move ahead more quickly take hold of them at the expense of others. When people did make mistakes, they would always accept responsibility, never trying to blame others for their own errors. Those who violated the law would be tried by juries who were astute thinkers, weighing the evidence judiciously and reaching fair-minded and well-supported verdicts.

On a personal level, you would be confident of your place in society and taken seriously by others who respected your special qualities. People would treat you with consideration, and you would reciprocate, with feelings of goodwill overwhelming any doubts or suspicions. You would think the best of people, and they would respond in kind. You would live your life under what philosophers used to call "the aspect of eternity," reflecting on the purpose of your existence and your connections to humanity and the universe. When working with others, your productive discussions would always move toward the most logical and informed conclusions. You would be able to navigate intelligently through the daily avalanche of information, separating the useful from the irrelevant. You would have a deep understanding of complex social issues and would enjoy exploring their nuances through constructive conversations. You would live your life creatively, expressing yourself freely without fear of social condemnation. Your life would be vibrant, filled with satisfying relationships and accomplishments in which you would take great pride. You would enjoy the admiration of others as you steered a purposeful course that reflected your profound self-understanding. You would feel secure, strong, loved, happy, and fulfilled.

What would a world populated with critical thinkers be like? It would be a sublime world, the kind of world you would love to live in, the kind of world you would want for your children. It would be a world in which all people were able to achieve their personal potential, echoing the words of the writer Henry Miller:

> We are all part of things,
> We are all part of creation, all kings, all poets, all musicians,
> We have only to open up, to discover what is already there.

Analyzing Issues

We live in a complex world filled with challenging and often perplexing issues that we are expected to make sense of. For example, the media inform us every day of issues related to abortion, AIDS, terrorism, animal experimentation, budget priorities, child custody, crime and punishment, drugs, environmental pollution, genetic engineering, human rights, individual rights, international conflicts, moral values, pornography, poverty, racism, reproductive technology, the right to die, sex education, and many others. Often these broad social issues intrude into our own personal lives, taking them from the level of abstract discussion into our immediate experience. As effective thinkers, we have an obligation to develop informed, intelligent opinions about these issues so that we can function as responsible citizens and also make appropriate decisions when confronted with these issues in our lives.

Almost everyone has opinions about these and other issues. Some opinions, however, are more informed and well supported than others. To make sense of complex issues, we need to bring to them a certain amount of background knowledge and an integrated set of thinking and language abilities.

What Is the Issue?

Many social issues are explored, analyzed, and evaluated through our judicial system. Imagine that you have been called for jury duty and subsequently impaneled on a jury that is asked to render a verdict on the following situation. (Note: This fictional case is based on an actual case that was tried in May 1990 in Minneapolis, Minnesota.)

> On January 23, the defendant, Mary Barnett, left Chicago to visit her fiancé in San Francisco. She left her six-month-old daughter, Alison, unattended in the apartment. Seven days later, Mary Barnett returned home to discover that her baby had died of dehydration. She called the police and initially told them that she had left the child with a baby sitter. She later stated that she knew she had left the baby behind, that she did not intend to come back, and that she knew Alison would die in a day or two. She has been charged with the crime of second-degree murder: intentional murder without pre-meditation. If convicted, she could face up to eighteen years in jail.

As a member of the jury, your role is to hear and weigh the evidence, evaluate the credibility of the witnesses, analyze the arguments presented by the prosecution and defense, determine whether the law applies specifically to this situation, and render a verdict on the guilt or innocence of the defendant. To perform these tasks with clarity and fairness, you will have to use a variety of sophisticated thinking and language abilities. To begin with, describe your initial assessment of whether the defendant is innocent or guilty and explain your reasons for thinking so.

As part of the jury selection process, you are asked by the prosecutor and defense attorney whether you will be able to set aside your initial reactions or preconceptions to render an impartial verdict. Identify any ideas or feelings related to this case that might make it difficult for you to view it objectively. Are you a parent? Have you ever had any experiences related to the issues in this case? Do you have any preconceived views concerning individual responsibility in situations like this? Then evaluate whether you will be able to go beyond your initial reactions to see the situation objectively, and explain how you intend to accomplish this.

What Is the Evidence?

The evidence at judicial trials is presented through the testimony of witnesses called by the prosecution and the defense. As a juror, your job is to absorb the information being presented, evaluate its accuracy, and assess the reliability of the individuals giving the testimony. The following are excerpts of testimony from some of the witnesses at the trial. Witnesses for the prosecution are presented first, followed by witnesses for the defense.

CAROLINE HOSPERS: On the evening of January 30, I was in the hallway when Mary Barnett entered the building. She looked distraught and didn't have her baby Alison with her. A little while later the police arrived and I discovered that she had left poor little Alison all alone to die. I'm not surprised this happened. I always thought that Ms. Barnett was a disgrace — I mean, she didn't have a husband. In fact, she didn't even have a steady man after that sailor left for California. She had lots of wild parties in her apartment, and that baby wasn't taken care of properly. Her garbage was always filled with empty whiskey and wine bottles. I'm sure that she went to California just to party and have a good time, and didn't give a damn about little Alison. She was thinking only of herself. It's obvious that she is entirely irresponsible and was not a fit mother.

OFFICER MITCHELL: We were called to the defendant's apartment at 11 P.M. on January 30 by the defendant, Mary Barnett. Upon entering the apartment, we found the defendant holding the deceased child in her arms. She was sobbing and was obviously extremely upset. She stated that she had left the deceased with a baby sitter one week before when she went to California, and had just returned to discover the deceased alone in the apartment. When I asked the defendant to explain in detail what had happened before she left, she stated: "I remember making airline reservations for my trip. Then I tried to find a baby sitter, but I couldn't. I knew that I was leaving Alison alone and that I wouldn't be back for a while, but I had to get to California at all costs. I visited my mother and then left." An autopsy was later performed that determined that the deceased had died of dehydration several days earlier. There were no other marks or bruises on the deceased.

DR. PARKER: I am a professional psychiatrist who has been involved in many judicial hearings on whether a defendant is mentally competent to stand trial, and I am familiar with these legal tests. At the request of the district attorney's office, I interviewed the defendant four times during the last three months. Ms. Barnett is suffering from depression and anxiety, possibly induced by the guilt she feels for what she did. These symptoms can be controlled with proper medication. Based on my interview, I believe that Ms. Barnett is competent to stand trial. She understands the charges against her, and the roles of her attorney, the prosecutor, the judge and jury, and can participate in her own defense. Further, I believe that she was mentally competent on January 23, when she left her child unattended. In my opinion she knew what she was doing and what the consequences of her actions would be. She was aware that she was leaving her child unattended and that the child would be in great danger. I think that she feels guilty for the decisions she made, and that this remorse accounts for her current emotional problems.

To be effective critical thinkers, we need to try to determine the accuracy of the information and evaluate the credibility of the people providing the information. Evaluate the credibility of the prosecution witnesses by identifying those factors that led you to believe their testimony and those factors that raised questions in your mind about the accuracy of the information presented. Use these questions to guide your evaluation:

- What information is the witness providing?
- Is the information relevant to the charges?
- Is the witness credible? What biases might influence the witness's testimony?
- To what extent is the testimony accurate?

Based on the testimony you have heard up to this point, do you think the defendant is innocent or guilty of intentional murder without premeditation? Explain the reasons for your conclusion.

Now let's review testimony from the witnesses for the defense.

ALICE JONES: I have known the defendant, Mary Barnett, for over eight years. She is a very sweet and decent woman, and a wonderful mother. Being a single parent isn't easy, and Mary has done as good a job as she could. But shortly after Alison's birth, Mary got depressed. Then her fiancé, Tim Stewart, was transferred to California. He's a navy engine mechanic. She started drinking to overcome her depression, but this just made things worse. She began to feel trapped in her apartment with little help raising the baby and few contacts with her family or friends. As her depression deepened, she clung more closely to Tim, who as a result became more distant and put off their wedding, which caused her to feel increasingly anxious and desperate. She felt that she had to go to California to get things straightened out, and by the time she reached that point I think she had lost touch with reality. I honestly don't think she realized that she was leaving Alison unattended. She loved her so much.

DR. BLOOM: Although I have not been involved in judicial hearings of this type, Mary Barnett has been my patient, twice a week for the last four months, beginning two months after she returned from California and was arrested.

In my professional opinion, she is mentally ill and not capable of standing trial. Further, she was clearly not aware of what she was doing when she left Alison unattended and should not be held responsible for her action. Ms. Barnett's problems began after the birth of Alison. She became caught in the grip of the medical condition known as postpartum depression, a syndrome that affects many women after the birth of their children, some more severely than others. Women feel a loss of purpose, a sense of hopelessness, and a deep depression. The extreme pressures of caring for an infant create additional anxiety. When Ms. Barnett's fiancé left for California, she felt completely overwhelmed by her circumstances. She turned to alcohol to raise her spirits, but this just exacerbated her condition. Depressed, desperate, anxious, and alcoholic, she lapsed into a serious neurotic state and became obsessed with the idea of reaching her fiancé in California. This single hope was the only thing she could focus on, and when she acted on it she was completely unaware that she was putting her daughter in danger. Since the trial has begun, she has suffered two anxiety attacks, the more severe resulting in a near-catatonic state necessitating her hospitalization for several days. This woman is emotionally disturbed. She needs professional help, not punishment.

MARY BARNETT: I don't remember leaving Alison alone. I would never have done that if I had realized what I was doing. I don't remember saying any of the things that they said I said, about knowing I was leaving her. I have tried to put the pieces together through the entire investigation, and I just can't do it. I was anxious, and I was real frightened. I didn't feel like I was in control, and it felt like it was getting worse. The world was closing in on me, and I had nowhere to turn. I knew that I had to get to Tim, in California, and that he would be able to fix everything. He was always the one I went to, because I trusted him. I must have assumed that someone was taking care of Alison, my sweet baby. When I was in California, I knew something wasn't right. I just didn't know what it was.

Based on this new testimony, do you think that the defendant is innocent or guilty of intentional murder without premeditation? Have your views changed? Explain the reasons for your current conclusion. Evaluate the credibility of the defense witnesses by identifying those factors that led you to believe their testimony and those factors that raised questions in your mind about the accuracy of the information being presented. Use the questions on page 76 as a guide.

What Are the Arguments?

After the various witnesses present their testimony through examination and cross-examination questioning, the prosecution and defense then present their final arguments and summations. The purpose of this phase of the trial is to tie together — or raise doubts about — the evidence that has been presented in order to persuade the jury that the defendant is guilty or innocent. Included here are excerpts from these final arguments.

PROSECUTION ARGUMENTS: Child abuse and neglect are a national tragedy. Every day thousands of innocent children are neglected, abused, and even killed. The parents responsible for these crimes are rarely brought to justice because their victims are usually not able to speak in their own behalf. In some sense, all of these abusers are emotionally disturbed, because it takes emotionally disturbed people to torture, maim, and kill innocent children. But these people are also responsible for their actions and they should be punished accordingly. They don't have to hurt these children. No one is forcing them to hurt these children. They can choose not to hurt these children. If they have emotional problems, they can choose to seek professional help. Saying you hurt a child because you have "emotional problems" is the worst kind of excuse.

The defendant, Mary Barnett, claims that she left her child unattended, to die, because she has "emotional problems" and that she is not responsible for what she did. This is absurd. Mary Barnett is a self-centered, irresponsible, manipulative, deceitful mother who abandoned her six-month-old daughter to die so that she could fly to San Francisco to party all week with her fiancé. She was conscious, she was thinking, she knew exactly what she was doing, and that's exactly what she told the police when she returned from her little pleasure trip. Now she claims that she can't remember making these admissions to the police, nor can she remember leaving little Alison alone to die. How convenient!

You have heard testimony from her neighbor, Caroline Hospers, that she was considerably less than an ideal mother: a chronic drinker who liked to party rather than devoting herself to her child. You have also heard the testimony of Dr. Parker, who stated that Mary Barnett was aware of what she was doing on the fateful day in January and that any emotional disturbance is the result of her feelings of guilt over the terrible thing she did, and her fear of being punished for it.

Mary Barnett is guilty of murder, pure and simple, and it is imperative that you find her so. We need to let society know that it is no longer open season on our children.

After reviewing these arguments, describe those points you find most persuasive and those you find least persuasive, and then review the defense arguments that follow.

DEFENSE ARGUMENTS: The district attorney is certainly correct — child abuse is a national tragedy. Mary Barnett, however, is not a child abuser. You heard the police testify that the hospital found no marks, bruises, or other indications of an abused child. You also heard her friend, Alice Jones, testify that Mary was a kind and loving mother who adored her child. But if Mary Barnett was not a child abuser, then how could she have left her child unattended? Because she had snapped psychologically. The combination of postpartum depression, alcoholism, the pressures of being a single parent, and the loss of her fiancé were too much for her to bear. She simply broke under the weight of all that despair and took off blindly for California, hoping to find a way out of her personal hell. How could she leave Alison unattended? Because she was completely unaware that she was doing so. She had lost touch with reality and had no idea what was happening around her.

You have heard the in-depth testimony of Dr. Bloom, who has explained to you the medical condition of postpartum depression and how this led to Mary's emotional breakdown. You are aware that Mary has had two severe anxiety attacks while this trial has taken place, one resulting in her hospitalization. And you have seen her desperate sobbing whenever her daughter Alison has been mentioned in testimony.

Alison Barnett is a victim. But she is not a victim of intentional malice from the mother who loves her. She is the victim of Mary's mental illness, of her emotional breakdown. And in this sense Mary is a victim also. In this enlightened society we should not punish someone who has fallen victim to mental illness. To do so would make us no better than those societies who used to torture and burn mentally ill people whom they thought were possessed by the devil. Mary needs treatment, not blind vengeance.

After reviewing the arguments presented by the defense, identify those points you find most persuasive and those you find least persuasive.

What Is the Verdict?

Following the final arguments and summations, the judge will sometimes give the jury specific instructions to clarify the issues to be considered. In this case the judge reminds the jury that they must focus on the boundaries of the law and determine whether the case falls within these boundaries or outside them. The jury then retires to deliberate the case and render a verdict.

For a defendant to be found guilty of second-degree murder, the prosecution must prove that he or she intended to kill someone, made a conscious decision to do so at that moment (without premeditation), and was aware of the consequences of his or her actions. In your discussion with the other jurors, you must determine whether the evidence indicates, beyond a reasonable doubt, that the defendant's conduct in this case meets these conditions. What does the qualification "beyond a reasonable doubt" mean? A principle like this is always difficult to define in specific terms, but in general the principle means that it would not make good sense for thoughtful men and women to conclude otherwise.

Based on your analysis of the evidence and arguments presented in this case, describe what you think the verdict ought to be and explain your reasons for thinking so.

Verdict: Guilty _____   Not Guilty _____

THINKING ACTIVITY 2.10

Analyzing Your Verdict

Exploring this activity has given you the opportunity to analyze the key dimensions of a complex court case. Synthesize your thoughts regarding this case in a two-page paper in which you explain the reasons and evidence that influenced your verdict. Be sure to discuss the important testimony and your evaluation of the credibility of the various witnesses.

THINKING PASSAGES

Jurors' and Judges' Reasoning Processes

The first of the following articles, "Jurors Hear Evidence and Turn It into Stories," by Daniel Goleman, author of the best-selling book *Emotional Intelligence*, describes recent research that gives us insight into the way jurors think and reason during the process of reaching a verdict. The second article, "Judicial Reasoning Is All Too Human," by Patricia Cohen, sheds light on the reasoning processes — and potential biases — of judges in court proceedings. As you read these articles, reflect on the reasoning process you engaged in while thinking about the Mary Barnett case, and then answer the questions found at the end of the articles.

JURORS HEAR EVIDENCE AND TURN IT INTO STORIES
by Daniel Goleman

Studies Show They Arrange Details to Reflect Their Beliefs

Despite the furor over the verdict in the Rodney G. King beating case, scientists who study juries say the system is by and large sound. Many also believe that it is susceptible to manipulation and bias, and could be improved in various specific ways suggested by their research findings.

If there is any lesson to be learned from the research findings, it is that juries are susceptible to influence at virtually every point, from the moment members are selected to final deliberation.

Much of the newest research on the mind of the juror focuses on the stories that jurors tell themselves to understand the mounds of disconnected evidence, often presented in a confusing order. The research suggests that jurors' unspoken assumptions about human nature play a powerful role in their verdicts.

"People don't listen to all the evidence and then weigh it at the end," said Dr. Nancy Pennington, a psychologist at the University of Colorado. "They process it as they go along, composing a continuing story throughout the trial that makes sense of what they're hearing."

That task is made difficult by the way evidence is presented in most trials, in an order dictated for legal reasons rather than logical ones. Thus, in a murder trial, the first witness is often a coroner, who establishes that a death occurred.

"Jurors have little or nothing to tie such facts to, unless an attorney suggested an interpretation in the opening statement," in the form of a story line to follow, Dr. Pennington said.

In an article in the November 1991 issue of *Cardozo Law Review,* Dr. Pennington, with Dr. Reid Hastie, also a psychologist at the University of Colorado, reported a series of experiments that show just how important jurors' stories are in determining the verdict they come to. In the studies, people called for jury duty but not involved in a trial were recruited for a simulation in which they were to act as jurors for a murder trial realistically reenacted on film.

In the case, the defendant, Frank Johnson, had quarreled in a bar with the victim, Alan Caldwell, who threatened him with a razor. Later that evening they went outside, got into a fight, and Johnson knifed Caldwell, who died.

Source: "Jurors Hear Evidence and Turn It into Stories," by Daniel Goleman, *The New York Times,* May 12, 1992. Copyright © 1992 by The New York Times Co. Reprinted by permission.

VISUAL THINKING

"Members of the Jury, Don't Be Deceived . . ."

- Courtroom dramas, like that depicted in this photo, provide rich contexts for sophisticated critical thinking. What crime do you think the defendant (in the witness chair) might have been charged with? Do you have any positive or negative bias toward him based on his appearance and facial expression? Do you think the woman addressing the jury is the prosecutor or defense attorney? Why?

Disputed points included whether or not Caldwell was a bully who had started the first quarrel when his girlfriend had asked Johnson for a ride to the racetrack, whether Johnson had stabbed Caldwell or merely held his knife out to protect himself, and whether Johnson had gone home to get a knife.

In detailed interviews of the jurors, Dr. Pennington found that in explaining how they had reached their verdicts, 45 percent of the references they made were to events that had not been included in the courtroom testimony. These included inferences about the men's motives and psychological states, and assumptions the jurors themselves brought to the story from their own experience.

The stories that jurors told themselves pieced together the evidence in ways that could lead to opposite verdicts. One common story among the jurors, which led to a verdict of first-degree murder, was that the threat with the razor by Caldwell had so enraged Johnson that he went home to get his knife — a point that was in dispute — with the intention of picking a fight, during which he stabbed him to death.

By contrast, just as many jurors told themselves a story that led them to a verdict of not guilty: Caldwell started the fight with Johnson and threatened him with a razor, and Caldwell ran into the knife that Johnson was using to protect himself.

Role of Jurors' Backgrounds

The study found that jurors' backgrounds could lead to crucial differences in the assumptions they brought to their explanatory stories. Middle-class jurors were more likely to find the defendant guilty than were working-class jurors. The difference mainly hinged on how they interpreted the fact that Johnson had a knife with him during the struggle.

Middle-class jurors constructed stories that saw Johnson's having a knife as strong evidence that he planned a murderous assault on Caldwell in their second confrontation. But working-class jurors said it was likely that a man like Johnson would be in the habit of carrying a knife with him for protection, and so they saw nothing incriminating about his having the knife.

"Winning the battle of stories in the opening statements may help determine what evidence is attended to, how it is interpreted, and what is recalled both during and after the trial," Dr. Richard Lempert, a psychologist at the University of Michigan Law School, wrote in commenting on Dr. Pennington's article.

Verdicts that do not correspond to one's own "story" of a case are shocking. In the King case, "We didn't hear the defense story of what was going on, but only saw the strongest piece of the prosecution's evidence, the videotape," said Dr. Stephen Penrod, a psychologist at the University of Minnesota Law School. "If we had heard the defense theory, we may not have been so astonished by the verdict."

In the contest among jurors to recruit fellow members to one or another version of what happened, strong voices play a disproportionate role. Most juries include some people who virtually never speak up, and a small number who dominate the discussion, typically jurors of higher social status, according to studies reviewed in *Judging the Jury* (Plenum Press, 1986) by two psychologists, Dr. Valerie Hans of the University of Delaware and Dr. Neil Vidmar of Duke University.

The research also reveals that "juries are more often merciful to criminal defendants" than judges in the same cases would be, said Dr. Hans.

Blaming the Victim

In recent research, Dr. Hans interviewed 269 jurors in civil cases and found that many tended to focus on the ability of victims to have avoided being injured. "You see the same kind of blaming the victim in rape cases, too, especially among female jurors," Dr. Hans said. "Blaming the victim is reassuring to jurors because if victims are responsible for the harm that befell them, then you don't have to worry about becoming a victim yourself because you know what to do to avoid it."

That tendency may have been at work among the King jurors, Dr. Hans said, "when the jurors said King was in control and that if he stopped moving the police would have stopped beating him."

"Of course, the more they saw King as responsible for what happened, the less the officers were to blame in their minds," Dr. Hans said.

Perhaps the most intensive research has focused on the selection of a jury. Since lawyers can reject a certain number of prospective jurors during jury selection without having to give a specific reason, the contest to win the mind of the jury begins with the battle to determine who is and is not on the jury.

The scientific selection of juries began in the early 1970s when social scientists volunteered their services for the defense in a series of political trials, including proceedings arising from the 1971 Attica prison uprising in upstate New York. One method used was to poll the community where the trial was to be held to search for clues to attitudes that might work against the defendant, which the defense lawyers could then use to eliminate jurors.

For example, several studies have shown that people who favor the death penalty are generally pro-prosecution in criminal cases, and so more likely to convict a defendant. Defense lawyers can ask prospective jurors their views on the death penalty, and eliminate those who favor it.

On the basis of such a community survey for a trial in Miami, Dr. Elizabeth Loftus, a psychologist at the University of Washington, found that as a group, whites trust the honesty and fairness of the police far more than blacks. "If you knew nothing else, you'd use that demographic variable in picking a jury in the King case," she said. "But in Ventura County, there's a jury pool with almost no blacks. It was a gift to the defense, in retrospect."

Over the last two decades, such methods have been refined to the point that 300 or more consulting groups now advise lawyers on jury selection.

JUDICIAL REASONING IS ALL TOO HUMAN
by Patricia Cohen

Forget the 14th Amendment and the peculiarities of California state law. The real inspiration behind Supreme Court Justice Antonin Scalia's vote to deny the child of an adulterous affair any contact with her natural father was the legend of King Arthur, Guinevere and Lancelot.

At least that's the way Anthony Amsterdam, a lawyer, and Jerome Bruner, a psychologist, see it. "Much judicial decision-making is driven by psychological processes," Mr. Amsterdam said, and "literature enters powerfully into cultural psychology."

So if you want to understand adultery, don't look merely at legal statutes, the two scholars insist. Examine a culture's narrative tradition, what psychologists call its "mythic patterns." Only then, they argue in their provocative book *Minding the Law* (Harvard University Press), can one "fully appreciate the power of the Guinevere legend in shaping Justice Scalia's portrayal of adultery."

In other words, stories are how we all make sense of marriage and fidelity, death and betrayal, accomplishment and revenge; how Iago eggs Othello to murder and how Tony Soprano can describe himself as a "captain-of-industry type" instead of a mob boss; how you decide whether a giant computer corporation is an unethical shark or simply a fierce competitor, and whether a mayor who wants to divorce his wife is a cheating cad or a henpecked husband.

Stories, and the way judges — intentionally or not — categorize and spin them, are as responsible for legal rulings as logic and precedent, Mr. Amsterdam and Mr. Bruner said. Their novel attempt to reach into the psyche of Justice Scalia and other members of the Supreme Court is part of a growing interest in a long-neglected and cryptic subject: the psychology of judicial decision-making.

Source: Patricia Cohen, "Judicial Reasoning Is All too Human," *The New York Times,* June 30, 2001. Copyright © 2001 by The New York Times Co. Reprinted by permission.

"The most exciting work in law schools right now is to try to bring an understanding of how people actually think in contact with the law," said Cass Sunstein, a law professor at the University of Chicago Law School and the editor of *Behavioral Economics and the Law* (Cambridge University Press, 2000). "It is just starting."

Of course, legal scholars have long recognized that the law is more than an antiseptic collection of rules, precedents and procedures that stand apart from the larger world of politics, culture, self-interest and morality. In the 1920's and 30's, the legal realists argued that people should pay attention to the social context of the law as well as human psychology. No one should assume that decisions are entirely rational, Jerome Frank declared in his seminal 1930 study, *Law and the Modern Mind,* because of the simple fact that "judges are human." But while the psychology of juries has been extensively studied, little research has been done on the psychology of judges.

"Judges are hard to study," said Stephan Landsman, a law professor at DePaul College of Law in Chicago. "We've had very few opportunities to ask them the sort of questions that we ask juries" all the time.

Not only are judges reluctant to participate in studies, he said, but few legal scholars have the necessary training to do this kind of research.

Jeffrey J. Rachlinski, a psychologist and law professor at Cornell Law School, is one who does. Working with Chris Guthrie, a law professor at the University of Missouri School of Law, and Judge Andrew J. Wistrich, a federal district judge in California, Mr. Rachlinski managed to corral 167 federal magistrate judges and convince them to answer a questionnaire intended to detect five common "cognitive illusions" or mental shortcuts, like perceiving past events to be more predictable than they actually were and overestimating their own ability. (A common example of this bias is a husband's estimate of how much housework he does; in this case, judges were asked to estimate whether they were overturned on appeal more or less frequently than their colleagues.) Do even highly trained judges suffer from the sort of psychological quirks that distort decision-making?

Although the judges were somewhat less susceptible to two of the five, these psychological illusions caused them to err again and again. As the authors wrote in the *Cornell Law Review* last month, "Wholly apart from political orientation and self-interest, the very nature of human thought can mislead judges confronted by particular types of situations into making consistent and predictable mistakes."

Yet the legal system takes no account of such mental mechanisms. Indeed, it assumes that judges, with their specialized training and their mastery of the rules of evidence, are much better equipped than jurors to put aside emotion and ignore evidence that might bias a decision. But are they?

In an early study on the subject, Mr. Landsman teamed up with a psychologist, Richard F. Rakos, in 1992 to test whether a group of Ohio judges could discount what they knew to be inadmissible information — like a defendant's prior conviction. It turned out they couldn't. Those who heard information that reflected badly on the defendant — but that the law says should be ignored — ended up voting against the defendant; judges who didn't hear it ruled the other way. Judges "make decisions in the same way that other people make decisions," Mr. Landsman said, but "getting that idea out and following up its implications has been very difficult because it threatens a judge's claim of authority and trustworthiness."

Rather than try to set up scientifically controlled experiments, Theodore Eisenberg, a law professor at Cornell Law School, looks to the real world, studying thousands of actual cases in an effort to discover how judges reach their decisions. He has examined whether juries are a softer touch than judges in product liability cases (they're not), and why bankruptcy judges think they rule more quickly than they actually do (they suffer from self-serving bias — just like everyone else). But such research is particularly tough to do, Mr. Eisenberg said, because of the way legal databases are organized.

Whatever the experimental design, "the pattern across all of these studies is strikingly consistent," writes Shari Seidman Diamond, a law professor and psychologist at Northwestern University Law School, who has reviewed what research there is for a forthcoming book. "Judges as well as laypersons are influenced by these cognitive biases."

Mr. Amsterdam and Mr. Bruner agree with that conclusion, although they take a more, well, idiosyncratic route to it. For more than 35 years, Mr. Amsterdam has been one of the country's leading capital defense lawyers; the man who persuaded the Supreme Court in 1972 to ban capital punishment on the ground that it was being arbitrarily administered. (The ban was lifted in 1976.) Mr. Bruner is considered a founder of cognitive psychology; after doing research on infant learning, he helped establish the nation's Head Start program.

Taking a page from Jungian and some cognitive psychologists, Mr. Bruner and Mr. Amsterdam believe that archetypal stories or myths unconsciously give shape to people's perceptions of their own lives. Universal themes and characters offer a kind of rough script or road map for today's bankers and janitors, salesclerks and toll collectors. As Joseph Campbell wrote in his 1949 classic, *The Hero with a Thousand Faces,* "The latest incarnation of Oedipus, the continued romance of Beauty and the Beast, stands this afternoon on the corner of 42d Street and Fifth Avenue, waiting for the traffic light to change."

They also sit in the witness box, at the defense and plaintiff tables, and in the judge's chair, Mr. Amsterdam and Mr. Bruner say.

Consider the 1989 adultery case, Michael H. v. Gerald D. Michael went to court to get permission to see his biological daughter Victoria, who was born during an on-and-off, six-year affair with Carole. Carole and her husband, Gerald, fought the request and the case worked its way up to the Supreme Court, where Michael lost, 5 to 4.

Justice Scalia wrote the majority opinion, and to the professors' ears, it retells an ancient combat myth that serves as the basis for the legend of King Arthur, Queen Guinevere and Lancelot, a tale of a married woman who is carried off by a ravisher and ultimately rescued by her husband. Justice Scalia presents the case, Mr. Amsterdam and Mr. Bruner contend, as a "winner-take-all struggle" in which the adulterous villain must be punished and the "sanctity" of the family restored. They dissect the opinion to show, for example, how Justice Scalia narrowly defines the category of "family" to mean only one father sanctioned by marriage, not two even if the second is the biological father. Then, they add, he artfully uses rhetoric — for example, talking about what "Nature requires" — to make any other definition of family, or any compromise that would take account of both fathers' rights, appear unnatural.

Richard A. Posner, chief judge for the United States Circuit Court of Appeals in Chicago, thinks much of Mr. Amsterdam and Mr. Bruner's analysis is hogwash. The topic is important, said Judge Posner, who wrote about psychology and the law in his recent book, *Frontiers of Legal Theory,* but he doubts whether "cognitive psychology or even rational choice theory has the tools to make much progress in the understanding of judicial psychology."

Yet even if it's not clear precisely how judges are affected by these psychological biases, it is clear that they are affected, researchers argue, so adjust the system to correct for them. Consider having a panel instead of a single judge rule on cases, as is regularly done on the appellate level, Mr. Landsman suggests. Rely on juries because they can be shielded from unlawful evidence, Ms. Diamond argues. Set up rules of thumb or guidelines to limit unconscious bias, Mr. Rachlinski says. For instance, doctors cannot be found liable unless their care strays from an established customary standard.

The first hurdle is to get judges to admit they are subject to the same psychological hiccups as everyone else, the field's pioneers say. Professionals can learn to adapt to cognitive biases, but only if they get constant feedback.

"Our whole book, in a sense, is a treatise for the proposition that judges have choices they do not acknowledge to themselves and the world," Mr. Amsterdam said. "They make many decisions under the delusion that those results are foreordained by rules of reason, but they are not."

That's not too surprising. After all, they're only human.

Questions for Analysis

1. Reflect back on your own deliberations of the Mary Barnett case and describe the reasoning process you used to reach a verdict. Did you find that you were composing a continuing story to explain the testimony you were reading? If so, was this story changed or modified as you learned more information or discussed the case with your classmates?

2. Explain how factors from your own personal experience (age, gender, experience with children, etc.) may have influenced your verdict and the reasoning process that led up to it.

3. Explain how your beliefs about human nature may have influenced your analysis of Mary Barnett's motives and behavior.

4. Explain whether you believe that the research strategies lawyers are using to select the "right" jury for their cases are undermining the fairness of the justice system.

5. According to this article, judges are vulnerable to the same psychological influences, biases, and errors in reasoning as jurors and the rest of the general population. To what five "cognitive illusions" are judges susceptible, as revealed in the research conducted by psychologist Jeffrey J. Rachlinski? Explain how cognitive illusions might play a role in determining the guilt or innocence of Mary Barnett.

6. Judges' reasoning processes are also influenced by universal cultural themes and mythic patterns, according to Anthony Amsterdam and Jerome Bruner. Think of two different archetypal stories, fairy tales, or myths, and explain how these might influence a judge to find Mary Barnett guilty or innocent.

3 Solving Problems

An Organized
Approach to Analyzing
Difficult Problems

Step 1: What Is the Problem?

What do I know about the situation?
What results am I aiming for?
How can I define the problem?

Step 2: What Are the Alternatives?

What are the boundaries?
What are possible alternatives?

Step 3: What Are the Advantages and/or Disadvantages of Each Alternative?

What are the advantages?
What are the disadvantages?
What additional information do I need?

Critical thinking can help creatively and constructively solve problems.

Step 4: What Is the Solution?

Which alternatives will I pursue?
What steps can I take?

Step 5: How Well Is the Solution Working?

What is my evaluation?
What adjustments are necessary?

Thinking Critically About Problems

Throughout your life, you are continually solving problems, including the many minor problems that you solve each day: negotiating a construction delay on the road, working through an unexpected difficulty at your job, helping an upset child deal with a disappointment. As a student, you are faced with a steady stream of academic assignments, quizzes, exams, and papers. Relatively simple problems like these do not require a systematic or complex analysis. For example, in order to do well on an exam, you need to *define* the problem (what areas will the exam cover, and what will be the format?), identify and evaluate various *alternatives* (what are possible study approaches?), and then put all these factors together to reach a *solution* (what will be your study plan and schedule?). But the difficult and complicated problems in life require more attention.

Problems are the crucible that forges the strength of our characters. When you are tested by life — forced to overcome adversity and think your way through the most challenging situations — you will emerge a more intelligent, resourceful, and resilient person. However, if you lead a sheltered existence that insulates you from life's trials, or if you flee from situations at the first sign of trouble — then you will be weak and unable to cope with the eruptions and explosions that are bound to occur. Adversity reveals the person you have become, the character you have created. As the Roman philosopher and poet Lucretius explained, "So it is more useful to watch a man in times of peril, and in adversity to discern what kind of man he is; for then, at last, words of truth are drawn from the depths of his heart, and the mask is torn off, reality remains."

The quality of your life can be traced in large measure to your competency as a problem-solver. The fact that some people are consistently superior problem-solvers is largely due to their ability to approach problems in an informed and organized way. Less competent problem-solvers just muddle through when it comes to confronting adversity, using hit-or-miss strategies that rarely provide the best results. How would you rate yourself as a problem-solver? Do you generally approach difficulties confidently, analyze them clearly, and reach productive solutions? Or do you find that you often get "lost" and confused in such situations, unable to understand the problem clearly and to break out of mental ruts? Of course, you may find that you are very adept at solving problems in one area of your life — such as your job — and miserable at solving problems in other areas, such as your love life or your relationships with your children.

Becoming an expert problem-solver is, for the most part, a learned skill that you can develop by practicing and applying the principles described in this chapter. You can learn to view problems as *challenges*, opportunities for growth instead of obstacles or burdens. You can become a person who attacks adversity with confidence and enthusiasm.

Introduction to Solving Problems

Consider the following problem:

> My best friend is addicted to drugs, but he won't admit it. Jack always liked to drink, but I never thought too much about it. After all, a lot of people like to drink socially, get relaxed, and have a good time. But over the last few years he's started using other drugs as well as alcohol, and it's ruining his life. He's stopped taking classes at the college and will soon lose his job if he doesn't change. Last week I told him that I was really worried about him, but he told me that he has no drug problem and that in any case it really isn't any of my business. I just don't know what to do. I've known Jack since we were in grammar school together and he's a wonderful person. It's as if he's in the grip of some terrible force and I'm powerless to help him.

In working through this problem, the student who wrote this will have to think carefully and systematically in order to reach a solution. To think effectively in situations like this, we usually ask ourselves a series of questions.

1. What is the *problem?*
2. What are the *alternatives?*
3. What are the *advantages* and/or *disadvantages* of each alternative?
4. What is the *solution?*
5. How well is the solution *working?*

Let's explore these questions further — and the thinking process that they represent — by applying them to the problem described here.

What Is the Problem?   There are a variety of ways to define the problem facing this student. Describe as specifically as possible what *you* think the problem is.

What Are the Alternatives?   In dealing with this problem, you have a wide variety of possible actions to consider before selecting the best choices. Identify some of the alternatives you might consider.

1. Speak to my friend in a candid and forceful way to convince him that he has a serious problem.

2.

etc.

What Are the Advantages and/or Disadvantages of Each Alternative?

Evaluate the strengths and weaknesses of each of the problems you identified so you can weigh your choices and decide on the best course of action.

1. Speak to my friend in a candid and forceful way to convince him that he has a serious problem.

   Advantage: He may respond to my direct emotional appeal, acknowledge that he has a problem, and seek help.

   Disadvantage: He may react angrily, further alienating me from him and making it more difficult for me to have any influence on him.

2.

   Advantage:

   Disadvantage:

etc.

What Is the Solution?   After evaluating the various alternatives, select what you think is the most effective alternative for solving the problem and describe the sequence of steps you would take to act on the alternative.

How Well Is the Solution Working?   The final step in the process is to review the solution and decide whether it is working. If it is not, you must be able to modify your solution. Describe what results would inform you that the alternative you had selected to pursue was working well or poorly. If you concluded that your alternative was working poorly, describe what your next action would be.

In this situation, trying to figure out the best way to help your friend recognize his problem and seek treatment requires making a series of decisions. If we understand the way our minds operate when we are thinking effectively, then we can apply this understanding to improve our thinking in new, challenging situations. In the remainder of this chapter, we will explore a more sophisticated version of this problem-solving approach and apply it to a variety of complex problems.

THINKING ACTIVITY 3.1

Analyzing a Problem You Solved

1. Describe in specific detail an important problem you have solved recently.
2. Explain how you went about solving the problem. What were the steps, strategies, and approaches you used to understand the problem and make an informed decision?
3. Analyze the organization exhibited by your thinking process by completing the five-step problem-solving method we have been exploring.
4. Share your problem with other members of the class and have them try to analyze and solve it. Then explain the solution you arrived at.

Solving Complex Problems

Imagine yourself in the following situations. What would your next move be, and what are your reasons for it?

Procrastination   I am a procrastinator. Whenever I have something important to do, especially if it's difficult or unpleasant, I tend to put it off. Though this chronic delaying bothers me, I try to suppress my concern and instead work on more trivial things. It doesn't matter how much time I allow for certain responsibilities, I always end up waiting until the last minute to really focus and get things done, or I overschedule too many things for the time available. I usually meet my deadlines, but not always, and I don't enjoy working under this kind of pressure. In many cases I know that I'm not producing my best work. To make matters worse, the feeling that I'm always behind is causing me to feel really stressed out and is undermining my confidence. I've tried every kind of schedule and technique, but my best intentions simply don't last, and I end up slipping into my old habits. I must learn to get my priorities in order and act on them in an organized way so that I can lead a well-balanced and happier life.

Losing Weight   My problem is the unwelcome weight that has attached itself to me. I was always in pretty good physical shape when I was younger, and if I gained a few extra pounds, they were easy to lose if I adjusted my diet slightly or exercised a little more. As I've gotten older, however, it seems easier to add the weight and more difficult to take it off. I'm eating healthier than I ever have before and getting just as much exercise, but the pounds just keep on coming.

My clothes are tight, I'm feeling slow and heavy, and my self-esteem is suffering. How can I lose this excess poundage?

Smoking One problem in my life that has remained unsolved for about twelve years is my inability to stop smoking. I know it is dangerous for my health, and I tell my children that they should not smoke. They then tell me that I should stop, and I explain to them that it is very hard to do. I have tried to stop many times without success. The only times I previously was able to stop were during my two pregnancies, because I didn't want to endanger my children's health. But after their births, I went back to smoking, although I realize that second-hand smoke can also pose a health hazard. I want to stop smoking because it's dangerous, but I also enjoy it. Why do I continue, knowing it can only damage me and my children?

Loss of Financial Aid I'm just about to begin my second year of college, following a very successful first year. To this point, I have financed my education through a combination of savings, financial aid, and a part-time job (sixteen hours per week) at a local store. However, I just received a letter from my college stating that it was reducing my financial aid package by half due to budgetary problems. The letter concludes, "We hope this aid reduction will not prove to be too great an inconvenience." From my perspective, this reduction in aid isn't an inconvenience — it's a disaster! My budget last year was already tight, and with my job, I had barely enough time to study, participate in a few college activities, and have a modest (but essential) social life. To make matters worse, my mother has been ill, a condition which has reduced her income and created financial problems at home. I'm feeling panicked! What in the world am I going to do?

When we first approach a difficult problem, it often seems a confused tangle of information, feelings, alternatives, opinions, considerations, and risks. The problem of the college student just described is a complicated situation that does not seem to offer a single simple solution. Without the benefit of a systematic approach, our thoughts might wander through the tangle of issues like this:

> I want to stay in school . . . but I'm not going to have enough money. . . . I could work more hours at my job . . . but I might not have enough time to study and get top grades . . . and if all I'm doing is working and studying, what about my social life? . . . And what about mom and the kids? . . . They might need my help. . . . I could drop out of school for a while . . . but if I don't stay in school, what kind of future do I have? . . .

VISUAL THINKING

"Eureka! I Found the Needle!"

● Why is this person's solution to finding the needle "creative"? Why do people usually settle for conventional alternatives when trying to solve problems, rather than pushing for truly innovative ideas? Describe a time when you were able to solve a difficult problem with a flash of creative insight that no one else was able to think of.

Very often when we are faced with difficult problems like this, we simply do not know where to begin in trying to solve them. Frustrated by not knowing where to take the first step, we often give up trying to understand the problem. Instead, we may

1. *Act impulsively* without thought or consideration (e.g., "I'll just quit school").
2. *Do what someone else suggests* without seriously evaluating the suggestion (e.g., "Tell me what I should do — I'm tired of thinking about this").
3. *Do nothing* as we wait for events to make the decision for us (e.g., "I'll just wait and see what happens before doing anything").

None of these approaches is likely to succeed in the long run, and they can gradually reduce our confidence in dealing with complex problems. An alternative to these reactions is to *think critically* about the problem, analyzing it with an organized approach based on the five-step method described earlier.

Although we will be using an organized method for working through diffi-cult problems and arriving at thoughtful conclusions, the fact is that our minds do not always work in such a logical, step-by-step fashion. Effective problem-solvers typically pass through all the steps we will be examining, but they don't always do so in the sequence we will be describing. Instead, the best problem-solvers have an integrated and flexible approach to the process in which they deploy a repertoire of problem-solving strategies as needed. Some-times exploring the various alternatives helps them go back and redefine the original problem; similarly, seeking to implement the solution can often sug-gest new alternatives.

The key point is that although the problem-solving steps are presented in a logical sequence here, you are not locked into following these steps in a mechanical and unimaginative way. At the same time, in learning a problem-solving method like this it is generally not wise to skip steps, because each step deals with an important aspect of the problem. As you become more proficient in using the method, you will find that you can apply its concepts and strate-gies to problem-solving in an increasingly flexible and natural fashion, just as learning the basics of an activity like driving a car gradually gives way to a more organic and integrated performance of the skills involved.

Before applying a method like the one just outlined above to your problem, however, you need first to prepare yourself by *accepting* the problem.

Accepting the Problem

To solve a problem, you must first be willing to *accept* the problem by *acknowl-edging* that the problem exists, *identifying* the problem, and *committing* yourself to trying to solve it.

Successful problem-solvers are highly motivated and willing to persevere through the many challenges and frustrations of the problem-solving process. How do you find the motivation and commitment that prepare you to enter the problem-solving process? There are no simple answers, but a number of strate-gies may be useful to you:

1. *List the benefits.* Make a detailed list of the benefits you will derive from successfully dealing with the problem. Such a process helps you clarify why you might want to tackle the problem, motivates you to get started, and serves as a source of encouragement when you encounter difficulties or lose momentum.

2. *Formalize your acceptance.* When you formalize your acceptance of a prob-lem, you are "going on record," either by preparing a signed declaration or by signing a "contract" with someone else. This formal commitment serves

Problem-Solving Method (Advanced)

1. Step 1: What is the problem?
   a. What do I know about the situation?
   b. What results am I aiming for in this situation?
   c. How can I define the problem?

2. Step 2: What are the alternatives?
   a. What are the boundaries of the problem situation?
   b. What alternatives are possible within these boundaries?

3. Step 3: What are the advantages and/or disadvantages of each alternative?
   a. What are the advantages of each alternative?
   b. What are the disadvantages of each alternative?
   c. What additional information do I need to evaluate each alternative?

4. Step 4: What is the solution?
   a. Which alternative(s) will I pursue?
   b. What steps can I take to act on the alternative(s) chosen?

5. Step 5: How well is the solution working?
   a. What is my evaluation?
   b. What adjustments are necessary?

as an explicit statement of your original intentions that you can refer to if your resolve weakens.

3. *Accept responsibility for your life.* Each one of us has the potential to control the direction of our lives, but to do so we must accept our freedom to choose and the responsibility that goes with it. As you saw in the last chapter, critical thinkers actively work to take charge of their lives rather than letting themselves be passively controlled by external forces.

4. *Create a "worst-case" scenario.* Some problems persist because you are able to ignore their possible implications. When you use this strategy, you remind yourself, as graphically as possible, of the potentially disastrous consequences of your actions. For example, using vivid color photographs and research conclusions, you can remind yourself that excessive smoking, drinking, or eating can lead to myriad health problems and social and psychological difficulties as well as an early demise.

5. *Identify what's holding you back.* If you are having difficulty accepting a problem, it is usually because something is holding you back. Whatever the

constraints, using this strategy involves identifying and describing all of the factors that are preventing you from attacking the problem and then addressing these factors one at a time.

Step 1: What Is the Problem?

The first step in solving problems is to determine exactly what the central issues of the problem are. If you do not clearly understand what the problem really is, then your chances of solving it are considerably reduced. For example, consider the different formulations of the following problems.

"School is boring." vs. "I feel bored in school."
"I'm a failure." vs. "I just failed an exam."

In each of these cases, a very general conclusion (left column) has been replaced by a more specific characterization of the problem (right column). The general conclusions ("I'm a failure") do not suggest productive ways of resolving the difficulties. On the other hand, the more specific descriptions of the problem situation ("I just failed an exam") *do* permit us to attack the problem with useful strategies. Correct identification of a problem is essential if you are going to perform a successful analysis and reach an appropriate conclusion.

Let us return to the problem of the college finances we encountered on page 95 and analyze it using our problem-solving method. *(Note:* As you work through this problem-solving approach, apply the steps and strategies to an unsolved problem in your own life. You will have an opportunity to write up your analysis when you complete Thinking Activity 3.2 on page 110.) In order to complete the first major step of this problem-solving approach — "What is the problem?" — address these three questions:

1. What do I know about the situation?
2. What results am I aiming for in this situation?
3. How can I define the problem?

Step 1A: What Do I Know About the Situation?   Solving a problem begins with determining what information you *know* to be the case and what information you *think* might be the case. Your need to have a clear idea of the details of your beginning circumstances to explore the problem successfully.

You can identify and organize what you know about the problem situation by using *key questions.* In Chapter 2, we examined six types of questions that can be used to explore situations and issues: *fact, interpretation, analysis, synthesis, evaluation,* and *application.* By asking — and trying to answer — questions of fact, you are establishing a sound foundation for the exploration of your problem. Answer the following questions of fact — who, what, where, when, how, why — about the problem described at the beginning of the chapter on page 92.

1. *Who* are the people involved in this situation?
   Who will benefit from solving this problem?
   Who can help me solve this problem?

2. *What* are the various parts or dimensions of the problem?
   What are my strengths and resources for solving this problem?
   What additional information do I need to solve this problem?

3. *Where* can I find people or additional information to help me solve the problem?

4. *When* did the problem begin?
   When should the problem be resolved?

5. *How* did the problem develop or come into being?

6. *Why* is solving this problem important to me?
   Why is this problem difficult to solve?

7. *Additional questions:*

Step 1B: What Results Am I Aiming for in This Situation?   The second part of answering the question "What is the problem?" consists of identifying the specific *results* or objectives you are trying to achieve and encourages you to look ahead to the future. The results are those goals that will eliminate the problem. In this respect, it is similar to the process of establishing and working toward your goals that you examined in Chapter 1. To identify your results, ask yourself: "What are the objectives that, once achieved, will solve this problem?"

Step 1C: How Can I Define the Problem?   Conclude Step 1 by defining the problem as clearly and specifically as possible. Defining the problem is a crucial task in the entire problem-solving process because this definition will determine the direction of the analysis. To define the problem, you need to identify its central issue(s). Often, identifying the central issue of a problem is a complex process. For example, the statement "My problem is relating to other people" suggests a complicated situation with many interacting variables that resists simple definition. In fact, you may only begin to develop a clear idea of the problem as you engage in the process of trying to solve it.

Although there are no simple formulas for defining challenging problems, you can pursue several strategies in identifying the central issue most effectively:

1. ***View the problem from different perspectives.*** As you saw in Chapter 2, perspective-taking is a key ingredient of thinking critically, and it can help you zero in on many problems as well. In the college finances problem, how would you describe the following perspectives?

   Your perspective:

   The college's perspective:

   Your parent's perspective:

2. ***Identify component problems.*** Larger problems are often composed of component problems. To define the larger problem, it is often necessary to identify and describe the subproblems that comprise it. For example, poor performance at school might be the result of a number of factors, such as ineffective study habits, inefficient time management, and preoccupation with a personal problem. Defining, and dealing effectively with, the larger problem means defining and dealing with the subproblems first. Identify possible subproblems in the sample problem:

   Subproblem a:

   Subproblem b:

3. ***State the problem clearly and specifically.*** A third defining strategy is to state the problem as clearly and specifically as possible, based on an examination of the results that need to be achieved to solve the problem. If you state the problem in *very general* terms, you won't have a clear idea of how best to proceed in dealing with it. But if you can describe your problem in more *specific terms*, then your description will begin to suggest actions you can take to solve the problem. Examine the differences between the statements of the following problem:

   General: "My problem is money."

   More specific: "My problem is budgeting my money so that I won't always run out near the end of the month."

   Most specific: "My problem is developing the habit and the discipline to budget my money so that I won't always run out near the end of the month."

Review your analysis of the sample problem and then define the problem as clearly and specifically as possible.

Step 2: What Are the Alternatives?

Once you have identified your problem clearly and specifically, your next move is to examine the possible actions that might help you solve the problem.

Before you list the alternatives, determine first which actions are possible and which are impossible. You can do this by exploring the *boundaries* of the problem situation.

Step 2A: What Are the Boundaries of the Problem Situation?   Boundaries are the limits in the problem situation that you cannot change. They are a part of the problem, and they must be accepted and dealt with. At the same time, you must be careful not to identify as boundaries circumstances that can actually be changed. For instance, in the sample problem you might assume that your problem must be solved in your current location without realizing that relocating to another, less expensive college is one of your options. Identify additional boundaries that might be a part of the sample situation and some of the questions you would want to answer regarding the boundary.

Step 2B: What Alternatives Are Possible Within These Boundaries?   After you have established a general idea of the boundaries of the problem situation, identify the courses of action possible within these boundaries. Of course, identifying all the possible alternatives is not always easy; in fact, it may be part of your problem. Often we do not see a way out of a problem because our thinking is fixed in certain perspectives. You can use several strategies to overcome such obstacles:

1. *Discuss the problem with other people.* Discussing possible alternatives with others uses a number of the aspects of critical thinking you explored in Chapter 2, such as being open to seeing situations from different viewpoints and discussing your ideas with others in an organized way. As critical thinkers we live — and solve problems — in a community. Other people can often suggest possible alternatives that we haven't thought of, in part because they are outside the situation and thus have a more objective perspective, and in part because they view the world differently than we do, based on their past experiences and their personalities. In addition, discussions are often creative experiences that generate ideas. The dynamics of these interactions often lead to ideas and solutions that are greater than the individual "sum" of those involved.

2. *Brainstorm ideas.* Brainstorming builds on the strengths of working with other people to generate ideas and solve problems. In a typical brainstorming session, a group of people work together to generate as many ideas as possible in a specific period of time. Ideas are not judged or evaluated, as this tends to inhibit the free flow of ideas and discourages people from making suggestions. Evaluation is deferred until a later stage. A useful visual

VISUAL THINKING

"I Have a Creative Idea!"

● Most problems have more than one possible solution, and to discover the most creative ideas we need to go beyond the obvious. Imagine that you are faced with the challenge depicted in the illustration; then describe your own creative solution for getting the ball out of the glass cannister without damaging either. Where did your creative idea come from? How does it compare with the solutions of other students in your class?

adjunct to brainstorming is creating mind maps, a process described in Chapter 8, "Relating and Organizing."

3. *Change your location.* Your perspective on a problem is often tied into its location. Sometimes you need a fresh perspective; getting away from the location of the problem situation lets you view it with more clarity. Using these strategies, identify alternatives to help solve the sample problem.

Step 3: What Are the Advantages and/or Disadvantages of Each Alternative?

Once you have identified the various alternatives, your next step is to *evaluate* them by using the evaluation questions described in Chapter 2. Each possible course of action has certain advantages in the sense that if you select that alternative, there will be some positive results. At the same time, each of the possible courses of action likely has disadvantages because selecting that alternative may involve a cost or a risk of negative results. Examine the potential advantages and/or disadvantages in order to determine how helpful each course of action would be.

Step 3A: What Are the Advantages of Each Alternative?   One alternative you may have listed in Step 2 for the sample problem ("Attend college part-time") might include the following advantages:

Alternatives:	*Advantages:*
Attend college part-time	This would remove some of the immediate time and money pressures I am experiencing while still allowing me to prepare for the future. I would have more time to focus on the courses that I am taking and to work additional hours.

Identify the advantages of each of the alternatives that you listed in Step 2. Be sure that your responses are thoughtful and specific.

Step 3B: What Are the Disadvantages of Each Alternative?   You also need to consider the disadvantages of each alternative. The alternative you listed for the sample problem might include the following disadvantages:

Alternatives:	*Disadvantages:*
Attend college part-time	It would take me much longer to complete my schooling, thus delaying my progress toward my goals. Also, I might lose motivation and drop out before completing school because the process was taking so long. Being a part-time student might even threaten my eligibility for financial aid.

Now identify the disadvantages of each of the alternatives that you listed. Be sure that your responses are thoughtful and specific.

Step 3C: What Additional Information Do I Need to Evaluate Each Alternative?   Determine what you must know *(information needed)* to best evaluate and compare the alternatives. In addition, you need to figure out where best to get this information *(sources)*.

To identify the information you need, ask yourself the question *"What if* I select this alternative?" For instance, one alternative in the sample problem was "Attend college part-time." When you ask yourself the question *"What if* I attend college part-time?" you are trying to predict what will occur if you select this course of action. To make these predictions, you must answer certain questions and find the information to answer them.

- How long will it take me to complete my schooling?
- How long can I continue in school without losing interest and dropping out?
- Will I threaten my eligibility for financial aid if I become a part-time student?

Possible sources for this information include the following: myself, other part-time students, school counselors, the financial aid office.

Identify the information needed and the sources of this information for each of the alternatives that you identified. Be sure that your responses are thoughtful and specific.

Step 4: What Is the Solution?

The purpose of Steps 1 through 3 is to analyze your problem in a systematic and detailed fashion — to work through the problem in order to become thoroughly familiar with it and the possible solutions to it. After breaking down the problem in this way, the final step should be to try to put the pieces back together — that is, to decide on a thoughtful course of action based on your increased understanding. Even though this sort of problem analysis does not guarantee finding a specific solution to the problem, it should *deepen your understanding* of exactly what the problem is about. And in locating and evaluating your alternatives, it should give you some very good ideas about the general direction you should move in and the immediate steps you should take.

Step 4A: Which Alternative(s) Will I Pursue?   There is no simple formula or recipe to tell you which alternatives to select. As you work through the different courses of action that are possible, you may find that you can immediately rule some out. For example, in the sample problem you may know with certainty that you do not want to attend college part- time (alternative 1) because you will forfeit your remaining financial aid. However, it may not be so simple

VISUAL THINKING

"Why Didn't I Think of That!"

- The figure on the right was able to solve this problem when the others weren't. Why? Recall a time in your life when you were able to use a similar thinking process to come up with a creative solution to a problem involving "time" or "money," and share your creative solution with your classmates.

to select which of the other alternatives you wish to pursue. How do you decide?

The decisions we make usually depend on what we believe to be most important to us. These beliefs regarding what is most important to us are known as *values*. Our values are the starting points of our actions and strongly influence our decisions. Our values help us *set priorities* in life. We might decide that, for the present, going to school is more important than having an active social life. In this case, going to school is a higher priority than having an active social life. Unfortunately, our values are not always consistent with each other — we may have to choose *either* to go to school or to have an active social life. Both activities may be important to us; they are simply not compatible with each other. Very often the *conflicts* between our values constitute the problem. Let's examine some strategies for selecting alternatives that might help us solve the problem.

1. ***Evaluate and compare alternatives.*** Although each alternative may have certain advantages and disadvantages, not all advantages are equally desirable or potentially effective. Thus it makes sense to evaluate and rank the various alternatives based on how effective they are likely to be and how they match up with your value system. A good place to begin is the "Results" stage, Step 1B. Examine each of the alternatives and evaluate how well it will contribute to achieving the results you are aiming for. Rank the alternatives or develop your own rating system to assess their relative effectiveness.

   After evaluating the alternatives in terms of their anticipated *effectiveness*, the next step is to evaluate them in terms of their *desirability*, based on your needs, interests, and value system. After completing these two separate evaluations, select the alternative(s) that seem most appropriate. Review the alternatives you identified in the sample problem and then rank or rate them according to their potential effectiveness and desirability.

2. ***Combine alternatives.*** After reviewing and evaluating the alternatives, you may develop a new alternative that combines the best qualities of several options while avoiding their disadvantages. In the sample problem, you might combine attending college part-time during the academic year with attending school during the summer session so that progress toward your degree won't be impeded. Examine the alternatives you identified and develop a new option that combines their best elements.

3. ***Try out each alternative in your imagination.*** Focus on each alternative and try to imagine, as concretely as possible, what it would be like if you actu-

ally selected it. Visualize what impact your choice would have on your problem and what the implications would be for your life as a whole. By trying out the alternative in your imagination, you can sometimes avoid unpleasant results or unexpected consequences. As a variation of this strategy, you can sometimes test alternatives on a very limited basis in a practice situation. For example, if you are trying to overcome your fear of speaking in groups, you can practice various speaking techniques with your friends or family until you find an approach you are comfortable with.

After trying out these strategies on the sample problem, select the alternative(s) you think would be most effective and desirable.

Step 4B: What Steps Can I Take to Act on the Alternative(s) Chosen?   Once you have decided on the correct alternative(s) to pursue, your next move is to *take action* by planning specific steps. In the sample problem, for example, imagine that one of the alternatives you have selected is "Find additional sources of income that will enable me to work part-time and go to school full-time." The specific steps you would want to take might include the following:

1. Contact the financial aid office at the school to see what other forms of financial aid are available and what you have to do to apply for them.
2. Contact some of the local banks to see what sort of student loans are available.
3. Look for a higher-paying job so that you can earn more money without working additional hours.
4. Discuss the problem with students in similar circumstances in order to generate new ideas.

Identify the steps you would have to take in pursuing the alternative(s) you identified on page 107.

Once you know what actions you have to take, you need to commit yourself to taking the necessary steps. This is where many people stumble in the problem-solving process, paralyzed by inertia or fear. Sometimes, to overcome these blocks and inhibitions, you need to reexamine your original acceptance of the problem, perhaps making use of some of the strategies you explored on pages 97–99. Once you get started, the rewards of actively attacking your problem are often enough incentive to keep you focused and motivated.

Step 5: How Well Is the Solution Working?

Any analysis of a problem situation, no matter how careful and systematic, is ultimately limited. You simply cannot anticipate or predict everything that is going to happen in the future. As a result, every decision you make is provisional in the sense that your ongoing experience will inform you if your decisions are working out or if they need to be changed and modified. As you saw in Chapter 2, this is precisely the attitude of the critical thinker — someone who is *receptive* to new ideas and experiences and *flexible* enough to change or modify beliefs based on new information. Critical thinking is not a compulsion to find the "right" answer or make the "correct" decision; it is an ongoing process of exploration and discovery.

Step 5A: What Is My Evaluation?   In many cases the relative effectiveness of your efforts will be apparent. In other cases it will be helpful to pursue a more systematic evaluation.

1. *Compare the results with the goals.* Compare the anticipated results of the alternative(s) you selected. To what extent will your choice(s) meet your goals? Are there goals that are not likely to be met by your alternative(s)? Which ones? Could they be addressed by other alternatives? Asking these and other questions will help you clarify the success of your efforts and provide a foundation for future decisions.

2. *Get other perspectives.* As you have seen throughout the problem-solving process, getting the opinions of others is a productive strategy at virtually every stage, and this is certainly true for evaluation. It is not always easy to receive the evaluations of others, but maintaining open-mindedness toward outside opinions will stimulate and guide you to produce your best efforts.

   To receive specific, practical feedback from others, ask specific, practical questions that will elicit this information. General questions ("What do you think of this?") typically result in overly general, unhelpful responses ("It sounds okay to me"). Be focused in soliciting feedback, and remember: You do have the right to ask people to be *constructive* in their comments, providing suggestions for improvement rather than flatly expressing what they think is wrong.

Step 5B: What Adjustments Are Necessary?   As a result of your review, you may discover that the alternative you selected is not feasible or is not leading to satisfactory results. At other times you may find that the alternative you selected is working out fairly well but still requires some adjustments as you continue to work toward your desired outcomes. In fact, this is a typical situation. Even when things initially appear to be working reasonably well, an active thinker continues to ask questions such as "What might I have overlooked?" and "How could I have done this differently?" Of course, asking — and trying to answer — questions like these is even more essential if solutions are hard to come by (as they usually are in real-world problems) and if you are to retain the flexibility and optimism you will need to tackle a new option.

THINKING ACTIVITY 3.2

Analyzing an Unsolved Problem

Select a problem from your own life. It should be one that you are currently grappling with and have not yet been able to solve. After selecting the problem you want to work on, strengthen your *acceptance* of the problem by using one or more of the strategies described on pages 97–99 and describing your efforts. Then analyze your problem using the problem-solving method described in this chapter. Discuss your problem with other class members to generate fresh perspectives and unusual alternatives that might not have occurred to you. Write your analysis in outline style, giving specific responses to the questions in each step of the problem-solving method. Although you might not reach a "guaranteed" solution to your problem, you should deepen your understanding of the problem and develop a concrete plan of action that will help you move in the right direction. Implement your plan of action and then monitor the results.

THINKING ACTIVITY 3.3

Analyzing College Problems

Analyze the following problems using the problem-solving approach presented in this chapter.

Problem 1: Background Information

The most important unsolved problem that exists for me is my inability to make that crucial decision of what to major in. I want to be secure with respect to both money and happiness when I make a career for myself, and I don't want to make a mistake in choosing a field of study. I want to make this decision before beginning the next semester so that I can start immediately in my career. I've been thinking about managerial studies. However, I often wonder if I have the capacity to make executive decisions when I can't even decide on what I want to do with my life.

Additional problems often encountered by college students that can be used for this activity are located on the companion web site.

Solving Nonpersonal Problems

The problems we have analyzed up to this point have been "personal" problems in the sense that they represent individual challenges encountered by us as we live our lives. We also face problems as members of a community, a society, and the world. As with personal problems, we need to approach these kinds of problems in an organized and thoughtful way in order to explore the issues, develop a clear understanding, and decide on an informed plan of action.

Making sense of a complex, challenging situation is not a simple process. Although the problem-solving method we have been using in this chapter is a powerful approach, its successful application depends on having sufficient information about the situation we are trying to solve. As a result, it is often necessary for us to research articles and other sources of information to develop informed opinions.

The famous newspaperman H. L. Mencken once said, "To every complex question there is a simple answer — and it's wrong!" We have seen in this chapter that complex problems do not admit simple solutions, whether they concern personal problems in our lives or larger social problems like racial prejudice or world hunger. We have also seen, however, that by working through these complex problems thoughtfully and systematically, we can achieve a deeper understanding of their many interacting elements as well as develop strategies for solving them.

Becoming an effective problem-solver does not merely involve applying a problem-solving method in a mechanical fashion any more than becoming a mature critical thinker involves mastering a set of thinking skills. Rather, solving problems, like thinking critically, reflects a total approach to making sense of experience. When we think like problem-solvers, we have the courage to meet difficult problems head-on and the determination to work through them. Instead of acting impulsively or relying exclusively on the advice of others, we are able to make sense of complex problems in an organized way and develop practical solutions and initiatives.

A sophisticated problem-solver employs all of the critical-thinking abilities that we have examined so far and those we will explore in the chapters ahead.

And while we might agree with H. L. Mencken's evaluation of simple answers to complex questions, we might endorse a rephrased version: "To many complex questions there are complex answers — and these are worth pursuing!"

THINKING ACTIVITY 3.4

Analyzing Social Problems

Identify an important local, national, or international problem that needs to be solved. Locate two or more articles that provide background information and analysis of the problem. Using these articles as a resource, analyze the problem using the problem-solving method developed in this chapter.

THINKING PASSAGES

Liberty Versus Security

In the months following the terrorist attacks of September 11, 2001, Americans began to confront the kinds of encroachments on personal freedoms long endured by citizens of other nations. From the comic inconvenience of having to remove your shoes for airport security checks to the inability of international artists and writers (from countries as benign as Australia) to obtain entrance visas to the United States, new laws and policies have been enacted that permit the federal government to more strictly (and covertly) monitor the comings and goings of American citizens and noncitizens alike as well as monitor everything from e-mail communications to library loans. For Americans of Muslim descent and visitors from Muslim countries, the years since 9/11 have been marked by increasing suspicion and periodic hate crimes. Although President George W. Bush and other leaders strongly condemned acts of anti-Muslim discrimination and violence after 9/11, such acts have continued. Muslim Americans have found themselves subjected to a kind of racial profiling in many areas of their lives. Some writers (including Eleanor Stein; see page 122) have even compared the most serious forms of profiling to the internment of Japanese Americans after Pearl Harbor in 1941. As you read the following essays, consider the compromises we make — collectively and individually — as we try to guard our safety yet protect our freedom.

For more information on the Patriot Act, which tremendously expanded the federal government's abilities to track and investigate anyone suspected of "terrorism" (as well as broadening the definition of *terrorism*), go to <http://thomas.loc.gov/cgi-bin/query/z?c107:H.R.3162.ENR:>. Section 105 and Title II deal specifically with electronic surveillance, which is discussed in Stein's essay and predicted by Lisa Guernsey ("Living Under an Electronic Eye," page 119).

Liberty v Security
by *The Economist*

The Current Emergency Justifies a Shifting of the Balance — But Under Clear Democratic Controls

George Bush correctly called the attack on America "an attack on freedom." It was also, to some extent, an "attack through freedom." The terrorists were able to strike at the world's most open society partly by exploiting its openness. Now, as western governments rush to block these loopholes, many fear that they will inadvertently finish what the terrorists began — and curtail the very freedoms which they are fighting to protect.

In America, Mr. Bush, who came to power hoping to reduce the reach of government, is overseeing an increase in its powers. Some of that is planned through new programmes and activities, but some has reflected immediate action by the FBI and police: more than 350 people have already been arrested under emergency rules. In Britain, the debate about introducing national identity cards has gained new vigour. In many countries, leaders are looking at tougher "anti-terrorism" laws ranging from surveillance and powers of arrest to financial disclosure and racial profiling. As one headline has it, "thousands dead, millions deprived of civil liberties." Politicians acidly reply that theoretical liberties were not of much use to the dead in the World Trade Centre.

Amid all this sound and fury, both sides need to consider the fundamental question: in light of the attack, where must the balancing point between security and liberty be set? Civil libertarians should begin by admitting that, contrary to much of their rhetoric, some sort of a balance has always had to be struck. Even fundamental freedoms — for instance, that of speech — are not absolute. People who shout fire in a crowded theatre can expect to be arrested. Defence is the area in which freedoms are most often restricted. Most democracies already grant some discretion to their policemen over

Source: From *The Economist*, September 29, 2001. Copyright © 2001 by The Economist Newspaper Ltd. All rights reserved. Reprinted with permission. Further reproduction prohibited. <www.economist.com>

V I S U A L   T H I N K I N G

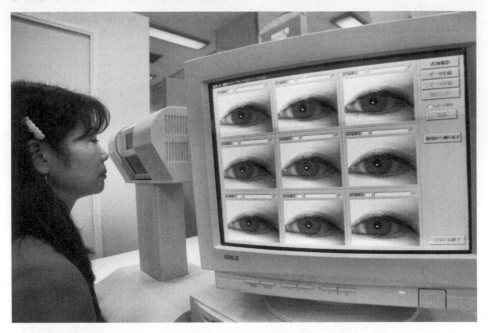

"You Have Beautiful Eyes . . . Let Me Read You Your Rights."

- A democratic society needs to balance personal liberties with the need for security. What do you think about security systems, like the one depicted in this photo, that can identify you instantly? Do you think these kinds of security procedures should be increased to make us safer? Or do you think they should be restricted in order to protect personal privacy? If you were in charge of national security, what policies would you advocate?

whom they investigate, and offer broad protections for secrecy. Many require their citizens to carry identity cards.

Next, libertarians need to accept that, from a security point of view, September 11th was genuinely a day when the world changed. To be sure, that change was most dramatic in America, a country which has had relatively few terrorist attacks of any sort. But even for western countries that have been exposed to bombs and bullets for longer, the bombings of the World Trade Centre and the Pentagon unveiled a new level of threat. The scale of the outrage (the death toll was ten times larger than any comparable tragedy), the use of suicide bombers, the lack of warning, the conversion of aircraft into flying missiles, all should serve as prompts to re-examine old procedures and question established liberties — be they "the freedom" to carry and buy knives at airports or "the freedom" to stash your money in a numbered account in Liechtenstein.

However, if libertarians must accept that something changed on September 11th, authoritarians need to accept that not everything did. Many of the failures of security were not connected to unrestrained liberty, and some measures currently being floated are only tangentially linked to the disaster. Most Britons would not worry too much about carrying identity cards, since they already carry many bits of plastic that serve to identify them; the main objection would be to being charged with a crime, or held on suspicion, simply if they have left their card at home. Nevertheless, supporters of identity cards have overlooked the fact that the hijackers did produce identity papers of one sort or another at the airport. Several were travelling under stolen passports. Identity theft is a growing crime in America — and presumably would be even worse in Britain, where records are appalling.

On the whole, the security lapses in America had less to do with liberty than inefficiency. Security was found wanting, partly because it had to deal with what once seemed an unimaginable threat and partly because, on the evidence available, it did not work well. In particular, America's lavishly funded intelligence services failed to spot that dozens of cohorts of the country's "public enemy number one" had entered the United States, were taking flying lessons and loitering around airports. Much of the failure can be ascribed to an old-fashioned lack of informants and poor collation of existing information, though restrictive laws on wiretapping and other surveillance methods cannot have helped.

The Emergency v the Longer Term

The most important distinction that will need to be drawn is between those measures that are necessary because of a current emergency and those that are desirable for the longer term. With military action likely to prompt further atrocities from terrorist groups, the case for greater emergency powers of surveillance and arrest is strong in any country in which retaliation could occur. Such powers should, however, be granted only with sunset clauses attached so that they need to be reconsidered in a democratic forum before they can be reinstated. Such powers should also remain subject to case-by-case judicial approval — when practical, in advance, but if necessary, in retrospect — in order both to avoid their misuse and to maintain public confidence.

The longer term will pose tougher issues, for even then the security will be needed not against a visible enemy such as another country but against an invisible, potential enemy which September 11th showed could come from many quarters. Efficient security, whether at airports or in any other public place, is itself a challenge to liberty for it steals away time, involves intrusive searches, and restricts freedoms of movement and behaviour. The likelihood must be that, as long as it is done in a way that is non-discriminatory and subject to legal controls, people in democratic countries will choose to accept such security in their own interests. But as this campaign proceeds and as the debate develops, they will have to be given that choice, either directly or through their elected representatives. Democracy is, after all, another of the values that the terrorists have sought to challenge.

NATIONAL I.D. CARDS: ONE SIZE FITS ALL
by Daniel J. Wakin

Imagine you were moving to a new state and the government required you to register at the local police precinct. Or that before the hospital let Mom leave with her newborn, Dad had to register the newly arrived citizen at a central office. Or that the police could stop you and demand to see your papers while you stepped out for a quart of milk.

Hard to accept? Not for Italians, because like most Europeans they live with these rules, though in Italy the chasm between theory and practice can be huge. Whatever the practice, though, scores of governments have the potential to wield strong monitoring powers over their citizens. Chief among their tools is the national identity card. In the post–Sept. 11 world, the idea of universal I.D. cards is being raised in this country, setting off a debate that touches on what it means to be American, and how to balance freedom with the need for security.

Polls in the weeks after the attacks show that Americans favor such identity cards. About 70 percent of those interviewed by the Pew Research Center from Sept. 13 to 17 said they approved of the requirement that all citizens carried one, to be produced on request by police. The following week, in a *New York Times*/CBS News poll, 56 percent said they would accept mandatory national electronic identification cards. A CNN/*Time* poll conducted on

Source: Daniel J. Wakin, "National I. D. Cards: One Size Fits All," The New York Times, October 7, 2001. Copyright © 2001 by *The New York Times* Co. Reprinted by permission.

Sept. 27 reported a similar figure. Helping fuel the debate was a widely published suggestion by Larry Ellison, the chief executive of the software maker Oracle, that the United States should establish a national I.D. system, embedding people's fingerprints on cards and creating a database so airport guards could check identities. Mr. Ellison offered to donate the software.

Similar ideas were floated in editorial and letters pages, with proponents saying the I.D.s could protect airline travelers at check-in and guard against identity theft. With the plethora of personal information already gathered by private industry, some argued, any threats to privacy would not matter that much anyway.

But given the nation's strong tradition of privacy protection, its innate resistance to government intrusion and a growing protest against the use of personal data by marketers, the I.D. idea still seems far off. The Bush administration has rejected the idea and the terrorism legislation now under consideration in Congress does not call for national I.D.s.

Nevertheless, at least one company that makes scanners has reportedly said several federal agencies had been in touch about using the devices in connection with I.D. cards. And some in Congress say the time could be ripe for a serious debate.

Other governments agree. Officials in Britain, Australia, the Netherlands and the Philippines have also raised the idea.

Privacy International, a watchdog group in London, estimates that about 100 countries — many of them developing nations — have compulsory national I.D.s. Some, like Denmark, issue I.D. numbers at birth around which a lifetime of personal information accretes. They are generally accepted among the citizenry of European countries, like France, with a tradition of centralized government and with extensive social welfare systems.

"In reality, the card is just the visible part of a vast information spectrum," said Simon Davies, the director of Privacy International. "To some it's a security icon; it represents the potential for a safer society. To others it represents a more efficient government. To others, it represents cracking down on illegal immigrants. But ultimately, the card is worthless without some sort of integrated computer system behind it." And that, he says, presents a danger to privacy, particularly in the developed world.

During the Apartheid era, South Africa produced the most nefarious sort of I.D.s, pass books that specified what areas blacks were allowed to circulate in and work. The pass laws allowed the police to arrest blacks without cards — a common form of harassment.

In the United States, resistance to a national I.D. dwells firmly in the deep-seated tradition of privacy protection, something that spans the ideological spectrum. "It is a traditional human rights notion that we see infusing many different constitutional doctrines in this country," said Nadine Strossen, president of the American Civil Liberties Union. "You do have a right to be left alone in the most literal sense."

A national I.D. could also become a powerful tool for ethnic profiling, Ms. Strossen argued, suggesting that the authorities would be more likely to stop Arab-Americans for an I.D. check. (The *Time*/CNN poll found that half of those surveyed favored requiring Arab-Americans as a group to carry federal I.D. cards.)

Other opponents argue that a national I.D. and the information behind it would only strengthen the power of bureaucracies. And they say it will offer little protection because forgers will inevitably catch up to the technology.

Right now, the United States has embarked on what could be considered a national I.D. pilot project — for Mexicans. The Immigration and Naturalization Service has approved four million cards under a new program for short-term, short-range border crossings. The new cards have fingerprint and personal information on an optically etched strip.

Actually, the best hope for proponents of national I.D.s may be sitting in our wallets. It is the driver's license. The American Association of Motor Vehicle Administrators has recommended to Congress that the nation adopt a standard proof of identity for the issuing of licenses. Such a program would cost up $35 million to develop, and up to $20 million a year to operate, the association says. At the same time, it is looking at national standards for drivers' licenses, including what sort of biometric data — like fingerprints and face recognition — to include.

Right now, 36 states and Washington, D.C., have or are planning drivers' licenses with two-dimensional bar codes that can contain 2,000 bytes of information, enough for a driving record, photograph and fingerprint data, said Nathan Root, who directs the association's standards program.

So now imagine this. A police officer stops you in your car, scans your license, matches your fingerprints with a central database and has immediate access to a plethora of information, including whether you are on a terrorist watch list.

What would the Italians think?

LIVING UNDER AN ELECTRONIC EYE
by Lisa Guernsey

In 1928 Justice Louis D. Brandeis made a prediction. Someday, he wrote in a dissent to a Supreme Court decision on wiretapping, the government may find ways to reproduce documents in court without removing them from "private drawers." Such methods, he warned, will expose "the most intimate occurrences of the home."

The dawn of computer technology, especially the Internet, has proved him right. With so much public and personal business being carried out electronically, it has become technically feasible for government agencies — or anyone with the proper tools — to find private electronic correspondence without ever breaking into secret drawers, or even entering a person's home or office.

And not just e-mail can be seized. The most mundane aspects of a person's life are now recorded digitally, often in databases beyond their control. With each new technology, more details of people's daily activities can potentially be scooped up by law enforcement officials and later presented in a courtroom.

But with such surveillance capabilities on tap, the question inevitably arises: Should the government be given the authority to use them?

In reaction to the terrorist attacks of Sept. 11, lawmakers and many of their constituents are saying yes. Several bills are being considered this week that would expand the ways in which the federal government could use technology not only as a law enforcement tool to track down terrorists or anyone suspected of committing a crime but also as a crime prevention tool to monitor suspicious activity and possibly anticipate any future attacks.

Officials, for example, are asking for broad authority to inspect logs of Internet use and the address fields of e-mail messages, which in addition to revealing the senders and the recipients could also divulge the messages' content through their subject lines. And they are seeking more latitude in listening to conversations of people on the move as they communicate by cellphone or other wireless technologies.

A wealth of new electronic information is already available to law enforcement agencies. With a court order, agents can retrieve records of credit-card purchases, peruse the logs kept by automated toll booths to

Source: Lisa Guernsey, "Living Under an Electronic Eye," *The New York Times,* September 27, 2001. Copyright © 2001 by The New York Times Co. Reprinted by permission.

determine which cars drove through, listen to voice mail left in databases, gather lists of library books checked out by patrons, watch videos recorded by public surveillance cameras and find out which television shows a subscriber has ordered on pay-per-view services.

"The problem that Brandeis feared is amplified," said Jeffrey Rosen, an associate professor of law at George Washington University and the author of *The Unwanted Gaze,* which traces the erosion of privacy. "The fact that so much more of our lives can be recorded and monitored in cyberspace makes the problem greater in degree and scope."

It is an open question, however, whether people view digital surveillance as intrusive, especially given their new fears about terrorism. By reviewing some of those seemingly mundane electronic records, investigators have been able to retrace the movements of terrorists who carried out the attacks on Sept. 11. Agents have searched computers at a public library and a Kinko's shop in Florida that appear to have been used by the hijackers to buy airline tickets. Videotape of automobile traffic at Logan Airport in Boston revealed that one of them, Mohamed Atta, drove through the area at least five times before the attacks, perhaps making dry runs.

A year ago, during the presidential election campaign, political pollsters were finding that voters seemed increasingly wary of privacy invasions by companies or by the government. Today, concerns about security are trumping such wariness. In a poll conducted on Sept. 13 and 14 by *The New York times* and CBS News, respondents were asked whether they believed that Americans would have to "give up some personal freedoms in order to make the country safe from terrorist attacks." "Yes" was the response of 74 percent. A week later that number rose to 79 percent.

The same poll showed a strengthening of support for governmental monitoring of e-mail and phone conversations of ordinary Americans on a regular basis. About 45 percent said they would be willing to allow such monitoring, up from 39 percent the week before; 56 percent of people also favored the idea of national electronic I.D. cards.

Steve and Paula Baumgardner, from Jacksonville, Fla., who visited New York City last week as tourists, echo the prevailing sentiments. "Freedom is not free," said Mr. Baumgardner, a business manager. "I'm not for Big Brother, but I don't mind paying a price for security and safety."

In national crises in the past, Americans have often declared their willingness to sacrifice some privacy in the name of security. When fears of Communism were running high in the 1950s, 65 percent of American adults surveyed in a Gallup poll said that the government should have the right to listen in on private telephone conversations.

After the bombing of the Oklahoma City federal building in 1995, *The Los Angeles Times* asked people if they thought that it would be necessary for the average person to give up some civil liberties to curb terrorism. Nearly half — 49 percent — answered yes. When the Pew Research Center revisited the security question in 1997 (using the same methodology as the 1995 *Times* poll), that figure had dropped to 29 percent.

It is difficult to gauge whether the support for governmental monitoring will outlast the immediate trauma of the Sept. 11 attacks. Nor have the recent polls determined exactly what kinds of freedoms most people would be willing to forgo.

Congress is considering several anti-terrorism measures, some of which involve eavesdropping on the Internet. Attorney General John Ashcroft has asked that the words "electronic communications" be added to existing laws governing telephone surveillance. His proposal implies the wider use of Carnivore, an Internet surveillance system that is used by the Federal Bureau of Investigation, although the system is not named in the proposal.

If the proposal becomes law, government agencies would be allowed to trace Web use under the same laws that govern their tracing of telephone numbers. Those laws call for less judicial oversight than laws for wiretaps, which involve the content of phone conversations.

But is a Web address equivalent to a telephone number? Some privacy advocates argue that Web addresses reveal far more information because some of them are made up of the words that a person keyed into a search engine. If the user enters the search terms "bomb" and "recipe" at Google, for example, the search yields the Web address *www.google.com/search?q=bomb+recipes&btnG=Google+Search*.

Similar concerns may apply to e-mail. The Ashcroft proposal appears to treat a message's addressing and routing information as if it were no more than a phone number, retrievable with the same low level of judicial oversight. But if that information were to include a message's subject line — a matter that is still up in the air — the government would essentially be peeking at personal correspondence, some privacy advocates say.

"We're not saying that law enforcement should not be able to gain access to that information," said Barry Steinhardt, associate director of the American Civil Liberties Union. What the A.C.L.U. is arguing, he said, is "that the information is content and that law enforcement should meet a higher standard to prove their need for it."

The changing technology of the telephone has also altered the politics of the wiretap. Mr. Ashcroft has proposed what analysts are calling "roving wiretaps," in which the government would have the authority to tap into a suspect's telephone calls regardless of what jurisdiction he was in or what phone he was using at a given moment. Before now, a criminal investigator had to get a separate court order for every jurisdiction in which a phone was tapped, which becomes more difficult as cellphones proliferate and can be used across borders.

"We need to be able to have the court authority to monitor not the phone but the telephone communications of a person," Mr. Ashcroft said at a recent news conference, "and to have that authority stay with one person."

Cellphones can also be used to locate people within a few city blocks. As long as a phone is turned on, it is communicating with the closest cell towers, sending signals about its whereabouts. If those signals are considered addressing or routing information, analysts say, they could easily be part of the records requested in a wiretap.

Aside from the legal questions, it is unclear how effective these forms of electronic surveillance may prove to be. For example, while some electronic information about the Sept. 11 terrorists has come to light via computer searches and video records, it is not known whether increased digital tracking would have helped head off the plot, since so few of the terrorists had come to the attention of the Central Intelligence Agency before the attacks.

Marc Rotenberg, director of the Electronic Privacy Information Center, said he wondered if law enforcement and intelligence agents might be better served by old-fashioned techniques like infiltrating suspected groups and code-breaking. "It may turn out that the problem was that we had too much electronic surveillance," he said.

Winn Schwartau, a security consultant in Seminole, Fla., and the author of the books *Information Warfare* and *Cybershock,* agrees that electronic surveillance should not be a substitute for proven labor-intensive techniques.

"We need human intelligence — a live human being on the ground, being a spy," Mr. Schwartau said. "And we've given up a huge amount of it."

CONSTRUCTION OF AN ENEMY
by Eleanor Stein

Remember the Nazi technique: "pit race against race, religion against religion, prejudice against prejudice. Divide and conquer!"

— President Franklin D. Roosevelt (January 1942) admonishing Americans not to discriminate against aliens, weeks before he signed the Japanese exclusion order (Greg Robinson, *By Order of the Presidency,* 2001).

The aggressive measures instituted by the Bush administration against immigrants and visitors of Muslim faith, or from primarily Muslim Arab and South Asian countries, seem aimed less at their putative foreign targets than at the hearts and minds of our domestic population. Packaged as post–September 11 law enforcement, the new racial profiling has netted few if any prosecutions for terrorist acts, but has done a great deal to demonize Arabs, South Asians, and Muslims, to dehumanize them, and to construct them as the enemy of America in the twenty-first century. Once the state successfully constructs an enemy group, it can justify detentions without charge, military occupation, and other drastic means of waging war against that other, the enemy.

Nativist and xenophobic identification of immigrants with national security threats is a theme coincident with the history of the United States. The Naturalization Act of 1790 prohibited citizenship and civil rights to immigrants of disfavored ethnicity. The Alien and Sedition Acts of 1798 placed restrictions on which ethnicities or nationalities could apply for citizenship, and authorized the president to order the deportation of all immigrants judged dangerous to national security. The "sedition" of concern in 1798 were the ideas of the French Revolution. The Chinese Exclusion (Geary) Act of 1882, in violation of the express terms of a treaty in force between China and the United States, forbade Chinese laborers from entering the United States.

The National Origins Act of 1924 established immigration quotas privileging "Nordic" immigrants. The Smith Act of 1940 required registration and fingerprinting of aliens, and added vague classifications of "subversives" and "excludables" to the list of deportable persons. The McCarran Walter Act of 1952 empowered the Department of Justice to deport immigrants or naturalized citizens engaging in "subversive" activities. The Anti-Terrorism and Effective Death Penalty Act of 1996 granted the executive the authority, based upon secret evidence, to designate any foreign organization a terrorist group and to deport noncitizens as terrorists.

But it was the internment of Japanese Americans during the Second World War that elevated xenophobia into national policy. And it was in the internment cases that the Supreme Court, upholding the internment as a matter of military necessity, wrote the requirement of strict judicial scrutiny of "invidious" distinction into American jurisprudence.

Source: Eleanor Stein, "Construction of an Enemy," *Monthly Review,* July–August 2003. Copyright © 2003 by Monthly Review Press. Reprinted by permission of Monthly Review Foundation.

Based upon reports by the military that it had intercepted radio and light signals between offshore locations and the California coast, the evacuation and internment orders forced persons of Japanese descent to leave their homes in specified control areas in California, Arizona, Oregon, and Washington, and move to internment camps. Over 120,000 persons, two-thirds of them U.S.–born citizens, spent the years of the war in such camps.

The internment order was rationalized not only by military necessity — the fear of sabotage and espionage — but also by the military's claim that the normal criminal investigatory work of the Justice Department had been overly slow and inadequate to guarantee U.S. security. The racist hysteria in which the roundups took place was fed by the Hearst press and by California economic interests — such as the White American Nurserymen — in competiton with small entrepreneurs of Japanese descent.

Two brave individuals, Fred Korematsu and Gordon Hirabayashi, refused to report for internment and sought to challenge the order in the Federal Courts. In a shameful decision, the U.S. Supreme Court upheld as constitutional this mass internment; included were 80,000 citizens deprived of liberty solely by reason of their ethnic origin. Forty years later, when the two whose refusal to report for internment had led to Supreme Court cases sought (and received) judicial exoneration, it was discovered that the military report, which was the justification for the internment order and the Supreme Court decision, was a complete fabrication. An archival researcher, working in conjunction with a congressional commission appointed to investigate the internment, found the original report. The supposed intercepted radio and light signals, dutifully repeated in the Supreme Court opinion, had never occurred.

The shadow of Manzanar — the California inter[n]ment camp — looms today over all of the current measures being taken against Arab and Muslim immigrants. These measures can be seen as internment for the twenty-first century — or to coin a more accurate term, externment.

Shortly after September 11, 2001, the "Ashcroft Raids" occurred, the secret detention and deportation of up [to] a thousand or more Arab or Muslim men. Some were held for months, even as long as one year, without access to lawyers and in some cases, to families. Ashcroft stated he intended to jail every terrorist he could find, and that net included thousands of Muslim noncitizens. What were the results of this dragnet? Not a single person charged with involvement in the September 11 attacks, and four indicted on charges of support for terrorism, with none of the indictments including any specific violent acts. The Justice Department now admits that at least 766 persons were detained on "special interest" charges after September 11 and held incommunicado; of these, 511 have been deported. The Justice Department claims that among those deported were some who could have been — but have not been — charged with terrorism offenses. This in turn has led to reported speculation that one purpose of the mass detention policy was the recruitment of intelligence agents *(www.law.com/jsp/article.jsp?id= 1052440755868)*. An additional six thousand were deported for violations of immigration status. Eight thousand were called for interviews on the sole ground that they were recent male immigrants from Arab countries.

The USA Patriot Act, enacted within six weeks of September 11, permits the Attorney General to detain noncitizens without a hearing; to bar foreign citizens from entering the United States because of their political opinions; and authorizes deportation based upon support of a disfavored group. None of these restrictions is tied to participation in any terrorist act. On April 29, 2003, the Supreme Court approved mandatory detention of "criminal aliens" pending deportation — that is, permanent resident aliens convicted of any of a list of crimes who are subject to deportation have no entitlement to a hearing to consider bail for the period they contest or await deportation.

Also coming soon may be Patriot Act II, which modifies the definiton of "foreign power" to include all persons, regardless of whether they are affiliated with an international terrorist group, who engage in international terrorism; and defines any person who engaged in clandestine intelligence[-]gathering activities for a foreign power as an agent of that power, regardless of whether those activities are federal crimes.

One of the most far-reaching forms of racial profiling is the requirement of the Immigration and Naturalization Service, now merged into the Office of Homeland Security, termed Special Registration. These new rules apply to any male, over the age of sixteen, who is not currently a permanent resident (green cardholder), from twenty-five countries: Afghanistan, Algeria, Bahrain, Eritrea, Iran, Iraq, Lebanon, Libya, Morocco, North Korea, Oman, Qatar, Somalia, Sudan, Syria, Tunisia, United Arab Emirates, Yemen, Pakistan, Saudi Arabia, Bangladesh, Egypt, Indonesia, Jordan, and Kuwait. These men were required to register in person at an immigration office during February and March 2003 on a few weeks notice, to be photographed, fingerprinted, and interviewed, in many cases about their political beliefs and associations. More than 125,000 registered; over 2,000 were detained. All must re-register annually and any time they leave the United States. A widespread panic resulted in immigrant communities, and thousands in the New York and New England areas traveled with their families to the Canadian border to seek asylum; however, the United States had closed the border. Hundreds were detained there, their families left without shelter or resources in the bitter New England winter. Local refugee assistance organizations, overwhelmed, were forced to close their doors.

Government profiling also contributed to a wave of popular violence against Arab, South Asian, and Muslim communities. The number of reported U.S. hate crimes against Muslims and Arabs in 2002 increased 1600 percent over the previous year.

The construction of an enemy, through government targeting with media complicity and a popular echo, endangers and dehumanizes millions of Arabs, Asians, and Muslims. Given a dehumanized enemy, bombing its cities and sacking its history was presented on U.S. TV as an extreme sport. The construction of an enemy provides an effective means of control of the domestic population, which visits its fears and frustrations on its Arab and Muslim neighbors. This control is, however, contested. In communities all over the country, towns and cities have passed local government resolutions criticizing and even refusing to enforce the Patriot Act.

Fred Korematsu and Gordon Hirabayashi waited forty years for vindication and reparations; and few outside the Japanese-American community, with the notable exception of the Quakers, had opposed internment. Hopefully we are doing better this time.

Interfaith groups are building bridges to Muslim communities. In upstate New York, Women Against War organized a toy drive for children of detainees and deportees to celebrate Eid, the end of Ramadan and, with national civil liberties organizations, recruited attorneys and other volunteers to assist men reporting for Special Registration and their families.

And shortly after September 11 the National Asian Pacific American Legal Consortium invited Arab Americans to join them at the National Japanese American Memorial to show solidarity in anticipation of racial profiling. Resistance as ever is based on acts of individual decency, which in these sad times appear as acts of courage. But the liberty interests of all U.S. residents are implicated; if we do not stand by our Muslim neighbors in their registration, detention, and deportation nightmare[,] we will have a yet harder time when these techniques are more widely applied.

Questions for Analysis

1. The editorial writer for *The Economist* ("Liberty v Security") asks: "In light of the attack, where must the balancing point between security and liberty be set?" How would you answer this question? Are you aware of any way in which your personal "liberty" has been somehow confined, restrained, or denied because of 9/11 and its aftermath?

2. Take an inventory of your wallet, your mail, and your incoming telephone calls. To what extent have you already given up your privacy to public records, banks, telemarketers, and others? If you're technically savvy, you might search your computer for cookies and other "hidden" software programs that silently track your movements from one web site to the next, building a profile for marketers. What do you find? To what extent is the fabric of society made up of these interconnections? Is it ever possible to opt out of them completely?

3. What are your responsibilities toward your neighbors and your community — watching over and keeping track of each other, or allowing everyone to go about their business? On the Web, or through an electronic database, search for information on the murder of Kitty Genovese in 1964 and the 1995 murder of Deletha Ward. Can you think of other examples of similar cases or behavior?

4. In the following poem, W. H. Auden satirizes the paradox of anonymity with a complete lack of privacy. To what extent was Auden, who published this poem in 1940, accurately predicting the future? How would any of the essayists in this section respond?

THE UNKNOWN CITIZEN
by W. H. Auden

He was found by the Bureau of Statistics to be
One against whom there was no official complaint,
And all the reports on his conduct agree
That, in the modern sense of an old-fashioned word, he was a saint,
For in everything he did he served the Greater Community.
Except for the War till the day he retired
He worked in a factory and never got fired,
But satisfied his employers, Fudge Motors Inc.

Source: "The Unknown Citizen," copyright 1940 and renamed 1968 by W. H. Auden, from *Collected Poems* by W. H. Auden. Used by permission of Random House, Inc.

Yet he wasn't a scab or odd in his views,
For his Union reports that he paid his dues,
(Our report on his Union shows it was sound)
And our Social Psychology workers found
That he was popular with his mates and liked a drink.
The Press are convinced that he bought a paper every day
And that his reactions to advertisements were normal in every way.
Policies taken out in his name provide that he was fully insured,
And his Health-card shows he was once in a hospital but left it cured.
Both Producers Research and High-Grade Living declare
He was fully sensible to the advantages of the Instalment Plan
And had everything necessary to the Modern Man,
A phonograph, a radio, a car and a frigidaire.
Our researchers into Public Opinion are content
That he held the proper opinions for the time of year;
When there was peace, he was for peace: when there was war, he went.
He was married and added five children to the population,
Which our Eugenist says was the right number for a parent of his generation.
And our teachers report that he never interfered with their education.
Was he free? Was he happy? The question is absurd:
Had anything been wrong, we should certainly have heard.

4

Perceiving

Organizing
sensations into a
design or pattern

Selecting
sensations to pay
attention to

Interpreting
what this pattern or
event means

Perceiving
Actively selecting, organizing,
and interpreting sensations

Experiences shape
our perceptions.

We construct beliefs
based on our perceptions.

We view the world
through our own unique
"lenses," which shape
and influence our
perceptions.

We construct
knowledge based
on our beliefs.

Thinking critically involves understanding how "lenses"
influence perceptions, beliefs, and knowledge.

Thinking is the way you make sense of the world. By thinking in an active, purposeful, and organized way, you are able to solve problems, work toward your goals, analyze issues, and make decisions. Your experience of the world comes to you by means of your *senses:* sight, hearing, smell, touch, and taste. These senses are your bridges to the world, making you aware of what occurs outside you, and the process of becoming aware of your world through your senses is known as *perceiving.*

In this chapter you will explore the way your perceiving process operates and how it relates to your ability to think effectively. In particular, you will discover the way you shape your personal experience by actively selecting, organizing, and interpreting the sensations provided by the senses. In a way, each of us views the world through a pair of individual "eyeglasses" or "contact lenses" that reflect our past experiences and unique personalities. As a critical thinker, you want to become aware of the nature of your own "lenses" to help eliminate any bias or distortion they may be causing. You also want to become aware of the "lenses" of others so that you can better understand why they view things the way they do.

At almost every waking moment of your life, your senses are being bombarded by a tremendous number of stimuli: images to see, noises to hear, odors to smell, textures to feel, and flavors to taste. The experience of all these sensations happening at once creates what the nineteenth-century American philosopher William James called "a bloomin' buzzin' confusion." Yet for us, the world usually seems much more orderly and understandable. Why is this so?

In the first place, your sense equipment can receive sensations only within certain limited ranges. For example, there are many sounds and smells that animals can detect but you cannot because their sense organs have broader ranges in these areas than yours do.

A second reason you can handle this sensory bombardment is that from the stimulation available, you *select* only a small amount on which to focus your attention. To demonstrate this, try the following exercise. Concentrate on what you can *see,* ignoring your other senses for the moment. Focus on sensations that you were not previously aware of and then answer the first question. Concentrate on each of your other senses in turn, following the same procedure.

1. What can you *see?* (For example, the shape of the letters on the page, the design of the clothing on your arm)
2. What can you *hear?* (For example, the hum of the air circulator, the rustling of a page)
3. What can you *feel?* (For example, the pressure of the clothes against your skin, the texture of the page on your fingers)

4. What can you *smell?* (For example, the perfume or cologne someone is wearing, the odor of stale cigarette smoke)

5. What can you *taste?* (For example, the aftereffects of your last meal)

Compare your responses with those of the other students in the class. Do your classmates perceive sensations that differ from the ones you perceived? If so, how do you explain these differences?

As you practice this simple exercise, it should become clear that for every sensation that you focus your attention on, there are countless other sensations that you are simply ignoring. If you were aware of *everything* that is happening at every moment, you would be completely overwhelmed. By selecting certain sensations, you are able to make sense of your world in a relatively orderly way. The activity of using your senses to experience and make sense of your world is known as *perceiving.*

perceiving *Actively selecting, organizing, and interpreting what is experienced by your senses*

Actively Selecting, Organizing, and Interpreting Sensations

It is tempting to think that your senses simply record what is happening out in the world as if you were a human camera or tape recorder. You are not, however, a passive receiver of information, a "container" into which sense experience is poured. Instead, you are an *active participant* who is always trying to understand the sensations you are encountering. As you perceive your world, your experience is the result of combining the sensations you are having with the way you understand these sensations. For example, examine the following collection of markings. What do you see?

If all you see is a collection of black spots, try looking at the group sideways. After a while, you will probably perceive a familiar animal.

From this example you can see that when you perceive the world, you are doing more than simply recording what your senses experience. Besides experiencing sensations, you are also *actively making sense* of these sensations. That is why this collection of black spots suddenly became the figure of an animal — because you were able actively to organize these spots into a pattern you recognized.

When you actively perceive the sensations you are experiencing, you are engaged in three distinct activities:

1. *Selecting* certain sensations to pay attention to

2. *Organizing* these sensations into a design or pattern

3. *Interpreting* what this design or pattern means to you

In the case of the figure on page 131, you were able to perceive an animal because you *selected* certain of the markings to concentrate on, *organized* these markings into a pattern, and *interpreted* this pattern as representing a familiar animal.

Of course, when you perceive, these three operations of selecting, organizing, and interpreting are usually performed quickly, automatically, and often simultaneously. Also, you are normally unaware that you are performing these operations because they are so rapid and automatic. This chapter is designed to help you slow down this normally automatic process of perceiving so that you can understand how the process works.

Let's explore more examples that illustrate how you actively select, organize, and interpret your perceptions of the world. Carefully examine the figure at the top of page 133.

Do you see both the young woman and the old woman? If you do, try switching back and forth between the two images. As you switch back and forth, notice how for each image you are

- *Selecting* certain lines, shapes, and shadings on which to focus your attention

- *Organizing* these lines, shapes, and shadings into different patterns

- *Interpreting* these patterns as representing things that you are able to recognize — a hat, a nose, a chin

Another way for you to become aware of your active participation in perceiving your world is to consider how you see objects. Examine the illustration that

follows. Do you perceive different-sized people or the same-sized people at different distances?

When you see someone who is far away, you usually do not perceive a tiny person. Instead, you perceive a normal-sized person who is far away from you. Your experience in the world has enabled you to discover that the farther things are from you, the smaller they look. The moon in the night sky appears about the size of a quarter, yet you perceive it as being considerably larger. As you look down a long stretch of railroad tracks or gaze up at a tall building, the boundary lines seem to come together. Even though these images are what your eyes "see," however, you do not usually perceive the tracks meeting or the building coming to a point. Instead, your mind actively organizes and interprets a world composed of constant shapes and sizes, even though the images you actually see usually vary, depending on how far you are from them and the angle from which you are looking at them.

In short, your mind actively participates in the way you perceive the world. By combining the sensations you are receiving with the way your mind selects, organizes, and interprets these sensations, you perceive a world of things that is stable and familiar, a world that usually makes sense to you.

The process of perceiving takes place at a variety of different levels. At the most basic level, the concept of "perceiving" refers to the selection, organization, and interpretation of sensations: for example, being able to perceive the various objects in your experience, like a basketball. However, you also perceive larger patterns of meaning at more complex levels, as when watching the action of a group of people engaged in a basketball game. Although these are very different contexts, both engage you in the process of actively selecting, organizing, and interpreting what is experienced by your senses — in other words, "perceiving."

People's Perceptions Differ

Your *active* participation in perceiving your world is something you are not usually aware of. You normally assume that what you are perceiving is what is actually taking place. Only when you find that your perception of the same event differs from the perceptions of others are you forced to examine the manner in which you are selecting, organizing, and interpreting the events in your world.

THINKING ACTIVITY 4.1

Analyzing Perceptions

Carefully examine the picture of a boy sitting at a desk on page 136. What do you think is happening in this picture?

1. Describe as specifically as possible what you perceive is taking place in the picture.
2. Describe what you think will happen next.
3. Identify the details of the picture that led you to your perceptions.
4. Compare your perceptions with the perceptions of other students in the class. List several perceptions that differ from yours.

In most cases, people in a group will have a variety of perceptions about what is taking place in the picture in Thinking Activity 4.1. Some will see the boy as frustrated because the work is too difficult. Others will see him concentrating on what has to be done. Still others may see him as annoyed because he is being forced to do something he does not want to do. In each case, the perception

VISUAL THINKING

The Investigation

- Explain why each witness describes the suspect differently. Have you ever been involved in a situation in which people described an individual or event in contrasting or conflicting ways? What is the artist saying about people's perceptions?

depends on how the person is actively using his or her mind to organize and interpret what is taking place. Since the situation pictured is by its nature somewhat puzzling, different people perceive it in different ways.

Additional examples that provide opportunities for you to analyze your perceptions can be found on the companion web site.

Viewing the World Through "Lenses"

To understand how various people can be exposed to the same stimuli or events and yet have different perceptions, it helps to imagine that each of us views the world through our own pair of "contact lenses." Of course, we are not usually aware of the lenses we are wearing. Instead, our lenses act as *filters* that select and shape what we perceive without our realizing it.

This concept of "lenses" explains why people can be exposed to the same stimuli or events and yet perceive different things. This happens because people are wearing *different lenses,* which influence what they are perceiving. F135example, in "The Investigation" on page 135, each witness is giving what he or she (or it!) believes is an accurate description of the man in the center, unaware that their descriptions are being influenced by who they are and the way that they see things. When members of your class had different perceptions of the boy at the desk in Thinking Activity 4.1, their different perceptions were the result of the different lenses through which each views the world.

To understand the way people perceive the world, you have to understand their individual lenses, which influence how they actively select, organize, and interpret the events in their experience. A diagram of the process might look like this:

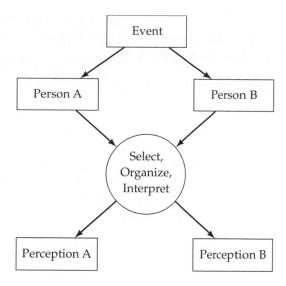

Consider the following pairs of statements. In each of these cases, both people are being exposed to the same basic *stimulus* or event, yet each has a totally different *perception* of the experience. Explain how you think the various perceptions might have developed.

1. a. That chili was much too spicy to eat.
   Explanation:

   b. That chili needed more hot peppers and chili powder to spice it up a little.
   Explanation:

2. a. People who wear lots of makeup and jewelry are very sophisticated.
   Explanation:

   b. People who wear lots of makeup and jewelry are overdressed.
   Explanation:

3. a. The music that young people enjoy listening to is a very creative cultural expression.
   Explanation:

   b. The music that young people enjoy listening to is obnoxious noise.
   Explanation:

To become an effective critical thinker, you have to become aware of the lenses that you — and others — are wearing. These lenses aid you in actively selecting, organizing, and interpreting the sensations in your experience. If you are unaware of the nature of your own lenses, you can often mistake your own perceptions for objective truth without bothering to examine either the facts or others' perceptions on a given issue.

Selecting Perceptions

We spend much of the time experiencing the world in a very general way, unaware of many of the details of the events that are taking place. For example, try to draw a picture of the face of a push-button phone, complete with numbers and letters. Then compare your drawing with an actual phone. Did you have any difficulty? Why? We also tend to select perceptions about subjects that have been called to our attention for some reason. For instance, at the age of three, my daughter suddenly became aware of beards. Upon entering a subway car, she would ask in a penetrating voice, "Any beards here?" and then would proceed to count them out loud. In doing this, she naturally focused my attention — as well as the attention of many of the other passengers — on beards.

As another aspect of our "perceiving" lenses, we tend to notice what we need, desire, or find of interest. When we go shopping, we focus on the items we are looking for. Walking down the street, we tend to notice certain kinds of people or events while completely ignoring others. Even while watching a movie or reading a book, we tend to concentrate on and remember the elements we find of interest. Another person can perform *exactly* the same actions — shop at the same store, walk down the same street with you, read the same book, or go to the same movie — and yet see and remember entirely different things. In other words, what you perceive depends largely on your interests, needs, and desires.

The way you are feeling — your mood or emotional state — can also affect the perceptions you select. For example, think back on the times when you have felt cranky, perhaps because you did not get enough sleep or were under pressure, and recall how you behaved. When we are in bad moods, we often seem ready to focus our attention on every potential insult or criticism made by others — and are ready to respond the same way.

Although we tend to focus on what is familiar to us, we are normally not aware that we are doing so. In fact, we often take for granted what is familiar to us — the taste of chili or eggs, the street that we live on, our family or friends — and normally do not think about our perception of it. But when something happens that makes the familiar seem strange and unfamiliar, we become aware of our perceptions and start to evaluate them.

To sum up, you actively select your perceptions based on what has been called to your attention, your needs or interests, your mood or feelings, and what seems familiar or unfamiliar. The way you select your perceptions is an important factor in shaping the lenses through which you view the world.

Organizing Perceptions

Not only do you actively *select* certain perceptions; you also actively *organize* these perceptions into meaningful relationships and patterns. Consider the following series of lines:

Did you perceive them as individual lines, or did you group them into pairs? We naturally try to organize our perceptions to create order and meaning. Consider the items pictured next and try to organize them into a pattern that is familiar to you:

As you perceive the world, you naturally try to order and organize what you are experiencing into patterns and relationships that make sense to you. And when you are able to do so, the completed whole means more to you than the sum of the individual parts. You are continually organizing your world in this way at virtually every waking moment.

We do not live in a world of isolated sounds, patches of color, random odors, and individual textures. Instead, we live in a world of objects and people, language and music — a world in which all these individual stimuli are woven together. We are able to perceive this world of complex experiences because we are able to organize the individual stimuli we are receiving into relationships that have meaning for us.

The way you organize your experience is an important part of the lenses through which you perceive the world. You are able to perceive objects, human expressions, and potential human action because of your ability to organize the lines, shapes, and shadings into meaningful patterns and complex relationships.

Interpreting Perceptions

Besides selecting and organizing your perceptions, you also actively *interpret* what you perceive. When you interpret, you are figuring out what something means. One of the elements that influences your interpretations of what you are perceiving is the *context*, or overall situation, within which the perception is occurring. For example, imagine that you see a man running down the street. Your interpretation of his action will depend on the specific context. For example, is there a bus waiting at the corner? Is a police officer running behind him? Is he wearing a jogging suit?

You are continually trying to interpret what you perceive, whether it is a design, someone's behavior, or a social situation. Like the example of someone running down the street, many of the perceptions you experience can be interpreted in more than one way. When a situation has more than one possible interpretation, you say that it is *ambiguous*. The more ambiguous a situation is, the greater the number of possible meanings or interpretations it has.

Think again about the picture you examined in Thinking Activity 4.1. Your description of what was happening — and what was about to happen — was based on your interpretation of the situation. Other members of the class may have given different descriptions of what was occurring because they interpreted the situation differently. Since this picture is by its nature puzzling and ambiguous, no one interpretation is necessarily more correct than another. Instead, each interpretation simply reveals the lenses through which this person views the world. Of course, you may feel that some interpretations make more sense than others, based on the details and the relationships that you perceive in the situation.

Similarly, the way you are feeling can influence your interpretations of what you are experiencing. When you feel happy and optimistic, the world often seems friendly and the future full of possibilities, and you interpret the problems you encounter as challenges to be overcome. But when you are depressed or unhappy, you may perceive your world entirely differently. The future can appear full of problems that are trying to overwhelm you. In both cases the outer circumstances may be very similar; it is your own interpretation of the world through your lenses that varies so completely.

What Factors Shape Perceptions?

Your perceptions of the world are dramatically influenced by your past experiences: the way you were brought up, the relationships you have had, and your training and education. Every dimension of "who" you are is reflected in your perceiving lenses. It takes critical reflection to become aware of these powerful influences on our perceptions of the world and the beliefs we construct based on them.

Your special interests and areas of expertise also affect how you see the world. Consider the case of two people who are watching a football game. One person, who has very little understanding of football, sees merely a bunch of grown men hitting each other for no apparent reason. The other person, who loves football, sees complex play patterns, daring coaching strategies, effective blocking and tackling techniques, and zone defenses with "seams" that the receivers are trying to "split." Both have their eyes focused on the same event, but they are perceiving two entirely different situations. Their perceptions differ because each person is actively selecting, organizing, and interpreting the available stimuli in different ways. The same is true of any situation in which you are perceiving something about which you have special knowledge or expertise. The following are examples:

- A builder examining the construction of a new house
- A music lover attending a concert
- A naturalist experiencing the outdoors
- A cook tasting a dish just prepared
- A lawyer examining a contract
- An art lover visiting a museum

Think about a special area of interest or expertise that you have and how your perceptions of that area differ from those of people who don't share your knowledge. Ask other class members about their areas of expertise. Notice how their perceptions of that area differ from your own because of their greater knowledge and experience.

In all these cases, the perceptions of the knowledgeable person differ substantially from the perceptions of the person who lacks knowledge of that area. Of course, you do not have to be an expert to have more fully developed perceptions. It is a matter of degree.

THINKING ACTIVITY 4.2

Thinking Critically About My Perceiving Lenses

This is an opportunity for you to think about the unique "prescription" of your perceiving lenses. Reflect on the elements in yourself and your personal history that you believe exert the strongest influence on the way that you view the world. These factors will likely include the following categories:

- Demographics (age, gender, race/ethnicity, religion, geographical location)
- Tastes in fashion, music, leisure activities
- Special knowledge, talents, expertise
- Significant experiences in your life, either positive or negative
- Values, goals, aspirations

Create a visual representation of the prescription for your perceiving lenses, highlighting the unique factors that have contributed to your distinctive perspective on the world. Then, compare your "prescription" to those of other students in your class, and discuss the ways in which your lenses result in perceptions and beliefs that are different from those produced by other prescriptions.

THINKING ACTIVITY 4.3

Analyzing Different Accounts of the Assassination of Malcolm X

Let's examine a situation in which a number of different people had somewhat different perceptions about an event they were describing — in this case, the assassination of Malcolm X as he was speaking at a meeting in Harlem. The following are five different accounts of what took place on that day. As you read through the various accounts, pay particular attention to the different perceptions each one presents of this event. After you have finished reading the accounts, analyze some of the differences in these perceptions by answering the questions that follow.

FIVE ACCOUNTS OF THE ASSASSINATION OF MALCOLM X

The *New York Times* (February 22, 1965)

Malcolm X, the 39-year-old leader of a militant Black Nationalist movement, was shot to death yesterday afternoon at a rally of his followers in a ballroom in Washington Heights. The bearded Negro extremist had said only a few words of greeting when a fusillade rang out. The bullets knocked him over backwards.

Source: "On the Assassination of Malcolm X," *The New York Times*, February 22, 1965. Copyright © 1965 by The New York Times Co. Reprinted by permission.

VISUAL THINKING

Witnessing a Martyrdom

● Have you ever been the witness to an event which other people present described in contrasting or conflicting ways? Why do you think this happens? What are the responsibilities of bearing witness?

A 22-year-old Negro, Thomas Hagan, was charged with the killing. The police rescued him from the ballroom crowd after he had been shot and beaten.

Pandemonium broke out among the 400 Negroes in the Audubon Ballroom at 160th Street and Broadway. As men, women and children ducked under tables and flattened themselves on the floor, more shots were fired. The police said seven bullets struck Malcolm. Three other Negroes were shot. Witnesses reported that as many as 30 shots had been fired. About two hours later the police said the shooting had apparently been a result of a feud between followers of Malcolm and members of the extremist group he broke with last year, the Black Muslims. . . .

Life (March 5, 1965)[1]

His life oozing out through a half dozen or more gunshot wounds in his chest, Malcolm X, once the shrillest voice of black supremacy, lay dying on the stage of a Manhattan auditorium. Moments before, he had stepped up to the lectern and 400 of the faithful had settled down expectantly to hear the sort of speech for which he was famous — flaying the hated white man. Then a scuffle broke out in the hall and Malcolm's bodyguards bolted from his side to break it up — only to discover that they had been faked out. At least two men with pistols rose from the audience and pumped bullets into the speaker, while a third cut loose at close range with both barrels of a sawed-off shotgun. In the confusion the pistol man got away. The shotgunner lunged through the crowd and out the door, but not before the guards came to their wits and shot him in the leg. Outside he was swiftly overtaken by other supporters of Malcolm and very likely would have been stomped to death if the police hadn't saved him. Most shocking of all to the residents of Harlem was the fact that Malcolm had been killed not by "whitey" but by members of his own race.

The *New York Post* (February 22, 1965)[2]

They came early to the Audubon Ballroom, perhaps drawn by the expectation that Malcolm X would name the men who firebombed his home last Sunday. . . . I sat at the left in the 12th row and, as we waited, the man next to me spoke of Malcolm and his followers: "Malcolm is our only hope. You can depend on him to tell it like it is and to give Whitey hell.". . .

There was a prolonged ovation as Malcolm walked to the rostrum. Malcolm looked up and said, "A salaam aleikum (Peace be unto you)," and the audience replied, "We aleikum salaam (And unto you, peace)."

Bespectacled and dapper in a dark suit, sandy hair glinting in the light, Malcolm said: "Brothers and sisters. . . ." He was interrupted by two men in the center of the ballroom, who rose and, arguing with each other, moved forward. Then there was a scuffle at the back of the room. I heard Malcolm X say his last words: "Now, brothers, break it up," he said softly. "Be cool, be calm."

Then all hell broke loose. There was a muffled sound of shots and Malcolm, blood on his face and chest, fell limply back over the chairs behind him. The two men who had approached him ran to the exit on my side of the room, shooting wildly behind them as they ran. I heard people screaming, "Don't let them kill him." "Kill those bastards." At an exit I saw some of

Sources: (1) Excerpt from "Assassination of Malcolm X," *Life* Magazine, March 5, 1965. © 1965 Time Inc. Reprinted by permission. (2) Excerpt *New York Post*, February 22, 1965. Reprinted by permission.

Malcolm's men beating with all their strength on two men. I saw a half dozen of Malcolm's followers bending over his inert body on the stage. Their clothes were stained with their leader's blood.

Four policemen took the stretcher and carried Malcolm through the crowd and some of the women came out of their shock and one said: "I hope he doesn't die, but I don't think he's going to make it."

Associated Press (February 22, 1965)

A week after being bombed out of his Queens home, Black Nationalist leader Malcolm X was shot to death shortly after 3 (P.M.) yesterday at a Washington Heights rally of 400 of his devoted followers. Early today, police brass ordered a homicide charge placed against a 22-year-old man they rescued from a savage beating by Malcolm X supporters after the shooting. The suspect, Thomas Hagan, had been shot in the left leg by one of Malcolm's bodyguards as, police said, Hagan and another assassin fled when pandemonium erupted. Two other men were wounded in the wild burst of firing from at least three weapons. The firearms were a .38, a .45 automatic and a sawed-off shotgun. Hagan allegedly shot Malcolm X with the shotgun, a double-barrelled sawed-off weapon on which the stock also had been shortened, possibly to facilitate concealment. Cops charged Reuben Frances, of 871 E. 179th St., Bronx, with felonious assault in the shooting of Hagan, and with Sullivan Law violation — possession of the .45. Police recovered the shotgun and the .45.

The *Amsterdam News* (February 27, 1965)

"We interrupt this program to bring you a special newscast . . . ," the announcer said as the Sunday afternoon movie on the TV set was halted temporarily. "Malcolm X was shot four times while addressing a crowd at the Audubon Ballroom on 166th Street." "Oh no!" That was my first reaction to the shocking event that followed one week after the slender, articulate leader of the Afro-American Unity was routed from his East Elmhurst home by a bomb explosion. Minutes later we alighted from a cab at the corner of Broadway and 166th St. just a short 15 blocks from where I live on Broadway. About 200 men and women, neatly dressed, were milling around, some with expressions of awe and disbelief. Others were in small clusters talking loudly and with deep emotion in their voices. Mostly they were screaming for vengeance. One woman, small, dressed in a light gray coat and her eyes

Source: From *The Amsterdam News*, February 27, 1965. Reprinted by permission of *N.Y. Amsterdam News*.

flaming with indignation, argued with a cop at the St. Nicholas corner of the block. "This is not the end of it. What they were going to do to the Statue of Liberty will be small in comparison. We black people are tired of being shoved around." Standing across the street near the memorial park one of Malcolm's close associates commented: "It's a shame." Later he added that "if it's war they want, they'll get it." He would not say whether Elijah Muhammed's followers had anything to do with the assassination. About 3:30 P.M. Malcolm X's wife, Betty, was escorted by three men and a woman from the Columbia Presbyterian Hospital. Tears streamed down her face. She was screaming, "They killed him!" Malcolm X had no last words. . . . The bombing and burning of the No. 7 Mosque early Tuesday morning was the first blow by those who are seeking revenge for the cold-blooded murder of a man who at 39 might have grown to the stature of respectable leadership.

Questions for Analysis

1. What details of the events has each writer *selected* to focus on?
2. How has each writer *organized* the details that have been selected? Bear in mind that most news organizations present what they consider the most important information first and the least important information last.
3. How does each writer *interpret* Malcolm X, his followers, the gunmen, and the significance of the assassination?
4. How has each writer used *language* to express his or her perspective and to influence the thinking of the reader? Which language styles do you find most effective?

THINKING ACTIVITY **4.4**

Analyzing Different Accounts of the 2001 World Trade Center and Pentagon Attacks

The terrorist attacks on September 11, 2001, were witnessed live around the world and documented by hundreds of media sources as well as on personal camcorders and other devices. In this activity, you will examine accounts — some raw, some "professional," some purely visual, and some real-time audio commentary — of the events of that day. Go to the companion web site for this activity and questions for analysis.

THINKING PASSAGE

Experiences Shape Your Perceptions

Your ways of viewing the world are developed over a long period of time through the experiences you have and your thinking about these experiences. As you think critically about your perceptions, you learn more from your experiences and about how you make sense of the world. Your perceptions may be strengthened by this understanding, or they may be changed by this understanding. For example, read the following student passage and consider the way the writer's experiences — and her reflection on these experiences — contributed to shaping her perspective on the world.

ACQUIRED KNOWLEDGE
by Anonymous

When news of the Acquired Immune Deficiency Syndrome first began to spread, it was just another one of those issues on the news that I felt did not really concern me. Along with cancer, leukemia, and kidney failure, I knew these diseases ran rampant across the country, but they didn't affect me.

Once the AIDS crisis became a prevalent problem in society, I began to take a little notice of it, but my interest only extended as far as taking precautions to insure that I would not contract the disease. Sure, I felt sorry for all the people who were dying from it, but again, it was not my problem.

My father was an intravenous drug user for as long as I can remember. This was a fact of life when I was growing up. I knew that what he was doing was wrong, and that eventually he would die from it, but I also knew that he would never change.

On July 27th, my father died. An autopsy showed his cause of death as pneumonia and tuberculosis, seemingly natural causes. However, I was later informed that these were two very common symptoms related to carriers of the HIV virus. My father's years of drug abuse had finally caught up with him. He had died from AIDS.

My father's death changed my life. Prior to that, I had always felt that as long as a situation did not directly affect me, it was really no concern of mine. I felt that somewhere, someone would take care of it. Having a crisis strike so close to me made me wake up to reality. Suddenly I became acutely aware of all the things that are wrong in the world. I began to see the problems of AIDS, famine, homelessness, unemployment, and others from a personal point of view, and I began to feel that I had an obligation to join the crusade to do something about these problems.

I organized a youth coalition called UPLIFT INC. In this group, we meet and talk about the problems in society, as well as the everyday problems that any of our members may have in their lives. We organize shows (talent shows, fashion shows) and give a large portion of our proceeds to the American Foundation for AIDS Research, the Coalition for the Homeless, and many other worthy organizations.

Now I feel that I am doing my duty as a human being by trying to help those who are less fortunate than myself. My father's death gave me insight into my own mortality. Now I know that life is too short not to only try to enjoy it, but to really achieve something worthwhile out of it. Material gains matter only if you are willing to take your good fortune and spread it around to those who could use it.

THINKING ACTIVITY 4.5

Describing a Shaping Experience

Think of an experience that has shaped your life. Write an essay describing the experience and the ways it changed your life and how you perceive the world. After writing, analyze your experience by answering the following questions.

1. What were your *initial* perceptions of the situation? As you began the experience, you brought into the situation certain perceptions about the experience and the people involved.

2. What previous experiences had you undergone? Identify some of the influences that helped to shape these perceptions. Describe the actions that you either took or thought about taking.

3. As you became involved in the situation, what experiences in the situation influenced you to question or doubt your initial perceptions?

4. In what new ways did you view the situation that would better explain what was taking place? Identify the revised perceptions that you began to form about the experience.

Thinking Critically About Perceptions

Because we actively participate in selecting, organizing, and interpreting the sensations we experience, our perceptions are often incomplete, inaccurate, or subjective. To complicate the situation even more, our own limitations in perceiving are not the only ones that can cause us problems. Other people often purposefully create perceptions and misperceptions. An advertiser who wants to sell a product may try to create the impression that your life will be changed if you use this product. Or a person who wants to discredit someone else may spread untrue rumors about her in order to influence others' perceptions of her.

The only way you can correct the mistakes, distortions, and incompleteness of your perceptions is to *become aware* of this process by which you perceive and make sense of your world. By becoming aware of this process, you can think critically and then correct your mistakes and distortions. Perception alone cannot be totally relied on, and if you remain unaware of how it operates and of your active role, then you will be unable to exert any control over it. And in that case, you will be convinced that the way *you see* the world is the way the world *is*, even when your perceptions are mistaken, distorted, or incomplete.

The first step in critically examining your perceptions is to be willing to *ask questions* about what you are perceiving. As long as you believe that the way you see things is the only way to see them, you will be unable to recognize when your perceptions are distorted or inaccurate.

Besides asking questions, you have to try to become aware of the personal factors your lenses bring to your perceptions. As you have seen, each of us brings to every situation a whole collection of expectations, interests, fears, and hopes that can influence what we are perceiving. Consider the following situations:

> You've been fishing all day without a nibble. Suddenly you get a strike! You reel it in, but just as you're about to pull the fish into the boat, it frees itself from the hook and swims away. When you get back home later that night, your friends ask you, "How large was the fish that got away?"

> The teacher asks you to evaluate the performance of a classmate who is giving a report to the class. You don't like this other student because he acts as if he's superior to the rest of the students in the class. How do you evaluate his report?

You are asked to estimate the size of an audience attending an event that your organization has sponsored. How many people are there?

In each of these cases, you can imagine that your perceptions might be influenced by certain hopes, fears, or prejudices that you brought to the situation, causing your observations to become distorted or inaccurate. Although you usually cannot eliminate the personal feelings that are influencing your perceptions, you can become aware of them and try to control them. For instance, if you are asked to evaluate a group of people, one of whom is a good friend, you should try to keep these personal feelings in mind when making your judgment in order to make your perceptions as accurate as possible.

As you saw in Chapter 2, critical thinkers strive to see things from different perspectives. One of the best ways to do so is by communicating with others and engaging in *dialogue* with them. This means exchanging and critically examining ideas in an open and organized way. Similarly, dialogue is one of the main ways that you check your perceptions — by asking others what their perceptions are and then comparing and contrasting these with your own. This is exactly what you did when you discussed the different possible interpretations of the boy at the computer and the ambiguous photograph. By exchanging your perceptions with the perceptions of other class members, you developed a more complete sense of how these different events could be viewed, as well as the reasons that support these different perspectives.

Looking for reasons that support various perceptions also involves trying to discover any independent proof or evidence regarding the perception. When evidence is available in the form of records, photographs, video, or experimental results, this information will help you evaluate the accuracy of your perceptions.

Thinking critically about your perceptions means trying to avoid developing impulsive or superficial perceptions that you are unwilling to change. As you saw in Chapter 2, critical thinkers are *thoughtful* in approaching the world and *open* to modifying their views in the light of new information or better insight. Consider the following perceptions:

- Women are very emotional.
- Politicians are corrupt.
- Teenagers are wild and irresponsible.
- People who are good athletes are usually poor students.
- Men are thoughtless and insensitive.

These types of general perceptions are known as *stereotypes* because they express a belief about an entire group of people without recognizing the indi-

VISUAL THINKING

Walking on Water?

● What is the artist saying about perceptions with this illustration? If you were writing a caption, what would it be? Describe a situation in which what you perceived to be taking place turned out to be something much different.

vidual differences among members of the group. Stereotypes affect your perception of the world because they encourage you to form an inaccurate and superficial idea of a whole group of people ("All teenagers are reckless drivers"). When you meet someone who falls into this group, you automatically perceive that person as having these stereotyped qualities ("This person is a teenager, so he is a reckless driver"). Even if you find that this person does not fit your stereotyped perception ("This teenager is not a reckless driver"), this sort of superficial and unthoughtful labeling does not encourage you to change your perception of the group as a whole. Instead, it encourages you to overlook the conflicting information in favor of your stereotyped perception ("All teenagers are reckless drivers — except for this one"). However, when you are perceiving in a thoughtful fashion, you try to see what a person is like as an individual, instead of trying to fit him or her into a pre-existing category.

THINKING ACTIVITY 4.6

Analyzing Stereotypes

1. Describe an incident in which you were perceived as a stereotype because of your age, ethnic or religious background, employment, accent, or place of residence.

2. Describe how it felt to be stereotyped in this way.

3. Explain what you think are the best ways to overcome stereotypes such as these.

THINKING PASSAGE

Plato's Allegory of the Cave: The Journey from Perception to Knowledge

As your mind develops through the experiences you have and your reflection on these experiences, your perceptions of the world should continue to develop as well. By thinking critically about your perceptions, by seeking to view our world from perspectives other than your own and to comprehend the reasons that support these perspectives, you should find that your understanding of the world becomes increasingly more accurate and complete. As you have seen in this chapter, much of your knowledge of the world begins with perceiving. But to develop knowledge and understanding, you must make use of your thinking abilities in order to examine this experience critically. Increased understanding of the way the world operates thus increases the accuracy and completeness of your perceptions and leads you to informed beliefs about what is happening.

You can view your efforts to think critically about what you are perceiving as an intellectual journey of discovery as you continually attempt to interpret your experiences in more enlightened ways in order to attain knowledge and truth. More than 2,500 years ago, the Greek philosopher Plato explored the very same themes. In an effort to describe the path to intellectual enlightenment, he created a powerful metaphor that has become an important part of Western thinking: "The Allegory of the Cave." In the following section, philosopher Sonja Tanner relates this powerful allegory and explains how we can use it to understand our own personal quests to achieve knowledge and truth. After reading the section, complete the questions that follow.

ON PLATO'S CAVE
by Sonja Tanner

In the seventh book of Plato's dialogue The Republic, he offers an image of education in which humans are likened to prisoners in a cave. To understand this fully, we can attempt to render this image.

> "Next, then," (Socrates) said, "make an image of our nature in its education and want of education, likening it to a condition of the following kind. See human beings as though they were in an underground cave-like dwelling with its entrance, a long one, open to the light across the whole width of the cave. They are in it from childhood with their legs and necks in bonds so that they are fixed, seeing only in front of them, unable because of the bond to turn their heads all the way around. Their light is from a fire burning far above and behind them. Between the fire and the prisoners there is a road above, along which we see a wall, built like the partitions puppet-handlers set in front of the human beings and over which they show the puppets."
>
> "I see," (Glaucon) said.
>
> "Then also see along this wall human beings carrying all sorts of artifacts, which project above the wall, and statues of men and other animals wrought from stone, wood, and every kind of material. . . ." (514a1–515a2, Allan Bloom, trans.)

We see persons at the bottom of a cave, chained so as to prevent them from leaving the cave and from turning around to see what is behind them. Positioned in this way, they can only watch the shadows projected onto the

Source: Sonja Tanner, "On Plato's Cave" is reprinted by kind permission of the author.

back wall of the cave, by the passing of the artifacts in front of the fire. Behind the prisoners is a low wall which obscures the persons carrying these artifacts. This projection is like those we create around campfires, or in front of slide projectors, where a set of hands may look like a barking dog or a flying bird. A similar distortion takes place in the cave. Further up the cave is a fire and beyond that lies the cave's opening to the sunlight.

Having sketched what is happening within the cave literally, we must now try to interpret what this image means figuratively. When Glaucon remarks upon how strange these prisoners are, Socrates tells him that they are like us. How are we like these passive and helpless prisoners? Do we ever receive information or entertainment without thinking about where it actually comes from? Although Plato was writing over two thousand years before the invention of cathode ray tubes, the modern example of television may show us what he meant. If the projected images are analogous to those televised to us, then what might the persons behind the wall represent? Acting as filters of information, they might be seen as television networks, advertisers, or the media in general. They and their motivations for presenting information about the world to us through their particular perceptual lenses are obscured from view like the persons who pass behind the wall in the cave. As the chains prevent the prisoners from turning to see what is causing the images they watch, we are sometimes prevented by ignorance or uncritical thinking from recognizing the interests and persons served by the way in which information is presented to us. When we are unaware as to how perceptual lenses shape what it is we then believe, the information we receive and the beliefs we build upon this information may be distorted, like the shadows projected onto the wall. Many other persons shape the information we receive and the beliefs we hold. Authorities of all sorts fulfill this function — politicians, journalists, parents, teachers, writers and sometimes even ourselves.

Plato does not think us doomed to this unreflective state, however. Escape from the cave, though mysterious, is possible. Someone is apparently released from their bonds, turns around, and despite the confusion and pain from the dazzling light and arduous ascent, both of which they are unaccustomed to, is able to leave the cave. Just as when we leave a matinee movie and enter bright sunlight, we are at first dazzled and our eyes need a few moments to adjust to the light, the ascendant may experience disorientation or confusion upon first turning around. Turning from the shadows, this person discovers the objects causing these projections and the persons carrying them and, once outside the cave, the beings which these artifacts are made to resemble. The journey upwards is one of turning from images to their originals, ending ultimately in one's view of the sun itself, which, as the earth's source of heat and light, is a cause of all of the beings described in this allegory.

But how is escape from chains which bind at the neck and legs possible? Does someone release the prisoner and force them up into the light, and if so, who is this and why do they do it? Perhaps we are taking this image too literally in seeing this as a physical journey. Taking a cue from the afore-mentioned example in which the projections represent beliefs and informa-tion we take on uncritically, perhaps this journey is not physical but mental. The chains may signify ignorance and the uncritical taking over of second-hand opinions or beliefs and, as such, the chains themselves may even be self-imposed. Such an intellectual journey begins with a recognition that what we see and believe are only images, and by turning away from such appearances towards reality.

If the ascent is intellectual, rather than physical, a problem presents itself. Although Plato describes the release of a prisoner as though she or he were dragged up and out of the cave by the scruff of their neck, this type of force seems unlikely to guide an intellectual journey. Could one truly be forced or compelled to think independently? What else would motivate the journey? This is a particularly difficult question given the description of both ascent and return back into the cave as arduous, painful, and as subjecting one to derision and danger from the prisoners. What benefit could make good of undergoing such difficulties to leave the cave? We have been assuming here that the compulsion Plato describes as motivating the ascent is a force exter-nal to the ascendant, but internal forces motivate us as well. Why take the treacherous journey out of the cave? Perhaps simply because we *want* to. Our motivation upwards may be a desire for knowledge, as opposed to mere beliefs. If desire is the impetus for the ascent, this places responsibility for one's education squarely on the shoulders of the individual. We may have assistance, encouragement and sometimes even external forces com-pelling us upwards, but ultimately, our success depends upon our own desire for knowledge and truth, and our willingness to give up what we are accustomed to — the passive life and familiar comforts of cave-dwelling — for the rewards of rational and grounded knowledge.

We are now able to locate ourselves on the trajectory of enlightenment. Looking at and discussing images are a first stage in education according to Plato and indeed that is precisely what we have done here thus far. The next step then seems to be turning away from the images we accept unreflec-tively and towards questions as to why we believe what we do, who or what are the sources of these beliefs, and how reliable are these sources, which can distinguish unfounded beliefs from substantiated knowledge. Maybe this ascent is undertaken by us on a regular basis, rather than simply once, in our lives.

Questions for Analysis

1. Create a diagram that illustrates Plato's cave allegory and exchange it with a classmate. Did you both understand the allegory in the summary?

2. Explain how the images projected on the back wall of Plato's cave are similar to the images we see on television or in newspapers, magazines, and books.

3. Why do the people in Plato's cave believe that the perceptual images they see projected on the wall are "real"? Why do many people who watch television and read information sources uncritically believe that what they are viewing or reading about is "real"?

4. At the start of our journey from the dark depths of ignorance toward the illumination of understanding, it is essential to recognize that the perceptions we encounter in our daily lives are often incomplete, inaccurate, and distorted. Explain why.

5. In Plato's allegory, discarding ignorant beliefs and embracing the truth can be a disturbing process, as we are forced to see things objectively, as they really are, rather than shrouded in bias and distortion. Describe an experience of your own in which achieving a knowledgeable, truthful insight was a disturbing experience.

6. Using the diagram you created for question 1, identify the stage in Plato's allegory at which you would place yourself at this point in your life, and explain why. If you don't agree with Plato's framework, create a new diagram that illustrates your own ideas on the subject.

THINKING PASSAGES

Perception and Global Conflict

That there are tensions between the Muslim world and the West — or between the Occidental and the Oriental worlds — is not surprising to students of history, and it is certainly not a recent development. Dating back to the medieval Crusades, Muslim and Judeo-Christian civilizations have existed in an uneasy distrust that has frequently flared into violence. For example, some have suggested that the terrorist attacks on Spanish com-

VISUAL THINKING

Would You Like to Supersize That?

● Why do cultures tend to create distorted and stereotypical perceptions of people in other cultures? What are some effective approaches for replacing negative judgments about other cultures with tolerance, and changing suspicion of the unfamiliar to trust?

muter trains in March 2004 could be related to the Moorish (Arab) occupation of Spain and the expulsion of the Moors in 1492. The perceptions of "difference" between nations, faiths, and cultures are often distorted by fear and lack of knowledge. The Rwandan genocide of 1994, the 1995 "ethnic cleansing" as a result of civil war in the former Yugoslavia, and certainly the persecution and extermination of European Jews during the Second World War depended a great deal on the use of media and propaganda to exploit old superstitions, fears, and ignorance.

On the world stage, it can seem like these ancient rivalries will never be completely extinguished; they smolder away, waiting for a spark, and no amount of considered and thoughtful reasoning can resolve the violence for good. But on a community and even on a personal level, the perceptions we have of one another's differences can be critically evaluated, and our relationships with one another can be made more tolerant, even compassionate. The following essays explore ancient rivalries and suggest ways in which cultures can come to tolerate and respect one another. As you read, think about the distorted perceptions some in your community might have of others.

A WORLD NOT NEATLY DIVIDED
by Amartya Sen

When people talk about clashing civilizations, as so many politicians and academics do now, they can sometimes miss the central issue. The inadequacy of this thesis begins well before we get to the question of whether civilizations must clash. The basic weakness of the theory lies in its program of categorizing people of the world according to a unique, allegedly commanding system of classification. This is problematic because civilizational categories are crude and inconsistent and also because there are other ways of seeing people (linked to politics, language, literature, class, occupation or other affiliations).

The befuddling influence of a singular classification also traps those who dispute the thesis of a clash: To talk about "the Islamic world" or "the Western world" is already to adopt an impoverished vision of humanity as unalterably divided. In fact, civilizations are hard to partition in this way, given the diversities within each society as well as the linkages among different countries and cultures. For example, describing India as a "Hindu civilization" misses the fact that India has more Muslims than any other country except Indonesia and possibly Pakistan. It is futile to try to understand Indian art, literature, music, food or politics without seeing the extensive interactions across barriers of religious communities. These include Hindus and Muslims, Buddhists, Jains, Sikhs, Parsees, Christians (who have been in India since at least the fourth century, well before England's conversion to Christianity), Jews (present since the fall of Jerusalem), and even atheists and agnostics. Sanskrit has a larger atheistic literature than exists in any other classical language. Speaking of India as a Hindu civilization may be comforting to the Hindu fundamentalist, but it is an odd reading of India.

A similar coarseness can be seen in the other categories invoked, like "the Islamic world." Consider Akbar and Aurangzeb, two Muslim emperors of the Mogul dynasty in India. Aurangzeb tried hard to convert Hindus into Muslims and instituted various policies in that direction, of which taxing the non-Muslims was only one example. In contrast, Akbar reveled in his multiethnic court and pluralist laws, and issued official proclamations insisting that no one "should be interfered with on account of religion" and that "anyone is to be allowed to go over to a religion that pleases him."

Source: Amartya Sen, "A World Not Neatly Divided," *The New York Times,* November 23, 2001.
Copyright © 2001 by The New York Times Co. Reprinted by permission.

If a homogeneous view of Islam were to be taken, then only one of these emperors could count as a true Muslim. The Islamic fundamentalist would have no time for Akbar; Prime Minister Tony Blair, given his insistence that tolerance is a defining characteristic of Islam, would have to consider excommunicating Aurangzeb. I expect both Akbar and Aurangzeb would protest, and so would I. A similar crudity is present in the characterization of what is called "Western civilization." Tolerance and individual freedom have certainly been present in European history. But there is no dearth of diversity here, either. When Akbar was making his pronouncements on religious tolerance in Agra, in the 1590's, the Inquisitions were still going on; in 1600, Giordano Bruno was burned at the stake, for heresy, in Campo dei Fiori in Rome.

Dividing the world into discrete civilizations is not just crude. It propels us into the absurd belief that this partitioning is natural and necessary and must overwhelm all other ways of identifying people. That imperious view goes not only against the sentiment that "we human beings are all much the same," but also against the more plausible understanding that we are diversely different. For example, Bangladesh's split from Pakistan was not connected with religion, but with language and politics.

Each of us has many features in our self-conception. Our religion, important as it may be, cannot be an all-engulfing identity. Even a shared poverty can be a source of solidarity across the borders. The kind of division highlighted by, say, the so-called "anti-globalization" protesters — whose movement is, incidentally, one of the most globalized in the world — tries to unite the underdogs of the world economy and goes firmly against religious, national or "civilizational" lines of division.

The main hope of harmony lies not in any imagined uniformity, but in the plurality of our identities, which cut across each other and work against sharp divisions into impenetrable civilizational camps. Political leaders who think and act in terms of sectioning off humanity into various "worlds" stand to make the world more flammable — even when their intentions are very different. They also end up, in the case of civilizations defined by religion, lending authority to religious leaders seen as spokesmen for their "worlds." In the process, other voices are muffled and other concerns silenced. The robbing of our plural identities not only reduces us; it impoverishes the world.

THE ORIGINS OF OCCIDENTALISM
by Ian Buruma

When the West is under attack, as it was on September 11, it is often assumed — not only in America — that the West means the United States. This goes for those on the left, who believe that U.S. foreign policy (or "imperialism") and U.S. corporate power (or "globalization") have brought the suicide bombers and holy warriors upon America by marginalizing and bullying the millions of people who have failed to benefit from the capitalist world order. But it also goes for conservatives, who think that Islamist radicalism, like Communism before, is an attack on "our values," that is, on the "American way of life."

There is some truth to those claims. The worldwide reach of Wall Street, Hollywood, and the U.S. armed forces invites resentment. And to the extent that those institutions represent the American way of life, they are indeed targets of the Islamist jihad. It is also true that U.S. foreign policy can be misguided, even brutal. And global capitalism can do a great deal of damage as well as good. Finally, the United States, as the only Western superpower, has indeed come to stand for the West as a whole. And countries, such as Israel, that are looked upon as U.S. proxies provoke violent hostility for that reason alone.

However, the kind of violence currently directed at targets associated with the West, from the World Trade Center to a discothèque in Bali, is not just about the United States. Nor can it be reduced to global economics. Even those who have good reason to blame their poverty on harsh forms of U.S.–backed capitalism do not normally blow themselves up in public places to kill the maximum number of unarmed civilians. We do not hear of suicide bombers from the slums of Rio or Bangkok.

Something else is going on, which my co-author, Avishai Margalit, and I call Occidentalism (the title of our new book): a war against a particular idea of the West, which is neither new nor unique to Islamist extremism. The current jihadis see the West as something less than human, to be destroyed, as though it were a cancer. This idea has historical roots that long precede any form of "U.S. imperialism." Similar hostility, though not always as lethal, has been directed in the past against Britain and France as much as against America. What, then, is the Occidentalist idea of the West?

Source: Ian Buruma, "The Origins of Occidentalism," *The Chronicle Review* 50, February 6, 2004. Copyright © 2004 by The Chronicle of Higher Education. Reprinted by permission.

That is the problem that vexed a group of prominent Japanese intellectuals who gathered for a conference in Kyoto in 1942. The attack on Pearl Harbor was not the ostensible reason for the conference, but the underlying idea was to find an ideological justification for Japan's mission to smash, and in effect replace, the Western empires in Asia. The topic of discussion was "how to overcome the modern." Modernity was associated with the West, and particularly with Western imperialism.

Westernization, one of the scholars said, was like a disease that had infected the Japanese spirit. The "modern thing," said another, was a "European thing." Others believed that "Americanism" was the enemy, and that Japan should make common cause with the Europeans to defend old civilizations against the New World (there would certainly have been takers in Europe). There was much talk about unhealthy specialization in knowledge, which had fragmented the wholeness of Oriental spiritual culture. Science was to blame. So were capitalism, the absorption into Japanese society of modern technology, and notions of individual freedom and democracy. These had to be "overcome."

All agreed that culture — that is, traditional Japanese culture — was spiritual and profound, whereas modern Western civilization was shallow, rootless, and destructive of creative power. The West, particularly the United States, was coldly mechanical, a machine civilization without spirit or soul, a place where people mixed to produce mongrel races. A holistic, traditional Orient united under divine Japanese imperial rule would restore the warm organic Asian community to spiritual health. As one of the participants put it, the struggle was between Japanese blood and Western intellect.

Precisely the same terms had been used by others, in other places, at other times. Blood, soil, and the spirit of the *Volk* were what German romantics in the late 18th and early 19th centuries invoked against the universalist claims of the French Enlightenment, the French Revolution, and Napoleon's invading armies. This notion of national soul was taken over by the Slavophiles in 19th-century Russia, who used it to attack the "Westernizers," that is, Russian advocates of liberal reforms. It came up again and again, in the 1930s, when European fascists and National Socialists sought to smash "Americanism," Anglo-Saxon liberalism, and "rootless cosmopolitanism" (meaning Jews). Aurel Kolnai, the great Hungarian scholar, wrote a book in the 1930s about fascist ideology in Austria and Germany. He called it *War Against the West.* Communism, too, especially under Stalin, although a bastard child of the Enlightenment and the French Revolution, was the sworn enemy of Western liberalism and "rootless cosmopolitanism." Many

Islamic radicals borrowed their anti-Western concepts from Russia and Germany. The founders of the Ba'ath Party in Syria were keen readers of prewar German race theories. Jalal Al-e Ahmad, an influential Iranian intellectual in the 1960s, coined the phrase "Westoxification" to describe the poisonous influence of Western civilization on other cultures. He, too, was an admirer of German ideas on blood and soil.

Clearly, the idea of the West as a malign force is not some Eastern or Middle Eastern idea, but has deep roots in European soil. Defining it in historical terms is not a simple matter. Occidentalism was part of the counter-Enlightenment, to be sure, but also of the reaction against industrialization. Some Marxists have been attracted to it, but so, of course, have their enemies on the far right. Occidentalism is a revolt against rationalism (the cold, mechanical West, the machine civilization) and secularism, but also against individualism. European colonialism provoked Occidentalism, and so does global capitalism today. But one can speak of Occidentalism only when the revolt against the West becomes a form of pure destruction, when the West is depicted as less than human, when rebellion means murder.

Wherever it occurs, Occidentalism is fed by a sense of humiliation, of defeat, Isaiah Berlin once described the German revolt against Napolean as "the original exemplar of the reaction of many a backward, exploited, or at any rate patronized society, which, resentful of the apparent inferiority of its status, reacted by turning to real or imaginary triumphs and glories in its past, or enviable attributes of its own national or cultural character."

The same thing might be said about Japan in the 1930s, after almost a century of feeling snubbed and patronized by the West, whose achievements it so fervently tried to emulate. It has been true of the Russians, who have often slipped into the role of inferior upstarts, stuck in the outer reaches of Asia and Europe. But nothing matches the sense of failure and humiliation that afflicts the Arab world, a once glorious civilization left behind in every respect by the post-Enlightenment West.

Humiliation can easily turn into a cult of the pure and the authentic. Among the most resented attributes of the hated Occident are its claims to universalism. Christianity is a universalist faith, but so is the Enlightenment belief in reason. Napoleon was a universalist who believed in a common civil code for all his conquered subjects. The conviction that the United States represents universal values and has the god-given duty to spread democracy in the benighted world belongs to the same universalist tradition. Some of these values may indeed be universal. One would like to think that all people could benefit from democracy or the use of reason. The *Code*

Napoleon brought many benefits. But when universal solutions are imposed by force, or when people feel threatened or humiliated or unable to compete with the powers that promote such solutions, that is when we see the dangerous retreat into dreams of purity.

Not all dreams of local authenticity and cultural uniqueness are noxious, or even wrong. As Isaiah Berlin also pointed out, the crooked timber of humanity cannot be forcibly straightened along universal standards with impunity. The experiments on the human soul by Communism showed how bloody universalist dreams can be. And the poetic romanticism of 19th-century German idealists was often a welcome antidote to the dogmatic rationalism that came with the Enlightenment.

It is when purity or authenticity, of faith or race, leads to purges of the supposedly inauthentic, of the allegedly impure, that mass murder begins. The fact that anti-Americanism, anti-Zionism, anti-Semitism, and a general hostility to the West often overlap is surely no coincidence. Even in Japan, where Jews play no part in national life, one of the participants at the 1942 Kyoto conference suggested that the war against the West was a war against the "poisonous materialist civilization" built on Jewish financial capitalist power. At the same time, European anti-Semites, not only in Nazi Germany, were blaming the Jews for Bolshevism.

Both Bolshevism and capitalism are universalist systems in the sense that they do not recognize national, racial, or cultural borders. Since Jews are traditionally regarded by the defenders of purity as the congenital outsiders, the archetypal "rootless cosmopolitans," it is no wonder that they are also seen as the main carriers of the universalist virus. To be sure, Jews had sound reasons to be attracted to such notions as equality before the law, secular politics, and internationalism, whether of a socialist or capitalist stamp. Exclusivity, whether racial, religious, or nationalist, is never good for minorities. Only in the Middle East have Jews brought their own form of exclusivity and nationalism. But Zionism came from the West. And so Israel, in the eyes of its enemies, is the colonial outpost of "Westoxification." Its material success only added to the Arab sense of historic humiliation.

The idea, however, that Jews are a people without a soul, mimics with no creative powers, is much older than the founding of the State of Israel. It was one of the most common anti-Semitic slurs employed by Richard Wagner. He was neither the first to do so, nor very original in this respect. Karl Marx, himself the grandson of a rabbi, called the Jews greedy parasites, whose souls were made of money. The same kind of thing was often said by 19th-century Europeans about the British. The great Prussian novelist Theodor Fontane, who rather admired England, nonetheless opined that "the cult of the Gold Calf is the disease of the English people." He was convinced that English society would be destroyed by "this yellow fever of gold, this sell-out of all souls to the devil of Mammon." And much the same is said today about the Americans.

Calculation — the accounting of money, interests, scientific evidence, and so on — is regarded as soulless. Authenticity lies in poetry, intuition, and blind faith. The Occidentalist view of the West is of a bourgeois society, addicted to creature comforts, animal lusts, self-interest, and security. It is by definition a society of cowards, who prize life above death. As a Taliban fighter once put it during the war in Afghanistan, the Americans would never win, because they love Pepsi-Cola, whereas the holy warriors love death. This was also the language of Spanish fascists during the civil war, and of Nazi ideologues, and Japanese kamikaze pilots.

The hero is one who acts without calculating his interests. He jumps into action without regard for his own safety, ever ready to sacrifice himself for the cause. And the Occidentalist hero, whether he is a Nazi or Islamist, is just as ready to destroy those who sully the purity of his race or creed. It is indeed his duty to do so. When the West is seen as the threat to authenticity, then it is the duty of all holy warriors to destroy anything to do with the "Zionist Crusaders," whether it is a U.S. battleship, a British embassy, a Jewish cemetery, a chunk of lower Manhattan, or a disco in Bali. The symbolic value of these attacks is at least as important as the damage inflicted.

What, then, is new about the Islamist holy war against the West? Perhaps it is the totality of its vision. Islamism, as an antidote to Westoxification, is an odd mixture of the universal and the pure: universal because all people can, and in the eyes of the believers should, become orthodox Muslims; pure because those who refuse the call are not simply lost souls but savages who must be removed from this earth.

Hitler tried to exterminate the Jews, among others, but did not view the entire West with hostility. In fact, he wanted to forge an alliance with the British and other "Aryan" nations, and felt betrayed when they did not see things his way. Stalinists and Maoists murdered class enemies and were opposed to capitalism. But they never saw the Western world as less than human and thus to be physically eradicated. Japanese militarists went to war against Western empires but did not regard everything about Western civilization as barbarous. The Islamist contribution to the long history of Occidentalism is a religious vision of purity in which the idolatrous West simply has to be destroyed.

The worship of false gods is the worst religious sin in Islam as well as in ancient Judaism. The West, as conceived by Islamists, worships the false

Thinking Critically About Images: Truth and Reality in Popular Culture

Throughout the ages, philosophers have urged people to look beyond superficial displays of wealth and beauty for deeper and more lasting virtues. Although he was addressing the citizens of Athens some 2,500 years ago, the words of Socrates could easily apply to a television-watching, mall-shopping consumer in contemporary America: "Are you not ashamed of heaping up the greatest amount of money and honor and reputation, and caring so little about wisdom and truth and the greatest improvement of the soul, which you never regard or heed at all?"

As many of the images in this portfolio demonstrate, the ways in which popular culture defines "honor" and "reputation" seem to have far more to do with six-pack abs and rolls of cash than a hard-earned understanding of life's perils and potentials. You could argue, of course, that it's not the job of "popular culture" to educate and challenge — that, indeed, popular culture exists only to entertain and distract. And yet the lines between what is "real" and "true" about life, and what is manufactured for prime-time television, have become increasingly blurred. Our culture re-creates idealized versions of cities, so that you no longer need to experience what it's "really" like to travel; we happily settle in to watch beautiful women and handsome men subject themselves to high-wire stunts, thus avoiding the depressing news from foreign battlefields; we even acknowledge the desire to change our faces and bodies to fit some superhuman ideal.

As you examine the following portfolio of images from popular culture, think about the *selection* of details in each image, the way those details are *organized*, and the manner in which a viewer or consumer is encouraged to *interpret* those details. Finally, as you begin thinking more critically about popular culture, remember that visual images are subject to the same criteria of "truth" and "reality" as all other beliefs and opinions. Before you simply accept as "true" an image that has been created or broadcast by the media, remember to think critically about the authority and credentials of those who created the image and to do some searching on your own to find alternate viewpoints and perspectives.

If You Can Make It There. . . .

- The New York-New York Hotel
  and Casino is just one of several
  Las Vegas casinos to re-create an
  idealized city (such as Paris and
  Venice) or historical era (such as
  ancient Egypt and classical
  Rome). After the terrorist
  attacks of September 11, 2001,
  the actual skyline of New York
  City seems haunted by the
  absence of the Twin Towers,
  which still appear in countless
  movies and television shows
  filmed in the city.

Thinking critically about the images

1. The contemporary American novelist Don DeLillo wrote: "To be a tourist is
   to escape accountability. Errors and failings don't cling to you the way they
   do back home. . . .Together with thousands, you are granted immunities and
   broad freedoms. You are an army of fools, wearing bright polyesters, riding
   camels, taking pictures of each other. . . .There is nothing to think about but
   the next shapeless event." Are tourists who visit an illusion or idealization of
   a real place searching for an escape from "errors and failings"?

2. Most of us travel to places we've longed to see for ourselves, after reading
   about them or seeing them in movies or hearing about other people's
   adventures there. But if you go someplace with a preconceived idea of what
   that place will be like (or look like or smell like), will your actual experience
   of that place be *true*?

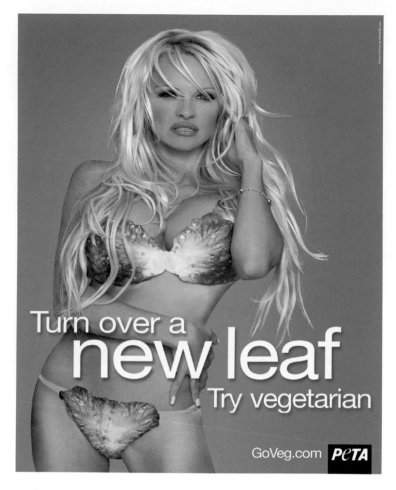

Brrrr. . . .

- Model, actress, and pinup Pamela Anderson makes fur seem very unfashionable (if not unnecessary) in this 1997 advertisement for the animal-rights activist organization People for the Ethical Treatment of Animals.

Thinking critically about the image

1. Many activist organizations gain publicity through the support of actors, musicians, and other figures of popular culture. When is it effective for a celebrity to lend "star power" to a cause, and when does it seem cynical? Give examples of both a successful and a not-so-successful campaign.

2. It's a given that "sex sells" — everything from cars to beer to chewing gum. Why is sex so effective — and ubiquitous — in advertising? This PETA campaign isn't trying to sell anything, and yet it is trying to influence consumer behavior. Are there other kinds of public-service messages that do (or could) use sex to get their point across?

Fear for Fun and Profit

- The NBC television "reality" program *Fear Factor* dares contestants to perform feats of bravery (or folly, depending on your perspective) ranging from scaling tall buildings to escaping from burning buildings or submerged automobiles. Other stunts involve gross-out challenges, such as getting into a box filled with scorpions or eating various disgusting (and, occasionally, still living) substances.

Thinking critically about the images

1. Dozens of "reality" television shows have been created and broadcast within the last five years. All of them seem to rely on our willingness to be voyeurs — to watch people scheme, plot, be humiliated, get scared, fall in love, act like idiots, and bare their souls for our amusement. What is "real" about "reality" television?

2. There are some "reality" shows, of course, that don't pre-screen contestants or promise cash prizes. Think about shows like *Cops* or *Greatest Police Chases*, which seem to catch people at their most miserable or embarrassed; or shows that follow someone through a surgical procedure or even giving birth. Are these a different kind of "reality" television? How so?

3. Why are the contestants on *Fear Factor* always young and attractive?

Real Bravery

- Firefighter Mike Kehoe running up the stairs of Tower 1 of the World Trade Center on September 11, 2001. This photo was taken by office worker John Labriola. Both Kehoe and Labriola survived; 343 New York City firefighters lost their lives in the collapse of the Twin Towers. For more on Kehoe's experiences that day — and his efforts to come to terms with its terrible costs — see *Time* magazine's coverage at <http://www.time.com/time/photoessays/kehoe/1.html>.

Thinking critically about the image

1. At the moment this photograph was taken, nobody in this stairwell was entirely sure of what had happened — and no one could guess what would happen next. If you didn't know the context of this photograph, what "story" would you tell about it? What does it suggest about "real" courage and bravery?

2. When you watch shows like *Survivor* or *Fear Factor,* do you ever think about people who are facing "real" struggles to find food and shelter, or to escape a "real" burning building? Is there a line of taste, decency, or compassion that these "reality" entertainment shows don't dare cross? Where would that line be?

Peace, Love, and a Whole Lot of Mud

• In August 1969, tens of thousands of young people converged on the tiny town of Bethel, New York, for the three-day Woodstock Music and Art Fair. The festival became a turning point in American popular culture and counterculture, combining music, politics, fashion, and alternative lifestyles in ways that continue to influence youth culture throughout the world.

Thinking critically about the images

In popular culture, and especially in consumer culture, we are what we wear. The kinds of clothes we buy and the way we wear those clothes are a kind of performance that lets other people know what we think of ourselves and our place in the world. Obviously, a culture has to be sufficiently wealthy and have enough leisure time to devote its energies to fashion. The photographs of these two pages illustrate "countercultural" fashion among young people in the 1960s and in the early twenty-first century. Think about the following passages from philosopher Friedrich Nietzsche and playwright David Mamet. Given their views on fashion, how would they explain the behavior and choices of the people in these photographs? Do you agree with either Nietzsche or Mamet's ideas about fashion, especially as you see it in contemporary popular culture?

1. "The obvious self-satisfaction of the individual with his own form stimu-lates imitation and gradually produces the form of the many — that is,

Never Mind the. . . .

- By the mid-1970s, a grimmer countercultural youth movement was forming in New York City's underground music clubs and the streets of London. Punk, with its anarchic politics and shock-value fashion and music, had a much more bleak view of the potential for social change. However, just like the bohemian styles of Woodstock's hippies, punk's signature fashion statements (the ripped clothes, black boots, brightly-colored hair, and unexpected piercings) soon became part of the fashion mainstream.

fashion. Through fashion, the many strive towards and even achieve that very same comforting self-satisfaction with their form. When you consider how many reasons each person has for anxiety and timid self-concealment, and how three-quarters of his energy and goodwill can be paralyzed and rendered fruitless by these reasons, you have to be very grateful to fashion to the extent that it sets that three-quarters free and communicates self-confidence and a mutual and cheerful cooperation to those who realize that they are all bound by its law. Even foolish laws confer freedom and emotional tranquility so long as enough people submit to them." Friedrich Nietzsche (1844–1900).

2. "The pursuit of Fashion is the attempt of the middle class to co-opt tragedy. In adopting the clothing, speech, and personal habits of those in straitened, dangerous, or pitiful circumstances, the middle class seeks to have what it feels to be the exigent and nonequivocal experiences had by those it emulates." David Mamet (b. 1947).

Ebony and Ivory?

- Pop star Michael Jackson's shifting facial structure, changing hair texture, and fading skin color have been a source of fascination and criticism for nearly twenty years.

Thinking critically about the images

1. Some ethnic groups feel that cosmetic surgery to change distinctive features wrongly promotes a Caucasian standard of "beauty" that rejects diversity. Other people argue that they have the right to make whatever changes they like to their own faces and bodies. How do you feel about the issue?

2. The *Twilight Zone* episodes "The Mask" and "Eye of the Beholder" (available on DVD) use plastic surgery as a metaphor to explore issues of conformity and "true" beauty. Because he is such an immensely famous celebrity, is there some larger moral significance to Michael Jackson's changing face? Would the "moral" of his story be different if he were just a private citizen?

gods of money, sex, and other animal lusts. In this barbarous world the thoughts and laws and desires of Man have replaced the kingdom of God. The word for this state of affairs is *jahiliyya,* which can mean idolatry, religious ignorance, or barbarism. Applied to the pre-Islamic Arabs, it means ignorance: People worshiped other gods because they did not know better. But the new *jahiliyya,* in the sense of barbarism, is everywhere, from Las Vegas and Wall Street to the palaces of Riyadh. To an Islamist, anything that is not pure, that does not belong to the kingdom of God, is by definition barbarous and must be destroyed.

Just as the main enemies of Russian Slavophiles were Russian Westernizers, the most immediate targets of Islamists are the liberals, reformists, and secular rulers in their own societies. They are the savage stains that have to be cleansed with blood. But the source of the barbarism that has seduced Saudi princes and Algerian intellectuals as much as the whores and pimps of New York (and in a sense all infidels are whores and pimps) is the West. And that is why holy war has been declared against the West.

Since the target of the holy warriors is so large, figuring out how to defend it is not easy. But it is not immediately apparent that a war against Iraq was the most effective way to fight the Islamist jihad. Saddam Hussein's Ba'ath regime was a murderous dictatorship that deserved to come to an end, but it was not in line with the holy revolution. There is no evidence that Saddam wished to destroy the West. Osama bin Laden clearly does, and *he* is still at large. It may even be that attacking Iraq, however gratifying in many ways, has made the defense against Islamist revolution harder. Moderate Muslims everywhere are cowed into silence by aggressive U.S. actions, for fear of being seen as traitors or, worse, barbarous idolators.

As even President Bush has been at pains to point out, the battle with religious terrorism is not a war against Islam, or even religion. Violent attempts to force secularism on Muslim societies in the past invited the problem of religious extremism and should not be seen as the solution now. Zealotry was in part a reaction against the aggressive secularism of such regimes as Reza Shah's in Iran during the 1930s. If political freedoms are to be guaranteed in the Muslim world through popular sovereignty, religion will have to be taken into account. The best chance for democracies to succeed in countries as varied as Indonesia, Turkey, and Iraq is if moderate Muslims can be successfully mobilized. But that will have to come from those countries themselves. Even though Western governments should back the forces for democracy, the hard political struggle cannot be won in Washington, or through the force of U.S. arms.

In the West itself, we must defend our freedoms against the holy warriors who seek to destroy them. But we must also be careful that in doing so we don't end up undermining them ourselves. In the balance between security and civil liberty, the latter should never be sacrificed to the former. We should also guard against the temptation to fight fire with fire, Islamism with our own forms of intolerance. To think that we are at war with Islamism in the name of Christianity, as some zealots believe, is a fatal error, for that is to conform precisely to the Manichaeistic view of those who seek to defeat us. Muslims living in the West should not be allowed to join the holy war against it. But their rights as Europeans or Americans must be respected. The survival of our liberties depends on our willingness to defend them against enemies outside, but also against the temptation of our own leaders to use our fears in order to destroy our freedoms.

WAR OF IDEAS, PART 6
by Thomas L. Friedman

DAVOS, Switzerland — For the past few weeks I've tried to lay out the tactics we in the West can adopt to strengthen the moderates in the Arab-Muslim world to fight the war of ideas against the forces of intolerance within their civilization — which is where the real war on terrorism will either be won or lost. But if there is one thing I've learned in examining this issue it's this: ideas don't just spread on their own. Ideas spread in a context. So often, since 9/11, people have remarked to me: "Wow, Islam, that's a really angry religion." I disagree. I do agree, though, that there are a lot of young Muslims who are angry, because they live in some of the most repressive societies, with the fewest opportunities for women and youth, and with some of the highest unemployment. Bad contexts create an environment where humiliation — and the anger, bad ideas and violence that flow from it — are rife. In short, it is impossible for us to talk about winning the war of ideas in the Arab-Muslim world without talking about the most basic thing that gives people dignity and hope: A job.

"For a long time now, I've felt that what we're really facing is not a clash of civilizations, but a clash of generations," argued David Rothkopf, a

Source: Thomas L. Friedman, "War of Ideas, Part 6," *The New York Times,* January 25, 2004. Copyright © 2004 by The New York Times Co. Reprinted by permission.

former acting U.S. undersecretary of commerce. "You have an aging developed world, particularly Europe, that is trying to protect its jobs, and you have a young, job-seeking, job-needing emerging world, particularly the Muslim world, that will go anywhere and do anything to either seize the job opportunities or express their frustration with not having opportunities."

Just read the numbers and weep: of the 90 million Arab youth today (between the ages of 15 and 24), 14 million are unemployed, many of them among the 15 to 20 million Muslims now living in Europe. "There's not enough jobs and not enough hope," Jordan's King Abdullah told the Davos economic forum. According to the 2003 Arab Human Development Report, between 1980 and 1999 the nine leading Arab economies registered 370 patents (in the U.S.) for new inventions. Patents are a good measure of a society's education quality, entrepreneurship, rule of law and innovation. During that same 20-year period, South Korea alone registered 16,328 patents for inventions. You don't run into a lot of South Koreans who want to be martyrs.

I was at Google's headquarters in Silicon Valley a few days ago, and they have this really amazing electronic global map that shows, with lights, how many people are using Google to search for knowledge. The region stretching from Morocco to the border of India had almost no lights. I attended a breakfast at Davos on the outsourcing of high-tech jobs from the U.S. and Europe to the developing world. There were Indian and Mexican businessmen there, and much talk about China. But not a word was spoken about outsourcing jobs to the Arab world. The context — infrastructure, productivity, education — just isn't there yet.

So what to do? A lot of help can and should come from Europe. Although America is often the target, Europe has been the real factory of Arab-Muslim rage. Europe has done an extremely poor job of integrating and employing its growing Muslim minorities, many of which have a deep feeling of alienation. And Europe has done a very poor job of investing in North Africa and the Middle East — its natural backyard.

America is far from perfect in this regard, but by forging the [NAFTA] free trade agreement with Mexico, the U.S. helped create a political and economic context there that not only spurred jobs and the modernization of Mexico, but created the environment for its democratization. Former Mexican President Ernesto Zedillo remarked to me: "I don't think I would have been successful in political reform without the decent economic growth we had [spurred by NAFTA] from 1996 to 2000. Those five years, we had average growth of 5 percent." It was in that optimistic environment that Mexico had its first democratic transition from the ruling party to the opposition.

So if you take anything away from this series, I hope it's this: The war of ideas among Arabs and Muslims can only be fought and won by their own forces of moderation, and those forces can only emerge from a growing middle class with a sense of dignity and hope for the future. Young people who grow up in a context of real economic opportunity, basic rule of law and the right to speak and write what they please don't usually want to blow up the world. They want to be part of it.

Questions for Analysis

1. In his essay "A World Not Neatly Divided," Amartya Sen criticizes the "crude and inconsistent" ways in which whole civilizations are classified, grouped, and defined. Often, these classification systems are based on outmoded and inaccurate perceptions. Do you agree with Sen? Examining your own cultural, economic, and religious background, can you describe any instances in which someone seemed to hold an ignorant or prejudiced view of you? Conversely, if you are an American citizen, do you feel any particular patriotism or other emotional identification with the idea of America, and if so, on what is that feeling based? Are there some kinds of fundamental differences between people — faiths, attitudes toward women, approaches to technology — that you think might be completely unresolvable?

2. Sen notes that "Each of us has many features in our self-conception." As you have worked through this chapter, you have evaluated how your beliefs and experiences shape your perceptions of the world around you. Now, consider how you perceive your *self*. Which of the "lenses" that you have explored in this chapter seems to have the greatest influence on how you "see" yourself?

3. Ian Buruma explores the historical roots of "Occidentalism," which he defines as "a war against a particular idea of the West." His provocative thesis is that this "particular idea of the West" grows not from Islamic fundamentalism but from an early modern European reaction against industrialization and global capitalism, and a "sense of humiliation, of defeat." Is it easier to distrust, fear, or even hate some people if you sense that they are in some way superior to you — or if you suspect that they are condescending to you, giddy with their own misguided superiority? Why is "envy" so poisonous in personal as well as in international relations?

4. Using an electronic database, look up the series of six essays Thomas L. Friedman published in *The New York Times* in late 2003 and early 2004. How well does he support his contention that economic opportunities for Arab youth will help to resolve tensions and violence in their region of the world? Do you agree with David Rothkopf's observation that "what we're really facing is not a clash of civilizations, but a clash of generations"? How do perceptual differences between generations lead to conflict in mainstream American culture? Could there be common ground between people who are similar in age but who have had very different experiences and have very different perspectives?

5 Believing and Knowing

Beliefs
Interpretations, evaluations, conclusions, and predictions about the world that we endorse as true

Beliefs based on indirect experience (oral or written sources of information)

Beliefs based on direct experience

How reliable is the information?

Evaluating online information

How reliable is the source of information?

Developing Knowledge
by thinking critically about our beliefs

Are the beliefs compelling and coherent explanations?

Are the beliefs based on reliable sources?

Are the beliefs consistent with other beliefs/knowledge?

Are the beliefs supported by reasons and evidence?

Are the beliefs accurate predictions?

It seems to be a natural human impulse to try to understand the world we live in. This is the overall goal of thinking, which we have defined as the mental process by which we make sense of the world. Perceiving is an important part of this thinking process, but your perceptions, taken by themselves, do not provide a reliable foundation for your understanding of the world. Your perceptions are often incomplete, distorted, and inaccurate. They are shaped and influenced by your perceiving "lenses," which reflect your own individual personality, experiences, biases, assumptions, and ways of viewing things. To clarify and validate your perceptions, you must critically examine and evaluate these perceptions.

Thinking critically about your perceptions results in the formation of your beliefs and ultimately in the construction of your knowledge about the world. For example, consider the following statements and answer "Yes," "No," or "Not sure" to each.

1. Humans need to eat to stay alive.
2. Smoking marijuana is a harmless good time.
3. Every human life is valuable.
4. Developing your mind is as important as taking care of your body.
5. People should care about other people, not just about themselves.

Your responses to these statements reflect certain beliefs you have, and these beliefs help you explain why the world is the way it is and how you ought to behave. In this chapter you will see that beliefs are the main tools you use to make sense of the world and guide your actions. The total collection of your beliefs represents your view of the world, your philosophy of life.

What exactly are "beliefs"? Beliefs represent an interpretation, evaluation, conclusion, or prediction about the nature of the world. For example, this statement — "I believe that the whale in the book *Moby Dick* by Herman Melville symbolizes a primal, natural force that men are trying to destroy" — represents an *interpretation* of that novel. To say, "I believe that watching soap operas is unhealthy because they focus almost exclusively on the seamy side of human life" is to express an *evaluation* of soap operas. The statement "I believe that one of the main reasons two out of three people in the world go to bed hungry each night is that industrially advanced nations like the United States have not done a satisfactory job of sharing their knowledge" expresses a *conclusion* about the problem of world hunger. To say, "If drastic environmental measures are not undertaken to slow the global warming trend, then I believe that the polar ice caps will melt and the earth will be flooded" is to make a *prediction* about events that will occur in the future.

Besides expressing an interpretation, evaluation, conclusion, or prediction about the world, beliefs also express an *endorsement* of the accuracy of the beliefs by the speaker or author. In the preceding statements the speakers are not simply expressing interpretations, evaluations, conclusions, and predictions; they are also indicating that they believe these views are *true*. In other words, the speakers are saying that they have adopted these beliefs as their own because they are convinced that they represent accurate viewpoints based on some sort of evidence. This "endorsement" by the speaker is a necessary dimension of beliefs, and we assume it to be the case even if the speaker doesn't directly say, "I believe." For example, the statement "Astrological predictions are meaningless because there is no persuasive reason to believe that the position of the stars and planets has any effect on human affairs" expresses a belief even though it doesn't specifically include the words "I believe. "

> **beliefs** *Interpretations, evaluations, conclusions, or predictions about the world that we endorse as true*

Describe beliefs you have that fall in each of these categories (interpretation, evaluation, conclusion, prediction) and then explain the reason(s) you have for endorsing the beliefs.

1. **Interpretation** (an explanation or analysis of the meaning or significance of something)
   My interpretation is that . . .
   Supporting reason(s):

2. **Evaluation** (a judgment of the value or quality of something, based on certain standards)
   My evaluation is that . . .
   Supporting reason(s):

3. **Conclusion** (a decision made or an opinion formed after consideration of the relevant facts or evidence)
   My conclusion is that . . .
   Supporting reason(s):

4. **Prediction** (a statement about what will happen in the future)
   My prediction is that . . .
   Supporting reason(s):

⊚ Believing and Perceiving

The relationship between the activities of believing and perceiving is complex and interactive. On the one hand, your perceptions form the foundation of many of your beliefs about the world. On the other hand, your beliefs about the world shape and influence your perceptions of it. Let's explore this interactive relationship by examining a variety of beliefs, including

1. *Interpretations* ("Poetry enables humans to communicate deep, complex emotions and ideas that resist simple expression.")
2. *Evaluations* ("Children today spend too much time watching television and too little time reading.")
3. *Conclusions* ("An effective college education provides not only mastery of information and skills, but also evolving insight and maturing judgment.")
4. *Predictions* ("With the shrinking and integration of the global community, there will be an increasing need in the future for Americans to speak a second language.")

These beliefs, for people who endorse them, are likely to be based in large measure on a variety of perceptual experiences: events that people have seen and heard. The perceptual experiences by themselves, however, do not result in beliefs — they are simply experiences. For them to become beliefs, *you must think about* your perceptual experiences and then organize them into a belief structure. This thinking process of constructing beliefs is known as *cognition*, and it forms the basis of your understanding of the world. What are some of the perceptual experiences that might have led to the construction of the beliefs just described?

> <u>Example:</u> *Many times I have seen that I can best express my feelings toward someone I care deeply about through a poem.*

As we noted in Chapter 4, "Perceiving," your perceptual experiences not only contribute to the formation of your beliefs; the beliefs you have formed also have a powerful influence on the perceptions you *select* to focus on, how you *organize* these perceptions, and the manner in which you *interpret* them. For example, if you come across a poem in a magazine, your perception of the poem is likely to be affected by your beliefs about poetry. These beliefs may influence whether you *select* the poem as something to read, the manner in which you *organize* and *relate* the poem to other aspects of your experience, and your *interpretation* of the poem's meaning. This interactive relationship holds true for most beliefs. Assume that you endorse the four beliefs previously listed. How might holding these beliefs influence your perceptions?

> *Example:* When I find a poem I like, I often spend a lot of time trying to understand how the author has used language and symbols to create and communicate meaning.

The belief systems you have developed to understand your world help you correct inaccurate perceptions. When you watch a magician perform seemingly impossible tricks, your beliefs about the way the world operates inform you that what you are seeing is really a misperception, an illusion. In this context, you expect to be tricked, and your question is naturally, "How did he or she do that?" Potential problems arise, however, in those situations in which it is not apparent that your perceptions are providing you with inaccurate information and you use these experiences to form mistaken beliefs. For example, you may view advertisements linking youthful, attractive, fun-loving people with cigarette smoking and form the apparently inaccurate belief that smoking cigarettes is an integral part of being youthful, attractive, and fun loving. As a critical thinker, you have a responsibility to continually monitor and evaluate both aspects of this interactive process — your beliefs and your perceptions — so that you can develop the most informed perspective on the world.

THINKING ACTIVITY 5.1

Analyzing a False Perception

Describe an experience of a perception you had that later turned out to be false, based on subsequent experiences or reflection. Address the following questions:

1. What qualities of the perception led you to believe it to be true?
2. How did this perception influence your beliefs about the world?
3. Describe the process that led you to conclude that the perception was false.

Believing and Knowing

The beliefs you develop help you explain why the world is the way it is, and they guide you in making decisions. But all beliefs are not equal. Some beliefs are certain ("I believe that someday I will die") because they are supported by compelling reasons. Other beliefs are less certain ("I believe that life exists on other planets") because the support is not as solid. As you form and revise your beliefs, based on your experiences and your reflection on these experiences, it is important to make them as accurate as possible. The more accurate your beliefs are, the better you are able to understand what is taking place and to predict what will occur in the future.

The beliefs you form vary tremendously in accuracy. The idea of *knowing* is the ability to distinguish beliefs supported by strong reasons or evidence from beliefs for which there is less support, as well as from beliefs disproved by evidence to the contrary (such as the belief that the earth is flat). This distinction between "believing" and "knowing" can be illustrated by replacing the word *believe* with the word *know* in statements. For example:

1. I *know* that I will die.
2. I *know* that there is life on other planets.
3. I *know* that working hard will lead me to a happy life.
4. I *know* that the earth is flat.

The only statement with which most people would agree it clearly makes sense to use the word *know* is the first one, because there is conclusive evidence that this belief is accurate. In the case of statement 2, we might say that, although life on other planets is a possibility, there does not seem to be *conclusive* evidence at present that supports this view. In the case of statement 3, we might say that, although for some people working hard leads to a happy life, this is not always the case. Statement 4 expresses a belief that we "know" is *not* true. In other words, when you say that "you know" something, you mean at least two different things.

1. I think this belief is completely accurate.
2. I can explain to you the reasons or evidence that support this belief.

If either of these standards is not met, we would usually say that you do not really "know." Or to state it another way, "You can *believe* what is not so, but you cannot *know* what is not so."

We work at evaluating the accuracy of our beliefs by examining the reasons or evidence that support them (known as the *justification* for the beliefs). As you learn more about the world and yourself, you try to form beliefs that are increasingly accurate and justified.

Determining the accuracy and justification of your beliefs is challenging. The key point is that as a critical thinker, you should continually try to form and revise your beliefs so that you can understand the world in increasingly effective ways. Even when you find that you maintain certain beliefs over a long period of time, your explorations will result in a deeper and fuller understanding of these beliefs.

THINKING ACTIVITY 5.2

Evaluating the Accuracy of Beliefs

State whether you think that each of the following beliefs is

- *Completely accurate* (so that you would say, "I know this is the case")
- *Generally accurate* but not completely accurate (so that you would say, "This is often, but not always, the case")
- *Generally not accurate* but sometimes accurate (so that you would say, "This is usually not the case but is sometimes true")
- *Definitely not accurate* (so that you would say, "I know that this is not the case")

After determining the *degree of accuracy* in this way, explain why you have selected your answer.

- *Example:* I believe that if you study hard, you will achieve good grades.
- *Degree of accuracy:* Generally, but not completely, accurate.
- *Explanation:* Although many students who study hard achieve good grades, this is not always true. Sometimes students have difficulty understanding the work in a certain subject, no matter how hard they study. And sometimes they just don't know how to study effectively. In other cases, students may lack adequate background or experience in a certain subject area (for example, English may be a second language), or they may have a personality conflict with the instructor.

1. I believe that essay exams are more difficult than multiple-choice exams.
2. I believe that longer prison sentences discourage people from committing crimes.
3. I believe that there are more people on the earth today than there were one hundred years ago.
4. I believe "fate" plays an important role in determining life's events.
5. I believe that people have the freedom to change themselves and their circumstances if they really want to.

Now write some of your most important beliefs on the following subjects and evaluate them in the same way:

- love
- physical health
- happiness
- religion

THINKING PASSAGE

Is the Earth Round or Flat?

In Chapter 2 you examined the process that led you to the conclusion that the earth is round, not flat. The following article, "Is the Earth Round or Flat?" by author and astrophysicist Alan Lightman, examines this process and provides a clear analysis of the difference between "believing" and "knowing." Read the article and answer the questions that follow.

IS THE EARTH ROUND OR FLAT?
by Alan Lightman

I propose that there are few of you who have personally verified that the Earth is round. The suggestive globe in the den or the Apollo photographs don't count. These are secondhand pieces of evidence that might be thrown out entirely in court. When you think about it, most of you simply believe what you hear. Round or flat, whatever. It's not a life-or-death matter, unless you happen to live near the edge.

A few years ago I suddenly realized, to my dismay, that I didn't know with certainty if the Earth were round or flat. I have scientific colleagues, geodesists they are called, whose sole business is determining the detailed shape of the Earth by fitting mathematical formulae to someone else's measurements of the precise locations of test stations on the Earth's surface. And I don't think those people really know either.

Aristotle is the first person in recorded history to have given proof that the Earth is round. He used several different arguments, most likely because he wanted to convince others as well as himself. A lot of people believed everything Aristotle said for 19 centuries.

His first proof was that the shadow of the Earth during a lunar eclipse is always curved, a segment of a circle. If the Earth were any shape but spher-

Source: "Is the Earth Round or Flat?" by Alan Lightman from Alan Lightman from *Time Travel and Papa Joe's Pipe,* reprinted in *Science,* March 1982, pp. 80–86. Copyright 1982 by the AAAS. Reprinted by permission of the American Association for the Advancement of Science and the author.

VISUAL THINKING

"The Earth Is Flat!"

● Why do you think people in earlier times believed the earth was
flat? If you were to travel back in time, how would you prove to
these "flat earthers" that the world is round? Do you think they
would believe you? Why or why not?

ical, the shadow it casts, in some orientations, would not be circular. (That
the normal phases of the moon are crescent-shaped reveals the moon is
round.) I find this argument wonderfully appealing. It is simple and direct.
What's more, an inquisitive and untrusting person can knock off the experiment alone, without special equipment. From any given spot on the Earth,
a lunar eclipse can be seen about once a year. You simply have to look up on
the right night and carefully observe what's happening. I've never done it.

Aristotle's second proof was that stars rise and set sooner for people in the East than in the West. If the Earth were flat from east to west, stars would rise as soon for Occidentals as for Orientals. With a little scribbling on a piece of paper, you can see that these observations imply a round Earth, regardless of whether it is the Earth that spins around or the stars that revolve around the Earth. Finally, northbound travelers observe previously invisible stars appearing above the northern horizon, showing the Earth is curved from north to south. Of course, you do have to accept the reports of a number of friends in different places or be willing to do some traveling.

Aristotle's last argument was purely theoretical and even philosophical. If the Earth had been formed from smaller pieces at some time in the past (or *could* have been so formed), its pieces would fall toward a common center, thus making a sphere. Furthermore, a sphere is clearly the most perfect solid shape. Interestingly, Aristotle placed as much emphasis on this last argument as on the first two. Those days, before the modern "scientific method," observational check wasn't required for investigating reality.

Assuming for the moment that the Earth is round, the first person who measured its circumference accurately was another Greek, Eratosthenes (276–195 B.C.). Eratosthenes noted that on the first day of summer, sunlight struck the bottom of a vertical well in Syene, Egypt, indicating the sun was directly overhead. At the same time in Alexandria, 5,000 stadia distant, the sun made an angle with the vertical equal to 1/50 of a circle. (A stadium equaled about a tenth of a mile.) Since the sun is so far away, its rays arrive almost in parallel. If you draw a circle with two radii extending from the center outward through the perimeter (where they become local verticals), you'll see that a sun ray coming in parallel to one of the radii (at Syene) makes an angle with the other (at Alexandria) equal to the angle between the two radii. Therefore Eratosthenes concluded that the full circumference of the Earth is $50 \times 5{,}000$ stadia, or about 25,000 miles. This calculation is within one percent of the best modern value.

For at least 600 years educated people have believed the Earth is round. At nearly any medieval university, the quadrivium was standard fare, consisting of arithmetic, geometry, music, and astronomy. The astronomy portion was based on the *Tractatus de Sphaera,* a popular textbook first published at Ferrara, Italy, in 1472 and written by a 13th century, Oxford-educated astronomer and mathematician, Johannes de Sacrobosco. The *Sphaera* proves its astronomical assertions, in part, by a set of diagrams with movable parts, a graphical demonstration of Aristotle's second method of proof. The round Earth, being the obvious center of the universe, provides a fixed pivot for the assembly. The cutout figures of the sun, the moon, and the stars revolve about the Earth.

By the year 1500, 24 editions of the *Sphaera* had appeared. There is no question that many people *believed* the Earth was round. I wonder how many *knew* this. You would think that Columbus and Magellan might have wanted to ascertain the facts for themselves before waving good-bye.

To protect my honor as a scientist, someone who is supposed to take nothing for granted, I set out with my wife on a sailing voyage in the Greek islands. I reasoned that at sea I would be able to calmly observe land masses disappear over the curve of the Earth and thus convince myself, firsthand, that the Earth is round.

Greece seemed a particularly satisfying place to conduct my experiment. I could sense those great ancient thinkers looking on approvingly, and the layout of the place is perfect. Hydra rises about 2,000 feet above sea level. If the Earth has a radius of 4,000 miles, as they say, then Hydra should sink down to the horizon at a distance of about 50 miles, somewhat less than the distance we were to sail from Hydra to Kea. The theory was sound and comfortable. At the very least, I thought, we would have a pleasant vacation.

As it turned out, that was all we got. Every single day was hazy. Islands faded from view at a distance of only eight miles, when the land was still a couple of degrees above the horizon. I learned how much water vapor was in the air but nothing about the curvature of the Earth.

I suspect that there are quite a few items we take on faith, even important things, even things we could verify without much trouble. Is the gas we exhale the same as the gas we inhale? (Do we indeed burn oxygen in our metabolism, as they say?) What is your blood made of ? (Does it indeed have red and white "cells"?) These questions could be answered with a balloon, a candle, and a microscope.

When we finally do the experiment, we relish the knowledge. At one time or another, we have all learned something for ourselves, from the ground floor up, taking no one's word for it. There is a special satisfaction and joy in being able to tell somebody something you have pieced together from scratch, something you really know. I think that exhilaration is a big reason why people do science.

Someday soon, I'm going to catch the Earth's shadow in a lunar eclipse, or go to sea in clear air, and find out for sure if the Earth is round or flat. Actually, the Earth is reported to flatten at the poles, because it rotates. But that's another story.

Questions for Analysis

1. Explain why Lightman states that, although he had always *believed* that the earth was round, "a few years ago I suddenly realized, to my dismay, that I didn't know with certainty if the Earth were round or flat."

2. In your own words, explain how you could prove to someone else that the earth is round.

3. Describe a conclusion about the world that you "believe" but do not "know," in Lightman's sense. Analyze your belief in terms of the criteria for determining the accuracy of beliefs.

   - How effectively do your beliefs *explain what is taking place?*

   - To what extent are these beliefs *consistent with other beliefs* you have about the world?

   - How effectively do your beliefs help you *predict what will happen* in the future?

   - To what extent are your beliefs supported by *sound reasons and compelling evidence* derived from *reliable sources?*

◎ Knowledge and Truth

Most people in our culture are socialized to believe that knowledge and truth are absolute and unchanging. One major goal of social institutions, including family, school system, and religion, is to transfer the knowledge that has been developed over the ages. Under this model, the role of learners is to absorb this information passively, like sponges. As you have seen in this text, achieving knowledge and truth is a complicated process. Instead of simply relying on the testimony of authorities like parents, teachers, textbooks, and religious leaders, critical thinkers have a responsibility to engage *actively* in the learning process and participate in developing their own understanding of the world.

The need for this active approach to knowing is underscored by the fact that authorities often disagree about the true nature of a given situation or the best course of action. It is not uncommon, for example, for doctors to disagree about a diagnosis, for economists to differ on the state of the economy, for researchers to present contrasting views on the best approach to curing cancer, for psychiatrists to disagree on whether a convicted felon is a menace to society or a harmless victim of social forces, and for religions to present conflicting approaches to achieving eternal life.

What do we do when experts disagree? As a critical thinker, you must analyze and evaluate all the available information, develop your own well-reasoned beliefs, and recognize when you don't have sufficient information to arrive at well-reasoned beliefs. You must realize that these beliefs may evolve over time as you gain information or improve your insight.

Although there are compelling reasons to view knowledge and truth in this way, many people resist it. Either they take refuge in a belief in the absolute, unchanging nature of knowledge and truth, as presented by the appropriate authorities, or they conclude that there is no such thing as knowledge or truth and that trying to seek either is a futile enterprise. Some beliefs *are* better than others, not because an authority has proclaimed them so but because they can be analyzed in terms of the following criteria:

- How effectively do your beliefs *explain what is taking place?*
- To what extent are these beliefs *consistent with other beliefs* you have about the world?
- How effectively do your beliefs help you *predict what will happen* in the future?
- To what extent are your beliefs supported by *sound reasons and compelling evidence* derived from *reliable sources?*

Another important criterion for evaluating your beliefs is that the beliefs are *falsifiable.* This means that you can state conditions — tests — under which the beliefs could be disproved and the beliefs nevertheless *pass* those tests. For example, if you believe that you can create ice cubes by placing water-filled trays in a freezer, it is easy to see how you can conduct an experiment to determine if your belief is accurate. If you believe that your destiny is related to the positions of the planets and stars (as astrologers do), it is not clear how you can conduct an experiment to determine if your belief is accurate. Since a belief that is not *falsifiable* can never be *proved,* such a belief is of questionable accuracy.

A critical thinker sees knowledge and truth as goals that we are striving to achieve, processes that we are all actively involved in as we construct our understanding of the world. Developing accurate knowledge about the world is often a challenging process of exploration and analysis in which our understanding grows and evolves over a period of time.

Stages of Knowing

The road to becoming a critical thinker is a challenging journey that involves passing through different Stages of Knowing, in order to achieve an effective understanding of the world. These stages, ranging from simple to complex, characterize people's thinking and the way they understand their world. A critical thinker is a person who has progressed through all of the stages to achieve a sophisticated understanding of the nature of knowledge. This framework is based on the work of Harvard psychologist Dr. William Perry (*Forms of Intellectual and Ethical Development in the College Years: A Scheme*), who used in-depth research to create a developmental model of human thought. I use a condensed three-stage version of Perry's framework.

Stage 1: The Garden of Eden
Stage 2: Anything Goes
Stage 3: Thinking Critically

An individual may be at different stages simultaneously, depending on the subject or area of experience. For example, a person may be at an advanced stage in one area of life (academic work) but at a less sophisticated stage in another area (romantic relationships or conception of morality). In general, however, people tend to operate predominantly within one stage in most areas of their lives.

Stage 1: The Garden of Eden   People in the Garden of Eden stage of thinking tend to see the world in terms of black and white, right and wrong. How do they determine what is right, what to believe? The "authorities" *tell* them. Just like in the biblical Garden of Eden, knowledge is absolute, unchanging, and in the sole possession of authorities. Ordinary people can never determine the truth for themselves; they must rely on the experts. If someone disagrees with what they have been told by their authorities, then that person *must* be wrong. There is no possibility of compromise or negotiation.

Who are the authorities? The first authorities we encounter are usually our parents. When parents are rooted in this stage of thinking, they expect children to do as they're told. Parents are the authorities, and the role of children is to benefit from their parents' years of experience, their store of knowledge, and their position of authority. Similarly, when children enter a school system built on the foundation of Stage 1 thinking (as most school systems are), they are likely to be told, "We have the questions and the answers; your role is to learn them, not ask questions of your own" — an approach that runs counter to children's natural curiosity.

People in this Garden of Eden stage of thinking become dissatisfied when they realize that they can't simply rely on authorities to tell them what to think and believe because in virtually every arena — medicine, religion, economics, psychology, education, science, law, child-rearing — authorities often disagree with each other. We explored this disturbing phenomenon earlier in the chapter, and it poses a mortal threat to Stage 1 thinking. If the authorities disagree with each other, then how do we figure out what (and whom) to believe? Stage 1 thinkers try to deal with this contradiction by maintaining that *my* authorities know more than *your* authorities. But if we are willing to think clearly and honestly, this explanation simply doesn't hold up: We have to explain *why* we choose to believe one authority over another. And as soon as that happens, we have transcended Stage 1 thinking. Just as Adam and Eve could not go back to blind, uncritical acceptance of authority once they had tasted the fruit of the Tree of the Knowledge of Good and Evil, so it is nearly impossible to return to Stage 1 after recognizing its oversimplifying inadequacies.

Why are some people able to go beyond Stage 1 thinking while others remain more or less stuck there throughout their lives? Part of the answer lies in how diverse their environment is. When people live in predominantly homogeneous environments, surrounded by people who think and believe the same way, it is much easier to maintain the artificially uniform world view of the Garden of Eden thinking.

However, when people are exposed to diverse experiences that challenge them with competing perspectives, it is much more difficult to maintain the unquestioned faith in authoritarian dictates of Stage 1 thinking. For example, in my philosophy of religion classes, the final term project is for students to visit five different places of religious worship selected from a list of thirty I provide; these range from Zen Buddhist to Pentecostal, Catholic to Southern Baptist, Jewish to Hindu. Students invariably report that this project transformed their thinking, stimulating them to view religion in a richer, more complex light. It gives them the opportunity to see other people who were just as serious and devout as themselves engage in very different religious practices.

However, simply providing people with diverse experiences does not guarantee that they will be stimulated to question and transcend the limiting confines of Stage 1 thinking. We need to have the *emotional willingness* to open ourselves to new possibilities and the *intellectual ability* to see issues from different perspectives. Very often people are so emotionally entangled in their point of view that they are simply unwilling to question its truth, and so the power of their emotional needs inhibits the potential illumination of their reasoning abilities. Additionally, many people have not developed the flexibility of thinking needed to extricate themselves from their own point of view and look at issues from different perspectives. To become a Stage 2 thinker, both of these conditions must be met: the emotional willingness *and* the cognitive ability to be open-minded.

Stage 2: Anything Goes   Once one has rejected the dogmatic, authoritarian framework of Stage 1, the temptation in Stage 2 is to go to the opposite extreme and believe that anything goes. The reasoning is something like this: If authorities are not infallible and we can't trust their expertise, then no one point of view is ultimately any better than any other. In Stage 1 the authorities could resolve such disputes, but if their opinion is on the same level as yours and mine, then there is no rational way to resolve differences.

In the tradition of philosophy, such a view is known as *relativism:* the truth is relative to any individual or situation, and there is no standard we can use to decide which beliefs make most sense. Take the example of fashion. You may believe that an attractive presentation includes loose-fitting clothing in muted colors, a natural hair style, and a minimum of makeup and jewelry. Someone else might prefer tight-fitting black clothing, gelled hair, tattoos, and body piercings. In Stage 2 thinking, there's no way to evaluate these or any other fashion preferences: They are simply "matters of taste." And, in fact, if you examine past photographs of yourself and what you considered to be "attractive" years ago, this relativistic point of view probably makes some sense.

Although we may be drawn to this seemingly open-minded attitude — anything goes — the reality is that we are often not so tolerant. We *do* believe that some appearances are more aesthetically pleasing than others. But there is an even more serious threat to Stage 2 thinking. Imagine the following scenario: As you are strolling down the street, you suddenly feel a gun pushed against your back accompanied by the demand for all your valuables. You protest, arguing with this would-be mugger that he has no right to your possessions. "On the contrary," your philosophically inclined mugger responds, "I believe that 'might makes right,' and since I have a weapon, I am entitled to your valuables. You have your beliefs, I have my beliefs, and as Stage 2 thinkers, there's no way for you to prove me wrong!" Preposterous? Nevertheless, this is the logical conclusion of Anything Goes thinking. If we truly believe this, then we cannot condemn *any* belief or action, no matter how heinous, and we cannot praise *any* belief or action, no matter how laudatory.

When we think things through, it's obvious that the Anything Goes level of thinking simply doesn't work because it leads to absurd conclusions that run counter to our deeply felt conviction that some beliefs *are* better than other beliefs. So while Stage 2 may represent a slight advance over Stage 1 in sophistication and complexity, it's clear to a discerning thinker that a further advance to the next stage is necessary.

Stage 3: Thinking Critically   The two opposing perspectives of Stages 1 and 2 find their synthesis in Stage 3, Thinking Critically. When people achieve this level of understanding, they recognize that some viewpoints *are* better than other viewpoints, not simply because authorities say so but because *there are compelling reasons to support these viewpoints.* At the same time, people in this

Stages of Knowing

Stage 1: The Garden of Eden
Knowledge is clear, certain, and absolute and is provided by authorities. Our role is to learn and accept information from authorities without question or criticism. Anyone who disagrees with the authorities must be wrong.

Stage 2: Anything Goes
Since authorities often disagree with each other, no one really "knows" what is true or right. All beliefs are of equal value, and there is no way to determine whether one belief makes more sense than another belief.

Stage 3: Thinking Critically
Some viewpoints *are* better than other viewpoints, not because authorities say so but because there are compelling reasons to support these viewpoints. We have a responsibility to explore every perspective, evaluate the supporting reasons of each, and develop our own informed conclusions that we are prepared to modify or change based on new information or better insight.

stage are open-minded toward other viewpoints, especially those that disagree with theirs. They recognize that there are often a number of legitimate perspectives on complex issues, and they accept the validity of these perspectives to the extent that they are supported by persuasive reasons and evidence.

Consider a more complicated issue, like euthanasia. A Stage 3 thinker approaches this as she approaches all issues: trying to understand all of the different viewpoints on the issue, evaluating the reasons that support each of these viewpoints, and then coming to her own thoughtful conclusion. When asked, she can explain the rationale for her viewpoint, but she also respects differing viewpoints that are supported by legitimate reasons, even though she feels her viewpoint makes more sense. In addition, a Stage 3 thinker maintains an open mind, always willing to consider new evidence that might convince her to modify or even change her position.

But while people in the Thinking Critically stage are actively open to different perspectives, they also *commit* themselves to definite points of view and are *confident* in explaining the reasons and evidence that have led them to their conclusions. Being open-minded is not the same thing as being intellectually wishy-washy. In addition to having clearly defined views, Stage 3 thinkers are always willing to listen to people who disagree with them. In fact, they actively seek out opposing viewpoints because they know that this is the only way to achieve the clearest, most insightful, most firmly grounded understanding. They recognize that their views may evolve over time as they learn more.

Becoming a Stage 3 thinker is a worthy goal, and it is the only way to adequately answer Socrates' challenge to examine our lives thoughtfully and honestly. To live a life of reflection and action, of open-mindedness and commitment, of purpose and fulfillment, requires the full development of our intellectual abilities and positive traits of character.

THINKING ACTIVITY 5.3

What Stage of Knowing Am I In?

1. Create a diagram to illustrate the three Stages of Knowing.

2. We all know people who illustrate each of these three Stages of Knowing. Think about the people in your life — professionally and personally — and identify which stage you think they mainly fall into.

3. Consider carefully your beliefs in each of the following areas, and evaluate in which of the three Stages of Knowing you predominantly think.

- education
- professional area of expertise
- science
- moral issues
- religion
- human nature
- social relationships
- child-rearing
- aesthetic areas (beauty)

Example: "My beliefs in the area of my academic classes tend to be Stage 1. I have always trusted the experts, whether they are my teachers or the textbooks we are learning. That's how I see the purpose of education: to learn the facts from those who know them." Or "My beliefs in my area of special interest, health, are Stage 3. When confronted with a set of symptoms, I consider all of the possible diagnoses, carefully evaluate the relevant evidence, get a second opinion if necessary, and then develop a plan that involves holistic and nutritional approaches as well as standard medical treatments."

Thinking Critically About Your Beliefs

The path to becoming a consistent Stage 3 thinker begins with evaluating the process you use to form beliefs and reach conclusions about the world. Some of your beliefs are deep and profound, with far-reaching implications, such as your belief (or disbelief) in a Supreme Being or your opinion on whether the Golden Rule should govern people's actions. Other beliefs are less significant, such as whether vitamin supplements improve your health or if having children wear school uniforms is beneficial. Your total collection of beliefs constitutes your philosophy of life, the guiding beacon you use to chart the course of your personal existence. As you become a more accomplished critical thinker, you will develop beliefs that will enhance the quality of your life, beliefs that are clearly conceived, thoughtfully expressed, and solidly supported. This is the first step in constructing an enlightened philosophy, painting a portrait of yourself that you can present to the world with pride and satisfaction.

Everybody has a collection of beliefs that she or he uses to guide her or his actions. What differentiates people is the *quality* of their beliefs, the strength of the reasons and evidence that support their beliefs. As a critical thinker, you should be striving to develop beliefs constructed through a process of thoughtful reflection and analysis. For example, here is a brief survey of some beliefs that may contribute to your philosophy of life. Briefly answer the statements in the following activity and note how comfortable you would feel in justifying your answers as well as the paths you pursued to arrive at them. Remember that these questions don't have a simple right or wrong answer.

THINKING ACTIVITY 5.4

Surveying Your Beliefs

Answer the following questions, based on what you believe to be true:

1. Is there a God?
2. Should research on the cloning of humans continue?
3. Should women have the legal right to decide to have an abortion?
4. Should the government take all steps to keep our society safe from terrorism, even if this means curtailing some of our personal liberties?
5. Is the death penalty justified for some convicted murderers?
6. Should health care workers and potential patients be tested for AIDS and if positive, be identified to each other?
7. Should the government provide public assistance to citizens who cannot support themselves and their families?
8. Should affirmative action programs be created to compensate for long-standing discrimination?
9. Have aliens visited earth in some form?

Thinking Critically About Evaluating Evidence

Authorities: Are the authorities knowledgeable in this area? Are they reliable? Have they ever given inaccurate information? Do other authorities disagree?

Written references: What are the credentials of the authors? Are there others who disagree with their opinions? On what evidence do the authors base their opinions?

Factual evidence: What are the source and foundation of the evidence? Can the evidence be interpreted differently? Does the evidence support the conclusion?

Personal experience: What were the circumstances under which the experience took place? Were distortions or mistakes in perception possible? Have other people had either similar or conflicting experiences? Are there other explanations for the experience?

10. Should parents be permitted to refuse conventional medical care for their children if their religious beliefs prohibit it?
11. Should certain "recreational" drugs, such as marijuana, be legalized?
12. Should people with terminal illnesses be permitted to end their lives with medical assistance, such as that provided by Dr. Jack Kevorkian?

Critical thinkers continually evaluate their beliefs by applying *intellectual standards* in order to assess the strength and accuracy of these beliefs. *Uncritical* thinkers generally adopt beliefs without thoughtful scrutiny or rigorous evaluation, letting these beliefs drift into their thinking for all sorts of superficial and illogical reasons. The most effective way for you to test the strength and accuracy of your beliefs is to evaluate evidence that supports them. There are four categories of evidence: authorities, written references, factual evidence, and personal experience.

Now you may be thinking, "Will I be called upon to apply this structure — these thinking tools — to every situation?" It may be overly optimistic to expect that we can take time out to step back and evaluate all our situations this way, especially because we already feel so overburdened and overextended. However, it is precisely because of this that we need to put on the brakes, or we risk losing ourselves in the frenetically accelerated flow of today's culture. What you are learning from these and further exercises is a way of *approaching* both small and large questions differently from the way you did before. By recognizing the *need* to impose these intellectual standards, you will eventually use them *habitually.*

THINKING ACTIVITY 5.5

Evaluating My Beliefs

1. Select several of your responses to the Belief Survey (Thinking Activity 5.4 on page 188), and explain the reasons, evidence, and experiences that led you to your conclusions. Be specific.

2. After you have recorded your evidence, use the questions under "Thinking Critically About Evaluating Evidence" to assess its accuracy and strength.

Example: I believe that aliens have visited the earth in some form.

Explanation: I have read a great deal about eyewitness sightings and evidence of a government cover-up, and I have met people who believe they have seen UFOs.

Reasons/Evidence:

- *Authorities:* Many reputable people have seen UFOs and had personal encounters with aliens. The government has documented these in secret files, which include the UFO crash at Roswell, New Mexico, in 1947. Government attempts at concealment and cover-up have been transparent.

- *References:* There are many books supporting alien visitations and alien abductions.

- *Factual evidence:* There are many photographs of UFOs and eyewitness accounts from people who have seen alien spacecraft. There have also been accounts of alien abductions. In addition, the movie *Alien Autopsy* purportedly shows an alien being dissected.

- *Personal experience:* I have personally spoken to several people who are convinced that they saw things in the sky that looked like flying saucers.

Let's examine the process of critical evaluation by thinking through a sample belief: "I believe that aliens have visited the earth in some form." Interestingly, a recent Gallup Poll found that 42 percent of American college graduates believe that flying saucers have visited earth in some form, and the popularity of shows like *The X Files* have highlighted people's fascination with this subject.

VISUAL THINKING

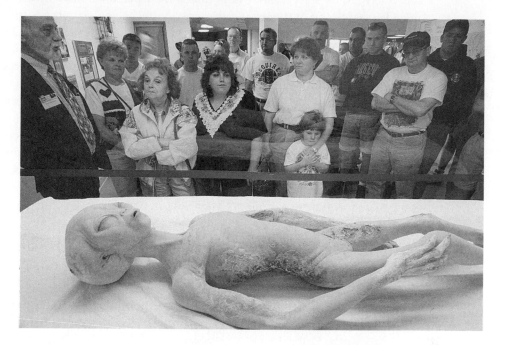

"I Knew That Aliens Existed!"

- Examining the faces and body language of people in the photo, do you think they believe that this "alien" corpse is real? Do you think it might be real? Do you believe that alien life has visited earth? Why or why not?

Reasons/Evidence

Authorities

Many reputable people have seen UFOs and had personal encounters with aliens. The government has documented these in secret files, which include the UFO crash at Roswell, New Mexico, in 1947. Government attempts at concealment and cover-up have been transparent.

    Thinking Critically About Authorities: Although there are many individuals who have testified to the existence of alien encounters over the years, virtually all scientific authorities have been extremely skeptical. They emphasize that all of the "evidence" is unsubstantiated, controversial, indirect, and murky — the markings of pseudoscientific fantasies. If aliens and UFOs exist, why haven't they announced their presence in an incontrovertible fashion? Some of the most intriguing evidence comes in the form of the government's belated and somewhat bizarre explanations for UFO sightings and the alleged Roswell incident. On June 25, 1997, the air force announced that the mysterious happenings in the New Mexico desert in the late 1940s and 1950s were in fact experiments involving crash dummies and weather balloons. Six weeks later, on August 3, 1997, the CIA "admitted" that the U.S. government had lied about alleged UFO sightings in the 1950s and 1960s in order to protect classified information regarding top-secret spy planes, the U-2 and SR-71. Why did the government suddenly attempt to explain these mysteries after all these years? And why does there appear to be contradictory testimony from different parts of the government? Why do the government explanations seem almost as fanciful and farfetched as the UFO stories?

References

There are many books supporting alien visitations and alien abductions.

Thinking Critically About References: Although many books regarding UFOs have been written, few have been more than unsubstantiated speculation. Recently, Philip J. Corso, who served on the National Security Council under President Dwight D. Eisenhower, contended in his book *The Day After Roswell* (Pocket Books, 1997) that he personally directed an army project that transferred to the military various types of technology recovered from the alien ship that crashed in the desert. To date, efforts to prove or disprove his account have been inconclusive. After reviewing written accounts and interviewing people claiming to be alien abductees, Dr. John Mack, a psychiatry professor at Harvard Medical School, came to the conclusion that many of these reports are true. Though he was harshly criticized by his colleagues, Dr. Mack became instantly popular on the UFO circuit, and he recently convened a conference at which 200 mental health professionals gathered to discuss alien abductions.

Factual Evidence

There are many photographs of UFOs and eyewitness accounts from people who have seen alien spacecraft. There have also been accounts of alien abductions. In addition, the movie *Alien Autopsy* purportedly shows an alien being dissected.

Thinking Critically About Factual Evidence: There have been innumerable UFO sightings, many of which can be explained by the presence of aircraft in the vicinity, meteors, or some other physical event. However, there is a core of sightings, sometimes by large groups of reputable people, that have not been satisfactorily explained. There are a number of photographs of "flying saucers" taken at a considerable distance, and though provocative in their possibilities, they are inconclusive. Most reports of alien abductions have been considered by the scientific establishment to be hoaxes or the result of mental illness or hallucinations — at least until Dr. Mack's analysis noted previously. Medical experts and movie-makers have derided *Alien Autopsy* as a crude hoax, although a small number of people knowledgeable about physiology and movie-making techniques find it persuasive. There is no documented history of where the film came from, a fact that undermines its credibility.

Personal Experience

I have personally spoken to several people who are convinced that they saw things in the sky that looked like flying saucers.

Thinking Critically About Personal Experience: The perceptions of eyewitness testimony are notoriously unreliable. People consistently mistake and misinterpret what they experience and often see what they want to see. In evaluating the testimony of personal experience, we must establish independent confirmation.

◎ Using Perspective-Taking to Achieve Knowledge

In Chapter 4, we examined contrasting media accounts of the assassination of Malcolm X. Each account, we found, viewed the event through its own perceiving lenses, which shaped and influenced the information the writer selected, the way the writer organized it, his or her interpretations of the event and the people involved, and the language used to describe it. We can see now that this type of organized evaluation of contrasting sources and opinions — "perspective-taking" — is an essential strategy of Stage 3 thinking and one of the most powerful ways to construct well-supported beliefs and genuine knowledge. The following activity, which centers on the events at Tiananmen Square in 1989 involving mainly Chinese college students, provides another opportunity to engage in perspective-taking critical thinking.

THINKING ACTIVITY 5.6

Analyzing Different Accounts of the Confrontation at Tiananmen Square

In the spring of 1989, a vigorous prodemocracy movement erupted in Beijing, the capital of China. Protesting the authoritarian control of the Communist regime, thousands of students staged demonstrations, engaged in hunger strikes, and organized marches involving hundreds of thousands of people. The geographical heart of these activities was the historic Tiananmen Square, taken over by the demonstrators who had erected a symbolic "Statue of Liberty." On June 4, 1989, the fledgling prodemocracy movement came to a bloody end when the Chinese army entered Tiananmen Square and seized control of it. Thinking Activity 5.6 on the companion web site includes various accounts of this event from different sources. After analyzing these accounts, construct your own version of what you believe took place on that day. Use these questions to guide your analysis of the varying accounts:

- Does the account provide a convincing description of what took place?
- What reasons and evidence support the account?
- How reliable is the source? What are the author's perceiving lenses, which might influence his or her account?
- Is the account consistent with other reliable descriptions of this event?

THINKING ACTIVITY 5.7

Analyzing Different Accounts of a Current Event

Locate three different newspaper or magazine accounts of an important event — a court decision, a crime, and a political demonstration are possible topics. Analyze each of the accounts with the questions listed next, and then construct your own version of what you believe took place.

- Does the account provide a convincing description of what took place?
- What reasons and evidence support the account?
- How reliable is the source? What are the author's perceiving lenses, which might influence his or her account?
- Is the account consistent with other reliable descriptions of this event?

VISUAL THINKING

Tiananmen Square Aftermath

- Once you have read various accounts of the Tiananmen Square incident, explain what you think is the point of view or perspective of the person who took this picture? What kinds of photos might result from other perspectives?

Beliefs Based on Direct Experience

As you attempt to make sense of the world, your thinking abilities give you the means to

- Ask questions about your experience
- Work toward forming beliefs that will enable you to answer these questions and make useful decisions

Asking questions encourages you to try to form more accurate beliefs to explain what is taking place. By questioning your experience, instead of passively accepting it, you are better able to understand the situation you are in and to take effective control of your life.

Let's explore how these activities of asking questions and forming beliefs enable you to make sense of your world. Read carefully the following passage, in which a student, Maria, describes her experiences with the "system."

A few years ago my oldest son went to a party. On his way home he was accosted by three individuals who tried to take his belongings. Seeing guns, my son's first reaction was to run away, which he did. While running he was shot and his wounds left him paralyzed from the neck down. As he lay in the intensive care unit of the hospital, I started to receive threatening phone calls telling me that if I identified them to the police, "they would finish the work."

I reported the phone calls to both the police and the telephone company, but I was irritated by the way the police handled the whole situation. They told me that there was no reason why the city should pay for having a police officer protect my son and they asked me what he was doing in the streets at this time. (The time was 11 P.M., and my son was almost eighteen years old.) Finally, I was told there was nothing that could be done. In my anger, I called the mayor's office, the senator's office, and the local councilman. I also wrote a letter to the police commissioner and mailed it registered, special delivery, as proof in case the situation didn't improve. Within a few hours, there was an officer at my son's bedside making sure that nothing further happened to him.

I learned that although there are many laws to protect citizens, if citizens don't fight for their rights, these laws will never be exercised. My opinion of the "system" changed after this experience. I believe that I shouldn't have had to go through so much red tape in order to have my legal rights. I feel that, if you don't take a stand, there is no one who will go out of the way to instruct you or to help out. I was never informed at the police headquarters about what to do and how to go about doing it. I was left standing without any hope at all. I feel sorry for those persons who are ignorant about how you can make the system work for you.

Throughout this experience, Maria's beliefs influenced her decisions. Before her son got shot, she had formed certain beliefs about the law, the police, and the legal system as a whole. After her son was shot, Maria tried to make sense of the situation in terms of her beliefs and to act on their basis. However, Maria began to discover that her beliefs did not seem to explain what was happening. As Maria came to doubt the accuracy of her initial beliefs, she began to form new beliefs to explain what was happening. After taking action based on her revised beliefs, Maria received responses that seemed to support her revised beliefs about the law, the police, and the system. These revised beliefs helped her to understand and control the situation in a way her initial beliefs had not, leading her to the following conclusion: "I learned that although there are many laws to protect citizens, if citizens don't fight for their rights, these laws will never be exercised." After reflecting critically on her experiences, Maria was convinced that the revised beliefs she had formed to explain her situation and guide her actions were more accurate than her initial beliefs. As a result, she advises those who find themselves in similar circumstances to "take a stand" and "make the system work" for them.

Maria's story illustrates the process by which we form and re-form our beliefs, a process that often follows this sequence:

1. We *form* beliefs to explain what is taking place. (These initial beliefs are often based on our past experiences.)
2. We *test* these beliefs by acting on them.
3. We *revise* (or re-form) these beliefs if our actions do not result in our desired goals.
4. We *retest* these revised beliefs by acting on them.

As you actively participate in this ongoing process of forming and re-forming beliefs, you are using your critical thinking abilities to identify and critically examine your beliefs by asking the following questions:

- How effectively do your beliefs *explain what is taking place?*
- To what extent are these beliefs *consistent with other beliefs* you have about the world?
- How effectively do your beliefs help you *predict what will happen* in the future?
- To what extent are your beliefs supported by *sound reasons and compelling evidence* derived from *reliable sources?*

This process of critical exploration enables you to develop a greater understanding of various situations in your experience and also gives you the means to exert more effective control in these situations.

THINKING ACTIVITY 5.8

Analyzing a Changed Belief

1. Interview another person about a belief he or she once held but no longer holds. Ask that person the following questions. (*Note:* Try asking the questions in the course of a conversation you have with the person rather

than confronting him or her with an intimidating series of formal questions. Most people like to be asked about their beliefs and are very coop-
erative.)

- What is the belief?
- On what evidence did you hold that belief? (Was it based on personal perception or oral or written sources? What were they?)
- What caused you to change the belief?
- What were your feelings or attitudes when you found that changing the belief was necessary?
- How do you feel now about changing the belief?

2. Next, write a summary of the interview. Begin by describing the person and explaining your relationship to him or her. Then give his or her answers to the questions. Be as detailed as possible.

3. Describe your reaction to the other person's experience. What did you learn about perception and belief from that experience?

THINKING PASSAGE

Why I Quit the Klan

Examine the process of forming and re-forming beliefs by reading the following interview, which Studs Terkel conducted with C. P. Ellis, once president
(Exalted Cyclops) of the Durham, North Carolina, chapter of the Ku Klux Klan.
The interview traces the evolution of Ellis's limited, racist beliefs through
thoughtful reflection and critical evaluation. Answer the questions that follow
the passage. The complete essay can be found on the companion web site.

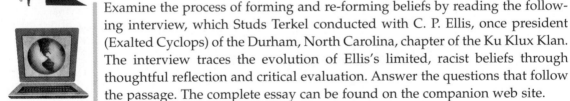

WHY I QUIT THE KLAN
by C. P. Ellis

All my life, I had work, never a day without work, worked all the overtime
I could get and still could not survive financially. I began to see there's something wrong with this country. I worked my butt off and just never seemed
to break even. I had some real great ideas about this nation. They say to abide
by the law, go to church, do right and live for the Lord, and everything'll
work out. But it didn't work out. It just kept gettin worse and worse. . . .

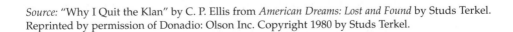

Source: "Why I Quit the Klan" by C. P. Ellis from *American Dreams: Lost and Found* by Studs Terkel.
Reprinted by permission of Donadio: Olson Inc. Copyright 1980 by Studs Terkel.

Tryin to come out of that hole, I just couldn't do it. I really began to get bitter. I didn't know who to blame. I tried to find somebody. Hatin America is hard to do because you can't see it to hate it. You gotta have somethin to look at to hate. The natural person for me to hate would be black people, because my father before me was a member of the Klan. . . .

So I began to admire the Klan. . . . To be part of somethin. . . . The first night I went with the fellas . . . I was led into a large meeting room, and this was the time of my life! It was thrilling. Here's a guy who's worked all his life and struggled all his life to be something, and here's the moment to be something. I will never forget it. Four robed Klansmen led me into the hall. The lights were dim and the only thing you could see was an illuminated cross. . . . After I had taken my oath, there was loud applause goin through-out the buildin, musta been at least four hundred people. For this one little ol person. It was a thrilling moment for C. P. Ellis. . . .

The majority of [the Klansmen] are low-income whites, people who really don't have a part in something. They have been shut out as well as blacks. Some are not very well educated either. Just like myself. We had a lot of support from doctors and lawyers and police officers.

Maybe they've had bitter experiences in this life and they had to hate somebody. So the natural person to hate would be the black person. He's beginnin to come up, he's beginnin to . . . start votin and run for political office. Here are white people who are supposed to be superior to them, and we're shut out. . . . Shut out. Deep down inside, we want to be part of this *great society.* Nobody listens, so we join these groups. . . .

We would go to the city council meetings, and the blacks would be there and we'd be there. It was a confrontation every time. . . . We began to make some inroads with the city councilmen and county commissioners. They began to call us friend. Call us at night on the telephone: "C. P., glad you came to that meeting last night." They didn't want integration either, but they did it secretively, in order to get elected. They couldn't stand up openly and say it, but they were glad somebody was sayin it. We visited some of the city leaders in their homes and talked to em privately. It wasn't long before councilmen would call me up: "The blacks are comin up tonight and makin outrageous demands. How about some of you people showin up and have a little balance?". . .

We'd load up our cars and we'd fill up half the council chambers, and the blacks the other half. During these times, I carried weapons to the meetings, outside my belt. We'd go there armed. We would wind up just hollerin and fussin at each other. What happened? As a result of our fightin one another, the city council still had their way. They didn't want to give up control to the blacks nor the Klan. They were usin us.

I began to realize this later down the road. One day I was walkin downtown and a certain city council member saw me comin. I expected him to shake my hand because he was talkin to me at night on the telephone. I had been in his home and visited with him. He crossed the street [to avoid me]. . . . I began to think, somethin's wrong here.

Most of em are merchants or maybe an attorney, an insurance agent, people like that. As long as they kept low-income whites and low-income blacks fightin, they're gonna maintain control. I began to get that feelin after I was ignored in public. I thought: . . . you're not gonna use me any more. That's when I began to do some real serious thinkin.

The same thing is happening in this country today. People are being used by those in control, those who have all the wealth. I'm not espousing communism. We got the greatest system of government in the world. But those who have it simply don't want those who don't have it to have any part of it. Black and white. When it comes to money, the green, the other colors make no difference.

I spent a lot of sleepless nights. I still didn't like blacks. I didn't want to associate with them. Blacks, Jews or Catholics. My father said: "Don't have anything to do with em." I didn't until I met a black person and talked with him, eyeball to eyeball, and met a Jewish person and talked to him, eyeball to eyeball. I found they're people just like me. They cried, they cussed, they prayed, they had desires. Just like myself. Thank God, I got to the point where I can look past labels. But at that time, my mind was closed.

I remember one Monday night Klan meeting. I said something was wrong. Our city fathers were using us. And I didn't like to be used. The reactions of the others was not too pleasant: "Let's just keep fightin them niggers."

I'd go home at night and I'd have to wrestle with myself. I'd look at a black person walkin down the street, and the guy'd have ragged shoes or his clothes would be worn. That began to do something to me inside. I went through this for about six months. I felt I just had to get out of the Klan. But I wouldn't get out. . . .

[Ellis was invited, as a Klansman, to join a committee of people from all walks of life to make recommendations on how to solve racial problems in the school system. He very reluctantly accepted. After a few stormy meetings, he was elected co-chair of the committee, along with Ann Atwater, a black woman who for years had been leading local efforts for civil rights.]

A Klansman and a militant black woman, co-chairmen of the school committee. It was impossible. How could I work with her? But it was in our hands. We had to make it a success. This give me another sense of belongin, a sense of pride. This helped the inferiority feeling I had. A man who has stood up publicly and said he despised black people, all of a sudden he was willin to work with em. Here's a chance for a low-income white man to be somethin. In spite of all my hatred for blacks and Jews and liberals, I accepted the job. Her and I began to reluctantly work together. She had as many problems workin with me as I had workin with her.

One night, I called her: "Ann, you and I should have a lot of differences and we got em now. But there's something laid out here before us, and if it's gonna be a success, you and I are gonna have to make it one. Can you lay aside some of these feelings?" She said: "I'm willing if you are." I said: "Let's do it."

My old friends would call me at night: "C. P., what the hell is wrong with you? You're sellin out the white race." This begin to make me have guilt feel-ins. Am I doin right? Am I doin wrong? Here I am all of a sudden makin an about-face and tryin to deal with my feeling, my heart. My mind was begin-nin to open up. I was beginnin to see what was right and what was wrong. I don't want the kids to fight forever. . . .

One day, Ann and I went back to the school and we sat down. We began to talk and just reflect. . . . I begin to see, here you are, two people from the far ends of the fence, havin identical problems, except hers bein black and me bein white. . . . The amazing thing about it, her and I, up to that point, has cussed each other, bawled each other, we hated each other. Up to that point, we didn't know each other. We didn't know we had things in com-mon. . . .

The whole world was openin up, and I was learning new truths that I had never learned before. I was beginning to look at a black person, shake hands with him, and see him as a human bein. I hadn't got rid of all this stuff. I've still got a little bit of it. But somethin was happenin to me. . . .

I come to work one mornin and some guys says: "You need a union." At this time I wasn't pro-union. My daddy was anti-labor too. We're not gettin paid much, we're havin to work seven days in a row. We're all starvin to death. . . . I didn't know nothin about organizin unions, but I knew how to organize people, stir people up. That's how I got to be business agent for the union.

When I began to organize, I began to see far deeper. I begin to see people again bein used. Blacks against whites. . . . There are two things manage-ment wants to keep: all the money and all the say-so. They don't want none of these poor workin folks to have none of that. I begin to see management fightin me with everythin they had. Hire anti-union law firms, badmouth unions. The people were makin $1.95 an hour, barely able to get through weekends. . . .

It makes you feel good to go into a plant and . . . see black people and white people join hands to defeat the racist issues [union-busters] use against people. . . .

I tell people there's a tremendous possibility in this country to stop wars, the battles, the struggles, the fights between people. People say: "That's an impossible dream. You sound like Martin Luther King." An ex-Klansman who sounds like Martin Luther King. I don't think it's an impossible dream. It's happened in my life. It's happened in other people's lives in America. . . .

. . . They say the older you get, the harder it is for you to change. That's not necessarily true. Since I changed, I've set down and listened to tapes of Martin Luther King. I listen to it and tears come to my eyes cause I know what he's sayin now. I know what's happenin.

Questions for Analysis

1. What were C. P. Ellis's most important *initial beliefs?* From where did his stereotypes originate?

2. What were some of the *experiences* that helped form these initial beliefs?

3. What *actions* did he take based on these initial beliefs?

4. What *experiences* raised doubts and questions about his initial beliefs? Why was he able to say: "Thank God, I got to the point where I can look past labels. . . . I was beginning to look at a black person, shake hands with him, and see him as a human bein"?

5. What *revised beliefs* did he form to better make sense of his experiences?

C. P. Ellis's powerful interview displays how the processes of perceiving and believing continually influence each other. On the one hand, our perceptions influence what we come to believe. Thus, for example, the fact that C. P. Ellis's friends and family insulted and disparaged African Americans, Jews, and Catholics led him to form racist beliefs about these groups. On the other hand, our beliefs influence the way we perceive things; that is, they influence the perceptual lenses we use to view the world. Thus, the racist beliefs that C. P. Ellis had formed were reflected in his perceptual stereotypes of African Americans, Jews, and Catholics.

Fortunately, beliefs do not stand still in the minds of critical thinkers. We continue to form and re-form our beliefs, based in part on what we are experiencing and how we think about what we are experiencing. For C. P. Ellis, the experience of meeting and working with people from other ethnic groups broke down his perceptual stereotypes of them, for he discovered: "I found they're people just like me. They cried, they cussed, they prayed, they had desires. Just like myself."

Beliefs Based on Indirect Experience

Until now, we have been exploring the way we form and revise beliefs based on our direct experiences. Yet no matter how much you have experienced in your life, the fact is that no one person's direct experiences are enough to establish an adequate set of accurate beliefs. We can only be in one place at one time — and with a limited amount of time at that. As a result, we depend on the direct experience of *other people* to provide us with beliefs and also to act as foundations for those beliefs. Consider the following questions. How would you go about explaining the reasons or evidence for your beliefs?

1. Were you really born on the day that you have been told you were?
2. Do germs really exist?
3. Do you have a brain in your head?
4. Does outer space extend infinitely in all directions?

In all probability, your responses to these questions reveal beliefs that are based on reasons or evidence beyond your direct experience. Of all the beliefs each one of us has, few are actually based on our direct experience. Instead, virtually all are founded on the experiences of others, who then communicated to us these beliefs and the evidence for them in some shape or form. As you reach beyond your personal experience to form and revise beliefs, you find that the information provided by other people is available in two basic forms: written and spoken testimony.

It is crucial that you use all your critical thinking abilities to examine what others suggest you believe. In critically examining the beliefs of others, you should pursue the same goals of accuracy and completeness that you seek when examining beliefs based on your personal experience. As a result, you should be interested in the reasons or evidence that support the information others are presenting. For example, when you ask directions from others, you try to evaluate how accurate the information is by examining the reasons or evidence that seems to support the information being given.

When you depend on information provided by others, however, there is a further question to be asked: How *reliable* is the person providing the information? For instance, what sort of people do you look for if you need to ask directions? Why do you look for these particular types of people? In most cases, when you need to ask directions, you try to locate someone who you think will be reliable — in other words, a person who you believe will give you *accurate* information.

During the remainder of this chapter, you will explore the various ways you depend on others to form and revise your beliefs. In each case you will try to evaluate the information being presented by asking the following questions:

1. How reliable (how accurate and justified) is the *information?*

2. How reliable is the *source* of the information?

How Reliable Are the Information and the Source?

One of the main goals of your thinking is to make sense of information, and there are key questions that you should ask when evaluating information being presented to you. As you saw in Chapter 4, each of us views the world through our own unique "lenses," which shape how we view the world and influence how we select and present information. Comparing different sources helps to make us aware of these lenses and highlights the different interests and purposes involved.

THINKING ACTIVITY 5.9

Evaluating Different Perspectives

Locate two different passages concerning the same topic, and then analyze each passage using the Information Evaluation Questions detailed on page 205. For example, you might choose two different reviews of a movie, a play, a book, an art exhibit, or a concert — or two different passages analyzing a topic of current interest, such as a criminal trial result or a U.S. foreign policy issue.

There are a variety of standards or criteria you can use to evaluate the reliability of the sources of information. The following criteria are useful for evaluating both written and spoken testimony:

- Was the source of the information able to make *accurate observations?*
- What do you know about the *past reliability* of the source of the information?
- How *knowledgeable or experienced* is the source of the information?

INFORMATION EVALUATION QUESTIONS

1. How reliable is the information?
   a. What are the main ideas being presented?
   b. What reasons or evidence supports the information?
   c. Is the information accurate? Is there anything you believe to be false?
   d. Is there anything that you believe has been left out?

2. How reliable is the source of the information?
   a. What is the source of the information?
   b. What are the interests or purposes of the source of this information?
   c. How have the interests and purposes of the source of the information influenced the information selected for inclusion?
   d. How have these interests and purposes influenced the way this information is presented?

Was the Source of the Information Able to Make Accurate Observations?
Imagine that you are serving as a juror at a trial in which two youths are accused of mugging an elderly person and stealing her social security check. During the trial the victim gives the following account of the experience:

> I was walking into the lobby of my building at about six o'clock. It was beginning to get dark. Suddenly these two young men rushed in behind me and tried to grab my pocketbook. However, my bag was wrapped around my arm, and I just didn't want to let go of it. They pushed me around, yelling at me to let go of the bag. They finally pulled the bag loose and went running out of the building. I saw them pretty well while we were fighting, and I'm sure that the two boys sitting over there are the ones who robbed me.

In evaluating the accuracy of this information, you have to try to determine how reliable the source of the information is. In doing this, you might ask yourself whether the person attacked was in a good position to make accurate observations. In the case of this person's testimony, what questions could you ask in order to evaluate the accuracy of the testimony?

Example: How sharp is the person's eyesight? (Does she wear glasses? Were the glasses knocked off in the struggle?)

When trying to determine the accuracy of testimony, you should try to use the same standards you would apply to yourself if you were in a similar situation. You would ask yourself questions: Was there enough light to see clearly?

Did the excitement of the situation influence my perceptions? Were my senses operating at full capacity?

As you work toward evaluating the reliability of the source of the information, it is helpful to locate whatever additional sources of information are available. For instance, if you can locate others who can identify the muggers, or if stolen items were found in their possession, this will serve as evidence to support the testimony given by the witness.

Finally, accurate observations depend on more than how well your senses are functioning. Accurate observations also depend on how well you understand the personal factors (your "lenses") you or someone else brings to a situation. These personal feelings, expectations, and interests often influence what you are perceiving without your being aware of it. Once you become aware of these influencing factors, you can attempt to make allowances for them in order to get a more accurate view of what is taking place. For example, imagine that you and your friends have sponsored an antiracism rally on your college campus. The campus police estimate the crowd to be 250, while your friends who organized the rally claim it was more than 500. How could you go about determining the reliability of your friends' information? What questions could you ask them to help clarify the situation? How could you go about locating additional information to gain a more accurate understanding of the situation?

What Do You Know About the Past Reliability of the Source of the Information?   As you work at evaluating the reliability of sources, it is useful to consider how accurate and reliable their information has been in the past. If someone you know has consistently given you sound information over a period of time, you gradually develop confidence in the accuracy of that person's reports. Police officers and newspaper reporters must continually evaluate the reliability of information sources. Over time, people in these professions establish information sources who have consistently provided reliable information. Of course, this works the other way as well. When people consistently give you inaccurate or incomplete information, you gradually lose confidence in their reliability and the reliability of their information.

Nevertheless, few people are either completely reliable or completely unreliable in the information they offer. You probably realize that your own reliability tends to vary, depending on the situation, the type of information you are providing, and the person you are giving the information to. Thus, in trying to evaluate the information offered by others, you have to explore each of these different factors before arriving at a provisional conclusion, which may then be revised in the light of additional information.

How Knowledgeable or Experienced Is the Source of the Information?   A further step in evaluating information is to determine how knowledgeable or experienced the person is in that particular area. When you seek information from others, you try to locate people who you believe will have a special understanding of the area in which you are interested. When asking directions, you look for a police officer, a cab driver, or a resident. When your car begins making strange noises, you search for someone who has knowledge of car engines. In each case, you try to identify a source of information who has special experience or understanding of a particular area because you believe that this person will be reliable in giving you accurate information. Of course, there is no guarantee that the information will be accurate, even when you carefully select knowledgeable sources. By seeking people who are experienced or knowledgeable rather than those who are not, however, you increase your chances of gaining accurate information. For example, suppose you are interested in finding out more information about the career you are planning to pursue. Who are some of the people you would select to gain further information? What are the reasons you would select these people? Are these sound reasons?

In seeking information from others whom you believe to be experienced or knowledgeable, it is important to distinguish between the opinions of "average" sources, such as ourselves, and the opinions of experts. Experts are people who have specialized knowledge in a particular area, based on special training and experience. Who qualifies as an expert? Someone with professional expertise as certified by the appropriate standards qualifies as an expert. For instance, you do not want someone working on your teeth just because he or she has always enjoyed playing with drills or is fascinated with teeth. Instead, you insist on someone who has graduated from dental college and has been professionally certified.

It is also useful to find out how up-to-date the expert's credentials are. If practitioners have not been keeping abreast of developments in their field, they will have gradually lost their expertise, even though they may have an appropriate diploma. For example, identify some experts whose information and services you rely on. How could you go about discovering how up-to-date and effective their expertise is?

You should also make sure that the experts are giving you information and opinions in their field of expertise. It is certainly all right for people like Tiger Woods or Julia Roberts to give their views on a product, but you should remember that they are speaking simply as human beings (and ones who have been paid a large sum of money and told exactly what to say), not as scientific experts. This is exactly the type of mistaken perception encouraged by advertisers who want to sell their products. For example, identify two "experts" in television or magazine advertising who are giving testimony *outside* their fields of expertise. Why do you think they were chosen for the particular products they are endorsing? Do you trust such expertise in evaluating the products?

Finally, you should not accept expert opinion without question or critical examination, even if the experts meet all the criteria that you have been exploring. Just because a mechanic assures you that your car needs a new transmission for $900 does not mean that you should accept that opinion at face value. Or simply because one doctor assures you that surgery is required for your ailment does not mean that you should not investigate further. In both cases, seeking a second (or even third) expert opinion makes sense.

@ Evaluating Online Information

The Internet is an incredibly rich source of information on virtually every subject that exists. But it's important to remember that information is not knowledge. Information doesn't become *knowledge* until we think critically about it. As a critical thinker, you should never accept information at face value without first establishing its accuracy, evaluating the credibility of the source, and determining the point of view or bias of the source. These are issues that we will explore throughout this book, but for now you can use the checklist on page 209 to evaluate the information on the Internet — and other sources as well.

Before You Search

The first stage of evaluating web sources should happen *before* you search the Internet!

Ask yourself what you are looking for. If you don't know what you're looking for, you probably won't find it!

You might want

- narratives
- facts
- opinions
- photographs or graphics
- arguments
- statistics
- eyewitness reports

Do you want new ideas, support for a position you already hold, or something entirely different? Once you decide, you will be better able to evaluate what you find on the Web.

✔ CHECKLIST   **Evaluating the Quality of Internet Resources**

Criterion 1: Authority

☑ Is it clear who sponsors the page and what the sponsor's purpose in maintaining the page is? Is there a respected, well-known organizational affiliation?

☑ Is it clear who wrote the material and what the author's qualifications for writing on this topic are?

☑ Is there a way of verifying the legitimacy of the page's sponsor? In particular, is there a phone number or postal address to contact for more information? (An e-mail address alone is not enough.)

☑ If the material is protected by copyright, is the name of the copyright holder given? Is there a date of page creation or version?

☑ *Beware!* Avoid anonymous sites and affiliations that you've never heard of or that can't be easily checked.

Criterion 2: Accuracy

☑ Are the sources for any factual information clearly listed so they can be verified in another source?

☑ Has the sponsor provided a link to outside sources (such as product reviews or reports filed with the SEC) that can be used to verify the sponsor's claims?

☑ Is the information free of grammatical, spelling, and other typographical errors? (These kinds of errors not only indicate a lack of quality control but can actually produce inaccuracies in information.)

☑ Are statistical data in graphs and charts clearly labeled and easy to read?

☑ Does anyone monitor the accuracy of the information being published?

☑ *Beware!* Avoid unverifiable statistics and claims not supported by reasons and evidence.

Criterion 3: Objectivity

☑ For any given piece of information, is it clear what the sponsor's motivation is for providing it?

☑ Is the information content clearly separated from any advertising or opinion content?

☑ Is the point of view of the sponsor presented in a clear manner, with its arguments well supported?

☑ *Beware!* Avoid sites offering "information" in an effort to sell a product or service as well as sites containing conflicts of interest, bias and one-sidedness, emotional language, and slanted tone.

Criterion 4: Timeliness

☑ Are there dates on the page to indicate when the page was written, first placed on the Web, and last revised?

☑ Are there any other indications that the material is kept current?

☑ If material is presented in graphs or charts, is there a clear statement as to when the data were gathered?

☑ Is there an indication that the page has been completed and is not still in the process of being developed?

☑ *Beware!* Avoid sites that lack any dates, sources, or references.

Choose Sources Likely to Be Reliable

Ask yourself, "What sources (or what kinds of sources) would be most likely to give me the kind of reliable information I'm looking for?"

Some sources are more likely than others to

- be fair
- be objective
- lack hidden motives
- show quality control

Sometimes a site's "address" (URL, or "uniform resource locator") suggests its reliability or its purpose. Sites ending in

- .edu indicate educational or research material
- .gov indicate government resources
- .com indicate commercial products or commercially sponsored sites

"~NAME" in a URL may indicate a "personal" home page without recognized affiliation.

Keep these considerations in mind; don't just accept the opinion of the first sources you locate.

Final Thoughts

In this chapter we have explored the ways people form and revise beliefs. Your ability to think critically about your beliefs guides you in asking the questions necessary to explore, evaluate, and develop your beliefs.

You use both direct and indirect experience to form and re-form your beliefs. As you evaluate beliefs based on your experience, you need to use the following criteria:

- How effectively do your beliefs *explain what is taking place?*
- To what extent are these beliefs *consistent with other beliefs* you have about the world?
- How effectively do your beliefs help you *predict what will happen* in the future?
- To what extent are your beliefs supported by *sound reasons and compelling evidence* derived from *reliable sources?*

Your indirect experiences are based on outside sources of information, both spoken and written. To evaluate critically these outside sources of information, you have to ask the following questions:

- How reliable (how accurate and justified) is the *information?*
- How reliable is the *source* of the information?

By thinking critically about the process by which you form and revise your beliefs about the world, you will be able to develop your understanding insightfully and creatively.

THINKING ACTIVITY 5.10

Analyzing Different Accounts of Dropping Atom Bombs on Japan

Chapter 4 emphasized the extent to which people's perceiving "lenses" shape and influence the way they see things, the conclusions they reach, and the decisions they make. Thinking critically involves becoming aware of these perceiving lenses and evaluating their validity when determining the accuracy of information and sources of information. One of the most powerful strategies for achieving this goal is to perform a comparative analysis of different perspectives. For example, one of the most controversial and still hotly debated events in U.S. history was our country's atomic bombing of the Japanese cities of Hiroshima and Nagasaki. Although the bombings ended World War II, they killed over 100,000 civilians and resulted in radiation poisoning that affected many thousands more at that time and in subsequent generations. In 1995, the Smithsonian Institute planned an exhibit to commemorate the fiftieth anniversary of the bombings, but controversy over whether the perspective of the exhibit was unbalanced led to its cancellation and the resignation of the Air and Space Museum's director.

The following activity developed by historian Kevin O'Reilly presents two contrasting analyses of this event, each supported by historical documentation. After reviewing the two accounts, answer the questions that follow.

WAS THE UNITED STATES JUSTIFIED IN DROPPING ATOMIC BOMBS ON JAPAN?

Background Information

For the United States, World War II began with a sneak attack by Japanese planes on American naval forces at Pearl Harbor. The war was fought in Europe against the Germans and their allies, and in the Pacific against the Japanese. During the war the secret Manhattan Project was commissioned to develop an atomic bomb for the United States. Germany surrendered (May 1945) before the bombs were completed, but on August 6, 1945, a single atomic bomb destroyed Hiroshima, and on the ninth, another atomic bomb destroyed Nagasaki.

In this lesson two viewpoints are presented on the controversial use of the atomic bombs. Read and evaluate them according to the criteria of critical thinking. Consider the relevant information that follows the two viewpoints.

Historian A

Some historians argue that dropping atomic bombs on Japan was justified because it shortened the war, thus saving lives in the end. This view is wrong. The United States was not justified in dropping the bombs.

In the summer of 1945, the Japanese were almost totally defeated. American ships and planes pounded the island without any response by the Japanese. Leaders in Japan were trying to surrender and American leaders knew it. Several times the Japanese went to the Russians to ask them to mediate a peace settlement with the United States.[1] (It is not unusual for a country that wants to surrender to ask another country to speak for it at first and help negotiate a settlement.) There was only one condition that the Japanese insisted on — they wanted to keep their emperor, the symbol of Japanese culture. The United States never even talked with the Japanese about surrender terms — American leaders kept demanding unconditional surrender. After we used the bombs and the Japanese surrendered, we let them keep their emperor anyway. We could have allowed the Japanese to surrender earlier and saved all those lives obliterated by the bombs by letting them have their one condition in the first place.

If the bombs were not used to bring about surrender, then why were they used? The plain truth is that they were used to scare Russia. In 1945 the United States disagreed with the Soviet Union in regard to Russia's actions in Europe. Our leaders felt that by showing the Russians we had a powerful weapon, we could get them to agree to our terms in Europe and Asia. As Secretary of War Stimson said in his diary, in diplomacy the bomb would be a "master card."[2]

President Truman had an important meeting scheduled with the Russian leader, Josef Stalin, at Potsdam, Germany, in July 1945. He wanted to have the bomb completed and successfully tested when he went into that meeting. Atomic scientist J. Robert Oppenheimer said, "We were under incredible pressure to get it [the bomb] done before the Potsdam meeting."[3] Truman hoped to have the bomb sticking out of his hip pocket, so to speak, when he negotiated with Stalin. Then he could make new demands of the Russians regarding eastern Europe. He told some of his friends at Potsdam before the final test, "If it explodes as I think it will, I'll certainly have a hammer on those boys."[4]

VISUAL THINKING

After the Bomb

● What point of view is represented in this photo of the aftereffect of dropping the bomb on Japan? According to the historians' accounts you read here, and your own thoughts and opinions, what kinds of photos might result from other perspectives?

While Truman was negotiating in Potsdam, the bomb was successfully tested in New Mexico, and he became more demanding with Stalin. Secretary of War Stimson stated, "He [Truman] said it [the bomb] gave him an entirely new feeling of confidence. . . ."[5]

But the Russians had to see the power of the bomb before the United States could intimidate them with it. This was accomplished at Hiroshima. Truman remarked, "This is the greatest thing in history!"[6]

A second motive for dropping the bomb was to end the war in Asia before the Russians could get involved. The Japanese were talking of surrender, but the United States wanted surrender within days, not a negotiated surrender taking weeks to complete. The Russians had agreed at Yalta to enter the war against Japan three months after the end of the war in Europe. This would be three months after May 9, or somewhere around August 9. If the Russians got involved in the war in Asia, they could spread Communism to China and other countries and possibly to Japan itself. American leaders did not want to see this happen.[7]

If the United States could speed up the Japanese surrender, we could avoid all these problems. We dropped the first bomb on August 6; Russia entered the war on the eighth, and we dropped the second bomb on the ninth. Don't these dates look suspicious? No country could surrender in only three days — it takes longer than that to make such an important decision. We would not wait longer because we wanted Japan to surrender before the Russians could get involved.

Some scientists who worked on the bomb recommended that it not be dropped on people. They proposed that the United States demonstrate the bomb's power to Japanese leaders by dropping it on an uninhabited island. American political leaders rejected this idea. The devastating effect of the bomb had to be shown by destroying a city.

Even top military leaders opposed the use of the atomic bomb.[8] The bomb would have little effect on the war, they argued, since the Japanese were already trying to surrender.

All this evidence shows that the atomic bombs were not used to end the war and save lives, but rather to scare the Russians and speed up the end of the war before Russian influence spread further into Asia. The killing of over 100,000 civilians in one country in order to scare the leaders of another country was wrong. The United States was not justified in dropping the atomic bombs.

Endnotes for Historian A

(All are quotes from the sources cited except bracketed portions.)

[1] Gar Alperovitz (a historian), *Atomic Diplomacy* (1965). (Direct quotations from *Foreign Relations Papers of the United States: Conference at Berlin*, Vol. II, pp. 1249, 1250, 1260, 1261.)

> "On July 17, the day of the first plenary session, another intercepted Japanese message showed that although the government felt that the unconditional surrender formula involved too great a dishonor, it was convinced that 'the demands of the times' made Soviet mediation to terminate the war absolutely essential. Further cables indicated that the one condition the Japanese asked was preservation of 'our form of government.' A message of July 25 revealed instructions to the [Japanese] Ambassador in Moscow to go anywhere to meet with [Soviet Foreign Minister] Molotov

during the recess of the Potsdam meeting so as to 'impress them with the sincerity of our desire' to terminate the war. He was told to make it clear that 'we should like to communicate to the other party [the United States] through appropriate channels that we have no objection to a peace based on the Atlantic Charter.' The only 'difficult point is the . . . formality of unconditional surrender.'"

James F. Byrnes (Secretary of State), *All in One Lifetime,* p. 297:

"July 28: Secretary Forrestal arrived and told me in detail of the intercepted messages from the Japanese government to Ambassador Sato in Moscow, indicating Japan's willingness to surrender."

[2] Stimson (Secretary of War) Diary, May 15:

"The trouble is that the President has now promised apparently to meet Stalin and Churchill on the first of July [at Potsdam] and at that time these questions will become burning and it may become necessary to have it out with Russia on her relations to Manchuria and Port Arthur and various other parts of North China, and also the relations of China to us. Over any such tangled web of problems the S-1 secret [the atomic bomb] would be dominant and yet we will not know until after . . . that meeting, whether this is a weapon in our hands or not. We think it will be shortly afterwards, but it seems a terrible thing to gamble with such big stakes in diplomacy without having your master card in your hand."

Leo Szilard (an atomic scientist who opposed use of the bombs on Japan), Conversation with Secretary of State Byrnes. Recorded on August 24, 1944, in Stewart to Bush, Atomic Energy Commission Document 200. Manhattan Engineering District — Top Secret, National Archives, Record Group 77, Box 7, folder 12; Box 14, folder 4:

[Szilard argued that we should not use the bomb.]

"Byrnes — Our possessing and demonstrating the bomb would make Russia more manageable in Europe."

"Szilard — [The] interests of peace might best be served and an arms race avoided by not using the bomb against Japan, keeping it secret, and letting the Russians think that our work on it had not succeeded."

"Byrnes — How would you get Congress to appropriate money for atomic energy research if you do not show results for the money which has been spent already?"

[3] Atomic Energy Commission, Oppenheimer Hearings, p. 31.

[4] Jonathan Daniels (biographer), *The Man of Independence* (1950), p. 266.

[5] *Foreign Relations Papers of the United States: Conference at Berlin*, 1945, Vol. II, p. 1361.

Stimson Diary, July 22:

"Churchill read Grove's report [on the successful testing of the atomic bomb in New Mexico] in full. . . . He said, 'Now I know what happened to Truman yesterday. I couldn't understand it. When he got to the meeting after having read this report he was a changed man. He told the Russians just where they got on and off and generally bossed the whole meeting.'"

[6] Harry S Truman, *Year of Decisions*, p. 421.

[7] Byrnes, *All in One Lifetime*, p. 300:

"Though there was an understanding that the Soviets would enter the war three months after Germany surrendered, the President and I hoped that Japan would surrender before then."

Secretary of War Stimson stated in his diary on August 10, 1945, that he urged the President that:

"The thing to do was to get this surrender through as quickly as we can before Russia should get down in reach of the Japanese homeland. . . . It was of great importance to get the homeland into our hands before the Russians could put in any substantial claim to occupy and help rule it."

[8] General Dwight Eisenhower, statement in "Ike on Ike," *Newsweek*, November 11, 1963, p. 107:

"I voiced to him [Secretary of War Stimson] my grave misgivings, first on the basis of my belief that Japan was already defeated and that dropping the bomb was completely unnecessary and secondly, because I thought our country should avoid shocking world opinion by the use of a weapon whose employment was, I thought, no longer necessary as a measure to save American lives. It was my belief that Japan was, at the very moment, seeking some way to surrender with a minimum loss of 'face.' . . . It wasn't necessary to hit them with that awful thing."

Admiral W. D. Leahy, *I Was There* (1950), p. 441:

"It was my opinion that the use of this barbarous weapon at Hiroshima and Nagasaki was of no material assistance in our war against Japan. The Japanese were already defeated and ready to surrender."

Air Force Chief of Staff LeMay, *New York Herald Tribune*, September 21, 1945:

"The atomic bomb had nothing to do with the end of the war."

Historian B

Dropping atomic bombs on Hiroshima and Nagasaki helped the United States avoid a costly invasion of Japan. It therefore saved lives in the long run, which makes it a justifiable action.

It is true that the United States received some indication in the summer of 1945 that Japan was trying to surrender. Japan would not surrender unconditionally, however, and that was very important to the United States. The Germans had not surrendered unconditionally at the end of World War I and, as a result, they rose again to bring on World War II. The United States was not going to let that mistake happen again. As President Roosevelt said, "This time there will be no doubt about who defeated whom."[1]

Although the Japanese military situation in July 1945 was approaching total defeat, many Japanese leaders hoped for one last ditch victory in order to get softer peace terms.[2] One of their hopes was to divide the Grand Alliance by getting Russia (which was not at the time at war with Japan) to be the intermediary for peace negotiations. Maybe the Allies would begin to disagree, the Japanese militarists reasoned, and Japan would get off easy. Their other hope was that they could inflict enough casualties on the American troops, or hold out long enough, to get the American public to pressure their leaders to accept something less than unconditional surrender.[3]

Some historians argue that the only issue which prevented the Japanese from accepting unconditional surrender was their fear that the emperor would be removed by the Americans. American leaders, however, believed that allowing this one condition would encourage the militarists in Japan to further resistance. Americans also felt that it would weaken the war effort in the United States since we would be deviating from our well-publicized policy of unconditional surrender.[4]

Some Japanese leaders wanted much more, however, than just the one condition of keeping their emperor. They wanted their troops to surrender to them, and they wanted no occupation of Japan or war crimes trials of Japanese leaders. Even on August 9, after the bombing of Hiroshima and Nagasaki, and after the Russian declaration of war against them, the Japanese leaders still could not agree to surrender.[5] This shows that the bombs were necessary — anything less than the bombs or invasion would not have brought about unconditional surrender.

Some people believe that the dates of dropping the bombs (August 6 and 9) show that the United States dropped them to stop Russian entry into the war (August 8). There are two problems with this line of reasoning. First, the United States did not know the exact date of Russian entry. Second, the bombs were to be dropped when a military officer decided that the weather was right.[6] If Truman wanted to beat the Russians, why didn't he order the bombs to be dropped sooner, or why didn't he give in on unconditional surrender?

The argument that the United States dropped the bombs in order to threaten the Russians is also weak. The fact that we were so unsuccessful in getting the Russians to agree to our policies in Europe shows that the bomb was not used for that reason. It must have been used to shorten the war. It certainly did not scare the Russians.

Some American scientists opposed using the bomb on civilian or military targets, preferring to demonstrate it on an uninhabited island. This recommendation was studied carefully by a committee (the Interim Committee) set up to consider how to use the bomb. The committee said that a demonstration could have had a lot of problems, which would have wasted one of the bombs and precious time. In light of the fact that it took two bombs dropped on cities to bring about a surrender, the demonstration idea does not seem like it would have been effective. The committee recommended the bombs be used against military targets.[7]

It is important to remember that on July 26, 1945, the United States warned the Japanese that we would use the atomic bomb against them unless they accepted unconditional surrender.[8] The fanatical Japanese leaders would not give in. They said they would ignore the warning.[9] Thus, the loss of life from atomic bombings was the responsibility of the Japanese leaders, not the Americans.

The United States was right in insisting on unconditional surrender. Since the Japanese would not surrender unconditionally, and since a demonstration bombing would not have been effective, the only alternative to using the atomic bombs was continuing the war. This would have cost hundreds of thousands more lives. In the long run, the use of the atomic bombs on Hiroshima and Nagasaki shortened the war and saved lives.

Endnotes for Historian B

(All are quotes from the sources cited except bracketed portions.)

[1] President Roosevelt at a press conference, *F.D.R.: Public Papers of the Presidents,* Vol. XIII, p. 210:

> "Practically all Germans deny the fact they surrendered in the last war, but this time they are going to know it. And so are the Japs."

[2] *Command Decisions* (a history of World War II), p. 504, quotes a study done by Brigadier General George A. Lincoln, June 4, 1945:

"In allied intelligence Japan was portrayed as a defeated nation whose military leaders were blind to defeat. . . . Japan was still far from surrender. She had ample reserves of weapons and ammunition and an army of 5,000,000 troops, 2,000,000 of them in the home islands. . . . In the opinion of the intelligence experts, neither blockade nor bombing alone would produce unconditional surrender before the date set for invasion [November 1945]. And the invasion itself, they believed, would be costly and possibly prolonged."

[3] *Command Decisions,* p. 517:

"The militarists [in the Japanese Government] could and did minimize the effects of the bomb, but they could not evade the obvious consequences of Soviet intervention, which ended all hope of dividing their enemies and securing softer peace terms."

[4] *Command Decisions,* pp. 512–13, summarizing former Secretary of State Cordell Hull, *Memoirs,* Vol. II, p. 1593:

"[Cordell] Hull's view . . . was the proposal [by Secretary of War Stimson to let the Japanese keep the Emperor] smacked of appeasement. . . . The proposal to retain the imperial system might well encourage resistance [by the Japanese] and have 'terrible political repercussions' in the United States."

[5] Robert Butow (a historian), *Japan's Decision to Surrender* (1959), pp. 161, 163, 164. (Describing the debate among the six Japanese leaders about whether to surrender, August 9, 1945.)

"While Suzuki [Prime Minister], Togo [Foreign Minister] and Yonai [Navy Minister] were committed in varying degrees to an outright acceptance [of the Potsdam Declaration demanding unconditional surrender] on the basis of the sole reservation that the Imperial house would be maintained, Anami [War Minister], Umezu [Army Chief of Staff], and Toyoda [Navy Chief of Staff], felt quite differently. . . . What gagged these men — all true 'Samurai' bred in an uncompromising tradition — were the other points Yonai had mentioned. They wanted either to prevent a security occupation entirely or to exclude at least the metropolis of Tokyo. . . . So far as war criminals were concerned, they felt it should be Japan and not the victorious enemy who must try such cases. In effect, they also wanted to accept the surrender of their own men. . . .

"From the standpoint of making postwar rationalizations and of 'opening up the future of the country' it was psychologically vital for the Japanese army and navy to make it appear as if they had voluntarily disbanded their military might in order to save the nation and the world at large from the continued ravages of war. If they could do this, they could very easily later plant an appealing suggestion to the effect that the imperial forces of Great Japan had not really suffered defeat at all. For this reason, too, a security occupation and war crimes trials conducted by Allied tribunals had to be avoided at all costs. . . .

"Togo pointedly asked whether Japan could win the war if a collapse of the type [of negotiations] occurred. To this the military heads could only reply that although they were not certain of ultimate victory, they were still capable of one more campaign — a 'decisive' battle in the homeland. . . . The Council was deadlocked."

[6] Memorandum to Major General I. R. Groves from Brigadier General T. F. Farrell

Subject: Report on Overseas Operations — Atomic Bomb:
     27 September 1945

"After the Hiroshima strike we scheduled the second attack for 11 August [local time]. On learning that bad weather was predicted for that time, we reviewed the status of the assembly work for the Fat Man [the second atomic bomb], our uncompleted test program, and readiness of the planes and crews. It was determined that with an all-out effort, everything could be ready for takeoff on the early morning of 9 August [local time], provided our final test of the Fat Man proved satisfactory, which it did. The decision turned out to be fortunate in that several days of bad weather followed 9 August."

[7] Interim Committee report, June 1, 1945, from Harry S Truman, *Year of Decisions*, p. 419:

"Recommend unanimously:

"1. The bomb should be used against Japan as soon as possible.

"2. It should be used against a military target surrounded by other buildings.

"3. It should be used without prior warning of the nature of the weapon."

[8] Proclamation for Unconditional Surrender, July 26, 1945. *Foreign Relations Papers of the United States: Potsdam Papers*, Vol. II, p. 1258:

"Section 13: We call upon the government of Japan to proclaim now the unconditional surrender of the Japanese armed forces, and to provide proper and adequate assurance of their good faith in such action. The alternative for Japan is prompt and utter destruction."

[9] *Foreign Relations Papers of the United States: Potsdam Papers,* Document 12518, July 28, 1945.

Japanese Prime Minister Suzuki to reporters:

"I believe the Joint Proclamation [the Potsdam Proclamation — warning Japan to accept unconditional surrender] by the three countries is nothing but a rehash of the Cairo Declaration [which also called on Japan to surrender]. As for the [Japanese] Government, it does not find any important value in it, and there is no other recourse but to ignore it entirely and resolutely fight for the successful conclusion of the war."

Questions for Analysis

1. Describe the main arguments, reasons, and evidence that support the perspective of Historian A.

2. Describe the main arguments, reasons, and evidence that support the perspective of Historian B.

3. Imagine that you were in the position of the U.S. president, Harry Truman. Explain what action you would have taken with respect to the atomic bombs and explain the rationale for your decision.

Language and Thought

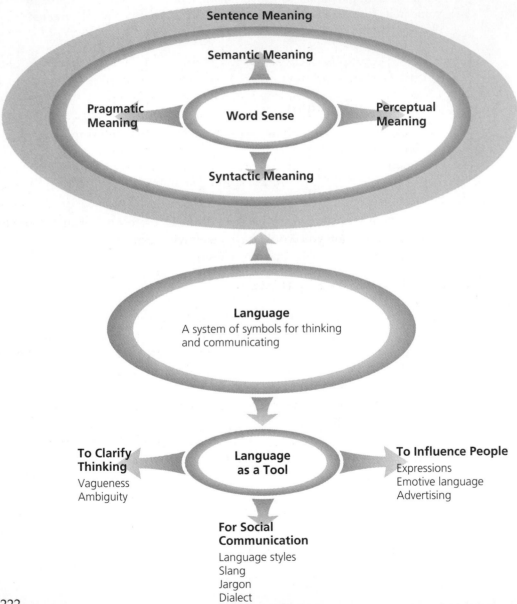

Sentence Meaning

Semantic Meaning

Pragmatic Meaning

Word Sense

Perceptual Meaning

Syntactic Meaning

Language
A system of symbols for thinking
and communicating

To Clarify Thinking
Vagueness
Ambiguity

Language as a Tool

To Influence People
Expressions
Emotive language
Advertising

For Social Communication
Language styles
Slang
Jargon
Dialect

Every time we use language, we send a message about our thinking. When we speak or write, we are conveying ideas, sharing feelings, and describing experiences. At the same time, language itself shapes and influences thinking. When language use is sloppy — vague, general, indistinct, imprecise, foolish, inaccurate — it leads to the same sort of thinking. The reverse is also true: Clear, precise language leads to clear, precise thinking, speaking, and writing. Thus, it is vital to use language with clarity and precision if other people are to understand the thoughts we are trying to communicate. And to use language effectively, we need to view language as a system, one with agreed-upon sets of rules and expectations.

To comprehend this essential tool more fully and use it more powerfully, we will consider both the development of languages and the symbolic nature of language. We will then examine strategies for using language effectively and for using language to clarify thinking. Finally, we will consider the social uses of language and how it can be used to influence thinking and behavior.

Throughout the chapter you will have opportunities to connect your ideas to these concepts. The various assignments place special emphasis on thinking and writing with precision: clearly conceptualizing what you want to say and discovering the best use of language to say it. You will also have the chance to explore the work of professional writers who have developed special expertise in thinking and communicating with language.

The Evolution of Language

Imagine a world without language. Imagine that you have suddenly lost your ability to speak, to write, to read. Imagine that your only means of expression are grunts, shrieks, and gestures. And finally, imagine that you soon discover that *everyone* in the world had also lost the ability to use language. What do you think such a world would be like?

As this exercise of the imagination illustrates, language forms the bedrock of your relations with others. It is the means you have to communicate your thoughts, feelings, and experiences to others, and they to you. This mutual sharing draws you together and leads to your forming relationships. Consider the social groups in your school, your neighborhood, or your community. Notice how language plays a central role in bringing people together into groups and in maintaining these groups. A loss of language would both limit the complexity of your individual relationships with others and drastically affect the entire way you live in society.

Linguists have ascertained that no single language was the parent of all languages. Rather, like people, languages belong to families. Languages in the same family share some characteristics with other members of their family, but they also demonstrate individual characteristics. We know that languages, like the human beings of whom they are a natural part, live, change, and die. Phrygian is no longer a living language, nor is Latin.

English, like Spanish, French, Chinese, Urdu, or any of the other languages that you may speak, is a living language — and it has changed over hundreds of years. The English language has gone through four major evolutionary stages: *Old English*, A.D. 700–1050; *Middle English*, A.D. 1050–1450; *Early Modern English*, A.D 1450–1700; and *Modern English*, 1700 to the present. Because languages are systems based on sound, these evolutionary stages of English reflect variations in how the language sounds. It is difficult to represent these sounds accurately for the older periods of English because of the absence of recordings. The written symbols demonstrating early versions of the Lord's Prayer that follow are approximations based on the consensus of linguistic scholars.

THE LORD'S PRAYER

Old English

Faeder ure
Thu the eart on heofonum,
Si thin name gehalgod.
Tobecume thin rice.
Gewurthe thin willa on eorthan swa swa on heofonum.
Urne gedaeghwamlican hlaf syle you to daeg.
And forgyf you urne gyltas, swa swa you forgyfath urum gyltendum.
And ne gelaed thu you on costnunge, ac alys you of yfele. Sothlice.

Middle English

Oure fadur
that art in hauenes,
halewid be thi name;
thi kyngdoom come to;
be thi wile don in erthe as in heuene;
zyue to vs this dai oure breed ouer othir substaunce;
and forzyue to vs oure dettis, as you forzyuen to oure dettouris;
and lede vs not in to temptacioun,
but delyuere vs from yeul. Amen.

Early Modern English

Our Father
which art in heaven,
hallowed be thy name.
Thy kingdom come.
Thy will be done, in earth, as it is in heaven.
Give us this day our daily bread.
And forgive us our debts, as we forgive our debtors.
And lead us not into temptation,
but deliver us from evil:
for Thine is the kingdom, and the power, and the glory for ever, Amen.

As you read these versions of the Lord's Prayer, think about the variations in sounds, words, and sentences. With the other members of your class, discuss variations in the language(s) you speak. Could any of these be considered evolutionary changes? Why or why not?

The Symbolic Nature of Language

As human beings, we are able to communicate with each other because of our ability to *symbolize,* or let one thing represent something else. Words are the most common symbols we use in our daily life. Although words are only sounds or written marks that have no meaning in and of themselves, they stand for objects, ideas, and other aspects of human experience. For example, the word *sailboat* is a symbol that represents a watergoing vessel with sails that is propelled by the wind. When you speak or write *sailboat,* you are able to communicate the sort of thing you are thinking about. Of course, if other people are to understand what you are referring to when you use this symbol, they must first agree that this symbol *(sailboat)* does in fact represent that wind-propelled vessel that floats on the water.

Language symbols (or words) can take two forms: They can be spoken sounds or written markings.* The symbol *sailboat* can be either written down or spoken aloud. Either way, it communicates the same idea. Since using language is so natural to us, we rarely stop to realize that our **language** is really a system of spoken sounds and written markings that we use to represent various aspects of our experience.

*A unique language case is posed by American Sign Language (ASL), which is now regarded by linguists as a full-fledged language, possessing its own grammar and syntax.

language *A system of symbols for thinking and communicating*

Language is like a set of symbolic building blocks. The basic blocks are sounds, which may be symbolized by letters. Sounds form the phonetic foundation of a language, and this process explains why different languages have distinctly different "sounds." Try having members of the class who speak other languages speak a word or a few sentences in the language they know. Listen to how the sound of each language differs from those of the others.

When humans are infants, they are able to make all the sounds of all languages. As they are continually exposed to the specific group of sounds of their society's language, they gradually concentrate on making only those sounds while discarding or never developing the others.

Sounds combine to form larger sets of blocks called *words*. Words are used to represent the various aspects of our experience — they symbolize objects, thoughts, feelings, actions, and concepts. When you read, hear, or think about a word, then it usually elicits in you a variety of ideas and feelings. Describe the ideas or feelings that the following words arouse in you: *college education, happiness, freedom, creative, love.*

The combination of all the ideas and feelings that a word arouses in your mind make up the "meaning" of that word to you. And although the meanings that these words have for you is likely to be similar in many respects to the meanings they have for other people, there are likely also many differences. Consider the different meanings these words have for the two people in the following dialogue:

A: For me, a **college education** represents the most direct path to my dreams. It's the only way I can develop the knowledge and abilities required for my career.

B: I can't agree with you. I pursued a **college education** for a while, but it didn't work out. I found that most of my courses consisted of large classes with professors lecturing about subjects that had little relation to my life. The value of a college education is overblown. I know many people with college degrees who have not been able to find rewarding careers.

A: Don't you see? An important part of achieving **happiness** is learning about things you aren't familiar with, expanding your horizons about the world, developing new interests. That's what college can give you.

B: I have enough interests. As far as I'm concerned, **happiness** consists of having the opportunity to do the things that I enjoy doing with the people I enjoy doing them with. For me, happiness is **freedom!**

VISUAL THINKING

Communicating (and Miscommunicating) with Language

- How does this illustration express the insight that words are complex carriers of meaning that evoke in people a variety of ideas and feelings? Why does miscommunication happen? How can we make our communication clearer?

A: **Freedom** to do what? Freedom is meaningful only when you have worthwhile options to select and the wisdom to select the right ones. And a college education can help provide you both!

B: That sounds very idealistic, but it's also naive. Many of the college graduates I have met are neither wise nor happy. In order to be truly happy, you have to be involved in **creative** activities. Every day should be a surprise, something different to look forward to. Many careers pay well, but they don't provide creative opportunities.

A: Being **creative** means doing things you **love.** When you really love something you're doing, you are naturally creative. For example, I love to draw and paint, and these activities provide a creative outlet for me. I don't need to be creative at work — I have enough creative opportunities outside of work.

B: You're wrong! **Creativity** doesn't simply mean being artistic. We should strive to be creative in every part of our lives, keep looking for new possibilities and unique experiences. And I think that you are misusing the word *love.* You can only really love things that are alive, like people and pets.

A: That's a very weird idea of **love** you have. As far as I'm concerned, *love* is a word that expresses a strong positive emotion that can be directed toward objects ("I love my car"), activities ("I love to dance"), or people. I don't see what's so complicated about that.

B: To be able to **love** in any meaningful sense, the object of your love has to be able to respond to you so that the two of you can develop a relationship together. When was the last time that your car responded to your love for it?

A: Very funny. I guess that we just have different ideas about the word **love** — as well as the words **happiness, freedom,** and **creative.**

As this dialogue suggests, words are not simple entities with one clear meaning that everyone agrees on. Instead, most words are complex, multidimensional carriers of meaning; their exact meaning often varies from person to person. These differences in meaning can lead to disagreements and confusion, as illustrated in the previous dialogue. To understand how words function in your language and your thinking, you have to examine the way words serve as vehicles to express meaning.

Words arouse in each of us a variety of ideas, feelings, and experiences. Taken together, these ideas, feelings, and experiences express the *total meaning* of the words for the individual. Linguists believe that this total meaning is actually composed of four different types of meaning:

- Semantic meaning
- Perceptual meaning
- Syntactic meaning
- Pragmatic meaning

Let us examine each of them in turn.

Semantic Meaning (Denotation)

The **semantic meaning** of a word expresses the relationship between a linguistic event (speaking or writing) and a nonlinguistic event (an object, idea, or feeling). For example, saying "chair" relates to an object you sit in, while saying "college education" relates to the experience of earning an academic degree through postsecondary study. What events (ideas, feelings, objects) relate to the word *happiness? Freedom? Creative? Love?*

The semantic meaning of a word, also referred to as its **denotative meaning,** expresses the general properties of the word, and these properties determine how the word is used within its language system. How do you discover the general properties that determine word usage? Besides examining your own knowledge of the meaning and use of words, you can also check dictionary definitions. They tend to focus on the general properties that determine word usage. For example, a dictionary definition of *chair* might be "a piece of furniture consisting of a seat, legs, and back, and often arms, designed to accommodate one person."

However, to understand clearly the semantic meaning of a word, you often need to go beyond defining its general properties to identifying examples of the word that embody those properties. If you are sitting in a chair or can see one from where you are, examine its design. Does it embody all the properties identified in the definition? (Sometimes unusual examples embody most, but not all, of the properties of a dictionary definition — for example, a "beanbag chair" lacks legs and arms.) If you are trying to communicate the semantic meaning of a word to someone, it is generally useful to provide both the general properties of the word and examples that embody those properties. Try identifying those properties and examples for the words *happiness, freedom, creative,* and *love.*

Perceptual Meaning (Connotation)

The total meaning of a word also includes its **perceptual meaning,** which expresses the relationship between a linguistic event and an individual's consciousness. For each of us, words elicit unique and personal thoughts and feelings based on previous experiences and past associations. For example, I might relate saying "chair" to my favorite chair in my living room or the small chair that I built for my daughter. Perceptual meaning also includes an individual's positive and negative responses to a word. For this reason, perceptual meaning is sometimes called **connotative meaning,** the literal or basic meaning of a word plus all it suggests, or connotes, to you.

Think about the words you considered earlier and describe what personal perceptions, experiences, associations, and feelings they evoke in your mind: *college education, happiness, freedom, creative, love.*

Syntactic Meaning

Another component of a word's total meaning is its **syntactic meaning,** which defines its relation to other words in a sentence. Syntactic relationships extend among all the words of a sentence that are spoken or written or that will be spoken or written. The syntactic meaning defines three relationships among words:

- *Content:* words that express the major message of the sentence
- *Description:* words that elaborate or modify the major message of the sentence
- *Connection:* words that join the major message of the sentence

For example, in the sentence "The two novice hikers crossed the ledge cautiously," *hikers* and *crossed* represent the content, or major message, of the sentence. *Two* and *novice* define a descriptive relationship to *hikers,* and *cautiously* elaborates *crossed.*

At first, you may think that this sort of relationship among words involves nothing more than semantic meaning. The following sentence, however, clearly demonstrates the importance of syntactic meaning in language: "Invisible fog rumbles in on lizard legs." Although *fog* does not *rumble,* and it is not *invisible,* and the concept of moving on *lizard legs* instinctively seems incompatible with *rumbling,* still the sentence "makes sense" at some level of meaning — namely, at the syntactic level. One reason it does is that in this sentence you still have three basic content words — *fog, rumbles,* and *legs* — and two descriptive words, namely, *invisible* and *lizard.*

A further major syntactic relationship is that of connection. You use connective words to join ideas, thoughts, or feelings being expressed. For example, you could connect content meaning to either of your two sentences in the following ways:

- "The two novice hikers crossed the ledge cautiously *after* one of them slipped."
- "Invisible fog rumbles in on lizard legs, *but* acid rain doesn't."

When you add content words such as *one slipped* and *rain doesn't,* you join the ideas, thoughts, or feelings they represent to the earlier expressed ideas, thoughts, or feelings *(hikers crossed* and *fog rumbles)* by using connective words like *after* and *but,* as in the previous sentences.

"Invisible fog rumbles in on lizard legs" also makes sense at the syntactic level of meaning because the words of that sentence obey the syntax, or order, of English. Most speakers of English would have trouble making sense of "Invisible rumbles legs lizard on fog in" — or "Barks big endlessly dog brown the," for that matter. Because of syntactic meaning, each word in the sentence derives part of its total meaning from its combination with the other words in that sentence.

Look at the following sentences and explain the difference in meaning between each pair of sentences:

1a. The process of achieving an *education at college* changes a person's future possibilities.
  b. The process of achieving a *college education* changes a person's future possibilities.

2a. She felt *happiness* for her long-lost brother.
  b. She felt the *happiness* of her long-lost brother.

3a. The most important thing to me is *freedom from* the things that restrict my choices.
  b. The most important thing to me is *freedom to* make my choices without restrictions.

4a. Michelangelo's painting of the Sistine Chapel represents his *creative* genius.
  b. The Sistine Chapel represents the *creative* genius of Michelangelo's greatest painting.

5a. I *love* the person I have been involved with for the past year.
  b. I am *in love* with the person I have been involved with for the past year.

Pragmatic Meaning

The last element that contributes to the total meaning of a word is its *pragmatic meaning*, which involves the person who is speaking and the situation in which the word is spoken. For example, the sentence "That student likes to borrow books from the library" allows a number of pragmatic interpretations:

1. Was the speaker outside looking at *that student* carrying books out of the library?

2. Did the speaker have this information because he was a classmate of *that student* and saw her carrying books?

3. Was the speaker in the library watching *that student* check the books out?

The correct interpretation or meaning of the sentence depends on what was actually taking place in the situation — in other words, its pragmatic meaning, which is also called its *situational meaning*. For each of the following sentences, try describing a pragmatic context that identifies the person speaking and the situation in which the words are being spoken.

1. A *college education* is currently necessary for many careers that formerly required only high school preparation.
2. The utilitarian ethical system is based on the principle that the right course of action is that which brings the greatest *happiness* to the greatest number of people.
3. The laws of this country attempt to balance the *freedom* of the individual with the rights of society as a whole.
4. "You are all part of things, you are all part of *creation*, all kings, all poets, all musicians, you have only to open up, to discover what is already there." (Henry Miller)
5. "If music be the food of *love*, play on." (William Shakespeare)

After completing the activity, compare your answers with those of your classmates. In what ways are the answers similar or different? Analyze the way different pragmatic contexts (persons speaking and situations) affect the meanings of the italicized words.

The four meanings you just examined — semantic, perceptual, syntactic, pragmatic — create the total meaning of a word. That is to say, all the dimensions of any word — all the relationships that connect linguistic events with nonlinguistic events, your consciousness, other linguistic events, and situations in the world — make up the meaning *you* assign to a word.

THINKING ACTIVITY 6.1

The Language of War*

During times of war and conflict, language takes on special significance, and political leaders take great care in selecting the key words related to the conflict. In the United States in late 2001, the significance of word meaning was thrust into the spotlight when words that were originally used to characterize the war against terrorism were found to be offensive to certain groups of people and were therefore replaced. Read the following texts by William

*Thanks to Nancy Erber for suggesting this activity.

Safire and Michael R. Gordon and then answer the questions at the conclusion.

> "You are about to embark upon a great *crusade*," General Eisenhower told his troops on the eve of D-Day; he later titled his memoirs "*Crusade* in Europe." American presidents liked that word: Thomas Jefferson launched "a crusade against ignorance," Theodore Roosevelt exhorted compatriots to "spend and be spent in an endless *crusade*" and F.D.R., calling for a "new deal" in his acceptance speech at the 1932 Democratic convention, issued "a call to arms," a "*crusade* to restore America to its own people."
>
> But when George W. Bush ad-libbed that "this *crusade*, this war on terrorism, is going to take a while," his figure of speech was widely criticized. That's because the word has a religious root, meaning "taking the cross," and was coined in the 11th century to describe the first military expedition of the Crusaders, European Christians sent to recover the Holy Land from the followers of Muhammad. The rallying-cry noun is offensive to many Muslims: three years ago, Osama bin Laden maligned U.S. forces in the Middle East as "*crusader* armies spreading like locusts." . . .
>
> In the same way, when the proposed Pentagon label for the antiterror campaign was floated out as "Operation Infinite Justice," a spokesman for the council on American-Islamic Relations noted that such eternal retribution was "the prerogative of God." Informed of this, Defense Secretary Donald Rumsfeld quickly pulled the plug on the pretentious moniker.
>
> Who coins these terms? Nobody will step forward; instead, software called "Code Word, Nickname and Exercise Term System" is employed to avoid responsibility; it spits out a list of random names from which commanders can choose. This avoidance of coinage responsibility leads to national embarrassment (which is finite justice). "Operations," said Winston Churchill, "ought not to be described by code words which imply a boastful and overconfident sentiment." . . .
>
> — *William Safire, "Every Conflict Generates Its Own Lexicon"*

LONDON, Oct. 26 — Britain said today that it was prepared to join the United States in ground combat inside Afghanistan and would provide 600 Royal Marine commandos for the American-led military operation. The allies have their own lexicon. While the United States calls the operation Enduring Freedom, the British name for the operation is Veritas. The Canadians call the operation Apollo. The Australians call it Operation Slipper. An Australian official said the term was derived from Australian slang and alluded to the ability of forces to stealthily "slip in and slip out." The original name for the United States' operation was Infinite Justice, but this was changed recently.

— *Michael R. Gordon,* The New York Times

1. For each of the following terms, identify the *origin, definition,* and *related word forms:*
   - crusade
   - infinite
   - justice
   - endure
   - apollo
   - *veritas*

2. Next, find a quotation from an anthology (Bartlett's or another source) to illustrate the use and meaning of the word. Be sure to write down the entire quotation and any information about it, such as the author and date.

3. Finally, compare the word meaning in these quotations with the word meanings you identified in question 1.

THINKING ACTIVITY 6.2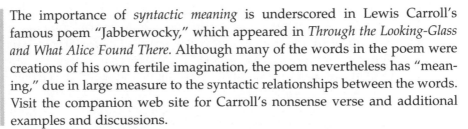

Understanding Nonsense Words

The importance of *syntactic meaning* is underscored in Lewis Carroll's famous poem "Jabberwocky," which appeared in *Through the Looking-Glass and What Alice Found There.* Although many of the words in the poem were creations of his own fertile imagination, the poem nevertheless has "meaning," due in large measure to the syntactic relationships between the words. Visit the companion web site for Carroll's nonsense verse and additional examples and discussions.

THINKING ACTIVITY 6.3

The Language of Cloning

Recent breakthroughs in human cloning have ignited a firestorm of debate. As described in articles at the conclusion of Chapter 10, "Constructing Arguments," many people are excited about the scientific benefits to human health that cloning techniques might provide. In contrast, many others feel that human cloning is ethically and/or religiously wrong and ought to be prohibited.

Not surprisingly, language plays a pivotal role in this debate, as it does with other controversial issues such as abortion and capital punishment. Read the following article, "That Scientific Breakthrough Thing," and then answer the questions that follow.

WASHINGTON

Dispatch from the cloning wars: When Advanced Cell Technology announced that it had created human embryos by cloning, a political uproar ensued. Now comes the fight over vocabulary.

Last week, the Senate held hearings on therapeutic cloning, in which DNA from an adult cell is inserted into a woman's egg — not to make a baby, but to generate specialized tissues to treat disease. Proponents of the technique, keenly aware that cloning has acquired a bad name in Washington, began offering new ones.

Dr. Bert Vogelstein of Johns Hopkins University proposed "nuclear transplantation." Senator Tom Harkin, Democrat of Iowa, suggested "therapeutic cellular transfer," or T.C.T. (Just what Washington needs, another abbreviation.)

And what to call the cloned embryos themselves? Dr. Ronald Green, the Dartmouth philosophy professor who heads Advanced Cell's ethics panel, said over the summer that he didn't like the term embryo because it implies the product of egg and sperm. And he pointed out that the entities created by cloning have no precedent in biology. "I'm tending personally to steer toward the term 'activated egg,'" he said then.

More recently, he has offered up "cleaving egg," to refer to the continuous cell division that follows the implantation of the DNA. Dr. Ann Kiessling, a Harvard University reproductive biologist who also serves on the ethics panel, has invented the word "ovasome" (rhymes with chromosome), reasoning that the experiments use an egg to make somatic, or body, cells.

"It's a marketing strategy," said Douglas Johnson, spokesman for the National Right to Life Committee, which strongly opposes cloning. "They are working overtime to develop linguistic cloaking devices."

Not so, says Dr. Kiessling, of Harvard. "The problem here," she said, "is accuracy of language. We don't have any words for this that don't mean something else to somebody."

Maybe so, but in announcing the experiment that created the ruckus, Advanced Cell Technology said that it had created the world's first cloned human embryos. Then again, what kind of splash would the news have made had the company declared itself the creator of the world's first human activated eggs?

— *Sheryl Gay Stolberg, "That Scientific Breakthrough Thing"**

*Sheryl Gay Stolberg, "That Scientific Breakthrough Thing," *The New York Times,* December 9, 2001. Copyright © 2001 by The New York Times Co. Reprinted by permission.

1. Explain the various word meanings (semantic, perceptual, pragmatic) associated with the following terms:

   The cloning process   *The cloning result*

      Human cloning   Cloned embryos

      Nuclear transplantation   Activated egg

      Therapeutic cellular transfer   Cleaving egg

      (T.C.T.)   Ovasome

2. Identify which terms you think are most appropriate (you can also create your own, like "ovasome") and explain the reasons for your selection.

Using Language Effectively

To develop your ability to use language effectively, you have to understand how language functions when it is used well. One way to do this is to read widely. By reading good writing, you get a "feel" for how language can be used effectively. You can get more specific ideas by analyzing the work of highly regarded writers, who use word meanings accurately. They also often use many action verbs, concrete nouns, and vivid adjectives to communicate effectively. By doing so, they appeal to your senses and help you understand clearly what is being communicated. Good writers may also vary sentence length to keep the reader's attention and create a variety of sentence styles to enrich meaning. Communicating your ideas effectively involves using the full range of words to express yourself. Writing is like painting a "word picture" of your thoughts: You need to use the full range of colors, not just a few basic ones. An equally important strategy is for you to write and then have others evaluate your writing and give you suggestions for improving it. You will be using both of these strategies in the pages that follow.

THINKING PASSAGE

Blue Highways

The following selection is from *Blue Highways,* a book written by a young man of Native American heritage named William Least Heat-Moon. After losing his teaching job at a university and separating from his wife, he decided to explore America. He outfitted his van (named "Ghost Dancing") and drove around the country using back roads (represented on the maps by blue lines) rather than superhighways. During his travels, he saw fascinating sights, met intriguing people, and developed some significant insights about himself. Read the passage carefully and then answer the questions that follow.

From *Blue Highways*
by William Least Heat-Moon

Back at Ghost Dancing, I saw a camper had pulled up. On the rear end, by the strapped-on aluminum chairs, was something like "The Wandering Watkins." Time to go. I kneeled to check a tire. A smelly furry white thing darted from behind the wheel, and I flinched. Because of it, the journey would change.

"Harmless as a stuffed toy." The voice came from the other end of the leash the dog was on. "He's nearly blind and can't hear much better. Down just to the nose now." The man, with polished cowboy boots and a part measured out in the white hair, had a face so gullied even the Soil Conservation Commission couldn't have reclaimed it. But his eyes seemed lighted from within.

"Are you Mr. Watkins?" I asked.

"What's left of him. The pup's what's left of Bill. He's a Pekingese. Chinese dog. In dog years, he's even older than I am, and I respect him for that. We're two old men. What's your name?"

"Same as the dog's."

"I wanted to give him a Chinese name, but old what's-her-face over there in the camper wouldn't have it. Claimed she couldn't pronounce Chinese names. I says, 'You can't say Lee?' She says, 'You going to name a dog Lee?' 'No,' I says, 'but what do you think about White Fong?' Now, she's not a reader unless it's a beauty parlor magazine with a Kennedy or Hepburn woman on the cover, so she never understood the name. You've read your Jack London, I hope. She says, 'When I was a girl we had a horse called William, but that name's too big for that itty-bitty dog. Just call him Bill.' That was that. She's a woman of German descent and a decided person. But when old Bill and I are out on our own, I call him White Fong."

Watkins had worked in a sawmill for thirty years, then retired to Redding; now he spent time in his camper, sometimes in the company of Mrs. Watkins.

"I'd stay on the road, but what's-her-face won't have it."

As we talked, Mrs. What's-her-face periodically thrust her head from the camper to call instructions to Watkins or White Fong. A finger-wagging woman, full of injunctions for man and beast. Whenever she called, I watched her, Watkins watched me, and the dog watched him. Each time he

Source: From *Blue Highways: A Journey into America* by William Least Heat-Moon. Copyright © 1982 by William Least Heat-Moon. By permission of Little, Brown and Company Inc.

would say, "Well, boys, there you have it. Straight from the back of the horse."

"You mind if I swear?" I said I didn't. "The old biddy's in there with her Morning Special — sugar doughnut, boysenberry jam, and a shot of Canadian Club in her coffee. In this beauty she sits inside with her letters."

"What kind of work you in?" he asked.

That question again. "I'm out of work," I said to simplify.

"A man's never out of work if he's worth a damn. It's just sometimes he doesn't get paid. I've gone unpaid my share and I've pulled my share of pay. But that's got nothing to do with working. A man's work is doing what he's supposed to do, and that's why he needs a catastrophe now and again to show him a bad turn isn't the end, because a bad stroke never stops a good man's work. Let me show you my philosophy of life." From his pressed Levi's he took a billfold and handed me a limp business card. "Easy. It's very old."

The card advertised a cafe in Merced when telephone numbers were four digits. In quotation marks was a motto: "Good Home Cooked Meals."

"'Good Home Cooked Meals' is your philosophy?"

"Turn it over, peckerwood."

Imprinted on the back in tiny, faded letters was this:

> I've been bawled out, balled up, held up, held down, hung up, bulldozed, blackjacked, walked on, cheated, squeezed and mooched; stuck for war tax, excess profits tax, sales tax, dog tax, and syntax, Liberty Bonds, baby bonds, and the bonds of matrimony, Red Cross, Blue Cross, and the double cross; I've worked like hell, worked others like hell, have got drunk and got others drunk, lost all I had, and now because I won't spend or lend what little I earn, beg, borrow or steal, I've been cussed, discussed, boycotted, talked to, talked about, lied to, lied about, worked over, pushed under, robbed, and damned near ruined. The only reason I'm sticking around now is to see WHAT THE HELL IS NEXT.

"I like it," I said.

"Any man's true work is to get his boots on each morning. Curiosity gets it done about as well as anything else."

Questions for Analysis

1. After reading the passage from *Blue Highways,* analyze Least Heat-Moon's use of language. Make three columns on a page. Use these headings: Action Verbs, Concrete Nouns, and Vivid Adjectives. List at least six examples of each from the reading.

2. Describe how the author uses dialogue and analogies to introduce us to Mr. Watkins.

3. According to Mr. Watkins, "A man's never out of work if he's worth a damn. It's just sometimes he doesn't get paid. . . . Any man's true work is to get his boots on each morning. Curiosity gets it done about as well as anything else." What do you think he's trying to say about the challenges posed by life to both men and women?

THINKING ACTIVITY 6.4

Communicating an Experience

Create your own description of an experience you have had while traveling. Use language as effectively as possible to communicate the thoughts, feelings, and impressions you wish to share. Be conscious of your use of action verbs, concrete nouns, and vivid adjectives. Ask other students to read your description and identify examples of these words. Then ask for feedback on ways to improve your description.

Using Language to Clarify Thinking

Language reflects thinking, and thinking is shaped by language. Previous sections of this chapter examine the creature we call *language.* You have seen that it is composed of small cells, or units, pieces of sound that combine to form larger units called *words.* When words are combined into groups allowed by the rules of the language to form sentences, the creature grows by leaps and bounds. Various types of sentence structure not only provide multiple ways of expressing the same ideas, thoughts, and feelings, but also help to structure those thoughts, weaving into them nuances of focus. In turn, your patterns of thinking breathe life into language, giving both processes power.

Language is a tool powered by patterns of thinking. With its power to represent your thoughts, feelings, and experiences symbolically, language is the most important tool your thinking process has. Although research shows that

VISUAL THINKING

Words Paint a Picture

● Describe a time when you were able to "paint a picture" with words. Why were you able to use language so effectively? How can we "paint" word pictures more frequently in our everyday lives?

thinking and communicating are two distinct processes, these two processes are so closely related that they are often difficult to separate or distinguish.*

Because language and thinking are so closely related, how well you perform one process is directly related to how well you perform the other. In most cases, when you are thinking clearly, you are able to express your ideas clearly in language. When you have unclear thoughts, it is usually because you lack a clear understanding of the situation, or you do not know the right language to give form to these thoughts. When your thoughts are truly clear and precise, this means that you know the words to give form to these thoughts and so are able to express them in language.

The relationship between thinking and language is *interactive*; both processes are continually influencing each other in many ways. This is particularly true in the case of language, as the writer George Orwell points out in the following passage from his classic essay "Politics and the English Language":

*Seminal works on this topic are *Thought and Language,* by Lev Vygotsky; and *Cognitive Development: Its Cultural and Social Foundation,* by A. R. Luria.

A man may take to drink because he feels himself to be a failure, and then fail all the more completely because he drinks. It is rather the same thing that is happening to the English language. It becomes ugly and inaccurate because our thoughts are foolish, but the slovenliness of our language makes it easier for us to have foolish thoughts. The point is that the process is reversible. Modern English, especially written English, is full of bad habits which spread by imitation and which can be avoided if one is willing to take the necessary trouble. If one gets rid of these habits one can think more clearly.

Just as a drinker falls into a vicious cycle that keeps getting worse, so too can language and thinking. When your use of language is sloppy — that is, vague, general, indistinct, imprecise, foolish, inaccurate, and so on — it leads to thinking of the same sort. And the reverse is also true. Clear and precise language leads to clear and precise thinking:

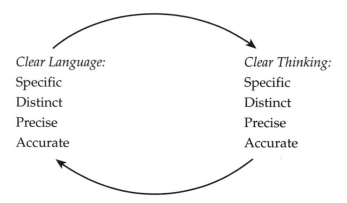

Clear Language:
Specific
Distinct
Precise
Accurate

Clear Thinking:
Specific
Distinct
Precise
Accurate

The opposite of clear, effective language is language that fails to help the reader (or listener) picture or understand what the writer (or speaker) means because it is vague or ambiguous. Most of us are guilty of using such ineffective language in speech ("It was a great party!"), but for college and work writing, we need to be as precise as possible. And our writing can gain clarity and power if we use our creative thinking skills to develop fresh, striking figures of speech to illuminate our ideas.

Improving Vague Language

Although our ability to name and identify gives us the power to describe the world in a precise way, often we tend to describe it using words that are imprecise and general. Such general and nonspecific words are called *vague* words. Consider the following sentences:

- I had a *nice* time yesterday.
- That is an *interesting* book.
- She is an *old* person.

In each of these cases, the italicized word is vague because it does not give a precise description of the thought, feeling, or experience that the writer or speaker is trying to communicate. A word (or group of words) is vague if its meaning is not clear and distinct. That is, vagueness occurs when a word is used to represent an area of experience without clearly defining it.

vague word *A word that lacks a clear and distinct meaning*

Most words of general measurement — *short, tall, big, small, heavy, light,* and so on — are vague. The exact meanings of these words depend on the specific situation in which they are used and on the particular perspective of the person using them. For example, give specific definitions for the following words in italics by filling in the blanks. Then compare your responses with those of other members of the class. Can you account for the differences in meaning?

1. A *middle-aged* person is one who is _____ years old.

2. A *tall* person is one who is over _____ feet _____ inches tall.

3. It's *cold* outside when the temperature is _____ degrees.

4. A person is *wealthy* when he or she is worth _____ dollars.

Although the vagueness of general measurement terms can lead to confusion, other forms of vagueness are more widespread and often more problematic. Terms such as *nice* and *interesting,* for example, are imprecise and unclear. Vagueness of this sort permeates every level of human discourse, undermines clear thinking, and is extremely difficult to combat. To use language clearly and precisely, you must develop an understanding of the way language functions and commit yourself to breaking the entrenched habits of vague expression.

For example, read the following opinion of a movie and circle all the vague, general words that do not express a clear meaning:

Pulp Fiction is a really funny movie about some really unusual characters in California. The movie consists of several different stories that connect up at different points. Some of the stories are nerve-racking and others are hilarious, but all of them are very well done. The plots are very interesting, and the main characters are excellent. I liked this movie a lot.

Because of the vague language in this passage, it expresses only general approval — it does not explain in exact or precise terms what the experience was like. Thus, the writer of the passage is not successful in communicating the experience.

Strong language users have the gift of symbolizing their experiences so clearly that you can actually relive those experiences with them. You can identify with them, sharing the same thoughts, feelings, and perceptions that they had when they underwent (or imagined) the experience. Consider how effectively the passage written by William Least Heat-Moon on pages 237–238 communicates the thoughts, feelings, and experiences of the author.

One useful strategy for clarifying vague language often used by journalists is to ask and try to answer the following questions: *Who? What? Where? When? How? Why?* Let's see how this strategy applies to the movie vaguely described previously.

- *Who* were the people involved in the movie? (actors, director, producer, characters portrayed)
- *What* took place in the movie? (setting, events, plot development)
- *Where* does the movie take place? (physical location, cultural setting)
- *When* do the events in the movie take place? (historical situation)
- *How* does the film portray its events? (How do the actors create their characters? How does the director use film techniques to accomplish his goals?)
- *Why* do I have this opinion of the film? (What are the reasons for my forming that opinion?)

Even if we don't give an elaborate version of our thinking, we can still communicate effectively by using language clearly and precisely. For example, examine this review summary of *Pulp Fiction* by the professional film critic David Denby. Compare and contrast it with the earlier review.

An ecstatically entertaining piece of suave mockery by Quentin Tarantino that revels in every manner of pulp flagrancy — murder and betrayal, drugs, sex, and episodes of sardonically distanced sadomasochism — all told in three overlapping tales. It's a very funky, American sort of pop masterpiece: improbable, uproarious, with bright colors and danger and blood right on the surface.

THINKING ACTIVITY 6.5

Reviewing a Movie

Write a review of a movie that you saw recently, concentrating on expressing your ideas clearly and precisely. Use the following questions to guide your analysis:

1. *Who* were the people involved with the movie?
2. *What* took place in the movie?
3. *Where* does the movie take place?
4. *When* do the events in the movie take place?
5. *How* does the film portray its events?
6. *Why* did you form this particular opinion about the film?

Most people use vague language extensively in day-to-day conversations. In many cases, it is natural that your immediate reaction to an experience would be fairly general ("That's nice," "She's interesting," etc.). If you are truly concerned with sharp thinking and meaningful communication, however, you should follow up these initial general reactions by more precisely clarifying what you really mean.

- I think that she is a nice person *because* . . .
- I think that he is a good teacher *because* . . .
- I think that this is an interesting class *because* . . .

Vagueness is always a matter of degree. In fact, you can think of your descriptive/informative use of language as falling somewhere on a scale between extreme generality and extreme specificity. For example, the following statements move from the general to the specific.

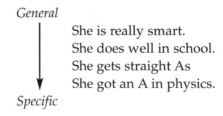

General

She is really smart.
She does well in school.
She gets straight As
She got an A in physics.

Specific

Although different situations require various degrees of specificity, you should work at becoming increasingly more precise in your use of language.

THINKING PASSAGE

An Account of Avianca Flight 52

Using language imprecisely can lead to miscommunication, sometimes with disastrous results. For example, on January 29, 1990, an Avianca Airlines flight from Colombia, South America, to New York City crashed, killing seventy-three persons. After circling Kennedy Airport for 45 minutes, the plane ran out of fuel before it could land, apparently the result of imprecise communication between the plane's pilot and the air traffic controllers. Read the following excerpts from the January 30, 1990, *The New York Times* account of the incident, and then answer the questions that follow.

AN ACCOUNT OF AVIANCA FLIGHT 52

The Federal Aviation Administration today defended the controllers who guided a Colombian jetliner toward Kennedy International Airport, releasing the first verbatim transcripts of communications in the hour before the jet crashed. The officials suggested that the plane's pilot should have used more precise language, such as the word "emergency," in telling controllers how seriously they were short of fuel. They made the statements a day after Federal investigators said that regional controllers never told local controllers the plane was short of fuel and had asked for priority clearance to land.

The transcripts show that the crew of Avianca Flight 52 told regional controllers about 45 minutes before the plane crashed that "we would run out of fuel" if the plane was redirected to Boston instead of being given priority to land at Kennedy. The crew said it would be willing to continue in its holding pattern 40 miles south of Kennedy for "about five minutes — that's all we can do" before the plane would have to move onward to Kennedy. But the regional controllers who gave that message to the local controllers who were to guide the plane on its final descent to Kennedy did not tell them that there was a problem with fuel supplies on the jet or that the plane had requested priority handling, the transcripts recorded by the FAA confirmed.

Taken by itself, the information that the plane could circle for just five more minutes would not make the immediate danger of the plane clear to the local controllers. Without being told that the plane did not have enough fuel to reach Boston or that its crew had asked for priority clearance, the

Source: "An Account of Avianca Flight 52," *The New York Times,* January 30, 1990. Copyright © 1990 by The New York Times Co. Reprinted by permission.

local controllers might have assumed that it had reached a point where it could still land with adequate reserves of fuel still on board.

Despite the apparent lapse in communications among controllers, an FAA spokesman said they acted properly because the plane's crew had not explicitly declared a fuel emergency. An emergency would require immediate clearance to land.

R. Steve Bell, president of the National Air Traffic Controllers Association, called the safety board's statements during its inquiry "highly misleading and premature." Mr. Bell, in a statement issued today, said the pilots of the plane should have made known to controllers the extent of their problem in order to obtain immediate clearance to land the plane. "The Avianca pilot never declared a 'fuel emergency' or 'minimum fuel,' both of which would have triggered an emergency response by controllers," he said. "Stating that you are low on fuel does not imply an immediate problem. In addition, this information would not necessarily be transmitted when one controller hands off to another."

Questions for Analysis

1. If the pilot of the airplane were alive (all crew died in the crash), how do you think he would analyze the cause of the crash?
2. How do the air traffic controllers and the FAA analyze the cause of the crash?
3. How do you analyze the cause of the crash? What reasons led you to that conclusion?
4. Describe a situation that you were involved in, or that you heard about, in which a misunderstanding resulted from an ambiguous use of language.

Using Language in Social Contexts

Language Styles

Language is always used in a context. That is, you always speak or write with an audience, whether a person or a group of people, in mind. The audience may include friends, coworkers, strangers, or only yourself! You also always use language in a particular situation. You may converse with your friends, meet with your boss, or carry out a business transaction at the bank or supermarket. In each of these cases, you use the *language style* that is appropriate to the social situation. For example, describe how you usually greet the following people when you see them:

A good friend:

A teacher:

A parent:

An employer:

A waiter/waitress:

Different social contexts call for different language responses. In a working environment, no matter how frequently you interact with coworkers or employers, your language style tends to be more formal and less abbreviated than it is in personal friendships. Conversely, the more familiar you are with someone and the better you know that person, the more abbreviated your *style* of language will be in that context, for you share a variety of ideas, opinions, and experiences with that person. The language style identifies this shared thinking and consequently *restricts* the group of people who can communicate within this context.

We all belong to social groups in which we use styles that separate "insiders" from "outsiders." On the one hand, when you use an abbreviated style of language with your friend, you are identifying that person as a friend and sending a social message that says, "I know you pretty well, and I can assume many common perspectives between us." On the other hand, when you are speaking to someone at the office in a more elaborate language style, you are sending a different social message, namely, "I know you within a particular context [this workplace], and I can assume only certain common perspectives between us."

In this way we use language to identify the social context and to define the relationship between the people communicating. Language styles vary from *informal,* in which we abbreviate not only sentence structure but also the sounds that form words — as in "ya" for *you* — to increasingly *formal,* in which we use more complex sentence structure as well as complete words in terms of sound patterns.

Standard American English

The language style used in most academic and workplace writing is called *Standard American English (SAE).* SAE follows the rules and conventions given in handbooks and taught in school. The ability to use SAE marks a person as part of an educated group that understands how and when to use it.

VISUAL THINKING

"What's Happening?"

- Using language effectively involves using the language style appropriate to the situation. What are some of the different language styles you use in your life? Which language styles do you feel least comfortable with? Why?

Unless otherwise specified, you should use SAE for college speaking and writing assignments, and your vocabulary should be appropriate for the intended audience. For example, social science students and instructors would immediately understand what *bell curve* means, but other audiences might need an explanation of this term. Again, if your literature teacher is the sole intended audience for your paper, you don't need to define a *literary symbol*.

But if the assignment asks you to write for fourth-grade students to encourage them to enjoy poetry, then you would want to define literary terms. Depending on your intended audience and purpose, you may or may not wish to employ slang, jargon, or dialect, but you should understand these forms of language.

Slang

Read the following dialogue and then rewrite it in your own style.

Girl 1: "Hey, did you see that new guy? He's a dime. I mean, really diesel."

Girl 2: "All the guys in my class are busted. They are tore up from the floor up. Punks, crack-heads, low-lifes. Let's exit. There's a jam tonight that is going to be the bomb, really fierce. I've got to hit the books so that I'll still have time to chill."

How would you describe the style of the original dialogue? How would you describe the style of your version of the dialogue? The linguist Shoshana Hoose writes:

> As any teen will tell you, keeping up with the latest slang takes a lot of work. New phrases sweep into town faster than greased lightning, and they are gone just as quickly. Last year's "hoser" is this year's "dweeb" (both meaning somewhat of a "nerd"). Some slang consists of everyday words that have taken on a new, hip meaning. "Mega," for instance, was used mainly by astronomers and mathematicians until teens adopted it as a way of describing anything great, cool, and unbelievable. Others are words such as *gag* that seem to have naturally evolved from one meaning (to throw up) to another (a person or thing that is gross to the point of making one want to throw up). And then there are words that come from movies, popular music, and the media. "Rambo," the macho movie character who single-handedly defeats whole armies, has come to mean a muscular, tough, adventurous boy who wears combat boots and fatigues.

> As linguists have long known, cultures create the most words for the things that preoccupy them the most. For example, Eskimos have more than seventy-six words for *ice* and *snow*, and Hawaiians can choose from scores of variations on the word *water*. Most teenage slang falls into one or two categories: words meaning "cool" and words meaning "out of it." A person who is really out of it could be described as a *nerd*, a *goober*, a *geek*, a *fade*, or a *pinhead*, to name just a few possibilities.

THINKING ACTIVITY 6.6

Thinking About Slang

Review the slang terms and definitions in the following glossary. How do your terms match up? For each term, list a word that you use or have heard of to mean the same thing.

Word	Your Word	Meaning
dime, buff, diesel, hot		good-looking (guy)
phat, shorty, fly, all that		good-looking (girl)
busted		gross, disgusting
punk, loser		unsuccessful person

Word	Your Word	Meaning
hip, fierce, cool		awesome
the bomb		really cool
trifling		showoff
played		out of date
exit, be out, step off, bounce, jet		leave

If your meanings did not match those in the glossary or if you did not recognize some of the words in the glossary, what do you think was the main reason for your lack of comprehension?

Slang is a restrictive style of language that limits its speakers to a particular group. As Hoose points out, age is usually the determining factor in using slang. But there are special forms of slang that are not determined by age; rather, they are determined by profession or interest group. Let's look at this other type of language style.

Jargon

Jargon is made up of words, expressions, and technical terms that are intelligible to professional circles or interest groups but not to the general public. Consider the following interchanges:

1. *A:* Breaker 1-9. Com'on, Little Frog.
   B: Roger and back to you, Charley.
   A: You got to back down; you got a Smokey ahead.

B: I can't afford to feed the bears this week. Better stay at 5-5 now.
A: That's a big 10-4.
B: I'm gonna cut the coax now.

2. OK A1, number six takes two eggs, wreck 'em, with a whiskey down and an Adam and Eve on a raft. Don't forget the Jack Tommy, express to California.

3. Please take further notice, that pursuant to and in accordance with Article II, Paragraph Second and Fifteen of the aforesaid Proprietary Lease Agreement, you are obligated to reimburse Lessor for any expense Lessor incurs including legal fees in instituting any action or proceeding due to a default of your obligations as contained in the Proprietary Lease Agreement.

Can you identify the groups that would understand the meaning of each of the previous examples?

Dialects

Within the boundaries of geographical regions and ethnic groups, the form of a language used may be so different from the usual (or standard) in terms of its sound patterns, vocabulary, and sentence structure that it cannot be understood by people outside the specific regional or ethnic group. In this case, we are no longer talking about variations in language *style;* we are talking instead about distinct *dialects.* Consider these sentences from two different dialects of English:

Dialect A: Dats allabunch of byoks at de license bureau. He fell out de rig and broke his leg boon.

Dialect B: I went out to the garden to pick the last of them Kentucky Wonder pole beans of mine, and do you know, there on the grass was just a little mite of frost.

Though you can recognize these sentences as English, you may not recognize all of the words, sentence structures, and sound patterns that these speakers used.

Dialects differ from language styles in being generally restricted to geographical and/or ethnic groups, but also in varying from the standard language to a greater degree than language styles do. Dialects vary not only in words but also in sound patterns and in syntax. If you speak a dialect, write one or two sentences in that dialect and share them with your classmates. How does your dialect vary from Standard American English in terms of words and syntactic forms?

The Social Boundaries of Language

Language is a system of communication, by sounds and markings, among given groups of people. Within each language community, members' thinking patterns are defined in many respects by the specific patterns of meaning that language imposes. Smaller groups within language communities display distinctive language patterns. When there are some differences from the norm, mainly in vocabulary and length of sentences, we say the speakers are using a specific *language style*. When the form of the language spoken by these smaller groups shows many differences from the "usual" or "regular" form in words and sentence structure, we call this language form a *dialect*. Often language style is determined by the context, but sometimes speakers who differ from each other in terms of age, sex, or social class will also differ from each other in their speech — even in the same social context. This is called *social variation*.

We cannot, however, ignore the way in which our thoughts about a social situation determine the variety of language we use. The connection between language and thought turns language into a powerful social force that separates us as well as binds us together. The language that you use and the way you use it serve as important clues to your social identity. For example, dialect identifies your geographical area or group, slang marks your age group and subculture, jargon often identifies your occupation, and accent typically suggests the place you grew up and your socioeconomic class. Social dimensions of language are important influences in shaping your response to others. Sometimes they can trigger stereotypes you hold about someone's interests, social class, intelligence, personal attributes, and so on. The ability to think critically gives you the insight and the intellectual ability to distinguish people's language use from their individual qualities, to correct inaccurate beliefs about people, and to avoid stereotypical responses in the future.

THINKING ACTIVITY 6.7

Analyzing Language Uses

1. Describe examples, drawn from individuals in your personal experience, of each of the following: dialect, accent, jargon, slang.

2. Describe your immediate responses to the examples you just provided. For example, what is your immediate response to someone speaking in each of the dialects on page 251? To someone with a British accent? To someone speaking "computerese"? To someone speaking a slang that you don't understand?

3. Analyze your responses. How were they formed? Do they represent an accurate understanding of the person or a stereotyped belief?

4. Identify strategies for using critical thinking abilities to overcome inaccurate and inappropriate responses to others based on their language usage.

◎ Using Language to Influence

The intimate relationship between language and thinking makes it natural that people use language to influence the thinking of others. As you have seen, within the boundaries of social groups, people use a given language style or dialect to emphasize shared information and experience. Not only does this sharing socially identify the members of the group; it also provides a base for them to influence each other's thinking. The expression "Now you're speaking my language!" illustrates this point. Some people make a profession of using language to influence people's thinking. In other words, many individuals and groups are interested in influencing — and sometimes controlling — your thoughts, your feelings, and (as a result) your behavior. To avoid being unconsciously manipulated by these efforts, you must have an understanding and an awareness of how language functions. Such an understanding will help you distinguish actual arguments, information, and reasons from techniques of persuasion that others use to try to get you to accept their viewpoint without critical thought. Two types of language are often used to promote the uncritical acceptance of viewpoints:

- Euphemistic language
- Emotive language

By developing insight into these language strategies, you will strengthen your abilities to function as a critical thinker.

Euphemistic Language

The term *euphemism* derives from a Greek word meaning "to speak with good words" and involves substituting a more pleasant, less objectionable way of saying something for a blunt or more direct way. For example, an entire collection of euphemisms exists to disguise the unpleasantness of death: "passed away," "went to her reward," "departed this life," and "blew out the candle."

Why do people use euphemisms? They do so probably to help smooth out the "rough edges" of life, to make the unbearable bearable and the offensive inoffensive. Sometimes people use them to make their occupations seem more important. For example, a garbage collector may be called a "sanitation engineer"; a traveling salesman, a "field representative"; and a police officer, a "law enforcement official."

Euphemisms can become dangerous when they are used to create misperceptions of important issues. For example, an alcoholic may describe himself as a "social drinker," thus ignoring the problem and the help he needs. Or a politician may indicate that one of her other statements was "somewhat at variance with the truth" — meaning that she lied. Even more serious examples include describing rotting slums as "substandard housing," making the deplorable conditions appear reasonable and the need for action less important. One of the most devastating examples of the destructive power of euphemisms was Nazi Germany's characterization of the slaughter of over 12 million men, women, and children by such innocuous phrases as the "final solution" and the "purification of the race."

George Orwell, the author of the futuristic novel *1984*, describes how governments often employ euphemisms to disguise and justify wrongful policies in the following passage taken from his classic essay "Politics and the English Language":

> In our time, political speech and writing are largely the defense of the indefensible. Things like the continuance of British rule in India, the Russian purges and deportations, [and] the dropping of the atom bombs on Japan can indeed be defended, but only by arguments which are too brutal for most people to face, and which do not square with the professed aims of political parties. Thus political language has to consist largely of euphemism, question-begging and sheer cloudy vagueness. Defenseless villages are bombarded from the air, the inhabitants driven out into the countryside, the cattle machine-gunned, the huts set on fire with incendiary bullets: this is called *pacification*. Millions of peasants are robbed of their farms and sent trudging along the roads with no more than they can carry: this is called *transfer of population* or *rectification of frontiers*. People are imprisoned for years without trial, or shot in the back of the neck or sent to die of scurvy in Arctic lumber camps: this is called *elimination of unreliable elements*. Such phraseology is needed if one wants to name things without calling up mental pictures of them.

Euphemisms crop up in every part of our lives, but bureaucracies are particularly prolific and creative "euphemisers." Every year the nation's English teachers present annual "Doublespeak Awards" to those institutions producing the most egregious euphemisms. Listed below are some past winners. Why do you think these organizations created these particular euphemisms? Can you add to the list euphemisms that you've heard or read recently?

Department of Defense

bombing	=	"servicing the target"
people to be killed	=	"soft targets"
buildings to be bombed	=	"hard targets"

U.S. Senate

voting a $23,200 raise for themselves	=	"pay equalization concept"

U.S. Government Economic Report

recession	=	"meaningful downturn in aggregate output"

Several Foreign Governments

assassinations	=	"active self-defense," "interception"
terrorist	=	"freedom fighter"
torture	=	"moderate physical pressure"

Companies are acutely sensitive to the power of language and often try to shape public perceptions and attitudes through the words they use to communicate. For example, consider the following excerpt from a *New York Times* article by John Schwartz that describes the decision by cigarette maker Philip Morris to change its name to "Altria Group." What euphemistic meanings do you think the company was trying to capture? Do you think it made a good choice? Why or why not? If you were the CEO of Philip Morris, what other names might you have considered?

Philip Morris, the owner of one of the world's best-known corporate names, plans to change that name next year to the Altria Group, company executives said yesterday.

The new name, which is subject to approval by shareholders at the company's annual meeting next April, is drawn from the Latin word "altus," meaning "high," and is supposed to suggest high performance, said Steven C. Parrish, the company's senior vice president for corporate affairs, in an interview at the company's headquarters in New York. . . .

"Call for Altria" doesn't have the ring of the company's "Call for Philip Morrrrrr-isssss!" slogan from radio's golden age. But that might be the point. The company has taken this action, its executives say, to reduce the drag on the company's reputation that association with the world's most famous cigarette maker has caused.

"When people say 'Philip Morris,' people don't know which company you're talking about," Mr. Parrish said. "We're more than a tobacco company, obviously, but there are a lot of people who don't understand that."

"They are running away from tobacco," countered David A. Kessler, former commissioner of the Food and Drug Administration and now the dean of the medical school at Yale University. . . .

A longtime opponent of the tobacco industry, however, said a new name would not change the fact that Philip Morris's Marlboro cigarettes are by far the favorite brand of underage smokers. "It's sort of like the line from the Dragnet TV show, 'This story is true, but the names have been changed to protect the innocent,'" said Matthew L. Myers, president of the National Center for Tobacco-Free Kids. "In this case it's 'The story is true, but the names have been changed to protect the guilty.'" In the end, he said, "this is quintessential Philip Morris practice."

"Instead of changing its business practices, Philip Morris has chosen a public relations campaign to divert attention away from what it does." . . .

— *John Schwartz*, The New York Times

THINKING ACTIVITY 6.8

Analyzing Euphemisms

Read the following essay by linguistics professor Robin Tolmach Lakoff about the use of euphemism to dehumanize the "enemy" in times of war. In what ways did George Orwell (see page 254) predict the use of euphemism to make the human costs of warfare more politically palatable? Can you think of other social policies with direct human consequences that are discussed, by politicians or the media, in euphemistic terms? Identify several euphemisms used to describe a policy or issue and explain how the euphemisms can lead to dangerous misperceptions and consequences. (For further discussion of how language can be used to influence, suppress, or direct behavior, see "Thinking Passages: Critical Thinking and Obedience to Authority" in Chapter 11.)

FROM *ANCIENT GREECE TO IRAQ, THE POWER OF WORDS IN WARTIME* by Robin Tolmach Lakoff

An American soldier refers to an Iraqi prisoner as "it." A general speaks not of "Iraqi fighters" but of "the enemy." A weapons manufacturer doesn't talk about people but about "targets."

Source: From "Ancient Greece to Iraq, the Power of Words in Wartime," by Robin Tolmach Lakoff. Copyright © 2004 by the New York Times Co. Reprinted by permission.

Bullets and bombs are not the only tools of war. Words, too, play their part.

Human beings are social animals, genetically hard-wired to feel compassion toward others. Under normal conditions, most people find it very difficult to kill.

But in war, military recruits must be persuaded that killing other people is not only acceptable but even honorable.

The language of war is intended to bring about that change, and not only for soldiers in the field. In wartime, language must be created to enable combatants and noncombatants alike to see the other side as killable, to overcome the innate queasiness over the taking of human life. Soldiers, and those who remain at home, learn to call their enemies by names that make them seem not quite human — inferior, contemptible and not like "us."

The specific words change from culture to culture and war to war. The names need not be obviously demeaning. Just the fact that we can name them gives us a sense of superiority and control. If, in addition, we give them nicknames, we can see them as smaller, weaker and childlike — not worth taking seriously as fully human.

The Greeks and Romans referred to everyone else as "barbarians" — etymologically those who only babble, only go "bar-bar." During the American Revolution, the British called the colonists "Yankees," a term with a history that is still in dispute. While the British intended it disparagingly, the Americans, in perhaps the first historical instance of reclamation, made the word their own and gave it a positive spin, turning the derisive song "Yankee Doodle" into our first, if unofficial, national anthem.

In World War I, the British gave the Germans the nickname "Jerries," from the first syllable of German. In World War II, Americans referred to the Japanese as "Japs."

The names may refer to real or imagined cultural and physical differences that emphasize the ridiculous or the repugnant. So in various wars, the British called the French "Frogs." Germans have been called "Krauts," a reference to weird and smelly food. The Vietnamese were called "slopes" and "slants." The Koreans were referred to simply as "gooks."

The war in Iraq has added new examples. Some American soldiers refer to the Iraqis as "hadjis," used in a derogatory way, apparently unaware that the word, which comes from the Arabic term for a pilgrimage to Mecca, is used as a term of respect for older Muslim men.

The Austrian ethologist Konrad Lorenz suggested that the more clearly we see other members of our own species as individuals, the harder we find it to kill them.

So some terms of war are collective nouns, encouraging us to see the enemy as an undifferentiated mass, rather than as individuals capable of suffering. Crusaders called their enemy "the Saracen," and in World War I, the British called Germans "the Hun."

American soldiers are trained to call those they are fighting against "the enemy." It is easier to kill an enemy than an Iraqi. The word "enemy" itself provides the facelessness of a collective noun. Its non-specificity also has a fear-inducing connotation; enemy means simply "those we are fighting," without reference to their identity.

The terrors and uncertainties of war make learning this kind of language especially compelling for soldiers on the front. But civilians back home also need to believe that what their country is doing is just and necessary, and that the killing they are supporting is in some way different from the killing in civilian life that is rightly punished by the criminal justice system. The use of the language developed for military purposes by civilians reassures them that war is not murder.

The linguistic habits that soldiers must absorb in order to fight make atrocities like those at Abu Ghraib virtually inevitable. The same language that creates a psychological chasm between "us" and "them" and enables American troops to kill in battle, makes enemy soldiers fit subjects for torture and humiliation. The reasoning is: They are not really human, so they will not feel the pain.

Once language draws that line, all kinds of mistreatment become imaginable, and then justifiable. To make the abuses at Abu Ghraib unthinkable, we would have to abolish war itself.

Emotive Language

What is your *immediate* reaction to the following words?

sexy	peaceful	disgusting	God	filthy
mouthwatering	bloodthirsty	whore	Nazi	

Most of these words probably stimulate certain feelings in you. In fact, this ability to evoke feelings in people accounts for the extraordinary power of language. As a stark illustration of the way people (in this case, politicians) use language to manipulate emotions, a political action committee named Gopac distributed a booklet several years ago entitled "Language: A Key Mechanism of Control" to the candidates they supported. The booklet urged members of

Congress to use words like "environment, peace, freedom, fair, flag, we-us-our, family, and humane" when speaking of themselves. When speaking of opponents, words like "betray, sick, pathetic, lie, liberal, hypocrisy, permissive attitude, and self-serving" were preferable. Think of a recent election: Do you recall candidates following these linguistic suggestions?

Making sense of the way that language can influence your thinking and behavior means understanding the emotional dimension of language. Special words (like those just listed) are used to stand for the emotive areas of your experience. These emotive words symbolize the whole range of human feelings, from powerful emotions ("I adore you!") to the subtlest of feeling.

Emotive language often plays a double role — it not only symbolizes and expresses our feelings but also arouses or *evokes* feelings in others. When you say, "I love you" to someone, you usually are not simply expressing your feelings toward that person — you also hope to inspire similar feelings in that person toward you. Even when you are communicating factual information, you make use of the emotive influence of language to interest other people in what you are saying. For example, compare the factually more objective account by the *New York Times* of Malcolm X's assassination with the more emotive/action account by *Life* magazine (pages 142–144). Which account do you find more engaging? Why?

Although an emotive statement may be an *accurate* description of how you feel, it is *not* the same as a factual statement because it is true only for you — not for others. For instance, even though you may feel that a movie is tasteless and repulsive, someone else may find it exciting and hilarious. By describing your feelings about the movie, you are giving your personal evaluation, which often differs from the personal evaluations of others (consider the case of conflicting reviews of the same movie). A factual statement, in contrast, is a statement with which all "rational" people will agree, providing that suitable evidence for its truth is available (for example, the fact that mass transit uses less energy than automobiles).

In some ways, symbolizing your emotions is more difficult than representing factual information about the world. Expressing your feelings toward a person you know well often seems considerably more challenging than describing facts about that person.

When emotive words are used in larger groups (such as in sentences, paragraphs, compositions, poems, plays, novels), they become even more powerful. The pamphlets of Thomas Paine helped inspire American patriots during the Revolutionary War, and Abraham Lincoln's Gettysburg Address has endured as an expression of our most cherished values. In fact, it was the impassioned oratory of Adolf Hitler that helped influence the German people before and during World War II.

One way to think about the meaning and power of emotive words is to see them on a scale or continuum from mild to strong. For example: *plump, fat, obese.* Philosopher Bertrand Russell used this feature of emotive words to show how we perceive the same trait in various people:

- I am firm.

- You are stubborn.

- He or she is pigheaded.

We usually tend to perceive ourselves favorably ("I am firm"). I am speaking to you face to face, so I view you only somewhat less favorably ("You are stubborn"). But since a third person is not present, you can use stronger emotive language ("He or she is pigheaded"). Try this technique with two other emotive words:

1. I am . . . .   You are . . . .   He or she is . . . .

2. I am . . . .   You are . . . .   He or she is . . . .

Finally, emotive words can be used to confuse opinions with facts, a situation that commonly occurs when we combine emotive uses of language with informative uses. Although people may appear to be giving *factual* information, they actually may be adding personal evaluations that are not factual. These opinions are often emotional, biased, unfounded, or inflammatory. Consider the following statement: "New York City is a filthy and dangerous pigpen — only idiots would want to live there." Although the speaker is pretending to give factual information, he or she is really using emotive language to advance an opinion. But emotive uses of language are not always negative. The statement "She's the most generous, wise, honest, and warm friend that a person could have" also illustrates the confusion of the emotive and the informative uses of language, except that in this case the feelings are positive.

The presence of emotive words is usually a sign that a personal opinion or evaluation rather than a fact is being stated. Speakers occasionally do identify their opinions as opinions with such phrases as "In my opinion . . ." or "I feel that . . . ." Often, however, speakers do *not* identify their opinions as opinions because they *want* you to treat their judgments as *facts*. In these cases the combination of the informative use of language with the emotive use can be misleading and even dangerous.

THINKING ACTIVITY 6.9

Analyzing Emotive Language

Identify examples of emotive language in the following passages, and explain how it is used by the writers to influence people's thoughts and feelings:

> I draw the line in the dust and toss the gauntlet before the heel of tyranny, and I say segregation now, segregation tomorrow, segregation forever.
> — *Governor George C. Wallace, 1963*

> We dare not forget today that we are heirs of that first revolution. Let the word go forth from this time and place, to friend and foe alike, that the torch has been passed to a new generation of Americans — born in this century, tempered by war, disciplined by a hard and bitter peace, proud of our ancient heritage — and unwilling to witness or permit the slow undoing of those human rights to which this nation has always been committed, and to which we are committed today at home and around the world.
> — *President John F. Kennedy, Inaugural Address, 1961*

> Every criminal, every gambler, every thug, every libertine, every girl ruiner, every home wrecker, every wife beater, every dope peddler, every moonshiner, every crooked politician, every pagan Papist priest, every shyster lawyer, every white slaver, every brothel madam, every Rome-controlled newspaper, every black spider — is fighting the Klan. Think it over. Which side are you on?
> — *from a Ku Klux Klan circular*

> We need another and a wiser and perhaps a more mystical concept of animals. Remote from universal nature, and living by complicated artifice, man in civilization surveys the creature through the glass of his knowledge and sees thereby a feather magnified and the whole image in distortion. We patronize them for their incompleteness, for their tragic fate of having taken form so far below ourselves. And therein we err, and greatly err. For the animal shall not be measured by man. In a world older and more complete than ours they move finished and complete, gifted with extensions of the senses you have lost or never attained, living by voices you shall never hear. They are not brethren, they are not underlings; they are other nations, caught with ourselves in the net of life and time, fellow prisoners of the splendour and travail of the earth.
> — *Henry Beston*, The Outermost House

THINKING PASSAGES

Persuading with Political Speeches

The central purpose of political speeches has traditionally been to persuade listeners to a particular point of view, using language as the vehicle. This has never been more true than in times of war or national crisis. For examples of this type of persuasion, go to the companion web site and read excerpts from political speeches given by the individuals listed below at critical moments in history:

- President Franklin D. Roosevelt speaking after the attack on Pearl Harbor by the Japanese military
- Prime Minister Winston Churchill speaking after the invasion and defeat of most of the countries of western Europe by Hitler's military
- President George W. Bush speaking ten days following the terrorist attacks on the World Trade Center and the Pentagon
- Prime Minister Tony Blair speaking several weeks after the terrorist attacks
- Al Qaeda leader Osama bin Laden's videotaped comments released worldwide several days following the terrorist attacks

After reading the selections, also answer the questions at the conclusion of the readings.

THINKING ACTIVITY 6.10

How E-mail Changes Communication

Elsewhere in this text we have looked at the differences between expressing ourselves in writing and expressing ourselves orally. When we express ourselves in writing, our audience is not able to hear our vocal inflections or see our gestures and body language. The impression we make depends completely upon what we write.

The same holds true for the use of electronic mail, which has changed the way many people communicate at work, in social settings, in the classroom, and at home.

- What are some of the differences between communicating via e-mail, the spoken word, or another form of writing?

- Do you think an e-mail is easier to misunderstand than other styles of writing? Why or why not?

Have you ever

- Received an e-mail you thought was sarcastic, cruel, or too blunt?
- Sent one that was misinterpreted?
- gotten "hoax" virus warnings?
- Gotten chain letters promising unbelievable rewards?
- Received jokes you didn't want?

In your opinion, has the popularity of e-mail changed the nature or frequency of these kinds of messages as compared to paper mail? If so, how has that happened?

How Do You "Come Across"?

Have you noticed that you speak differently to different groups of people in different situations? Depending upon whether and where you work, you may notice that your choice of words and even grammatical constructions vary from those you use when speaking with, for example, family members. For that matter, how you speak to children is probably different from how you speak to siblings or to parents and other elders. You have a different "speaking personality" in different situations.

What different e-mail personalities do you have? What steps can you take to ensure that you come across as you intend when you use e-mail?

Final Thoughts

This chapter on language explores the essential role of language in developing sophisticated thinking abilities. The goal of clear, effective thinking and communication — avoiding ambiguity and vagueness — is accomplished through the joint efforts of thought and language. Learning to use the appropriate language style, depending on the social context in which you are operating, requires both critical judgment and flexible expertise with various language forms. Critically evaluating the pervasive attempts of advertisers and others to bypass your critical faculties and influence your thinking involves insight into the way language and thought create and express meaning.

Its link with thinking makes language so powerful a tool that we not only rely on it as a vehicle for expressing our thoughts and feelings and for influencing others, but we also use language to provide a structure for learning. Like a choreographer who creates a dance, language shapes and forms our thoughts. It organizes them. It relates one idea to another so that their combinations, many and varied, can be reported with strength and vitality, creating meaning that no one idea could convey alone. Used expertly, language *expresses* our thinking in a way that clearly evokes the images, feelings, and ideas that we as speakers and writers want to present. It also *communicates* our thinking in such a way that others can comprehend our meaning, in turn making appropriate inferences and judgments and thereby expanding their own thinking. We will be examining these further relationships between language and thought in the ensuing chapters.

THINKING PASSAGE

Gender Differences in Language

Recently, gender differences in language use have reached the forefront of social research, even though variations in language use between the sexes has been observed for centuries. Proverbs such as "A woman's tongue wags like a lamb's tail" historically attest to supposed differences — usually inferiorities — in women's speech and, by implication, in their thinking when compared with men's. Vocabulary, swearing and use of taboo language, pronunciation, and verbosity have all been said to illustrate gender differences in language. Only within the last two decades, however, have scholars of the social use of language paid serious attention to the variation between men's and women's language and the social factors that contribute to these differences. The following passage from the work of Deborah Tannen reflects the current interest in sociolinguistic variations between the "languages" used by women and men. After reading the selection, answer the questions that follow.

SEX, LIES AND CONVERSATION: WHY IS IT SO HARD FOR MEN AND WOMEN TO TALK TO EACH OTHER?
by Deborah Tannen

I was addressing a small gathering in a suburban Virginia living room — a women's group that had invited men to join them. Throughout the evening, one man had been particularly talkative, frequently offering ideas and anecdotes, while his wife sat silently beside him on the couch. Toward the end of

Source: "Sex, Lies and Conversation" by Deborah Tannen, *Washington Post,* June 14, 1990. Reprinted by permission of the author.

VISUAL THINKING

"You're Not Going to Believe This . . . ."

● Each of us uses a variety of communication styles in our lives, depending on the people we're with. What is the communication style displayed in this photo? What are some of the communication styles that you use on a regular basis? How would you communicate the same message to different audiences?

the evening, I commented that women frequently complain that their husbands don't talk to them. This man quickly concurred. He gestured toward his wife and said, "She's the talker in our family." The room burst into laughter; the man looked puzzled and hurt. "It's true," he explained. "When I come home from work I have nothing to say. If she didn't keep the conversation going, we'd spend the whole evening in silence."

This episode crystallizes the irony that although American men tend to talk more than women in public situations, they often talk less at home. And this pattern is wreaking havoc with marriage.

The pattern was observed by political scientist Andrew Hacker in the late '70s. Sociologist Catherine Kohler Riessman reports in her new book *Divorce Talk* that most of the women she interviewed — but only a few of the men — gave lack of communication as the reason for their divorces. Given the current divorce rate of nearly 50 percent, that amounts to millions of cases in the United States every year — a virtual epidemic of failed conversation.

In my own research, complaints from women about their husbands most often focused not on tangible inequities such as having given up the chance for a career to accompany a husband to his, or doing far more than their share of daily life-support work like cleaning, cooking, social arrangements and errands. Instead, they focused on communication: "He doesn't listen to me," "He doesn't talk to me." I found, as Hacker observed years before, that most wives want their husbands to be, first and foremost, conversational partners, but few husbands share this expectation of their wives.

In short, the image that best represents the current crisis is the stereotypical cartoon scene of a man sitting at the breakfast table with a newspaper held up in front of his face, while a woman glares at the back of it, wanting to talk.

Linguistic Battle of Sexes

How can women and men have such different impressions of communication in marriage? Why the widespread imbalance in their interests and expectations?

In the April issue of *American Psychologist,* Stanford University's Eleanor Maccoby reports the results of her own and others' research showing that children's development is most influenced by the social structure of peer interactions. Boys and girls tend to play with children of their own gender, and their sex-separate groups have different organizational structures and interactive norms.

I believe these systematic differences in childhood socialization make talk between women and men like cross-cultural communication, heir to all the attraction and pitfalls of that enticing but difficult enterprise. My research on men's and women's conversations uncovered patterns similar to those described for children's groups.

For women, as for girls, intimacy is the fabric of relationships, and talk is the thread from which it is woven. Little girls create and maintain friendships by exchanging secrets; similarly, women regard conversation as the cornerstone of friendship. So a woman expects her husband to be a new and improved version of a best friend. What is important is not the individual subjects that are discussed but the sense of closeness, a life shared, that emerges when people tell their thoughts, feelings, and impressions.

Bonds between boys can be as intense as girls', but they are based less on talking, more on doing things together. Since they don't assume talk is the cement that binds a relationship, men don't know what kind of talk women want, and they don't miss it when it isn't there.

Boys' groups are larger, more inclusive, and more hierarchical, so boys must struggle to avoid the subordinate position in the group. This may play a role in women's complaints that men don't listen to them. Some men really don't like to listen, because being the listener makes them feel one-down, like a child listening to adults or an employee to a boss.

But often when women tell men, "You aren't listening," and the men protest, "I am," the men are right. The impression of not listening results from misalignments in the mechanics of conversation. The misalignment begins as soon as a man and a woman take physical positions. This became clear when I studied videotapes made by psychologist Bruce Dorval of children and adults talking to their same-sex best friends. I found that at every age, the girls and women faced each other directly, their eyes anchored on each other's faces. At every age, the boys and men sat at angles to each other and looked elsewhere in the room, periodically glancing at each other. They were obviously attuned to each other, often mirroring each other's movements. But the tendency of men to face away can give women the impression they aren't listening even when they are. A young woman in college was frustrated: Whenever she told her boyfriend she wanted to talk to him, he would lie down on the floor, close his eyes, and put his arm over his face. This signaled to her, "He's taking a nap." But he insisted he was listening extra hard. Normally, he looks around the room, so he is easily distracted. Lying down and covering his eyes helped him concentrate on what she was saying.

Analogous to the physical alignment that women and men take in conversation is their topical alignment. The girls in my study tended to talk at length about one topic, but the boys tended to jump from topic to topic. Girls exchanged stories about people they knew. The second-grade boys teased, told jokes, noticed things in the room and talked about finding games to play. The sixth-grade girls talked about problems with a mutual friend. The sixth-grade boys talked about *55* different topics, none of which extended over more than a few turns.

Listening to Body Language

Switching topics is another habit that gives women the impression men aren't listening, especially if they switch to a topic about themselves. But the evidence of the 10th-grade boys in my study indicates otherwise. The 10th-grade boys sprawled across their chairs with bodies parallel and eyes straight ahead, rarely looking at each other. They looked as if they were riding in a car, staring out the windshield. But they were talking about their feelings. One boy was upset because a girl had told him he had a drinking problem, and the other was feeling alienated from all his friends.

Now, when a girl told a friend about a problem, the friend responded by asking probing questions and expressing agreement and understanding. But the boys dismissed each other's problems. Todd assured Richard that his drinking was "no big problem" because "sometimes you're funny when you're off your butt." And when Todd said he felt left out, Richard responded, "Why should you? You know more people than me."

Women perceive such responses as belittling and unsupportive. But the boys seemed satisfied with them. Whereas women reassure each other by implying, "You shouldn't feel bad because I've had similar experiences," men do so by implying, "You shouldn't feel bad because your problems aren't so bad."

There are even simpler reasons for women's impression that men don't listen. Linguist Lynette Hirschman found that women make more listener-noise, such as "mhm," "uhuh," and "yeah," to show "I'm with you." Men, she found, more often give silent attention. Women who expect a stream of listener-noise interpret silent attention as no attention at all.

Women's conversational habits are as frustrating to men as men's are to women. Men who expect silent attention interpret a stream of listener-noise as overreaction or impatience. Also, when women talk to each other in a close, comfortable setting, they often overlap, finish each other's sentences and anticipate what the other is about to say. This practice, which I call "participatory listenership," is often perceived by men as interruption, intrusion and lack of attention.

A parallel difference caused a man to complain about his wife, "She just wants to talk about her own point of view. If I show her another view, she gets mad at me." When most women talk to each other, they assume a conversationalist's job is to express agreement and support. But many men see their conversational duty as pointing out the other side of an argument. This is heard as disloyalty by women, and refusal to offer the requisite support. It is not that women don't want to see other points of view, but that they prefer them phrased as suggestions and inquiries rather than as direct challenges.

In his book *Fighting for Life,* Walter Ong points out that men use "agonistic," or warlike, oppositional formats to do almost anything; thus discussion becomes debate, and conversation a competitive sport. In contrast, women see conversation as a ritual means of establishing rapport. If Jane tells a problem and June says she has a similar one, they walk away feeling closer to each other. But this attempt at establishing rapport can backfire when used with men. Men take too literally women's ritual "troubles talk," just as women mistake men's ritual challenges for real attack.

The Sounds of Silence

These differences begin to clarify why women and men have such different expectations about communication in marriage. For women, talk creates intimacy. Marriage is an orgy of closeness: you can tell your feelings and thoughts, and still be loved. Their greatest fear is being pushed away. But men live in a hierarchical world, where talk maintains independence and status. They are on guard to protect themselves from being put down and pushed around.

This explains the paradox of the talkative man who said of his silent wife, "She's the talker." In the public setting of a guest lecture, he felt challenged to show his intelligence and display his understanding of the lecture. But at home, where he has nothing to prove and no one to defend against, he is free to remain silent. For his wife, being home means she is free from the worry that something she says might offend someone, or spark disagreement, or appear to be showing off; at home she is free to talk.

The communication problems that endanger marriage can't be fixed by mechanical engineering. They require a new conceptual framework about the role of talk in human relationships. Many of the psychological explanations that have become second nature may not be helpful, because they tend to blame either women (for not being assertive enough) or men (for not being in touch with their feelings). A sociolinguistic approach by which male-female conversation is seen as cross-cultural communication allows us to understand the problem and forge solutions without blaming either party.

Once the problem is understood, improvement comes naturally, as it did to the young woman and her boyfriend who seemed to go to sleep when she wanted to talk. Previously, she had accused him of not listening, and he had refused to change his behavior, since that would be admitting fault. But then she learned about and explained to him the differences in women's and men's habitual ways of aligning themselves in conversation. The next time she told him she wanted to talk, he began, as usual, by lying down and covering his eyes. When the familiar negative reaction bubbled up, she reassured herself that he really was listening. But then he sat up and looked at her. Thrilled, she asked why. He said, "You like me to look at you when you talk, so I'll try to do it." Once he saw their differences as cross-cultural rather than right and wrong, he independently altered his behavior.

Women who feel abandoned and deprived when their husbands won't listen to or report daily news may be happy to discover their husbands trying to adapt once they understand the place of small talk in women's relationships. But if their husbands don't adapt, the women may still be comforted that for men, this is not a failure of intimacy. Accepting the difference, the wives may look to their friends or family for that kind of talk. And husbands who can't provide it shouldn't feel their wives have made unreasonable demands. Some couples will still decide to divorce, but at least their decisions will be based on realistic expectations.

In these times of resurgent ethnic conflicts, the world desperately needs cross-cultural understanding. Like charity, successful cross-cultural communication should begin at home.

Questions for Analysis

1. Identify the distinctive differences between the communication styles of men and women, according to Deborah Tannen, and explain how these differences can lead to miscommunication and misunderstanding.

2. Based on your experience, explain whether you believe Dr. Tannen's analysis of these different communication styles is accurate. Provide specific examples to support your viewpoint.

3. Describe a situation in which you had a miscommunication with a person of the opposite sex. Analyze this situation based on what you read in the Tannen article.

4. Identify strategies that both men and women can use to help avoid the miscommunication that can result from these contrasting styles.

CHAPTER 7

Forming and Applying Concepts

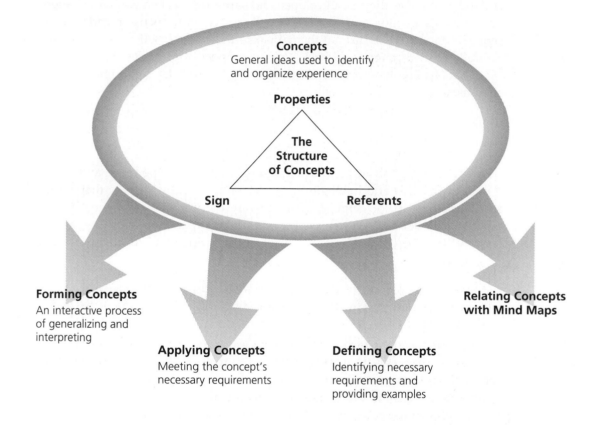

Concepts
General ideas used to identify and organize experience

Properties

The Structure of Concepts

Sign

Referents

Forming Concepts
An interactive process of generalizing and interpreting

Applying Concepts
Meeting the concept's necessary requirements

Defining Concepts
Identifying necessary requirements and providing examples

Relating Concepts with Mind Maps

We live in a world filled with concepts. A large number of the words you use to represent your experience express concepts you have formed. *Music video, person, education, computer, sport, situation comedy, elated,* and *thinking* are only a few examples of concepts. Your academic study involves learning new concepts as well, and in order to be successful in college and your career, you need to master the conceptualizing process. For example, when you read textbooks or listen to lectures and take notes, you are required to grasp the key concepts and follow them as they are developed and supported. When you write papers or homework assignments, you are usually expected to focus on certain concepts, develop a thesis around them, present the thesis (itself a concept!) with carefully argued points, and back it up with specific examples. Many course examinations involve applying key concepts you have learned to new sets of circumstances.

◎ What Are Concepts?

Concepts are general ideas you use to organize your experience and, in so doing, bring order and intelligibility to your life. In the same way that words are the vocabulary of language, concepts are the vocabulary of thought. As organizers of your experience, concepts work in conjunction with language to identify, describe, distinguish, and relate all the various aspects of your world.

> **concepts** *General ideas that we use to identify and organize our experience*

To become a sophisticated thinker, you must develop expertise in the conceptualizing process, improving your ability to *form, apply, define,* and *relate* concepts. This complex conceptualizing process is going on all the time in your mind, enabling you to think in a distinctly human way.

How do you use concepts to organize and make sense of experience? Think back to the first day of the semester. For most students, this is a time to evaluate their courses by trying to determine which concepts apply.

- Will this course be interesting? Useful? A lot of work?

- Is the teacher stimulating? Demanding? Entertaining?

- Are the students friendly? Intelligent? Conscientious?

Each of these words or phrases represents a concept you are attempting to apply so that you can understand what is occurring at the moment and also anticipate what the course will be like in the future. As the course progresses, you gather further information from your actual experiences in the class. This information may support your initial concepts, or it may conflict with these initial concepts. If the information you receive supports these concepts, you tend to maintain them ("Yes, I can see that this is going to be a difficult course"). But if the information you receive conflicts with these concepts, you tend to form new concepts to explain the situation ("No, I can see that I was wrong — this course isn't going to be as difficult as I thought at first"). A diagram of this process might look something like this:

Experience: Attending the first day of class

↓

   leads to

↓

Applying a concept to explain the situation: This course will be very difficult, and I might not do very well.

↓

   leads to

↓

Looking for information to support or conflict with my concept

↙   ↘

Supporting Information	*Conflicting Information*
The teacher is very demanding.	I find that I am able to keep up with the work.
	↓
There are lots of writing assignments.	leads to
	↓
The reading is challenging.	Forming a new concept to explain the situation: This course is difficult, but I will be able to handle the work and do well.
	↓
	leads to
	↓
	Action: I'm going to remain in the course, work to the best of my ability, and expect to do well.

VISUAL THINKING

Organizing Our World

● How does this illustration express the insight that we use concepts to organize our experience and bring intelligibility to our lives? Identify a concept you frequently use to make sense of your world. Why is this concept so powerful for you?

   To take another example, imagine that you are a physician and that one of your patients comes to you complaining of shortness of breath and occasional pain in his left arm. After he describes his symptoms, you would ask a number of questions, examine him, and perhaps administer some tests. Your ability to *identify* the underlying problem would depend on your knowledge of various human diseases. Each disease is identified and described by a different concept. Identifying these various diseases means that you can *distinguish* different concepts and that you know in what situations to apply a given concept correctly. In addition, when the patient asks, "What's wrong with me, doctor?" you are able to describe the concept (for example, heart disease) and explain how it is related to his symptoms. Fortunately, modern medicine has developed (and is continuing to develop) remarkably precise concepts to describe and explain the diseases that afflict us. In the patient's case, you may conclude that the problem is heart disease. Of course, there are different kinds of heart disease, represented by different concepts, and success in treating the patient will depend on figuring out exactly which type of heart disease is involved.

THINKING ACTIVITY 7.1

Forming New Concepts Through Experience

Identify an initial concept you had about an event in your life (starting a new job, attending college, etc.) that changed as a result of your experiences. After identifying your initial concept, describe the experiences that led you to change or modify the concept, and then explain the new concept you formed to explain the situation. Your response should include the following elements: *an initial concept, new information provided by additional experiences,* and *a new concept formed to explain the situation.*

Learning to master concepts will help you in every area of your life: academic, career, and personal. In college study, each academic discipline or subject is composed of many different concepts that are used to organize experience, give explanations, and solve problems. Here is a sampling of college-level concepts: *entropy, subtext, Gemeinschaft, cell, metaphysics, relativity, unconscious, transformational grammar, aesthetic, minor key, interface, health, quantum mechanics, schizophrenia.* To make sense of how disciplines function, you need to understand what the concepts of that discipline mean, how to apply them, and the way they relate to other concepts. You also need to learn the methods of investigation, patterns of thought, and forms of reasoning that various disciplines use to form larger conceptual theories and methods. We will be exploring these subjects in the next several chapters of the text.

Regardless of specific knowledge content, all careers require conceptual abilities, whether you are trying to apply a legal principle, develop a promotional theme, or devise a new computer program. Similarly, expertise in forming and applying concepts helps you make sense of your personal life, understand others, and make informed decisions. The Greek philosopher Aristotle once said that the intelligent person is a "master of concepts."

@ The Structure of Concepts

Concepts are general ideas you use to identify, distinguish, and relate the various aspects of your experience. Concepts allow you to organize your world into patterns that make sense to you. This is the process by which you discover and create meaning in your life.

In their role as organizers of experience, concepts act to group aspects of your experience based on their similarity to one another. Consider the thing that you usually write with: a pen. The concept *pen* represents a type of object that you use for writing. But look around the classroom at all the other instruments people are using to write with. You use the concept *pen* to identify these things as well, even though they may look very different from the one you are using.

Thus, the concept *pen* not only helps you make distinctions in your experience by indicating how pens differ from pencils, crayons, or magic markers, but it also helps you determine which items are similar enough to each other to be called *pens*. When you put items into a group with a single description — like "pen" — you are focusing on the *similarities* among the items:

- They use ink.
- They are used for writing.
- They are held with a hand.

Being able to see and name the similarities among certain things in your experience is the way you form concepts and is crucial for making sense of your world. If you were not able to do this, then everything in the world would be different, with its own individual name.

The process by which you group things based on their similarities is known as *classifying*. The process of classifying is one of the main ways that you order, organize, and make sense of your world. Because no two things or experiences are exactly alike, your ability to classify things into various groups is what enables you to recognize things in your experience. When you perceive a pen, you recognize it as a *kind of thing* you have seen before. Even though you may not have seen this particular pen, you recognize that it belongs to a group of things that you are familiar with.

The best way to understand the structure of concepts is to visualize them by means of a model. Examine the following figure:

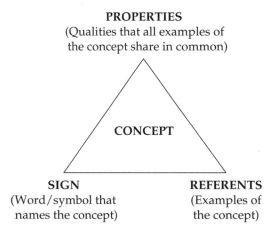

PROPERTIES
(Qualities that all examples of
the concept share in common)

CONCEPT

SIGN
(Word/symbol that
names the concept)

REFERENTS
(Examples of
the concept)

The *sign* is the word or symbol used to name or designate the concept; for example, the word *triangle* is a sign. The *referents* represent all the various examples of the concept; the three-sided figure we are using as our model is an example of the concept *triangle*. The *properties* of the concept are the features that all things named by the word or sign share in common; all examples of the concept *triangle* share the characteristics of being a polygon and having three sides. These are the properties that we refer to when we *define* concepts; thus, "a triangle is a three-sided polygon."

Let's take another example. Suppose you wanted to explore the structure of the concept *automobile*. The *sign* that names the concept is the word *automobile* or the symbol 🚗 . *Referents* of the concept include the 1954 MG "TF" currently residing in the garage as well as the Ford Explorer parked in front of the house. The *properties* that all things named by the sign *automobile* include are wheels, a chassis, an engine, and seats for passengers. The following figure is a conceptual model of the concept *automobile:*

PROPERTIES
Wheels, Chassis, Engine,
Seats for passengers

SIGN
"Automobile"

REFERENTS
1954 MG-TF
Ford Explorer

THINKING ACTIVITY 7.2

Diagramming the Structure of Concepts

Using the model we have developed, diagram the structure of the following concepts, as well as two concepts of your own choosing: *table, dance, successful, student, religion, music, friend,* _____, _____.

⊚ Forming Concepts

Throughout your life you are engaged in the process of forming — and applying — concepts to organize your experience, make sense of what is happening at the moment, and anticipate what may happen in the future. You form concepts by the interactive process of *generalizing* (focusing on the common properties shared by a group of things) and *interpreting* (finding examples of the concept). The common properties form the necessary requirements that must be met in order to apply the concept to your experience. If you examine the diagrams of concepts in the last section, you can see that the process of forming concepts involves moving back and forth between the *referents* (examples) of the concept and the *properties* (common features) shared by all examples of the concept. Let's explore further the way this interactive process of forming concepts operates.

Consider the following sample conversation between two people trying to form and clarify the concept *philosophy*:

A: What is your idea of what *philosophy* means?

B: Well, I think philosophy involves expressing important beliefs that you have — like discussing the meaning of life, assuming that there is a meaning.

A: Is explaining my belief about who's going to win the Super Bowl engaging in philosophy? After all, this is a belief that is very important to me — I've got a lot of money riding on the outcome!

B: I don't think so. A philosophical belief is usually a belief about something that is important to everyone — like what standards we should use to guide our moral choices.

A: What about the message that was in my fortune cookie last night: "Eat, drink, and be merry, for tomorrow we diet!"? This is certainly a belief that most people can relate to, especially during the holiday season! Is this philosophy?

B: I think that's what my grandmother used to call "foolosophy"! Philosophical beliefs are usually deeply felt views that we have given a great deal of thought to — not something plucked out of a cookie.

A: What about my belief in the Golden Rule: "Do unto others as you would have them do unto you"? After all, we all want to be treated well by others, and it's only fair — and reasonable — to conclude that we should treat other people the same way. Doesn't that have all of the qualities that you mentioned?

B: *Now* you've got it!

As we review this dialogue, we can see that *forming* the concept *philosophical belief* works hand in hand with *applying* the concept to different examples. When two or more things work together in this way, we say that they interact. In this case, there are two parts of this interactive process.

We form concepts by generalizing, by focusing on the similar features among different things. In the dialogue just given, the things from which generalizations are being made are kinds of beliefs — beliefs about the meaning of life or standards we use to guide our moral choices. By focusing on the similar features among these beliefs, the two people in the dialogue develop a list of properties philosophical beliefs share, including

- Beliefs that deal with important issues in life about which everyone is concerned
- Beliefs that reflect deeply felt views to which we have given a great deal of thought

These common properties act as the *requirements* an area must meet to be considered a philosophical belief.

We apply concepts by interpreting, by looking for different examples of the concept and seeing if they meet the requirements of the concept we are developing. In the conversation, one of the participants attempts to apply the concept *philosophical belief* to the following examples:

- A belief about the outcome of the Super Bowl
- A fortune cookie message: "Eat, drink, and be merry, for tomorrow we diet!"

Each of the proposed examples suggests the development of new requirements for the concept to help clarify how the concept can be applied. Applying a concept to different possible examples thus becomes the way we develop and gradually sharpen our idea of the concept. Even when a proposed example turns out *not* to be an example of the concept, our understanding of the concept is often clarified. For example, although the proposed example — a belief about the outcome of the Super Bowl — in the dialogue turns out not to be an example of the concept *philosophical belief,* examining it as a possible example helps clarify the concept and suggests other examples.

The process of developing concepts involves a constant back-and-forth movement between these two activities:

generalizing *Focusing on certain similar features among things to develop the requirements for the concept*

interpreting *Looking for different things to apply the concept to in order to determine if they "meet the requirements" of the concept we are developing*

As the back-and-forth movement progresses, we gradually develop a specific list of requirements that something must have to be considered an example of the concept and, at the same time, to give ourselves a clearer idea of how it is defined. We are also developing a collection of examples that embody the qualities of the concept and demonstrate situations in which the concept applies. This *interactive* process is illustrated in the following figure:

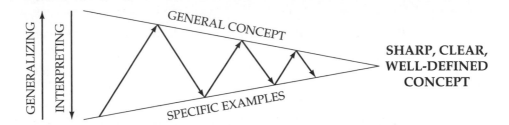

GENERALIZING
INTERPRETING

GENERAL CONCEPT

SPECIFIC EXAMPLES

SHARP, CLEAR, WELL-DEFINED CONCEPT

THINKING ACTIVITY 7.3

Forming New Concepts Through Generalizing and Interpreting

Select a type of music with which you are familiar (e.g., jazz) and write a dialogue similar to the one just examined. In the course of the dialogue, be sure to include

1. Examples from which you are generalizing (e.g., cool, big band)

2. General properties shared by various types of this music (e.g., jazz's audience spans many generations)

3. Examples to which you are trying to apply the developing concept (e.g., the music of Miles Davis or of Thelonius Monk)

Forming concepts involves performing both of these operations (generalizing and interpreting) together, because

- You cannot form a concept unless you know how it might apply. If you have absolutely no idea what *jazz* or *philosophy* might be examples of, then you cannot begin to form the concept, even in vague or general terms.

- You cannot gather up examples of the concept unless you know what they might be examples of. Until you begin to develop some idea of what the concepts *jazz* or *philosophy* might be (based on certain similarities among various things), you will not know where to look for examples of the concept (or how to evaluate them).

This interactive process is the way that you usually form all concepts, particularly the complicated ones. In school, much of your education is focused on carefully forming and exploring key concepts such as *democracy, dynamic equilibrium,* and *personality.* This book has also focused on certain key concepts, such as

- Thinking critically
- Solving problems
- Perceiving

- Believing
- Knowing
- Language

In each case, you have carefully explored these concepts through the interactive process of generalizing the properties/requirements of the concept and interpreting the concept by examining examples to which the concept applies.

◎ Applying Concepts

Making sense of our experience means finding the right concept to explain what is going on. To determine whether the concept we have selected fits the situation, we have to determine whether the requirements that form the concept are being met. For example, the original television series *Superman* used to begin with the words "Look — up in the sky! It's a bird! It's a plane! No! It's Superman!"

To figure out which concept applies to the situation (so that we can figure out what is going on), we have to

1. Be aware of the properties that form the boundaries of the concept
2. Determine whether the experience meets those requirements, for only if it does can we apply the concept to it

In the opening line from *Superman,* what are some of the requirements for using the concepts being identified?

- Bird:
- Plane:
- Superman:

If we have the requirements of the concept clearly in mind, we can proceed to figure out which of these requirements are met by the experience — whether it is a bird, a plane, or the "man of steel" himself. This is the way we apply concepts, which is one of the most important ways we figure out what is going on in our experience.

In determining exactly what the requirements of the concept are, we can ask ourselves, *"Would something still be an example of this concept if it did not meet this requirement?"* If the answer to this question is *no* — that is, something would not be an example of this concept if it did not meet this requirement — then we can say the requirement is a necessary part of the concept.

Consider the concept *dog*. Which of the following descriptions are requirements of the concept that must be met to say that something is an example of the concept *dog?*

1. Is an animal

2. Normally has four legs and a tail

3. Bites the mail carrier

It is clear that descriptions 1 and 2 are requirements that must be met to apply the concept *dog* because if we apply our test question — "Would something still be an example of this concept if it did not meet this requirement?" — we can say that something would not be an example of the concept *dog* if it did not fit the first two descriptions: if it were not an animal and did not normally have four legs and a tail.

This does not seem to be the case, however, with description 3. If we ask ourselves the same test question, we can see that something might still be an example of the concept *dog* even if it did not bite the mail carrier. This is because even though some dogs do in fact bite, this is not a requirement for being a dog.

Of course, there may be other things that meet these requirements but are not dogs. For example, a cat is an animal (description 1) that normally has four legs and a tail (description 2). What this means is that the requirements of a concept tell us only what something *must* have to be an example of the concept. As a result, we often have to identify additional requirements that will define the concept more sharply. This point is clearly illustrated as children form concepts. Not identifying a sufficient number of the concept's requirements leads to such misconceptions as "All four-legged animals are doggies" or "All yellow-colored metal is gold."

This is why it is so important for us to have a very clear idea of the greatest possible number of specific requirements of each concept. These requirements determine when the concept can be applied and indicate those things that qualify as examples of it. When we are able to identify *all* of the requirements of the concept, we say these requirements are both *necessary* and *sufficient* for applying the concept.

Although dealing with concepts like *dog* and *cat* may seem straightforward, the situation quickly becomes more confusing when you start analyzing the more complex concepts that you encounter in your academic study. For example, consider the concepts of *masculinity* and *femininity*, two of the more emotionally charged and politically contentious concepts in our culture. There are many different perspectives on what these concepts mean, what they should mean, or whether we should be using them at all. Identify what you consider to be the essential properties (specific requirements that must be met to apply the concept) for each of these concepts, as well as examples of people or behavior that illustrate these properties. For example, you might identify "physical strength" as a property of the concept *masculinity* and identify Arnold Schwarzenegger as a person who illustrates this quality. Or you might identify "intuition" as a property of the concept *femininity* and illustrate this with the behavior of "being able to predict what someone is going to do or say before it occurs." Then compare your responses with those of the other students in the class. What are the similarities and differences in your concepts? What factors might account for these similarities and differences?

THINKING PASSAGES

Femininity and Masculinity

The following passages by Susan Brownmiller and Patricia Leigh Brown deal with the concepts of *masculinity* and *femininity*. After reading the passages, analyze the authors' concepts of *masculinity* and *femininity* by answering the questions that follow. How do their perspectives on these concepts compare and contrast with your concepts and those of the other members of the class?

FROM *FEMININITY*
by Susan Brownmiller

It is fashionable in some quarters to describe the feminine and masculine principles as polar ends of the human continuum, and to sagely profess that both polarities exist in all people. Sun and moon, yin and yang, soft and hard, active and passive, etcetera, may indeed be opposites, but a linear

Source: Excerpt from Susan Brownmiller, *Femininity,* Simon & Schuster, January 1984.

VISUAL THINKING

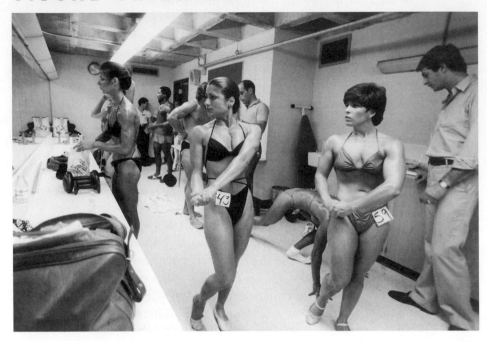

"Pose!"

- What's your reaction to the women in this photograph? Do you think that the concepts of *masculinity* and *femininity* are outdated relics of earlier cultures? Or do you believe that these concepts reflect basic qualities of the human species that are still relevant today?

continuum does not illuminate the problem. What, then, is the basic distinction? The masculine principle is better understood as a driving ethos of superiority designed to inspire straightforward, confident success, while the feminine principle is composed of vulnerability, the need for protection, the formalities of compliance and the avoidance of conflict — in short, an appeal of dependence and good will that gives the masculine principle its romantic validity and admiring applause. Femininity pleases men because it makes them appear more masculine by contrast; and, in truth, conferring an extra portion of unearned gender distinction on men, and unchallenged space in which to breathe freely and feel stronger, wiser, more competent, is femininity's special gift. One could say that masculinity is often an effort to please women, but masculinity is known to please by displays of mastery and competence while femininity pleases by suggesting that these concerns, except in small matters, are beyond its intent. Whimsy, unpredictability and patterns of thinking and behavior that are dominated by emotion, such as tearful expressions of sentiment and fear, are thought to be feminine precisely because they lie outside the established route to success.

THE RETURN OF MANLY MEN
By Patricia Leigh Brown

They are the knights in shining fire helmets. They are the welders, policemen and businessmen with can-do attitudes who are unafraid to tackle armed hijackers — even if it means bringing down an airplane.

The operative word is men. Brawny, heroic, manly men.

After a few iffy decades in which manliness was not the most highly prized cultural attribute, men — stoic, muscle-bound and exuding competence from every pore — are back. Since Sept. 11, the male hero has been a predominant cultural image, presenting a beefy front of strength to a nation seeking steadiness and emotional grounding. They are the new John Waynes. They are, as the former Reagan speechwriter Peggy Noonan wrote in the *Wall Street Journal* recently, "men who charge up the stairs in a hundred pounds of gear and tell everyone else where to go to be safe."

Of course, war has traditionally brought out America's inner Schwarzenegger. But since the September attacks, the firefighter coated with ash and soot has provided a striking contrast to the now prehistoric-seeming male archetype of such a short time ago: the casually dressed dot-commer in khakis and a BMW.

"Before Sept. 11, ruggedness was an affectation you put on like an outfit," said David Granger, the editor in chief of *Esquire* magazine. "Now there's a selflessness being attributed to rugged men. After a decade of prosperity that made us soft, metaphorically and physically, there's a longing for manliness. People want to regain what we had in World War II. They want to believe in big, strapping American boys."

To be sure, there is a small measure of preening in the resurrected male hero. Men who have donned the same uniform every day with little fanfare — from local politicians in Brooks Brothers suits to cops in catalog-issue blues — are aware enough of the camera and their own testosterone to

Source: Patricia Leigh Brown, "The Return of Manly Men," *The New York Times,* October 28, 2001. Copyright © 2001 by The New York Times Co. Reprinted by permission.

fervently seize masculinity's newfound moment. From the Gang of Five (Bush, Gephardt, Daschle, Lott and Hastert) making decisions over breakfast on Capitol Hill, to the Special Ops forces blazing forth in Afghanistan, images of masculinity in full flex have played to maximum effect on television screens for weeks. So much so that, in the manner of football trading cards, the physical characteristics of the heroes aboard United Flight 93 (Todd Beamer, 6 feet, 200 pounds) have become an intrinsic part of the media retelling of that awful ordeal.

And of course, some observers like Carol Gilligan, the Graham professor of gender studies at Harvard and a visiting professor at the New York University School of Law, have noted that men's rising star has all but eclipsed that of the many heroic women who have risen to the occasion, be they firefighters or police officers.

Still, to cultural defenders of manliness who have deplored the last decade's gender-neutral sex roles, nirvana has arrived. "I can't help noticing how robustly, dreamily masculine the faces of the firefighters are," said Camille Paglia, the conservative social critic. "These are working-class men, stoical, patriotic. They're not on Prozac or questioning their gender."

In contrast to past eras of touchy-feeliness (Alan Alda) and the vaguely feminized, rakish man-child of the 1990's (Leonardo DiCaprio), the notion of physical prowess in the service of patriotic duty is firmly back on the pedestal.

"A few years ago, a lot of fashionable academics wrote about 'the end of the male project,' the idea that, due to technological advances, men no longer needed physical strength," said David Blankenhorn, president of the Institute for American Values, a New York organization that researches family issues. "Doesn't that look different now," he asked, "when 'the project' at hand is wrestling hijackers, pulling people out of buildings and hunting down terrorists in Afghanistan caves?"

As the country comes to grips with the possibility of deadly spores lurking in the mailbox and other fears, it may be that traditional images of manliness serve as emotional anchors. "We're all very afraid," said the writer Susan Faludi, whose most recent book, "Stiffed: The Betrayal of the American Man," was an examination of the country's masculinity crisis. "There's a great desire to feel protected, to feel Daddy is going to take care of us. The image of firefighters and rescuers is a healing and satisfying vision of masculinity."

Cultural notions of manliness have, of course, worn very different faces over the last several weeks. The dark side has been on abundant display as information about the lives of the hijackers, as well as Osama bin Laden himself, come to light, revealing a society in which manhood is equated with violent conquest and women have been ruthlessly prevented from participating in almost every aspect of life. "The common thread in violent societies is the polarization of sex roles," said the feminist pioneer Gloria Steinem.

Part of understanding terrorism, in fact, often involves getting to the root of what is masculine. In her 1990 book, "The Demon Lover: The Roots of Terrorism," which is being rushed back into print, the feminist author Robin Morgan examines the cyclical breeding of masculine aggression in some cultures. "The intersection of glamorized, eroticized violence with what is considered manhood forms the central knot of terrorism," she said.

But in this country, the most profound and hopeful changes to have emerged since Sept. 11 may include a new definition of manliness forged from the depths of sorrow and loss. "The good news," Ms. Morgan said, "is that the perception of the quote-unquote hero has moved from athletes and movie stars to people, largely men, who have an element of tenderness and self-sacrifice in them."

Or as the veteran television producer Norman Lear noted, the tough-tender hero that normally occupies the fictional world of television drama has been, quite suddenly, made real. "Now we're looking at real people, real heroes," he said. "That's an astonishingly good thing."

Questions for Analysis

1. According to Susan Brownmiller, what are the properties of the concept of *femininity?* What are some examples of this concept?

2. Explain whether you agree with the conceptual properties Brownmiller has identified. What properties of the concept of *femininity* do you think should be included that she has not addressed? Give at least one example of each property you identify.

3. According to Patricia Leigh Brown, what are the properties of the concept of *masculinity?* What are some examples of this concept?

4. Explain whether you agree with the conceptual properties she has identified. What properties of the concept of *masculinity* do you think should be included that Brown has not addressed? For each property you identify, give at least one example.

5. Some people feel that the concepts of *masculinity* and *femininity* were formed by earlier cultures, are outdated in our current culture, and should be revised. Other people believe that these concepts reflect basic qualities of the human species, just like the sexual differences in other species, and should

not be excessively tampered with. Explain where you stand on this issue, and describe the reasons that support your position.

Using Concepts to Classify

When you apply a concept to an object, idea, or experience, you are *classifying* the object, idea, or experience by placing it into the group of things defined by the properties/requirements of the concept. The individual objects, ideas, or experiences belong to no particular class until you classify them. In fact, the same things can often be classified in many different ways. For example, if someone handed you a tomato and asked, "Which class does this tomato belong in: fruit or vegetable?" how would you respond? The fact is a tomato can be classified as *both* a fruit and a vegetable, depending on your purposes.

Let us consider another example. Imagine that you are walking on undeveloped land with some other people when you come across an area of soggy ground with long grass and rotting trees. One person in your group surveys the parcel and announces: "That's a smelly marsh. All it does is breed mosquitoes. It ought to be covered with landfill and built on so that we can use it productively." Another member of your group disagrees with the classification "smelly marsh," stating: "This is a wetland of great ecological value. There are many plants and animals that need this area and other areas like it to survive. Wetland areas also help prevent the rivers from flooding by absorbing excess water during heavy rains." Which person is right? Should the wet area be classified as a "smelly marsh" or a "valuable wetland"? Actually, the wet area can be classified both ways. The classification that you select depends on your needs and your interests. Someone active in construction and land development may tend to view the parcel through perceptual lenses that reflect her interests and experience and classify it accordingly. Someone involved in preserving natural resources will tend to view the same parcel through different lenses and place it in a different category. The diagram on page 289 illustrates how a tree might be "seen" from a variety of perspectives, depending on the interest and experience of those involved.

These examples illustrate that the way you classify reflects and influences the way you see the world, the way you think about the world, and the way you behave in the world. This is true for virtually all the classifications you make. Consider the racehorse Secretariat, who won the Triple Crown in 1973 and was one of the most famous racehorses that ever lived. Which classification should Secretariat be placed into?

- A magnificent thoroughbred
- A substantial investment

VISUAL THINKING

THE TREE, as seen by...

the planner...   the parks department...   the publisher...

400 LUXURY HOMES TO BE ERECTED ON THIS SITE

the highways department...   the developer...   the landscape architect.

Hellman

"A Tree Is Just a Tree, Is Just a Tree. . . ."

● Create a caption for this illustration. Then draw a symbolic picture of your favorite tree.

- An animal ill equipped for farming
- A descendant of Bold Ruler
- A candidate for the glue factory

You classify many of the things in your experience differently than others do because of your individual needs, interests, and values. For instance, smoking marijuana might be classified by some as "use of a dangerous drug" and by others as a "harmless good time." Some view large cars as "gas guzzlers"; others see the same cars as "safer, more comfortable vehicles." Some people categorize the latest music as "meaningless noise" while others think of it as "creative expression." The way you classify aspects of your experience reflects the kind of individual you are and the way you think and feel about the world.

You also place people into various classifications. The specific classifications you select depend on who you are and how you see the world. Similarly, each of us is placed into a variety of classifications by different people. For example, here are some of the classifications into which certain people placed me:

Classification	People Who Classify Me
First-born son	My parents
Taxpayer	Internal Revenue Service
Tickler	My son/daughter
Bagel with cream cheese	Restaurant where I pick up my breakfast

List some of the different ways that you can be classified, and identify the people who would classify you that way.

Finally, besides classifying the same thing or event in a variety of different ways, you can classify most *collections* of things in various ways. For example, consider the different ways the members of your class can be classified. You could group them according to their majors, their ages, their food preferences, and so on. The specific categories you would use would depend on the purposes of your classification. If you were trying to organize career counseling, then classifying according to majors makes sense. If you were trying to plan the menu for a class party, then food preferences would be the natural category for classification.

Not only do you continually classify things and people into various groups based on the common properties you choose to focus on, you also classify ideas, feelings, actions, and experiences. Explain, for instance, why the killing of another person might be classified in different ways, depending on the circumstances.

Classification	Circumstance	Example
1. Manslaughter	Killing someone accidentally	Driving while intoxicated
2. Self-defense		
3. Premeditation		
4. Mercy killing		
5. Diminished capacity		

Each of these classifications represents a separate legal concept, with its own properties and referents (examples). Of course, even when you understand clearly what the concept means, the complexity of the circumstances often makes it difficult to determine which concept applies. For example, in Chapter 2,

"Thinking Critically," you considered a court case that raised complex and disturbing issues. In circumstances like these, trying to identify the appropriate concepts and then to determine which of the further concepts, "guilty" or "innocent," also applies, is a challenging process. This is true of many of life's complex situations: You must work hard at identifying the appropriate concepts to apply to the situations you are trying to make sense of and then be prepared to change or modify these concepts based on new information or better insight.

Defining Concepts

When you define a concept, you usually identify the necessary properties/requirements that determine when the concept can be applied. In fact, the word *definition* is derived from the Latin word meaning "boundary" because that is exactly what a definition does: It gives the boundaries of the territory in your experience that can be described by the concept. For example, a definition of the concept *horse* might include the following requirements:

- Large, strong animal
- Four legs with solid hoofs
- Flowing mane and tail
- Domesticated long ago for drawing or carrying loads, carrying riders, and so on

By understanding the requirements of the concept *horse*, you understand what conditions must be met in order for something to qualify as an example of the concept. This lets you know in what situations you can apply the concept: to the animals running around the racetrack, the animals pulling wagons and carriages, the animals being ridden on the range, and so on. In addition, understanding the requirements lets you know to which things the concept can be applied. No matter how much a zebra looks like a horse, you won't apply the concept *horse* to it if you really understand the definition of the concept involved.

Definitions also often make strategic use of *examples* of the concept being defined. Consider the following definition by Ambrose Bierce:

An edible: Good to eat and wholesome to digest, as a worm to a toad, a toad to a snake, a snake to a pig, a pig to a man, and a man to a worm.

Contrast this definition with the one illustrated in the following passage from Charles Dickens's *Hard Times:*

"Bitzer," said Thomas Gradgrind. "Your definition of a horse." "Quadruped. Graminivorous. Forty teeth, namely twenty-four grinders, four eye teeth, and twelve incisive. Sheds coat in the spring; in marshy countries shed hoofs, too. Hoofs hard, but requiring to be shod with iron. Age known by marks in mouth." That (and much more) Bitzer. "Now girl number twenty," said Mr. Gradgrind, "you know what a horse is."

Although Bitzer has certainly done an admirable job of listing some of the necessary properties/requirements of the concept *horse*, it is unlikely that "girl number twenty" has any better idea of what a horse is than she had before because the definition relies exclusively on a technical listing of the properties characterizing the concept *horse* without giving any examples that might illustrate the concept more completely. Definitions that rely exclusively on a technical description of the concept's properties are often not very helpful unless you already know what the concept means. A more concrete way of communicating the concept *horse* would be to point out various animals that qualify as horses and other animals that do not. You could also explain why they do not (for example, "That can't be a horse because it has two humps and its legs are too long and skinny").

Although examples do not take the place of a clearly understood definition, they are often useful in clarifying, supplementing, and expanding such a definition. If someone asked you, "What is a horse?" and you replied by giving examples of different kinds of horses (thoroughbred racing horses, plow horses for farming, quarter horses for cowboys, hunter horses for fox hunting, circus horses), you certainly would be communicating a good portion of the meaning of *horse*. Giving examples of a concept complements and clarifies the necessary requirements for the correct use of that concept. For example, provide a dictionary definition for each of the following concepts, and describe ways you could supplement and expand each definition:

Example: Smile

a. Definition: a facial expression characterized by an upward curving of the corners of the mouth and indicating pleasure, amusement, or derision.

b. Ways to expand the definition: smiling at someone or drawing a picture of a smiling face.

- ambivalent
- intelligent
- art
- thinking
- work
- create

The process of providing definitions of concepts is thus the same process you use to develop concepts. Of course, this process is often difficult and complex,

Defining a Concept

Giving an effective definition of a concept means both

- Identifying the general qualities of the concept, which determine when it can be correctly applied

- Using appropriate examples to demonstrate actual applications of the concept — that is, examples that embody the general qualities of the concept

and people don't always agree on how concepts should be defined. For example, consider the concepts *masculinity* and *femininity* that you explored earlier through the passages by Susan Brownmiller and Patricia Leigh Brown. Notice how, although areas of overlap exist between both authors' definitions, there are also significant differences in the defining properties and examples that they identify.

THINKING ACTIVITY 7.4

Analyzing the Concept of Responsibility

Review the ideas we have explored in this chapter by analyzing the concept *responsibility*. "Responsibility" is a complex idea that has an entire network of meaning. The word comes from the Latin word *respondere,* which means "to pledge or promise."

Generalizing

1. Describe two important responsibilities you have in your life, and identify the qualities they embody that lead you to think of them as "responsibilities."

2. Describe a person in your life whom you think is responsible, and then describe a person in your life whom you think is irresponsible. In reflecting on these individuals, identify the qualities they embody that lead you to think of them as "responsible" and "irresponsible."

Interpreting

3. Consider the following situations. In each case, describe what you consider to be examples of responsible behavior and irresponsible behavior. Be sure to explain the reasons for your answers.

a. You are a member of a group of three students who are assigned the task of writing a report on a certain topic. Your life is very hectic and in addition, you find the topic dull. What is your response? Why?

b. You are employed at a job in which you observe your supervisor and other employees engaged in activities that break the company rules. You are afraid that if you "blow the whistle," you might lose your job. What is your response? Why?

Defining

4. Using these activities of generalizing and interpreting as a foundation, define the concepts *responsible* and *irresponsible* by listing the qualities that make up the boundaries of each concept and identifying the key examples that embody and illustrate the qualities of the concept.

THINKING ACTIVITY 7.5

The Concepts of *Information* and *Ownership*

The Internet allows information to be easily and cheaply manipulated, duplicated, and shared. In this new environment, what happens to the concept of "ownership" of information, music, text, or other online material? What are the ethics of using such material for personal enjoyment or enrichment? For additional readings about music file-sharing, online plagiarism, and related issues, visit the companion web site.

THINKING PASSAGE

Identify Yourself: Who's American?

To be "an American" is a complex, diverse concept that has had a variety of meanings at different points in America's history. Unlike most countries, where the majority populations tend to be more homogeneous and national identity is generally built around shared ancestry or common ethnic heritage, America is a country that has been built on diversity of every sort. Who's American? The following article by Gregory Rodriguez explores this complex concept in order to provide us with a coherent, intelligible answer.

IDENTIFY YOURSELF: WHO'S AMERICAN?
By Gregory Rodriguez

American national identity is not based on shared ancestry or common ethnic heritage. Though it has become a dirty word in the past few decades,
assimilation — in which people of different backgrounds come to consider
themselves part of a larger national family — has long been the basis of citizenship. Because America is a nation of immigrants, its history was a constant struggle by outsiders seeking to become insiders. Yet America's very
diversity always made it particularly uncomfortable with the idea of the
"other."

Now, the terrorist attacks in New York and Washington are making
Americans more wary of outsiders than they have been in decades — and
are having profound implications for the debate over what it means to be
American.

Assimilation was long viewed as a process of subtraction — newcomers
displayed their loyalty by discarding the language and customs of their
native lands. Immigrants were criticized for congregating and finding
mutual support.

Not until the 1960's was it permissible for immigrants to adhere to their
cultural heritages. This new understanding tested and broadened the
nation's collective notions of what it meant to be an American. The definition of citizenship shifted from the belief in a common culture to following
shared ideals. Since the 1970's, multiculturalism helped nurture an unprecedented level of public tolerance of ethnic and racial differences and new
respect for hyphenated identities.

In some quarters, a rigid form of multiculturalism also arose that challenged the need for immigrants and other minorities to identify with America at all. By the end of the 20th century, some scholars speculated that being
American simply meant participation in the search for wealth and stability.

Now, however, after the attacks, not only is the drive for unity bound to
tilt the nation's ethnic balance back in favor of the American side of the
hyphen, it could permanently undermine the more extreme forms of multiculturalism. In the worst-case scenario, it could also dampen the nation's
recent appreciation of diversity.

Source: Gregory Rodriguez, "Aftermath: Melting Pot; Identify Yourself: Who's American?" *The
New York Times*, September 23, 2001. Copyright © 2001 by The New York Times Co. Reprinted by
permission.

VISUAL THINKING

Who Is an American?

How would you define an American? Does examining this photo help you define the concept of *American?* Why or why not? Is America different from other countries in the way it defines its citizens?

"Historically, war and the crises associated with it have been instrumental in terms of nation-building," said Gary Gerstle, a historian at the University of Maryland. Before the Civil War, for example, Americans spoke of the United States in the plural ("the United States are"), because each state was considered a discrete unit. Only after the crucible of the war did the public begin to refer to the nation in the singular ("the United States is").

The United States is currently experiencing a greater sense of national unity across racial and ethnic lines than it has since the early 1960's. External threats to any country tend to crystallize the collective identity and encourage citizens to distinguish themselves from the enemy. Yet while wars and other national crises have served as catalysts to unite a diverse population, they have also incited some of the worst incidents of repression against minorities the public associated with the enemy.

Since the Sept. 11 attacks, there has been a notable number of hate crimes against Arab-Americans and Muslims. Frightened by a wave of violence, American Sikhs are explaining to the public that despite their turbans and beards, they are not Muslims. President Bush visited a Washington mosque on Monday, in an attempt to discourage retaliation against Arab-Americans. He showed that, at the very least, wartime repression this time around would not be government-scanctioned. But Muslim leaders are already discussing plans for Muslim women to change the way they dress, perhaps exchanging head scarves for hats and turtlenecks. On Monday, a woman trekked to the New York Health Department headquarters trying to change her son's surname from "Mohammed" to "Smith."

The catastrophe in New York and Washington and the talk of war is already hastening the assimilation — in both negative and positive ways — of immigrants into American society. Many of the newest Americans, some of whom may have considered themselves marginalized just weeks ago, are going to great lengths to show solidarity with their adopted nation.

Pakistani taxi drivers in New York are displaying the Stars and Stripes in their cabs. Last Saturday in Los Angeles, two Spanish-language radio stations hosted thousands of Spanish-speaking immigrants at one of the city's largest solidarity rallies. The widespread sense of a common fate is giving many immigrants a sense of belonging to a national community.

But the hardening of the national identity also induces subtle shifts in the country's racial and ethnic hierarchy. On Tuesday, at an alternative school in Washington, eight black teenagers who were not strangers to the criminal justice system expressed their anger and fear of Arab-Americans, and for the first time spoke for the other side of the racial profiling debate. In Southern California, a dark-complected Moroccan immigrant comforts himself with the fact that many people assume he is Mexican, a group that felt itself under attack only a few years ago.

"Pearl Harbor made Chinese into Americans for the first time since the 1880's," said Philip Kasinitz, a sociologist at the Graduate Center of the City University of New York. "But it excluded the Japanese-Americans regardless of how long they had been in America." In some crude way, the reforging of American identity under fire produces winners and losers.

Perhaps in their desire to establish their credentials as insiders and to distinguish themselves from the enemy, minority Americans are sometimes the most zealous in excluding whoever has been deemed the new outsiders. The Arizona man arrested last week for allegedly murdering a Sikh gas station operator has a Spanish surname. He asserted to police as he was arrested, "I'm a damn American all the way." During World War I, Poles and other Eastern Europeans were particularly active in their repression of German-Americans. In World War II, there were incidents of Filipinos attacking Japanese-Americans.

The most egregious example of an American minority being targeted because of its association with the foreign enemy was the internment of 110,000 Japanese-Americans (two-thirds of whom were U.S. citizens) during World War II.

Earlier, the outbreak of World War I intensified Americans' already strong suspicions of foreigners, which, in turn, gave rise to a campaign to rid the country of foreign influences.

Because they shared the same ethnicity as the enemy and because many Teutonic organizations lobbied heavily to keep America neutral in the early years of the war, German-Americans suffered one of the most dramatic reversals of fortunes of any group in American history. The German language, its culture, customs, and even food came under attack. In 1918, nearly half the states had restricted or eliminated German-language instruction; several stripped citizens of the freedom of speaking German in public.

But while national solidarity during World War I was characterized by coercion, World War II engendered what one scholar has called "patriotic assimilation." "By the end of the war," writes Eric Foner, a historian at Columbia University, "the new immigrant groups had been fully accepted as ethnic Americans, rather than members of distinct and inferior races."

On the level of everyday life, the war was a great common experience, particularly for the 12 million men and women who served in the armed forces, but also for much of the rest of the population, which shared the losses, privations and ultimately, the joys of victory. Wartime "fox hole" movies didn't seek to deny ethnic distinctions but affirmed the American-ness of the Irish, Jewish, Polish, and Okie soldiers who were "all in it together."

African-Americans, of course, have fought in every war in American history, and were still not recognized as full Americans when they returned. But it was at the end of World War II that blacks first saw the beginnings of integration, a process that accelerated in the postwar years. Still, just as the Japanese-American units in World War II became the most decorated in American military history, many black soldiers have sought to express and prove their "Americanness" through valor. "It is a refusal to be left out of the definition of whatever it is that comprises American identity," said Debra Dickerson, a writer and 12-year Air Force veteran.

But wartime can also reinvigorate the public's appreciation for the country's most cherished values. "It compels an articulation of American ideals, those things that America stands for," said Professor Gerstle. Just as the need for tightened security will at times conflict with the nation's belief in broad civil liberties, the quest for unity is bound to clash with another American ideal: tolerance.

Questions for Analysis

1. Before reading this article, what was your answer to the question "Who's American?" How did you develop this concept of being an American? If you or your parents were born in another country, how would you define the national identity of that country? (For example, what does it mean to be Dominican or Chinese?)

2. How did the events of September 11, 2001, affect the debate over what it means to be American?

3. How would you relate the concept of *multiculturalism* to that of being an American? Do you think these concepts are in potential conflict with each other? Why or why not?

4. How have wars traditionally influenced the general perception of being an American?

5. How can the concept of a national identity both unite and divide people?

6. After reflecting on these issues via this article, these questions, and class discussions, has your concept of what it means to be an American changed? If so, in what ways?

Relating Concepts with Mind Maps

A *mind map* is is a visual presentation of the ways in which concepts can be related to one another. For example, each chapter in this book opens with a diagram — what we will call a "mind map" or "cognitive map" — that visually summarizes the chapter's basic concepts as well as the way in which these concepts are related to one another. These maps are a reference guide that reveals basic themes and chapter organization. Because they clearly articulate various patterns of thought, mind maps are effective tools for helping us understand complex bodies of information. For examples of mind-mapping strategies to help you with your study skills and decision-making, visit the companion web site.

Analogously, a mapping approach offers some clear advantages in organizing the information you receive from oral communication. For instance, when you as a student take notes of what a teacher is saying, it's difficult to write down whole sentences and quotations from the lecture or class discussion. Taking notes by mapping enables you to identify the key ideas and articulate the various relationships among them. Similarly, mapping is also an effective aid in preparing for oral presentations because by organizing the information you want to present in this way, you have all the key ideas and their relationships in a single whole.

Along with reading, listening, and speaking, mapping is also useful for writing. First, the organization grows naturally, reflecting the way your mind naturally makes associations and organizes information. Second, the organization can be easily revised on the basis of new information and your developing understanding of how this information should be organized. Third, you can express a range of relationships among the various ideas, and each idea can remain an active part of the overall pattern, suggesting new possible relationships. Fourth, you do not have to decide initially on a beginning, sub-points, sub-subpoints, and so on; you can do this after your pattern is complete, saving time and avoiding frustration.

The companion web site for this text includes an extensive section on mind mapping that includes examples, activities, and links to related web sites. Mind mapping is a flexible and effective tool that can be used in nearly every part of the learning and thinking process.

THINKING ACTIVITY 7.6

Creating and Applying Mind Maps

Suppose someone handed you a pencil and a piece of paper with the request "Please draw me a detailed map that shows how to get to where you live from where we are now." Draw such a map on a separate sheet of paper.

Maps, like the one you just drew, are really groups of symbols organized in certain relationships. In creating your visual map, you tried both to represent and to organize various aspects of your experience into a pattern that made sense to you and to others. As you constructed your map, you probably traveled the route home "in your mind," trying to recall the correct turns, street names, buildings, and so on. You then symbolized these experiences and organized the symbols into a meaningful pattern — your map.

You can see that the activity of making maps draws on two skills needed for making sense of your world:

- Representing your experience with symbols
- Organizing and relating these symbols into various patterns to gain an increased understanding of your experience

Creating maps is thus a way to represent and organize experience so that you can make sense of it, and it is a strategy you can apply to many different areas of your world. For example, you can create maps of your mind — "mind maps" that express the patterns of your thinking processes.

Final Thoughts

In the same way that words are the vocabulary of language, concepts are the vocabulary of thought. Concepts are general ideas that we use to bring order and intelligibility to our experience. As organizers of our experience, concepts work in conjunction with language to identify, describe, distinguish, and relate all the various aspects of our world. They give us the means to understand our world and make informed decisions, to think critically and act intelligently.

To become a sophisticated thinker, you must develop expertise in the conceptualizing process, improving your ability to

- *Form* concepts through the interactive process of generalizing and interpreting
- *Apply* concepts by matching their necessary requirements to potential examples
- *Relate* concepts to each other in various patterns

This complex conceptualizing process is going on all the time in our minds, enabling us to think in a distinctly human way.

By understanding the conceptualizing process, you can more fully appreciate the integral relationship between language and thought that you have been exploring in these last two chapters, the way in which these two processes work as one to create meaning and understanding. In the same way that words are combined according to the rules of language to produce an infinite variety of linguistic expression, so concepts are related according to the patterns of thought to create the infinite dimensions of thinking.

The remaining chapters of this text will focus on the rules and patterns of thought that determine the way concepts are combined and organized in complex relationships to produce the highest, most sophisticated levels of human thinking.

THINKING PASSAGE

What Is Religion?

There are few concepts more complex and emotionally charged than the concept of *religion*. The following passage, "What Is Religion?" is taken from the book *Ways of Being Religious,* and it presents a provocative introduction to the concepts of *religion* and *religious experience.* After reading the selection, answer the questions that follow.

WHAT IS RELIGION?
By Frederick J. Streng

An African proverb, from the Ganda tribe in central Uganda, states, "He who never visits thinks his mother is the only cook." As with most proverbs, its meaning is larger than the explicit subjects referred to — in this case food and visiting. It suggests that a person is much the poorer for not having had exposure to and acquaintance with the ways of other people.

All of us have had some acquaintance with religious people, just as we have tasted our mother's food. But do we really understand very well what it means to be religious? The "Father of the Scientific Study of Religion," Max Mueller, once said: "He who knows one religion understands none." That is perhaps too extreme a statement as it stands, and yet it says about the study of religion what the African proverb says about the knowledge of life in general — that we sacrifice much if we confine ourselves to the familiar.

If a visit is to be fruitful, the "traveler" must do more than just move from place to place. He must respond to what he sees. But what is it that shapes the way we respond to new experiences? Our perception of things is often colored by our previous attitudes toward them. In this case, what do you, the reader, expect from an exposure to various expressions of religion? What sorts of things do you expect to see? How do you think you will respond to them? If you were asked to define, illustrate, or to characterize religious behavior, how would you do so? The answers to these questions, of course,

Source: Ways of Being Religious: Readings for a New Approach to Religion, by Frederick J. Streng. © 1973. Reprinted by permission of Prentice-Hall, Inc., Upper Saddle River, NJ.

VISUAL THINKING

What Is Religion?

- How would you define *religion?* What are some of the religious elements — objects and rituals — in this photo that are common to your religion? What are some different elements? Do you think that there are some things common to all religions? Why or why not?

reflect your preconceptions. To become conscious of your preconceptions, ask yourself the following four questions:

Does your definition* reduce *religion to what you happen to be acquainted with by accident of birth and socialization? Perhaps that goes without saying. It may be true of anyone's "off-the cuff" definition of religion. However, we ask this question to encourage you to consider whether your definition has sufficient *scope.* Is it broad enough to include the religious activities of human beings throughout the world? In surveying university students we have commonly gotten responses to the question, "What is religion?" as follows: "Being Christian, I would define it [religion] as personal relationship with Christ." "Religion [is]: God, Christ, and Holy Ghost and their meaning to each individual." Other students think of worship rather than belief. In this vein, one edition of Webster's dictionary, in the first of its definitions, describes religion as "the service and adoration of God or a god as expressed in forms of worship." If we were to accept any of the above definitions, many people in the world would be excluded — people who regard some of their most important activities as religious, but who do not focus upon a deity. That is to say, not all religions are theistic. It remains to be seen, of course, whether and to what extent this is true. But let us all be warned of taking our habits or our dictionary as the sole resource for defining religion. In some areas, the main lines of significant understanding are already well established. Therefore we have no serious quarrel with Webster's definition of food as "nutritive material taken into an organism for growth, work, or repair and for maintaining the vital processes." But in religion, interpretive concepts are more problematical. Therefore we are suspicious of the adequacy of the dictionary's definition of religion.

Another common way to define religion is to regard it as "morality plus stories," or "morality plus emotion." These are ways of asserting that religion has to do mainly with ethics, or that its myths merely support the particular views of a people. There are, of course, persons for whom religion has been reduced to ethics, as when Thomas Paine stated (in *The Rights of Man*): "My country is the world, and my religion is to do good." But we should be cautious in assuming that this testimony would do for all religious people.

A final example of a definition that begins with personal experience is one that claims: "Religion is a feeling of security"; or, as one student put it: "Religion is an aid in coping with that part of life which man does not understand, or in some cases a philosophy of life enabling man to live more deeply." In locating the basis of religion in man's need for a sense of security, this approach suggests that the deepest study of religion is through psychology. It has been dramatically expressed by the psychiatrist and writer C. G. Jung when he wrote: "Religion is a relationship to the highest or strongest value . . . the value by which you are possessed unconsciously. That psychological fact which is the greatest power in your system is the god, since it is always the overwhelming psychic factor which is called 'god.'" Although this understanding of religion expresses a very important point, many theologians and religious philosophers point out that an interpretation that reduces all of religious experience to psychological, biological, or social factors omits the central reality exposed in that experience — the Sacred or Ultimate Reality. Thus, a student of religion should keep open the question of whether a familiar interpretation of religious life that fits into a conventional, social science perspective of man is adequate for interpreting the data.

Does your definition reflect a **bias** *on your part — positive or negative — toward religion as a whole, or toward a particular religion?* There are many examples of biased definitions that could be cited. Some equate religion with superstition, thus reflecting a negative evaluation. One man defined religion as "the sum of the scruples which impede the free exercise of the human faculties." Another hostile view of religion is to see religion as a device of priests to keep the masses in subjection and themselves in comfort. Similarly, Karl Marx, while not actually attempting to define religion, called it "the opiate of the people," again reflecting a bias against (all) religion.

Still others, in defining religion, are stating their concept of *true* religion as opposed to what they regard as false or pagan faiths. Henry Fielding, in his novel *Tom Jones*, has the provincial parson Mr. Thwackum saying, "When I mention religion I mean the Christian religion; and not only the Christian religion, but the Protestant religion; and not only the Protestant religion; but the Church of England." Some Christians assume that their personal conviction comprises a definition of religion, so that religion is regarded as "the worship of God through His Son Jesus Christ,"or "a personal relationship with Christ." A Muslim can point out that the essence of religion is to make peace with God through complete submission to God's will, a submission that he will insist is brought to fulfillment in Islam. (In Arabic the word "Islam" means "submission," "peace," "safety," and "salvation.")

Therefore the student interested in reflecting on religious experience that includes more than a single institutional or cultural expression should remember the distinction between descriptive (neutral) and evaluative definitions. A descriptive definition attempts to be as inclusive as possible about a class of items, such as religious forms. An evaluative definition, on the other hand, reflects one's own criteria for truth or falsity, for reality or illusion. In "visiting" religious people, we suggest that you delay making an evaluation until you have understood why their expressions and processes have profound meaning for them — however strange those expressions may seem to you. In the final analysis, each person must evaluate different religious alternatives; but one of our goals in bringing together the material in this volume is to provide you with a variety of options — a variety that is reduced if you limit religion to any single historical expression.

Obviously the believer who advocates one religion to the exclusion of all others differs sharply from one who rejects all. Nevertheless, if either accepts his own convictions about what is best or worst in religion as a description of what religion in fact is everywhere and for everyone, he exhibits a common indifference to unfamiliar, and therefore potentially surprising, religious patterns. As a believer (or skeptic), you have a right to declare your own understanding of what is most important, most real, in religion. This declaration is, in fact, essential, for it guides you in your quest for whatever is most real in life. As a student, on the other hand, you have an obligation to carry your studies as far as necessary to include relevant data. In this role, your obligation is not only to your own perception of value but also to a common world of understanding in which men of many religious persuasions can converse with each other.

Does your definition **limit** *religion to what it has been in the past, and nothing else, or does your definition make it possible to speak of emerging forms of religion?* In asking this question, we should observe two striking facts of the history of religion: there was a time when some present religions did not exist, and some of the religions which once emerged no longer exist (for example, the Egyptian and Babylonian religions). Human history, then, has witnessed the emergence and abandonment of several religions.

Even religious traditions that have maintained a sense of continuity over vast stretches of time (Hinduism, Buddhism, Judaism, Christianity, for example) have undergone important changes. Is it really as obvious as we tend to think that they are essentially the same now as they were at their origins? Do the terms naming these traditions even today point to a single entity, however complex? You are familiar with at least some instances of religious warfare *within* the Christian tradition. Roman Catholics have persecuted and killed Lutherans; Lutherans have persecuted and killed Calvinists; Calvinists, Anglicans; Anglicans, Quakers; and most have returned the act with interest. Are all of these groups expressions of "the one true church"? Are some more Christian than others? Is there only one form of Christianity? Are new movements violations of the tradition? Or is the one who speaks to his own time the one who is most faithful to the genius of his tradition? These questions can be asked of all religious traditions. All have experienced change and diversity. Furthermore, it seems likely that this will continue, and that new religious traditions will emerge. Therefore, the conventions of the past cannot be regarded as the limits of future religious forms.

In part because history has witnessed the emergence and internal changes of many religions, anthropologists and cultural historians commonly suggest that religion (and human culture in general) has attained only its adolescence. Likewise, philosophers and religious thinkers in both East and West point to the anxiety and tensions today that are expressed in political, social, economic, and intellectual upheaval. They raise a question of whether or not man's moral, psychic, and evaluative resources can catch up with his self-destructive potential seen in technologically advanced weapons and psychological-chemical techniques for social control. The most hopeful of these philosophers perceive the present turmoil as a lack of "maturity" in human consciousness, and express the hope that it is not too late (quite) to change the direction of man from self-destruction to self-fulfillment.

From this perspective most of mankind's experience is still in the future. The history of religious life to the present is only a beginning. But the basis of these projections is the recognition that man's survival requires him to recognize religious dynamics and processes for evaluations as major forces in human life. Should not a definition of religion aid us in looking at contemporary phenomena to see if any new ways of being religious are emerging? At least it should not inhibit persons with an interest in this matter, and we think an introduction to religion should encourage such reflection.

***Does your definition have sufficient* precision?** Are there any limits to the scope of religion, or are the limits so vague that they fail to mark out an object of study? In an attempt to be as broadminded as possible, many definitions are like a student's statement that religion is "the means man has of coping with his world." Or they are similar to the claim that religion is "believing in a way of life which involves understanding and caring for others," or "religion is love." Such definitions tell us a good deal, but without some qualification they might refer to many other expressions of human life than specifically religious ones. In order to find a focus and a set of limitations at the outer circumference of that focus, we need to designate what are those essential elements of religion that will expose the *religious* meaning of the evidence we look at.

When one has "visited" (seen) a wide range of religious life, from all parts of the world and throughout human history, it becomes apparent that religion is a way of life that involves many processes — all of which, in different ways, are directed toward a common end. The goal is to reach a state of being that is conceived to be the highest possible state or condition. Religion is the general term for the various ways by which people seek to become changed into that highest state. We understand *religion as a means toward ultimate transformation.* By this we are not claiming that every activity you think of as religious will in fact transform you ultimately. It might, but that is not our point. We mean that *any* reasonably specific means that *any* person adopts with the serious hope and intention of moving toward ultimate transformation should be termed "religious." We think it possible to speak of all religious activity (Eastern and Western, past, present, and emerging) without reducing religion to what is merely familiar to us and without putting a value judgment on one or more religions.

Questions for Analysis

1. Describe your concept of *religion* as specifically as possible. Where did the concept originate for you? How did it evolve as you have matured? Explain the reasons or experiences that support your concept.

2. Evaluate your concept of *religion* by answering the four questions posed in the Thinking Passage:

   - "Does your definition *reduce* religion to what you happen to be acquainted with by accident of birth and socialization?"

   - "Does your definition reflect a *bias* on your part — positive or negative — toward religion as a whole, or toward a particular religion?"

   - "Does your definition *limit* religion to what it has been in the past, and nothing else, or does your definition make it possible to speak of emerging forms of religion?"

   - "Does your definition have sufficient *precision?*"

3. Compare your definition of religion to the definitions of other students in your class. What are the similarities? What are the differences? How do you explain these similarities and differences?

4. In the Thinking Passage, religion is defined as a "means toward ultimate transformation." What do you think this definition means? Explain how this definition relates to your definition.

8 Relating and Organizing

Relating and Organizing
Using thinking patterns to make sense of the world

Chronological and Process Relationships

Organizing events or ideas in terms of time

Comparative and Analogical Relationships

Focusing on the similarities and/or dissimilarities among different objects, events, or ideas

Causal Relationships

Relating events in terms of the influence or effect they have on one another

Throughout this book we have been considering and experiencing the insight that each one of us is a "creator." Our world does not exist as a finished product, waiting for us to perceive it, think about it, and describe it with words and pictures. Instead, we are *active participants* in composing the world that seems so familiar to us.

The goal of this composing process is to organize your world into meaningful patterns that will help you figure out what is going on and what you ought to do. Composing your world involves all the activities that we have been exploring, including

perceiving	symbolizing	interpreting
believing	describing	conceptualizing
knowing	classifying	defining
solving problems	generalizing	analyzing

Your ability to think critically gives you the means to examine the different ways by which you are making sense of the world so that you can develop and sharpen your understanding. As you actively discover and compose various patterns, you are exploring the ways in which different aspects of your experience *relate* to each other.

Ideas, things, and events in the world can be related and organized in a variety of ways. For example, different individuals might take the same furniture and decorations in the same space and arrange them in many different ways, reflecting each person's needs, ways of thinking, and aesthetic preferences. Or, to take another example, a class of students may write essays about the same subject and yet create widely differing results.

All these ways of relating and organizing reflect basic thinking patterns that you rely on constantly when you think, act, or use language. These basic thinking patterns are an essential part of your process of composing and making sense of the world. We will explore three basic ways of relating and organizing in this chapter.

Chronological and Process Relationships

- Chronological — relating events in time sequence
- Process — relating aspects of the growth or development of an event or object

Comparative and Analogical Relationships

- Comparative — relating things in the same general category in terms of similarities and dissimilarities

- Analogical — relating things belonging to different categories in terms of each other

Causal Relationships

- Causal — relating events in terms of the way some event(s) is/are responsible for bringing about other event(s)

These basic thinking patterns (and others besides) play an active role in the way you perceive, shape, and organize your world to make it understandable to you. The specific patterns you use to organize your ideas in thinking, writing, and speaking depend on the subject you are exploring, the goals you are aiming for, the type of writing or speaking you are doing, and the audience who will be reading or listening to your work. In most cases, you will use a variety of basic patterns in thinking, writing, and speaking to organize and relate the ideas you are considering.

Chronological and Process Relationships

Chronological and process patterns of thinking organize events or ideas in terms of their occurrence in time, though the two patterns tend to differ in focus or emphasis. The *chronological* pattern of thinking organizes something into a series of events in the sequence in which they occurred. The *process* mode of thinking organizes an activity into a series of steps necessary for reaching a certain goal.

Chronological Relationships

The simplest examples of chronological descriptions are logs or diaries, in which people record things that occurred at given points in time. The oldest and most universal form of chronological expression is the *narrative*, a way of thinking and communicating in which someone tells a story about experiences he or she has had. (Of course, the person telling the story can be a *fictional* character created by a writer who is using a narrative form.) Every human culture has used narratives to pass on values and traditions from one generation to the next, exemplified by such enduring works as the *Odyssey* and the Bible. The word *narrative* is derived from the Latin word for "to know." Narrators are people who "know" what happened because they were there to experience it firsthand (or spoke to people who were there) and who now share this experience with you.

One of America's great storytellers, Mark Twain, once said that a good story has to accomplish something and arrive somewhere. In other words, if a story is to be effective in engaging the interest of the audience, it has to have a purpose. The purpose may be to provide more information on a subject, to illustrate an idea, to lead us to a particular way of thinking, or merely to entertain us. An effective story does not merely record the complex, random, and often unrelated events of life. Instead, it has focus and purpose, possesses an ordered structure (a *plot),* and expresses a meaningful point of view.

THINKING PASSAGE

Back, but Not Home

Review the following narrative by Maria Muniz, which uses chronological examples of thinking and expression, and then answer the questions that follow.

BACK, BUT NOT HOME
by Maria Muniz

With all the talk about resuming diplomatic relations with Cuba, and with the increasing number of Cuban exiles returning to visit friends and relatives, I am constantly being asked, "Would you ever go back?" In turn, I have asked myself, "Is there any reason for me to go?" I have had to think long and hard before finding my answer. Yes.

I came to the United States with my parents when I was almost five years old. We left behind grandparents, aunts, uncles and several cousins. I grew up in a very middle-class neighborhood in Brooklyn. With one exception, all my friends were Americans. Outside of my family, I do not know many Cubans. I often feel awkward visiting relatives in Miami because it is such a different world. The way of life in Cuban Miami seems very strange to me and I am accused of being too "Americanized." Yet, although I am now an American citizen, whenever anyone has asked me my nationality, I have always and unhesitatingly replied, "Cuban."

Outside American, inside Cuban.

I recently had a conversation with a man who generally sympathizes with the Castro regime. We talked of Cuban politics and although the discussion was very casual, I felt an old anger welling inside. After 16 years of living an "American" life, I am still unable to view the revolution with

Source: Back, but Not Home" by Mark Muniz. Originally published in *The New York Times,* July 13, 1979 (Op-Ed). Copyright © 1979 by The New York Times Co. Reprinted by permission.

detachment or objectivity. I cannot interpret its results in social, political or economic terms. Too many memories stand in my way.

And as I listened to this man talk of the Cuban situation, I began to remember how as a little girl I would wake up crying because I had dreamed of my aunts and grandmothers and I missed them. I remembered my mother's trembling voice and the sad look on her face whenever she spoke to her mother over the phone. I thought of the many letters and photographs that somehow were always lost in transit. And as the conversation continued, I began to remember how difficult it often was to grow up Latina in an American world.

It meant going to kindergarten knowing little English. I'd been in this country only a few months and although I understood a good deal of what was said to me, I could not express myself very well. On the first day of school I remember one little girl's saying to the teacher: "But how can we play with her? She's so stupid she can't even talk!" I felt so helpless because inside I was crying, "Don't you know I can understand everything you're saying?" But I did not have words for my thoughts and my inability to communicate terrified me.

As I grew a little older, Latina meant being automatically relegated to the slowest reading classes in school. By now my English was fluent, but the teachers would always assume I was somewhat illiterate or slow. I recall one teacher's amazement at discovering I could read and write just as well as her American pupils. Her incredulity astounded me. As a child, I began to realize that Latina would always mean proving I was as good as the others. As I grew older, it became a matter of pride to prove I was better than the others.

As an adult I have come to terms with these memories and they don't hurt as much. I don't look or sound very Cuban. I don't speak with an accent and my English is far better than my Spanish. I am beginning my career and look forward to the many possibilities ahead of me.

But a persistent little voice is constantly saying, "There's something missing. It's not enough." And this is why when I am now asked, "Do you want to go back?" I say "yes" with conviction.

I do not say to Cubans, "It is time to lay aside the hurt and forgive and forget." It is impossible to forget an event that has altered and scarred all our lives so profoundly. But I find I am beginning to care less and less about politics. And I am beginning to remember and care more about the child (and how many others like her) who left her grandma behind. I have to return to Cuba one day because I want to know that little girl better.

When I try to review my life during the past 16 years, I almost feel as if I've walked into a theater right in the middle of a movie. And I'm afraid I won't fully understand or enjoy the rest of the movie unless I can see and understand the beginning. And for me, the beginning is Cuba. I don't want to go "home" again; the life and home we all left behind are long gone. My home is here and I am happy. But I need to talk to my family still in Cuba.

Like all immigrants, my family and I have had to build a new life from almost nothing. It was often difficult, but I believe the struggle made us strong. Most of my memories are good ones.

But I want to preserve and renew my cultural heritage. I want to keep "la Cubana" within me alive. I want to return because the journey back will also mean a journey within. Only then will I see the missing piece.

Questions for Analysis

1. Because chronological thinking patterns represent a sequence of events in time, they can be visually represented with mind maps structured like the diagram on page 316. Using this form as a guide, create a mind map that expresses the key events in the author's life and their relationship to one another.

2. Explain the purpose(s) you think the narrator is trying to achieve in writing this essay.

3. Identify the key points the author makes in trying to achieve her purpose(s).

THINKING ACTIVITY 8.1

Creating a Narrative Description

Using a mind map that you create as a guide, like the diagram on page 316, write a narrative describing an event or experience that had special significance in your life. After completing your narrative, explain what you think is the most important point that you are trying to share with your audience. Read your narrative to the other members of the class, and then discuss it with them, comparing the meaning you intended with the meaning they derived.

Process Relationships

Another type of time-ordered thinking is the process relationship, which focuses on relating aspects of the growth and development of an event or expe-

CHRONOLOGICAL RELATIONSHIPS

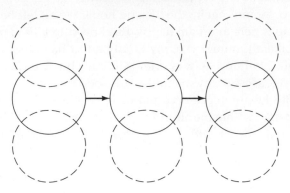

rience. From birth onward, you are involved with processes in every facet of your life. These processes can be classified in various ways: natural (e.g., growing in height), mechanical (e.g., assembling a bicycle), physical (e.g., learning a sport), mental (e.g., developing your thinking), creative (e.g., writing a poem), and so on.

Performing a *process analysis* involves two basic steps. The first step is to divide the process or activity you are analyzing into parts or stages. The second step is to explain the movement of the process through these parts or stages from beginning to end. The stages you have identified should be separate and distinct and should involve no repetition or significant omissions.

In performing a process analysis, you are typically trying to achieve one or both of two goals. The first goal is to give people step-by-step instruction in how to perform an activity, such as taking a photograph, changing a tire, or writing an essay. The second goal is simply to give information about a process, not to teach someone how to perform it. For example, your biology teacher might explain the process of photosynthesis to help you understand how green plants function, not to teach you how to go about transforming sunlight into chlorophyll!

THINKING ACTIVITY 8.2

Analyzing Process Relationships

Review the following passages, which are examples of the process-analysis pattern of thinking. For each passage do the following:

1. Identify the purpose of the passage.

2. Describe the main stages in the process identified by the author.

3. List questions you still have about how the process operates.

Jacketing was a sleight-of-hand I watched with wonder each time, and I have discovered that my father was admired among sheepmen up and down the valley for his skill at it: *He was just pretty catty at that, the way he could get that ewe to take on a new lamb every time.* Put simply, jacketing was a ruse played on a ewe whose lamb had died. A substitute lamb quickly would be singled out, most likely from a set of twins. Sizing up the tottering newcomer, Dad would skin the dead lamb, and into the tiny pelt carefully snip four leg holes and a head hole. Then the stand-in lamb would have the skin fitted onto it like a snug jacket on a poodle. The next step of disguise was to cut out the dead lamb's liver and smear it several times across the jacket of pelt. In its borrowed and bedaubed skin, the new baby lamb then was presented to the ewe. She would sniff the baby impostor endlessly, distrustful but pulled by the blood-smell of her own. When in a few days she made up her dim sheep's mind to accept the lamb, Dad snipped away the jacket and recited his victory: *Mother him like hell now, don't ye? See what a hellava dandy lamb I got for ye, old sister? Who says I couldn't jacket day onto night if I wanted to, now-I-ask-ye?*

— Ivan Doig, *This House of Sky*

If you are inexperienced in relaxation techniques, begin by sitting in a comfortable chair with your feet on the floor and your hands resting easily in your lap. Close your eyes and breathe evenly, deeply, and gently. As you exhale each breath let your body become more relaxed. Starting with one hand direct your attention to one part of your body at a time. Close your fist and tighten the muscles of your forearm. Feel the sensation of tension in your muscles. Relax your hand and let your forearm and hand become completely limp. Direct all your attention to the sensation of relaxation as you continue to let all tension leave your hand and arm. Continue this practice once or several times each day, relaxing your other hand and arm, your legs, back, abdomen, chest, neck, face, and scalp. When you have this mastered and can relax completely, turn your thoughts to scenes of natural tranquility from your past. Stay with your inner self as long as you wish, whether thinking of nothing or visualizing only the loveliest of images. Often you will become completely unaware of your surroundings. When you open your eyes you will find yourself refreshed in mind and body.

— Laurence J. Peter, *The Peter Prescription*

The stages of mourning are universal and are experienced by people from all walks of life. Mourning occurs in response to an individual's own terminal illness or to the death of a valued being, human or animal. There are five stages of normal grief.

In our bereavement, we spend different lengths of time working through each step and express each stage more or less intensely. The five stages do not necessarily occur in order. We often move between stages before achieving a more peaceful acceptance of death. Many of us are not afforded the luxury of time required to achieve this final stage of grief. The death of a loved one might inspire you to evaluate your own feelings or mortality. Throughout each stage, a common thread of hope emerges. As long as there is life, there is hope. As long as there is hope, there is life.

1. *Denial and isolation:* The first reaction to learning of terminal illness or death of a cherished pet is to deny the reality of the situation. It is a normal reaction to rationalize overwhelming emotions. It is a defense mechanism that buffers the immediate shock. We block out the words and hide from the facts. This is a temporary response that carries us through the first wave of pain.

2. *Anger:* As the masking effects of denial and isolation begin to war, reality and its pain re-emerge. We are not ready. The intense emotion is deflected from our vulnerable core, redirected and expressed instead as anger. The anger may be aimed at inanimate objects, complete strangers, friends or family. Anger may be directed at our dying or deceased loved one. Rationally, we know the person is not to be blamed. Emotionally, however, we may resent it for causing us pain or for leaving us. We feel guilty for being angry, and this makes us more angry. The doctor who diagnosed the illness and was unable to cure the disease might become a convenient target.

3. *Bargaining:* The normal reaction to feelings of helplessness and vulnerability is often a need to regain control. If only we had sought medical attention sooner or secured a second opinion from another doctor. Secretly, we may make a deal with God or our higher power in an attempt to postpone the inevitable. This is a weaker line of defense to protect us from the painful reality.

4. *Depression:* Two types of depression are associated with mourning. The first one is a reaction to practical implications relating to the loss. Sadness and regret predominate. We worry that, in our grief, we have spent less time with others that depend on us. This phase may be eased by simple clarification and reassurance. We may need a bit of helpful cooperation and a few kind words. The second type of depression is more subtle and, in a sense, perhaps more private. It is our quiet preparation to separate and to bid our loved one farewell.

5. *Acceptance:* Reaching this stage of mourning is a gift not afforded to everyone. Death may be sudden and unexpected or we may never see beyond our anger or denial. It is not necessarily a mark of bravery to resist the inevitable and to deny ourselves the opportunity to make our peace. This phase is marked by withdrawal and calm. This is not a period of happiness and must be distinguished from depression.

THINKING ACTIVITY 8.3

Creating a Process Description

We tend to be most acutely aware of process analysis when we are learning a new activity for the first time, such as preparing formula for an infant or installing a new oil filter in a car. Identify such an occasion in your own life and then complete the following activities:

1. Create a mind map of the process, similar in form to the diagram on page 320.
2. Describe the steps or stages in the process.
3. Write a passage explaining how the stages fit together in an overall sequence.
4. Describe any special problems you had to solve, the manner in which you went about solving them, and the feelings you experienced in learning this process.

Comparative and Analogical Relationships

Comparative and analogical patterns of thinking focus on the similarities and/or dissimilarities among different objects, events, or ideas. Comparative modes of thinking relate things in the *same* general category in terms of their similarities and differences. For example, when you shop for something important, like a car, you generally engage in a process of organized comparing (evaluating similarities and differences) as you examine the various makes and models. However, analogical modes of thinking relate things in entirely different categories in terms of their similarities. For example, on your shopping expedition for a car, you might say of a used car badly in need of repair, "That car is a real lemon." Obviously cars and lemons are in different categories, but

PROCESS RELATIONSHIPS

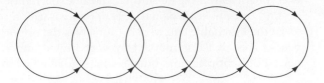

the analogy brings out some similarities between the two (a sense of "sour-ness" or "bitterness").

Comparative Relationships

Think of an item you shopped for and bought in the past month. It might have been an article of clothing, a good book, a new CD, or a DVD player. Identify the item you selected, noting as much specific information about it as you can remember — brand, color, size, cost, and so on. When you went shopping, you probably spent a fair amount of time examining other items of the same type, things that you looked at but did not buy. As you made your decision to purchase the item you did, you probably compared the various brands before making your selection. Identify some of the factors you took into consideration in comparing the different items. For example, if you were shopping for jeans:

Item Purchased	Comparative Factors	Item Not Purchased
Levi's jeans	Brand	Girbaud jeans
$39.00	Price	$50.00
Straight cut	Style	Designer cut
Unwashed denim	Material	Prewashed denim

You compare in this way all the time, usually without even realizing it. Whenever you select an item on a menu or in a store, or a seat in a theater or on a bus, you are automatically looking for similarities and differences among the various items from which you are selecting, and these similarities and differences guide you in making your decision.

Of course, you do not always engage in a systematic process of comparison. In many cases, the selections and decisions you make seem to be unconscious. This may be so because you have already performed an organized comparison at some time in the past and already know what you want and why you want it (e.g., "I always choose an aisle seat so that I don't have to climb over people").

Sometimes, however, you make decisions impulsively, without any thought or comparative examination. Maybe someone told you to, maybe you were influenced by a commercial you saw, or maybe you simply said, "What the heck, let's take a chance." Sometimes these impulsive decisions work out for you, but often they do not because they are simply a result of rolling the dice. In contrast, when you engage in a critical and comparative examination, you gain information that can help you make intelligent decisions.

Standards for Comparison   Naturally, not all of the factors you use in comparing are equally important in your decision-making. How do you determine which factors are more important than others and which information is more relevant than other information? Unfortunately, there is no simple formula for answering these questions. For example, review the lists you completed previously and place a check next to the factors that played an important part in your decision to buy the item. These factors represent the comparative information you found to be most important and relevant and probably reflect your needs and purposes. If you are on a limited budget, price differences may play a key role in your decision. If money is no object, your decision may have been based solely on the quality of the item or on some other consideration.

Even though there is no hard and fast way to determine which areas of comparison are most important, it does help you to become *aware* of the factors that are influencing your perceptions and decisions. These areas of comparison represent the standards you use to come to conclusions, and a critical and reflective examination of these standards can help you sharpen, clarify, and improve them.

When making comparisons, there are pitfalls you should try to avoid:

- *Incomplete comparisons.* This difficulty arises when you focus on too few points of comparison. For example, in looking for a competent surgeon to operate on you, you might decide to focus only on the fee that each doctor charges. Even though this may be an important area for comparative analysis, you would be foolish to overlook other areas of comparison, such as medical training, experience, recommendations, and success rates.

- *Selective comparisons.* This problem occurs when you take a one-sided view of a comparative situation — when you concentrate on the points favoring one side of the things being compared but overlook the points favoring the other side. For example, in selecting a dependable friend to perform a favor for you, you may focus on Bob because he is your best friend and you have known him the longest, but you may overlook the fact that he let you down the last few times you asked him to do something for you.

THINKING ACTIVITY 8.4

Analyzing Comparative Relationships

Review the following passages, which use comparative patterns of thinking to organize the ideas being presented. For each passage do the following:

1. Identify the key ideas being compared.
2. Analyze the points of similarity and dissimilarity between the ideas being presented by using a mind map like the diagram on page 323.
3. Describe the conclusions to which the passage leads you.

The difference between an American cookbook and a French one is that the former is very accurate and the second exceedingly vague. American recipes look like doctors' prescriptions. Perfect cooking seems to depend on perfect dosage. You are told to take a teaspoon of this and a tablespoon of that, then to stir them together until thoroughly blended. A French recipe seldom tells you how many ounces of butter to use to make *crêpes suzette,* or how many spoonfuls of oil should go into a salad dressing. French cookbooks are full of unusual measurements such as a *pinch* of pepper, a *suspicion* of garlic, or a *generous sprinkling* of brandy. There are constant references to seasoning *to taste,* as if the recipe were merely intended to give a general direction, relying on the experience and art of the cook to make the dish turn out right.

— Raoul de Roussy de Sales, "American and French Cookbooks"

The rapidity of change and the speed with which new situations are created follow the impetuous and heedless pace of man rather than the deliberate pace of nature. Radiation is no longer merely the background radiation of rocks, the bombardment of cosmic rays, the ultraviolet rays of the sun that have existed before there was any life on earth; radiation is now the unnatural creation of man's tampering with the atom. The chemicals to which life is asked to make its adjustment are no longer merely the calcium and silica and copper and all the rest of the minerals washed out of the rocks and carried in rivers to the sea; they are the synthetic creations of man's inventive mind, brewed in his laboratories, and having no counterparts in nature. To adjust to these chemicals would require time on the scale that is nature's; it would require not merely the years of a man's life but the life of generations. And even this, were it by some miracle possible, would be futile, for the new chemicals come from our laboratories in an endless stream; almost five hundred annually find their way into actual use in the United States alone.

— Rachel Carson, *Silent Spring*

COMPARATIVE RELATIONSHIPS

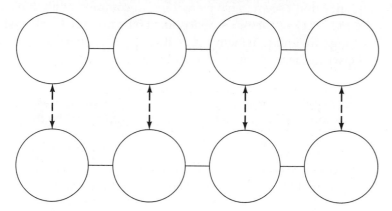

Analogical Relationships

We noted earlier that comparative relationships involve examining the similarities and differences of two items in the same general category, such as items on a menu or methods of birth control. There is another kind of comparison, however, that does not focus on things in the same category. Such comparisons are known as *analogies*, and their goal is to clarify or illuminate a concept from one category by saying that it is the same as a concept from a very different category.

The purpose of an analogy is not the same as the purpose of the comparison we considered in the last section. At that time, we noted that the goal of comparing similar things is usually to make a choice and that the process of comparing can provide you with information on which you can base an intelligent decision. The main goal of analogies, however, is not to choose or decide; it is to illuminate our understanding. Identifying similarities between very different things can often stimulate you to see these things in a new light, from a different perspective than you are used to. This can result in a clearer and more complete understanding of the things being compared. Consider the following example:

Life's but a walking shadow, a poor player
That struts and frets his hour upon the stage
And then is heard no more.

— William Shakespeare, *Macbeth*

In this famous quotation, Shakespeare is comparing two things that at first glance don't seem to have anything in common at all: life and an actor. Yet as you look closer at the comparison, you begin to see that even though these two things are unlike in many ways, there are also some very important similarities between them. What are some of these similarities?

> **analogy** *A comparison between things that are basically dissimilar made for the purpose of illuminating our understanding of the things being compared*

We ourselves often use analogies to get a point across to someone else. Used appropriately, analogies can help you illustrate and explain what you are trying to communicate. This is particularly important when you have difficulty in finding the right words to represent your experiences. Powerful or complex emotions can make you speechless or make you say things like "Words cannot describe what I feel." Imagine that you are trying to describe your feelings of love and caring for another person. To illustrate and clarify the feelings you are trying to communicate, you might compare your feelings of love to "the first rose of spring," noting the following similarities:

- Like the first rose, this is the first great love of my life.
- Like the fragile yet supple petals of the rose, my feelings are tender and sensitive.
- Like the beauty of the rose, the beauty of my love should grow with time.

What are some other comparisons of love to a rose?

- Like the color of the rose, . . .
- Like the fragrance of the rose, . . .
- Like the thorns of the rose, . . .

Another favorite subject for analogies is the idea of the meaning or purpose of life, which the simple use of the word *life* does not communicate. You have just seen Shakespeare's comparison of life to an actor. Here are some other popular analogies involving life. What are some points of similarity in each of these comparisons?

- Life is just a bowl of cherries.
- Life is a football game.
- Life is like a box of chocolates.
- "Life is a tale told by an idiot, full of sound and fury, signifying nothing." (Shakespeare)

VISUAL THINKING

"Nice Umbrella!" "Nice Raft!"

- How does this illustration depict the role of analogical thinking? Think of a vivid analogy and then sketch a picture of the two concepts being related.

Create an analogy for life representing some of your feelings, and explain the points of similarity.

- Life is . . . .

In addition to communicating experiences that resist simple characterization, analogies are useful when you are trying to explain a complicated concept. For instance, you might compare the eye to a camera lens or the immunological system of the body to the National Guard (corpuscles are called to active duty and rush to the scene of danger when undesirable elements threaten the well-being of the organism).

Analogies possess the power to bring things to life by evoking images that illuminate the points of comparison. Consider the following analogies and explain the points of comparison that each author is trying to make:

- "Laws are like cobwebs, which may catch small flies, but let wasps and hornets break through." (Jonathan Swift)
- "I am as pure as the driven slush." (Tallulah Bankhead)
- "He has all the qualities of a dog, except its devotion." (Gore Vidal)

Similes and Metaphors   From the examples discussed so far, you can see that analogies have two parts: an *original subject* and a *compared subject* (what the original is being likened to). In comparing your love to the first rose of spring, the original subject is your feelings of love and caring for someone whereas the compared subject is what you are comparing those feelings to in order to illuminate and express them — namely, the first rose of spring.

In analogies, the connection between the original subject and the compared subject can either be obvious (explicit) or implied (implicit). For example, you can echo the lament of the great pool hustler Minnesota Fats and say, "A pool player in a tuxedo is like a hotdog with whipped cream on it." This is an obvious analogy (known as a *simile*) because you have explicitly noted the connection between the original subject (pool player in a tuxedo) and the compared subject (hotdog with whipped cream) by using the comparative term *like*. (Sometimes the structure of the sentence calls for *as* in a similar position.)

> **simile** *An explicit comparison between basically dissimilar things made for the purpose of illuminating our understanding of the things being compared*

You could also have used other forms of obvious comparison, such as "is similar to," "reminds me of," or "makes me think of." In this case, you could say, "A pool player in a tuxedo is a hotdog with whipped cream on it." Here, you are making an implied analogy (known as a *metaphor*) because you have not included any words that point out that you are making a comparison. Instead, you are stating that the original subject *is* the compared subject. Naturally, you are assuming that most people will understand that you are making a comparison between two different things and not describing a biological transformation.

> **metaphor** *An implied comparison between basically dissimilar things made for the purpose of illuminating our understanding of the things being compared*

Create a *simile* (obvious analogy) for a subject of your own choosing, noting at least two points of comparison.

Subject

1.

2.

Create a *metaphor* (implied analogy) for a subject of your own choosing, noting at least two points of comparison.

Subject

1.

2.

THINKING ACTIVITY 8.5

Analyzing Analogical Relationships

Read the following passage, which uses an analogical pattern of thinking. Identify the major ideas being compared and describe the points of similarity between them. Explain how the analogy helps illuminate the subject being discussed.

> The mountain guide, like the true teacher, has a quiet authority. He or she engenders trust and confidence so that one is willing to join the endeavor. The guide accepts his leadership role, yet recognizes that success (measured by the heights that are scaled) depends upon the close cooperation and active participation of each member of the group. He has crossed the terrain before and is familiar with the landmarks, but each trip is new and generates its own anxiety and excitement. Essential skills must be mastered; if they are lacking, disaster looms. The situation demands keen focus and rapt attention; slackness, misjudgment, or laziness can abort the venture. The teacher is not a pleader, not a performer, not a huckster, but a confident, exuberant guide on expeditions of shared responsibility into the most exciting and least-understood terrain on earth — the mind itself.
>
> — Nancy K. Hill, "Scaling the Heights:
> The Teacher as Mountaineer"

THINKING ACTIVITY 8.6

Creating Analogies to Capture Life

Analogies are powerful tools to capture our thoughts and emotions about events in our lives that are profound or traumatic. The authors of the articles describing the terrorist attacks on the World Trade Center towers and the Pentagon (which can be found on the companion web site) use a variety of analogies to communicate their intense feelings, including

- A hellish storm of ash, glass, smoke, and leaping victims
- The twisted, smoking, ash-choked carcasses of the twin towers
- The similarity to the special effects in the Hollywood film *Independence Day*
- The deeply scarred Pentagon, still on fire, suggesting the loss of America's collective sense of security
- The intense heat causing the seemingly invincible steel beams of the towers to melt like cotton candy
- The scenario of a Tom Clancy thriller or Spielberg blockbuster now unfolding live on the world's television screens
- In a grotesque parody of the tickertape parades that characterize New York celebrations, thousands of pieces of office paper being carried on the gusting wind

Select an event that you have personally experienced that has an intense and profound meaning to you. Compose a description of that experience that makes use of powerful analogies to communicate your thoughts and feelings.

Causal Relationships

Causal patterns of thinking involve relating events in terms of the influence or effect they have on one another. For example, if you were right now to pinch yourself hard enough to feel it, you would be demonstrating a cause and effect relationship. Stated very simply, a *cause* is anything that is responsible for bringing about something else — usually termed the *effect*. The cause (the pinch) brings about the effect (the feeling of pain). When you make a causal statement, you are merely stating that a causal relationship exists between two or more things: The pinch *caused* the pain in my arm.

Of course, when you make (or think) causal statements, you do not always use the word *cause*. For example, the following statements are all causal statements. In each case, underline the cause and circle the effect.

- Since I was the last person to leave, I turned off the lights.
- Taking lots of vitamin C really cured me of that terrible cold I had.
- I accidentally toasted my hand along with the marshmallows by getting too close to the fire.

In these statements, the words *turned off, cured,* and *toasted* all point to the fact that something has caused something else to take place. Our language contains thousands of these causal "cousins."

You make causal statements all the time, and you are always thinking in terms of causal relationships. In fact, the goal of much of your thinking is to figure out why something happened or how something came about, for if you can figure out how and why things occur, you can then try to predict what will happen in the future. These predictions of anticipated results form the basis of many of your decisions. For example, the experience of toasting your hand along with the marshmallows might lead you to choose a longer stick for toasting — simply because you are able to figure out the causal relationships involved and then make predictions based on your understanding (namely, a longer stick will keep your hand farther away from the fire, which will prevent it from getting toasted).

Consider the following activities, which you probably performed today. Each activity assumes that certain causal relationships exist, which influenced your decision to perform them. Explain one such causal relationship for each activity.

- Brushing your teeth. The *causal relationship* is
- Locking the door. The *causal relationship* is
- Studying for an exam. The *causal relationship* is

Causal Chains

Although you tend to think of causes and effects in isolation — *A* caused *B* — in reality causes and effects rarely appear by themselves. Causes and effects generally appear as parts of more complex patterns, including three that we will examine here:

- Causal chains

- Contributory causes

- Interactive causes

Consider the following scenario: Your paper on the topic "Is there life after death?" is due on Monday morning. You have reserved the whole weekend to work on it and are just getting started when the phone rings — your best friend from childhood is in town and wants to stay with you for the weekend. You say yes. By Sunday night, you've had a great weekend but have made little progress on your paper. You begin writing, when suddenly you feel stomach cramps — it must have been those raw oysters that you had for lunch!

Three hours later, you are ready to continue work. You brew a pot of coffee and get started. At 3:00 A.M. you are too exhausted to continue. You decide to get a few hours of sleep and set the alarm clock for 6:00 A.M., giving you plenty of time to finish up. When you wake up, you find that it's 9:00 A.M. — the alarm failed to go off! Your class starts in forty minutes, and you have no chance of getting the paper done on time. As you ride to school, you go over the causes for this disaster in your mind. You are no longer worried about life after death — you are now worried about life after this class!

- What causes in this situation are responsible for your paper being late?
- What do you think is the single most important cause?
- What do you think your teacher will identify as the most important cause? Why?

A *causal chain,* as you can see from these examples, is a situation in which one thing leads to another, which then leads to another, and so on. There is not just *one* cause for the resulting effect; there is a whole string of causes. Which cause in the string is the "real" cause? Your answer often depends on your perspective on the situation. In the example of the unfinished paper on the topic "Is there life after death?" you might see the cause as a faulty alarm clock. The teacher, however, might see the cause as an overall lack of planning. Proper planning, she might say, does not involve leaving things until the last minute, when unexpected problems can prevent you from reaching your goal. You can illustrate this causal structure with the following diagram:

CAUSAL CHAIN

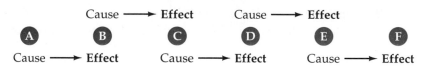

THINKING ACTIVITY 8.7

Creating a Causal Chain

1. Create a similar scenario of your own, detailing a chain of causes that results in being late for class, standing someone up for a date, failing an exam, or producing another effect of your own choosing.

2. Review the scenario you have just created. Explain how the "real" cause of the final effect could vary, depending on your perspective on the situation.

Contributory Causes

In addition to operating in causal chains over a period of time (*A* leads to *B*, which leads to *C*, which leads to *D*, and so on), causes can act simultaneously to produce an effect. When this happens (as it often does), you have a situation in which a number of different causes are instrumental in bringing something about. Instead of working in isolation, each cause *contributes* to bringing about the final effect. When this situation occurs, each cause serves to support and reinforce the action of the other causes, a structure illustrated in the following diagram:

CONTRIBUTORY CAUSES

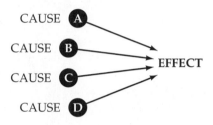

Consider the following situation: It is the end of the term, and you have been working incredibly hard at school — writing papers, preparing for exams, finishing up course projects. You haven't been getting enough sleep, and you haven't been eating regular or well-balanced meals. To make matters worse, you have been under intense pressure in your personal life, having serious arguments with the person you have been dating. You find that this situation is constantly on your mind. It is also the middle of the flu season, and many of the people you know have been sick with various bugs. Walking home from school one evening, you get soaked by an unexpected shower. By the time you get home, you are shivering. You soon find yourself in bed with a thermometer in your mouth — you are sick!

What was the "cause" of your getting sick? In this situation, you can see it probably was not just *one* thing that brought about your illness. It was probably *a combination* of different factors that led to your physical breakdown: having low resistance, getting wet and chilled, being exposed to various germs and viruses, being physically exhausted, not eating properly, and so on. Taken by itself, no one factor might have been enough to cause your illness. Working together, they all contributed to the final outcome.

VISUAL THINKING

"The Birds and the Bees, the Flowers and the Trees"

● How is the natural causal order being thwarted in this illustration? Describe an incident in which your cause and effect plan didn't happen as you expected. What went wrong?

THINKING ACTIVITY 8.8

Creating a Scenario of Contributory Causes

Create a similar scenario of your own, detailing the contributory causes that led to asking someone for a date, choosing a major, losing or winning a game you played in, or producing an effect of your own choosing.

Interactive Causes

Our examination of causal relationships has revealed that causes rarely oper-ate in isolation but instead often influence (and are influenced by) other fac-tors. Imagine that you are scheduled to give a speech to a large group of people. As the time for your moment in the spotlight approaches, you become anxious, which results in a dry mouth and throat, making your voice sound more like a croak. The prospect of sounding like a bullfrog increases your anx-iety, which in turn dries your mouth and constricts your throat further, reduc-ing your croak to something much worse — silence.

This not uncommon scenario reveals the way different factors can relate to one another through reciprocal influences that flow back and forth from one to the other. This type of causal relationship, which involves an *interactive* think-ing pattern, is an extremely important way to organize and make sense of your experiences. For example, to understand social relationships, such as families, teams, or groups of friends, you have to understand the complex ways each individual influences — and is influenced by — all the other members of the group.

Understanding biological systems and other systems is similar to under-standing social systems. To understand and explain how an organ like your heart, liver, or brain functions, you have to describe its complex, interactive relationships with all the other parts of your biological system.

THINKING ACTIVITY 8.9

Analyzing Causal Relationships

Read the following passage, which deals with the collapse of the World Trade Center. What are the causal relationships that resulted in the collapse?

Additional examples of causal relationships can be found on the com-panion web site which also has a portfolio of images of the World Trade Center.

. . . Since the collapse of the World Trade Center towers, on September 11th, structural engineers and their profession have received a great deal of public attention. . . .

Of course, you don't need an engineer to tell you why the towers fell down: two Boeing 767s, travelling at hundreds of miles an hour, and car-rying more than ten thousand gallons of jet fuel each (if you converted the energy in the Oklahoma City bomb into jet fuel, it would amount to only

VISUAL THINKING

Why . . . ?

● What is the emotional impact of this photograph on you? How does the juxtaposition of the World Trade Center wreckage with a New York City fireman affect your perception? When you see photographs like this of the WTC remnant forked into the ground, do they have any special symbolic meaning for you?

fifty-one gallons), crashed into the north and south buildings at 8:45 A.M. and 9:06 A.M., respectively, causing them to fall — the south tower at 9:59 A.M. and the north tower at ten-twenty-eight. Nor do we need a government panel to tell us that the best way to protect tall buildings is to keep airplanes out of them. Nevertheless, there is considerable debate among experts about precisely what order of events precipitated the collapse of each building, and whether the order was the same in both towers. Did the connections between the floors and the columns give way first or did the vertical supports that remained after the impact lose strength in the fire, and, if so, did the exterior columns or the core columns give way first? . . .

Was there any way for the structural engineers and architects involved in building the towers to know that they were going to collapse, and how quickly? . . .

Among the dozens of people I have spoken to recently who are experts in the construction of tall buildings (and many of whom witnessed the events of September 11th as they unfolded), only one said that he knew immediately, upon learning, from TV, of the planes' hitting the buildings, that the towers were going to fall. This was Mark Loizeaux, the president of Controlled Demolition Incorporated, a Maryland-based family business that specializes in reducing tall buildings to manageable pieces of rubble. "Within a nanosecond," he told me. "I said, 'It's coming down. And the second tower will fall first, because it was hit lower down.'" . . .

Loizeaux said he had an enhanced video of the collapses, and he talked about them in a way that indicated he had watched the video more than once. "First of all, you've got the obvious damage to the exterior frame from the airplane — if you count the number of external columns missing from the sides the planes hit, there are about two thirds of the total. And the buildings are still standing, which is amazing — even with all those columns missing, the gravity loads have found alternate pathways. O.K., but you've got fires — jet-fuel fires, which the building is not designed for, and you've also got lots of paper in there. Now, paper cooks. A paper fire is like a coal-mine fire: it keeps burning as long as oxygen gets to it. And you're high in the building, up in the wind, plenty of oxygen. So you've got a hot fire. And you've got these floor trusses, made of fairly thin metal, and fire protection has been knocked off most of them by the impact. And you have all this open space — clear span from perimeter to core — with no columns or partition walls, so the airplane is going to skid right through that space to the core, which doesn't have any reinforced concrete in it. Just sheetrock covering steel, and the fire is going to spread everywhere immediately, and no fire-protection systems are working — the sprinkler heads shorn off by the airplanes, the water pipes in the core are likely cut. So what's going to happen? Floor A is going to fall onto floor B, which falls onto floor C; the unsupported columns will buckle; and the

> weight of everything above the crash site falls onto what remains below — bringing loads of two thousand pounds per square foot, plus the force of the impact, onto floors designed to bear one hundred pounds per square foot. It has to fall." . . .
>
> — John Seabrook, "The Tower Builder"

Final Thoughts

Concepts are the vocabulary of thought, the general ideas that we use to represent our world; thinking patterns are the vehicles we use to relate and organize concepts so that we can make sense of our world. In this chapter you have examined a number of basic thinking patterns that can enable you to organize your experiences into relationships that have meaning to you:

- Chronological and process relationships
- Comparative and analogical relationships
- Causal relationships

Each of these thinking patterns helps you figure out what has happened in the past, what is occurring in the present, and what will happen in the future. You use these patterns to reveal the way the world is and also to impose your own interpretation on the events of your experience. In this sense we are all scientists and artists, both deciphering the mysteries of the world and composing our own unique perspectives on it. All of us perform these activities in distinctive ways and construct a view of the world that is uniquely our own. As you refine your abilities to relate and organize the conceptual vocabulary of your mind, you are improving the power and creativity of your thinking processes while at the same time developing a more accurate understanding of the world.

THINKING PASSAGES

Environmental Issues

The impact of human civilization on the environment has taken on increasing urgency as global warming, the razing of rain forests, the search for sustainable fuel sources, and our dependence on "factory-farmed" or genetically modified food are discussed and debated in the media and affect the most basic aspects of our lives, from the quality of our air to the safety of our next meal. The writers here consider the various and complicated causal relationships between humans and the natural world. As you read, watch for each writer's development of causal chains and evaluate the clarity and effectiveness of their arguments.

WORRIED? US?
by Bill McKibben

For fifteen years now, some small percentage of the world's scientists and diplomats and activists has inhabited one of those strange dreams where the dreamer desperately needs to warn someone about something bad and imminent; but somehow, no matter how hard he shouts, the other person in the dream — standing smiling, perhaps, with his back to an oncoming train — can't hear him. This group, this small percentage, knows that the world is about to change more profoundly than at any time in the history of human civilization. And yet, so far, all they have achieved is to add another line to the long list of human problems — people think about "global warming" in the way they think about "violence on television" or "growing trade deficits," as a marginal concern to them, if a concern at all. Enlightened governments make smallish noises and negotiate smallish treaties; enlightened people look down on America for its blind piggishness. Hardly anyone, however, has fear in their guts.

Why? Because, I think, we are fatally confused about time and space. Though we know that our culture has placed our own lives on a demonic fast-forward, we imagine that the earth must work on some other timescale. The long slow accretion of epochs — the Jurassic, the Cretaceous, the Pleistocene — lulls us into imagining that the physical world offers us an essentially stable background against which we can run our race. Humbly, we believe that the world is big and that we are small. This humility is attractive, but also historic and no longer useful. In the world as we have made it, the opposite is true. Each of us is big enough, for example, to produce our own cloud of carbon dioxide. As a result, we — our cars and our industry — have managed to raise the atmospheric level of carbon dioxide, which had been stable at 275 parts per million throughout human civilization, to about 380 parts per million, a figure that is climbing by one and a half parts per million each year. This increase began with the Industrial Revolution in

Source: Bill McKibben, "Worried? Us?" *Granta, 83,* Fall 2003. Reprinted by permission of Bill McKibben, author of *The End of Nature.*

the eighteenth century, and it has been accelerating ever since. The consequence, if we take a median from several respectable scientific projections, is that the world's temperature will rise by five degrees Fahrenheit (roughly two and a half degrees Celsius) over the next hundred years, to make it hotter than it has been for 400 million years. At some level, these are the only facts worth knowing about our earth.

Fifteen years ago, it was a hypothesis. Those of us who were convinced that the earth was warming fast were a small minority. Science was skeptical, but set to work with rigour. Between 1988 and 1995, scientists drilled deep into glaciers, took core samples from lake bottoms, counted tree rings, and, most importantly, refined elaborate computer models of the atmosphere. By 1995, the almost impossibly contentious world of science had seen enough. The world's most distinguished atmospheric chemists, physicists and climatologists, who had organized themselves into a large collective called the Intergovernmental Panel on Climate Change, made their pronouncement: "The balance of evidence suggests that there is a discernible human influence on global climate." In the eight years since, science has continued to further confirm and deepen these fears, while the planet itself has decided, as it were, to peer-review their work with a succession of ominously hot years (1998 was the hottest ever, with 2002 trailing by only a few hundredths of a degree). So far humanity has raised the planet's temperature by about one degree Fahrenheit, with most of that increase happening after 1970 — from about fifty-nine degrees Fahrenheit, where it had been stuck since the first cities rose and the first crops grew, to about sixty degrees. Five more degrees in the offing, as I have said, but already we understand, with an almost desperate clarity, how finely balanced our world has been. One degree turns out to be a lot. In the cryosphere — the frozen portions of the planet's surface — glaciers are everywhere in rapid retreat (spitting out Bronze Age hunter-gatherers). The snows of Kilimanjaro are set to become the rocks of Kilimanjaro by 2015. Montana's Glacier National Park is predicted to lose its last glaciers by 2030. We know how thick Arctic ice is — we know it because Cold War nuclear-powered submarines needed the information for their voyages under the ice cap. When the data was declassified in the waning days of the Clinton administration, it emerged that Arctic ice was forty per cent thinner than it had been forty years before. *Perma*frost is melting. Get it?

"Global warming" can be a misleading phrase — the temperature is only the signal that extra solar radiation is being trapped at the earth's surface. That extra energy drives many things: wind-speeds increase, a reflection of the increasing heat-driven gradients between low and high pressure; sea level starts to rise, less because of melting ice caps than because warm air holds more water vapour than cold; hence evaporation increases and with it drought, and then, when the overloaded clouds finally part, deluge and flood. Some of these effects are linear. A recent study has shown that rice fertility drops by ten per cent for each degree Celsius that the temperature rises above thirty degrees Celsius during the rice plant's flowering. At forty degrees Celsius, rice fertility drops to zero. But science has come to understand that some effects may not follow such a clear progression. To paraphrase Orwell, we may all be hot, but some will be hotter than others. If the Gulf Stream fails because of Arctic melting, some may, during some seasons, even be colder.

The success of the scientific method underlines the failure of the political method. It is clear what must happen — the rapid conversion of our energy system from fossil to renewable fuels. And it is clear that it could happen — much of the necessary technology is no longer quixotic, no longer the province of backyard tinkerers. And it is also clear that it isn't happening. Some parts of Europe have made material progress — Denmark has built great banks of windmills. Some parts of Europe have made promises — the United Kingdom thinks it can cut its carbon emissions by sixty per cent by 2050. But China and India are still building power plants and motorways, and the United States has made it utterly clear that nothing will change soon. When Bill Clinton was President he sat by while American civilians traded up from cars to troop-transport vehicles; George Bush has not only rejected the Kyoto treaty, he has ordered the Environmental Protection Agency to replace "global warming" with the less ominous "climate change," and issued a national energy policy that foresees ever more drilling, refining and burning. Under it, American carbon emissions will grow another forty per cent in the next generation.

As satisfying as it is to blame politicians, however, it will not do. Politicians will follow the path of least resistance. So far there has not been a movement loud or sustained enough to command political attention. Electorates demand economic prosperity — more of it — above all things. Gandhianism, the political philosophy that restricts material need, is now only a memory even in the country of its birth. And our awareness that the world will change in every aspect, should we be so aware, is muted by the future tense, even though that future isn't far away, so near in fact that preventing global warming is a lost cause — all we can do now is to try to keep it from getting utterly out of control.

This is a failure of imagination, and in this way a literary failure. Global warming has still to produce an Orwell or a Huxley, a Verne or a Wells, a *Nineteen Eighty-Four* or a *War of the Worlds*, or in film any equivalent of *On the Beach* or *Doctor Strangelove*. It may never do so. It may be that because — fingers crossed — we have escaped our most recent fear, nuclear annihilation via the Cold War, we resist being scared all over again. Fear has its uses, but fear on this scale seems to be disabling, paralysing. Anger has its uses too, but the rage of anti-globalization demonstrators has yet to do more than alienate majorities. Shame sends a few Americans shopping for small cars, but on the whole America, now the exemplar to the world, is very nearly unshameable.

My own dominant feeling has always been sadness. In 1989, I published *The End of Nature*, the first book for a lay audience about global warming. Half of it was devoted to explaining the science, the other half to my unease. It seemed, and still seems, to me that humanity has intruded into and altered every part of the earth (or very nearly) with our habits and economies. Thoreau once said that he could walk half an hour from his home in Concord, Massachusetts, and come to a place where no man stood from one year to the next, and "there consequently politics are not, for politics are but the cigar smoke of a man." Now that cigar smoke blows everywhere.

Paradoxically, the world also seems more lonely. Everything else exists at our sufferance. Biologists guess that the result of a rapid warming will be the greatest wave of extinction since the last asteroid crashed into the earth. Now we are the asteroid. The notion that we live in a God-haunted world is harder to conjure up. God rebuked Job: "Were you there when I wrapped the ocean in clouds . . . and set its boundaries, saying, 'Here you may come but no farther. Here shall your proud waves break . . . Who gathers up the stormclouds, slits them and pours them out?'" Job, and everyone else until our time, had the sweet privilege of shutting up in the face of that boast — it was clearly God or gravity or some force other than us. But as of about 1990 we can answer back, because we set the sea level now, and we run the storm systems. The excretion of our economy has become the most important influence on the planet we were born into. We're what counts.

Our ultimate sadness lies in the fact that we know that this is not a preordained destiny; it isn't fate. New ways of behaving, of getting and spending, can still change the future; there is, as the religious evangelist would say, still time, though not much of it, and a miraculous conversion is called for — Americans in the year 2000 produced fifteen per cent more carbon dioxide than they had ten years before.

The contrast between two speeds is the key fact of our age: between the pace at which the physical world is changing and the pace at which human

Thinking Critically About Images: Truth and Reality in the Media

As a critical thinker, you are learning to consider many different sources of information and to test those sources against your own experience of the world. You are careful to evaluate the authority and credibility of those sources; you are aware of the different kinds of appeals that are made in order to persuade you to buy something or vote for someone; and you maintain a healthy skepticism about anyone who claims to be totally in the right or to have the only correct answer. The goal of thinking critically is to develop the most informed perspective possible, by examining various perspectives (including our own!) and then critically evaluating their strengths and weaknesses.

The word "media" is the plural of "medium;" it means, simply, something that is "in the middle," something that conveys something else from one place to another. At its most fundamental level, then, the term "media" seems perfectly neutral. But we know that the "media" is not neutral at all; anyone, or anything, claiming to be perfectly impartial and omniscient would probably be dismissed as insane! In our time, "media" has come to mean any way of conveying information, be it through newspapers, cable news networks, web sites, or blogs. As critical thinkers, we must learn to recognize the ways in which the media present biased or incomplete information, and develop strategies so that we can be sure of getting "the whole story" if not the "truth" behind the news.

Everything that you see in this portfolio of images — just like everything you see on the news — *happened*. And yet the creators of these photos and web sites were keenly aware of the power of these images to make a persuasive argument about a particular *version* of that truth. The late media analyst and scholar Marshall McLuhan, who famously declared that "the medium is the message," also noted that "only puny secrets need protection. Big discoveries are protected by public incredulity." McLuhan made his observations decades before the Internet; he died just as cable television was becoming a more constant presence in American lives. How likely are you to believe that something is "true" because you read about it in a newspaper, or on a web site? Now, more than ever, is it "true" that a picture is worth a thousand words?

Mission Accomplished?

- President George W. Bush arrived on the aircraft carrier *USS Lincoln* on board a Navy fighter jet on May 1, 2003. Despite the banner reading "Mission Accomplished" and his speech in which the President declared the war in Iraq a "victory" and said that the United States and its allies had "prevailed," American soldiers continued to fight and die in Iraq through 2004.

Thinking critically about the image

1. Using the information in the photo caption above, conduct an online and database search to locate at least five different articles describing this event. The articles you select should offer different perspectives and interpretations. Apply the same questions and critical thinking skills to this exercise that you used in your comparisons of different accounts of 9/11 and Tiananmen Square.

2. Locate the text of the speech that President Bush gave on this occasion. What visual elements of the day's events seem to complement or underscore his rhetoric?

A Hidden Homecoming

- In March 2004, a Freedom of Information Act filing compelled the Pentagon to release photographs of the coffins of United States soldiers killed in Iraq being returned to Dover Air Force Base. These photographs were taken by Air Force photographers. In June 2004, the United States Senate voted to uphold a ban on the future release of such photos.

Thinking critically about the image

1. Editors of television news programs as well as newspapers and magazines are very attentive to the effect that images have when they are placed next to each other. What is the effect of seeing these two photographs on facing pages? Is there an argument being made by the placement of these two images next to each other? Is that argument fair?

2. Look up the full text of the Freedom of Information Act online (one source is at Legal Information Institute, <http://www4.law.cornell.edu/uscode/5/552.html>), and find other examples of the use of this act by individuals seeking information from government agencies.

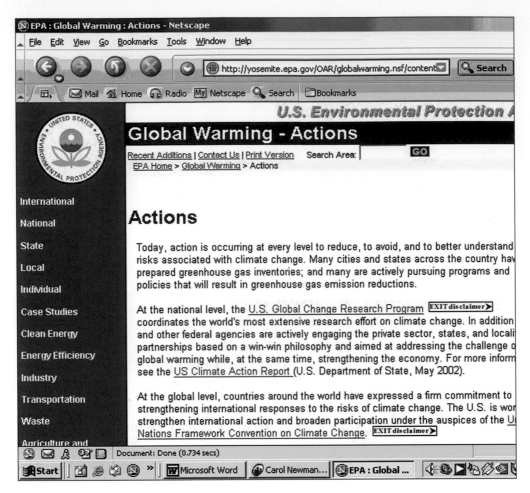

Government Keeps Its Cool . . .

- The web sites on these two pages were both found through the search engine Google, using the search term "global warming." The U.S. Environmental Protection Agency (EPA) sponsors this web site; this particular page (captured in 2004) describes how state and federal governments are responding to global warming under the Bush administration.

Thinking critically about the image

1. Using Google, conduct your own search using the term "global warming." How many sites does Google find? How could you refine your search to come up with a more useful source list for a research paper?

2. Compare the language and priorities of this web page with that of the Union of Concerned Scientists. What is a "win-win" situation? Which site stresses economic considerations, and why? What is each site's opinion about global warming, and how can you tell?

. . . While Scientists Feel the Heat

- The Union of Concerned Scientists was founded by students and faculty at the Massachusetts Institute of Technology. A nonprofit alliance of scientists and concerned citizens, the organization lobbies government about global warming issues.

Thinking critically about the image

1. Compare the rhetoric and images on the Union of Concerned Scientists page to that of the EPA. To whom is each site appealing, and how does it get a reader's attention? (Review the discussions of various kinds of argumentative appeals in Chapter 11.)

2. Of these two pages, which urges the reader to take direct action? What kind of action is urged, and how can you tell?

3. Would you be able to base a well-reasoned argument about global warming on either the Union of Concerned Scientists web site or the EPA web site alone? Why, or why not?

Love, Honor, and Cherish

- The officiant presiding over this August 2003 wedding ceremony in Massachusetts proclaimed: "Through no power invested in me by the state or any religious institution, but instead through the power invested in me by your family, friends, and the two of you." In 2004, the Massachusetts Supreme Judicial Court finally ruled that same-sex couples have the same right to apply for marriage licenses as straight couples.

Thinking critically about the image

1. Photojournalists often take dozens of images of an event or person; the images eventually selected to complement a story are chosen by an editor, sometimes without the input of the photojournalist or the reporter writing the story. As a consumer of news media, what qualities do you think make for an effective, compelling, and accurate image?

2. Does this image seem to make an argument for or against same-sex marriage? In what way?

For Better or Worse

- *The Saturday Evening Post,* founded in 1728, is the oldest continuously publishing magazine in America. In the mid-twentieth century, its cover illustrations by artists such as Norman Rockwell depicted a sunny, mythic America. This 1953 illustration, by Constantin Alajalov, is entitled "Wedding Recessional."

Thinking critically about the image

1. The issue of same-sex marriage is just one of many challenges to traditional ideas about the family in contemporary American culture. Were you to make an argument about marriage in America today, what kinds of illustrations would you use to support your claims?

2. Who is the "gay young bachelor" of this magazine's headline? How would a celebrity or politician today react to being called a "gay young bachelor" — whether he was gay or not? How does language shape, inform, and describe a changing social issue like marriage?

3. Are there any similarities between the images on these two pages? What are the key differences between these images? How can those similarities and/or differences be used to support an argument about the changing nature of the American marriage?

Tracking Santa

- The North American Aerospace Defense Command, a joint operation of the Canadian and American armed forces to "Deter, Detect, Defend" North American airspace against hostile actions. The original intent of NORAD was to protect against potential Cold War–era enemy action; according to its main web site at <www.norad.mil>, NORAD's mission has changed since the terrorist attacks of 9/11 to focus on the potential threat to North American airspace from within the borders of the United States and Canada.

Thinking critically about the image

1. "NORAD Tracks Santa" is one of the options available at the "For Kids Only" link on the NORAD web site. (You might remember similar broadcasts by your local news channel's weather service on Christmas Eve.) Locate the web pages of other government and military institutions, such as the Central Intelligence Agency and the National Institutes of Health. What kinds of sites and activities are offered for children? Are you surprised?

2. Examine the graphics of this web page. What do the wings and the swords signify? What do they have to do with Santa?

society is reacting to this change. In history, if it exists, we shall be praised or damned.

～～～～

THE CONUNDRUM OF CONSUMPTION
by Alan Thein Durning

For Sidney Quarrier of Essex, Connecticut, Earth Day 1990 was Judgment Day — the day of ecological reckoning. While tens of millions of people around the world were marching and celebrating in the streets, Sidney was sitting at his kitchen table with a yellow legal pad and a pocket calculator. The task he set himself was to tally up the burden he and his family had placed on the planet since Earth Day 1970.[1]

Early that spring morning he began tabulating everything that had gone into their house — oil for heating, nuclear-generated electricity, water for showers and watering the lawn, cans of paint, appliances, square footage of carpet, furniture, clothes, food, and thousands of other things — and everything that had come out — garbage pails of junk mail and packaging, newspapers and magazines by the cubic meter, polluted water, and smoke from the furnace. He listed the resources they had tapped to move them around by car and airplane, from fuel and lubricants to tires and replacement parts. "I worked on that list most of the day," Sid remembers. "I dug out wads of old receipts, weighed trash cans and the daily mail, excavated the basement and shed, and used triangulation techniques I hadn't practiced since graduate school to estimate the materials we used in the roofing job.[2]

Manufacturing and delivering each of the objects on his list, Sid knew, had required additional resources he was unable to count. National statistics suggested, for example, that he should double the energy he used in his house and car to allow for what businesses and government used to provide him with goods and services. He visualized a global industrial network of factories making things for him, freighters and trucks transporting them, stores selling them, and office buildings supervising the process. He wondered how much steel and concrete his state needed for the roads, bridges, and parking garages he used. He wondered about resources used by the hospital that cared for him, the air force jets and police cars that protected

---

Source: Alan Durning, "The Conondrum of Consumption," from *How Much Is Enough?* Alan Durning directs Northwest Environment Watch in Seattle, Washington.

him, the television stations that entertained him, and the veterinary office that cured his dog.

As his list grew, Sid was haunted by an imaginary mountain of discarded televisions, car parts, and barrels of oil — all piling up toward the sky on his lot. "It was a sober revisiting of that period. . . . It's only when you put together all the years of incremental consumption that you realize the totality." That totality hit him like the ton of paper packaging he had hauled out with the trash over the years: "The question is," Sid said, "Can the earth survive the impact of Sid, and can the Sids of the future change?"[3]

That *is* the question. Sidney Quarrier and his family are no gluttons. "During those years, we lived in a three-bedroom house on two and a half acres in the country, about 35 miles from my job in Hartford," Sidney recounts. "But we have never been rich," he insists. "What frightened me was that our consumption was typical of the people here in Connecticut."[4]

Sid's class — the American middle class — is the group that, more than any other, defines and embodies the contemporary international vision of the good life. Yet the way the Quarriers lived for those 20 years is among the world's premier environmental problems, and may be the most difficult to solve.

Only population growth rivals high consumption as a cause of ecological decline, and at least population growth is now viewed as a problem by many governments and citizens of the world. Consumption, in contrast, is almost universally seen as good — indeed, increasing it is the primary goal of national economic policy. The consumption levels exemplified in the two decades Sid Quarrier reviewed are the highest achieved by any civilization in human history. They manifest the full flowering of a new form of human society: the consumer society.

This new manner of living was born in the United States, and the words of an American best capture its spirit. In the age of U.S. affluence that began after World War II, retailing analyst Victor Lebow declared: "Our enormously productive economy . . . demands that we make consumption our way of life, that we convert the buying and use of goods into rituals, that we seek our spiritual satisfaction, our ego satisfaction, in consumption. . . . We need things consumed, burned up, worn out, replaced, and discarded at an ever increasing rate." Most citizens of western nations have responded to Lebow's call, and the rest of the world appears intent on following.[5]

In industrial lands, consumption now permeates social values. Opinion surveys in the world's two largest economies — Japan and the United States — show that people increasingly measure success by the amount they consume. The Japanese speak of the "new three sacred treasures": color television, air conditioning, and the automobile. One fourth of Poles deem "Dynasty," which portrays the life-style of the richest Americans, their favorite television program, and villagers in the heart of Africa follow "Dallas," the television series that portrays American oil tycoons. In Taiwan, a billboard demands "Why Aren't You a Millionaire Yet?" A *Business Week* correspondent beams: "The American Dream is alive and well . . . in Mexico." Indeed, the words "consumer" and "person" have become virtual synonyms.[6]

The life-style made in the United States is emulated by those who can afford it around the world, but many cannot. The economic fault lines that fracture the globe defy comprehension. The world has 202 billionaires and more than 3 million millionaires. It also has 100 million homeless people who live on roadsides, in garbage dumps, and under bridges. The value of luxury goods sales worldwide — high-fashion clothing, top-of-the-line autos, and the other trappings of wealth — exceeds the gross national products of two thirds of the world's countries. Indeed, the world's average income, about $5,000 a year, is below the U.S. poverty line.[7]

The gaping divide in material consumption between the fortunate and unfortunate stands out starkly in their impacts on the natural world. The soaring consumption lines that track the rise of the consumer society are, from another perspective, surging indicators of environmental harm. The consumer society's exploitation of resources threatens to exhaust, poison, or unalterably disfigure forests, soils, water, and air. We, its members, are responsible for a disproportionate share of all the global environmental challenges facing humanity.

Ironically, high consumption is a mixed blessing in human terms too. People living in the nineties are on average four-and-a-half times richer than their great-grandparents were at the turn of the century, but they are not four-and-a-half times happier. Psychological evidence shows that the relationship between consumption and personal happiness is weak. Worse, two primary sources of human fulfillment — social relations and leisure — appear to have withered or stagnated in the rush to riches. Thus many of us in the consumer society have a sense that our world of plenty is somehow hollow — that, hoodwinked by a consumerist culture, we have been fruitlessly attempting to satisfy with material things what are essentially social, psychological, and spiritual needs.[8]

Of course, the opposite of overconsumption — destitution — is no solution to either environmental or human problems. It is infinitely worse for people and bad for the natural world too. Dispossessed peasants slash-and-burn their way into the rain forests of Latin America, hungry nomads turn their herds out onto fragile African rangeland, reducing it to desert, and small farmers in India and the Philippines cultivate steep slopes, exposing them to the erosive powers of rain. Perhaps half the world's billion-plus absolute poor are caught in a downward spiral of ecological and economic impoverishment. In desperation, they knowingly abuse the land, salvaging the present by savaging the future.[9]

If environmental destruction results when people have either too little or too much, we are left to wonder, How much is enough? What level of consumption can the earth support? When does having more cease to add appreciably to human satisfaction? Is it possible for all the world's people to live comfortably without bringing on the decline of the planet's natural health? Is there a level of living above poverty and subsistence but below the consumer life-style — a level of sufficiency? Could all the world's people have central heating? Refrigerators? Clothes dryers? Automobiles? Air conditioning? Heated swimming pools? Airplanes? Second homes?

Many of these questions cannot be answered definitively, but for each of us in the consumer society, asking is essential nonetheless. Unless we see that more is not always better, our efforts to forestall ecological decline will be overwhelmed by our appetites. Unless we ask, we will likely fail to see the forces around us that stimulate these appetites, such as relentless advertising, proliferating shopping centers, and social pressures to "keep up with the Joneses." We may overlook forces that make consumption more destructive than it need be, such as subsidies to mines, paper mills, and other industries with high environmental impacts. And we may not act on opportunities to improve our lives while consuming less, such as working fewer hours to spend more time with family and friends.

Still, the difficulty of transforming the consumer society into a sustainable one can scarcely be overestimated. We consumers enjoy a life-style that almost everybody else aspires to, and why shouldn't they? Who would just as soon *not* have an automobile, a big house on a big lot, and complete control over indoor temperature throughout the year? The momentum of centuries of economic history and the material cravings of 5.5 billion people lie on the side of increasing consumption.

We may be, therefore, in a conundrum — a problem admitting of no satisfactory solution. Limiting the consumer life-style to those who have already attained it is not politically possible, morally defensible, or ecologically sufficient. And extending that life-style to all would simply hasten the ruin of the biosphere. The global environment cannot support 1.1 billion of us living like American consumers, much less 5.5 billion people, or a future population of at least 8 billion. On the other hand, reducing the consumption levels of the consumer society, and tempering material aspirations elsewhere, though morally acceptable, is a quixotic proposal. It bucks the trend of centuries. Yet it may be the only option.

If the life-supporting ecosystems of the planet are to survive for future generations, the consumer society will have to dramatically curtail its use of resources — partly by shifting to high-quality, low-input durable goods and partly by seeking fulfillment through leisure, human relationships, and other nonmaterial avenues. We in the consumer society will have to live a technologically sophisticated version of the life-style currently practiced lower on the economic ladder. Scientific advances, better laws, restructured industries, new treaties, environmental taxes, grassroots campaigns — all can help us get there. But ultimately, sustaining the environment that sustains humanity will require that we change our values.

–1992

Notes

1. Sidney Quarrier, geologist, Connecticut Geological & Natural History Survey, Hartford, Conn., private communication, February 25, 1992.
2. Ibid.
3. Ibid.
4. Ibid.
5. Lebow in *Journal of Retailing,* quoted in Vance Packard, *The Waste Makers* (New York: David Mckay, 1960).
6. Sepp Linhart, "From Industrial to Postindustrial Society: Changes in Japanese Leisure-Related Values and Behavior," *Journal of Japanese Studies,* Summer 1988; Richard A. Easterlin and Eileen M. Crimmins, "Recent Social Trends: Changes in Personal Aspirations of American Youth," *Sociology and Social Research,* July 1988; "Dynasty" from "Harper's Index," *Harper's,* December 1990; "Dallas" from Jerry Mander, *In the Absence of the Sacred* (San Francisco: Sierra Club Books, 1991); Taiwan from "Asian Century," *Newsweek,* February 22, 1988; Stephen Baker and S. Lynne Walker, "The American Dream Is Alive and Well — in Mexico," *Business Week,* September 30, 1991.
7. Billionaires from Jennifer Reese, "The Billionaires: More Than Ever in 1991," *Fortune,* September 9, 1991; millionaires estmated from Kevin R. Phillips, "Reagan's America: A Capital Offense," *New York Times Magazine,* June 18, 1990; homelessness from U.N. Centre for Human Settlements, New York, private communication, November 1, 1989; luxury goods from "The Lapse of Luxury," *Economist,* January 5, 1991; gross national product from United Nations Development Programme, *Human Development Report 1991* (New York: Oxford University Press,

1991); member countries in United Nations from U.N. Information Center, Washignton, D.C., private communication, January 14, 1992; world average income from 1987, in 1987 U.S. dollars adjusted for international variations in purchasing power, from Ronald V. A. Sprout and James H. Weaver, "International Distribution of Income: 1960–1987," Working Paper No. 159, Department of Economics, American University, Washington, D.C., May 1991; U.S. 1987 poverty line for an individual from U.S. Bureau of the Census, *Statistical Abstract of the United States: 1990* (Washington, D.C.: U.S. Government Printing Office, 1990).

8. Four-and-a-half times richer from Angus Maddison, *The World Economy in the 20th Century* (Paris: Organisation for Economic Co-operation and Development, 1989).

9. Alan Durning, *Poverty and the Environment: Reversing the Downward Spiral,* Worldwatch Paper 92 (Washington, D.C.: Worldwatch Institute, November 1989).

Questions for Analysis

1. Both McKibben and Durning imply an ethical obligation, both individual and collective, to change our habits of consumption. What do these authors think about the effects of American consumer culture on the natural environment and on our relationships with each other? What evidence does each author offer to support his causal claim(s)? How would you balance their ethical demands with the practical (and, frankly, recreational) needs of your own life?

2. Create a diagram that illustrates the various causes of industrialism (as Durning sees it) that lead to a particular effect. (This is a kind of summary; it may be a more effective way for you to work through and understand a complex reading.)

3. In paragraph 12, Durning notes that "we have been fruitlessly attempting to satisfy with material things what are essentially social, psychological, and spiritual needs." Do you agree, or disagree? Are there different kinds of satisfaction to be had in life, and are any of them more virtuous or important than the others?

4. Think about the most recent meal you ate. Where did it come from? Who grew it, harvested it, shipped it, and sold it? Should you know? Should you care?

Reporting, Inferring, and Judging

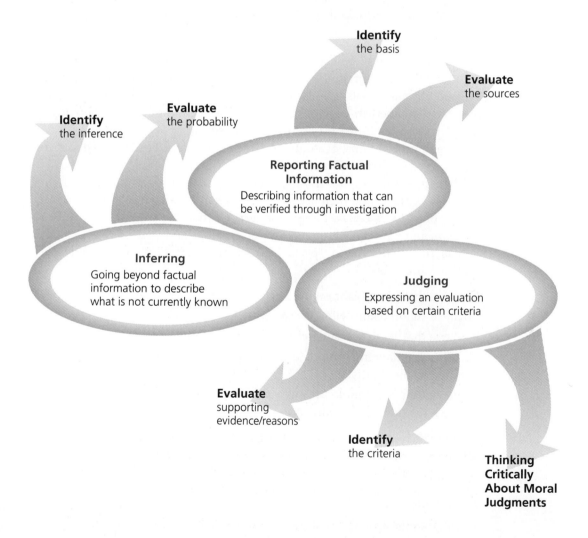

Identify
the basis

Evaluate
the sources

Evaluate
the probability

Identify
the inference

Reporting Factual Information
Describing information that can be verified through investigation

Inferring
Going beyond factual information to describe what is not currently known

Judging
Expressing an evaluation based on certain criteria

Evaluate
supporting evidence/reasons

Identify
the criteria

Thinking Critically About Moral Judgments

The main goal of your thinking process is to organize the world into intelligible relationships that help you understand what is going on. The relationships that you compose and discover express the basic thinking patterns you use to make sense of the world. In the last chapter we critically examined the following basic thinking patterns:

- Chronological and process
- Comparative and analogical
- Causal

In this chapter we will be exploring the way that we use these thinking patterns, and others, to organize our beliefs and knowledge about the world. Beliefs are the main tools you use to make sense of the world and guide your actions, as explained in Chapter 5. The total collection of your beliefs represents your view of the world and your philosophy of life. More specifically, beliefs are interpretations, evaluations, conclusions, and predictions about the world that you endorse as true.

All beliefs are not equal. In fact, beliefs differ from one another in many kinds of ways, including their accuracy. The belief "The earth is surrounded by stars and planets" is considerably more certain than the belief "The positions of the stars and planets determine our personalities and destinies."

Beliefs differ in other respects besides accuracy. Review the following beliefs, and then describe some of their differences:

1. I believe that I have hair on my head.
2. I believe that the sun will rise tomorrow.
3. I believe that there is some form of life after death.
4. I believe that dancing is more fun than jogging and that jogging is preferable to going to the dentist.
5. I believe that you should always act toward others in ways that you would like to have them act toward you.

In this chapter you will be thinking critically about three basic types of beliefs you use to make sense of the world:

- Reports
- Inferences
- Judgments

These beliefs are expressed in both your thinking and your use of language, as illustrated in the following sentences:

1. My bus was late today.
   Type of belief: reporting
2. My bus will probably be late tomorrow.
   Type of belief: inferring
3. The bus system is unreliable.
   Type of belief: judging

Now try the activity with a different set of statements.

1. Each modern atomic warhead has over one hundred times the explosive power of the bomb dropped on Hiroshima.
   Type of belief:
2. With all of the billions of planets in the universe, the odds are that there are other forms of life in the cosmos.
   Type of belief:
3. In the long run, the energy needs of the world will best be met by solar energy technology rather than nuclear energy or fossil fuels.
   Type of belief:

As you examine these statements, you can see that they provide you with different types of information about the world. For example, the first statement in each list reports aspects of the world that you can verify — that is, check for accuracy. By doing the appropriate sort of investigating, you can determine whether the bus was actually late today and whether modern atomic warheads really have the power attributed to them. When you describe the world in ways that can be verified through investigation, you are said to be *reporting* factual information about the world.

> **reporting factual information** *Describing the world in ways that can be verified through investigation*

Looking at the second statement in each list, you can see immediately that each provides a different sort of information from the first one. These statements cannot be verified. There is no way to investigate and determine with certainty whether the bus will indeed be late tomorrow or whether there is in fact life on other planets. Although these conclusions may be based on factual information, they go beyond factual information to make statements about what is not currently known. When you describe the world in ways that are based on factual information yet go beyond this information to make statements regarding what is not currently known, you are said to be *inferring* conclusions about the world.

> **inferring** *Describing the world in ways that are based on factual information yet going beyond this information to make statements about what is not currently known*

Finally, as you examine the third statement in both lists, it is apparent that these statements are different from both factual reports and inferences. They describe the world in ways that express the speaker's evaluation — of the bus service and of energy sources. These evaluations are based on certain standards (criteria) that the speaker is using to judge the bus service as unreliable and solar energy as more promising than nuclear energy or fossil fuels. When you describe the world in ways that express your evaluation based on certain criteria, you are said to be *judging*.

> **judging** *Describing the world in ways that express an evaluation based on certain criteria*

You continually use these various ways of describing and organizing your world — reporting, inferring, judging — to make sense of your experience. In most cases, you are not aware that you are actually performing these activities, nor are you usually aware of the differences among them. Yet these three activities work together to help you see the world as a complete picture.

THINKING ACTIVITY 9.1

Identifying Reports, Inferences, and Judgments

1. Compose six sentences that embody these three types of beliefs: two reports, two inferences, and two evaluations.
2. Locate a short article from a newspaper or magazine and identify the reports, inferences, and judgments it contains.

VISUAL THINKING

Observing a Street Scene

● Carefully examine this photograph of a street scene. Then write five statements based on your observations of the scene. Identify each statement as reporting, inferring, or judging, and explain why you classify each one as such.

Reporting Factual Information

The statements that result from the activity of reporting express the most accurate beliefs you have about the world. Factual beliefs have earned this distinction because they are verifiable, usually with one or more of your senses. For example, consider the following factual statement:

That young woman is wearing a brown hat in the rain.

This statement about an event in the world is considered to be factual because it can be verified by your immediate sense experience — what you can (in principle or in theory) see, hear, touch, feel, or smell. It is important to say *in principle* or *in theory* because you often do not use all of your relevant senses to check out what you are experiencing. Look again at your example of a factual statement: You would normally be satisfied to *see* this event, without insisting on touching the hat or giving the person a physical examination. If necessary, however, you could perform these additional actions — in principle or in theory.

You use the same reasoning when you believe factual statements from other people that you are not in a position to check out immediately. For instance:

- The Great Wall of China is more than fifteen hundred miles long.
- There are large mountains and craters on the moon.
- Your skin is covered with germs.

You consider these to be factual statements because, even though you cannot verify them with your senses at the moment, you could in principle or in theory verify them with your senses *if* you were flown to China, *if* you were rocketed to the moon, or *if* you were to examine your skin with a powerful microscope. The process of verifying factual statements involves *identifying* the sources of information on which they are based and *evaluating* the reliability of these sources, topics examined in some detail in Chapter 5.

You communicate factual information to others by means of reports. A *report* is a description of something experienced that is communicated in as accurate and complete a way as possible. Through reports you can share your sense experiences with other people, and this mutual sharing enables you to learn much more about the world than if you were confined to knowing only what you experience. The *recording* (making records) of factual reports also makes possible the accumulation of knowledge learned by previous generations.

Because factual reports play such an important role in our exchange and accumulation of information about the world, it is important that they be as accurate and complete as possible. This brings us to a problem. We have already seen in previous chapters that our perceptions and observations are often *not* accurate or complete. What this means is that often when we think we are making true, factual reports, our reports are actually inaccurate or incomplete. For instance, consider our earlier "factual statement":

That young woman is wearing a brown hat in the rain.

Here are some questions you could ask concerning the accuracy of the statement:

- Is the woman really young, or does she merely look young?
- Is the woman really a woman, or a man disguised as a woman?

- Is that really a hat the woman/man is wearing or something else (e.g., a paper bag)?

Of course, there are methods you could use to clear up these questions with more detailed observations. Can you describe some of these methods?

Besides difficulties with observations, the "facts" that you see in the world actually depend on more general *beliefs* that you have about how the world operates. Consider the question "Why did the man's body fall from the top of the building to the sidewalk?" Having had some general science courses, you might say something like "The body was simply obeying the law of gravity," and you would consider this to be a "factual statement." But how did people account for this sort of event before Newton formulated the law of gravity? Some popular responses might have included the following:

- Things always fall down, not up.

- The spirit in the body wanted to join with the spirit of the earth.

When people made statements like these and others, such as "Humans can't fly," they thought that they were making "factual statements." Increased knowledge and understanding have since shown these "factual beliefs" to be inaccurate, and so they have been replaced by "better" beliefs. These "better beliefs" are able to explain the world in a way that is more accurate and predictable. Will many of the beliefs you now consider to be factually accurate also be replaced in the future by beliefs that are *more* accurate and predictable? If history is any indication, this will most certainly happen. (Already Newton's formulations have been replaced by Einstein's, based on the latter's theory of relativity. And Einstein's have been refined and modified as well and may be replaced someday.)

THINKING ACTIVITY 9.2

Evaluating Factual Information

1. Locate and carefully read an article that deals with an important social issue.
2. Summarize the main theme and key points of the article.
3. Describe the factual statements that are used to support the major theme.
4. Evaluate the accuracy of the factual information.
5. Evaluate the reliability of the sources of the factual information.

VISUAL THINKING

Telescoping Visions

- What concept is the artist depicting in this illustration? What do you think he means to suggest by the woman standing on one telescope and holding another in her hands?

THINKING ACTIVITY 9.3

"Real" and Manipulated Images in Film

In Chapter 4 we examined the process of perceiving, so we know that the cliché "Seeing is believing" is not always true. The increasing popularity and affordability of digital photography and image enhancement software have directly demonstrated to many people the degree to which images can be manipulated to create pictures of people and events with no counterpart in "real" life.

Special effects in movies were much easier to identify as "unreal" before recent advances in computer modeling. The success of full-length animated feature films has led some motion picture industry experts to predict that films in the near future may feature animated "synthetic actors." If computer techniques continue to grow in sophistication, will the audience be able to distinguish "real" from "synthetic" actors?

For examples of special effects in film, go to the companion web site.

THINKING PASSAGE

The End of My Childhood

The following essay by N. Scott Momaday, "The End of My Childhood," illustrates the way in which reporting factual information can help us understand memorable experiences and the spiritual mystery of certain places. After reading the selection, answer the questions that follow.

THE END OF MY CHILDHOOD
by N. Scott Momaday

At Jemez I came to the end of my childhood. There were no schools within easy reach. I had to go nearly thirty miles to school at Bernalillo, and one year I lived away in Albuquerque. My mother and father wanted me to have the benefit of a sound preparation for college, and so we read through many high school catalogues. After long deliberation we decided that I should spend my last year of high school at a military academy in Virginia.

The day before I was to leave I went walking across the river to the red mesa, where many times before I had gone to be alone with my thoughts. And I had climbed several times to the top of the mesa and looked among the old ruins there for pottery. This time I chose to climb the north end, perhaps because I had not gone that way before and wanted to see what it was. It was a difficult climb, and when I got to the top I was spent. I lingered among the ruins for more than an hour, I judge, waiting for my strength to return. From there I could see the whole valley below, the fields, the river, and the village. It was all very beautiful, and the sight of it filled me with longing.

Source: N. Scott Momaday, "The End of My Childhood," from *Names: A Memoir,* Harper & Row, 1976. Reprinted by permission of the author.

I looked for an easier way to come down, and at length I found a broad, smooth runway of rock, a shallow groove winding out like a stream. It appeared to be safe enough, and I started to follow it. There were steps along the way, a stairway, in effect. But the steps became deeper and deeper, and at last I had to drop down the length of my body and more. Still it seemed convenient to follow in the groove of rock. I was more than halfway down when I came upon a deep, funnel-shaped formation in my path. And there I had to make a decision. The slope on either side was extremely steep and forbidding, and yet I thought that I could work my way down on either side. The formation at my feet was something else. It was perhaps ten or twelve feet deep, wide at the top and narrow at the bottom, where there appeared to be a level ledge. If I could get down through the funnel to the ledge, I should be all right; surely the rest of the way down was negotiable. But I realized that there could be no turning back. Once I was down in that rocky chute I could not get up again, for the round wall which nearly encircled the space there was too high and sheer. I elected to go down into it, to try for the ledge directly below. I eased myself down the smooth, nearly vertical wall on my back, pressing my arms and legs outward against the sides. After what seemed a long time I was trapped in the rock. The ledge was no longer there below me; it had been an optical illusion. Now, in this angle of vision, there was nothing but the ground, far, far below, and jagged boulders set there like teeth. I remember that my arms were scraped and bleeding, stretched out against the walls with all the pressure that I could exert. When once I looked down I saw that my legs, also spread out and pressed hard against the walls, were shaking violently. I was in an impossible situation: I could not move in any direction, save downward in a fall, and I could not stay beyond another minute where I was. I believed then that I would die there, and I saw with a terrible clarity the things of the valley below. They were not the less beautiful to me. It seemed to me that I grew suddenly very calm in view of that beloved world. And I remember nothing else of that moment. I passed out of my mind, and the next thing I knew I was sitting down on the ground, very cold in the shadows, and looking up at the rock where I had been within an eyelash of eternity. That was a strange thing in my life, and I think of it as the end of an age. I should never again see the world as I saw it on the other side of that moment, in the bright reflection of time lost. There are such reflections, and for some of them I have the names.

Questions for Analysis

1. Momaday begins his essay with the statement "At Jemez I came to the end of my childhood." Identify the descriptions of his experience at Jemez that lead him to this conclusion.

2. His essay concludes with this passage: "That was a strange thing in my life, and I think of it as the end of an age. I should never again see the world as I saw it on the other side of that moment, in the bright reflection of time lost." Explain why Momaday sees the world differently as a result of his experiences.

3. Think about an experience that had special meaning for you, one that transformed the way you see the world. Write a passage in which you use descriptive reports to create the atmosphere and meaning that this experience had for you.

Inferring

Imagine yourself in the following situations:

1. Your roommate has just learned that she passed a math exam for which she had done absolutely no studying. Humming the song "I Did It My Way," she comes bouncing over to you with a huge grin on her face and says, "Let me buy you dinner to celebrate!" What do you conclude about how she is feeling?

2. It is midnight and the library is about to close. As you head for the door, you spy your roommate shuffling along in an awkward waddle. His coat bulges out in front like he's pregnant. When you ask, "What's going on?" he gives you a glare and hisses, "Shhh!" Just before he reaches the door, a pile of books slides from under his coat and crashes to the floor. What do you conclude?

In these examples, it would be reasonable to make the following conclusions:

1. Your roommate is happy.
2. Your roommate is stealing library books.

Although these conclusions are reasonable, they are not factual reports; they are *inferences*. You have not directly experienced your roommate's "happiness" or "stealing." Instead, you have inferred it based on your roommate's behavior and the circumstances. What are the clues in these situations that might lead to these conclusions?

One way of understanding the inferential nature of these views is to ask yourself the following questions:

1. Have you ever pretended to be happy when you weren't? Could other people tell?
2. Have you ever been accused of stealing something when you were perfectly innocent? How did this happen?

From these examples you can see that whereas factual beliefs can in principle be verified by direct observation, *inferential beliefs* go beyond what can be directly observed. For instance, in the examples given, your observation of certain of your roommate's actions led you to infer things that you were *not* observing directly — "She's happy"; "he's stealing books." Making such simple inferences is something you do all the time. It is so automatic that usually you are not even aware that you are going beyond your immediate observations, and you may have difficulty drawing a sharp line between what you *observe* and what you *infer*. Making such inferences enables you to see the world as a complete picture, to fill in the blanks and round out the fragmentary sensations being presented to your senses. In a way, you become an artist, painting a picture of the world that is consistent, coherent, and predictable.

Your picture also includes *predictions* of what will be taking place in the near future. These predictions and expectations are also inferences because you attempt to determine what is currently unknown from what is already known.

Of course, your inferences may be mistaken, and in fact they frequently are. You may infer that the woman sitting next to you is wearing two earrings and then discover that she has only one. Or you may expect the class to end at noon and find that the teacher lets you go early — or late. In the last section we concluded that not even factual beliefs are ever absolutely certain. Comparatively speaking, inferential beliefs are a great deal more uncertain than factual beliefs, and it is important to distinguish between the two.

Consider the following situations, analyzing each one by asking these questions: Is the action based on a factual belief or an inference? In what ways might the inference be mistaken? What is the degree of risk involved?

- Placing your hand in a closing elevator door to reopen it
- Taking an unknown drug at a party
- Jumping out of an airplane with a parachute on
- Riding on the back of a motorcycle
- Taking a drug prescribed by your doctor

Having an accurate picture of the world depends on your being able to evaluate how *certain* your beliefs are. Therefore, it is crucial that you *distinguish* infer-

VISUAL THINKING

"Only Two More Steps . . . ?"

● What aspect of working with inferences does this illustration fancifully depict?

ences from factual beliefs and then *evaluate* how certain or uncertain your inferences are. This is known as "calculating the risks," and it is very important to solving problems successfully and deciding what steps to take.

The distinction between what is observed and what is inferred is paid particular attention in courtroom settings, where defense lawyers usually want witnesses to describe *only what they observed* — not what they *inferred* — as part of the observation. When a witness includes an inference such as "I saw him steal it," the lawyer may object that the statement represents a "conclusion of the witness" and move to have the observation stricken from the record. For example, imagine that you are a defense attorney listening to the following testimony. At what points would you make the objection "This is a conclusion of the witness"?

I saw Harvey running down the street, right after he knocked the old lady down. He had her purse in his hand and was trying to escape as fast as he could. He was really scared. I wasn't surprised because Harvey has always taken advantage of others. It's not the first time that he's stolen either, I can tell you that. Just last summer he robbed the poor box at St. Anthony's. He was bragging about it for weeks.

Finally, you should be aware that even though in *theory* facts and inferences can be distinguished, in *practice* it is almost impossible to communicate with others by sticking only to factual observations. A reasonable approach is to state your inference along with the observable evidence on which the inference is based (e.g., John *seemed* happy because . . .). Our language has an entire collection of terms *(seems, appears, is likely,* and so on) that signal when we are making an inference and not expressing an observable fact.

Many of the predictions that you make are inferences based on your past experiences and on the information that you presently have. Even when there appear to be sound reasons to support these inferences, they are often wrong due to incomplete information or unanticipated events. The fact that even people considered by society to be "experts" regularly make inaccurate predictions with absolute certainty should encourage you to exercise caution when making your own inferences. Here are some examples; more can be found on the companion web site, along with links to related sites.

- *"So many centuries after the Creation, it is unlikely that anyone could find hitherto unknown lands of any value."* — the advisory committee to King Ferdinand and Queen Isabella of Spain, before Columbus's voyage in 1492

- *"The energy produced by the breaking down of the atom is a very poor kind of thing. Anyone who expects a source of power from the transformation of the atom is talking moonshine."* — Lord Rutherford, Nobel laureate, after the first experimental splitting of the atom, 1933

- *"The [atom] bomb will never go off, and I speak as an expert in explosives."* — Vannevar Bush, presidential adviser, 1945

- *"Among the really difficult problems of the world, [the Arab-Israeli conflict is] one of the simplest and most manageable."* — Walter Lippmann, newspaper columnist, 1948

- *"You ain't goin' nowhere, son. You ought to go back to driving a truck."* — Jim Denny, Grand Ole Opry manager, firing Elvis Presley after one performance, 1954

Examine the following list of statements, noting which statements are *factual beliefs* (based on observations) and which are *inferential beliefs* (conclusions that go beyond observations). For each factual statement, describe how you might go about verifying the information. For each inferential statement, describe a factual observation on which the inference could be based. (*Note:* Some statements may contain both factual beliefs and inferential beliefs.)

- When my leg starts to ache, that means snow is on the way.
- The grass is wet — it must have rained last night.
- I think that it's pretty clear from the length of the skid marks that the accident was caused by that person's driving too fast.
- Fifty men lost their lives in the construction of the Queensboro Bridge.
- Nancy said she wasn't feeling well yesterday — I'll bet that she's out sick today.

Now consider the following situations. What inferences might you be inclined to make based on what you are observing? How could you investigate the accuracy of your inference?

- A student in your class is consistently late for class.
- You see a friend of yours driving a new car.
- A teacher asks the same student to stay after class several times.
- You don't receive any birthday cards.

So far we have been exploring relatively simple inferences. Many of the inferences people make, however, are much more complicated. In fact, much of our knowledge about the world rests on our ability to make complicated inferences in a systematic and logical way. However, just because an inference is more complicated does not mean that it is more accurate; in fact, the opposite is often the case. One of the masters of inference is the legendary Sherlock Holmes. In the following passage, Holmes makes an astonishing number of inferences upon meeting Dr. Watson. Study carefully the conclusions he comes to. Are they reasonable? Can you explain how he reaches these conclusions?

"You appeared to be surprised when I told you, on our first meeting, that you had come from Afghanistan."

"You were told, no doubt."

"Nothing of the sort. I *knew* you came from Afghanistan. From long habit the train of thoughts ran so swiftly through my mind that I arrived at the conclusion without being conscious of intermediate steps. There were such steps, however. The train of reasoning ran, 'Here is a gentleman of a medical type, but with the air of a military man. Clearly an army doctor, then. He is just come from the tropics, for his face is dark, and that is not the natural tint of his skin, for his wrists are fair. He has undergone hardship and sickness, as his haggard face says clearly. His left arm has been injured. He holds it in a stiff and unnatural manner. Where in the tropics could an English army doctor have seen much hardship and got his arm wounded? Clearly in Afghanistan.' The whole train of thought did not occupy a second. I then remarked that you came from Afghanistan, and you were astonished."

— Sir Arthur Conan Doyle, *A Study in Scarlet*

THINKING ACTIVITY 9.4

Analyzing an Incorrect Inference

Describe an experience in which you made an *in*correct inference that resulted in serious consequences. For example, it might have been a situation in which you mistakenly accused someone, you were in an accident because of a miscalculation, or you made a poor decision based on an inaccurate prediction. Analyze that experience by answering the following questions:

1. What was (were) your mistaken inference(s)?
2. What was the factual evidence on which you based your inference(s)?
3. Looking back, what could you have done to avoid the erroneous inference(s)?

Judging

Identify and describe a friend you have, a course you have taken, and the college you attend. Be sure your descriptions are specific and include *what you think* about the friend, the course, and the college.

1. _____ is a friend whom I have.
   He or she is . . .

2. _____ is a course I have taken.
   It was . . .

3. _____ is the college I attend.
   It is . . .

Now review your responses. Do they include factual descriptions? For each response, note any factual information that can be verified.

In addition to factual reports, your descriptions may contain inferences based on factual information. Can you identify any inferences? In addition to inferences, your descriptions may include judgments about the person, course, and school — descriptions that express your evaluation based on certain criteria. Facts and inferences are designed to help you figure out what is actually happening (or will happen); the purpose of judgments is to express your evaluation about what is happening (or will happen). For example:

- My new car has broken down three times in the first six months. *(Factual report)*
- My new car will probably continue to have difficulties. *(Inference)*
- My new car is a lemon. *(Judgment)*

When you pronounce your new car a "lemon," you are making a judgment based on certain criteria you have in mind. For instance, a "lemon" is usually a newly purchased item — generally an automobile — with which you have repeated problems.

To take another example of judging, consider the following statements:

- Carla always does her work thoroughly and completes it on time. *(Factual report)*
- Carla will probably continue to do her work in this fashion. *(Inference)*
- Carla is a very responsible person. *(Judgment)*

By judging Carla to be responsible, you are evaluating her on the basis of the criteria or standards that you believe indicate a responsible person. One such criterion is completing assigned work on time. Can you identify additional criteria for judging someone to be responsible?

Review your previous descriptions of a friend, a course, and your college. Can you identify any judgments in your descriptions?

1. Judgments about your friend:

2. Judgments about your course:

3. Judgments about your college:

For each judgment you have listed, identify the criteria on which the judgment is based.

1. Criteria for judgments about your friend:

2. Criteria for judgments about your course:

3. Criteria for judgments about your college:

When we judge, we are often expressing our feelings of approval or disapproval. Sometimes, however, we make judgments that conflict with what we personally approve of. For example:

- I think a woman should be able to have an abortion if she chooses to, although I don't believe abortion is right.
- I can see why you think that person is very beautiful, even though she is not the type that appeals to me.

In fact, at times it is essential to disregard your personal feelings of approval or disapproval when you judge. For instance, a judge in a courtroom should render evaluations based on the law, not on his or her personal preferences.

Differences in Judgments

Many of our disagreements with other people focus on differences in judgments. As a critical thinker, you need to approach such differences in judgments intelligently. You can do so by following these guidelines:

- Make explicit the criteria or standards used as a basis for the judgment.
- Try to establish the reasons that justify these criteria.

For instance, if I make the judgment "Professor Andrews is an excellent teacher," I am basing my judgment on certain criteria of teaching excellence. Once these standards are made explicit, we can discuss whether they make sense and what the justification is for them. Identify some of your standards for teaching excellence.

Of course, your idea of what makes an excellent teacher may be different from someone else's, a conclusion you can test by comparing your criteria with those of other class members. When these disagreements occur, your only hope for resolution is to use the two steps previously identified:

- Make explicit the standards you are using.
- Give reasons that justify these standards.

For example, "Professor Andrews really gets my mind working, forcing me to think through issues on my own and then defend my conclusions. I earn what I learn, and that makes it really 'mine.'"

In short, not all judgments are equally good or equally poor. The credibility of a judgment depends on the criteria used to make the judgment and the evidence or reasons that support these criteria. For example, there may be legitimate disagreements about judgments on the following points:

- Who was the greatest U.S. president?
- Which movie deserves the Oscar this year?
- Who should win the Miss America Pageant or the Mr. America Contest?

- Which is the best baseball team this year?
- Which music is best for dancing?

However, in these and countless other cases, the quality of your judgments depends on your identifying the criteria used for the competing judgments and then demonstrating that your candidate best meets those criteria by providing supporting evidence and reasons. With this approach, you can often engage in intelligent discussion and establish which judgments are best supported by the evidence.

Understanding how judgments function also encourages you to continue thinking critically about a situation. For instance, the judgment "This course is worthless!" does not encourage further exploration and critical analysis. In fact, it may prevent such an analysis by discouraging further exploration. And because judgments are sometimes made before you have a clear and complete understanding of the situation, they can serve to prevent you from seeing the situation as clearly and completely as you might. Of course, if you understand that all judgments are based on criteria that may or may not be adequately justified, you can explore these judgments further by making the criteria explicit and examining the reasons that justify them.

THINKING ACTIVITY 9.5

Analyzing Judgments

Review the following passages, which illustrate various judgments. For each passage

1. Identify the evaluative criteria on which the judgments are based.
2. Describe the reasons or evidence the author uses to support the criteria.
3. Explain whether you agree or disagree with the judgments and give your rationale.

One widely held misconception concerning pizza should be laid to rest. Although it may be characterized as fast food, pizza is *not* junk food. Especially when it is made with fresh ingredients, pizza fulfills our basic nutritional requirements. The crust provides carbohydrates; from the cheese and meat or fish comes protein; and the tomatoes, herbs, onions, and garlic supply vitamins and minerals.

— Louis Philip Salamone, "Pizza: Fast Food, Not Junk Food"

Let us return to the question of food. Responsible agronomists report that before the end of the year millions of people if unaided might starve to death. Half a billion deaths by starvation is not an uncommon estimate. Even though the United States has done more than any other nation to feed the hungry, our relative affluence makes us morally vulnerable in the eyes of other nations and in our own eyes. Garrett Hardin, who has argued for a "lifeboat" ethic of survival (if you take all the passengers aboard, everybody drowns), admits that the decision *not* to feed all the hungry requires of us "a very hard psychological adjustment." Indeed it would. It has been estimated that the 3.5 million tons of fertilizer spread on American golf courses and lawns could provide up to 30 million tons of food in overseas agricultural production. The nightmarish thought intrudes itself. If we as a nation allow people to starve while we could, through some sacrifice, make more food available to them, what hope can any person have for the future of international relations? If we cannot agree on this most basic of values — feed the hungry — what hopes for the future can we entertain?

— James R. Kelly, "The Limits of Reason"

Thinking Critically About Moral Judgments

Many of the judgments with which you are involved are moral judgments, decisions regarding "right" and "wrong" behavior in your relationships with others. These judgments are often based on criteria that you have absorbed from your parents and the surrounding culture. If you have critically examined the ethical beliefs with which you were raised, however, you may have found that some of your views diverge from the views of those around you. Of course, critical evaluation may also strengthen your endorsement of the beliefs with which you were raised by deepening your understanding of the reasons on which they are based. These influences create a "moral compass" that each of us possesses to guide our decisions in moral situations.

Your Moral Compass

One research study that analyzed the moral compasses young people use to guide their decision-making in moral situations asked, "If you were unsure of what was right or wrong in a particular situation, how would you decide what to do?" (Describe how *you* would respond to this question.) According to the researcher, here's how the students interviewed responded:

- 23 percent: I would do what is best for everyone involved.
- 20 percent: I would follow the advice of an authority, such as a parent or teacher.
- 18 percent: I would do whatever made me happy.
- 16 percent: I would do what God or the Scriptures say is right.
- 10 percent: I would do whatever would improve my own situation.
- 9 percent: I do not know what I would do.
- 3 percent: I would follow my conscience.

Each of these guiding principles represents a different moral theory that describes the way people reason and make decisions about moral issues. However, moral values not only *describe* the way people behave; they also suggest that this is the way people *ought to* behave. For example, if I say, "Abusing children is morally wrong," I am not simply describing what *I* believe; I am also suggesting that abusing children is morally wrong for *everyone*. Let's briefly examine the moral theories represented by each of the responses just listed.

I Would Follow My Conscience   We could describe this as a *psychological* theory of morality because it holds that we should determine right and wrong based on our psychological moral sense. Our "conscience" is that part of our mind formed by internalizing the moral values we were raised with, generally from our parents, but from other authority figures and peers as well. If that moral upbringing has been intelligent, empathic, and fair-minded, then our conscience can serve as a fairly sound moral compass to determining right and wrong. The problem with following our conscience occurs when the moral values we have internalized are *not* intelligent, empathic, or fair-minded. For example, if we were raised in an environment that encouraged racist beliefs or condoned child abuse, then our conscience might tell us that these are morally acceptable behaviors.

I Do Not Know What I Would Do   This statement expresses a *morally agnostic* theory of morality that holds there is no way to determine clearly what is right or wrong in moral situations. This view is a form of relativism because it suggests that there is no universal common standard to determine how we ought to behave toward each other. Although there are often times when we are confused about the right course of action in complex moral situations, the moral agnostic theory is problematic because it does not permit us to evaluate the conduct of others. For example, if someone robs you and beats you up, you have no basis on which to say, "That was a morally wrong thing for that person to do." Instead, you have to tolerate such conduct because there is no ultimate right or wrong.

I Would Do Whatever Would Improve My Own Situation   We could describe this viewpoint as a *pragmatic* theory of morality because the right action is based on what works well for advancing the speaker's interests, while the wrong action is determined by what works against the speaker's interests. For example, if you are trying to decide whether you should do volunteer work at a local drug treatment center, you might conclude that this is the right thing to do because it will help you in your training as a psychologist and will look good on your résumé. The problem with this sort of moral reasoning is that you could also use it to justify cheating on an upcoming exam (if you were assured of not getting caught!) or hurting someone's reputation so that you could get ahead. At its heart, the pragmatic theory of morality can be used to justify any actions that serve the individual interests of anyone, ranging from Mother Teresa to Adolf Hitler!

I Would Do What God or the Scriptures Say Is Right   This statement expresses a *theist* theory of morality that holds that right and wrong are determined by a supernatural supreme being ("God"). We determine what this supreme being wants us to do through divinely inspired writings (Scriptures or Holy Books) or through divinely inspired messengers (priests, ministers, prophets, the pope). As an "absolutist" moral theory, this view holds that there are absolute moral principles that all humans should follow, determined by the supreme being that created them. The strength of this moral theory lies in the fact that many religions embody values that are intelligent, empathic, and fair-minded, and the devotion of these religions' followers encourages them to act in these morally upright ways. The potential problem with this moral perspective is that all religions don't agree regarding moral values, and so we are left to determine which religion is the right one on which to base our moral views. In addition, there have been many historical instances in which religion has been used to justify actions that by any standard are cruel and inhuman, including torture, murder, and human sacrifice. There is always a danger when we surrender our critical thinking faculties completely to another authority, as is shown by the actions of those who joined cults.

I Would Do Whatever Made Me Happy   This statement reflects a slightly more refined version of the *hedonist* moral theory, which advises people to do whatever brings them pleasure. Although this is certainly an understandable goal in life — almost everybody wants to be "happy," whatever *that* means — there are significant problems when we apply this way of thinking to the moral realm and our relationships with other people. For example, suppose you are contemplating an action that will make you very happy — stealing a new BMW convertible, for example — but will make someone else very *un*happy, namely, the owner of the car. According to this moral theory, the right thing to do might be to steal the car, assuming that you didn't experience feelings of guilt or risk getting caught, feelings that would interfere with your happiness. In other words, the trouble with doing whatever makes you happy is the same difficulty we saw with doing whatever improves your situation. Neither moral theory takes into account the interests or rights of other people, and so when your interests conflict with someone else's, your interests always prevail. If everyone thought this way, then our world would be an even more dangerous and unpleasant place to live!

I Would Follow the Advice of an Authority, Such As a Parent or Teacher This *authoritarian* moral theory is analogous to the *theist* moral theory ("I would do what God or the Scriptures say is right") in the sense that according to both theories, there are clear values of right and wrong and we should ask authorities to find out what these are. The difference is, of course, that in the theist view this authority is a supreme being, while the authoritarian view holds that the authority is human. And the same difficulties that the theist view brings carry over to the authoritarian perspective, for although the values of parents and teachers often reflect wisdom and insight, many times they do not. How can we tell the difference between the appropriate and inappropriate values of these authorities? And what do we do when these authorities disagree with each other, as they often do? If we have deferred our critical judgment to the authorities, then we are at their mercy. But if we are prepared to evaluate critically the values of authorities, accepting what makes sense and discarding what doesn't, then we need another source for our moral values.

I Would Do What Is Best for Everyone Involved This response expresses an *altruistic* moral theory, a view in which the interests of other people are held to be as important as our own when we are trying to decide what to do. For example, if you are trapped with other students in a burning theater, the morally right course of action is to work for everyone's safe escape, not simply for your own. This moral perspective is an important part of many of the prominent world religions, and it is embodied in the Golden Rule: "Do unto others as you would have them do unto you." In other words, deciding on the morally right thing to do requires that we mentally and emotionally place ourselves in the positions of other people who might be affected by our action and then make our decision based on what will be best for their interests *as well as* for our interests. By adopting this moral view, we eliminate many of the difficulties of other moral theories. For example, we will be reluctant to act in ways that harm other people because if we were in their position, we wouldn't want to be harmed that way ourselves. However, it is often difficult to determine what's best for everyone involved. Even more problematic is the question, What action should we take when the best interests of people *conflict* with one another? — a very common moral dilemma.

THINKING ACTIVITY 9.6

Analyzing Moral Dilemmas

The following are several dilemmas that ask you to respond with decisions based on moral reasoning. After thinking carefully about each situation, do the following:

- Describe the decision that you would make in this situation and explain why.

- Identify the moral value(s) or principle(s) on which you based your decision.

- At the conclusion of the activity, compare the moral values that you used. Did you find that you consistently used the same values to make decisions, or did you use different values? If you used different ones, how did the various values relate to one another?

- Based on this analysis, describe your general conclusions about your own "moral compass."

1. *The Lifeboat:* You are the captain, and your ship struck an iceberg and sank. There are thirty survivors, but they are crowded into a lifeboat designed to hold just seven. With the weather stormy and getting worse, it is obvious that many of the passengers will have to be thrown out of the lifeboat, or it will sink and everyone will drown. Will you have people thrown over the side? If so, on what basis will you decide who will go? Age? Health? Strength? Gender? Size?

2. *The Whistle-Blower:* You are employed by a large corporation that manufactures baby formula. You suspect that a flaw in the manufacturing process has resulted in contamination of the formula in a small number of cases. This contamination can result in serious illness, even death. You have been told by your supervisor that "everything is under control" and warned that if you "blow the whistle" by going public, you will be putting the entire company in jeopardy from multimillion-dollar lawsuits. You will naturally be fired and blackballed in the industry. As the sole provider in your household, your family depends on you.

3. *The Mad Bomber:* You are a police lieutenant heading up an investigation of a series of bombings that have resulted in extensive damage, injuries, and deaths. Your big break comes when you capture the person who you are certain is the "mad bomber." However, he tauntingly tells you that he has placed a number of devices in public locations that will explode at the cost of many innocent lives and injuries. You believe that your only chance of extracting the location of these bombs is to torture this person until he tells. If you decide to do this, both your career and the legal case against the bomber will be placed in jeopardy. What do you do?

4. *The Patient:* As a clinical psychologist, you are committed to protecting the privacy of your patients. One afternoon a patient tells you that her husband, who has been abusing her physically and mentally for years, has threatened to kill her, and she believes he would. You try to convince her to leave him, but she tells you that she has decided to kill *him*. She is certain that he would find her wherever she went and feels that she will be safe only when he is dead. What do you do?

5. *The Friend:* As the director of your department, you are in charge of filling an important vacancy. Many people have applied, including your best friend, who has been out of work for over a year and needs a job desperately. Although your friend would likely perform satisfactorily, there are several more experienced and talented candidates who would undoubtedly perform better. You have always prided yourself on hiring the best people, and you have earned a reputation as someone with high standards who will not compromise your striving for excellence. Whom do you hire?

As you think your way through these moral dilemmas, you will probably find yourself appealing to the basic moral principles that you typically use to guide your actions. Of course, what makes these examples moral *dilemmas* is the fact that they involve a *conflict* of traditional moral principles.

1. The Lifeboat involves a conflict between these moral beliefs:

   - It is wrong to take any innocent life.
   - It is right to save *some* lives rather than threaten *all* the lives on board.

2. The Whistle-Blower involves a conflict between these moral beliefs:

   - It is wrong to knowingly jeopardize the health of children.
   - It is right to protect the welfare of your family and your career.

3. The Mad Bomber involves a conflict between these moral beliefs:

- It is wrong to harm a human being.
- It is right to save the lives of many innocent people.

4. The Patient involves a conflict between these moral beliefs:

- It is wrong to violate the confidentiality of a professional relationship.
- It is right to prevent someone from committing murder.

5. The Friend involves a conflict between these moral beliefs:

- It is wrong to hire someone who is not the best-qualified candidate for the job.
- It is right to try to help and support your friends.

A moral dilemma is a situation in which at least two different moral principles to which you are appealing seem ethically sound and appropriate; the problem is that they contradict each other. What should you do when this happens? How do you decide which principle is *more* right? There is no simple answer to this question, just as there is no easy answer to the question "What do you do when experts disagree?" In both cases, you need to *think critically* in order to arrive at intelligent and informed conclusions.

Moral dilemmas can provoke intense angst and vigorous debate. For example, you might be faced with the decision of which employees to fire in order to keep your company afloat. Employees working for companies that manufacture baby formula, contraceptives like the Dalkon Shield, and tobacco products have often found themselves in a moral dilemma: Do they risk their own job and those of their coworkers by alerting the public to the dangers of a product? You yourself may have been in a job situation in which telling the truth or objecting to an unethical practice would have jeopardized your position or opportunity for advancement. Many therapists, clergy, lawyers, and doctors wrestle daily with issues of confidentiality. We all have to deal with the question of under what circumstances it is morally appropriate to break our promises to avoid a greater evil or achieve a greater good. There are countless instances in which we are forced to balance our feelings of personal obligation with our objective or professional analysis.

In addition to these kinds of ethical situations, you will undoubtedly confront other types of moral dilemmas that are at least as problematic. It is possible that at some point in your life you will have to make a "right to die" decision regarding a loved one nearing the end of life. You might also find yourself in a situation in which you are torn between ending a difficult marriage or remaining as a full-time parent of young children. Or you might be tempted to take advantage of an investment opportunity that, while not completely illegal, is clearly unethical. Dealing with complicated, ambiguous moral challenges is an inescapable part of the human condition. Since these situations can't be avoided, you need to develop the insight and conceptual tools to deal with them effectively.

The Thinker's Guide to Moral Decision-Making

After wrestling with the moral dilemmas presented in the previous section, you might be wondering exactly how we *do* develop a clear sense of right and wrong to guide us through complex moral situations. The answer is found by applying to moral issues the same critical thinking abilities we have been developing in the activities presented throughout this book to create **The Thinker's Guide to Moral Decision-Making.** Consider this guide a moral blueprint for constructing your own personal moral code. Using the concepts and principles provided by this guide, you can create a moral philosophy to analyze successfully virtually any moral situation and to make informed decisions that you can justify with confidence.

Make Morality a Priority   To live a life that achieves your moral potential, you must work to *become aware* of the moral issues that you face and strive to make choices that are grounded in thoughtful reflection and supported by persuasive reasoning. By living a morally enlightened life, you are defining yourself as a person of substance, a person with a vision that informs the quality of your relationships with others.

> ***Strategy:***   *During the next week, identify the moral issues that you encounter in your daily life that involve other people — choices related to right and wrong, good and evil, matters just and unjust. Select several of these moral choices, and think about the approach that you used in making each decision: What was the issue? What choices could you have made? Why did you make the choice that you did? If you had it to do over again, would you make the same choice? Why or why not?*

Adopt the "Ethic of Justice"   A critical thinking approach to ethics is founded on the principle of *justice* or *impartiality:* It is our moral obligation to treat everyone equally, with the same degree of consideration and respect, unless there is some persuasive reason not to do so. This is the basic principle of the ethic of justice. For example, differences among people that are based on race, religion, gender, or sexual orientation pose no threat to society as a whole. Therefore, people whose traits, beliefs, or practices differ from those of the majority deserve to be treated with the same respect to which everyone is enti-

VISUAL THINKING

"What Homeless Person?"

● How is the couple in this photo behaving in relation to the homeless woman on the sidewalk? Why? What kinds of moral judgments do people make about homeless people? Do you think these judgments are justified? Why or why not?

tled. The ethic of justice emphasizes the *intentions* of or *motivation* for an action. It expresses the conviction that you affirm when, confronted with a moral decision, you respond: "I have to do my duty to act justly. Regardless of the consequences, it's important for me to do what's right." It is both illogical and immoral to discriminate against other people.

Strategy: *Think about your own biases toward others and begin working to treat these people with the respect they are due.*

Adopt the "Ethic of Care"   The ethic of care expresses a moral responsibility to others that is based on your ability to empathize — to put yourself in other people's situations and view the world from their perspectives. This ability to empathize enables you to feel compassion and sympathy toward others and serves as the foundation of all your healthy relationships. According to an empathic point of view, achieving happiness and fulfillment in life involves pursuing your aspirations in a context of genuine understanding of other people. When you actively work to transcend your own perspective and think within other points of view, particularly those with which you disagree, you are gaining a deeper and richer understanding of others. You need to listen carefully to people who disagree with you and try to appreciate what thinking has brought them to their conclusions. Perspective-taking is the cornerstone of many of the world's ethical systems, such as the Golden Rule: "Do unto others as you would have them do unto you."

Strategy: *Increase your ability to empathize by making a special effort to transcend your own perspective and to place yourself in other people's "shoes." In your dealings with others, use your imagination to experience what you believe they are thinking and feeling, and observe whether this viewpoint influences your attitudes and actions toward them.*

Universalize Your Moral Choices   A very effective strategy to employ during your moral deliberations is to ask yourself if you would be willing for everyone in situations similar to your own to make the same choice that you are making — in other words, to "universalize" your choice. This moral principle was best articulated by the German philosopher Immanuel Kant in the "categorical imperative" that he believed every virtuous person should obey: "Act only according to that maxim by which you can at the same time will that it should become a universal law." Should you spread unflattering gossip about an unpopular acquaintance or coworker because you think the person "deserves" it? By applying this principle, you would determine that you should do so only if you believe that all people in all situations should spread unflattering gossip. Most people would be reluctant to sign on to this sort of universal rule.

But why should you go along with the categorical imperative in the first place? Being first and foremost a rational creature, you are necessarily committed to a belief in *logical consistency.* How could you defend doing something that you would condemn other people for doing? What qualities make you so unique, so superior to everyone else, that you are not subject to the same rules and requirements by which others are bound? Objectively speaking, there are no such special qualities. Your intrinsic value is no greater and no less than that of any other rational person. Reason dictates that everyone's interests must be treated in the same way, without special consideration. We should all be willing to make every personal choice a universal law.

> **Strategy:**   *As you deliberate the various moral choices in your life, both small ("Should I cut ahead in line?") and large ("Should I pursue my own self-interest at the risk of hurting someone else?"), make a conscious effort to universalize your anticipated actions. Would you be willing to have everyone take this same action in similar circumstances? If not, evaluate whether the action is truly morally justified and consistent with the other moral values you hold.*

Treat People as Ends, Not Means   Kant also formulated a second version of the categorical imperative: "Act so that you treat humanity, whether in your own person or in that of another, always as an end and never as a means only." Since all people possess the same *intrinsic value,* a value that is defined by the ability to understand their options and to make free choices, we should always act in a way that respects their inherent dignity as rational agents. Imagine, for example, that you want to sell something. Is it all right to manipulate people's feelings so that they will buy your product? Or suppose that your child or friend is planning to do something that you don't think is in her best interests. Is it permissible to manipulate her thinking indirectly so that she will make a different choice? According to Kant, both of these actions are morally wrong because you are not treating the people involved as "ends" — that is, as rational agents who are entitled to make their own choices. Instead, you are treating them as *means to an end,* even though you may believe that your manipulation is in their best interests. The morally correct thing to do is to tell them exactly what you are thinking and then give them the opportunity to reason through the situations and make their own choices. The idea of *always* treating people as "ends" and *never* as "means" to achieving our own ends may seem extreme. Perhaps we should begin by taking Kant's recommendation more seriously than we normally would. By respecting someone else's right — even a child's — to make free choices, we are bringing out the best in that person as we simultaneously enhance our own moral stature.

> **Strategy:**   *Think about some recent instances in which you attempted to influence someone's thoughts, feelings, or behavior. Did you make a clear case for your recommendation, respecting the person's right to make a free choice? Or did you try to manipulate him or her by using techniques designed to influence the person without his or her knowledge or to coerce the person against his or her wishes? If you discover examples of such manipulation, try to imagine how things would have turned out if you had taken a more forthright approach.*

Accept Responsibility for Your Moral Choices   From a critical thinking perspective, morality makes sense only if we assume that people are able to make free choices for which they are responsible. When people choose courses of action that we consider to be right, we judge them as morally good. When they choose courses of action that we consider to be wrong, we condemn them as morally evil. It is impossible to achieve genuine moral stature without admitting responsibility for the choices that you make. If you are to create yourself as a person of moral integrity, you must have the courage to acknowledge your own moral failures as well as the humility to accept your moral successes. And in order to exercise your freedom fully, you need to have insight into your options, your motivations, and the consequences of your actions. This is the uniquely human gift: We have the intelligence, the imagination, and the reflective insight to consider a range of options and to make choices. Sometimes we choose wisely, sometimes we choose poorly, but in all instances we are responsible for the choices that we ourselves make.

> **Strategy:**   *Strengthen your moral integrity by actively seeking to acknowledge your moral failings and then by committing yourself to improve. Self-honesty will build your inner strength and moral fiber, and you will find that moral integrity of this sort is both rewarding and habit forming.*

Seek to Promote Human Happiness   Promoting human happiness and its corollary, diminishing human suffering, have been mainstays of many ethical systems through the ages. Most people are perfectly willing to pursue their own happiness. However, moral recognition is typically earned by devoting your time and resources to enhancing the happiness of others, sometimes at the expense of your own interests. This moral value is founded on the principle of perspective-taking, which we explored earlier. Identifying with another's predicament can generate the desire to assist the person whose situation could just as easily have been yours ("There but for the grace of God . . ."). This, then, is the wellspring of charitable acts toward others.

But this moral concept is also relevant in your ordinary dealings with people. Happiness breeds happiness in the same way that aggression escalates aggression and negativity inspires more negativity. When you actively employ your words and actions to help other people become happy, their happiness will reflect back onto you, instilling a sense of satisfaction and fulfillment. Happiness and goodwill are not limited commodities. There are, in fact, inexhaustible supplies.

> **Strategy:**   *Think about specific ways in which you can increase the happiness of the people in your life. These may involve bestowing a small kindness on someone you know casually or making a more significant commitment to someone to*

whom you are very close. Create and implement a plan for doing this during the next few days and then evaluate the results of your efforts. How did applying the extra effort to make others happy make you feel? How did they respond? Doesn't it make sense to continue this effort and even to increase it?

Develop an Informed Moral Intuition   An informed moral intuition is the product of thoughtful exploration and reflection on moral issues throughout your life. Developing an informed, reliable moral intuition involves achieving insight into the essential nature of humans: What are the basic qualities that define what kind of individuals we ought to be and how we should treat others?

Once you have developed an intuition in which you have confidence, you need to *use* it to help you think your way through moral dilemmas. If your moral intuition is *informed,* the product of a great deal of thought and reflection, then it will have a high degree of credibility. But if your moral intuition is *uninformed,* the product of inaccurate information or inadequate experience, then your intuition will not be credible. People with depraved and underdeveloped moral sensibilities will have instincts and intuitions that reflect their diminished moral understanding. There is nothing magical or infallible about your conscience or moral understanding. If you have consciously worked at becoming a moral person, a person of character and integrity, then your intuitions will largely be trustworthy. But if you have not consciously striven to develop and refine your moral sensibilities, or if you have been raised in an environment saturated with destructive values that promote prejudice and violence, then you should be very suspicious of your moral intuitions.

> **Strategy:** *Imagine an ideal, perfect human being. What personal qualities would such a person possess? How would such a person treat other people? What moral vision and specific moral values would such a person display? Using these explorations, construct a composite portrait of an ideal person that you can use to guide your own moral intuitions.*

Choose to Be a Moral Person   Just as a person can possess an array of critical thinking abilities and yet choose not to use them, so also can a person be a walking compendium of moral theory and yet choose not to apply it to her or his own life. To achieve an enlightened moral existence in your own life, you need to decide to be a moral person struggling to live a moral life. You need to *value* morality, to aspire to an enhanced moral awareness, to exert the motivation and commitment required to reach this lofty but attainable goal.

Once you have developed a clear understanding of your own moral code, the struggle has just begun. Becoming a morally enlightened person — a person of character, compassion, and integrity — is a hard-won series of accomplishments, not a one-time award. As a reflective critical thinker, you will be conscious of the choices you are making and the reasons that you are making them, and you will "learn from experience," refining your code of ethics and improving your moral choices through self-exploration. Achieving moral enlightenment is an ongoing process, and it is a struggle that is not for the faint-hearted. But it is a struggle that cannot be avoided if you are to live a life of purpose and meaning, one created by a self that is authentic and, as Aristotle would say, "great souled."

> **Strategy:**   *Develop the habit of conducting a regular appraisal of your self and your life. Ask — and answer — questions such as these: Am I achieving my goals as a moral person? As a critical thinker? As a creative individual? Then use this evaluation regularly to maintain a much-needed perspective on your life, reminding yourself of the "big picture" and applying it to guide your evolution into the most worthy person you can become.*

Why Be Moral?

The considerations that we have been discussing provide a convincing answer to a pertinent question: Why be moral? As it turns out, becoming a moral person can help you become a psychologically healthy person; promoting the happiness of others frequently enhances your own happiness. Often adages are clichéd and empty of meaning, but in this case "Virtue is its own reward" contains a substantial measure of truth, a point noted by Socrates in his observation that doing wrong "will harm and corrupt that part of ourselves that is improved by just actions and destroyed by unjust actions."

As a free individual, you create yourself through the choices that you make, much as a sculptor gradually forms a figure through countless cuts of the chisel. If you create yourself as a moral person, you create a person of character and worth, someone with an acute sense of right and wrong and the power to make appropriate choices. But if you *don't* choose to create yourself as a moral person, you will gradually become corrupted. You will lose your moral sensitivity, developing a moral blindness that will handicap your ability to see yourself or the world clearly. It is no wonder that Socrates believed that "it is better to suffer wickedness than to commit it." You gain true power when you possess the unfettered and unrestrained ability to choose freely. Conversely, choosing immorality binds your hands, one loop of thread at a time, until your freedom of movement disappears. In the same way that substance abusers gradually surrender their freedom of choice to their destructive cravings, so also do immoral people have only the illusion of genuine freedom in their lives. While moral people enjoy healthy personalities and spiritual wholeness, immoral people are corrupted at their core, progressively ravaged by a disease of the spirit.

THINKING ACTIVITY 9.7

Nurturing Your Moral Growth

No matter how highly evolved you are as a moral person, you can achieve a more enlightened state by choosing to nurture your moral growth. Your critical thinking abilities will give you the means to explore the moral dimensions of your experience with insight, and your personal dedication to moral improvement will provide you with the ongoing motivation. Remember that becoming a moral person is both a daily and a lifetime project. Nurture your continued moral growth by cultivating the qualities that we have been exploring in this section.

- Make morality a priority.
- Adopt the "ethic of justice."
- Adopt the "ethic of care."
- Universalize your moral choices.
- Treat people as ends, not means.
- Accept responsibility for your moral choices.
- Seek to promote human happiness.
- Develop an informed moral intuition.
- Choose to be a moral person.

Final Thoughts

This chapter has explored the thinking processes that create three of the fundamental types of beliefs that you use to make sense of your world. These processes are

Reporting	Describing information that can be verified through investigation
Inferring	Going beyond factual information to describe what is not known
Judging	Expressing an evaluation based on certain criteria

Each of these types of beliefs has an important and distinctive role to play in your ongoing efforts to organize and make sense of your world. As a critical thinker, you must learn to recognize each of these different types of beliefs and use them properly. Of course, it is often difficult and confusing to distinguish among these types of beliefs because you rarely make an effort to try to separate them. Instead, the thinking activities of reporting, inferring, and judging tend to be woven together, organizing your world into a seamless fabric. Only when you make a special effort to reflect and think critically are you able to recognize these activities as being distinct.

In addition to recognizing and using these types of beliefs appropriately, thinking critically about these beliefs involves evaluating their basis and reliability: What is the reliability of the sources providing information for the *factual reports?* What is the probability that the *inference* is correct? What are the evidence and reasons that support the criteria used in the *judgment?* By distinguishing and critically evaluating these fundamental types of beliefs, you will be able to improve their accuracy and effectiveness as you seek to make sense of your world.

THINKING PASSAGE

Evolution as Fact and Theory

The following essay entitled "Evolution as Fact and Theory" was written by Stephen Jay Gould, a professor of geology at Harvard University who also wrote widely on scientific themes for nonscientific audiences. This essay illustrates the ongoing process by which natural scientists use inferences to discover factual information and to construct theories explaining this factual information. Read the selection carefully and then answer the questions that follow.

EVOLUTION AS FACT AND THEORY
by Stephen Jay Gould

Kirtley Mather, who died last year at age 89, was a pillar of both science and the Christian religion in America and one of my dearest friends. The difference of half a century in our ages evaporated before our common interests. The most curious thing we shared was a battle we each fought at the same age. For Kirtley had gone to Tennessee with Clarence Darrow to testify for evolution at the Scopes trial of 1925. When I think that we are enmeshed again in the same struggle for one of the best documented, most compelling and exciting concepts in all of science, I don't know whether to laugh or cry.

Source: "Evolution as Fact and Theory," selection from *Discover* 1981. Reprinted by permission of Steven J. Gould.

According to idealized principles of scientific discourse, the arousal of dormant issues should reflect fresh data that give renewed life to abandoned notions. Those outside the current debate may therefore be excused for suspecting that creationists have come up with something new, or that evolutionists have generated some serious internal trouble. But nothing has changed; the creationists have not a single new fact or argument. Darrow and Bryan were at least more entertaining than we lesser antagonists today.* The rise of creationism is politics, pure and simple; it represents one issue (and by no means the major concern) of the resurgent evangelical right. Arguments that seemed kooky just a decade ago have re-entered the mainstream.

Creationism Is Not Science

The basic attack of the creationists falls apart on two general counts before we even reach the supposed factual details of their complaints against evolution. First, they play upon a vernacular misunderstanding of the word "theory" to convey the false impression that we evolutionists are covering up the rotten core of our edifice. Second, they misuse a popular philosophy of science to argue that they are behaving scientifically in attacking evolution. Yet the same philosophy demonstrates that their own belief is not science, and that "scientific creationism" is therefore meaningless and self-contradictory, a superb example of what Orwell† called "newspeak."‡

In the American vernacular, "theory" often means "imperfect fact" — part of a hierarchy of confidence running downhill from fact to theory to hypothesis to guess. Thus the power of the creationist argument: evolution is "only" a theory, and intense debate now rages about many aspects of the theory. If evolution is less than a fact, and scientists can't even make up their minds about the theory, then what confidence can we have in it? Indeed, President Reagan echoed this argument before an evangelical group in Dallas when he said (in what I devoutly hope was campaign rhetoric): "Well, it is a theory. It is a scientific theory only, and it has in recent years been challenged in the world of science — that is, not believed in the scientific community to be as infallible as it once was."

---

*Darrow and Bryan: Clarence Darrow (1857–1938) was the defense attorney in the 1925 trial of John Thomas Scopes for teaching evolution; William Jennings Bryan (1860–1925) was an orator and politician who aided the prosecution in the Scopes trial. [Eds.]

†"George Orwell (1903–1950): English journalist and novelist, author of *Animal Farm* and *1984*. [Eds.]

‡"Newspeak": the official language in Orwell's *1984*, devised to meet the ideological needs of the ruling party and to make all other modes of thought impossible. [Eds.]

Well, evolution *is* a theory. It is also a fact. And facts and theories are different things, not rungs in a hierarchy of increasing certainty. Facts are the world's data. Theories are structures of ideas that explain and interpret facts. Facts do not go away when scientists debate rival theories to explain them. Einstein's theory of gravitation replaced Newton's, but apples did not suspend themselves in mid-air pending the outcome. And human beings evolved from apelike ancestors whether they did so by Darwin's proposed mechanism or by some other, yet to be discovered.

Moreover, "fact" does not mean "absolute certainty." The final proofs of logic and mathematics flow deductively from stated premises and achieve certainty only because they are *not* about the empirical world. Evolutionists make no claim for perpetual truth, though creationists often do (and then attack us for a style of argument that they themselves favor). In science, "fact" can only mean "confirmed to such a degree that it would be perverse to withhold provisional assent." I suppose that apples might start to rise tomorrow, but possibility does not merit equal time in physics classrooms.

Evolutionists have been clear about this distinction between fact and theory from the very beginning, if only because we have always acknowledged how far we are from completely understanding the mechanisms (theory) by which evolution (fact) occurred. Darwin continually emphasized the difference between his two great and separate accomplishments: establishing the fact of evolution, and proposing a theory — natural selection — to explain the mechanism of evolution. He wrote in *The Descent of Man:* "I had two distinct objects in view; firstly, to show that species had not been separately created, and secondly, that natural selection had been the chief agent of change. . . . Hence if I have erred in . . . having exaggerated its [natural selection's] power . . . I have at least, as I hope, done good service in aiding to overthrow the dogma of separate creations."

Thus Darwin acknowledged the provisional nature of natural selection while affirming the fact of evolution. The fruitful theoretical debate that Darwin initiated has never ceased. From the 1940s through the 1960s, Darwin's own theory of natural selection did achieve a temporary hegemony that it never enjoyed in his lifetime. But renewed debate characterizes our decade, and while no biologist questions the importance of natural selection, many now doubt its ubiquity. In particular, many evolutionists argue that substantial amounts of genetic change may not be subject to natural selection and may spread through populations at random. Others are challenging Darwin's linking of natural selection with gradual, imperceptible change through all intermediary degrees; they are arguing that most evolutionary events may occur far more rapidly than Darwin envisioned.

Scientists regard debates on fundamental issues of theory as a sign of intellectual health and a source of excitement. Science is — and how else can I say it? — most fun when it plays with interesting ideas, examines their implications, and recognizes that old information may be explained in surprisingly new ways. Evolutionary theory is now enjoying this uncommon vigor. Yet amidst all this turmoil no biologist has been led to doubt the fact that evolution occurred; we are debating *how* it happened. We are all trying to explain the same thing: the tree of evolutionary descent linking all organisms by ties of genealogy. Creationists pervert and caricature this debate by conveniently neglecting the common conviction that underlies it, and by falsely suggesting that we now doubt the very phenomenon we are struggling to understand.

Using another invalid argument, creationists claim that "the dogma of separate creations," as Darwin characterized it a century ago, is a scientific theory meriting equal time with evolution in high school biology curricula. But a prevailing viewpoint among philosophers of science belies this creationist argument. Philosopher Karl Popper has argued for decades that the primary criterion of science is the falsifiability of its theories. We can never prove absolutely, but we can falsify. A set of ideas that cannot, in principle, be falsified is not science.

The entire creationist argument involves little more than a rhetorical attempt to falsify evolution by presenting supposed contradictions among its supporters. Their brand of creationism, they claim, is "scientific" because it follows the Popperian model in trying to demolish evolution. Yet Popper's argument must apply in both directions. One does not become a scientist by the simple act of trying to falsify another scientific system; one has to present an alternative system that also meets Popper's criterion — it too must be falsifiable in principle.

"Scientific creationism" is a self-contradictory, nonsense phrase precisely because it cannot be falsified. I can envision observations and experiments that would disprove any evolutionary theory I know, but I cannot imagine what potential data could lead creationists to abandon their beliefs. Unbeatable systems are dogma, not science. Lest I seem harsh or rhetorical, I quote creationism's leading intellectual, Duane Gish, Ph.D., from his recent (1978) book *Evolution? The Fossils Say No!* "By creation we mean the bringing into being by a supernatural Creator of the basic kinds of plants and animals by the process of sudden, or flat, creation. We do not know how the Creator created, what processes He used, *for He used processes which are not now operating anywhere in the natural universe* [Gish's italics]. This is why we refer to creation as special creation. We cannot discover by scientific investigations anything about the creative processes used by the Creator." Pray tell, Dr. Gish, in the light of your last sentence, what then is "scientific" creationism?

The Fact of Evolution

Our confidence that evolution occurred centers upon three general arguments. First, we have abundant, direct, observational evidence of evolution in action, from both the field and the laboratory. It ranges from countless experiments on change in nearly everything about fruit flies subjected to artificial selection in the laboratory to the famous British moths that turned black when industrial soot darkened the trees upon which they rest. (The moths gain protection from sharp-sighted bird predators by blending into the background.) Creationists do not deny these observations; how could they? Creationists have tightened their act. They now argue that God only created "basic kinds," and allowed for limited evolutionary meandering within them. Thus toy poodles and Great Danes come from the dog kind and moths can change color, but nature cannot convert a dog to a cat or a monkey to a man.

The second and third arguments for evolution — the case for major changes — do not involve direct observation of evolution in action. They rest upon inference, but are no less secure for that reason. Major evolutionary change requires too much time for direct observation on the scale of recorded human history. All historical sciences rest upon inference, and evolution is no different from geology, cosmology, or human history in this respect. In principle, we cannot observe processes that operated in the past. We must infer them from results that still survive: living and fossil organisms for evolution, documents and artifacts for human history, strata and topography for geology.

The second argument — that the imperfection of nature reveals evolution — strikes many people as ironic, for they feel that evolution should be most elegantly displayed in the nearly perfect adaptation expressed by some organisms — the chamber of a gull's wing, or butterflies that cannot be seen in ground litter because they mimic leaves so precisely. But perfection could be imposed by a wise creator or evolved by natural selection. Perfection covers the tracks of past history. And past history — the evidence of descent — is our mark of evolution.

Evolution lies exposed in the *imperfections* that record a history of descent. Why should a rat run, a bat fly, a porpoise swim, and I type this essay with structures built of the same bones unless we all inherited them from a common ancestor? An engineer, starting from scratch, could design better limbs in each case. Why should all the large native mammals of Australia be marsupials, unless they descended from a common ancestor isolated on this island continent? Marsupials are not "better," or ideally suited for Australia; many have been wiped out by placental mammals imported by man from other continents. This principle of imperfection extends to all historical sciences. When we recognize the etymology of September, October, November, and December (seventh, eighth, ninth, and tenth, from the Latin), we know that two additional items (January and February) must have been added to an original calendar of ten months.

The third argument is more direct: transitions are often found in the fossil record. Preserved transitions are not common — and should not be, according to our understanding of evolution . . . — but they are not entirely wanting, as creationists often claim. The lower jaw of reptiles contains several bones, that of mammals only one. The nonmammalian jawbones are reduced, step by step, in mammalian ancestors until they become tiny nubbins located at the back of the jaw. The "hammer" and "anvil" bones of the mammalian ear are descendants of these nubbins. How could such a transition be accomplished? the creationists ask. Surely a bone is either entirely in the jaw or in the ear. Yet paleontologists have discovered two transitional lineages or therapsids (the so-called mammal-like reptiles) with a double jaw joint — one composed of the old quadrate and articular bones (soon to become the hammer and anvil), the other of the squamosal and dentary bones (as in modern mammals). For that matter, what better transitional form could we desire than the oldest human, *Australopithecus afarensis*, with its apelike palate, its human upright stance, and a cranial capacity larger than any ape's of the same body size but a full 1,000 cubic centimeters below ours? If God made each of the half dozen human species discovered in ancient rocks, why did he create an unbroken temporal sequence of progressively more modern features — increasing cranial capacity, reduced face and teeth, larger body size? Did he create a mimic evolution and test our faith thereby?

Conclusion

I am both angry at and amused by the creationists; but mostly I am deeply sad. Sad for many reasons. Sad because so many people who respond to creationist appeals are troubled for the right reason, but venting their anger at the wrong target. It is true that scientists have often been dogmatic and elitist. It is true that we have often allowed the white-coated, advertising image to represent us — "Scientists say that Brand X cures bunions ten times faster than. . . ." We have not fought it adequately because we derive benefits from appearing as a new priesthood. It is also true that faceless bureaucratic state power intrudes more and more into our lives and removes choices that should belong to individuals and communities. I can understand that requiring that evolution be taught in the schools might be seen as one more insult on all these grounds. But the culprit is not, and cannot be, evolution or any other fact of the natural world. Identify and fight your legitimate enemies by all means, but we are not among them.

I am sad because the practical result of this brouhaha will not be expanded coverage to include creationism (that would also make me sad), but the reduction or excision of evolution from high school curricula. Evolution is one of the half dozen "great ideas" developed by science. It speaks to the profound issues of genealogy that fascinate all of us — the "roots" phenomenon writ large. Where did we come from? Where did life arise? How did it develop? How are organisms related? It forces us to think, ponder, and wonder. Shall we deprive millions of this knowledge and once again teach biology as a set of dull and unconnected facts, without the thread that weaves diverse material into a supple unity?

But most of all I am saddened by a trend I am just beginning to discern among my colleagues. I sense that some now wish to mute the healthy debate about theory that has brought new life to evolutionary biology. It provides grist for creationist mills, they say, even if only by distortion. Perhaps we should lie low and rally round the flag of strict Darwinism, at least for the moment — a kind of old-time religion on our part.

But we should borrow another metaphor and recognize that we too have to tread a straight and narrow path, surrounded by roads to perdition. For if we ever begin to suppress our search to understand nature, to quench our own intellectual excitement in a misguided effort to present a united front where it does not and should not exist, then we are truly lost.

Questions for Analysis

1. According to Gould, evolution is both a scientific "fact" and a scientific "theory" asserting that all life forms are the result of a process of gradual development and differentiation over time, much like the progressive growth of tree branches from the central trunk. In contrast, creationism asserts that all basic forms of life were brought into being in a sudden act by a supernatural creator. Explain what you understand about the theory of evolution and about creationism based on your reading of the article.

2. Gould defines "facts" as the "world's data," like observing an apple fall from a tree, as Isaac Newton is alleged to have done. Describe some of the facts Gould gives as evidence to support the theory of evolution.

3. Gould defines "theories" as "structures of ideas that explain and interpret facts," such as Newton's theory of gravitation introduced to explain facts like falling apples. In addition to facts, Gould states that the theory of evolution is supported by reasonable inferences. Describe the inferences he cites as evidence.

4. According to Gould, creationism is neither a scientific fact nor a scientific theory. Describe the reasons he gives to support this belief.

5. At the beginning of the article, Gould gives the example of Kirtley Mather as "a pillar of both science and the Christian religion." Explain how you think it might be possible to believe in both of these viewpoints with respect to the origins of life.

10 Constructing Arguments

Recognizing Arguments
Cue words

Constructing Arguments
Decide
Explain
Predict
Persuade

Argument
A form of thinking in which certain reasons are offered to support a conclusion

Constructing Extended Arguments
Identifying a thesis
Conducting research
Evaluating sources
Organizing ideas

Understanding Deductive Arguments
Application of a general rule
Modus ponens
Modus tollens
Disjunctive syllogism

Evaluating Arguments
Truth
Validity
Soundness

Consider carefully the following dialogue about whether marijuana should be legalized:

Dennis: Did you hear about the person who was sentenced to fifteen years in prison for possessing marijuana? I think this is one of the most outrageously unjust punishments I've ever heard of! In most states, people who are convicted of armed robbery, rape, or even murder don't receive fifteen-year sentences. And unlike the possession of marijuana, these crimes violate the rights of other people.

Caroline: I agree that this is one case in which the punishment doesn't seem to fit the crime. But you have to realize that drugs pose a serious threat to the young people of our country. Look at all the people who are addicted to drugs, who have their lives ruined, and who often die at an early age of overdoses. And think of all the crimes committed by people to support their drug habits. As a result, sometimes society has to make an example of someone — like the person you mentioned — to convince people of the seriousness of the situation.

Dennis: That's ridiculous. In the first place, it's not right to punish someone unfairly just to provide an example. At least not in a society that believes in justice. And in the second place, smoking marijuana is nothing like using drugs such as heroin or even cocaine. It follows that smoking marijuana should not be against the law.

Caroline: I don't agree. Although marijuana might not be as dangerous as some other drugs, smoking it surely isn't good for you. And I don't think that anything that is a threat to your health should be legal.

Dennis: What about cigarettes and alcohol? We *know* that they are dangerous. Medical research has linked smoking cigarettes to lung cancer, emphysema, and heart disease, and alcohol damages the liver. No one has proved that marijuana is a threat to our health. And even if it does turn out to be somewhat unhealthy, it's certainly not as dangerous as cigarettes and alcohol.

Caroline: That's a good point. But to tell you the truth, I'm not so sure that cigarettes and alcohol should be legal. And in any case, they are already legal. Just because cigarettes and alcohol are bad for your health is no reason to legalize another drug that can cause health problems.

Dennis: Look — life is full of risks. We take chances every time we cross the street or climb into our car. In fact, with all of these loonies on the road, driving is a lot more hazardous to our health than any of the drugs around. And many of the foods we eat can kill. For example, red meat contributes to heart disease, and artificial sweeteners can cause cancer. The point is if people want to take chances with their health, that's up to them. And many people

VISUAL THINKING

"Let Herbs Grow Free!"

● Would you be inclined to join a "Legalize Marijuana" protest like this one? Why do some people believe that marijuana should be legalized? Why do others believe that it shouldn't?

in our society like to mellow out with marijuana. I read somewhere that over 70 percent of the people in the United States think that marijuana should be legalized.

Caroline: There's a big difference between letting people drive cars and letting them use dangerous drugs. Society has a responsibility to protect people from themselves. People often do things that are foolish if they are encouraged or given the opportunity to. Legalizing something like marijuana encourages people to use it, especially young people. It follows that many more people would use marijuana if it were legalized. It's like society saying, "This is all right — go ahead and use it."

Dennis: I still maintain that marijuana isn't dangerous. It's not addictive — like heroin is — and there is no evidence that it harms you. Consequently, anything that is harmless should be legal.

Caroline: Marijuana may not be physically addictive like heroin, but I think that it can be psychologically addictive because people tend to use more and more of it over time. I know a number of people who spend a lot of their time getting high. What about Carl? All he does is lie around and get high. This shows that smoking it over a period of time definitely affects your mind. Think about the people you know who smoke a lot — don't they seem to be floating in a dream world? How are they ever going to make anything of their lives? As far as I'm concerned, a pothead is like a zombie — living but dead.

Dennis: Since you have had so little experience with marijuana, I don't think that you can offer an informed opinion on the subject. And anyway, if you do too much of anything, it can hurt you. Even something as healthy as exercise can cause problems if you do too much of it. But I sure don't see anything wrong with toking up with some friends at a party or even getting into a relaxed state by yourself. In fact, I find that I can even concentrate better on my schoolwork after taking a little smoke.

Caroline: If you believe that, then marijuana really *has* damaged your brain. You're just trying to rationalize your drug habit. Smoking marijuana doesn't help you concentrate — it takes you away from reality. And I don't think that people can control it. Either you smoke and surrender control of your life, or you don't smoke because you want to retain control. There's nothing in between.

Dennis: Let me point out something to you: Because marijuana is illegal, organized crime controls its distribution and makes all the money from it. If marijuana were legalized, the government could tax the sale of it — like cigarettes and alcohol — and then use the money for some worthwhile purpose. For example, many states have legalized gambling and use the money to support education. In fact, the major tobacco companies have already copyrighted names for different marijuana brands — like "Acapulco Gold." Obviously, they believe that marijuana will soon become legal.

Caroline: Just because the government can make money out of something doesn't mean that they should legalize it. We could also legalize prostitution or muggings and then tax the proceeds. Also, simply because the cigarette companies are prepared to sell marijuana doesn't mean that it makes sense to. After all, they're the ones who are selling us cigarettes.

Continue this dialogue, incorporating other views on the subject of legalizing marijuana.

⊚ Recognizing Arguments

The preceding discussion is an illustration of two people engaging in *dialogue,* which we have defined (in Chapter 2) as the systematic exchange of ideas. Participating in this sort of dialogue with others is one of the keys to thinking critically because it stimulates you to develop your mind by carefully examining the way you make sense of the world. Discussing issues with others encourages you to be mentally active, to ask questions, to view issues from different perspectives, and to develop reasons to support conclusions. It is this last quality of thinking critically — supporting conclusions with reasons — that we will focus on in this chapter and the next.

When we offer reasons to support a conclusion, we are considered to be presenting an *argument.*

> **argument** *A form of thinking in which certain statements (reasons) are offered in support of another statement (a conclusion)*

At the beginning of the dialogue, Dennis presents the following argument against imposing a fifteen-year sentence for possession of marijuana (argument 1):

Reason: Possessing marijuana is not a serious offense because it hurts no one.

Reason: There are many other more serious offenses in which victims' basic rights are violated — such as armed robbery, rape, and murder — for which the offenders don't receive such stiff sentences.

Conclusion: Therefore, a fifteen-year sentence is an unjust punishment for possessing marijuana.

Can you identify an additional reason that supports this conclusion?

Reason:

The definition of *argument* given here is somewhat different from the meaning of the concept in our ordinary language. In common speech, "argument" usually refers to a dispute or quarrel between people, often involving intense feelings (for example: "I got into a terrible argument with the idiot who hit the back of my car"). Very often these quarrels involve people presenting arguments in the sense in which we have defined the concept, although the arguments are usually not carefully reasoned or clearly stated because the people are so angry. Instead of this common usage, in this chapter we will use the word's more technical meaning.

Using our definition, we can define the main ideas that make up an argument.

> **reasons** *Statements that support another statement (known as a conclusion), justify it, or make it more probable*

> **conclusion** *A statement that explains, asserts, or predicts on the basis of statements (known as reasons) that are offered as evidence for it*

The type of thinking that uses argument — reasons in support of conclusions — is known as *reasoning,* and it is a type of thinking you have been doing throughout this book, as well as in much of your life. We are continually trying to explain, justify, and predict things through the process of reasoning.

Of course, our reasoning — and the reasoning of others — is not always correct. For example, the reasons someone offers may not really support the conclusion they are supposed to. Or the conclusion may not really follow from the reasons stated. These difficulties are illustrated in a number of the arguments contained in the discussion on marijuana. Nevertheless, whenever we accept a conclusion as likely or true based on certain reasons or whenever we offer reasons to support a conclusion, we are using arguments to engage in reasoning — even if our reasoning is weak or faulty. In this chapter and the next, we will be exploring both the way we construct effective arguments and the way we evaluate arguments to develop and sharpen our reasoning ability.

Let us return to the discussion about marijuana. After Dennis presents the argument with the conclusion that the fifteen-year prison sentence is an unjust punishment, Caroline considers that argument. Although she acknowledges that in this case "the punishment doesn't seem to fit the crime," she goes on to offer another argument (argument 2), giving reasons that lead to a conclusion that conflicts with the one Dennis drew:

Reason: Drugs pose a very serious threat to the young people of our country.

Reason: Many crimes are committed to support drug habits.

Conclusion: As a result, sometimes society has to make an example of someone to convince people of the seriousness of the situation.

Can you identify an additional reason that supports this conclusion?

Reason:

Cue Words for Arguments

Our language provides guidance in our efforts to identify reasons and conclusions. Certain key words, known as *cue words*, signal that a reason is being offered in support of a conclusion or that a conclusion is being announced on the basis of certain reasons. For example, in response to Caroline's conclusion that society sometimes has to make an example of someone to convince people of the seriousness of the situation, Dennis gives the following argument (argument 3):

Reason: In the first place, it's not right to punish someone unfairly just to provide an example.

Reason: In the second place, smoking marijuana is nothing like using drugs such as heroin or even cocaine.

Conclusion: It follows that smoking marijuana should not be against the law.

In this argument, the phrases *in the first place* and *in the second place* signal that reasons are being offered in support of a conclusion. Similarly, the phrase *it follows that* signals that a conclusion is being announced on the basis of certain reasons. Here is a list of the most commonly used cue words for reasons and conclusions:

❋ *Cue Words Signaling Reasons*

since	in view of
for	first, second
because	in the first (second) place
as shown by	may be inferred from
as indicated by	may be deduced from
given that	may be derived from
assuming that	for the reason that

❋ *Cue Words Signaling Conclusions*

therefore	then
thus	it follows that
hence	thereby showing
so	demonstrates that
(which) shows that	allows us to infer that
(which) proves that	suggests very strongly that

implies that	you see that
points to	leads me to believe that
as a result	allows us to deduce that
consequently	

Of course, identifying reasons, conclusions, and arguments involves more than looking for cue words. The words and phrases listed here do not always signal reasons and conclusions, and in many cases arguments are made without the use of cue words. However, cue words do help alert us that an argument is being made.

THINKING ACTIVITY 10.1

Identifying Arguments with Cue Words

1. Review the discussion on marijuana and underline any cue words signaling that reasons are being offered or that conclusions are being announced.

2. With the aid of cue words, identify the various arguments contained in the discussion on marijuana. For each argument, describe

   a. The *reasons* offered in support of a conclusion

   b. The *conclusion* announced on the basis of the reasons

   Before you start, review the three arguments we have examined thus far in this chapter.

3. Go back to the additional arguments you wrote on page 392. Reorganize and add cue words if necessary to clearly identify your reasons as well as the conclusion you drew from those reasons.

THINKING PASSAGES

Legalizing Drugs

Two essays that discuss the issue of whether drugs should be legalized are located on the companion web site. The first passage, "Drugs," is written by Gore Vidal, a well-known essayist and novelist. The second, "The Case for Slavery," is authored by The *New York Times* editor and columnist A. M. Rosenthal. After carefully reading the essays, answer the questions that follow.

Arguments Are Inferences

When you construct arguments, you are composing and relating to the world by means of your ability to infer. As you saw in Chapter 9, *inferring* is a thinking process that you use to reason from what you already know (or believe to be the case) to form new knowledge or beliefs. This is usually what you do when you construct arguments. You work from reasons you know or believe in to form conclusions based on these reasons.

Just as you can use inferences to make sense of different types of situations, so you can also construct arguments for different purposes. In a variety of situations, you construct arguments to do the following:

- decide
- explain
- predict
- persuade

An example of each of these different types of arguments follows. After examining each example, construct an argument of the same type related to issues in your own life.

We Construct Arguments to Decide

Reason: Throughout my life, I've always been interested in all different kinds of electricity.

Reason: There are many attractive job opportunities in the field of electrical engineering.

Conclusion: I will work toward becoming an electrical engineer.

Reason:

Reason:

Conclusion:

We Construct Arguments to Explain

Reason: I was delayed in leaving my house because my dog needed an emergency walking.

Reason: There was an unexpected traffic jam caused by motorists slowing down to view an overturned chicken truck.

Conclusion: Therefore, I was late for our appointment.

Reason:

Reason:

Conclusion:

We Construct Arguments to Predict

Reason: Some people will always drive faster than the speed limit allows, no matter whether the limit is 55 or 65 mph.

Reason: Car accidents are more likely to occur at higher speeds.

Conclusion: It follows that the newly reinstated 65-mph limit will result in more accidents.

Reason:

Reason:

Conclusion:

We Construct Arguments to Persuade

Reason: Chewing tobacco can lead to cancer of the mouth and throat.

Reason: Boys sometimes are led to begin chewing tobacco by ads for the product that feature sports heroes they admire.

Conclusion: Therefore, ads for chewing tobacco should be banned.

Reason:

Reason:

Conclusion:

Evaluating Arguments

To construct an effective argument, you must be skilled in evaluating the effectiveness, or soundness, of arguments that have already been constructed. You must investigate two aspects of each argument independently to determine the soundness of the argument as a whole:

1. How true are the reasons being offered to support the conclusion?
2. To what extent do the reasons support the conclusion, or to what extent does the conclusion follow from the reasons offered?

We will first examine each of these ways of evaluating arguments separately and then see how they work together.

Truth: How True Are the Supporting Reasons?

The first aspect of the argument you must evaluate is the truth of the reasons that are being used to support a conclusion. Does each reason make sense? What evidence is being offered as part of each reason? Do you know each reason to be true based on your experience? Is each reason based on a source that

VISUAL THINKING

Sound Construction

● The scene in this illustration evokes two popular instructional tales — one from children's stories and one from the Bible (New Testament) — to depict the soundness of arguments. What other metaphors or symbols could be pictured to show the same concept?

can be trusted? You use these questions and others like them to analyze the reasons offered and to determine how true they are. As you saw in Chapter 5, evaluating the sort of beliefs usually found as reasons in arguments is a complex and ongoing challenge. Let us evaluate the truth of the reasons presented in the discussion at the beginning of this chapter about whether marijuana should be legalized.

Argument 1

Reason: Possessing marijuana is not a serious offense.

Evaluation: As it stands, this reason needs further evidence to support it. The major issue of the discussion is whether possessing (and using) marijuana is in fact a serious offense or no offense at all. This reason would be strengthened by stating: "Possessing marijuana is not as serious an offense as armed robbery, rape, and murder, according to the overwhelming majority of legal statutes and judicial decisions."

Reason: There are many other more serious offenses — such as armed robbery, rape, and murder — for which criminals don't receive such stiff sentences.

Evaluation: The accuracy of this reason is highly doubtful. It is true that there is wide variation in the sentences handed down for the same offense. The sentences vary from state to state and also vary within states and even within the same court. Nevertheless, on the whole, serious offenses like armed robbery, rape, and murder do receive long prison sentences.

The real point here is that a fifteen-year sentence for possessing marijuana is extremely unusual when compared with other sentences for marijuana possession.

Argument 2

Reason: Drugs pose a very serious threat to the young people of our country.

Evaluation: As the later discussion points out, this statement is much too vague. "Drugs" cannot be treated as being all the same. Some drugs (such as aspirin) are beneficial while other drugs (such as heroin) are highly dangerous. To strengthen this reason, we would have to be more specific, stating, "Drugs like heroin, amphetamines, and cocaine pose a very serious threat to the young people of our country." We could increase the accuracy of the reason even more by adding the qualification "*some* of the young people of our country" because many young people are not involved with dangerous drugs.

Reason: Many crimes are committed to support drug habits.

Evaluation:

Argument 3

Reason: It's not right to punish someone unfairly just to provide an example.

Evaluation: This reason raises an interesting and complex ethical question that has been debated for centuries. The political theorist Machiavelli stated that "the ends justify the means," which implies that if we bring about desirable results, it does not matter how we go about doing so. He would therefore probably disagree with this reason since using someone as an example might bring about desirable results, even though it might be personally unfair to the person being used as an example. In our society, however, which is based on the idea of fairness under the law, most people would probably agree with this reason.

Reason: Smoking marijuana is nothing like using drugs such as heroin or even cocaine.

Evaluation:

THINKING ACTIVITY 10.2

Evaluating the Truth of Reasons

Review the other arguments from the discussion on marijuana that you identified in Thinking Activity 10.1 (p. 396). Evaluate the truth of each of the reasons contained in the arguments.

Validity: Do the Reasons Support the Conclusion?

In addition to determining whether the reasons are true, evaluating arguments involves investigating the *relationship* between the reasons and the conclusion. When the reasons support the conclusion so that the conclusion follows from the reasons being offered, the argument is *valid.** If, however, the reasons do *not* support the conclusion so that the conclusion does *not* follow from the reasons being offered, the argument is *invalid.*

> **valid argument** *An argument in which the reasons support the conclusion so that the conclusion follows from the reasons offered*

> **invalid argument** *An argument in which the reasons do not support the conclusion so that the conclusion does* not *follow from the reasons offered*

One way to focus on the concept of validity is to *assume* that all the reasons in the argument are true and then try to determine how probable they make the conclusion. The following is an example of one type of valid argument:

---

* In formal logic, the term *validity* is reserved for deductively valid arguments in which the conclusions follow necessarily from the premises. (See the discussion of deductive arguments later in this chapter.)

Reason: Anything that is a threat to our health should not be legal.

Reason: Marijuana is a threat to our health.

Conclusion: Therefore, marijuana should not be legal.

This is a valid argument because if we assume that the reasons are true, then the conclusion necessarily follows. Of course, we may not agree that either or both of the reasons are true and thus not agree with the conclusion. Nevertheless, the *structure* of the argument is valid. This particular form of thinking is known as *deduction,* and we will examine deductive reasoning more closely in the pages ahead.

The following is a different type of argument:

Reason: As part of a project in my social science class, we selected 100 students in the school to be interviewed. We took special steps to ensure that these students were representative of the student body as a whole (total students: 4,386). We asked the selected students whether they thought the United States should actively try to overthrow foreign governments that the United States disapproves of. Of the 100 students interviewed, 88 students said the United States should definitely *not* be involved in such activities.

Conclusion: We can conclude that most students in the school believe the United States should not be engaged in attempts to actively overthrow foreign governments that the United States disapproves of.

This is a persuasive argument because if we assume that the reason is true, then it provides strong support for the conclusion. In this case, the key part of the reason is the statement that the 100 students selected were representative of the entire 4,386 students at the school. To evaluate the truth of the reason, we might want to investigate the procedure used to select the 100 students to determine whether this sample was in fact representative of all the students. This particular form of thinking is an example of *induction,* and we will explore inductive reasoning more fully in Chapter 11.

The following argument is an example of an invalid argument:

Reason: George W. Bush believes that the "Star Wars" missile defense shield should be built to ensure America's national defense because it provides the capability to intercept incoming nuclear missiles.

Reason: George W. Bush is the president of the United States.

Conclusion: Therefore, the "Star Wars" missile defense shield should be built.

This argument is *not* valid because even if we assume that the reasons are true, the conclusion does not follow. Although George W. Bush is the president of the United States, that fact does not give him any special expertise on the subject of sophisticated radar designs for weapons systems. Indeed, this is a subject of such complexity and global significance that it should not be based on any one person's opinion, no matter who that person is. This form of invalid thinking is a type of *fallacy,* and we will investigate fallacious reasoning in Chapter 11.

The Soundness of Arguments

When an argument includes both true reasons and a valid structure, the argument is considered to be *sound.* When an argument has either false reasons or an invalid structure, however, the argument is considered to be *unsound.*

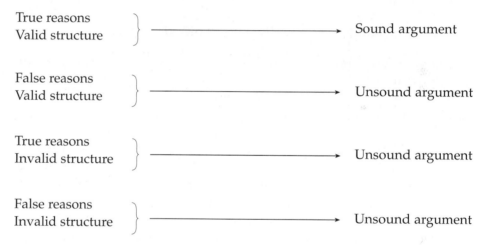

True reasons
Valid structure ⟶ Sound argument

False reasons
Valid structure ⟶ Unsound argument

True reasons
Invalid structure ⟶ Unsound argument

False reasons
Invalid structure ⟶ Unsound argument

From this chart, we can see that in terms of arguments "truth" and "validity" are not the same concepts. An argument can have true reasons and an invalid structure or false reasons and a valid structure. In both cases the argument is *unsound.* To be sound, an argument must have both true reasons and a valid structure. For example, consider the following argument:

Reason: For a democracy to function most effectively, its citizens should be able to think critically about the important social and political issues.

Reason: Education plays a key role in developing critical thinking abilities.

Conclusion: Therefore, education plays a key role in ensuring that a democracy is functioning most effectively.

A good case could be made for the soundness of this argument because the reasons are persuasive, and the argument structure is valid. Of course, someone might contend that one or both of the reasons are not completely true, which illustrates an important point about the arguments we construct and evaluate.

Many of the arguments we encounter in life fall somewhere between complete soundness and complete unsoundness because we are often not sure if our reasons are completely true. Throughout this book we have found that developing accurate beliefs is an ongoing process and that our beliefs are subject to clarification and revision. As a result, the conclusion of any argument can be only as certain as the reasons supporting the conclusion.

To sum up, evaluating arguments effectively involves both the truth of the reasons and the validity of the argument's structure. The degree of soundness an argument has depends on how accurate our reasons turn out to be and how valid the argument's structure is.

◎ Understanding Deductive Arguments

We use a number of basic argument forms to organize, relate to, and make sense of the world. As already noted, two of the major types of argument forms are *deductive arguments* and *inductive arguments.* In the remainder of this chapter, we will explore various types of deductive arguments, reserving our analysis of inductive arguments for Chapter 11.

The deductive argument is the one most commonly associated with the study of logic. Though it has a variety of valid forms, they all share one characteristic: If you accept the supporting reasons (also called *premises*) as true, then you must necessarily accept the conclusion as true.

> **deductive argument** *An argument form in which one reasons from premises that are known or assumed to be true to a conclusion that follows necessarily from these premises*

For example, consider the following famous deductive argument:

Reason/Premise: All men are mortal.

Reason/Premise: Socrates is a man.

Conclusion: Therefore, Socrates is mortal.

In this example of deductive thinking, accepting the premises of the argument as true means that the conclusion necessarily follows; it cannot be false. Many deductive arguments, like the one just given, are structured as *syllogisms,* an argument form that consists of two supporting premises and a conclusion.

There are also, however, a large number of *invalid* deductive forms, one of which is illustrated in the following syllogism:

Reason/Premise: All men are mortal.

Reason/Premise: Socrates is a man.

Conclusion: Therefore, all men are Socrates.

In the next several pages, we will briefly examine some common valid deductive forms.

Application of a General Rule

Whenever we reason with the form illustrated by the valid Socrates syllogism, we are using the following argument structure:

Premise: All *A* (men) are *B* (mortal).

Premise: *S* is an *A* (Socrates is a man).

Conclusion: Therefore, *S* is *B* (Socrates is mortal).

This basic argument form is valid no matter what terms are included. For example:

Premise: All politicians are untrustworthy.

Premise: Bill White is a politician.

Conclusion: Therefore, Bill White is untrustworthy.

Notice again that with any valid deductive form, *if* we assume that the premises are true, then we must accept the conclusion. Of course, in this case there is considerable doubt that the first premise is actually true.

When we diagram this argument form, it becomes clear why it is a valid way of thinking:

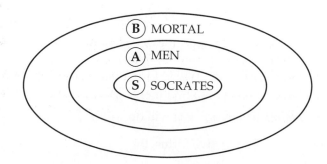

The *first premise* states that classification *A* (men) falls within classification *B* (mortal).

The *second premise* states that *S* (Socrates) is a member of classification *A* (men).

The *conclusion* simply states what has now become obvious — namely, that *S* (Socrates) must fall within classification *B* (mortal).

Although we are usually not aware of it, we use this basic type of reasoning whenever we apply a general rule in the form *All A is B*. For instance:

Premise: All children eight years old should be in bed by 9:30 P.M.

Premise: You are an eight-year-old child.

Conclusion: Therefore, you should be in bed by 9:30 P.M.

Review the dialogue at the beginning of this chapter and see if you can identify a deductive argument that uses this form.

Premise:

Premise:

Conclusion:

Describe an example from your own experience in which you use this deductive form.

Modus Ponens

A second valid deductive form that we commonly use in our thinking goes by the name *modus ponens* — that is, "affirming the antecedent" — and is illustrated in the following example:

Premise: If I have prepared thoroughly for the final exam, then I will do well.

Premise: I prepared thoroughly for the exam.

Conclusion: Therefore, I will do well on the exam.

When we reason like this, we are using the following argument structure:

Premise: If *A* (I have prepared thoroughly), then *B* (I will do well).

Premise: *A* (I have prepared thoroughly).

Conclusion: Therefore, *B* (I will do well).

Like all valid deductive forms, this form is valid no matter what specific terms are included. For example:

Premise: If the Democrats are able to register 20 million new voters, then they will win the presidential election.

Premise: The Democrats were able to register more than 20 million new voters.

Conclusion: Therefore, the Democrats will win the presidential election.

As with other valid argument forms, the conclusion will be true *if* the reasons are true. Although the second premise in this argument expresses information that can be verified, the first premise would be more difficult to establish.

Review the dialogue at the beginning of this chapter and see if you can identify any deductive arguments that use this form.

Modus Tollens

A third commonly used valid deductive form has the name *modus tollens* — that is, "denying the consequence" — and is illustrated in the following example:

Premise: If Michael were a really good friend, he would lend me his car for the weekend.

Premise: Michael refuses to lend me his car for the weekend.

Conclusion: Therefore, Michael is not a really good friend.

When we reason in this fashion, we are using the following argument structure:

Premise: If A (Michael is a really good friend), then B (He will lend me his car).

Premise: Not B (He won't lend me his car).

Conclusion: Therefore, not A (He's not a really good friend).

Again, like other valid reasoning forms, this form is valid no matter what subject is being considered. For instance:

Premise: If Iraq were genuinely interested in world peace, it would not have invaded Kuwait.

Premise: Iraq did invade Kuwait (that is, Iraq did not "not invade" Kuwait).

Conclusion: Therefore, Iraq is not genuinely interested in world peace.

This conclusion — and any other conclusion produced by this form of reasoning — can be considered accurate if the reasons are true. In this case, the second premise would be easier to verify than the first.

Review the dialogue at the beginning of this chapter and see if you can identify any deductive arguments that use this reasoning form.

Disjunctive Syllogism

A fourth common form of a valid deductive argument is known as a *disjunctive syllogism*. The term *disjunctive* means presenting several alternatives. This form is illustrated in the following example:

Premise: Either I left my wallet on my dresser, or I have lost it.

Premise: The wallet is not on my dresser.

Conclusion: Therefore, I must have lost it.

When we reason in this way, we are using the following argument structure:

Premise: Either A (I left my wallet on my dresser) or B (I have lost it).

Premise: Not A (I didn't leave it on my dresser).

Conclusion: Therefore, B (I have lost it).

This valid reasoning form can be applied to any number of situations and still yield valid results. For example:

Premise: Either your stomach trouble is caused by what you are eating, or it is caused by nervous tension.

Premise: You tell me that you have been taking special care with your diet.

Conclusion: Therefore, your stomach trouble is caused by nervous tension.

To determine the accuracy of the conclusion, we must determine the accuracy of the premises. If they are true, then the conclusion must be true.

Review the dialogue at the beginning of this chapter and see if you can identify any deductive arguments that use this reasoning form.

All these basic argument forms — application of a general rule, *modus ponens, modus tollens,* and disjunctive syllogism — are found not only in informal, everyday conversations but also at more formal levels of thinking. They appear in academic disciplines, in scientific inquiry, in debates on social issues, and elsewhere. Many other argument forms — both deductive and inductive — also constitute human reasoning. By sharpening your understanding of these ways of thinking, you will be better able to make sense of the world by constructing and evaluating effective arguments.

THINKING ACTIVITY 10.3

Evaluating Arguments

Analyze the following arguments by completing these steps:

1. Summarize the reasons and conclusions given.

2. Identify which, if any, of the following deductive argument forms are used.

- Application of a general rule
- *Modus ponens* (affirming the antecedent)
- *Modus tollens* (denying the consequence)
- Disjunctive syllogism

3. Evaluate the truth of the reasons that support the conclusion.

For if the brain is a machine of ten billion nerve cells and the mind can somehow be explained as the summed activity of a finite number of chemical and electrical reactions, [then] boundaries limit the human prospect — we are biological and our souls cannot fly free.

— Edward O. Wilson, *On Human Nature*

The state is by nature clearly prior to the family and to the individual, since the whole is of necessity prior to the part.

— Aristotle, *Politics*

There now is sophisticated research that strongly suggests a deterrent effect [of capital punishment]. Furthermore, the principal argument against the deterrent effect is weak. The argument is that in most jurisdictions where capital punishment has been abolished there has been no immediate, sharp increase in what had been capital crimes. But in those jurisdictions, the actual act of abolition was an insignificant event because for years the death penalty had been imposed rarely, if at all. Common sense — which deserves deference until it is refuted — suggests that the fear of death can deter some premeditated crimes, including some murders.

— George F. Will, *Cleveland Plain-Dealer,* March 13, 1981

If the increased power which science has conferred upon human volitions is to be a boon and not a curse, the ends to which these volitions are directed must grow commensurately with the growth of power to carry them out. Hitherto, although we have been told on Sundays to love our neighbor, we have been told on weekdays to hate him, and there are six times as many weekdays as Sundays. Hitherto, the harm that we could do to our neighbor by hating him was limited by our incompetence, but in the new world upon which we are entering there will be no such limit, and the indulgence of hatred can lead only to ultimate and complete disaster.

— Bertrand Russell, "The Expanding Mental Universe"

The extreme vulnerability of a complex industrial society to intelligent, targeted terrorism by a very small number of people may prove the fatal challenge to which Western states have no adequate response. Counterforce alone will never suffice. The real challenge of the true terrorist is to the basic values of a society. If there is no commitment to shared values in Western society — and if none are imparted in our amoral institutions of higher learning — no increase in police and burglar alarms will suffice to preserve our society from the specter that haunts us — not a bomb from above but a gun from within.

— James Billington, "The Gun Within"

To fully believe in something, to truly understand something, one must be intimately acquainted with its opposite. One should not adopt a creed by default, because no alternative is known. Education should prepare students for the "real world" not by segregating them from evil but by urging full confrontation to test and modify the validity of the good.

— Robert Baron, "In Defense of 'Teaching' Racism, Sexism, and Fascism"

The inescapable conclusion is that society secretly *wants* crime, *needs* crime, and gains definite satisfactions from the present mishandling of it! We condemn crime; we punish offenders for it; but we need it. The crime and punishment ritual is a part of our lives. We need crimes to wonder at, to enjoy vicariously, to discuss and speculate about, and to publicly deplore. We need criminals to identify ourselves with, to envy secretly, and to punish stoutly. They do for us the forbidden, illegal things we *wish* to do and, like scapegoats of old, they bear the burdens of our displaced guilt and punishment — "the iniquities of us all."

— Karl Menninger, "The Crime of Punishment"

THINKING ACTIVITY 10.4

Freedom of Speech on the Internet

Some people argue that the Internet should not be regulated in any form; people should be free to do and say whatever they wish on their web pages, in chat rooms, and via e-mail. Others say that new technologies enable new possibilities for abuse and call for new regulations. For arguments and information about this issue, go to the companion web site.

Constructing Extended Arguments

The purpose of mastering the forms of argument is to become a sophisticated critical thinker who can present her or his ideas to others effectively. The art of discussing and debating ideas with others was explored in Chapter 2. We saw then that effective discussion involves

- Listening carefully to other points of view
- Supporting views with reasons and evidence
- Responding to the points being made
- Asking — and trying to answer — appropriate questions
- Working to increase understanding, not simply to "win the argument"

Although learning to discuss ideas with others in an organized, productive fashion is crucial for thinking critically, it is equally important to be able to present your ideas in written form. Term papers, interoffice memos, research analyses, grant proposals, legal briefs, evaluation reports, and countless other situations that you are likely to encounter require that you develop the skills of clear, persuasive writing. Composing your ideas develops your mind in distinctive, high-level ways. When you express your ideas in writing, you tend to organize them into more complex relationships, select your terms with more care, and revise your work after an initial draft. As a result, your writing is often a more articulate and comprehensive expression of your ideas than you could achieve in verbal discussions. And the process of expressing your ideas in such a clear and coherent fashion has the simultaneous effect of sharpening your thinking. As you saw in Chapter 6, language and thinking are partners that work together to create meaning and communicate ideas. How well you perform one of these activities is directly related to how well you perform the other.

Writing an Extended Argument

Learning to construct extended arguments is one of the most important writing skills that you need to develop. Since an argument is a form of thinking in which you are trying to present reasons to support a conclusion, it is likely that much of your writing will fall into this category. Composing thoughtfully reasoned and clearly written arguments is very challenging, and few people are able to do it well. In the same way that many discussions are illogical, disorganized, and overly emotional, much of argumentative writing is also ineffective. In the section "Constructing Extended Arguments" on the companion web site, you will examine how to present your ideas in this essential form.

T H I N K I N G   A C T I V I T Y   10.5

Composing an Extended Argument

Select a current issue of interest to you. (Possible choices are animal rights, mandatory HIV testing, human cloning, and so on.) Following the guidelines in the section "Constructing Extended Arguments" on the companion web site, create an extended argument that explores the issue by

- Defining a thesis
- Conducting research (Locate at least two articles about the issue you have selected and use them as resources.)
- Organizing ideas (List arguments on both sides of the issue, organizing them into premises and conclusions. Make notes evaluating the strengths and weaknesses of each argument. Identify the most important arguments and make an outline.)

Before composing your essay, examine the two sets of extended arguments, one on legalizing drugs on the companion web site and one on human cloning (page 413). Note how each author organizes the essay and examine the types of arguments used. Your essay should begin with a paragraph that introduces the issue and should end with a paragraph that sums up and concludes it.

◉ Final Thoughts

In this chapter we have focused mainly on deductive arguments, an argument form in which it is claimed that the premises constitute conclusive evidence for the truth of the conclusion. In a correct deductive argument, which is organized into a valid deductive form, if the premises are true, the conclusion must

be true; it cannot be false.

Although *deductive* forms of reasoning are crucial to our understanding the world and making informed decisions, much of our reasoning is nondeductive. The various nondeductive argument forms are typically included under the general category of *inductive* reasoning. In contrast to deductive arguments, inductive arguments rarely provide conclusions that are totally certain. The premises offer evidence in support of the conclusion, but the conclusion does not follow necessarily from the premises. We will explore the area of inductive reasoning more fully in the next chapter.

THINKING PASSAGES

Human Cloning

Read the news report by Maggie Fox about the first successful experiment in cloning a human embryo. Then evaluate the two arguments that follow, each of which carefully examines the repercussions. "No Fear," written by Richard T. Hull, a philosophy professor, articulates a perspective that focuses on the positive aspects and scientific potential of cloning human cells. "Even If It Worked, Cloning Wouldn't Bring Her Back," by Thomas H. Murray, president of the Hastings Center, a bioethics research institute, argues that cloning is an imprecise science that cannot "change the fact of death nor deflect the pain of grief."

U.S. COMPANY SAYS IT CLONED HUMAN EMBRYO FOR CELLS
by Maggie Fox

Washington (Reuters) — A U.S. company said on Sunday it had cloned a human embryo for the first time ever in a breakthrough aimed not at creating a human being but at mining the embryo for stem cells used to treat diseases.

Biotechnology company Advanced Cell Technology Inc. (ACT), based in Worcester, Massachusetts, said it hopes the experiment will lead to tailored treatments for diseases ranging from Parkinson's to juvenile diabetes.

It also coaxed a woman's egg cell into becoming an early embryo on its own, without any kind of fertilization.

Although animals have been cloned repeatedly since Dolly the sheep made her appearance in 1997, and although there were no real technical barriers to making a cloned human embryo, the research crosses a line that may leave many around the world uneasy and even hostile.

Source: Maggie Fox, Reuters, "U.S. Company Says It Cloned Human Embryo for Cells," November 25, 2001. Copyright Reuters Limited 2001. Reprinted by permission.

V I S U A L   T H I N K I N G

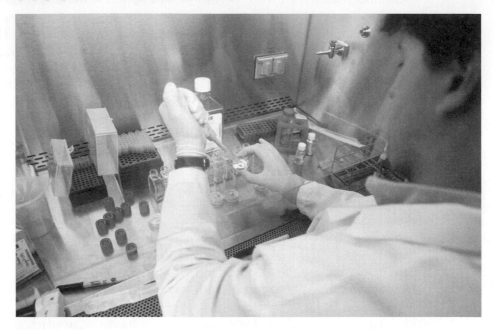

Cloning in the Lab

● In this photo you are looking at the process of creating cloned life — what is your reaction? Should limited cell cloning be pursued if it can help cure serious human illnesses? Why or why not? Should the actual cloning of people be permitted? Why or why not?

The company was at pains to stress that it did not intend to create ranks of genetically identical babies.

"Our intention is not to create cloned human beings, but rather to make lifesaving therapies for a wide range of human disease conditions, including diabetes, strokes, cancer, AIDS, and neurodegenerative disorders such as Parkinson's and Alzheimer's disease," Dr. Robert Lanza, a vice president at ACT, said in a statement.

The goal is to take a piece of skin and grow a new heart for a heart patient, or some brain tissue for an Alzheimer's patient, or vital pancreatic cells for a diabetes patient. But the announcement quickly drew criticism from those fearing the step would lead to the cloning of a human being.

The U.S. Congress has moved to outlaw all human cloning. A proposed new law is under consideration by the Senate, where lawmakers expressed some alarm at Sunday's news.

Michael West, chief executive officer of ACT, hinted that moves in Congress were why the company moved so quickly to report its findings. Federal law prohibits the use of taxpayer money for experimenting on human embryos but ACT is a privately funded company and can do as it pleases — for now.

The House has already backed a broad ban on this type of research, and President Bush has praised the bill. The Senate has not yet taken up companion legislation, and several senators said they did not want to rush into legislation without fully understanding the scientific implications.

Source of Stem Cells

Advanced Cell Technology said it had used cloning technology to grow a tiny ball of cells that could then be used as a source of stem cells. Embryonic stem cells are a kind of master cell that can grow into any kind of cell in the body.

"Scientifically, biologically, the entities we are creating are not an individual. They're only cellular life," West told NBC's "Meet the Press."

ACT Vice President Joe Cibelli, who led the research, said his team had used classic cloning technology using a human egg and a human skin cell. They removed the DNA from the egg cell and replaced it with DNA from the nucleus of the adult cell.

The egg began dividing as if it had been fertilized by a sperm, but was stopped from becoming a baby — at the stage at which it was still a ball of cells. The same technology has been used to clone sheep, cattle and monkeys.

The company did not say whether it had successfully removed embryonic stem cells from the cloned embryo.

The company also reported a second breakthrough in its paper, published in the online journal "E-biomed: Journal of Regenerative Medicine." Researchers took a human egg cell and got it to progress to the embryo stage without any kind of fertilization, either by sperm or outside genetic material.

The process is known as parthenogenesis, and occurs in insects and microbes but not naturally in higher animals.

Second Breakthrough — "Virgin" Conception

"You hesitate to describe it as a virgin birth, but it is sort of in that vein," John Rennie, editor-in-chief of "Scientific American" magazine, which publishes an article by ACT scientists in its January issue and whose reporter watched some of ACT's work in progress, said in a phone interview.

"That is an amazing accomplishment in its own right and, like cloning, something that people once thought was impossible in mammals."

Both cloning and stem cell technology are highly controversial areas of research in the United States. Stem cells are valued by scientists because they could be used to treat many diseases, including cancer and AIDS.

They can come from adults but the most flexible sources so far seem to be very early embryos — so small they are only a ball of a few cells. Such embryos, usually left over from attempts to make test-tube babies, are destroyed in the process, so many people oppose it.

President Bush decided earlier this year that federal funds could be used for research on embryonic stem cells, but only on those that had been created before August, found at 11 different academic and private laboratories.

When combined with cloning technology, the hope is that patients could be the source of their own tissue or organs, a technology known as therapeutic cloning.

"Human therapeutic cloning could be used for a host of age-related diseases," said West.

Reproduction Now in Hands of Men

Groups that have traditionally opposed abortion and embryo experimentation were quick to condemn the research.

"Some may call it a medical breakthrough. I believe it is a moral breakdown," Raymond Flynn, president of the National Catholic Alliance and a former U.S. ambassador to the Vatican, said in a statement.

"Human reproduction is now in the hands of men, when it rightfully belongs in the hands of God."

But the Biotechnology Industry Organization supported the research.

"Those of us who have testified before Congress on BIO's behalf regarding this issue have stated repeatedly that reproductive cloning is untested, unsafe, and morally repugnant," BIO president Carl Feldbaum said in a statement.

"BIO does, however, support therapeutic applications of cloning of cells and tissues — techniques that would not result in cloned children, but could produce treatments and cures for some of humanity's most vexing diseases and disabilities, especially and most immediately diabetes and Parkinson's."

The company said it had grown only a single embryo as far as the six-cell stage. But West said that had the embryo been placed in a woman's womb, it could possibly have grown into a human being.

"We took extreme measures to ensure that a cloned human could not result from this technology," he said.

In August, three researchers considered mavericks in the scientific community said they planned to clone people to help infertile couples, but experts told a meeting of the National Academy of Scientists that they lacked the needed skills.

NO FEAR
by Richard T. Hull

My typical reaction to noteworthy scientific advances is amazement and joy: amazement at the complexity of scientific knowledge and its rate of expansion, joy at living in a time when there is so much promise offered by science for having a major impact on human destiny. As a humanist, I see the ability of my species to manage its own evolution to be one of its most wonderful emerging properties, an ability that distinguishes humans from every other species. So I am deeply suspicious of attempts to impose bans on specific efforts to extend to humans new technologies achieved in animal models.

The Power of Science

The modern biological journey we are on, viewed unclouded by irrational fears and sweeping theological generalizations, is truly extraordinary. The cloning of a female sheep in Scotland stands as testimony to the power of the scientific method. Again and again, things we seem to know are overturned by the scientific testing of those knowledge claims. The cloning of Dolly from nucleus material taken from a cell of her progenitor's udder and inserted into an unfertilized egg (sans nucleus) was stunning. It refuted the widely held belief that the specialization of cells that goes on through the development and maintenance of an organism is an irreversible, linear process.

Such a belief underlies the distinction many held between a fertilized ovum and a body cell. People found it tempting to call the former an individual human being, the latter merely an individual human cell because of

Source: From Richard T. Hull, "No Fear," *Free Inquiry*, Summer 1997. Council for Democratic and Secular Humanists. Reprinted by permission.

the supposed difference in potential. But now we know that most of our cells have the potential, if situated and manipulated appropriately, to generate an individual human being. We have yet to hear from the theologians on this point, but my guess is that the status of the fertilized ovum in such circles is going to have to be fundamentally rethought as a result of this advance. Once again, when science and faith have been put to the test, beliefs generated by faith have not survived. The production of Dolly is on a par with Galileo pointing his telescope at the moon and seeing mountains and craters.

Nor do I view kindly the efforts of the Clinton administration to block the extension of this technology to humans. I hope the intent was a temporary moratorium to permit the President's Commission on Bioethics time to assemble the testimony of a variety of experts and commentators to quiet the fears fanned by the media's sensationalism. But I fear that the result may be a chilling effect on our most advanced researchers in this field.

The similar knee-jerk reaction of the British government in ending the grant to Dr. Ian Wilmut under which Dolly was brought about was alarming. It is implausible to say that the aims of the grant have been completed when the experiment produced but a single sheep out of several hundred attempts. Such a success is but a first indicator of possibilities, not the perfection of a technology. Withdrawal of funding in the face of the initial reports of the media must give any scientist in this field serious doubts about continuing investigations, even on the remaining questions to be answered in animal models.

Undeterred Inquiry

Those remaining questions, of course, should be answered before proceeding to human applications. They include the question of whether the DNA of an adult animal's cells has "aged." We know that errors of transcription in the DNA of specialized body cells accumulate as those cells divide and are replaced during the animal's life. Such mutations come from environmental factors (radiation, exposure to chemicals) that produce genetic breakage and from errors caused by imperfect replication. And there seems to be a theoretical limit in humans of about 50 cell divisions, after which division of a line of cells ceases and the cells simply age and die. The question these facts pose, then, is whether the DNA of Dolly's progenitor cell, taken from a six-year-old adult ewe's udder, carries with it such signs of aging. We simply don't know whether Dolly was born "six years old" or whether she faces the prospect of a life as lengthy as that of a sheep produced sexually. And we don't know whether Dolly will contract earlier the kinds of cancers and other age-related diseases that sheep produced sexually will.

Moreover, Dolly was the only ewe born of several hundred attempts at the same procedure. Why the procedure worked in roughly 0.3% of the cases and none of the others needs to be understood. The technology of cloning must be improved before it is commercially viable in animal husbandry, let alone appropriate to try in humans. . . .

Should such matters be controlled by governmental panels? Governmental panels are poor substitutes for the good sense and open communications of scientists working towards the same goal. What possible expertise does a congressman or senator have that is relevant to the question of whether the technology is good enough to try on a human? Such "solons" — wise lawgivers — are not dedicated to the rational advance of scientific questions — at least, not as their prime mission. They are, for the most part, motivated to reflect the interests of the strongest contributors among the groups they represent. And the presidency is also subject to pressures of media sensationalism, special interest groups, and polls.

False Alarms

Contrast the humanistic view of cloning with some of the more irrational concerns raised about Dolly and the prospect of cloning humans.

Handicapped infants will surely be the unavoidable result of early cloning attempts. If the standard of producing no damaged, handicapped infants were the litmus test of a method of human reproduction, the species should have stopped sexual reproduction long ago since it is the chief source of such unfortunates!

Cloning humans will contravene nature's wisdom in constantly mixing the human gene pool. The claim here is that having children genetically identical with their parents and grandparents and greatgrandparents will eventually weaken human diversity and deny future generations the benefits of what in the plant world is called "hybrid vigor." I have mentioned the two questions that are related to the genetic health and longevity of cloned individuals, and they must surely be answered before we proceed to introduce the technology into human reproduction. But just as the presence of carrots in the human diet doesn't mean we will necessarily all turn yellow from overindulgence in carotene-bearing foods, so the presence of cloning in medicine's arsenal doesn't mean that at some future date all humans will be clones of past generations. As an expensive medical therapy, cloning will have a small number of takers. And the worry associated with its development is no greater than the worries associated with the development of *in vitro* fertilization, or artificial inseminations, and probably considerably less than those associated with surrogacy.

No Exact Copies

Egomaniacal individuals will have themselves cloned to achieve a kind of immortality. We already know enough about the interaction between heredity and environment to know that it's impossible to reproduce all the influences that go into the making of an individual. Big egos may seize upon cloning as a kind of narcissistic self-recreation just as individuals now seize upon sexual reproduction as a kind of narcissistic self-recreation. When people do have children for narcissistic reasons, they are usually disappointed that the children don't turn out as their parents did. Because of the essentially unreproducible nature of environmental influences, cloning won't be any more successful at producing copies of their progenitors than sexual reproduction is. Yet another disappointment for big egos!

Cloning will be used to create embryos that can be frozen, then thawed and gestated as organ farms for their progenitors to harvest when facing major organ failure. This interesting worry — interesting because it may have some basis — deserves serious reflection. Given the way the fact of cloning transforms the question of the special status of the fertilized ovum, we may be on the verge of rethinking the whole question of what abortion is. If even the most conservative positions must now reopen the question of when the individual human begins, we may come to see harvesting fetal organs to be more like taking specialized cells from a culture than like taking organs from a baby.

Mastering the Genetic Code

But the more interesting possibility is that the development of cloning technology will be accompanied by mastery of the genetic code by which genes are turned on or off to sequence specialization. It may be possible in the future to clone individual organs without having to employ the medium of the fetus. Such a process should be faster than a nine-month gestation, and the availability of artificial womb technology (or some equivalent suitable for organ cloning) would make possible enormously important advances in organ transplantation that would be free of the complications of immune system suppression necessary for transplanting genetically non-identical organs. So while there are potential moral problems and temptations along the way, we should not recoil from them. As is nearly always the case with scientific advances, the likely potential benefits vastly outweigh the possible risks.

Those with religious scruples concerning cloning and other future bio-medical technologies need not employ them. Plenty of existing children need adoption; a more rational routine retrieval practice for transplantable organs would increase the supply; real wombs, whether owned or rented, will continue to provide an ample supply of human babies. Those of us who see the future of humankind in evolving greater and greater control over our destinies, who see human strivings and human achievements as the source of humanity's value, say this: cancel the executive orders, unchain our science, minimize its regulation, and let us rejoice in its fruits.

EVEN IF IT WORKED, CLONING WOULDN'T BRING HER BACK
by Thomas H. Murray

Eleven days ago, as I awaited my turn to testify at a congressional hearing on human reproductive cloning, one of five scientists on the witness list took the microphone. Brigitte Boisselier, a chemist working with couples who want to use cloning techniques to create babies, read aloud a letter from "a father, (Dada)." The writer, who had unexpectedly become a parent in his late thirties, describes his despair over his 11-month-old son's death after heart surgery and 17 days of "misery and struggle." The room was quiet as Boisselier read the man's words: "I decided then and there that I would never give up on my child. I would never stop until I could give his DNA — his genetic make-up — a chance."

I listened to the letter writer's refusal to accept the finality of death, to his wish to allow his son another opportunity at life through cloning, and I was struck by the futility and danger of such thinking. I had been asked to testify as someone who has been writing and teaching about ethical issues in medicine and science for more than 20 years; but I am also a grieving parent. My 20-year-old daughter's murder, just five months ago, has agonizingly reinforced what I have for years argued as an ethicist: Cloning can neither change the fact of death nor deflect the pain of grief.

Only four years have passed since the birth of the first cloned mammal — Dolly the sheep — was announced and the possibility of human cloning became real. Once a staple of science fiction, cloning was now the stuff of

Source: Thomas H. Murray, "Even If It Worked, Cloning Wouldn't Bring Her Back," by *The Washington Post,* April 8, 2001. Reprinted by permission of the author.

scientific research. A presidential commission, of which I am a member, began to deliberate the ethics of human cloning; scientists disavowed any interest in trying to clone people; and Congress held hearings but passed no laws. A moratorium took hold, stable except for the occasional eruption of self-proclaimed would-be cloners such as Chicago-based physicist Richard Seed and a group led by a man named Rael who claims that we are all clones of alien ancestors.

Recently, Boisselier, Rael's chief scientist, and Panos Zavos, an infertility specialist in Kentucky, won overnight attention when they proclaimed that they would indeed create a human clone in the near future. The prospect that renegade scientists might try to clone humans reignited the concern of lawmakers, which led to the recent hearings before the House Energy and Commerce subcommittee on oversight and investigations.

Cloning advocates have had a difficult time coming up with persuasive ethical arguments. Indulging narcissism — so that someone can create many Mini-Me's — fails to generate much support for their cause. Others make the case that adults should have the right to use any means possible to have the child they want. Their liberty trumps everything else; the child's welfare barely registers, except to avoid a life that would be worse than never being born, a standard akin to dividing by zero — no meaningful answer is possible. The strategy that has been the most effective has been to play the sympathy card — and who evokes more sympathy than someone who has lost a child?

Sadly, I'm in a position to correct some of these misunderstandings. I'm not suggesting that my situation is the same as that of the letter's author. Not better. Not worse. Simply different. His son was with him for less than a year, our daughter for 20; his son died of disease in a hospital; Emily, daughter to Cynthia and me, sister to Kate and Matt, Nicky and Pete, was reported missing from her college campus in early November. Her body was found more than five weeks later. She had been abducted and shot.

As I write those words, I still want to believe they are about someone else, a story on the 11 o'clock news. Cynthia and I often ask each other, how can this be our life? But it is our life. And Emily, as a physical, exuberant, loving presence, is not in the same way a part of it anymore. Death changes things and, I suspect, the death of a child causes more wrenching grief than any other death. So I am told; so my experience confirms.

I want to speak, then, to the author of that letter, father to father, grieving parent to grieving parent; and to anyone clinging to unfounded hope that cloning can somehow repair the arbitrariness of disease, unhappiness and death. I have nothing to sell you, I don't want your money, and I certainly don't want to be cruel. But there are hard truths here that some people, whether through ignorance or self-interest, are obscuring.

The first truth is that cloning does not result in healthy, normal offspring. The two scientific experts on animal cloning who shared the panel with Boisselier reported the results of the cattle, mice and other mammals cloned thus far: They have suffered staggering rates of abnormalities and death; some of the females bearing them have been injured and some have died. Rudolf Jaenisch, an expert on mouse cloning at MIT's Whitehead Institute for Biomedical Research, told the subcommittee that he did not believe there was a single healthy cloned mammal in existence — not even Dolly, the sheep that started it all, who is abnormally obese.

Scientists do not know why cloning fails so miserably. One plausible explanation begins with what we already know — that as the cells of an embryo divide and begin to transform into the many varieties of tissue that make up our bodies, most of the genes in each cell are shut down, leaving active only those that the cell needs to perform its specific role. A pancreatic islet cell, for example, needs working versions of the genes that recognize when a person needs the hormone insulin, then cobble it together and shunt it into the bloodstream. All of that individual's other genetic information is in that islet cell, but most of it is chemically locked, like an illegally parked car immobilized by a tire boot.

To make a healthy clone, scientists need to unlock every last one of those tire boots in the cell that is to be cloned. It is not enough to have the genes for islet cells; every gene will be needed sometime, somewhere. Unless and until scientists puzzle out how to restore all the genes to their original state, we will continue to see dead, dying and deformed clones.

You do not need to be a professional bioethicist, then, to see that trying to make a child by cloning, at this stage in the technology, would be a gross violation of international standards protecting people from overreaching scientists, a blatant example of immoral human experimentation.

Some scientists claim they can avoid these problems. Zavos, who spoke at the hearing, has promised to screen embryos and implant only healthy ones. But Zavos failed to give a single plausible reason to believe that he can distinguish healthy from unhealthy cloned embryos.

Now for the second truth: Even if cloning produced a healthy embryo, the result would not be the same person as the one whose genetic material was used. Each of us is a complex amalgam of luck, experience and heredity. Where in the womb an embryo burrows, what its mother eats or drinks, what stresses she endures, her age — all these factors shape the developing fetus. The genes themselves conduct an intricately choreographed dance, turning on and off, instructing other genes to do the same in response to their interior rhythms and to the pulses of the world outside. How we become who we are remains a mystery.

About the only thing we can be certain of is that we are much more than the sum of our genes. As I said in my testimony, perhaps the best way to extinguish the enthusiasm for human cloning would be to clone Michael Jordan. Michael II might well have no interest in playing basketball but instead long to become an accountant. What makes Michael I great is not merely his physical gifts, but his competitive fire, his determination, his fierce will to win.

Yet another hard truth: Creating a child to stand in for another — dead — child is unfair. No child should have to bear the oppressive expectation that he or she will live out the life denied to his or her idealized genetic avatar. Parents may joke about their specific plans for their children; I suspect their children find such plans less amusing. Of course, we should have expectations for our children: that they be considerate, honest, diligent, fair and more. But we cannot dictate their temperament, talents or interests. Cloning a child to be a reincarnation of someone else is a grotesque, fun-house mirror distortion of parental expectations.

Which brings me to the final hard truth: There is no real escape from grief.

Cynthia and I have fantasized about time running backward so that we could undo Emily's murder. We would give our limbs, our organs, our lives to bring her back, to give her the opportunity to live out her dream of becoming an Episcopal priest, of retiring as a mesmerizing old woman sitting on her porch on Cape Cod, surrounded by her grandchildren and poodles.

But trying to recreate Emily from her DNA would be chasing an illusion. Massive waves of sorrow knock us down, breathless; we must learn to live with them. When our strength returns we stagger to our feet, summon whatever will we can, and do what needs to be done. Most of all we try to hold each other up. We can no more wish our grief away than King Canute could stem the ocean's tide.

So I find myself wanting to say to the letter writer, and to the scientists who offer him and other sorrowing families false hope: There are no technological fixes for grief; cloning your dear dead son will not repair the jagged hole ripped out of the tapestry of your life. Your letter fills me with sadness for you and your wife, not just for the loss of your child but also for the fruitless quest to quench your grief in a genetic replica of the son you lost. It would be fruitless even — especially — if you succeeded in creating a healthy biological duplicate. But there is little chance of that.

Emily lived until a few months shy of her 21st birthday. In those years our lives became interwoven in ways so intricate that I struggle for words to describe how Cynthia and I now feel. We were fortunate to have her with us long enough to see her become her own person, to love her wholeheartedly and to know beyond question that she loved us. Her loss changes us forever. Life flows in one direction; science cannot reverse the stream or reincarnate the dead.

The Emily we knew and loved would want us to continue to do what matters in our lives, to love each other, to do good work, to find meaning. Not to forget her, ever: We are incapable of that. Why would we want to? She was a luminous presence in our family, an extraordinary friend, a promising young philosopher. And we honor her by keeping her memory vibrant, not by trying to manufacture a genetic facsimile. And that thought makes me address the letter's author once more: I have to think that your son, were he able to tell you, would wish for you the same.

Questions for Analysis

For each article on human cloning, do the following:

1. Identify the arguments that were used and summarize the reasons and conclusion for each.

2. Describe the types of argument forms that you identified.

3. Evaluate the *truth* of the reasons that support the conclusion for each of the arguments that you identified and the *validity* of the logical form.

4. Imagine that you have been asked by the president to prepare a position paper on human cloning that he can use to shape the government's policy. Construct an extended argument regarding human cloning, using the format described on the companion web site. Be sure to include arguments on both sides of the issue and conclude with your own reasoned analysis and conclusion. Be sure to include specific policy recommendations that you believe the government should take with respect to cloning.

11 Reasoning Critically

Inductive Reasoning

Reasoning from premises assumed to be true to a conclusion supported (but not logically) by the premises

Empirical Generalization

Drawing conclusions about a target population based on observing a sample population

Is the sample known?
Is the sample sufficient?
Is the sample representative?

Causal Reasoning

Concluding that an event is the result of another event

Scientific Method

1. Identify an event for investigation
2. Gather information
3. Develop a theory/hypothesis
4. Test/experiment
5. Evaluate results

Fallacies

Unsound arguments that can appear logical

Fallacies of False Generalization

Hasty generalization
Sweeping generalization
False dilemma

Causal Fallacies

Questionable cause
Misidentification of the cause
Post hoc ergo propter hoc
Slippery slope

Fallacies of Relevance

Appeal to authority
Appeal to tradition
Bandwagon
Appeal to pity
Appeal to fear
Appeal to flattery
Special pleading
Appeal to ignorance
Begging the question
Straw man
Red herring
Appeal to personal attack
Two wrongs make a right

The Critical Thinker's Guide to Reasoning

Reasoning is the type of thinking that uses arguments — reasons in support of conclusions — to decide, explain, predict, and persuade. Effective reasoning involves using all of the intellectual skills and critical attitudes we have been developing in this book, and in this chapter we will further explore various dimensions of the reasoning process.

Inductive Reasoning

Chapter 10 focused primarily on *deductive reasoning*, an argument form in which one reasons from premises that are known or assumed to be true to a conclusion that follows necessarily from the premises. In this chapter we will examine *inductive reasoning*, an argument form in which one reasons from premises that are known or assumed to be true to a conclusion that is supported by the premises but does not follow logically from them.

> **inductive reasoning** *An argument form in which one reasons from premises that are known or assumed to be true to a conclusion that is supported by the premises but does not necessarily follow from them*

When you reason inductively, your premises provide evidence that makes it more or less probable (but not certain) that the conclusion is true. The following statements are examples of conclusions reached through inductive reasoning.

1. A recent Gallup poll reported that 74 percent of the American public believes that abortion should remain legalized.
2. On the average, a person with a college degree will earn over $1,140,000 more in his or her lifetime than a person with just a high school diploma.
3. In a recent survey twice as many doctors interviewed stated that if they were stranded on a desert island, they would prefer Bayer Aspirin to Extra Strength Tylenol.
4. The outbreak of food poisoning at the end-of-year school party was probably caused by the squid salad.
5. The devastating disease AIDS is caused by a particularly complex virus that may not be curable.
6. The solar system is probably the result of an enormous explosion — a "big bang" — that occurred billions of years ago.

The first three statements are forms of inductive reasoning known as *empirical generalization*, a general statement about an entire group made on the basis of observing some members of the group. The final three statements are examples of *causal reasoning*, a form of inductive reasoning in which it is claimed that an event (or events) is the result of the occurrence of another event (or events). We will be exploring the ways each of these forms of inductive reasoning functions in our lives and in various fields of study.

In addition to examining various ways of reasoning logically and effectively, we will also explore certain forms of reasoning that are not logical and, as a result, are usually not effective. These ways of pseudo-reasoning (false reasoning) are often termed *fallacies:* arguments that are not sound because of various errors in reasoning. Fallacious reasoning is typically used to influence others. It seeks to persuade not on the basis of sound arguments and critical thinking but rather on the basis of emotional and illogical factors.

fallacies *Unsound arguments that are often persuasive and appearing to be logical because they usually appeal to our emotions and prejudices, and because they often support conclusions that we want to believe are accurate*

⊙ Empirical Generalization

One of the most important tools used by both natural and social scientists is empirical generalization. Have you ever wondered how the major television and radio networks can accurately predict election results hours before the polls close? These predictions are made possible by the power of *empirical generalization*, a first major type of inductive reasoning that is defined as reasoning from a limited sample to a general conclusion based on this sample.

empirical generalization *A form of inductive reasoning in which a general statement is made about an entire group (the "target population") based on observing some members of the group (the "sample population")*

Network election predictions, as well as public opinion polls that occur throughout a political campaign, are based on interviews with a select number of people. Ideally, pollsters would interview everyone in the *target population* (in this case, voters), but this, of course, is hardly practical. Instead, they select a relatively small group of individuals from the target population, known as a *sample*, who they have determined will adequately represent the group as a whole. Pollsters believe that they can then generalize the opinions of this smaller group to the target population. And with a few notable exceptions (such as in the 1948 presidential election, when New York governor Thomas Dewey went to bed believing he had been elected president and woke up a loser to Harry Truman, and the 2000 election, when Al Gore was briefly declared the presidential winner over George W. Bush), these results are highly accurate.

There are three key criteria for evaluating inductive arguments:

- Is the sample known?
- Is the sample sufficient?
- Is the sample representative?

Is the Sample Known?

An inductive argument is only as strong as the sample on which it is based. For example, sample populations described in vague and unclear terms — "highly placed sources" or "many young people interviewed," for example — provide a treacherously weak foundation for generalizing to larger populations. In order for an inductive argument to be persuasive, the sample population should be explicitly *known* and clearly identified. Natural and social scientists take great care in selecting the members in the sample groups, and this is an important part of the data that is available to outside investigators who may wish to evaluate and verify the results.

Is the Sample Sufficient?

The second criterion for evaluating inductive reasoning is to consider the *size* of the sample. It should be sufficiently large enough to give an accurate sense of the group as a whole. In the polling example discussed earlier, we would be concerned if only a few registered voters had been interviewed, and the results of these interviews were then generalized to a much larger population. Overall, the larger the sample, the more reliable the inductive conclusions. Natural and social scientists have developed precise guidelines for determining the size of the sample needed to achieve reliable results. For example, poll results are often accompanied by a qualification such as "These results are subject to an error factor of ± 3 percentage points." This means that if the sample reveals that 47 percent of those interviewed prefer candidate X, then we can reliably state that 44 to 50 percent of the target population prefer candidate X. Because a sample is usually a small portion of the target population, we can rarely state that the two match each other exactly — there must always be some room for variation. The exceptions to this are situations in which the target population is completely homogeneous. For example, tasting one cookie from a bag of cookies is usually enough to tell us whether or not the entire bag is stale.

Is the Sample Representative?

The third crucial element in effective inductive reasoning is the *representativeness* of the sample. If we are to generalize with confidence from the sample to the target population, then we have to be sure the sample is similar to the larger group from which it is drawn in all relevant aspects. For instance, in the polling example the sample population should reflect the same percentage of men and women, of Democrats and Republicans, of young and old, and so on, as the target population. It is obvious that many characteristics, such as hair color, favorite food, and shoe size, are not relevant to the comparison. The better the sample reflects the target population in terms of *relevant* qualities, the better the accuracy of the generalizations. However, when the sample is *not* representative of the target population — for example, if the election pollsters interviewed only females between the ages of thirty and thirty-five — then the sample is termed *biased*, and any generalizations about the target population will be highly suspect.

How do we ensure that the sample is representative of the target population? One important device is *random selection*, a selection strategy in which every member of the target population has an equal chance of being included in the sample. For example, the various techniques used to select winning lottery tickets are supposed to be random — each ticket is supposed to have an equal chance of winning. In complex cases of inductive reasoning — such as polling — random selection is often combined with the confirmation that all of the important categories in the population are adequately represented. For example, an election pollster would want to be certain that all significant geographical areas are included and then would randomly select individuals from within those areas to compose the sample.

Understanding the principles of empirical generalization is of crucial importance to effective thinking because we are continually challenged to construct and evaluate this form of inductive argument in our lives.

THINKING ACTIVITY 11.1

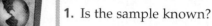

Evaluating Inductive Arguments

Review the following examples of inductive arguments. (Additional examples are included on the companion web site.) For each argument, evaluate the quality of the thinking by answering the following questions:

1. Is the sample known?
2. Is the sample sufficient?
3. Is the sample representative?
4. Do you believe the conclusions are likely to be accurate? Why or why not?

Link Between Pornography and Antisocial Behavior?   In a study of a possible relationship between pornography and antisocial behavior, questionnaires went out to 7,500 psychiatrists and psychoanalysts whose listing in the directory of the American Psychological Association indicated clinical experience. Over 3,400 of these professionals responded. The result: 7.4 percent of the psychiatrists and psychologists had cases in which they were convinced that pornography was a causal factor in antisocial behavior; an additional 9.4 percent were suspicious; 3.2 percent did not commit themselves; and 80 percent said they had no cases in which a causal connection was suspected.

To Sleep, Perchance to Die?   A survey by the Sleep Disorder Clinic of the VA hospital in La Jolla, California (involving more than one million people), revealed that people who sleep more than ten hours a night have a death rate 80 percent higher than those who sleep only seven or eight hours. Men who sleep less than four hours a night have a death rate 180 percent higher, and women with less [than four hours] sleep have a rate 40 percent higher. This might be taken as indicating that too much or too little sleep causes death.

THINKING ACTIVITY 11.2

Designing a Poll

Select an issue that you would like to poll a group of people about — for example, the population of your school or your neighborhood. Describe in specific terms how you would go about constructing a sample both large and representative enough for you to generalize the results to the target population accurately.

Fallacies of False Generalization

In Chapter 7 we explored the way that we form concepts through the interactive process of generalizing (identifying the common qualities that define the boundaries of the concept) and interpreting (identifying examples of the concept). This generalizing and interpreting process is similar to the process involved in constructing empirical generalizations, in which we seek to reach a general conclusion based on a limited number of examples and then apply this conclusion to other examples. Although generalizing and interpreting are useful in forming concepts, they also can give rise to fallacious ways of thinking, including the following:

- Hasty generalization
- Sweeping generalization
- False dilemma

Hasty Generalization

Consider the following examples of reasoning. Do you think that the arguments are sound? Why or why not?

> My boyfriends have never shown any real concern for my feelings. My conclusion is that men are insensitive, selfish, and emotionally superficial.

> My mother always gets upset over insignificant things. This leads me to believe that women are very emotional.

In both of these cases, a general conclusion has been reached that is based on a very small sample. As a result, the reasons provide very weak support for the conclusions that are being developed. It just does not make good sense to generalize from a few individuals to all men or all women. The conclusions are *hasty* because the samples are not large enough and/or not representative enough to provide adequate justification for the generalization.

Of course, many generalizations are more warranted than the two given here because the conclusion is based on a sample that is larger and more representative of the group as a whole. For example:

> I have done a lot of research in a variety of automotive publications on the relationship between the size of cars and the gas mileage they get. In general, I think it makes sense to conclude that large cars tend to get fewer miles per gallon than smaller cars.

In this case, the conclusion is generalized from a larger and more representative sample than those in the preceding two arguments. As a result, the reason for the last argument provides much stronger support for the conclusion.

Sweeping Generalization

Whereas the fallacy of hasty generalization deals with errors in the process of generalizing, the fallacy of *sweeping generalization* focuses on difficulties in the process of interpreting. Consider the following examples of reasoning. Do you think that the arguments are sound? Why or why not?

> Vigorous exercise contributes to overall good health. Therefore, vigorous exercise should be practiced by recent heart attack victims, people who are out of shape, and women who are about to give birth.

> People should be allowed to make their own decisions, providing that their actions do not harm other people. Therefore, people who are trying to commit suicide should be left alone to do what they want.

In both of these cases, generalizations that are true in most cases have been deliberately applied to instances that are clearly intended to be exceptions to the generalizations because of special features that the exceptions possess. Of course, the use of sweeping generalizations stimulates us to clarify the generalization, rephrasing it to exclude instances, like those given here, that have special features. For example, the first generalization could be reformulated as "Vigorous exercise contributes to overall good health, *except for* recent heart attack victims, people out of shape, and women who are about to give birth." Sweeping generalizations become dangerous only when they are accepted without critical analysis and reformulation.

Review the following examples of sweeping generalizations, and in each case (a) explain *why* it is a sweeping generalization and (b) reformulate the statement so that it becomes a legitimate generalization.

1. A college education stimulates you to develop as a person and prepares you for many professions. Therefore, all persons should attend college, no matter what career they are interested in.

2. Drugs such as heroin and morphine are addictive and therefore qualify as dangerous drugs. This means that they should never be used, even as painkillers in medical situations.

3. Once criminals have served time for the crimes they have committed, they have paid their debt to society and should be permitted to work at any job they choose.

False Dilemma

The fallacy of the *false dilemma* — also known as the "either/or" fallacy or the "black-or-white" fallacy — occurs when we are asked to choose between two extreme alternatives without being able to consider additional options. For example, we may say, "Either you're for me or against me," meaning that a choice has to be made between these alternatives. Sometimes giving people only two choices on an issue makes sense ("If you decide to swim the English Channel, you'll either make it or you won't"). At other times, however, viewing situations in such extreme terms may be a serious oversimplification — for it would mean viewing a complicated situation in terms that are too simple.

The following statements are examples of false dilemmas. After analyzing the fallacy in each case, suggest different alternatives than those being presented.

> **Example:**   *"Everyone in Germany is a National Socialist — the few outside the party are either lunatics or idiots." (Adolf Hitler, quoted by* The New York Times, *April 5, 1938)*
>
> **Analysis:**   *This is an oversimplification. Hitler is saying that if you are not a Nazi, then you are a lunatic or an idiot. By limiting the population to these groups, Hitler was simply ignoring all the people who did not qualify as Nazis, lunatics, or idiots.*

1. America — love it or leave it!

2. She loves me; she loves me not.

3. Live free or die.

4. If you're not part of the solution, then you're part of the problem. (Eldridge Cleaver)

5. If you know about BMWs, you either own one or you want to.

THINKING PASSAGE

Detecting Fallacies of False Generalization

In the article entitled "She's Not Really Ill . . . ," columnist (and humorist) Maureen Dowd acknowledges at the outset that she's likely guilty of making a sweeping generalization with her statement "All women have gone crazy." After reading the article, answer the questions that follow.

SHE'S NOT REALLY ILL . . .
by Maureen Dowd

Washington — I usually avoid sweeping generalizations.

Lately, however, I have come to the unavoidable conclusion that all women have gone crazy. O.K., maybe not all. But certainly most.

Sure, it's a little inflammatory to claim that most women are nuts and on drugs and that the drugs are clearly not working. But I have some anecdotal evidence to back it up.

First of all, I noticed that a lot of women I know are wacko-bango.

Then a doctor pal confided that she's surprised at how many of her female patients act loony even though they're on mood-smoothing pills — sometimes multiple meds.

Then another friend who took a bunch of high school seniors on a spring vacation mentioned that all the girls were on anti-anxiety and antidepression drugs, some to get an extra edge as they aimed for Ivy League colleges. (Let's not even start on the kiddie hordes on Ritalin.)

And finally, another friend told me she goes to a compounding pharmacy in L.A. where she gets testosterone to jump her libido, or sensurround, a cocktail with ingredients like estrogen, progesterone, DHEA, pregnenelone and tryptophan.

The sequel to "Valley of the Dolls" is being published later this month. Jacqueline Susann, it turned out, was Cassandra in Pucci.

It isn't only neurotic Hollywood beauties any more. Now America is the Valley of the Dolls.

In Ms. Susann's 1966 book, the women had to go to third-rate hotels on New York's West Side to medical offices with dirty windows and sweet-talk doctors into giving them little red, yellow or blue dolls. Now doctors and pharmaceutical companies sweet-talk patients into feel-good pills.

When I mentioned to a doctor a while ago that I was not in a serious relationship, he asked brightly, "Would you like antidepressants?"

Young professional women in Washington tell girlfriends in a tizzy: "Take a Paxil."

Source: Copyright © 2001 by The New York Times Co. Reprinted with Permission.

It isn't just women, of course. A young guy I know went in for a check-up last week and told his internist he was on edge because he's getting married and moving out of the country for a big new job.

The doctor proposed an antidepressant called Serzone. My friend refused, pointing out that you're supposed to be nervous before you get married and start a new job.

Doctors now want to medicate you for living your life.

"We're treating a level of depression that would not have been considered a serious illness in the past," says Peter Kramer, who wrote "Listening to Prozac." Now we're listening to ads touting "Prozac Weekly."

Women have always popped mood-altering pills more than men. Studies show that women in most cultures have twice the rates of depression that men do. And now they feel entitled to speak up about their suffering.

A top psychiatrist told me women take more dolls because they're "hormonally more complicated and biologically more vulnerable. Depression is the downside of attachment, and women are programmed to attach more strongly and punished more when they lose attachments."

There's an antidepressant for women who compulsively shop called Celexa. The "Washington Post" reported recently that Eli Lilly repackaged Prozac as the angelic Sarafem, in a pink and lavender capsule, and launched a multimillion-dollar ad campaign, with a woman irritably yanking a grocery cart, suffering from a new malady ominously called PMDD, premenstrual dysphoric disorder, an uber-PMS psychiatrists say may not be real.

Sales soared for "Prozac in drag," as Dr. Kramer calls it, adding: "The liltingly soft name Sarafem sounds like Esperanto for a beleaguered husband's fantasy — a serene wife."

He finds it ironic that Prozac, the drug that was supposed to help career women assert themselves, has morphed into Sarafem, a mother's little helper to soothe anxious housewives, as Miltown and Valium did in the Stepford wife era.

"Cooking fresh food for a husband's just a drag, so she buys an instant cake and she burns her frozen steak," the Rolling Stones sang in 1966.

So women began taking mood dolls because they felt bored and dissatisfied, home with the kids.

And now that women can have a family and a career, they need mood dolls to give them the confidence and energy to juggle all that stress.

Progress. Don't ya love it?

Questions for Analysis

1. Identify all of the sweeping generalizations, hasty generalizations, and false dilemmas that Dowd includes in her article.

2. What is the major point that Dowd is making in the article? Why do you think she decided to use generalization fallacies to make her point? Do you think the approach is effective? Why or why not?

3. Do you think that drugs are being overprescribed and overused to deal with psychological and emotional problems? If so, provide an example of what you consider to be an excessive use of prescription medications.

4. Why do you think our society is turning increasingly to pharmaceutical solutions for emotional and behavioral problems? For example, Ritalin and other drugs are increasingly being prescribed to deal in school with such children's behavioral and emotional problems as "attention deficit hyperactivity disorder." In 2001, doctors wrote almost twenty million monthly prescriptions for stimulant drugs for children, especially boys, a 13 percent increase over the previous year. In many cases the schools recommended or insisted that the drugs be taken. Some people believe that this is a dangerous trend, that these drugs may have long-term consequences for children, and that there is no scientific basis for the diagnosis of the disorder for which the drugs are prescribed. What do you think?

Causal Reasoning

A second major type of inductive reasoning is *causal reasoning*, a form in which an event (or events) is claimed to be the result of the occurrence of another event (or events).

As you use your thinking abilities to try to understand the world you live in, you often ask the question "Why did that happen?" For example, if the engine of your car is running roughly, your natural question is "What's wrong?" If you wake up one morning with an upset stomach, you usually ask yourself, "What's the cause?" Or maybe the softball team you belong to has been losing recently. You typically wonder, "What's going on?" In each of these cases you assume that there is some factor (or factors) responsible for what is occurring, some *cause* (or causes) that results in the *effect* (or effects) you are observing (the rough engine, the upset stomach, the losing team).

causal reasoning *A form of inductive reasoning in which an event (or events) is claimed to be the result of another event (or events)*

As you saw in Chapter 8, causality is one of the basic patterns of thinking we use to organize and make sense of our experience. For instance, imagine how bewildered you would feel if a mechanic looked at your car and told you there was no explanation for the poorly running engine. Or suppose you take your upset stomach to the doctor, who examines you and then concludes that there is no possible causal explanation for the malady. In each case you would be understandably skeptical of the diagnosis and would probably seek another opinion.

The Scientific Method

Causal reasoning is also the backbone of the natural and social sciences; it is responsible for the remarkable understanding of our world that has been achieved. The *scientific method* works on the assumption that the world is constructed in a complex web of causal relationships that can be discovered through systematic investigation. Scientists have devised an organized approach for discovering causal relationships and testing the accuracy of conclusions. The sequence of steps is as follows:

1. Identify an event or a relationship between events to be investigated.
2. Gather information about the event (or events).
3. Develop a hypothesis or theory to explain what is happening.
4. Test the hypothesis or theory through experimentation.
5. Evaluate the hypothesis or theory based on experimental results.

How does this sequence work when applied to the situation of the rough-running engine mentioned earlier?

1. *Identify an event or a relationship between events to be investigated.* In this case, the event is obvious — your car's engine is running poorly, and you want to discover the cause of the problem so that you can fix it.
2. *Gather information about the event (or events).* This step involves locating any relevant information about the situation that will help solve the problem. You initiate this step by asking and trying to answer a variety of questions: When did the engine begin running poorly? Was this change abrupt or gradual? When did the car last have a tune-up? Are there other mechanical difficulties that might be related? Has anything unusual occurred with the car recently?
3. *Develop a hypothesis or theory to explain what is happening.* After reviewing the relevant information, you will want to identify the most likely explanation of what has happened. This possible explanation is known as a

VISUAL THINKING

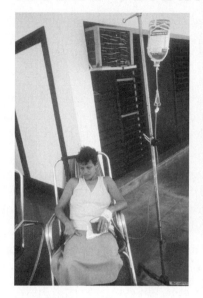

Curing Disease

- The woman in the photo on the left is an AIDS patient living under quarantine. As depicted in the photo on the right, many thousands of scientists around the world are actively seeking cures for a wide range of human illnesses, including AIDS, the plague of our times. Do you know anyone who is engaged in disease-related research?

hypothesis. (A *theory* is normally a more complex model that involves a number of interconnected hypotheses, such as the theory of quantum mechanics in physics.)

hypothesis *A possible explanation that is introduced to account for a set of facts and that can be used as a basis for further investigation*

Although your hypothesis may be suggested by the information you have, it goes beyond the information as well and so must be tested before you commit yourself to it. In this case the hypothesis you might settle on is "water in the gas." This hypothesis was suggested by your recollection that the engine troubles began right after you bought gas in the pouring rain. This hypothesis may be correct or it may be incorrect — you have to test it to find out.

When you devise a plausible hypothesis to be tested, you should keep three general guidelines in mind:

- *Explanatory power:* The hypothesis should effectively explain the event you are investigating. The hypothesis that damaged windshield wipers are causing the engine problem doesn't seem to provide an adequate explanation of the difficulties.

- *Economy:* The hypothesis should not be unnecessarily complex. The explanation that your engine difficulty is the result of sabotage by an unfriendly neighbor is possible but unlikely. There are simpler and more direct explanations you should test first.

- *Predictive power:* The hypothesis should allow you to make various predictions to test its accuracy. If the "water in the gas" hypothesis is accurate, you can predict that removing the water from the gas tank and gas line should clear up the difficulty.

4. *Test the hypothesis or theory through experimentation.* Once you identify a hypothesis that meets these three guidelines, the next task is to devise an experiment to test its accuracy. In the case of your troubled car, you would test your hypothesis by pouring several containers of "dry gas" into the tank, blowing out the gas line, and cleaning the carburetor. By removing the moisture in the gas system, you should be able to determine whether your hypothesis is correct.

5. *Evaluate the hypothesis or theory based on experimental results.* After reviewing the results of your experiment, you usually can assess the accuracy of your hypothesis. If the engine runs smoothly after you remove moisture from the gas line, then this strong evidence supports your hypothesis. If the engine does *not* run smoothly after your efforts, then this persuasive evidence suggests that your hypothesis is not correct. There is, however, a third possibility. Removing the moisture from the gas system might improve the engine's performance somewhat but not entirely. In that case you might want to construct a *revised* hypothesis along the lines of "Water in the gas system is partially responsible for my rough-running engine, but another cause (or causes) might be involved as well."

If the evidence does not support your hypothesis or supports a revised version of it, you then begin the entire process again by identifying and testing a new hypothesis. The natural and social sciences engage in an ongoing process of developing theories and hypotheses and testing them through experimental design. Many theories and hypotheses are much more complex than our "moisture in the gas" example and take years of generating, revising, and testing. Determining the subatomic structure of the universe and finding cures for various kinds of cancers, for example, have been the subjects of countless theories and hypotheses, as well as experiments to test their accuracy. We might diagram this operation of the scientific process as follows:

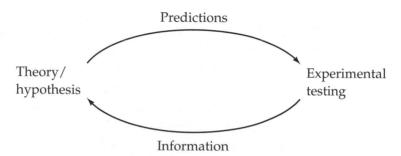

Predictions

Theory/
hypothesis   Experimental
                                             testing

Information

**Acceptance, rejection, or revision
of the theory/hypothesis**

THINKING ACTIVITY 11.3

Applying the Scientific Method

Select one of the following situations or describe a situation of your own choosing. Then analyze the situation by working through the various steps of the scientific method listed directly after.

- Situation 1: You wake up in the morning with an upset stomach.
- Situation 2: Your grades have been declining all semester.
- Situation 3: (Your own choosing)

1. *Identify an event or a relationship between events to be investigated.* Describe the situation you have selected.

2. *Gather information about the event (or events).* Elaborate the situation by providing additional details. Be sure to include a variety of possible causes for the event. (For example, an upset stomach might be the result of food poisoning, the flu, anxiety, etc.).

3. *Develop a theory or hypothesis to explain what is happening.* Based on the information you have described, identify a plausible hypothesis that (a) explains what occurred, (b) is clear and direct, and (c) leads to predictions that can be tested.

4. ***Test the theory or hypothesis through experimentation.*** Design a way of testing your hypothesis that results in evidence proving or disproving it.
5. ***Evaluate the theory or hypothesis.*** Describe the results of your experiment and explain whether the results lead you to accept, reject, or revise your hypothesis.

In designing the experiment in Thinking Activity 11.3, you may have used one of two common reasoning patterns.

> ***Reasoning Pattern 1:***   *A caused B because A is the only relevant common element shared by more than one occurrence of B.*

For example, imagine that you are investigating your upset stomach, and you decide to call two friends who had dinner with you the previous evening to see if they have similar symptoms. You discover they also have upset stomachs. Because dining at "Sam's Seafood" was the only experience shared by the three of you that might explain the three stomach problems, you conclude that food poisoning may in fact be the cause. Further, although each of you ordered a different entrée, you all shared an appetizer, "Sam's Special Squid," which suggests that you may have identified the cause. As you can see, this pattern of reasoning looks for the common thread linking different occurrences of the same event to identify the cause; stated more simply, "The cause is the common thread."

> ***Reasoning Pattern 2:***   *A caused B because A is the only relevant difference between this situation and other situations in which B did not take place.*

For example, imagine that you are investigating the reasons that your team, which has been winning all year, has suddenly begun to lose. One way of approaching this situation is to look for circumstances that might have changed at the time your team's fortunes began to decline. Your investigation yields two possible explanations. First, your team started wearing new uniforms about the time it started losing. Second, one of your regular players was sidelined with a foot injury. You decide to test the first hypothesis by having the team begin wearing the old uniforms again. When this doesn't change your fortunes, you conclude that the missing player may be the cause of the difficulties, and you anxiously await the player's return to see if your reasoning is accurate. As you can see, this pattern of reasoning looks for relevant differences linked to the situation you are trying to explain; stated more simply, "The cause is the difference."

Controlled Experiments

Although our analysis of causal reasoning has focused on causal relationships between specific events, much of scientific research concerns causal factors influencing populations composed of many individuals. In these cases the causal relationships tend to be much more complex than the simple formulation *A causes B.* For example, on every package of cigarettes sold in the United States appears a message such as "Surgeon General's Warning: Smoking Causes Lung Cancer, Heart Disease, Emphysema, and May Complicate Pregnancy." This does not mean that every cigarette smoked has a direct impact on one's health, nor does it mean that everyone who smokes moderately, or even heavily, will die prematurely of cancer, heart disease, or emphysema. Instead, the statement means that if you habitually smoke, your chances of developing one of the diseases normally associated with smoking are significantly higher than are those of someone who does not smoke or who smokes only occasionally. How were scientists able to arrive at this conclusion?

The reasoning strategy scientists use to reach conclusions like this one is the *controlled experiment,* and it is one of the most powerful reasoning strategies ever developed. There are three different kinds of controlled experiment designs:

1. Cause-to-effect experiments (with intervention)

2. Cause-to-effect experiments (without intervention)

3. Effect-to-cause experiments

Cause-to-Effect Experiments (with Intervention) The first of these forms of reasoning, known as *cause-to-effect experiments (with intervention),* is illustrated by the following example. Imagine that you have developed a new cream you believe will help cure baldness in men and women and you want to evaluate its effectiveness. What do you do? To begin with, you have to identify a group of people who accurately represent all of the balding men and women in the United States because testing the cream on all balding people simply isn't feasible. This involves following the guidelines for inductive reasoning described in the last section. It is important that the group you select to test be *representative* of all balding people (known as the *target population*) because you hope your product will grow hair on all types of heads. For example, if you select only men between the ages of twenty and thirty to test, the experiment will establish only whether the product works for men of these ages. Additional experiments will have to be conducted for women and other age groups. This representative group is known as a *sample.* Scientists have developed strategies for selecting sample groups to ensure that they fairly mirror the larger group from which they are drawn.

Once you have selected your sample of balding men and women — say, you have identified 200 people — the next step is to divide the sample into two groups of 100 people that are alike in all relevant respects. The best way to ensure that the groups are essentially alike is through the technique we examined earlier called *random selection*, which means that each individual selected has the same chance of being chosen as everyone else. You then designate one group as the *experimental group* and the other group as the *control group*. You next give the individuals in the experimental group treatments of your hair-growing cream, and you give either no treatments or a harmless, non-hair-growing cream to the control group. At the conclusion of the testing period, you compare the experimental group with the control group to evaluate hair gain and hair loss.

Suppose that a number of individuals in the experimental group do indeed show evidence of more new hair growth than the control group. How can you be sure this is because of the cream and not simply a chance occurrence? Scientists have developed a formula for statistical significance based on the size of the sample and the frequency of the observed effects. For example, imagine that thirteen persons in your experimental group show evidence of new hair growth, whereas no one in the control group shows any such evidence. Statisticians have determined that we can say with 95 percent certainty that the new hair growth was caused by your new cream — that the results were not merely the result of chance. This type of experimental result is usually expressed by saying that the experimental results were significant at the 0.05 level, a standard criterion in experimental research. The diagram below shows the cause-to-effect experiment (with intervention).

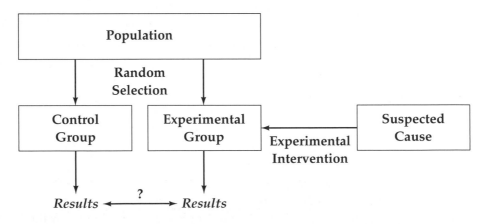

CAUSE-TO-EFFECT EXPERIMENTS (WITH INTERVENTION)

Cause-to-Effect Experiments (Without Intervention)   A second form of controlled experiment is known as the *cause-to-effect experiment (without intervention)*. This form of experimental design is similar to the one just described except that the experimenter does not intervene to expose the experimental group to a proposed cause (like the hair-growing cream). Instead, the experimenter identifies a cause that a population is already exposed to and then constructs the experiment. For example, suppose you suspect that the asbestos panels and insulation in some old buildings cause cancer. Because it would not be ethical to expose people intentionally to something that might damage their health, you would search for already existing conditions in which people are being exposed to the asbestos. Once located, these individuals (or a representative sample) could be used as the experimental group. You could then form a control group of individuals who are not exposed to asbestos but who match the experimental group in all other relevant respects. You could then investigate the health experiences of both groups over time, thereby evaluating the possible relationship between asbestos and cancer. The diagram at the bottom of this page illustrates the procedure used in cause-to-effect experiments (without intervention).

Effect-to-Cause Experiments   A third form of reasoning employing the controlled experimental design is known as the *effect-to-cause experiment.* In this case the experimenter works backward from an existing effect to a suspected cause. For example, imagine that you are investigating the claim by many Vietnam veterans that exposure to the chemical defoliant Agent Orange has resulted in significant health problems for them and for children born to them. Once again, you would not want to expose people to a potentially harmful substance just to test a hypothesis. And unlike the asbestos case we just exam-

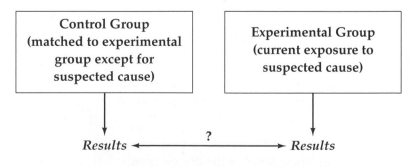

**CAUSE-TO-EFFECT EXPERIMENTS
(WITHOUT INTERVENTION)**

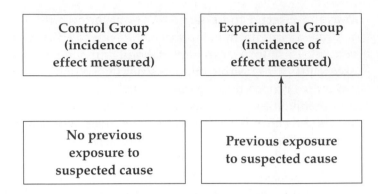

EFFECT-TO-CAUSE EXPERIMENTS

ined, people are no longer being exposed to Agent Orange as they were during the Vietnam War. As a result, investigating the claim involves beginning with the effect (health problems) and working back to the suspected cause (Agent Orange). In this case the target population would be Vietnam veterans who were exposed to Agent Orange, so you would draw a representative sample from this group. You would form a matching control group from the population of Vietnam veterans who were not exposed to Agent Orange. Next, you would compare the incidence of illnesses claimed to have been caused by Agent Orange in the two groups and evaluate the proposed causal relation. The diagram above illustrates the procedure used in effect-to-cause experiments.

THINKING ACTIVITY 11.4

Evaluating Experimental Results

Read the following experimental situations. (Additional situations are included on the companion web site.) For each situation

1. Describe the proposed causal relationship (the theory or hypothesis).
2. Identify which kind of experimental design was used.
3. Evaluate
   a. The representativeness of the sample
   b. The randomness of the division into experimental and control groups
4. Explain how well the experimental results support the proposed theory or hypothesis.

Mortality Shown to Center Around Birthdays   A new study, based on 2,745,149 deaths from natural causes, has found that men tend to die just before their birthdays, while women tend to die just after their birthdays. Thus an approaching birthday seems to prolong the life of women and precipitate death in men. The study, published in the journal *Psychosomatic Medicine,* found 3 percent more deaths than expected among women in the week after a birthday and a slight decline the week before. For men, deaths peaked just before birthdays and showed no rise above normal afterward.

A Shorter Life for Lefties   A survey of 5,000 people by Stanley Coren found that while 15 percent of the population at age ten was left-handed, there was a pronounced drop-off as people grew older, leaving 5 percent among fifty-year-olds and less than 1 percent for those age eighty and above. Where have all the lefties gone? They seem to have died. Lefties have a shorter life expectancy than righties, by an average of 9 years in the general population, apparently due to the ills and accidents they are more likely to suffer by having to live in a "right-handed world."

Nuns Offer Clues to Alzheimer's and Aging   The famous "Nun Study" is considered by experts on aging to be one of the most innovative efforts to answer questions about who gets Alzheimer's disease and why. Studying 678 nuns at seven convents has shown that folic acid may help stave off Alzheimer's disease, and that early language ability may be linked to lower risk of Alzheimer's because nuns who packed more ideas into the sentences of their early autobiographies were less likely to get Alzheimer's disease six decades later. Also, nuns who expressed more positive emotions in their autobiographies lived significantly longer — in some cases 10 years longer — than those expressing fewer positive emotions.

THINKING ACTIVITY 11.5

Designing a Scientific Experiment

Construct an experimental design to investigate a potential causal relationship of your own choosing. Be sure that your experimental design follows the guidelines established.

- A clearly defined theory or hypothesis expressing a proposed relationship between a cause and an effect in a population of individuals
- Representative samples
- Selection into experimental and control groups

- A clear standard for evaluating the evidence for or against the theory or hypothesis

THINKING PASSAGE

Researching Cures and Prevention

Human history is filled with examples of misguided causal thinking — bleeding people's veins and applying leeches to reduce fever, beating and torturing emotionally disturbed people to drive out the devils thought to possess them, sacrificing young women to ensure the goodwill of the gods, and so on. When the bubonic plague ravaged Europe in the fourteenth century, the lack of scientific understanding led to causal explanations like "God's punishment of the unholy" and "the astrological position of the planets."

Contrast this fourteenth-century plague with what some people have termed the plague of the twentieth and twenty-first centuries — acquired immune deficiency syndrome (AIDS). We now have the knowledge, reasoning, and technical capabilities to investigate the disease in an effective fashion, though no cure or preventative inoculation has yet been developed. Read the following excerpt from a World Health Organization report describing the political, social, and medical responses to the ongoing AIDS epidemic, and then answer the questions that follow.

"3 x 5" PROGRESS REPORT
by World Health Organization/UNAIDS

Changing Contexts and Responses

Despite the increasing political attention paid to HIV/AIDS, more than 8000 people are still dying every day from a disease that can be treated and prevented. However, some important progress is being made. Significant new resources are flowing to support the scaling up of antiretroviral therapy and are not simply being diverted from core prevention activities. More and more countries accept the need to provide antiretroviral therapy to the people who need it, and international and national partners across a diverse range of groups and agencies are coming together to support scale-up in accordance with "3 by 5" targets.

Source: World Health Organization. "'3x5' Progress Report: December 2003 Through June 2004." http://www.who.int/3by5/en/ Reprinted by permission of the World Health Organization.

The unprecedented momentum for access to treatment poses challenges for many countries. Coordination around a common set of goals and objectives at the national level is critical. Accordingly, UNAIDS developed the "three ones" principles to highlight the need for one national programme, one coordinating body and one monitoring and evaluation framework. Partnerships have been an increasing focus of work for WHO, as "3 by 5" is increasingly embraced as a global target owned by everyone. "3 by 5" clearly cannot be the project of one or even several agencies; the task is far too large and complex.

The "3 by 5" target has been widely discussed and sometimes misinterpreted. A time-limited target is a proven method for mobilizing action and resources. Some people remain uncomfortable with the ambitious agenda of having 3 million people receiving treatment in the next 18 months. But WHO and UNAIDS believe that the target is achievable and are committed to supporting all Member States to achieve it. Anything less falls short of an appropriate response to the greatest global public health challenge of our times. Beyond 2005, the ultimate goal of providing treatment to everyone who needs it as a human right has not been questioned.

The WHO Response to Helping Countries

In the past six months, WHO has worked strenuously to respond to the overwhelming demand from countries for urgent assistance. The original intention was to recruit "3 by 5" country officers and "3 by 5" country teams as soon as possible for each of the WHO-identified focus countries. Given the initial shortfall of funds to recruit new staff for these key positions, WHO instead focused on sending its existing staff to countries to provide interim support. Twenty-four teams from WHO headquarters and regional offices were sent in response to requests from countries. These missions mapped the local situation, identified key partners and technical assistance needs, prompted and reinforced political commitment and supported the process of developing national scale-up plans. In addition, 37 staff members from headquarters and regional offices were sent for 4 to 8 weeks to countries that had requested urgent support, especially those preparing applications for Round Four funding from the Global Fund to Fight AIDS, Tuberculosis and Malaria. Deployed staff also helped countries to identify obstacles to expanding access to the entire range of HIV/AIDS prevention, treatment and care services and, in some cases, began to develop initial plans for scaling up treatment. Much of this work has led to the creation of detailed country profiles developed with national counterparts and partners in each country. These profiles will be a practical tool to help guide countries in their scale-up efforts, to monitor progress and to clarify roles and responsibilities among the various actors at the country level.

Meanwhile, at WHO headquarters, at WHO regional offices and in consultation with partners, other key elements of the strategy were taking shape. The AIDS Medicines and Diagnostics Service (AMDS) was established as a multi-agency network linking WHO and the UNAIDS Secretariat more closely with other UNAIDS cosponsors the United Nations Children's Fund (UNICEF), the World Bank and the United Nations Population Fund (UNFPA), and now, the United Nations Development Programme (UNDP). Twenty-nine countries have already procured antiretroviral medicines through a combination of existing and new services under the AMDS umbrella. Member States have broadly endorsed WHO's prequalification process, which assesses the quality, safety and efficacy of drugs submitted by participating manufacturers. Further, WHO's Expert Committee on the Selection and Use of Essential Medicines has strongly recommended the use of fixed-dose combinations (fixed amounts of two or more active ingredients in one tablet or capsule), which simplify procurement and treatment and improve adherence.[1] Finally, the country-by-country availability of drugs and the related supply chain management issues are currently being mapped to identify specific gaps and technical assistance needs.

Technical and policy tools and guidelines were developed with unprecedented speed to help countries, donors and other partners in scaling up antiretroviral therapy within the context of a comprehensive health system response. Simplified and standardized approaches have facilitated the development of basic antiretroviral therapy training materials, and training packages and modules for health care and community workers have been under accelerated development. Key stakeholders have also agreed on a harmonized set of measures and tools to monitor progress on the implementation of antiretroviral therapy scale-up.

Extensive work has also been undertaken to establish, broaden and engage more extensively a broad network of partners including donors, United Nations organizations, business and trade unions, pharmaceutical manufacturers, faith-based organizations, people living with HIV/AIDS, nongovernmental organizations and treatment activists supporting "3 by 5". Three major international meetings have been held during which a wide range of partners have committed to working towards the "3 by 5" target and the ultimate goal of universal access to HIV/AIDS treatment for every-

---

[1]For more information on the WHO Prequalification Project, please visit the website, http://mednet3.who.int/prequal/

one who needs it. The roles of UNAIDS Cosponsors have been clearly delineated. However, many of these partnerships have not yet been formalized but are based on a mutual commitment to the goal of increasing the access of people living with HIV/AIDS to treatment, support and care services.

Although this work has successfully built on the initial commitment of countries, donors and international organizations to the goal of increasing access to antiretroviral therapy, it has not yet led to a sharp rise in the number of people living with HIV/AIDS receiving treatment. This is disappointing but not a reason to hesitate. Increased resources combined with progress in addressing the barriers to scaling up identified during the past six months auger well for this number to rise significantly over the next six months. There are many reasons for optimism: a rapid increase in the number of countries developing and refining their national HIV/AIDS treatment plans, coupled with increased resource flows, is accelerating progress on access. For the first time, specific plans are now in place to strengthen WHO country offices in focus countries with dedicated "3 by 5" country officers, national programme officers, administrative staff and appropriate activity budgets. Negotiations underway should lead to further cuts in the price of antiretroviral medicines. Training courses have been designed, health workers are being trained and the certification of health workers competent to deliver and monitor antiretroviral therapy has been agreed upon.

Nevertheless, the modest increase in the number of people being treated over the past year clearly shows that progress is not rapid enough. To this end, WHO is taking steps to improve the documentation and reapplication of knowledge and best practices in accelerating the scaling up of antiretroviral therapy. A system for information and knowledge management to support antiretroviral therapy scale-up will begin in Uganda in 2004. The scope of this work includes collecting data about the people receiving antiretroviral therapy, collecting qualitative information about treatment and health systems performance and implementing processes to share information and learning across multiple treatment sites using collaborative quality improvement techniques. In September 2004, a team of experts will visit countries such as Brazil and Thailand that have successfully scaled up to document key lessons from their experience. The members of this team will then provide direct and immediate assistance in reapplying these approaches to several countries ready to scale up nationally.

Questions for Analysis

1. Name and explain the different processes that the World Health Organization's "3 by 5" initiative is taking to address the AIDS epidemic in developing countries.

2. Construct an experimental design that would test the distribution of anti-retroviral therapy in developing countries described in paragraphs 5 and 6. Be sure that your experimental design follows the guidelines detailed in Thinking Activity 11.5 on page 447.

3. Go to the United Nations Programme on HIV/AIDS web site at <http://www.unaids.org/en/default.asp>. Look up information about how UNAIDS is addressing the epidemic in a specific country. What are the unique obstacles to fighting HIV/AIDS in that country? What steps is UNAIDS taking to help overcome those obstacles? Think about HIV/AIDS prevention efforts in your own community. What kinds of obstacles do educators and health care workers face in combating AIDS in your community? (For example, students might be too embarrassed or reluctant to discuss safe sex with a health care worker.) What would you propose as an effective, unique way to teach you and your peers about HIV/AIDS safety and prevention?

THINKING PASSAGE

Treating Breast Cancer

Scientific discovery is rarely a straightforward, uninterrupted line of progress. Rather, it typically involves confusing and often contradictory results, false starts and missteps, and results that are complex and ambiguous. It is only in retrospect that we are able to fit all of the pieces of the scientific puzzle into their proper places.

The race to discover increasingly effective treatments for breast cancer is a compelling example of the twisted path of scientific exploration. One American woman in eight develops breast cancer, and it is the health threat women fear most, although heart disease is by far the leading cause of death (ten times more lethal than breast cancer). But women have been receiving conflicting advice on the prevention and cure of breast cancer, based on scientific studies that have yielded seemingly confusing results: For example, one study concluded that support groups for women with advanced breast cancer extended their lives an average of eighteen months whereas another found that such groups had no impact on life expectancy.

But it is a recent study on the efficacy of mammograms that is causing the widest and most disturbing confusion. This study, reported in a British medical journal, asserts that the promise of regular mammograms is an illusion: Mammograms have no measurable impact on reducing risk of death or avoiding mastectomies! The article entitled "Study Sets off Debate over Mammograms' Value," which is located on the companion web site, provides an analysis of this bewildering situation and provides a window into the complex process of scientific discovery. After reading the article, respond to the questions that follow.

Causal Fallacies

Because causality plays such a dominant role in the way we make sense of the world, it is not surprising that people make many mistakes and errors in judgment in trying to determine causal relationships. The following are some of the most common fallacies associated with causality:

- Questionable cause
- Misidentification of the cause
- *Post hoc ergo propter hoc*
- Slippery slope

Questionable Cause

The fallacy of *questionable cause* occurs when someone presents a causal relationship for which no real evidence exists. Superstitious beliefs, such as "If you break a mirror, you will have seven years of bad luck," usually fall into this category. Some people feel that astrology, a system of beliefs tying one's personality and fortunes in life to the position of the planets at the moment of birth, also falls into this category.

Consider the following passage from St. Augustine's *Confessions*. Does it seem to support or deny the causal assertions of astrology? Why or why not?

Firminus had heard from his father that when his mother had been pregnant with him, a slave belonging to a friend of his father's was also about to bear. It happened that since the two women had their babies at the same instant, the men were forced to cast exactly the same horoscope for each newborn child down to the last detail, one for his son, the other for the little slave. Yet Firminus, born to wealth in his parents' house, had one of the more illustrious careers in life whereas the slave had no alleviation of his life's burden.

Other examples of this fallacy include explanations like those given by fourteenth-century sufferers of the bubonic plague who claimed that "the Jews are poisoning the Christians' wells." This was particularly nonsensical since an equal percentage of Jews were dying of the plague as well. The evidence did not support the explanation.

Misidentification of the Cause

In causal situations we are not always certain about what is causing what — in other words, what is the cause and what is the effect. *Misidentifying the cause* is easy to do. For example, which are the causes and which are the effects in the following pairs of items? Why?

- Poverty and alcoholism
- Headaches and tension
- Failure in school and personal problems
- Shyness and lack of confidence
- Drug dependency and emotional difficulties

Of course, sometimes a third factor is responsible for both of the effects we are examining. For example, the headaches and tension we are experiencing may both be the result of a third element — such as some new medication we are taking. When this occurs, we are said to commit the fallacy of *ignoring a common cause*. There also exists the fallacy of *assuming a common cause* — for example, assuming that both a sore toe and an earache stem from the same cause.

Post Hoc Ergo Propter Hoc

The translation of the Latin phrase *post hoc ergo propter hoc* is "After it, therefore because of it." It refers to those situations in which, because two things occur close together in time, we assume that one caused the other. For example, if your team wins the game each time you wear your favorite shirt, you might be tempted to conclude that the one event (wearing your favorite shirt) has some influence on the other event (winning the game). As a result, you might continue to wear this shirt "for good luck." It is easy to see how this sort of mistaken thinking can lead to all sorts of superstitious beliefs.

Consider the causal conclusion arrived at by Mark Twain's fictional character Huckleberry Finn in the following passage. How would you analyze the conclusion that he comes to?

I've always reckoned that looking at the new moon over your left shoulder is one of the carelessest and foolishest things a body can do. Old Hank

Bunker done it once, and bragged about it; and in less than two years he got drunk and fell off a shot tower and spread himself out so that he was just a kind of layer. . . . But anyway, it all come of looking at the moon that way, like a fool.

Can you identify any of your own superstitious beliefs or practices that might have been the result of *post hoc* thinking?

Slippery Slope

The causal fallacy of *slippery slope* is illustrated in the following advice:

Don't miss that first deadline, because if you do, it won't be long before you're missing all your deadlines. This will spread to the rest of your life, as you will be late for every appointment. This terminal procrastination will ruin your career, and friends and relatives will abandon you. You will end up a lonely failure who is unable to ever do anything on time.

Slippery slope thinking asserts that one undesirable action will inevitably lead to a worse action, which will necessarily lead to a worse one still, all the way down the "slippery slope" to some terrible disaster at the bottom. Although this progression may indeed happen, there is certainly no causal guarantee that it will. Create slippery slope scenarios for one of the following warnings:

- If you get behind on one credit card payment . . .
- If you fail that first test . . .
- If you eat that first fudge square . . .

Review the causal fallacies just described and then identify and explain the reasoning pitfalls illustrated in the following examples:

- The person who won the lottery says that she dreamed the winning numbers. I'm going to start writing down the numbers in my dreams.
- Yesterday I forgot to take my vitamins, and I immediately got sick. That mistake won't happen again!
- I'm warning you — if you start missing classes, it won't be long before you flunk out of school and ruin your future.
- I always take the first seat in the bus. Today I took another seat, and the bus broke down. And you accuse me of being superstitious!
- I think the reason I'm not doing well in school is that I'm just not interested. Also, I simply don't have enough time to study.

V I S U A L   T H I N K I N G

Slipping and Sliding

- The fallacy of slippery slope suggests that one undesirable action will inevitably lead to others, taking you down the "slippery slope" to some unavoidable terrible disaster at the bottom. Can you think of an example in which you have used this kind of thinking ("If you continue to _____, then things will get progressively worse until you ultimately find yourself _____")? What are some strategies for clarifying this sort of fallacious thinking?

Many people want us to see the cause and effect relationships that they believe exist, and they often utilize questionable or outright fallacious reasoning. Consider the following examples:

- Politicians assure us that a vote for them will result in "a chicken in every pot and a car in every garage."
- Advertisers tell us that using this detergent will leave our wash "cleaner than clean, whiter than white."
- Doctors tell us that eating a balanced diet will result in better health.
- Educators tell us that a college degree is worth an average of $1,140,000 additional income over an individual's life.
- Scientists inform us that nuclear energy will result in a better life for all.

In an effort to persuade us to adopt a certain point of view, each of these examples makes certain causal claims about how the world operates. As critical thinkers, it is our duty to evaluate these various causal claims in an effort to figure out whether they are sensible ways of organizing the world.

Explain how you might go about evaluating whether each of the following causal claims makes sense:

Example: *Taking the right vitamins will improve health.*

Evaluation: *Review the medical research that examines the effect of taking vitamins on health; speak to a nutritionist; speak to a doctor.*

- Sweet Smell deodorant will keep you drier all day long.
- Allure perfume will cause people to be attracted to you.
- Natural childbirth will result in a more fulfilling birth experience.
- Aspirin Plus will give you faster, longer-lasting relief from headaches.
- Listening to loud music will damage your hearing.

Fallacies of Relevance

Many fallacious arguments appeal for support to factors that have little or nothing to do with the argument being offered. In these cases, false appeals substitute for sound reasoning and a critical examination of the issues. Such appeals, known as *fallacies of relevance*, include the following kinds of fallacious thinking, which are grouped by similarity into "fallacy families":

- Appeal to authority
- Appeal to tradition
- Bandwagon

- Appeal to pity
- Appeal to fear
- Appeal to flattery
- Special pleading

- Appeal to ignorance
- Begging the question
- Straw man
- Red herring
- Appeal to personal attack
- Two wrongs make a right

Appeal to Authority

In Chapter 5, we explored the ways in which we sometimes *appeal to authorities* to establish our beliefs or prove our points. At that time, we noted that to serve as a basis for beliefs, authorities must have legitimate expertise in the area in which they are advising — like an experienced mechanic diagnosing a problem with your car. People, however, often appeal to authorities who are not qualified to give an expert opinion. Consider the reasoning in the following advertisements. Do you think the arguments are sound? Why or why not?

> Hi. You've probably seen me out on the football field. After a hard day's work crushing halfbacks and sacking quarterbacks, I like to settle down with a cold, smooth Maltz beer.

> SONY. Ask anyone.

> Over 11 million women will read this ad. Only 16 will own the coat.

Each of these arguments is intended to persuade us of the value of a product through appeal to various authorities. In the first case, the authority is a well-known sports figure; in the second, the authority is large numbers of people; and in the third, the authority is a select few, appealing to our desire to be exclusive ("snob appeal"). Unfortunately, none of these authorities offer legitimate expertise about the product. Football players are not beer experts; large numbers of people are often misled; exclusive groups of people are frequently mistaken in their beliefs. To evaluate authorities properly, we have to ask:

- What are the professional credentials on which the authorities' expertise is based?
- Is their expertise in the area they are commenting on?

Appeal to Tradition

A member of the same fallacy family as appeal to authority, *appeal to tradition* argues that a practice or way of thinking is "better" or "right" simply because it is older, it is traditional, or it has "always been done that way." Although traditional beliefs often express some truth or wisdom — for example, "Good nutrition, exercise, and regular medical check-ups are the foundation of good health" — traditional beliefs are often misguided or outright false. Consider, for example, the belief that "intentional bleeding is a source of good health because it lets loose evil vapors in the body" or traditional practices like Victorian rib-crushing corsets or Chinese footbinding. How do we tell which traditional beliefs or practices have merit? We need to think critically, evaluating the value based on informed reasons and compelling evidence. Critically evaluate the following traditional beliefs:

- Spare the rod and spoil the child.
- Children should be seen and not heard.
- Never take "no" for an answer.
- I was always taught that a woman's place was in the home, so pursuing a career is out of the question for me.
- Real men don't cry — that's the way I was brought up.

Bandwagon

Joining the illogical appeals to authority and tradition, the fallacy *bandwagon* relies on the uncritical acceptance of others' opinions, in this case because "everyone believes it." People experience this all the time through "peer pressure," when an unpopular view is squelched and modified by the group opinion. For example, you may change your opinion when confronted with the threat of ridicule or rejection from your friends. Or you may modify your point of view at work or in your religious organization in order to conform to the prevailing opinion. In all of these cases your views are being influenced by a desire to "jump on the bandwagon" and avoid getting left by yourself on the side of the road. The bandwagon mentality also extends to media appeals based on views of select groups such as celebrities or public opinion polls. Again, critical thinking is the tool that you have to distinguish an informed belief from a popular but uninformed belief. Critically evaluate the following bandwagon appeals:

- I used to think that _____ was my favorite kind of music. But my friends convinced me that only losers enjoy this music. So I've stopped listening to it.
- Hollywood celebrities and supermodels agree: Tattoos in unusual places are very cool. That's good enough for me!
- In the latest Gallup poll 86 percent of those polled believe that economic recovery will happen in the next six months, so I must be wrong.

Appeal to Pity

Consider the reasoning in the following arguments. Do you think that the arguments are sound? Why or why not?

I know that I haven't completed my term paper, but I really think that I should be excused. This has been a very difficult semester for me. I caught every kind of flu that came around. In addition, my brother has a drinking problem, and this has been very upsetting to me. Also, my dog died.

I admit that my client embezzled money from the company, your honor. However, I would like to bring several facts to your attention. He is a family man, with a wonderful wife and two terrific children. He is an important member of the community. He is active in the church, coaches a little league baseball team, and has worked very hard to be a good person who cares about people. I think that you should take these things into consideration in handing down your sentence.

In each of these *appeal to pity* arguments, the reasons offered to support the conclusions may indeed be true. They are not, however, relevant to the conclusion. Instead of providing evidence that supports the conclusion, the reasons are designed to make us feel sorry for the person involved and therefore agree with the conclusion out of sympathy. Although these appeals are often effective, the arguments are not sound. The probability of a conclusion can be established only by reasons that support and are relevant to the conclusion.

Of course, not every appeal to pity is fallacious. There *are* instances in which pity may be deserved, relevant, and decisive. For example, if you are soliciting a charitable donation, or asking a friend for a favor, an honest and straightforward appeal to pity may be appropriate.

Appeal to Fear

Consider the reasoning in the following arguments. Do you think that the arguments are sound? Why or why not?

I'm afraid I don't think you deserve a raise. After all, there are many people who would be happy to have your job at the salary you are currently receiving. I would be happy to interview some of these people if you really think that you are underpaid.

If you continue to disagree with my interpretation of *The Catcher in the Rye,* I'm afraid you won't get a very good grade on your term paper.

In both of these arguments, the conclusions being suggested are supported by an *appeal to fear*, not by reasons that provide evidence for the conclusions. In the first case, the threat is that if you do not forgo your salary demands, your job may be in jeopardy. In the second case, the threat is that if you do not agree with the teacher's interpretation, you will fail the course. In neither instance are the real issues — Is a salary increase deserved? Is the student's interpretation legitimate? — being discussed. People who appeal to fear to support their conclusions are interested only in prevailing, regardless of which position might be more justified.

Appeal to Flattery

Flattery joins the emotions of pity and fear as a popular source of fallacious reasoning. This kind of "apple polishing" is designed to influence the thinking of others by appealing to their vanity as a substitute for providing relevant evidence to support your point of view. Of course, flattery is often a harmless lubricant for social relationships, and it can also be used in conjunction with compelling reasoning. But *appeal to flattery* enters the territory of fallacy when it is the main or sole support of your claim, such as "This is absolutely the best course I've ever taken. And I'm really hoping for an A to serve as an emblem of your excellent teaching." Think critically about the following examples:

- You have a great sense of humor, boss, and I'm particularly fond of your racial and homosexual jokes. They crack me up! And while we're talking, I'd like to remind you how much I'm hoping for the opportunity to work with you if I receive the promotion that you're planning to give to one of us.
- You are a beautiful human being, inside and out. Why don't you stay the night?
- You are *so* smart. I wish I had a brain like yours. Can you give me any hints about the chemistry test you took today? I'm taking it tomorrow.

Special Pleading

This fallacy occurs when someone makes himself or herself a special exception, *without sound justification,* to the reasonable application of standards, principles, or expectations. For example, consider the following exchange:

"Hey, hon, could you get me a beer? I'm pooped from work today."

"Well, I'm exhausted from working all day, too! Why don't you get it yourself?"

"I need you to get it because I'm really thirsty."

As we saw in Chapter 4, we view the world through our own lenses, and these lenses tend to see the world as tilted toward our interests. That's why *special pleading* is such a popular fallacy: We're used to treating our circumstances as unique and deserving of special consideration when compared to the circumstances of others. Of course, other people tend to see things from a very different perspective. Critically evaluate the following examples:

- I know that the deadline for the paper was announced several weeks ago and that you made clear there would be no exceptions, but I'm asking you to make an exception because I experienced some very bad breaks.
- I really don't like it when you check out other men and comment on their physiques. I know that I do that toward other women, but it's a "guy thing."
- Yes, I would like to play basketball with you guys, but I want to warn you: As a woman, I don't like getting bumped around, so keep your distance.
- I probably shouldn't have used funds from the treasury for my own personal use, but after all I *am* the president of the organization.

Appeal to Ignorance

Consider the reasoning in the following arguments. Do you think that the arguments are sound? Why or why not?

> You say that you don't believe in God. But can you prove that He doesn't exist? If not, then you have to accept the conclusion that He does in fact exist.

> Greco Tires are the best. No others have been proved better.

> With me, abortion is not a problem of religion. It's a problem of the Constitution. I believe that until and unless someone can establish that the unborn child is not a living human being, then that child is already protected by the Constitution, which guarantees life, liberty, and the pursuit of happiness to all of us.

When the *appeal to ignorance* argument form is used, the person offering the conclusion is asking his or her opponent to *disprove* the conclusion. If the opponent is unable to do so, then the conclusion is asserted to be true. This argument form is not valid because it is the job of the person proposing the argument to prove the conclusion. Simply because an opponent cannot *dis-*prove the conclusion offers no evidence that the conclusion is in fact justified. In the first example, for instance, the fact that someone cannot prove that God does not exist provides no persuasive reason for believing that he does.

Begging the Question

This fallacy is also known as *circular reasoning* because the premises of the argument assume or include the claim that the conclusion is true. For example:

"How do I know that I can trust you?"

"Just ask Adrian; she'll tell you."

"How do I know that I can trust Adrian?"

"Don't worry; I'll vouch for her."

Begging the question is often found in self-contained systems of belief, such as politics or religion. For example:

"My religion worships the one true God."

"How can you be so sure?"

"Because our Holy Book says so."

"Why should I believe this Holy Book?"

"Because it was written by the one true God."

In other words, the problem with this sort of reasoning is that instead of providing relevant evidence in support of a conclusion, it simply "goes in a circle" by assuming the truth of what it is supposedly proving. Critically evaluate the following examples:

- Smoking marijuana has got to be illegal. Otherwise, it wouldn't be against the law.

- Of course, I'm telling you the truth. Otherwise, I'd be lying.

Straw Man

This fallacy is best understood by visualizing its name: You attack someone's point of view by creating an exaggerated *straw man* version of the position, and then you knock down the straw man you just created. For example, consider the following exchange:

"I'm opposed to the missile defense shield because I think it's a waste of money."

"So you want to undermine the security of our nation and leave the country defenseless. Are you serious?"

The best way to combat this fallacy is to point out that the straw man does not reflect an accurate representation of your position. For instance:

"On the contrary, I'm very concerned about national security. The money that would be spent on a nearly useless defense shield can be used to combat terrorist threats, a much more credible threat than a missile attack. Take your straw man somewhere else!"

How would you respond to the following arguments?

VISUAL THINKING

Fallacies in Action

- What fallacies do you think are being put forward by the two debaters in this illustration? How persuasive have you found those techniques to be in your own life, from your perspectives as both a speaker and a listener?

- You're saying that the budget for our university has to be reduced by 15 percent to meet state guidelines. That means reducing the size of the faculty and student population by 15 percent, and that's crazy.
- "I think we should work at keeping the apartment clean; it's a mess."

  "So you're suggesting that we discontinue our lives and become full-time maids so that we can live in a pristine, spotless, antiseptic apartment. That's no way to live!"

Red Herring

Also known as "smoke screen" and "wild goose chase," the *red herring* fallacy is committed by introducing an irrelevant topic in order to divert attention from the original issue being discussed. So, for example:

I'm definitely in favor of the death penalty. After all, overpopulation is a big problem in our world today.

Although this is certainly a novel approach to addressing the problem of over-population, it's not really relevant to the issue of capital punishment. Critically evaluate the following examples:

- I think all references to sex should be eliminated from films and music. Premarital sex and out-of-wedlock childbirths are creating moral decay in our society.
- I really don't believe that grade inflation is a significant problem in higher education. Everybody wants to be liked, and teachers are just trying to get students to like them.

Appeal to Personal Attack

Consider the reasoning in the following arguments. Do you think that the arguments are valid? Why or why not?

Your opinion on this issue is false. It's impossible to believe anything you say.

How can you have an intelligent opinion about abortion? You're not a woman, so this is a decision that you'll never have to make.

Appeal to personal attack has been one of the most frequently used fallacies through the ages. Its effectiveness results from ignoring the issues of the argument and focusing instead on the personal qualities of the person making the argument. By trying to discredit the other person, this argument form tries to discredit the argument — no matter what reasons are offered. This fallacy is also referred to as the *"ad hominem"* argument, which means "to the man" rather than to the issue, and *"poisoning the well,"* because we are trying to ensure that any water drawn from our opponent's well will be treated as undrinkable.

The effort to discredit can take two forms, as illustrated in the preceding examples. The fallacy can be *abusive* in the sense that we are directly attacking the credibility of our opponent (as in the first example). The fallacy can be *circumstantial* in the sense that we are claiming that the person's circumstances, not character, render his or her opinion so biased or uninformed that it cannot be treated seriously (as in the second example). Other examples of the circumstantial form of the fallacy would include disregarding the views on nuclear plant safety given by an owner of one of the plants or ignoring the views of a company comparing a product it manufactures with competing products.

Two Wrongs Make a Right

This fallacy attempts to justify a morally questionable action by arguing that it is a response to another wrong action, either real or imagined, in fact, that *two wrongs make a right.* For example, someone undercharged at a store might justify keeping the extra money by reasoning that "I've probably been overcharged many times in the past, and this simply equals things out." Or he or she might even speculate, "I am likely to be overcharged in the future, so I'm keeping this in anticipation of being cheated." This is a fallacious way of thinking because each action is independent and must be evaluated on its own merits. If you're overcharged and knowingly keep the money, that's stealing. If the store knowingly overcharges you, that's stealing as well. If the store inadvertently overcharges you, that's a mistake. Or as expressed in a common saying, "Two wrongs *don't* make a right." Critically evaluate the following examples:

- Terrorists are justified in killing innocent people because they and their people have been the victims of political repression and discriminatory policies.
- Capital punishment is wrong because killing murderers is just as bad as the killings they committed.

THINKING ACTIVITY 11.6

Identifying Fallacies

Locate (or develop) an example of each of the following kinds of false appeals. For each example, explain why you think that the appeal is not warranted.

1. Appeal to authority
2. Appeal to pity
3. Appeal to fear
4. Appeal to ignorance
5. Appeal to personal attack

The Critical Thinker's Guide to Reasoning

This book has provided you with the opportunity to explore and develop many of your critical thinking and reasoning abilities. As you have seen, these abilities are complex and difficult to master. The process of becoming an accomplished critical thinker and effective reasoner is a challenging quest that requires ongoing practice and reflection. This section will present a critical thinking/reasoning model that will help you pull together the important themes of this book into an integrated perspective. This model is illustrated on page 470. In order to become familiar with the model, you will be thinking through an important issue that confronts every human being: Are people capable of choosing freely?

What Is My Initial Point of View?

Reasoning always begins with a point of view. As a critical thinker, it is important for you to take thoughtful positions and express your views with confidence. Using this statement as a starting point, respond as specifically as you can:

- *I believe (or don't believe) that people can choose freely because . . .*

Here is a sample response:

> *I believe that people are capable of choosing freely because when I am faced with choosing among a number of possibilities, I really have the feeling that it is up to me to make the choice that I want to.*

How Can I Define My Point of View More Clearly?

After you state your initial point of view, the next step is to define the issues more clearly and specifically. As you have seen, the language that we use has multiple levels of meaning, and it is often not clear precisely what meaning(s) people are expressing. To avoid misunderstandings and sharpen your own thinking, it is essential that you clarify the key concepts as early as possible. In this case the central concept is "choosing freely." Respond by beginning with the following statement:

- *From my point of view, the concept of "choosing freely" means . . .*

Here is a sample response:

From my point of view, the concept of "choosing freely" means that when you are faced with a number of alternatives, you are able to make your selection based solely on what you decide, not on force applied by other influences.

What Is an Example of My Point of View?

Once your point of view is clarified, it's useful to provide an example that illustrates your meaning. As you saw in Chapter 7, the process of forming and defining concepts involves the process of generalizing (identifying general qualities) and the process of interpreting (locating specific examples). Respond to the issue we have been considering by beginning with the following statement:

- *An example of a free choice I made (or was unable to make) is . . .*

Here is a sample response:

An example of a free choice I made was deciding what area to major in. There are a number of career directions I could have chosen to go out with, but I chose my major entirely on my own, without being forced by other influences.

What Is the Origin of My Point of View?

To fully understand and critically evaluate your point of view, it's important to review its history. How did this point of view develop? Have you always held this view, or did it develop over time? This sort of analysis will help you understand how your perceiving "lenses" regarding this issue were formed. Respond to the issue of free choice by beginning with the following statement:

- *I formed my belief regarding free choice . . .*

Here is a sample response:

I formed my belief regarding free choice when I was in high school. I used to believe that everything happened because it had to, because it was determined. Then when I was in high school, I got involved with the "wrong crowd" and developed some bad habits. I stopped doing schoolwork and even stopped attending most classes. I was on the brink of failing when I suddenly came to my senses and said to myself, "This isn't what I want for my life." Through sheer willpower, I turned everything around. I changed my friends, improved my habits, and ultimately graduated with flying colors. From that time on, I knew that I had the power of free choice and that it was up to me to make the right choices.

What Are My Assumptions?

Assumptions are beliefs, often unstated, that underlie your point of view. Many disputes occur and remain unresolved because the people involved do not recognize or express their assumptions. For example, in the very emotional debate over abortion, when people who are opposed to abortion call their opponents "murderers," they are assuming the fetus, at *any* stage of development from the fertilized egg onward, is a "human life" since murder refers to the taking of a human life. When people in favor of abortion call their opponents "moral fascists," they are assuming that antiabortionists are merely interested in imposing their narrow moral views on others.

Thus, it's important for all parties to identify clearly the assumptions that form the foundation of their points of view. They may still end up disagreeing, but at least they will know what they are arguing about. Thinking about the issue that we have been exploring, respond by beginning with the following statement:

- *When I say that I believe (or don't believe) in free choice, I am assuming . . .*

Here is a sample response:

When I say that I believe in free choice, I am assuming that people are often presented with different alternatives to choose from, and I am also assuming that they are able to select freely any of these alternatives independent of any influences.

What Are the Reasons, Evidence, and Arguments That Support My Point of View?

Everybody has opinions. What distinguishes informed opinions from uninformed opinions is the quality of the reasons, evidence, and arguments that support the opinions. Respond to the issue of free choice by beginning with the following statement:

- *There are a variety of reasons, evidence, and arguments that support my belief (or disbelief) in free choice. First, . . . Second, . . . Third, . . .*

Here is a sample response:

There are a variety of reasons, evidence, and arguments that support my belief in free choice. First, I have a very strong and convincing personal intuition when I am making choices that my choices are free. Second, freedom is tied to responsibility. If people make free choices, then they are responsible for the consequences of their

ORIGIN

How did I
form this point
of view?

LOOK BEHIND

**OTHER POINT
OF VIEW**

Strong? | Reasons
Evidence
Arguments | Valid?

Relevant?

*LOOK TO
ONE SIDE*

POINT OF VIEW

Initial description
Clear definition
Examples

SUPPORT

Strong? | Reasons
Evidence
Arguments | Valid?

Relevant?

Inference

**CONCLUSION
DECISION
SOLUTION
PREDICTION**

Prediction

CONSEQUENCES

What will happen
if the conclusion
is adopted?

ASSUMPTIONS

What are
my unstated
beliefs?

LOOK BEHIND

**OTHER POINT
OF VIEW**

Strong? | | Valid?

Relevant?

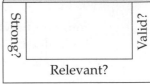

*LOOK TO THE
OTHER SIDE*

A modified version of a schema
originally devised by Ralph H.
Johnson; design and layout by
J. A. Blair.

choices. Since we often hold people responsible, that means that we believe that their choices are free. Third, if people are not free, and all of their choices are determined by external forces, then life would have little purpose and there would be no point in trying to improve ourselves. But we do believe that life has purpose, and we do try to improve ourselves, suggesting that we also believe that our choices are free.

What Are Other Points of View on This Issue?

One of the hallmarks of critical thinkers is that they strive to view situations from perspectives other than their own, to "think empathically" within other viewpoints, particularly those of people who disagree with their own. If we stay entrenched in our own narrow ways of viewing the world, the development of our minds will be severely limited. This is the only way to achieve a deep and full understanding of life's complexities. In working to understand other points of view, we need to identify the reasons, evidence, and arguments that have brought people to these conclusions. Respond to the issue we have been analyzing by beginning with the following statement:

- *A second point of view on this issue might be . . . A third point of view on this issue might be . . .*

Here is a sample response:

A second point of view on this issue might be that many of our choices are conditioned by experiences that we have had in ways that we are not even aware of. For example, you might choose a career because of someone you admire or because of the expectations of others, although you may be unaware of these influences on your decision. Or you might choose to date someone because he or she reminds you of someone from your past, although you believe you are making a totally free decision. A third point of view on this issue might be that our choices are influenced by people around us, although we may not be fully aware of it. For example, we may go along with a group decision of our friends, mistakenly thinking that we are making an independent choice.

What Is My Conclusion, Decision, Solution, or Prediction?

The ultimate purpose of reasoning is to reach an informed and successful conclusion, decision, solution, or prediction. Chapters 1 and 3 described reasoning approaches for making decisions and solving problems; Chapters 2 and 5 analyzed reaching conclusions; Chapter 9 explored the inferences we use to make predictions. With respect to the sample issue we have been considering — determining whether we can make free choices — the goal is to achieve a thoughtful conclusion. This is a complex process of analysis and synthesis in which we consider all points of view; evaluate the supporting reasons, evidence, and arguments; and then construct our most informed conclusion. Respond to our sample issue by using the following statement as a starting point:

- *After examining different points of view and critically evaluating the reasons, evidence, and arguments that support the various perspectives, my conclusion about free choice is . . .*

Here is a sample response:

> *After examining different points of view and critically evaluating the reasons, evidence, and arguments that support the various perspectives, my conclusion about free choice is that we are capable of making free choices but that our freedom is sometimes limited. For example, many of our actions are conditioned by our past experience, and we are often influenced by other people without being aware of it. In order to make free choices, we need to become aware of these influences and then decide what course of action we want to choose. As long as we are unaware of these influences, they can limit our ability to make free, independent choices.*

What Are the Consequences?

The final step in the reasoning process is to determine the *consequences* of our conclusion, decision, solution, or prediction. The consequences refer to what is likely to happen if our conclusion is adopted. Looking ahead in this fashion is helpful not simply for anticipating the future but also for evaluating the present. Identify the consequences of your conclusion regarding free choice by beginning with the following statement:

- *The consequences of believing (or disbelieving) in free choice are . . .*

Here is a sample response:

> *The consequences of believing in free choice are taking increasing personal responsibility and showing people how to increase their freedom. The first consequence is that if people are able to make free choices, then they are responsible for the results of their choices. They can't blame other people, bad luck, or events "beyond their control." They have to accept responsibility. The second consequence is that, although our freedom can be limited by influences of which we are unaware, we can increase our freedom by becoming aware of these influences and then deciding what we want to do. If people are not able to make free choices, then they are not responsible for what they do, nor are they able to increase their freedom. This could lead people to adopt an attitude of resignation and apathy.*

THINKING ACTIVITY 11.7

Applying the "Guide to Reasoning"

Identify an important issue in which you are interested, and apply "The Critical Thinker's Guide to Reasoning" to analyze it.

- What is my initial point of view?
- How can I define my point of view more clearly?
- What is an example of my point of view?
- What is the origin of my point of view?
- What are my assumptions?
- What are the reasons, evidence, and arguments that support my point of view?
- What are other points of view on this issue?
- What is my conclusion, decision, solution, or prediction?
- What are the consequences?

THINKING PASSAGES

Critical Thinking and Obedience to Authority

The following reading selections demonstrate graphically the destructive effects of *failing* to think critically and suggest ways to avoid these failures. After reading these provocative selections, answer the questions that follow.

CRITICAL THINKING AND OBEDIENCE TO AUTHORITY
by John Sabini and Maury Silver

In his 1974 book, *Obedience to Authority*, Stanley Milgram reports experiments on destructive obedience. In these experiments the subjects are faced with a dramatic choice, one apparently involving extreme pain and perhaps injury to someone else. When the subject arrives at the laboratory, the experimenter tells him (or her) and another subject — a pleasant, avuncular, middle-aged gentleman (actually an actor) — that the study concerns the effects of punishment on learning. Through a rigged drawing, the lucky subject wins the role of teacher and the experimenter's confederate becomes the "learner."

Source: From "Critical Thinking and Obedience to Authority" by John Sabini and Maury Silver, reprinted from *National Forum: The Phi Kappa Phi Journal*, Winter 1985, pp. 13–17, by permission.

VISUAL THINKING

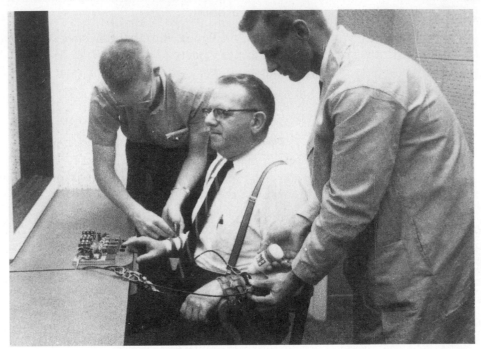

Milgram's Experiment

● In this actual photo from Milgram's obedience study, the man being strapped into the chair for the experiment is one of Milgram's research assistants and will receive no shock. What do you think the research assistant thought of the experiment? In his place, would you have been surprised by the findings?

In the next stage of the experiment, the teacher and learner are taken to an adjacent room; the learner is strapped into a chair and electrodes are attached to his arm. It appears impossible for the learner to escape. While strapped in the chair, the learner diffidently mentions that he has a heart condition. The experimenter replies that while the shocks may be painful, they cause no permanent tissue damage. The teacher is instructed to read to the learner a list of word pairs, to test him on the list, and to administer punishment — an electric shock — whenever the learner errs. The teacher is given a sample shock of 45 volts (the only real shock administered in the course of the experiment). The experimenter instructs the teacher to increase the level of shock one step on the shock generator for each mistake.

The generator has thirty switches labeled from 15 to 450 volts. Beneath these voltage readings are labels ranging from "SLIGHT SHOCK" to "DANGER: SEVERE SHOCK," and finally "XX."

The experiment starts routinely. At the fifth shock level, however, the confederate grunts in annoyance, and by the time the eighth shock level is reached, he shouts that the shocks are becoming painful. Upon reaching the tenth level (150 volts), he cries out, "Experimenter, get me out of here! I won't be in the experiment any more! I refuse to go on!" This response makes plain the intensity of the pain and underscores the learner's right to be released. At the 270-volt level, the learner's response becomes an agonized scream, and at 300 volts the learner refuses to answer further. When the voltage is increased from 300 volts to 330 volts, the confederate shrieks in pain at each shock and gives no answer. From 330 volts on, the learner is heard from no more, and the teacher has no way of knowing whether the learner is still conscious or, for that matter, alive (the teacher also knows that the experimenter cannot tell the condition of the victim since the experimenter is in the same room as the teacher).

Typically the teacher attempts to break off the experiment many times during the session. When he tries to do so, the experimenter instructs him to continue. If he refuses, the experimenter insists, finally telling him, "You must continue. You have no other choice." If the subject still refuses, the experimenter ends the experiment.

We would expect that at most only a small minority of the subjects, a cross section of New Haven residents, would continue to shock beyond the point where the victim screams in pain and demands to be released. We certainly would expect that very, very few people would continue to the point of administering shocks of 450 volts. Indeed, Milgram asked a sample of psychiatrists and a sample of adults with various occupations to predict whether they would obey the orders of the experimenter. All of the people asked claimed that they would disobey at some point. Aware that people would be unwilling to admit that they themselves would obey such an unreasonable and unconscionable order, Milgram asked another sample of middle-class adults to predict how far other people would go in such a procedure. The average prediction was that perhaps one person in a thousand would continue to the end. The prediction was wrong. In fact, 65 percent (26/40) of the subjects obeyed to the end.

It is clear to people who are not in the experiment what they should do. The question is, *What features of the experimental situation make this clear issue opaque to subjects?* Our aim is to suggest some reasons for such a failure of thinking and action and to suggest ways that people might be trained to avoid such failures — not only in the experiment, of course, but in our practical, moral lives as well. What are some of the sources of the failure?

The experimental conditions involve entrapment, and gradual entrapment affects critical thought. One important feature inducing obedience is the gradual escalation of the shock. Although subjects in the end administered 450-volt shocks, which is clearly beyond the limits of common morality and, indeed, common sense, they began by administering 15-volt shocks, which is neither. Not only did they begin with an innocuous shock, but it increased in innocuous steps of 15 volts. This gradualness clouds clear thinking: we are prepared by our moral training to expect moral problems to present themselves categorically, with good and evil clearly distinguished. But here they were not. By administering the first shock, subjects did two things at once — one salient, the other implicit. They administered a trivial shock, a morally untroublesome act, and they in that same act committed themselves to a policy and procedure which ended in clear evil.

Surely in everyday life, becoming entrapped by gradual increases in commitment is among the most common ways for us to find ourselves engaging in immoral acts, not to mention simple folly. The corrective cannot be, of course, refusing to begin on any path which *might* lead to immorality, but rather to foresee where paths are likely to lead, and to arrange for ourselves points beyond which we will not go. One suspects that had the subjects committed themselves — publicly — to some shock level they would not exceed, they would not have found themselves pushing the 450-volt lever. We cannot expect to lead, or expect our young to lead, lives without walking on slopes: our only hope is to reduce their slipperiness.

Distance makes obedience easier. Another force sustaining obedience was the *distance* between the victim and the subject. Indeed, in one condition of the experiment, subjects were moved physically closer to the victim; in one condition they had to hold his hand on the shock plate (through Mylar insulation to protect the teachers from shock). Here twelve out of forty subjects continued to the end, roughly half the number that did so when the subjects were farther from their victim.

Being closer to the victim did not have its effect by making subjects think more critically or by giving them more information. Rather it intensified their *discomfort* at the victim's pain. Still, being face to face with someone they were hurting probably caused them at least to focus on their victim, which might well be a first step in their taking seriously the pain they were causing him.

Both the experimenter's presence and the objective requirements of the situation influenced decisions to obey authority. The experimenter's *presence* is crucial to the subjects' obedience. In one version of the experiment he issued his commands at a distance, over the phone, and obedience was significantly reduced — to nine out of forty cases. The experimenter, then, exerts powerful *social influence* over the subjects.

One way to think about the experimenter's influence is to suppose that subjects uncritically cede control of their behavior to him. But this is too simple. We suggest that if the experimenter were to have told the subjects, for example, to shine his shoes, every subject would have refused. They would have refused because shining shoes is not a sensible command within the experimental context. Thus, the experimenter's ability to confuse and control subjects follows from his issuing commands which make sense given the ostensible purpose of the experiment; he was a guide, for them, to the experiment's objective requirements.

This interpretation of the experimenter's *role* is reinforced by details of his behavior. For example, his language and demeanor were cold — bureaucratic rather than emotional or personal. The subjects were led to see his commands to them as his dispassionate interpretations of something beyond them all: the requirements of the experiment.

Embarrassment plays a key role in decisions to obey authority. The experimenter entrapped subjects in another way. Subjects could not get out of the experiment without having to explain and justify their abandoning their duty to the experiment and to him. And how were they to do this?

Some subjects attempted to justify their leaving by claiming that they could not bear to go on, but such appeals to "personal reasons" were rebutted by the experimenter's reminding them of their duty to stay. If the subjects could not escape the experiment by such claims, then how could they escape? *They could fully escape his power only by confronting him on moral grounds.* It is worth noting that this is something that virtually none of the hundreds of subjects who took part in one condition or another fully did. Failing to address the experimenter in moral terms, even "disobedient" subjects just passively resisted; they stayed in their seats refusing to continue until the experimenter declared the experiment over. They did *not* do things we might expect them to: leave, tell the experimenter off, release the victim from his seat, and so on. Why did even the disobedient subjects not confront the experimenter?

One reason seems too trivial to mention: confronting the experimenter would be embarrassing. This trivial fact may have much to do with the subjects' obedience. To confront the experimenter directly, on moral grounds, would be to disrupt in a profound way implicit expectations that grounded this particular, and indeed most, social interaction: namely, that the subject and experimenter would behave as competent moral actors. Questioning these expectations is on some accounts, at least, the source of embarrassment.

Subjects in Milgram's experiment probably did not realize that it was in part embarrassment that [was] keeping them in line. Had they realized that — had they realized that they were torturing someone to spare themselves embarrassment — they might well have chosen to withstand the embarrassment to secure the victim's release. But rather we suspect that subjects experience their anticipation of embarrassment as a nameless force, a distressing emotion they were not able to articulate. Thus the subjects found themselves unable to confront the experimenter on moral grounds and unable to comprehend why they could not confront the experimenter.

Emotional states affect critical thought. Obviously the emotions the subjects experienced because of the embarrassment they were avoiding and the discomfort produced by hearing the cries of the victim affected their ability to reason critically. We do not know much about the effects of emotion on cognition, but it is plausible that it has at least one effect — a focusing of attention. Subjects seem to suffer from what Milgram has called "Tunnel Vision": they restricted their focus to the technical requirements of the experimental task, for these, at least, were clear. This restriction of attention is both a consequence of being in an emotional state more generally, and it is a strategy subjects used to avoid unwanted emotional intrusions. This response to emotion is, no doubt, a formidable obstacle to critical thought. To reject the experimenter's commands, subjects had to view their situation in a perspective different from the technical one the experimenter offered them. But their immediate emotional state made it particularly difficult for them to do just that: to look at their own situation from a broader, moral perspective.

How can we train individuals to avoid destructive obedience? Our analysis leads to the view that obedience in the Milgram experiment is not primarily a result of a failure of knowledge, or at least knowledge of the crucial issue of what is right or wrong to do in this circumstance. People do not need to be told that torturing an innocent person is something they should not do — even in the context of the experiment. Indeed, when the experimenter turns his back, most subjects are able to apply their moral principles and disobey. The subjects' problem instead is not knowing how to break off, how to make the moral response without social stickiness. If the subjects' defect is not primarily one of thinking correctly, then how is education, even education in critical thinking, to repair the defect? We have three suggestions.

First, we must teach people how to confront authority. We should note as a corollary to this effort that teaching has a wide compass: we teach people how to ride bikes, how to play the piano, how to make a sauce. Some teaching of how to do things we call education: we teach students how to do long division, how to parse sentences, how to solve physics problems. We inculcate these skills in students not by, or not only by, giving them facts or even strategies to remember, but also by giving them certain sorts of experiences, by correcting them when they err, and so on. An analogy would be useful here. Subjects in the Milgram experiment suffered not so much from a failure to remember that as center fielders they should catch fly balls as they did from an inability to do so playing under lights at night, with a great deal of wind, and when there is ambiguity about whether time-out has been called. To improve the players' ability to shag fly balls, in game conditions, we recommend practice rather than lectures, and the closer the circumstances of practice to the conditions of the actual game, the more effective the practice is likely to be.

Good teachers from Socrates on have known that the intellect must be trained; one kind of training is in criticizing authority. We teachers are authorities and hence can provide practice. Of course, we can only do that if we *remain* authorities. Practice at criticizing us if we do not respect our own authority is of little use. We do not have a recipe for being an authority who at the same time encourages criticism, but we do know that is what is important. And sometimes we can tell when we are either not encouraging criticism or when we have ceased being an authority. Both are equally damaging.

Practice with the Milgram situation might help too; it might help for students to "role play" the subjects' plight. If nothing else, doing this might bring home in a forcible way the embarrassment that subjects faced in confronting authority. It might help them develop ways of dealing with this embarrassment. Certainly, it would at least teach them that doing the morally right thing does not always "feel" right, comfortable, natural. There is no evidence about whether such experiences generalize, but perhaps they do.

If they are to confront authority assertively, individuals must also be taught to use social pressure in the service of personal values. Much of current psychology and education sees thought, even critical thought, as something that goes on within individuals. But we know better than this. Whether it be in science, law, or the humanities, scholarship is and must be a public, social process. To train subjects to think critically is to train them to expose their thinking to others, to open *themselves* to criticism, from their peers as well as from authority. We insist on this in scholarship because we know that individual thinking, even the best of it, is prey to distortions of all kinds, from mere ignorance to "bad faith."

Further, the support of others is important in another way. We know that subjects who saw what they took to be two other naive subjects disobey, and thus implicitly criticize the action of continuing, were very likely to do so themselves. A subject's sense that the experimenter had the correct reading was undermined by the counter reading offered by the "other subjects." Public reinforcement of our beliefs can liberate us from illegitimate pressure. The reason for this is twofold.

Agreement with others clarifies the cognitive issue and helps us see the morally or empirically right answer to questions. But it also can have another effect — a nonrational one.

We have claimed that part of the pressure subjects faced in disobeying was produced by having to deal with the embarrassment that might emerge from confrontation. Social support provides a counter-pressure. Had the subjects committed themselves publicly to disobedience before entering the experiment then they could have countered pressures produced by disobedience (during the experiment) by considering the embarrassment of admitting to others (after the experiment) that they had obeyed. Various self-help groups like Alcoholics Anonymous and Weight Watchers teach individuals to manage social pressures to serve good ends.

Social pressures are forces in our lives whether we concede them or not. The rational person, the person who would keep his action in accord with his values, must learn to face or avoid those pressures when they act to degrade his action, but equally important he ought to learn to *employ* the pressure of public commitment, the pressure implicit in making clear to others what he values, in the service of his values.

Students should know about the social pressures that operate on them. They should also learn how to use those pressures to support their own values. One reason we teach people to think critically is so that they may take charge of their own creations. We do not withhold from engineers who would create buildings knowledge about gravity or vectors or stresses. Rather we teach them to enlist this knowledge in their support.

A second area requires our attention. We need to eliminate intellectual illusions fostering nonintellectual obedience. These are illusions about human nature which the Milgram experiment renders transparent. None of these illusions is newly discovered; others have noticed them before. But the Milgram experiment casts them in sharp relief.

The most pernicious of these illusions is the belief, perhaps implicit, that only evil people do evil things and that evil announces itself. This belief, in different guises, bewildered the subjects in several ways.

First, the experimenter looks and acts like the most reasonable and rational of people: a person of authority in an important institution. All of this is, of course, irrelevant to the question of whether his commands are evil, but it does not seem so to subjects. The experimenter had no personally corrupt motive in ordering subjects to continue, for he wanted nothing more of them than to fulfill the requirements of the experiment. So the experimenter was not seen as an evil man, as a man with corrupt desires. He was a man, like Karl Adolf Eichmann, who ordered them to do evil because he saw that evil as something required of him (and of them) by the requirements of the situation they faced together. Because we expect our morality plays to have temptation and illicit desire arrayed against conscience, our ability to criticize morally is subverted when we find evil instructions issued by someone moved by, of all things, duty. [For a fuller discussion of this point, see Hannah Arendt's *Eichmann in Jerusalem* (1965), where the issue is placed in the context of the Holocaust.]

And just as the experimenter escaped the subjects' moral criticism because he was innocent of evil desire, the subjects escaped their own moral criticism because *they too* were free of evil intent: they did not *want* to hurt the victim; they really did not. Further, some subjects, at least, took action to relieve the victim's plight — many protested the experimenter's commands, many tried to give the victim hints about the right answers — thus further dramatizing their purity of heart. And because they acted out of duty rather than desire, the force of their conscience against their own actions was reduced. But, of course, none of this matters in the face of the evil done.

The "good-heartedness" of people, their general moral quality, is something very important to us, something to which we, perhaps rightly, typically pay attention. But if we are to think critically about the morality of our own and others' acts, we must see through this general fact about people to assess the real moral quality of the acts they do or are considering doing.

A second illusion from which the subjects suffered was a confusion about the notion of responsibility. Some subjects asked the experimenter who was responsible for the victim's plight. And the experimenter replied that he was. We, and people asked to predict what they would do in the experiment, see that this is nonsense. We see that the experimenter cannot discharge the subjects' responsibility — no more than the leader of a bank-robbing gang can tell his cohorts, "Don't worry. If we're caught, I'll take full responsibility." We are all conspirators when we participate in planning and executing crimes.

Those in charge have the right to assign *technical* responsibility to others, responsibility for executing parts of a plan, but moral responsibility cannot be given, taken away, or transferred. Still, these words — mere words — on the part of the experimenter eased subjects' "sense of responsibility." So long as the institutions of which we are a part are moral, the need to distinguish technical from moral responsibility need not arise. When those institutions involve wanton torture, we are obliged to think critically about this distinction.

There is a third illusion illustrated in the Milgram experiment. When subjects threatened to disobey, the experimenter kept them in line with prods, the last of which was, "You have no choice; you must go on." Some subjects fell for this, believed that they had no choice. But this is also nonsense. There may be cases in life when we *feel* that we have no choice, but we know we always do. Often feeling we have no choice is really a matter of believing that the cost of moral action is greater than we are willing to bear — in the extreme we may not be willing to offer our lives, and sometimes properly so. Sometimes we use what others have done to support the claim that we have no choice; indeed, some students interpret the levels of obedience in the Milgram experiment as proof that the subjects had no choice. But we all know they did. Even in extreme situations, we have a choice, whether we choose to exercise it or not. The belief that our role, our desires, our past, or the actions of others preclude our acting morally is a convenient but illusory way of distancing ourselves from the evil that surrounds us. It is an illusion from which we should choose to disabuse our students.

PRESSURE TO GO ALONG WITH ABUSE IS STRONG, BUT SOME SOLDIERS FIND STRENGTH TO REFUSE
by Anahad O'Connor

The images of prisoner abuse still trickling out of Iraq show a side of human behavior that psychologists have sought to understand for decades. But the murky reports of a handful of soldiers who refused to take part bring to light a behavior psychologists find even more puzzling: disobedience.

Buried in his report earlier this year on Abu Ghraib prison in Iraq, Maj. Gen. Antonio M. Taguba praised the actions of three men who tried to stop the mistreatment of Iraqi detainees. They are nowhere to be seen in the portraits of brutality that have touched off outrage around the world.

Source: Anahad O'Connor, "Pressure to Go Along With Abuse Is Strong, but Some Soldiers Find Strength to Refuse," *The New York Times,* May 14, 2004. Copyright © 2004 by The New York Times Co. Reprinted by permission.

Although details of their actions are sketchy, it is known that one soldier, Lt. David O. Sutton, put an end to one incident and alerted his commanders. William J. Kimbro, a Navy dog handler, "refused to participate in improper interrogations despite significant pressure" from military intelligence, according to the report. And Specialist Joseph M. Darby gave military police the evidence that sounded the alarm.

In numerous studies over the past few decades, psychologists have found that a certain percentage of people simply refuse to give in to pressure — by authorities or by peers — if they feel certain actions are wrong.

The soldiers have been reluctant to elaborate on what they saw and why they came forward. In an interview with *The Virginian-Pilot* in Norfolk, [VA], Lieutenant Sutton, a Newport News police sergeant, said, "I don't want to judge, but yes, I witnessed something inappropriate and I reported it."

The public will assume that there was widespread corruption, he told another local paper, "when in reality, it's just one bad apple."

In the noted experiment 40 years ago when Dr. Stanley Milgram showed that most people will deliver a lethal dose of electricity to another subject if instructed to do so by a scientist in a white lab coat, a minority still said no.

"These people are rare," said Dr. Elliot Aronson, a professor of psychology at the University of California, Santa Cruz, who studies social influence. "It's really hard for us to predict in advance who is going to resist by looking at things like demographic data or religious background."

The men singled out by General Taguba dissented despite the threat of being ridiculed or even court-martialed for not following orders. Psychologists believe they may have been guided by a strong moral compass and past experiences with conformity.

"It is sometimes the case that they themselves have been scapegoated or turned on by the crowd," said Dr. John Darley, a professor of psychology and public affairs at Princeton. "If you go back into the lives of these people you can often find some incident that has made very vivid to them the pressures of conformity working on the others in the group."

People who break from the crowd to blow the whistle, history shows, are often the most psychologically distanced from the situation. In 1968, Hugh Thompson, a helicopter pilot, was flying over Vietnam as G.I.'s were killing civilians. The soldiers on the ground had been told that the vil[l]age, My Lai, was a Vietcong stronghold. But from above Mr. Thompson could see there was no enemy fire. He landed his helicopter, rescued some villagers, and told his commanders about the massacre.

What happened there, and what o[c]curred at Abu Ghraib, Dr. Darley said, was a slow escalation.

Referring to reports that the guards were told to "soften up" the prisoners for interrogation, he said that it apparently "drifted more and more toward humiliation."

"Perhaps they thought they were doing the right thing," he said. "But someone who didn't get caught up at the start, someone who walks in and hasn't been involved in the escalation, like the pilot Thompson, can see the process for what it really is."

Mr. Thompson was supported by his gunner, Larry Colburn, who helped him round up civilians and radioed for help.

It is not clear when the three men cited in General Taguba's report tried to interfere with the interrogations or whether they had contact with one another. But a transcript of a court-martial hearing on May 1 suggests that additional officers who knew one another also tried to pass reports of the scandal up the chain of command.

Dr. Solomon E. Asch showed in experiments on compliance half a century ago that people are more likely to break from a group if they have an ally. Subjects in his experiment were asked to look at different lines on a card and judge their lengths. Each subject was unknowingly placed in a group of "confederates" who deliberately chose a line that was obviously wrong. About a third of the time, the subjects would give in and go along with the majority.

But if one confederate broke from the group and gave another answer, even a wrong answer, the subjects were more likely to give the repsonse they knew was correct.

"The more you feel support for your dissent, the more likely you are to do it," said Dr. Danny Axsom, an associate professor of psychology at Virginia Tech.

A lack of supervision, which General Taguba pointed out in his report, and confusion over the chain of command, Dr. Axsom said, may have also emboldened the three soldiers.

"There was less perceived legitimacy," he said. "If it's clear who the authority is, then you're more likely to obey. If it's not, then the legitimacy of the whole undertaking is undermined."

The power to resist coercion reflects what psychologists call internal locus of control, or the ability to determine one's own destiny. People at the other end of the scale, with external locus of control, are more heavily influenced by authority figures. They prefer to put their fate in the hands of others.

"If they fail a test, it's the teacher's fault; if they do poorly at a job, it's the boss's fault," said Dr. Thomas Ollendick, a professor of psychology at Virginia Tech. "They put the blame for everything outside of themselves. They are high in conformity because they believe someone else [is] in charge."

The average person, research shows, falls somewhere in the middle of the scale. People who voluntarily enlist in the military, knowing they will take orders, Dr. Ollendick suggested, may be more likely to conform. "These are people who are being told what to do," he said. "The ones who are conforming from the outset feel they can't change the system they're in. Those who blow the whistle can go above the situation and survive. They can basically endure whatever negative consequences might come from their actions."

Questions for Analysis

1. Sabini and Silver describe the reasons they believe that the majority of subjects in the Stanley Milgram experiment were willing to inflict apparent pain and injury on an innocent person. Explain what you believe were the most significant reasons for the absence of critical thinking and moral responsibility by many individuals.
2. The O'Connor article focuses on three individuals who were able to resist the pressures to inflict pain on Iraqi prisoners at Abu Ghraib prison. Why were these individuals able to retain their critical thinking abilities and sense of moral responsibility in the face of powerful pressures to do otherwise, including the obedience to authority?
3. Sabini and Silver argue that the ability to think critically must be developed within a social context, that we must expose our thinking to the criticism of others because "individual thinking, even the best of it, is prey to distortions of all kinds, from mere ignorance to 'bad faith'" Explain how "allies" were helpful in enabling those at Abu Ghraib prison to resist the pressure to conform to the prevailing norm of prisoner abuse.
4. Sabini and Silver contend that in order to act with critical thinking and moral courage, people must be taught to confront authority, and the individuals highlighted in the O'Connor article demonstrated precisely this ability. Explain how you think people can be taught and encouraged to confront authority in a constructive way.
5. "Even in extreme situations, we have a choice, whether we choose to exercise it or not. The belief that our role, our desires, our past, or the actions of others preclude our acting morally is a convenient but illusory way of distancing ourselves from the evil that surrounds us." Evaluate this claim in light of the behavior of the military and intelligence personnel at Abu Ghraib prison, both those who participated in prisoner abuse and those who resisted such participation.

12 Thinking Critically, Living Creatively

Living Creatively
Developing ideas that are unique, useful, and worthy of further elaboration

Thinking Critically
Carefully examining our thinking in order to clarify and improve understanding

Creating a Life Philosophy

Establishing Harmonious Relationships

Choosing Freely

Choosing a Meaningful Life

Choosing a Satisfying Career

Ⓔ Living a Life Philosophy

As the artist of your own life, your brush strokes express your philosophy of life, a vision that incorporates your most deeply held values, aspirations, and convictions. The challenge you face is to create a coherent view of the world that expresses who you are as well as the person you want to become. It should be a vision that not only guides your actions but also enables you to understand the value of your experiences, the significance of your relationships, and the meaning of your life.

The quality of your life philosophy is a direct result of your abilities to think critically and think creatively, abilities that you have been developing while working on activities presented throughout this book. But a life philosophy is incomplete until it is acted upon through the decisions you make, decisions made possible by your ability to choose freely. These are the three life principles of human transformation upon which this book is based. These three principles are interlocking pieces of the puzzle of your life. Working together as a unified force, these principles can illuminate your existence: answering questions, clarifying confusion, creating meaning, and providing fulfillment.

- *Think critically:* When used properly, your thinking process acts like a powerful beacon of light, illuminating the depths of your personality and the breadth of your experience. Clear thinking is a tool that helps you disentangle the often-confused jumble of thoughts and feelings that compose much of your waking consciousness. By becoming a more powerful critical thinker, you are acquiring the abilities you need to achieve your goals, solve problems, and make intelligent decisions. Critical thinkers are people who have developed thoughtful and well-founded beliefs to guide their choices in every area of their lives. In order to develop the strongest and most accurate beliefs possible, you need to become aware of your own biases, explore situations from many different perspectives, and develop sound reasons to support your points of view.

- *Live creatively:* Creativity is a powerful life force that can infuse your existence with meaning. Working in partnership with critical thinking, creative thinking helps you transform your life into a rich tapestry of productivity and success. When you approach your life with a mindful sense of discovery and invention, you can continually create yourself in ways limited only by your imagination. A creative lens changes everything for the better: Problems become opportunities for growth, mundane routines become challenges for inventive approaches, relationships become intriguing adventures. When you give free rein to your creative impulses, every aspect of your life takes on a special glow. You are able to break out of unthinking habitual responses and live fully in every minute, responding naturally and spontaneously. It sounds magical, and it is.

- *Choose freely:* People can transform themselves only if they choose to take different paths in their lives — and only if their choices are truly free. To exercise genuine freedom, you must have the insight to understand all of your options and the wisdom to make informed choices. When you fully accept your freedom, you redefine your daily life and view your future in a new light. By working to neutralize the constraints on your autonomy and guide your life in positive directions, you see alternatives that were not previously visible, having been concealed by the limitations of your previous vision. Your future becomes open, a field of rich possibilities that you can explore and choose among. A life that is free is one that is vital and exciting, suffused with unexpected opportunities and the personal fulfillment that comes from a life well lived.

Your "self" is, in its essence, a dynamic life force that is capable of thinking critically, creating, and choosing freely. These three essential dimensions of your self exist optimally when they work together in harmonious unity. When working together, these three basic elements create a person who is intelligent, creative, and determined — the ingredients for success in any endeavor. But consider the disastrous consequences of subtracting any of these elements from the dynamic equation. If you lack the ability to think critically, you won't be able to function very well in most challenging careers because you will have difficulty thinking clearly, solving complex problems, and making intelligent decisions. What's more, whatever creative ideas you come up with will be rootless, lacking an intelligible framework or practical strategies for implementing them. You will be an impractical dreamer, condemned to a life of frustrated underachieving. Without insight into yourself, your freedom will be imprisoned since you won't be able to see your choices clearly or to liberate yourself from the influences that are constraining you.

If you lack the ability to think creatively, then your thinking abilities may enable you to perform in a solid, workmanlike fashion, but your work will lack imagination, you will be afraid to try original approaches because of the risk of failure, and your personality will be lacking the spontaneous sparkle that people admire and are drawn to. You will in time become a competent but unimaginative "worker-bee," performing your duties with predictable adequacy but never rising to the lofty heights that you are capable of attaining. Your choices will be as limited as your imagination, and your habitual choices of safe and secure paths will eventually create a very small canvas for your personal portrait.

If you lack the ability to choose freely, then your abilities to think critically or creatively cannot save you from a life of disappointment. Though you may be able to clearly analyze and understand, you will lack the will to make the difficult choices and stay the course when you encounter obstacles and adversities. And though you may develop unique and valuable ideas, your inability to focus your energies and make things happen will doom these ideas to anonymity. Because you lack the will to create yourself as a strong individual of character and integrity, the people you encounter will come to view you as a shallow-rooted reed that bends with the wind of superficial trends, not as someone deserving of authority and responsibility.

Think of what you aspire to have: a life of purpose and meaning, the respect and devotion of those around you, success and fulfillment in your chosen endeavors, and a secure sense of who you are, a person with the courage and vision to accomplish great things. These aspirations are within your grasp, but only if you develop all of these fundamental dimensions of your self to their fullest potential: the abilities to think critically, think creatively, and choose freely.

Choosing Freely

You have the power to create yourself through the choices that you make, but only if your choices are truly free. To exercise genuine freedom, you must possess the insight to understand all of your options and the wisdom to make informed choices. In many instances passive, illogical, and superficial thinking inhibits people's abilities to make intelligent choices and erodes their motivation to persevere when obstacles are encountered. You can learn to redefine your daily life in a new light and enhance its value through free choices derived from thinking critically and creatively. The problem is that we get so caught up in routine, so mired in the day-to-day demands of reality and the pressures of conformity, that we don't even *see* alternatives to our condition, much less act on them. Our complaints often far outnumber our shining moments as we tend to focus on the forces and people who have thwarted our intentions:

If only that person hadn't sabotaged my career, I would have . . .
If only I had had a chance to meet the right person . . .

If only I had gotten the breaks now and then . . .

If only I could get rid of my habitual tendency to ———, I would . . .

If only other people were as dependable and caring as I am . . .

If only I had been given the advantages of a different background . . .

If only the world had not become so competitive . . .

If only I had been given the opportunity to show what I could do . . .

These complaints, and the millions of others like them, bitterly betray W. E. Henley's notion that *"I am the master of my fate, I am the captain of my soul."* It is much more common for people to believe that fate mastered them and that they never had sufficient opportunity to live life "their way." Instead of feeling free, we often feel beleaguered, trying desperately to prevent our small dinghy from getting swamped in life's giant swells rather than serenely charting a straight course in our sleek sailboat.

The end result is that when people think of "being free," they often conjure up a romantic notion of "getting away" from their concerns and responsibilities, imagining a world where anything is possible, and there is plenty of money to pay for it. However appealing this fantasy may be, it is a misconceived and unrealistic notion of freedom. Genuine freedom consists of making thoughtful choices from among the available options, choices that reflect your genuine desires and deepest values, and resisting the pressures to surrender your autonomy to external pressures *or* internal forces. How can you accomplish this?

To begin with, you need to *make freedom a priority* in your life. Achieving greater freedom for yourself is based on placing a high value on personal freedom. If you are primarily focused on meeting your needs within the existing structure of your life, then maximizing your choices and enlarging the scope of your life may not be a top priority. However, if you feel dissatisfied with the status quo and long to increase your options and your ability to choose them, increasing your personal freedom will be a very important goal.

> *Strategy:*   *Complete a brief inventory of your life, identifying some of the areas you would like to change as well as those you are basically satisfied with but would like to enrich. Think about the ways in which increasing your personal freedom and making different choices could help you achieve these life goals.*

A second strategy for increasing your personal freedom is to *willingly accept your freedom and responsibility.* The most important and disturbing element of personal freedom is that it necessarily involves personal responsibility. And personal responsibility is the main reason that people are so reluctant to embrace their freedom and, in fact, actively seek to "escape" from it. If you acknowledge that your choices are free, then you must accept that you are responsible for the outcomes resulting from your choices. When people are successful, it is easy for them to take full responsibility for their accomplishments. But when failure occurs, people tend to dive for cover, blaming others or forces beyond their control. This is exactly what's going on in all the "if only" statements listed previously and any others like them: They each express the belief that if only some outside force had not intervened, the person would have achieved the goal she or he had set. However, in many instances, these explanations are bogus, and these efforts to escape from freedom are illegitimate. They represent weak and inauthentic attempts to deny freedom *and* responsibility.

Your reaction to responsibility is an effective barometer of your attitude toward freedom. If you are comfortable with your personal responsibility, able openly to admit your mistakes as well as to take pleasure in your successes, this attitude is an indication that you accept your freedom. Similarly, if you take pride in your independence, welcoming the opportunity to make choices for which you are solely responsible, this attitude also reveals a willing embracing of your freedom.

> **Strategy:** *Create a "responsibility chart" that evaluates your acceptance of responsibility (and freedom) in various areas of your life. On one side of the page, describe common activities in which you are engaged ("Decisions at work," "Conflicts with my partner"), and on the other side, list typical judgments that you make ("I am solely responsible for that mistaken analysis"; "You made me do that embarrassing thing, and I can't forgive you"). After several days of record-keeping and reflection, you should begin to get an increasingly clear picture of the extent to which you accept (or reject) your personal freedom.*

A third way to increase your freedom is to *emphasize your ability to create yourself.* Although you may not be fully aware of it, you have your own psychological theory of human nature, which is expressed in how you view yourself and deal with other people. Do you believe that your personality is determined by your genetic history or by the environmental circumstances that have shaped you? Or do you believe that people are able to transcend their histories and choose freely?

> **Strategy:** *Instead of explaining your (and others') behavior entirely in terms of genes and environmental conditioning, develop the habit of analyzing your behavior in terms of the choices you make. Many people triumph over daunting odds while others fail miserably, despite having every advantage in life. What are the key ingredients of such triumphs? They are an unshakable belief in the ability to choose one's destiny and the determination to do so.*

Increasing your freedom necessarily involves a fourth strategy, *becoming aware of constraints on your freedom and willing yourself to break free from them.* Freedom consists of making thoughtful choices that reflect your authentic self, your genuine desires and deepest values. But there are many forces that threaten to limit your freedom and even repress it altogether. The limits to your freedom can either come from outside yourself (*external constraints*) or they can come from within yourself (*internal constraints*). While external factors may limit your freedom — for example, being incarcerated or working at a dead-end job — the more challenging limits are imposed by yourself through internal constraints. For instance, people don't generally procrastinate, smoke, suffer anxiety attacks, feel depressed, or engage in destructive relationships because someone is coercing them to do so. Instead, they are victimizing themselves in ways that they are often unaware of. How can you tell if your choice originates from your genuine self or from an internal constraint? There is no simple answer. You have to think critically about your situation in order to understand it fully, but here are some questions to guide your reflective inquiry:

- Do you feel that you are making a free, unconstrained choice and that you could easily "do otherwise" if you wanted to? Or do you feel that your choice is in some sense beyond your conscious control, that you are in the grip of a force that does not reflect your genuine self, a compulsion that has in some way "taken possession" of you?

- Does your choice add positive qualities to your life: richness of experience, success, happiness? Or does your choice have negative results that undermine many of the positive goals that you are striving for?

- If you are asked why you are making a certain choice, are you able to provide a persuasive, rational explanation? Or are you at a loss to explain why you are behaving this way, other than to say, "I can't help myself."

In order to remove constraints, you first have to become aware that they exist. For example, if someone is manipulating you to think or feel a certain way, you can't begin to deal with the manipulation until you first become aware of it. Similarly, you can't solve a personal problem, such as insecurity or emotional immaturity, without first acknowledging that it *is* a problem and then developing insight into the internal forces that are driving your behavior. Once you have achieved this deeper level of understanding, you are then in a position to choose a different path for yourself, using appropriate decision-making and problem-solving approaches such as those that we have been developing and addressing throughout this book.

Strategy: *Identify the external limitations (people or circumstances) on your freedom, and think about ways to remove these constraints. Then identify — as best you can — the internal compulsions that are influencing you to act in ways at variance with your genuine desires. Use the critical and creative thinking abilities you have been developing to diminish or eliminate their influence.*

Finally, maximizing your freedom involves *creating new options to choose from* instead of passively accepting the choices that are initially presented to you. The most vigorous exercise of freedom involves actively creating alternatives that may not be on the original menu of options. This talent involves both thinking critically by taking active initiatives and thinking creatively by generating unique possibilities. For example, if you are presented with a project at work, you should not restrict yourself to considering the conventional alternatives for meeting the goals; instead, actively seek improved possibilities. If you are enmeshed in a problem situation with someone else, you should not permit the person to establish the alternatives from which to choose; instead, work to formulate new or modified ways of solving the problem. Too often people are content to sit back and let the situation define their choices instead of taking the initiative to shape the situation in their own way. Critical and creative thinkers view the world as a malleable environment that they have a responsibility to form and shape. This perspective liberates them to exercise their freedom of choice to the fullest extent possible.

Active thinking, like passive thinking, is habit forming. But once you develop the habit of looking beyond the information given — to transcend consistently the framework within which you are operating — you will be increasingly unwilling to be limited by the alternatives determined by others. Instead, you will seek to create new possibilities and actively shape situations to fit your needs.

Strategy: *When you find yourself in situations with different choices, make a conscious effort to identify alternatives that are different from those explicitly presented. You don't necessarily have to choose the new options you have created if they are not superior to the others, but you do want to start developing the habit of using your imagination to look beyond the circumstances as presented.*

Deciding on a Career

"Work is a search for daily meaning as well as daily bread, for recognition as well as cash . . . in short, for a life rather than a Monday through Friday sort of dying."

— Studs Terkel, *Working*

VISUAL THINKING

Weighing Your Decision Carefully

● Why do many people tend to make quick decisions rather than approaching their decisions thoughtfully and analytically? Describe a decision you made that was based on thoughtful analysis. How did it turn out?

Let's apply these insights about personal freedom to a very important decision in your life. Choosing a professional career is one of the key decisions you will make in life, and you should use your thinking abilities to make the most informed decision possible.

"What are you going to be when you grow up?" In childhood this question is fun to contemplate because life is an adventure, and the future is unlimited. However, now that you are "grown up," this question may elicit more anxiety than enjoyment. "What am I going to be?" "Who am I going to be?" Enrolling in college is certainly an intelligent beginning. The majority of professional careers require a college education, and the investment is certainly worthwhile in monetary terms. But having entered college, many students react by asking, "Now what?"

Perhaps you entered college right out of high school, or perhaps you are returning to college after raising a family, working in a variety of jobs, or serving in the armed forces. The question is the same: "What is the right decision to make about your career future?" Some people have no idea how to answer this question; others have a general idea about a possible career (or careers) but aren't sure exactly which career they want or precisely how to achieve their career goals. Even if you feel sure about your choice, it makes sense to engage in some serious career exploration to ensure that you fully understand your interests and abilities as well as the full range of career choices that match up with your talents.

Most college students will change their majors a number of times before graduating. Although many students are concerned that these changes reveal instability and confusion, in most cases they are a healthy sign. They suggest that the students are actively engaged in the process of career exploration: considering possible choices, trying them out, and revising their thinking to try another possibility. Often we learn as much from discovering what we don't want as from what we do want. The student who plans to become a veterinarian may end up concluding, "I never want to see a sick animal the rest of my life," as one of my students confided after completing a three-month internship at a veterinary hospital.

The best place to begin an intelligent analysis of your career future is by completing a review of what you already know about your career orientation. Your personal history contains clues regarding which career directions are most appropriate for you. By examining the careers you have considered in your life, and by analyzing the reasons that have motivated your career choices, you can begin creating a picture of yourself that will help you define a fulfilling future. With these considerations in mind, complete the following activity as a way to begin creating your own individual "career portrait." Start by describing two careers that you have considered for yourself in the past few years along with the reason(s) for your choices, and then complete the following Thinking Activity.

THINKING ACTIVITY 12.1

Thinking About Your Career Plans

Describe in a two-page paper your current thoughts and feelings about your career plans. Be very honest, and include the following:

1. A specific description of the career(s) you think you might enjoy

2. A description of the history of this choice(s) and the reasons why you think you would enjoy it (them)

3. The doubts, fears, and uncertainties you have concerning your choice(s)

4. The problems you will have to solve and the challenges you will have to overcome in order to achieve your career goal

Thinking Errors in Career Decisions

Too often, people choose careers for the wrong reasons, including the following:

- They consider only those job opportunities with which they are familiar and fail to discover countless other career possibilities.

- They focus on certain elements — such as salary or job security — while ignoring others — like job satisfaction or opportunities for advancement.

- They choose careers because of pressure from family or peers rather than selecting careers that they really want.

- They drift into jobs by accident or circumstance and never reevaluate their options.

- They fail to understand fully their abilities and long-term interests, and what careers will match these.

- They don't pursue their "dream jobs" because they are afraid that they will not succeed.

- They are reluctant to give up their current unsatisfactory job for more promising possibilities because of the risk and sacrifice involved.

Whatever the reasons, the sad fact is that too many people wind up with dead-end, unsatisfying jobs that seem more like lifetime prison sentences than their "field of dreams." However, such depressing outcomes are not inevitable. This text is designed to help you develop the thinking abilities, knowledge, and insight you will need to achieve the appropriate career.

Creating Your Dream Job

One of the powerful thinking abilities you possess is the capacity to think imaginatively. In order to discover the career that is right for you, it makes sense to use your imagination to create an image of the job that you believe would make you feel most fulfilled. Too often people settle for less than they have to because they don't believe they have any realistic chance to achieve their dreams. Using this self-defeating way of thinking virtually guarantees failure in a career quest. Another thinking error occurs when people decide to pursue a career simply because it pays well, even though they have little interest in the work itself. This approach overlooks the fact that in order to be successful over a long period of time, you must be continually motivated — otherwise you may "run out of gas" when you most need it. Interestingly enough, when people pursue careers that reflect their true interests, their success often results in financial reward because of their talents and accomplishments, even though money wasn't their main goal!

So the place to begin your career quest is with your dreams, not with your fears. In order to get started, it's best to imagine an ideal job in as much detail as possible. Of course, any particular job is only one possibility within the field of your career choice. It is likely that you will have a number of different jobs as you pursue your career. However, your imagination works more effectively when conjuring up specific images, rather than images in general. You can begin this exploratory process by completing Thinking Activity 12.2.

THINKING ACTIVITY 12.2

Describing Your Dream Job

Write a two-page description of your ideal job. Spend time letting your imagination conjure up a specific picture of your job, and don't let negative impulses ("I could never get a job like that!") interfere with your creative vision. Be sure to address each of the four dimensions of your ideal job:

1. Physical setting and environment in which you would like to spend your working hours
2. Types of activities and responsibilities you would like to spend your time performing
3. Kinds of people you would like to be working with
4. Personal goals and accomplishments you would like to achieve as part of your work

VISUAL THINKING

A Bad Hair Day?

● There are countless careers that people don't consider because they are unfamiliar. What unusual occupation do you think is depicted in this photo? What would you expect to be the educational background and training of this person? What are three of the most unusual careers that you can think of? After sharing with the class, were you surprised at some of the unusual careers other students identified? Are any of interest to you?

Finding the Right Match

In Chapter 1 you learned how to use your thinking abilities to begin identifying your interests, abilities, and values. Discovering who you are is one part of identifying an appropriate career. The second part involves researching the careers that are available in order to determine which ones match up with your interests, abilities, and values. There are literally thousands of different careers, most of which you probably have only a vague notion about. How do you find out about them? There are a number of tools at your disposal. To begin with, your college probably has a career resource center that likely contains many reference books, periodical publications, videotapes, and software programs describing various occupations. Career counselors are also available either at your school or in your community. Speaking to people working in various careers is another valuable way to learn about what is really involved in a particular career. Work internships, summer jobs, and volunteer work are other avenues for learning about career possibilities and whether they might be right for you.

As you begin your career explorations, don't lose sight of the fact that your career decisions will likely evolve over time, reflecting your growth as a person and the changing job market. Many people alter their career paths often, so you should avoid focusing too narrowly. Instead, concentrate on preparing for broad career areas and developing your general knowledge and abilities. For example, by learning to think critically, solve problems, make intelligent decisions, and communicate effectively, you are developing the basic abilities needed in virtually any career. As an "educated thinker," you will be able to respond quickly and successfully to the unplanned changes and unexpected opportunities that you will encounter as you follow — and create — the unfolding path of your life.

THINKING PASSAGES

Finding Meaning in Work

Do you work to live, or live to work? In difficult economic times, "work" becomes a necessity and an anxiety; we search for (and stay in) jobs that may not fulfill us creatively or intellectually but may simply keep us solvent and insured. In the previous pages, you worked through a series of thinking exercises designed to help you balance your natural talents and skills with your need to find a career path. The following readings describe attitudes about, and approaches to, kinds of "work" that seem more like vocations than mere jobs. A *vocation* is, literally, a calling; when you have a vocation to do something, you simply cannot imagine yourself doing anything else. In the first reading, Annie Dillard describes the extraordinary bravery of a stunt pilot named Dave Rahm. A geologist by training and profession, Rahm saw stunt piloting as a vocation, not just an expensive and risky hobby. Dillard observes that anything performed so bravely and whole-heartedly is elevated to the level of art. The second essay might surprise you, too. College teacher Carlo Rotella describes the fierce commitment of his student Russell to the art and science of boxing. The dedication and discipline Russell develops in the ring will serve him well in any career or, indeed, in any sphere of his life. Finally, physicist Alan Lightman describes the joy of "patient, brilliant, solitary work" that motivates many scientists.

THE STUNT PILOT
by Annie Dillard

Dave Rahm lived in Bellingham, Washington, north of Seattle. Bellingham, a harbor town, lies between the alpine North Cascade Mountains and the San Juan Islands in Haro Strait above Puget Sound. The latitude is that of Newfoundland. Dave Rahm was a stunt pilot, the air's own genius.

In 1975, with a newcomer's willingness to try anything once, I attended the Bellingham Air Show. The Bellingham airport was a wide clearing in a forest of tall Douglas firs; its runways suited small planes. It was June. People wearing blue or tan zipped jackets stood loosely on the concrete walkways and runways outside the coffee shop. At that latitude in June, you stayed outside because you could, even most of the night, if you could think up something to do. The sky did not darken until ten o'clock or so, and it never got very dark. Your life parted and opened in the sunlight. You tossed your dark winter routines, thought up mad projects, and improvised everything from hour to hour. Being a stunt pilot seemed the most reasonable thing in the world; you could wave your arms in the air all day and night, and sleep next winter.

I saw from the ground a dozen stunt pilots; the air show scheduled them one after the other, for an hour of aerobatics. Each pilot took up his or her plane and performed a batch of tricks. They were precise and impressive. They flew upside down, and straightened out; they did barrel rolls, and straightened out; they drilled through dives and spins, and landed gently on a far runway.

For the end of the day, separated from all other performances of every sort, the air show director had scheduled a program titled "Dave Rahm." The leaflet said that Rahm was a geologist who taught at Western Washington University. He had flown for King Hussein in Jordan. A tall man in the

Source: "The Stunt Pilot" first published in *Esquire*. Copyright © 1989 by Annie Dillard. Reprinted by permission of this author.

crowd told me Hussein had seen Rahm fly on a visit the king made to the United States; he had invited him to Jordan to perform at ceremonies. Hussein was a pilot, too. "Hussein thought he was the greatest thing in the world."

Idly, paying scant attention, I saw a medium-sized, rugged man dressed in brown leather, all begoggled, climb in a black biplane's open cockpit. The plane was a Bücker Jungman, built in the thirties. I saw a tall, dark-haired woman seize a propeller tip at the plane's nose and yank it down till the engine caught. He was off; he climbed high over the airport in his biplane, very high until he was barely visible as a mote, and then seemed to fall down the air, diving headlong, and streaming beauty in spirals behind him.

The black plane dropped spinning, and flattened out spinning the other way; it began to carve the air into forms that built wildy and musically on each other and never ended. Reluctantly, I started paying attention. Rahm drew high above the world an inexhaustibly glorious line; it piled over our heads in loops and arabesques. It was like a Saul Steinberg fantasy; the plane was the pen. Like Steinberg's contracting and billowing pen line, the line Rahm spun moved to form new, punning shapes from the edges of the old. Like a Klee line, it smattered the sky with landscapes and systems.

The air show announcer hushed. He had been squawking all day, and now he quit. The crowd stilled. Even the children watched dumbstruck as the slow, black biplane buzzed its way around the air. Rahm made beauty with his whole body; it was pure pattern, and you could watch it happen. The plane moved every way a line can move, and it controlled three dimensions, so the line carved massive and subtle slits in the air like sculptures. The plane looped the loop, seeming to arch its back like a gymnast; it stalled, dropped, and spun out of it climbing; it spiraled and knifed west on one side's wings and back east on another; it turned cartwheels, which must be physically impossible; it played with its own line like a cat with yarn. How did the pilot know where in the air he was? If he got lost, the ground would swat him.

Rahm did everything his plane could do: tailspins, four-point rolls, flat spins, figure eights, snap rolls, and hammerheads. He did pirouettes on the plane's tail. The other pilots could do these stunts too, skillfully, one at a time. But Rahm used the plane inexhaustibly, like a brush marking thin air.

He was pure energy and naked spirit. I have thought about it for years. Rahm's line unrolled in time. Like music, it split the bulging rim of the future along its seam. It pried out the present. We watchers waited for the split-second curve of beauty in the present to reveal itself. The human pilot,

Dave Rahm, worked in the cockpit right at the plane's nose; his very body tore into the future for us and reeled it down upon us like a curling peel.

Like any fine artist, he controlled the tension of the audience's longing. You desired, unwittingly, a certain kind of roll or climb, or a return to a certain portion of the air, and he fulfilled your hope slantingly, like a poet, or evaded it until you thought you would burst, and then fulfilled it surprisingly, so you gasped and cried out.

The oddest, most exhilarating and exhausting thing was this: he never quit. The music had no periods, no rests or endings; the poetry's beautiful sentence never ended; the line had no finish; the sculptured forms piled overhead, one into another without surcease. Who could breathe, in a world where rhythm itself had no periods?

It had taken me several minutes to understand what an extraordinary thing I was seeing. Rahm kept all that embellished space in mind at once. For another twenty minutes I watched the beauty unroll and grow more fantastic and unlikely before my eyes. Now Rahm brought the plane down slidingly, and just in time, for I thought I would snap from the effort to compass and remember the line's long intelligence; I could not add another curve. He brought the plane down on a far runway. After a pause, I saw him step out, an ordinary man, and make his way back to the terminal.

The show was over. It was late. Just as I turned from the runway, something caught my eye and made me laugh. It was a swallow, a blue-green swallow, having its own air show, apparently inspired by Rahm. The swallow climbed high over the runway, held its wings oddly, tipped them, and rolled down the air in loops. The inspired swallow. I always want to paint, too, after I see the Rembrandts. The blue-green swallow tumbled precisely, and caught itself and flew up again as if excited, and looped down again, the way swallows do, but tensely, holding its body carefully still. It was a stunt swallow.

I went home and thought about Rahm's performance that night, and the next day, and the next.

I had thought I knew my way around beauty a little bit. I knew I had devoted a good part of my life to it, memorizing poetry and focusing my attention on complexity of rhythm in particular, on force, movement, repetition, and surprise, in both poetry and prose. Now I had stood among dandelions between two asphalt runways in Bellingham, Washington, and begun learning about beauty. Even the Boston Museum of Fine Arts was never more inspiriting than this small northwestern airport on this time-killing Sunday afternoon in June. Nothing on earth is more gladdening than knowing we must roll up our sleeves and move back the boundaries of the humanly possible once more.

Later I flew with Dave Rahm; he took me up. A generous geographer, Dick Smith, at Western Washington University, arranged it, and came along. Rahm and Dick Smith were colleagues at the university. In geology, Rahm had published two books and many articles. Rahm was handsome in a dull sort of way, blunt-featured, wide-jawed, wind-burned, keen-eyed, and taciturn. As anyone would expect. He was forty. He wanted to show me the Cascade Mountains; these enormous peaks, only fifty miles from the coast, rise over nine thousand feet; they are heavily glaciated. Whatcom County has more glaciers than the lower forty-eight states combined; the Cascades make the rocky mountains look like hills. Mount Baker is volcanic, like most Cascade peaks. That year, Mount Baker was acting up. Even from my house at the shore I could see, early in the morning on clear days, volcanic vapor rise near its peak. Often the vapor made a cloud that swelled all morning and hid the snows. Every day the newspapers reported on Baker's activity: Would it blow? (A few years later, Mount St. Helens did blow.)

Rahm was not flying his trick biplane that day, but a faster enclosed plane, a single-engine Cessna. We flew from a bumpy grass airstrip near my house, out over the coast and inland. There was coastal plain down there, but we could not see it for clouds. We were over the clouds at five hundred feet and inside them too, heading for an abrupt line of peaks we could not see. I gave up on everything, the way you do in airplanes; it was out of my hands. Every once in a while Rahm saw a peephole in the clouds and buzzed over for a look. "That's Larsen's pea farm," he said, or "That's Nooksack Road," and he changed our course with a heave.

When we got to the mountains, he slid us along Mount Baker's flanks sideways.

Our plane swiped at the mountain with a roar. I glimpsed a windshield view of dirty snow traveling fast. Our shaking, swooping belly seemed to graze the snow. The wings shuddered; we peeled away and the mountain fell back and the engines whined. We felt flung, because we were in fact flung; parts of our faces and internal organs trailed pressingly behind on the curves. We came back for another pass at the mountain, and another. We dove at the snow headlong like suicides; we jerked up, down, or away at the last second, so late we left our hearts, stomachs, and lungs behind. If I forced myself to hold my heavy head up against the G's, and to raise my eyelids, heavy as barbells, and to notice what I saw, I could see the wrinkled green crevasses cracking the glaciers' snow.

Pitching snow filled all the windows, and shapes of dark rock. I had no notion which way was up. Everything was black or gray or white except the fatal crevasses; everything made noise and shook. I felt my face smashed sideways and saw rushing abstractions of snow in the windshield. Patches of cloud obscured the snow fleetingly. We straightened out, turned, and dashed at the mountainside for another pass, which we made, apparently, on our ear, an inch or two away from the slope. Icefalls and cornices jumbled and fell away. If a commercial plane's black box, such as the FAA painstakingly recovers from crash sites, could store videotapes as well as pilots' last words, some videotapes would look like this: a mountainside coming up at the windows from all directions, ice and snow and rock filling the screen up close and screaming by.

Rahm was just being polite. His geographer colleague wanted to see the fissure on Mount Baker from which steam escaped. Everybody in Bellingham wanted to see that sooty fissure, as did every geologist in the country; no one on earth could fly so close to it as Rahm. He knew the mountain by familiar love and feel, like a face; he knew what the plane could do and what he dared to do.

When Mount Baker inexplicably let us go, he jammed us into cloud again and soon tilted. "The Sisters!" someone shouted, and I saw the windshield fill with red rock. This mountain looked infernal, a drear and sheer plane of lifeless rock. It was red and sharp; its gritty blades cut through the clouds at random. The mountain was quiet. It was in shade. Careening, we made sideways passes at these brittle peaks too steep for snow. Their rock was full of iron, somebody shouted at me then or later; the iron had rusted, so they were red. Later, when I was back on the ground, I recalled that, from a distance, the two jagged peaks called the Twin Sisters looked translucent against the sky; they were sharp, tapered, and fragile as arrowheads.

I talked to Rahm. He was flying us out to the islands now. The islands were fifty or sixty miles away. Like many other people, I had picked Bellingham, Washington, by looking at an atlas. It was clear from the atlas that you could row in the salt water and see snow-covered mountains; you could scale a glaciated mountainside with an ice ax in August, skirting green crevasses two hundred feet deep, and look out on the islands in the sea. Now, in the air, the clouds had risen over us; dark forms lay on the glinting water. There was almost no color to the day, just blackened green and some yellow. I knew the islands were forested in dark Douglas firs the size of skyscrapers. Bald eagles scavenged on the beaches; robins the size of herring gulls sang in the clearings. We made our way out to the islands through the layer of air between the curving planet and its held, thick clouds.

"When I started trying to figure out what I was going to do with my life, I decided to become an expert on mountains. It wasn't much to be, it wasn't everything, but it was something. I was going to know everything about mountains from every point of view. So I started out in geography." Geography proved too pedestrian for Rahm, too concerned with "how many bushels of wheat an acre." So he ended up in geology. Smith had told me that geology departments throughout the country used Rahm's photographic slides — close-ups of geologic features from the air.

"I used to climb mountains. But you know, you can get a better feel for a mountain's power flying around it, flying all around it, than you can from climbing it tied to its side like a flea."

He talked about his flying performances. He thought of the air as a line, he said. "This end of the line, that end of the line — like a rope." He improvised. "I get a rhythm going and stick with it." While he was performing in a show, he paid attention, he said, to the lighting. He didn't play against the sun. That was all he said about what he did.

In aerobatic maneuvers, pilots pull about seven positive G's on some stunts and six negative G's on others. Some gyrations push; others pull. Pilots alternate the pressures carefully, so they do not gray out or black out.

Later I learned that some stunt pilots tune up by wearing gravity boots. These are boots made to hook over a doorway; wearing them, you hang in the doorway upside down. It must startle a pilot's children to run into their father or mother in the course of their home wanderings — the parents hanging wide-eyed, upside down in the doorway like a bat.

We were landing; here was the airstrip on Stuart Island — that island to which Ferrar Burn was dragged by the tide. We put down, climbed out of the plane, and walked. We wandered a dirt track through fields to a lee shore where yellow sandstone ledges slid into the sea. The salt chuck, people there called salt water. The sun came out. I caught a snake in the salt chuck; the snake, eighteen inches long, was swimming in the green shallows.

I had a survivor's elation. Rahm had found Mount Baker in the clouds before Mount Baker found the plane. He had wiped it with the fast plane like a cloth and we had lived. When we took off from Stuart Island and gained altitude, I asked if we could turn over — could we do a barrel roll? The plane was making a lot of noise, and Dick Smith did not hear any of this, I learned later. "Why not?" Rahm said, and added surprisingly, "It won't hurt the plane." Without ado he leaned on the wheel and the wing went down and we went somersaulting over it. We upended with a roar. We stuck to the plane's sides like flung paint. All the blood in my body bulged on my face; it piled between my skull and skin. Vaguely I could see the chrome sea twirling over Rahm's head like a baton, and the dark islands sliding down the skies like rain.

The G's slammed me into my seat like thugs and pinned me while my heart pounded and the plane turned over slowly and compacted each organ in turn. My eyeballs were newly spherical and full of heartbeats. I seemed to hear a crescendo; the wing rolled shuddering down the last 90 degrees and settled on the flat. There were the islands, admirably below us, and the clouds, admirably above. When I could breathe, I asked if we could do it again, and we did. He rolled the other way. The brilliant line of the sea slid up the side window bearing its heavy islands. Through the shriek of my blood and the plane's shakes I glimpsed the line of the sea over the windshield, thin as a spear. How in performance did Rahm keep track while his brain blurred and blood roared in his ears without ceasing? Every performance was a tour de force and a show of will, a *Machtspruch.* I had seen the other stunt pilots straighten out after a trick or two; their blood could drop back and the planet simmer down. An Olympic gymnast, at peak form, strings out a line of spins ten stunts long across a mat, and is hard put to keep his footing at the end. Rahm endured much greater pressure on his faster spins using the plane's power, and he could spin in three dimensions and keep twirling till he ran out of sky room or luck.

When we straightened out, and had flown straightforwardly for ten minutes toward home, Dick Smith, clearing his throat, brought himself to speak. "What was that we did out there?"

"The barrel rolls?" Rahm said. "They were barrel rolls." He said nothing else. I looked at the back of his head; I could see the serious line of his cheek and jaw. He was in shirtsleeves, tanned, strong-wristed. I could not imagine loving him under any circumstance; he was alien to me, unfazed. He looked like GI Joe. He flew with that matter-of-fact, bored gesture pilots use. They click overhead switches and turn dials as if only their magnificent strength makes such dullness endurable. The half circle of wheel in their big hands looks like a toy they plan to crush in a minute; the wiggly stick the wheel mounts seems barely attached.

A crop-duster pilot in Wyoming told me the life expectancy of a crop-duster pilot is five years. They fly too low. They hit buildings and power lines. They have no space to fly out of trouble, and no space to recover from a stall. We were in Cody, Wyoming, out on the north fork of the Shoshone River. The crop duster had wakened me that morning flying over the ranch house and clearing my bedroom roof by half an inch. I saw the bolts on the wheel assembly a few feet from my face. He was spraying with pesticide the plain old grass. Over breakfast I asked him how long he had been dusting crops. "Four years," he said, and the figure stalled in the air between us for a moment. "You know you're going to die at it someday," he added. "We all know it. We accept that; it's part of it."

I think now that, since the crop-duster was in his twenties, he accepted only that he had to say such stuff; privately he counted on skewing the curve.

I suppose Rahm knew the fact too. I do not know how he felt about it. "It's worth it," said the early French aviator Mermoz. He was Antoine de Saint-Exupéry's friend. "It's worth the final smashup."

Rahm smashed up in front of King Hussein, in Jordan, during a performance. The plane spun down and never came out of it; it nosedived into the ground and exploded. He bought the farm. I was living then with my husband out on that remote island in the San Juans, cut off from everything. Battery radios picked up the Canadian Broadcasting Company out of Toronto, half a continent away; island people would, in theory, learn if the United States blew up, but not much else. There were no newspapers. One friend got the Sunday *New York Times* by mail boat on the following Friday. He saved it until Sunday and had a party, every week; we all read the Sunday *Times* and no one mentioned that it was last week's.

One day, Paul Glenn's brother flew out from Bellingham to visit; he had a seaplane. He landed in the water in front of the cabin and tied up to our mooring. He came in for coffee, and he gave out news of this and that, and — Say, did we know that stunt pilot Dave Rahm had cracked up? In Jordan, during a performance; he never came out of a dive. He just dove right down into the ground, and his wife was there watching. "I saw it on CBS News last night." And then — with a sudden sharp look at my filling eyes — "What, did you know him?" But no, I did not know him. He took me up once. Several years ago. I admired his flying. I had thought that danger was the safest thing in the world, if you went about it right.

Later, I found a newspaper. Rahm was living in Jordan that year; King Hussein invited him to train the aerobatics team, the Royal Jordanian Falcons. He was also visiting professor of geology at the University of Jordan. In Amman that day he had been flying a Pitt Special, a plane he knew well. Katy Rahm, his wife of six months, was sitting beside Hussein in the viewing stands, with her daughter. Rahm died performing a Lomcevak combined with a tail slide and hammerhead. In a Lomcevak, the pilot brings the plane up on a slant and pirouettes. I had seen Rahm do this: the falling plane twirled slowly like a leaf. Like a ballerina, the plane seemed to hold its head back stiff in concentration at the music's slow painful beauty. It was one of Rahm's favorite routines. Next the pilot flies straight up, stalls the plane, and slides down the air on his tail. He brings the nose down — the hammerhead — kicks the engine, and finishes with a low loop.

It is a dangerous maneuver at any altitude, and Rahm was doing it low. He hit the ground on the loop; the tail side had left him no height. When Rahm went down, King Hussein dashed to the burning plane to pull him out, but he was already dead.

A few months after the air show, and a month after I had flown with Rahm, I was working at my desk near Bellingham, where I lived, when I heard a sound so odd it finally penetrated my concentration. It was the buzz of an airplane, but it rose and fell musically, and it never quit; the plane never flew out of earshot. I walked out on the porch and looked up: it was Rahm in the black and gold biplane, looping all over the air. I had been wondering about his performance flight: could it really have been so beautiful? It was, for here it was again. The little plane twisted all over the air like a vine. It trailed a line like a very long mathematical proof you could follow only so far, and then it lost you in its complexity. I saw Rahm flying high over the Douglas firs, and out over the water, and back over farms. The air was a fluid, and Rahm was an eel.

It was as if Mozart could move his body through his notes, and you could walk out on the porch, look up, and see him in periwig and breeches, flying around in the sky. You could hear the music as he dove through it; it streamed after him like a contrail.

I lost myself; standing on the firm porch, I lost my direction and reeled. My neck and spine rose and turned, so I followed the plane's line kinesthetically. In his open-cockpit black plane, Rahm demonstrated curved space. He slid down ramps of air, he vaulted and wheeled. He piled loops in heaps and praised height. He unrolled the scroll of air, extended it, and bent it into Möbius strips; he furled line in a thousand new ways, as if he were inventing a script and writing it in one infinitely recurring utterance until I thought the bounds of beauty must break.

From inside, the looping plane had sounded tinny, like a kazoo. Outside, the buzz rose and fell to the Doppler effect as the plane looped near or away. Rahm cleaved the sky like a prow and tossed out time left and right in his wake. He performed for forty minutes; then he headed the plane, as small as a wasp, back to the airport inland. Later I learned Rahm often practiced acrobatic flights over this shore. His idea was that if he lost control and was going to go down, he could ditch in the salt chuck, where no one else would get hurt.

If I had not turned two barrel rolls in an airplane, I might have fancied Rahm felt good up there, and playful. Maybe Jackson Pollock felt a sort of playfulness, in addition to the artist's usual deliberate and intelligent care. In my limited experience, painting, unlike writing, pleases the senses while you do it, and more while you do it than after it is done. Drawing lines with an airplane, unfortunately, tortures the senses. Jet bomber pilots black out. I knew Rahm felt as if his brain were bursting his eardrums, felt that if he let his jaws close as tight as centrifugal force pressed them, he would bite through his lungs.

"All virtue is a form of acting," Yeats said. Rahm deliberately turned himself into a figure. Sitting invisible at the controls of a distant airplane, he became the agent and the instrument of art and invention. He did not tell me how he felt when we spoke of his performance flying; he told me instead that he paid attention to how his plane and its line looked to the audience against the lighted sky. If he had noticed how he felt, he could not have done the work. Robed in his airplane, he was as featureless as a priest. He was lost in his figural aspect like an actor or a king. Of his flying, he had said only, "I get a rhythm and stick with it." In its reticence, this statement reminded me of Veronese's "Given a large canvas, I enhanced it as I saw fit." But Veronese was ironic, and Rahm was not; he was as literal as an astronaut; the machine gave him tongue.

When Rahm flew, he sat down in the middle of art and strapped himself in. He spun it all around him. He could not see it himself. If he never saw it on film, he never saw it at all — as if Beethoven could not hear his final symphonies not because he was deaf but because he was inside the paper on which he wrote. Rahm must have felt it happen, that fusion of vision and metal, motion and idea. I think of this man as a figure, a college professor with a Ph.D. upside down in the loud band of beauty. What are we here for? *Propter chorum,* the monks say: for the sake of the choir.

"Purity does not lie in separation from but in deeper penetration into the universe," Teilhard de Chardin wrote. It is hard to imagine a deeper penetration into the universe than Rahm's last dive in his plane, or than his inexpressible wordless selfless line's inscribing the air and dissolving. Any other art may be permanent. I cannot recall one Rahm sequence. He improvised. If Christo wraps a building or dyes a harbor, we join his poignant and fierce awareness that the work will be gone in days. Rahm's plane shed a ribbon

510 Chapter Twelve: *Reasoning Critically, Thinking Creatively*

in space, a ribbon whose end unraveled in memory while its beginning unfurled as surprise. He may have acknowledged that what he did could be called art, but it would have been, I think, only in the common misusage, which holds art to be the last extreme of skill. Rahm rode the point of the line to the possible; he discovered it and wound it down to show. He made his dazzling probe on the run. "The world is filled, and filled with the Absolute," Teilhard de Chardin wrote. "To see this is to be made free."

<center>~~~~~~~</center>

CUT TIME
by Carlo Rotella

Russell, a pleasant young man who split his time between the college on the hill (where I taught) and the boxing gym down below, came up at the end of class one day to tell me that a card of fights would be held in a couple of weeks in nearby Allentown, Pennsylvania. He knew I was interested in boxing and thought I might like to go; also he needed a ride.

I had figured he was not stopping by to continue our discussion of "Bartleby the Scrivener." Seated front and center, in a posture of polite interest but not taking many notes, Russell followed the action in class without committing to it. Some students, infighters, sit up front to get your attention, but others do it for the opposite reason: one way to avoid getting hit is to get in too close, nestled cozily against your opponent's clavicle, where he cannot apply the leverage to hurt you (unless he fouls by head-butting, ear-biting, or calling on people who do not raise their hands). Russell did the reading and wrote his papers, but he was not swept up by fictions and make-believe characters. The class met in the afternoon just before he headed down the hill to the Larry Holmes Training Center, and I suspected that he daydreamed about the imminent shock of punching rather than concentrating on the literary matters at hand.

Every once in a while, though, Russell would say something that reminded me that he was paying attention. Impressed by Frederick Douglass's late-round TKO of the overseer Covey, he spoke up to remind us that this scene dramatized the red-blooded ideal of self-making with one's own two hands. But he had also been moved to speak by Melville's Bartleby, who comprehensively rejects one of the fight world's foundational princi-

Source: Excerpt from *Cut Time: An Education at the Fights* by Carlo Rotella. Compright © 2003 by Carlo Rotella. Reprinted by permission of Houghton Mifflin Company. All rights reserved.

ples: protect yourself at all times. Russell, breaking form, had his hand up first and initiated the discussion of Bartleby with references to Gandhi, Martin Luther King, and the difficult principle of moral inaction. Russell encouraged us to consider whether the pacific Bartleby, by preferring to do nothing, was acting decisively against the grain of his situation, or was simply not much good with his hands and therefore destined to be acted upon by a world that kept the hard knocks coming in a steady stream. At least that is what I took him to mean, and I got busy parlaying it into a general discussion in which Russell, having said his piece, declined to participate further.

Once the other students had risen to the bait and were doing the talking, I had a chance to look Russell over for new damage: this week it was a thick, dark line, resembling lavishly applied lampblack, that ran under his right eye from nose to cheekbone. Another black eye, and this one a prizewinner. One of the quiet dramas of having Russell in class was seeing what kind of punishment he had incurred of late. He was so placid in his manner, so Bartleby-like in his pale decency, that I was always jarred by the various lumps, welts, and bruises that passed over his face like weather fronts. Having seen him spar in the gym, I should not have been surprised. He was strong but not quick; and he came straight at his antagonist, equally accepting blows as the price of getting into range to deliver the one-twos he favored. I knew that Russell's style ensured that he would get hit often, even on his best days; but when I saw the marks of his latest lesson on his face, a little click of alarmed recognition still ran through me — registering somewhere in a roped-off area of my mind devoted to boxing — as I managed the discussion and scrawled on the blackboard, chalk dust all over my hands and on the thighs of my pants where I wiped them.

I gestured at the new black eye when Russell stopped to talk with me after class. He just said, "Sterling," looked at the floor, and shook his head, smiling faintly. Sterling was one of the gym's rising stars, a teenager already poised and smooth in the ring. Russell had several years and a few pounds on Sterling, although neither advantage did him much good. Sterling was so preternaturally fast and clever that he had fallen half in love with the idea of his own genius; that — and a tendency to switch back and forth too promiscuously between right- and left-handed stances in order to baffle his opponents — was his only evident weakness. He was the kind of evasive, willowy counterpuncher that solid hitters long to pummel. Russell, for one, believed with doctrinaire intensity that he could hurt Sterling if only he could catch him. I had not seen the two of them spar together, but I had seen Russell's face after their sessions and I had seen both of them spar with others, so I could imagine the encounters: Russell following Sterling doggedly around the ring, absorbing jabs and the occasional speed-blurred combination as he sought to fix the skinny body and weaving head in his sights long enough to throw a meaningful punch. When Russell drifted far away in thought during class, I assumed he was pursuing Sterling in his mind's eye in the hope of finally nailing him with a big right hand.

On our drive down to the fights later that month, Russell described himself as discouraged about boxing. He had been scheduled to make his first amateur fight in the Golden Gloves, but he had canceled it. He knew he was not ready. I asked if Sterling was still beating him up in the sparring ring, and he said, "Well, yeah, him, but also everybody else. A while ago I was walking around with two black eyes and loose cartilage in my nose and I started to get . . . *discouraged* thinking about it." Russell's stated ambition was to win an official boxing match, not just to spar or fight creditably, but the accumulating pain and damage made him worry that he might be foolish to pursue this goal any further. At the same time, he was wary of giving up too easily, of mistaking for perpetual futility what might be only a difficult period of his fistic education. He said, "When I spar I'm getting really beat up, like, humiliated, in there. I can't get better until I practice more, but I can't practice without getting beat up." I asked why he could not stop now, with no significant damage done, having learned the basics of boxing, having done much to inculcate in himself the generally applicable virtue of disciplined hard work, and having absorbed an instructive dose of the kind of violent extremity from which college usually shelters a young man or woman.

Russell had two answers to that. First, the ever-present threat of pain and humiliation in boxing inspired him to rigor in his training, and he worried that if he stopped going to the gym he would backslide in other endeavors that also required discipline. "When I first got to college," he said, "I slacked off a lot, just hung out and messed around, and it really affected me — my school work, my life. But once I found boxing, I got disciplined about everything. School, eating, sleeping, everything. This week I was getting really discouraged and I didn't go down to the gym at all, and I already felt myself letting things go. You know, falling back into bad habits." Second, he said, discipline aside, "It could turn out that pain and damage are important just by themselves. That's a kind of life experience you can't get as a middle-class college student. Maybe it's worth getting banged up to learn about yourself and, you know, the rest of the world." There were guys down at the gym who had been in jail, who had been addicted to drugs, who had given and taken beatings in and out of the ring, who had been out on the streets broke and without prospects. That was what Russell meant by "life experience."

He seemed to want an argument, so I gave him one. Boxing was not the only way to sample the world beyond College Hill. Most experience of that world fell somewhere between the extremes of reading about it in books and insisting on getting punched out over and over by experts. Warming to the task, I argued that his fixation on getting hurt as the key to authentic "life experience" took the school out of the school of hard knocks, reducing an education in pugilism to an elaborate form of self-abuse. If ritual humiliation and physical damage became his antidote to slacking off and a sheltered upbringing, wouldn't that formula for gaining "life experience" give him no reason to improve as a boxer? And, anyway, what made boxing necessarily a better path to "life experience" than college? Wasn't college, ideally, supposed to be about exactly the things he saw in boxing: rigorous self-knowledge, encounters with the wider world, the inculcation of discipline? After all, Frederick Douglass presents himself as a student first and a wordsmith last — a reader, writer, and speaker. He disdains boxing, like whiskey drinking, as a waste of a Sabbath day better spent in learning to read, and he fights only twice — when cornered, rather than going in search of beatings — in a definitively unsheltered life.

Russell said "I see that" and "Right, right" in the way a person does when he means that he has stated his position, he is pleased that you agree it is worth discussing, and there is nothing more to discuss. . . .

In the months that followed, Russell found a teacher, a retired fighter who sometimes worked with novices, and eventually declared himself ready to try the Golden Gloves. He was wrong. Russell described his amateur debut as a sort of out-of-body nightmare. He felt himself submerged in a flatfooted torpor in which he moved with desperately inappropriate serenity while the other fighter, unspeakably quick and confident, pounded him at will. Russell was not badly hurt, but he was thoroughly beaten. After the first round, the referee came to Russell's corner to ask if he wished to continue, and he did, but the referee stopped the bout in the second. Feeling himself profoundly out of place in the ring and in his own body, sustained only by courage once his craft had deserted him, seemingly unable to defend himself or fight back, Russell had frozen in the ring, as novices sometimes do. "I never got started," he told me. "It was like I wasn't even there."

I moved away from Easton soon after, but, back to visit a year later, I dropped by the Larry Holmes Training Center one afternoon. The fighters poured sweat in the late September heat. Stripped to a black tank top and shorts, Art was hitting a heavy bag steadily and well — first the left hand twice, a jab and a hook, then a right cross. Somebody was hitting the other heavy bag very hard; it jumped with each blow, and the thump-crack of sharp punching filled the long, low room. When the second hitter moved around his bag and out from behind Art, I could see it was Russell. There was a new weight and speed in his punching, and he had his legs and shoulders into the making of each punch. His diligence and his teacher's efforts had evidently paid off in an improved command of leverage. He was working on power shots: his left hooks made a perfect L from shoulder to glove, staving in the bag on one side; his straight rights imparted the illusion of animate sensitivity to the bag as it leapt away from the impact. He looked bigger than before, having begun to fill out, but, more than that, he looked looser, more competent, more alert. He had lost the quality of undersea abstraction that had always surrounded him in the gym. There was confident vigor in the way he shoved the bag away so it would swing back at him: he looked forward to its arrival because he was going to hit it just right, with all of himself behind the gloved fist.

I raised an eyebrow at Jeff, a stocky gym regular who worked for the grounds crew up at the college in the mornings and for Larry Holmes in the afternoons. He looked over at Russell, smiled and nodded, and said, "Yeah, Russ has been getting it together. He can *hit*, man. He was in sparring with one of those boys last week and the guy's head was just going like this: bop! bop! bop!" With each *bop!* Jeff threw his head back, chin up, like a fighter getting tagged. One of Holmes's seconds, a round-bodied, characteristically surly fellow named Charlie, chimed in: "Russ can hit. No doubt about it. He had his problems for a while, he got beat up, but he stayed with it and he's getting good. He gets in there this time, he'll surprise some people. Hurt 'em." This was unlooked-for, wildly enthusiastic praise coming from Charlie, who usually ignored the younger fighters in the gym except to shoo them out of the ring when Holmes was ready to work out.

Loyal to one of the gym's most diligent regulars, if not one of its most talented, Jeff and Charlie were talking Russell up to one of his professors, but anyone could see that he had made an important step forward on the way from dabbler to fighter. It looked as if he had arrived at a sense of belonging in the gym, not because he was training next to Art, but because he was doing it right and knew himself to be doing it right. Maybe the Golden Gloves beating had helped to drive home the lesson that just wanting to be in the ring is not a good enough reason to be there; you have to accept responsibility for your part in the mutual laying on of hands. I expected that

Russell would not freeze up in his next fight. He was still slow and hittable, and he might well lose; if he did, however, it would not be because he felt out of place in the ring but because he was outboxed or made mistakes or was simply not quick enough. And if the other guy let Russell start throwing punches, Russell might just give him a beating, or at least a stiff punch or two to remember him by.

When I got back home to Boston I sent Russell an e-mail saying I was pleased to see that he had made such progress in the gym. I admitted I had worried in the past that he would get seriously hurt, perhaps even in a life-changing way, because he was in the gym for the wrong reasons — to absorb "life experience" passively rather than to train actively at a craft — but I was less worried now that he had evidently got down to work in earnest. I was initially surpised, then, when Russell wrote back a couple of weeks later to announce a retirement of sorts:

> In earnest, I have become somewhat disenchanted with boxing. There seems to be a level, which I have reached, at which it has lost to some extent its seductive and mesmorizing effect. While I will always retain an interest and awe in the sport, I feel that I can understand the subtleties of the sport and could even execute them given the proper conditioning and practice. While I regard Larry and other successful boxers with the utmost respect and admiration, there seems to be a lack of transcendence into a higher state of more complete perfection in the human realm. Financial gain does not take the fighter out of the street and its culture, nor does it provide him with any solace or real advancement. I may be sounding somewhat highbrow, however, I now realize that I have bigger fish to fry. With my college education quickly coming to a close I need to focus the resource of my time on things which will propel my advancement after graduation. I will certainly remain active in training and boxing but I realistically can no longer give it my full commitment (and just when I was starting to see the fruit of my labor) . . .
>
> Still in need of an appropriate nickname,
> Russell

SPELLBOUND BY THE ETERNAL RIDDLE,
SCIENTISTS REVEL IN THEIR CAPTIVITY
by Alan Lightman

From an early age, I loved to solve puzzles. When my math teachers assigned homework, most students groaned, but I relished the job. I would save my math problems for last, right before bedtime, like bites of chocolate cake awaiting me after a long and dutiful meal of history and Latin. Then, I would devour my cake.

In geometry, I took pleasure in finding the inexorable and irrefutable relations between lines, angles and curves. In algebra, I delighted in the idea of abstraction, letting x's and y's stand for the number of nickels in a jar or the distance traveled by a train. And then solving a set of connected equations, one logical step after another. Sometimes, when the assigned problems were not challenging enough, I would make up my own problems and seek the solutions.

The biologist Barbara McClintock also enjoyed solving puzzles. In an interview with Evelyn Fox Keller, McClintock recalled that as a child she "used to love to be alone . . . just thinking about things." In high school science classes in Brooklyn, "I would solve some of the problems in ways that weren't the answers the instructor expected," she said. "It was a tremendous joy, the whole process of finding that answer, just pure joy."

Still pursuing that childlike joy in her early 40's, McClintock wondered why some kernels of Indian corn have a mixture of colors, with scattered spots of blue, red and brown. An odd puzzle, seemingly unimportant to anyone except a geneticist.

Realizing that the peculiar phenomenon could not be explained by the standard principles of genetic heredity, she began experiments to find an explanation. After five years of work — patient, brilliant, solitary work during which McClintock sometimes spent the fitful nights sleeping on a cot in her lab — she was led to the unorthodox conclusion that genes are not fixed links in the chain of a chromosome, but instead can change positions, rearrange themselves, and in doing so alter their function. For this revelation, she was awarded a Nobel Prize in 1983.

I believe that scientists of average abilities, like myself, and the great scientists, like McClintock, are propelled by the same forces. Why do I enjoy

Source: Copyright © 2003 by The New York Times Co. Reprinted by permission.

solving puzzles? I love the mental freedom, letting my mind roam and play. Like an athlete who gets pleasure simply from jogging around the quarter-mile track, I delight in letting my mind run. It feels good to use a machine for what it was designed to do.

I love the purity of problems with a logical solution. And the certainty, which contrasts with so much that is ambiguous and bedraggled in the world of people and society. I guiltily admit that sometimes I have closed the door on a screaming daughter, refused to listen to a dejected friend, and escaped to my little desk with its white pad of paper and lovely equations.

With most problems in mathematics and science, you are guaranteed an answer, as clean and crisp as a new $20 bill. Ever wonder how busy the traffic is on your street at different times of the day? When a scientist ponders such a question, he or she sits by the window with a pencil, paper and clock and records the number of passing cars in each minute interval throughout the day.

Even though science is constantly revising itself, constantly adapting to new information and ideas, at any moment a scientist is studying a more or less definite problem, formulated to lead to a definite answer. That answer is waiting, beckoning, challenging the scientist to find it.

In looking back on his early days in science, Einstein wrote that "the nothingness of the hopes and strivings which chases most men restlessly through life came to my consciousness with considerable vitality."

"Out yonder," he continued, "there was this huge world, which exists independently of us human beings and which stands before us like a great, eternal riddle, at least partially accessible to our inspections and thinking. The contemplation of this world beckoned like a liberation . . ."

In addition to the joy of solving riddles, there is the pleasure in craftsmanship. The pleasure in building good and useful things with one's hands. As a professional scientist, I've built only ideas, with equations, but as a child I often built various gadgets, using resistors and capacitors, coils of wire, batteries, switches, photoelectric cells, magnets, chemicals of various kinds. With a thermostat, a light bulb and a padded cardboard box, I constructed an incubator for the cell cultures in my biology experiments.

After seeing the Boris Karloff "Frankenstein" movie, I felt compelled to build a spark-generating induction coil, requiring tedious weeks upon weeks of winding a mile's length of wire around an iron core. Every night, I asked myself the question: Could I make the thing work?

It was a personal question. And that is a paradox of science. Although the truths of science lie outside of human beings, as Einstein said, the motivations for doing science are not only human but intensely personal. Each scientist challenges him or herself at a personal level. Each scientist seeks that challenge, indeed craves that challenge. Each scientist wants to feel his or her own machine revving and rumbling under the hood. Can I build this induction coil? Can I solve this equation? Can I discover the organization of genes?

It is a curious I. It is an I that comes in the warm-ups but oddly not during the heat of the race. And there lies another paradox of science. Although some scientists do indeed have astronomical egos and launch themselves toward honors and fame, during the actual moments of scientific discovery, as in all creative discoveries, the ego magically vanishes.

Something else gets under your skin, keeps you working days and nights at the sacrifice of your sleeping and eating and attention to your family and friends, something beyond the love of puzzle solving. And that other force is the anticipation of understanding something about the world that no one has ever understood before you.

Einstein wrote that when he first realized that gravity was equivalent to acceleration — an idea that would underlie his new theory of gravity — it was the "happiest thought of my life." On projects of far smaller weight, I have experienced that pleasure of discovering something new. It is an exquisite sensation, a feeling of power, a rush of the blood, a sense of living forever. To be the first vessel to hold this new thing.

All of the scientists I've known have at least one more quality in common: they do what they do because they love it, and because they cannot imagine doing anything else. In a sense, this is the real reason a scientist does science. Because the scientist must. Such a compulsion is both blessing and burden. A blessing because the creative life, in any endeavor, is a gift filled with beauty and not given to everyone, a burden because the call is unrelenting and can drown out the rest of life.

This mixed blessing and burden must be why the astrophysicist Chandrasekhar continued working until his mid-80's, why a visitor to Einstein's apartment in Bern found the young physicist rocking his infant with one hand while doing mathematical calculations with the other. This mixed blessing and burden must have been the "sweet hell" that Walt Whitman referred to when he realized at a young age that he was destined to be a poet. "Never more," he wrote, "shall I escape."

Questions for Analysis

1. What characteristics do Dave Rahm (the stunt pilot) and Russell (the boxer) share? What motivates them to excel in their sports? Are these motivations innate, or can they be developed through practice and discipline? Explain your answer with reference to your own extracurricular endeavors — for example, perhaps you're a gifted mechanic or a determined, disciplined marathoner.

2. Would you describe Dave Rahm's flying or Russell's boxing as "work"? Why or why not? If you wouldn't classify it as *work*, what would you call either the flying or the boxing? In an e-mail at the end of "Cut Time," Russell notes of boxing that "there seems to be a lack of transcendence into a higher state of more complete perfection in the human realm." Why is he ultimately disenchanted with boxing, and what is he looking for? What are *you* looking for in anything to which you dedicate much of your time, talent, and energy?

3. How would the stunt pilot and the boxer define *success?* How would you define it? Return to your description of your "dream job" that you developed in Thinking Activity 12.2. How would you determine success in that dream job? If you let go of that definition of *success,* would your dream job be something completely different?

4. In paragraph 15 of his essay, Alan Lightman describes the "curious I." Throughout this book, we have been examining curiosity as a key characteristic of a critical thinker. How does Lightman demonstrate his own curiosity? How does curiosity keep Russell and Rahm working toward their goals?

5. Does Lightman convince you — if you needed convincing — that scientists are just as creative as artists? How about stunt pilots, or even boxers? In what areas of your life are you creative, and how can you use that creativity to help you find fulfillment in your work?

Thinking Critically About Personal Relationships

Another crucial area in your life that requires full use of your abilities to think critically, live creatively, and choose freely is establishing healthy relationships with others. Relating to other people is by far the most complicated and challenging kind of relating that we do. Your thinking abilities provide you with the power to untangle the complex mysteries of the relationships in your life. By thinking clearly about your social connections, you can avoid miscommunications and solve interpersonal problems when they arise. Many emotional difficulties — including insecurity, depression, anger, jealousy, selfishness, rigidity, insensitivity, narrow-mindedness, and immaturity — are the product of confused thinking. Since it is these "negative" emotions that are responsible for the majority of relationship problems, transforming these "negatives" into "positives" — security, optimism, love, respect, support, generosity, flexibility, empathy, creativity, and maturity — makes it possible for you to have a wide range of positive, healthy relationships. Clear thinking can't make you fall in love with someone you judge to be a good candidate. But clear thinking will make it possible for you to fall in love and have a sustained, nurturing, intimate relationship. Clear thinking will make it possible for others to appreciate your best qualities, for them to experience you as a thoughtful, caring, intellectually vital person.

In order to understand the enigma of the human mind and the mystery of human relationships, we need to employ a logic that captures the organic connections between people. Human relationships are dynamic encounters between living persons, and virtually every significant encounter changes all participants, for better or for worse. As Carl Jung observed, "The meeting of two personalities is like the contact of two chemical substances: if there is any reaction, both are transformed."

The transformational nature of human encounters occurs in less intimate relationships as well. For example, think of someone you have dealings with on a daily basis with whom you are not personally close — perhaps a coworker or supervisor at your workplace or a staff member at the school where you donate your time. Even relatively straightforward encounters with such a person typically involve complex communication, practical negotiations, emotional reactions, and all of the other basic elements of relationships. Over time these encounters, and your reflections on them, change you as a person, influencing your ongoing creation of who you are. Even momentary encounters with others affect you: the Good Samaritan who shows you an unexpected kindness or the enraged motorist who tailgates your car's bumper, flashing his lights and making obscene gestures. The Good Samaritan's kindness may stimulate you to consider your moral responsibilities to others, even strangers, and strengthen your resolve to act more charitably. The enraged motorist may get you thinking about the pressures of modern life that cause such hostile behavior in people, insights that may help you control your own frustrations in more positive ways. When you encounter someone different from yourself, the interaction of ideas, emotions, and attitudes creates a "relationship," a living social creation that is continually changing and evolving.

The Thinker's Guide to Healthy Relationships

Though you may not have realized it, you have been developing all of the abilities needed for healthy relationships as you have worked through the ideas presented in the various chapters of this book. Here is an outline of the approach to those relationships that we will be using:

The Thinker's Guide to Healthy Relationships

- Establish goals.
- Communicate clearly.
- View your relationships from all perspectives.
- Build trust through reason.
- Foster creativity.
- Value freedom and responsibility.
- Problem-solve.

Establish Goals

Every relationship is unique and mysterious in its own way, but it is possible, if you make an effort to think clearly, to understand a great deal about what is going on, why it is happening, and how it will influence what will occur in the future. To begin, identify what goals you have for the relationship. There are general goals that apply to most relationships — being congenial, having clear communication — but there are also goals specific to the relationship in question, whether it is a relationship with a coworker, a parent, a close friend, a supervisor, a client, a niece, a babysitter, a former spouse, a doctor, or a new romantic interest. Too often, however, people don't identify objectives or stick to a plan, so as a result they end up spending too much time with people they don't want to be with and not enough time with those they do. Or they may wreck a potentially good relationship by piling on more expectations than one person can possibly fulfill: lover, best friend, therapist, roommate, career counselor — and more! If you define the goals of the relationship more narrowly — and more realistically — the relationship might function more successfully, whereas imposing excessive expectations might serve as its death warrant.

Communicate Clearly

Faulty communication is responsible for more problems in relationships than any other factor. How often have you heard — or uttered — the lament "We just don't seem to communicate"? Clear communication involves a complex blending of thinking, language, and social skills. For example, people often talk at each other, not really listening to the other person because they are concentrating on what they're going to say next.

In order to engage in a productive discussion, you have to articulate your viewpoint clearly, listen carefully to the other person's response, and then respond to it or ask for clarification. When both people approach the dialogue in this fashion, within a context of mutual respect and caring, meaningful communication can take place. Also, people do have different communication styles that need to be acknowledged in order to avoid misunderstanding, conflict, and fractured relationships.

Another essential dimension of communicating effectively is using language that is clear and precise, a skill we explored in Chapter 6. When language is vague or ambiguous, people tend to read into the vagueness their own personal meanings, assuming that their meanings are universally shared. They are often mistaken in this assumption, and as a result, trouble follows closely behind. A simple expression like "I love you" can express an astonishing number of different meanings, depending on the individual and the particular context. And if for one person "I love you" means "I think you are an engaging person to whom I am attracted," while the other person is thinking, "You are the perfect mate for me, and I expect us to spend eternity together," then there's trouble on the horizon that's likely to hit the relationship sooner or later. Disciplining yourself to speak and behave in ways that are clear, precise, and unambiguous will work wonders in avoiding miscommunications that can begin as small problems but then snowball into much larger ones.

View Your Relationships from All Perspectives

The success of most close relationships — romantic, familial, professional, and friendly — is directly related to the extent to which you can imaginatively place yourself in the other person's situation and fully appreciate what he or she is experiencing. This in-depth empathy is what emotionally close relationships are all about. In contrast, when two people are both excessively concerned with their own self-interests — with what the other person can do for "me" — then the relationship is in serious trouble. Healthy relationships are based on shared interests, not only on self-interest.

Think back to the last significant altercation you had with someone you are close to. You undoubtedly believed that you possessed a clarity that the other person didn't and that, despite your reason and restraint, the other person was trying to coerce you into accepting his or her confused point of view. Naturally, the other person probably felt the same way. Once two (or more) people establish these one-sided and self-serving postures, things generally deteriorate until a culminating crisis forces each person to become truly aware of the other.

As a critical thinker, you can make an extra effort to view things differently by asking the other person why he or she has arrived at that point of view and then placing yourself in that position. Then you can ask the other person, "If you were in my position, how would you view the situation, and what would you do?" Exchanging roles in this way, thinking and feeling as the other person does, changes the entire tone of the discussion. Instead of exchanges becoming increasingly more rancorous ("You don't understand anything"; "You are insensitive and blind"), there is an excellent chance that both of you will work together in a more harmonious and collaborative way to achieve mutual understanding.

Build Trust Through Reason

Of course, relationships cannot be fully understood through reason any more than reason can fully disclose the mysteries of an exquisite work of art, a moving musical passage, a transcendent spiritual experience, or the spontaneous eruption of delight occasioned by humor. Your reasoning ability is powerful, but it has limits as well, and it is important to appreciate those limits and to respect them. People who try to reduce every dimension of the rich tapestry of human experience to logical categories and rational explanations are pursuing fool's gold. Still, reason helps you make sense of the contours and patterns of your emotional life as well as many other elements that form the phenomenon of human relationships.

Suppose someone whom you feel close to does something that wounds you deeply. When you confront the friend and ask why he did what he did, further imagine that his response is, "I can't give you any reason — I just did it." How would you feel? You would probably feel bewildered and angry, and for good "reason." That's because we expect people — including ourselves — to try to understand their motivations so that they can exert some control over their choices. People hurt those close to them for many different reasons: They may have been acting thoughtlessly, selfishly, stupidly, callously, unconsciously, or sadistically. There are reasons that people behave as they do, and your confidence and trust in others depends on this conviction. If your friend says to you, "I hurt you, and I'm very sorry. I was only thinking of myself during that moment and did not fully appreciate how my actions might affect you. It was a mistake, and I won't repeat it in the future," then you have a foundation upon which you can build the future of your relationship. But if your friend says to you, "I hurt you for no reason that I can identify, and I don't know if it will happen again," then you will have difficulty trusting him in the future.

Reason is the framework that makes relationships possible. The more intimate the relationship, the more important the role reason plays. This is so because in intimate relationships you are most vulnerable; your emotions are laid bare. Reason is the safety net that gives you the courage to take those halting and dangerous steps on the high wire. You build trust in the other person because you believe his or her choices are governed, or at least are influenced, by reason, and you depend on that assurance. Of course, even the best intentions can be overwhelmed by mindless passion, unruly emotions, or unexpected compulsions. But even though emotions may erupt and temporarily swamp your rational faculties, your will and determination can once again set things right, reasserting the primacy of reason in directing your emotions so that your choices reflect your highest values. That's why thoughtful people get onto the high wire again, even after they have fallen, because they have confidence that the rule of reason guides well-intentioned people.

Foster Creativity

The abilities to think critically and to think creatively work together to produce accomplished thinking and an enriched life. This is a theme explored more fully in Chapter 1, and it applies directly to fostering healthy relationships. For example, think back to the last time you began a new relationship. Wanting to make a good impression, you probably invested a great deal of creative energy in nurturing the budding romance or friendship. Now reflect on the long-term relationships in which you are currently involved: Do you find that a certain staleness has set in? Have you fallen into routine patterns of activity, doing the same things on a fixed schedule? Do your conversations revolve around the same few topics, with the same comments being made with predictable regularity? If so, don't be too hard on yourself: This deterioration is very common in relationships.

The expression "Familiarity breeds contempt" points to the chronic human trait of taking for granted the people who are most important to us, letting habit and routine sap the vitality of our relationships. Since relationships are dynamic and alive, treating them as if they were machines running on past momentum will eventually cause them to become rusty and stop working altogether. In many cases, however, they can be revived by your choosing to again bring the same creative energy to them that you invested at the beginning of the relationship and by encouraging your partner to realize his or her creative potential. The result can be creative fusion between the two of you that will inspire you both with its power.

Value Freedom and Responsibility

Healthy relationships are ones in which the participants willingly take responsibility for themselves and value the freedom of others. Responsibility is the logical consequence of freedom, and while people cherish their personal freedom, they tend to flee from responsibility when things don't go according to plan. Consider the following situations:

- You are working collaboratively with a number of other colleagues on an important project. When your project turns out to be an embarrassing failure, your supervisor wants to know who's to blame for the fiasco. With your career on the line, what do you say?
- You are the parent of a child with an approaching birthday. You promised to purchase tickets to a special concert, but you procrastinate, and by the time you get around to buying the tickets, they're sold out. What explanation do you give your child?

If you found yourself instinctively trying to minimize your personal responsibility in these situations (and to maximize the responsibility of other people), it's not surprising. These are common human reactions. But healthy relationships are based on a willingness to assume responsibility, not evade it. By fully acknowledging your responsibility, you gain stature in the eyes of others and encourage them to accept responsibility for their own actions as well. However, if you chronically avoid taking responsibility for your mistakes and failings, you erode the trust and goodwill in relationships, and you shrink in stature.

Accepting responsibility means promoting freedom. Pursuing your own personal freedom is a natural and appropriate thing to do. But to foster healthy relationships with others, it is equally important to promote and respect their freedom. To maintain healthy relationships, you must value the autonomy of other people to make their own decisions, independent of your own wishes. Once others discover, as they likely will, that you are trying to pressure or manipulate them, you run the risk of undermining the mutual trust on which relationships are based.

Problem-Solve

Critical thinkers are problem-solvers, as we saw in Chapter 3. Problems are a natural part of life, and they are an unavoidable reality in relationships. The only question is how you are going to deal with the problems that you will inevitably encounter. You can approach problems with fear and loathing, letting them intimidate you and contaminate your relationships. Or you can approach these same problems with the confidence of a critical thinker, viewing them as opportunities to clarify important issues and improve your relationships. Friedrich Nietzsche's observation "What doesn't kill you, makes you stronger" applies to relationships as well. The strongest, most resilient relationships are those that have been tested, have overcome adversity, and ultimately have triumphed through the efforts of all parties. The most vulnerable relationships are those that have not been tested because the participants have denied themselves the opportunity to develop coping skills and the confidence that "the first serious wave won't capsize the boat." Repeated successes with problems both large and small will breed confidence in your problem-solving abilities — and in the resilience of your most significant relationships.

THINKING ACTIVITY 12.3

Improving Your Relationships

Select one of the important relationships in your life that you would like to improve. Using the strategies described in "The Thinker's Guide to Healthy Relationships," develop a plan to improve your relationship. Ask yourself the following questions:

- What are my goals?
- In what ways can I communicate more clearly?
- What is the other person's perspective?
- How can I build more trust through reason?
- In what ways can I approach this relationship more creatively?
- How can I accept more responsibility?
- What problems exist, and how can we solve them?

⊚ Choosing "the Good Life"

What is the ultimate purpose of your life? What is "the good life" that you are trying to achieve?

Psychologist Carl Rogers, who has given a great deal of thought to these issues, has concluded that the good life is

- *not* a fixed state like virtue, contentment, nirvana, or happiness
- *not* a condition like being adjusted, fulfilled, or actualized
- *not* a psychological state like drive or tension reduction

Instead, the good life is a *process* rather than a state of being, a *direction* rather than a destination. But what direction? According to Rogers, "The direction which constitutes the Good Life is that which is selected by the total organism when there is psychological freedom to move in any direction." In other words, the heart of the good life is creating yourself through genuinely free choices once you have liberated yourself from external and internal constraints. When you are living such a life, you are able to fulfill your true potential in every area of your existence. You are able to be completely open to your experience, becoming better able to listen to yourself, to experience what is going on within yourself. You are more aware and accepting of feelings of fear, discouragement, and pain, but also more open to feelings of courage, tenderness, and awe. You are more able to live your experiences fully instead of shutting them out through defensiveness and denial.

How do you know what choices you should make, what choices will best create the self you want to be and help you achieve your good life? As you achieve psychological freedom, your *intuitions* become increasingly more trustworthy since they reflect your deepest values, your genuine desires, your authentic self. It is when we are hobbled by constraints on ourselves that our intuitions are distorted and often self-destructive. As previously noted, you need to think clearly about yourself, to have an optimistic, self-explanatory style that enables you to approach life in the most productive way possible. When you have achieved this clarity of vision and harmony of spirit, what "feels right" — the testimony of your reflective consciousness and common sense — will serve as a competent and trustworthy guide to the choices you ought to make. The choices that emerge from this enlightened state will help you create a life that is enriching, exciting, challenging, stimulating, meaningful, and fulfilling. It will enable you to stretch and grow, to become more and to attain more of your potentialities. As author Albert Camus noted, "Freedom is nothing else but a chance to be better, whereas enslavement is a certainty of the worst."

The good life is different for each person, and there is no single path or formula for achieving it. It is the daily process of creating yourself in ways that express your deepest desires and highest values — your authentic self. Thinking critically and thinking creatively provide you with the insight to clearly see the person you want to become while choosing freely gives you the power actually to create the person you have envisioned.

Strategy: *Describe your ideal "good life." Make full use of your imagination, and be specific regarding the details of the life you are envisioning for yourself. Compare this imagined good life with the life you have now. What different choices do you have to make in order to achieve your good life?*

The Meaning of Your Life

According to psychiatrist and concentration camp survivor Victor Frankl, "Man's search for meaning is the primary motivation in his life." A well-known Viennese psychiatrist in the 1930s, Dr. Frankl and his family were arrested by the Nazis, and he spent three years in the Auschwitz concentration camp. Every member of his family, including his parents, siblings, and pregnant wife, were killed. He himself miraculously survived, enduring the most unimaginably abusive and degrading conditions. Following his liberation by the Allied troops, he wrote *Man's Search for Meaning,* an enduring and influential work, which he began on scraps of paper during his internment. Since its publication in 1945, it has become an extraordinary bestseller, read by millions of people and translated into twenty languages. Its success reflects the profound hunger for meaning that people have continually been experiencing, trying to answer a question that, in the author's words, "burns under their fingernails." This hunger expresses the pervasive *meaninglessness* of our age, the "existential vacuum" in which many people exist.

Dr. Frankl discovered that even under the most inhumane conditions, it is possible to live a life of purpose and meaning. But for the majority of prisoners at Auschwitz, a meaningful life did not seem possible. Immersed in a world that no longer recognized the value of human life and human dignity, that robbed prisoners of their will and made them objects to be exterminated, most people suffered a loss of their values. If a prisoner did not struggle against this spiritual destruction with a determined effort to save his or her self-respect, the person lost the feeling of being an individual, a being with a mind, with inner freedom and personal value. The prisoner's existence descended to the level of animal life, plunging him or her into a depression so deep that he or she became incapable of action. No entreaties, no blows, no threats would have any effect on the person's apathetic paralysis, and he or she soon died, underscoring Russian novelist Fyodor Dostoyevsky's observation, "Without a firm idea of himself and the purpose of life, man cannot live, and would sooner destroy himself than remain on earth, even if he was surrounded with bread."

Dr. Frankl found that the meaning of his life in this situation was to try to help his fellow prisoners restore their psychological health. He had to find ways for them to look forward to the future: a loved one waiting for the person's return, a talent to be used, or perhaps work yet to be completed. These were the threads he tried to weave back into the patterns of meaning in these devastated lives. His efforts led him to the following insight:

> We had to learn ourselves, and furthermore we had to teach the despairing men, that it did not matter what we expected from life, but rather *what life expected from us*. We needed to stop asking about the meaning of life but instead to think of ourselves as those who were being questioned by life, daily and hourly. Our answer must consist not in talk and meditation, but in right action and in right conduct. Life ultimately means taking the responsibility to find the right answer to its problems and to fulfill the tasks which it constantly sets for each individual.

We each long for a life of significance, to feel that in some important way our life has made a unique contribution to the world and to the lives of others. We each strive to create our self as a person of unique quality, someone who is admired by others as extraordinary. We hope for lives characterized by unique accomplishments and lasting relationships that will distinguish us as memorable individuals both during and after our time on earth.

The purpose of this book has been to help provide you with the thinking abilities you will need to guide you on your personal journey of self-discovery and self-transformation. Its intention has *not* been to provide you with answers but to equip you with the thinking abilities, conceptual tools, and personal insights to find your own answers. Each chapter has addressed an essential dimension of the thinking process, and the issues raised form a comprehensive blueprint for your life, a life that you wish to be clear in purpose and rich in meaning.

In order for you to discover the meaning of your life, you need to seek meaning actively, to commit yourself to meaningful projects, to meet with courage and dignity the challenges that life throws at you. You will have little chance of achieving meaning in your life if you simply *wait* for meaning to present itself to you or if you persist in viewing yourself as a *victim* of life. If you squander your personal resources by remaining trapped in unproductive patterns, then there will be no room left in your life for genuine meaning.

Reversing this negative orientation requires a radical shift of perspective from complaining about what life "owes" you to accepting the responsibility of meeting life's expectations, whether they be rewarding or cruel. Even in the dire conditions of the concentration camp, there were men like Victor Frankl who chose to act heroically, devoting themselves to comforting others or giving away their last piece of bread. They were living testament to the truth that even though life may take everything away from a person, it cannot take away "the last of the human freedoms — to choose one's attitude in any given set of circumstances, to choose one's own way."

Though you may have to endure hardship and personal tragedy, you still have the opportunity to invest your life with meaning by the way that you choose to respond to your suffering: whether you let it defeat you or whether you are able to rise above it triumphantly. Your ultimate and irreducible freedom to freely choose your responses to life's situations defines you as a person and determines the meaningfulness of your existence.

But how do you determine the "right" way to respond, select the path that will infuse your life with meaning and fulfillment? You need to think critically, think creatively, and make enlightened choices — all of the thinking abilities and life attitudes that you have been cultivating throughout your work with this book. They will provide you with the clear vision and strength of character that will enable you to create yourself as a worthy individual living a life of purpose and meaning. Your explorations of issues presented throughout this book have given you the opportunity to become acquainted with yourself and with the potential that resides within you: your unique intellectual gifts, imaginative dreams, and creative talents. As psychologist Abraham Maslow notes, you are so constructed that you naturally press toward fuller and fuller being, realizing your potentialities, becoming fully human, everything that you can become. But you alone can determine what choices you will make among all of the possibilities: which will be condemned to nonbeing and which will be actualized, creating your immortal portrait, the monument to your existence.

Clearly, the ultimate meaning of your life can never be fully realized within the confines of your own self. Meaning is encountered and created through your efforts to *go beyond* yourself. In the same way that "happiness" and "success" are the outgrowths of purposeful and productive living rather than ends in themselves, so your life's meaning is a natural by-product of reaching beyond yourself to touch the lives of others. This self-transcendence may take the form of a creative work or a heroic action that you display to the human community. It may also be expressed through your loving and intimate relationships with other people, your contribution to individual members of your human community.

What is the meaning of your life? It is the truth that you will discover as you strive, through your daily choices, to create yourself as an authentic individual, committed to enhancing the lives of others, fulfilling your own unique potential, and attuning yourself to your spiritual nature and the mysteries of the universe. It is the reality you will find as you choose to respond to both the blessings and the suffering in your life with courage and dignity. Joy and suffering, fulfillment and despair, birth and death — these are the raw materials that life provides you. Your challenge and responsibility are to shape these experiences into a meaningful whole — guided by a philosophy of life that you have constructed with your abilities to think critically, think creatively, and choose freely. This is the path you must take in order to live a life that is rich with meaning, lived by a person who is noble and heroic — a life led as an enlightened thinker.

GLOSSARY

accomplishment   Something completed successfully; an achievement. Also, an acquired skill or expertise.

accurate   Conforming exactly to fact; errorless; deviating only slightly or within acceptable limits from a standard.

active learner   One who takes initiative in exploring one's world, thinks independently and creatively, and takes responsibility for the consequences of one's decisions.

active participant   One who is always trying to understand the sensations one encounters instead of being a passive receiver of information, a "container" into which sense experience is poured.

alternative   A choice between two mutually exclusive possibilities, a situation presenting such a choice, or either of these possibilities.

altruistic   Showing unselfish concern for the welfare of others.

ambiguous   Open to more than one interpretation; doubtful or uncertain.

analogical relationships   Relationships which relate things belonging to different categories in terms of each other.

analogy   A comparison between things that are basically dissimilar made for the purpose of illuminating our understanding of the things being compared.

analysis   The study of the parts of an intellectual or material whole and their interrelationships in making up a whole.

appeal to authority   A type of fallacious thinking in which the argument is intended to persuade through the appeal to various authorities with legitimate expertise in the area in which they are advising.

appeal to fear   An argument in which the conclusion being suggested is supported by a reason invoking fear and not by a reason that provides evidence for the conclusion.

appeal to flattery   A source of fallacious reasoning designed to influence the thinking of others by appealing to their vanity as a substitute for providing relevant evidence to support a point of view.

appeal to ignorance   An argument in which the person offering the conclusion calls upon his or her opponent to disprove the conclusion. If the opponent is unable to do so, then the conclusion is asserted to be true.

appeal to personal attack   A fallacy that occurs when the issues of the argument are ignored and focus is instead directed to the personal qualities of the person making the argument in an attempt to discredit the argument. Also referred to as the "ad hominem" argument ("to the man" rather than to the issue) or "poisoning the well."

appeal to pity   An argument in which the reasons offered to support the conclusions are designed to invoke sympathy toward the person involved.

appeal to tradition   A misguided way of reasoning that argues that a practice or way of thinking is "better" or "right" simply because it is older, traditional, or has "always been done that way."

application   The act of putting something to a special use or purpose.

argument   A form of thinking in which certain statements (reasons) are offered in support of another statement (a conclusion).

assumption   Something taken for granted or accepted as true without proof.

authoritarian moral theory   A moral theory in which there are clear values of "right" and "wrong," with authorities determining what these are.

authority   An accepted source of expert information or advice.

* Glossary definitions have been adapted and reproduced by permission of *The American Heritage Dictionary of the English Language,* Fourth Edition. Copyright © 2000 by Houghton Mifflin Company.

bandwagon A fallacy that relies on the uncritical acceptance of others' opinions because "everyone believes it."

begging the question A circular fallacy that assumes in the premises of the argument that the conclusion about to be made is already true. Also known as "circular reasoning."

beliefs Interpretations, evaluations, conclusions, or predictions about the world that we endorse as true.

bias A preference or an inclination, especially one that inhibits impartial judgment.

blueprint A detailed plan of action, model, or prototype.

Boolean logic A system of symbolic logic devised by George Boole; used in computers.

brainstorming A method of shared problem solving in which all members of a group spontaneously contribute ideas.

call-outs Numbers in parentheses that appear within an essay to direct the reader to a note that credits the source of either the information used or the language quoted.

causal chain A situation in which one thing leads to another, which then leads to another, and so on.

causal fallacies Mistakes and errors made in judgment in trying to determine causal relationships.

causal reasoning A form of inductive reasoning in which it is claimed that an event (or events) is the result of the occurrence of another event (or events).

causal relationship A relationship that involves relating events in terms of the influence or effect they have on one another.

cause Anything that is responsible for bringing about something else — usually termed the *effect*.

cause-to-effect experiment (with intervention) A form of controlled experiment in which the conditions of one designated "experimental group" are altered while those of a distinct "control group" (both within a target population) remain constant.

cause-to-effect experiment (without intervention) A form of experimental design, similar to cause-to-effect experiment (with intervention), except that the experimenter does not intervene to expose the experimental group to a proposed cause.

certain Established beyond doubt or question; indisputable.

challenge A test of one's abilities or resources in a demanding but stimulating undertaking.

choose freely To choose to take different paths in life by exercising genuine freedom.

chronological Arranged in order of time of occurrence.

chronological relationship A relationship that relates events in time sequence.

circumstantial Of, relating to, or dependent on the conditions or details accompanying or surrounding an event.

classify To arrange or organize according to class or category.

cognition The thinking process of constructing beliefs that forms the basis of one's understanding of the world.

commit To pledge or obligate one's own self.

comparative relationship A relationship which relates things in the same general category in terms of similarities and dissimilarities.

compared subject In an analogy, the object or idea that the original subject is being likened to.

comparing Evaluating similarities and differences.

concepts General ideas that we use to identify and organize our experience.

conclusion   A statement that explains, asserts, or predicts on the basis of statements (known as reasons) that are offered as evidence for it. The result or outcome of an act or process.

conflict   To be in or come into opposition; differ.

consequence   Something that logically or naturally follows from an action or condition.

constructive criticism   Analysis that serves to develop a better understanding of what is going on.

context   The circumstances in which an event occurs; a setting.

contradict   To be contrary to; be inconsistent with.

contribute   To give or supply in common with others; give to a common fund or for a common purpose.

controlled experiment   A powerful reasoning strategy used by scientists.

creative   Able to break out of established patterns of thinking and approach situations from innovative directions.

creative thinking   The act or habit of using our thinking process to develop ideas that are unique, useful, and worthy of further elaboration.

criteria   A set of standards, rules, or tests on which a judgment or decision can be based.

critical analysis   Analysis characterized by careful, exact evaluation and judgment.

critical thinking   The act or habit of carefully exploring the thinking process, in order to clarify our understanding and make more intelligent decisions.

cue words   Key words that signal that a reason is being offered in support of a conclusion or that a conclusion is being announced on the basis of certain reasons.

curious   Willing to explore situations with probing questions which penetrate beneath the surface of issues, instead of being satisfied with superficial explanations.

database   A collection of data arranged for ease and speed of search and retrieval.

deductive argument   An argument form in which one reasons from premises that are known or assumed to be true to a conclusion that follows necessarily from these premises.

deep Web   Information stored on databases which are not directly available to search engines.

define   To describe the nature or basic qualities of; explain.

desirability   The degree to which something is worth having, seeking, doing, or achieving, as by being useful, advantageous, or pleasing.

dialect   A regional or social variety of a language distinguished by pronunciation, grammar, or vocabulary, especially a variety of speech differing from the standard literary language or speech pattern of the culture in which it exists.

dialogue   A systematic exchange of ideas or opinions.

dilemma   A situation that requires a choice between options that are or seem equally unfavorable or mutually exclusive.

disadvantage   Something that places one in an unfavorable condition or circumstance.

disjunctive   Presenting several alternatives.

disprove   To prove to be false, invalid, or in error; refute.

distinguish   To perceive as being different or distinct.

effect   Something brought about by a cause or agent; a result.

effectiveness   The degree to which something produces an intended or expected effect.

effect-to-cause experiment A form of reasoning employing the controlled experimental design in which the experimenter works backward from an existing effect to a suspected cause.

e-mail A system for sending and receiving messages electronically over a computer network, as between personal computers.

empirical generalization A form of inductive reasoning in which a general statement is made about an entire group (the "target population") based on observing some members of the group (the "sample population").

endorsement The act of giving approval or support.

euphemism The act or an example of substituting a mild, indirect, or vague term for one considered harsh, blunt, or offensive.

evaluate To examine and judge carefully, based on specified criteria.

evidence A thing or things helpful in forming a conclusion or judgment.

external constraints Limits to one's freedom that come from outside oneself.

fact Knowledge or information based on real-world occurrences.

factual beliefs Beliefs based on observations.

factual evidence Evidence derived from a concrete, reliable source or foundation.

fallacies Unsound arguments that are often persuasive and can appear to be logical because they usually appeal to our emotions and prejudices, and because they often support conclusions that we want to believe are accurate.

fallacy of relevance A fallacious argument which appeals for support to factors that have little or nothing to do with the argument being offered.

false dilemma A fallacy that occurs when we are asked to choose between two extreme alternatives without being able to consider additional options. Also known as the "either/or fallacy" or the "black-or-white fallacy."

falsifiable beliefs Beliefs that pass a set of tests or stated conditions formulated to test the beliefs.

fictional Relating to or characterized by an imaginative creation or a pretense that does not represent actuality but has been invented.

file transfer protocol (FTP) A communications protocol governing the transfer of files from one computer to another over a network. An FTP site uses the FTP method to transfer data.

flexible Responsive to change; adaptable.

form To develop in the mind; conceive.

generalize To focus on the common properties shared by a group of things.

genuine Honestly felt or experienced.

hasty generalization A general conclusion reached that is based on a very small sample.

hedonism A moral theory which advises people to do whatever brings them pleasure.

home page The opening or main page of a web site, intended chiefly to greet visitors and provide information about the site or its owner.

hypertext A computer-based text retrieval system that enables a user to access particular locations in web pages or other electronic documents by clicking on links within specific web pages or documents.

hypothesis A possible explanation that is introduced to account for a set of facts and that can be used as a basis for further investigation.

identify To ascertain the origin, nature, or definitive characteristics.

illumination Spiritual or intellectual enlightenment; clarification; elucidation.

incomplete comparison A comparison in which focus is placed on too few points of comparison.

independent thinkers Those who are not afraid to disagree with the group opinion. They develop well-supported beliefs through thoughtful analysis, instead of uncritically "borrowing" the beliefs of others.

inductive reasoning An argument form in which one reasons from premises that are known or assumed to be true to a conclusion that is supported by the premises but does not necessarily follow from them.

infer To conclude from evidence or premises.

inference The act or process of deriving logical conclusions from premises known or assumed to be true; the act of reasoning from factual knowledge or evidence.

inferential beliefs Beliefs that are based on inferences, that go beyond what can be directly observed.

inferring Going beyond factual information to describe what is not known.

informed Well acquainted with knowledge of a subject.

insightful Displaying an incisive understanding of a complex event.

interactive Acting or capable of acting on each other.

internal constraints Limits to one's freedom that come from within oneself.

Internet An interconnected system of networks that connects computers around the world via the TCP/IP protocol.

Internet service provider (ISP) A company such as America Online that provides its subscribers with access to the Internet.

interpret To explain the meaning of; to conceive the significance of; construe.

interpretation The result of conceiving or explaining the meaning of.

intuition A sense of something not evident or deducible; an impression.

invalid argument An argument in which the reasons do not support the conclusion so that the conclusion does not follow from the reasons offered.

jargon A style of language made up of words, expressions, and technical terms that are intelligible to professional circles or interest groups but not to the general public.

judging Expressing an evaluation based on certain criteria.

justification The act of demonstrating or proving to be just, right, or valid.

key questions Questions that can be used to explore situations and issues systematically.

knowledge Familiarity, awareness, or understanding gained through experience or study. Information doesn't become knowledge until it has been thought about critically.

knowledgeable Perceptive or well-informed.

language A system of symbols for thinking and communicating.

link A segment of text or a graphical item that serves as a cross-reference between parts of a hypertext document or between files or hypertext documents. Also called hotlink, hyperlink. By clicking on a link, one might more directly access a web site or homepage.

live creatively To approach life with a mindful sense of discovery and invention, enabling one to continually create oneself in ways limited only by the imagination.

mentally active Those who take initiative and actively use intelligence to confront problems and meet challenges, instead of responding passively to events.

metaphor An implied comparison between basically dissimilar things made for the purpose of illuminating our understanding of the things being compared.

mindful Making use of our responsive, perceptive faculties, thus avoiding rigid, reflexive behavior in favor of a more improvisational and intuitive response to life.

mind map A visual presentation of the ways concepts can be related to one another.

misidentification of the cause An error that occurs in causal situations when identification of the cause and the effect are unclear.

modus ponens "Affirming the antecedent"; a valid deductive form commonly used in our logical thinking.

modus tollens "Denying the consequence"; a commonly used valid deductive form.

moral Of or concerned with the judgment of the goodness or badness of human action and character.

moral agnosticism A theory of morality that holds there is no way to determine clearly what is "right" or "wrong" in moral situations.

narrative A way of thinking and communicating in which someone tells a story about experiences he or she has had.

necessary Needed to achieve a certain result or effect; requisite.

open-minded Listening carefully to every viewpoint, evaluating each perspective carefully and fairly.

organize To put together into an orderly, functional, structured whole.

original subject In an analogy, the primary object or idea being described or compared.

paradox A seemingly contradictory statement that may nonetheless be true.

passionate Having a passion for understanding; always striving to see issues and problems with more clarity.

perceiving Actively selecting, organizing, and interpreting what is experienced by your senses.

perceptual meaning A component of a word's total meaning that expresses the relationship between a linguistic event and an individual's consciousness.

personal experience Examples from one's own life; one of the four categories of evidence.

perspective Point-of-view or vista.

post hoc ergo propter hoc "After it, therefore because if it"; refers to situations in which, because two things occur close together in time, an assumption is made that one causes the other.

pragmatic Dealing or concerned with facts or actual occurrences; practical.

pragmatic meaning A component of a word's total meaning that involves the person who is speaking and the situation in which the word is spoken. Also known as situational meaning.

precision The state or quality of being specific, detailed, and exact.

prediction The act of stating, telling about, or making known in advance, especially on the basis of special knowledge.

premise A proposition upon which an argument is based or from which a conclusion is drawn.

principle A plausible or coherent scenario that has yet to be applied to experience.

prioritize To organize things in order of importance.

process analysis A method of analysis involving two steps: (1) to divide the process or activity being analyzed into parts or stages, (2) to explain the movement of the process through these parts or stages from beginning to end.

process relationships Relationships based on the relation of aspects of the growth or development of an event or object.

procrastinate To put off doing something, especially out of habitual carelessness or laziness; to postpone or delay needlessly.

properties Qualities or features that all things named by a word or sign share in common.

psychological Of, relating to, or arising from the mind or emotions.

quality An inherent or distinguishing characteristic; property; essential character or nature.

questionable cause A causal fallacy that occurs when someone presents a causal relationship for which no real evidence exists.

random selection A selection strategy in which every member of the target population has an equal chance of being included in the sample.

reasoning The type of thinking that uses argument — reasons in support of conclusions.

reasons Statements that support another statement (known as a conclusion), justify it, or make it more probable.

red herring A fallacy that is committed by introducing an irrelevant topic in order to divert attention from the original issue being discussed. Also known as "smoke screen" and "wild goose chase."

referents All the various examples of a concept.

relate To bring into or link in logical or natural association; to establish or demonstrate a connection between.

relativism A view according to the tradition of philosophy that says that the truth is relative to any individual or situation, that there is no standard we can use to decide which beliefs make most sense.

relevant Having a bearing on or connection with the matter at hand.

reliable Offering dependable information.

reporting Describing information in ways that can be verified through investigation.

representative In statistical sampling, when the sample is considered to accurately reflect the larger whole, or target population, from which the sample is taken.

revise To reconsider and change or modify.

role The characteristic and expected social behavior of an individual.

sample A portion, piece, or segment that is intended to be representative of a whole.

scientific method An organized approach devised by scientists for discovering causal relationships and testing the accuracy of conclusions.

selective comparisons A problem that occurs in making comparisons when a one-sided view of a comparative situation is taken.

self-aware Those who are aware of their own biases and are quick to point them out and take them into consideration when analyzing a situation.

semantic meaning A component of a word's total meaning of a word that expresses the relationship between a linguistic event and a nonlinguistic event.

senses Sight, hearing, smell, touch, and taste; means through which you experience your world, aware of what occurs outside you.

sign The word or symbol used to name or designate a concept.

simile An explicit comparison between basically dissimilar things made for the purpose of illuminating our understanding of the things being compared.

skilled discussants Those who are able to discuss ideas in an organized and intelligent way. Even when the issues are controversial, they listen carefully to opposing viewpoints and respond thoughtfully.

slang A kind of language occurring chiefly in casual and playful speech, made up typically of short-lived coinages and figures of speech that are deliberately used in place of standard terms for added raciness, humor, irreverence, or other effect.

slippery slope A causal fallacy that asserts that one undesirable action will inevitably lead to a worse action, which will necessarily lead to a worse one still, all the way down the "slippery slope" to some terrible disaster at the bottom.

social variation Variation of language style due to differences in the age, sex, or social class of the speakers.

solution The answer to or disposition of a problem.

sound argument A deductive argument in which the premises are true and the logical structure is valid.

source A person or document that supplies information needed.

special pleading A fallacy that occurs when someone makes themselves a special exception, without sound justification, to the reasonable application of standards, principles, or expectations.

standard American English (SAE) The style of the English language used in most academic and workplace writing, following the rules and conventions given in handbooks and taught in school.

standards Degrees or levels of requirement, excellence, or attainment.

stereotype A conventional, formulaic, and oversimplified conception, opinion, or image.

stimulus Something causing or regarded as causing a response.

straw man A fallacy in which a point of view is attacked by first creating a "straw man" version of the position and then "knocking down" the straw man created. The fallacy lies in that the straw man does not reflect an accurate representation of the position being challenged.

subject directory Created by universities, libraries, companies, organizations, and even volunteers, consisting of links to Internet resources.

surfing the Web Following pages "linked" to other related pages.

sweeping generalization A general conclusion reached that overlooks exceptions to the generalizations because of special features that the exceptions possess.

syllogism A form of deductive reasoning consisting of a major premise, a minor premise, and a conclusion.

symbolize To represent something else.

syntactic meaning A component of a word's total meaning which defines its relation to other words in the sentence.

synthesis The combining of separate elements or substances to form a coherent whole.

target population The entire group regarding which conclusions are drawn through statistical sampling and inductive reasoning.

telnet An Internet communications protocol that enables a computer to function as a terminal working from a remote computer.

testimony A declaration by a witness under oath, as that given before a court or deliberative body.

theist moral theory A theory of morality that holds that "right" and "wrong" are determined by a supernatural Supreme Being ("God").

theory   A plausible or coherent scenario that has yet to be applied to experience.

theory   A set of statements or principles devised to explain a group of facts or phenomena, normally involving a number of interconnected hypotheses.

thesis   A proposition that is maintained by argument; the issue on which an argument takes position.

thinking   A purposeful, organized cognitive process that we use to understand the world and make informed decisions.

thinking creatively   Using our thinking process to develop ideas that are unique, useful, and worthy of further elaboration.

thinking critically   The cognitive process we use to carefully examine our thinking (and the thinking of others) in order to clarify and improve our understanding.

total meaning   The meaning of a word believed by linguists to be composed of the semantic meaning, perceptual meaning, syntactic meaning, and pragmatic meaning.

two wrongs make a right   A fallacy that attempts to justify a morally questionable action by arguing that it is a response to another wrong action, either real or imagined.

uninformed decision   A decision that is the product of inaccurate information or inadequate experience.

uniform resource locator (URL)   An Internet address (for example, <http://www.hmco.com/trade/>), usually consisting of the access protocol (*http*), the domain name (*www.hmco .com*), and optionally the path to a file or resource residing on that server (*trade*).

unsound argument   A deductive argument in which the premises are false, the logical structure is invalid, or both.

vague word   A word that lacks a clear and distinct meaning.

valid argument   An argument in which the reasons support the conclusion so that the conclusion follows from the reasons offered.

values   Beliefs regarding what is most important to us.

Web   Abbreviation for World Wide Web.

web browser   A program such as Netscape Navigator or Microsoft's Internet Explorer that uses the URL to identify and retrieve the file from the host computer on which it resides, displaying Web pages in a convenient manner to the user.

web search engine   A program such as Yahoo! or Google that retrieves information about Internet sites containing user-entered keywords.

web site   A set of interconnected web pages, usually including a homepage, generally located on the same server, and prepared and maintained as a collection of information by a person, group or organization.

written references   Evidence derived from the written opinions of another person; one of the four categories of evidence.

CREDITS

(continued from page iv)

p. 3: Illustration by Warren Gebert

p. 5: Illustration by Warren Gebert

p. 14: Illustration by Warren Gebert

p. 21: Illustration by Warren Gebert

p. 36: Illustration by Warren Gebert

p. 39: David Young Wolff/PhotoEdit Inc.

p. 50: Michael Newman/PhotoEdit Inc.

p. 60: Illustration by Warren Gebert

p. 63: Cartoon © Steve Kelley/The Times-Picayune

p. 82: Bob Daemmrich/Stock Boston

p. 96: Illustration by Warren Gebert

p. 103: Illustration by Warren Gebert

p. 106: Illustration by Warren Gebert

p. 114: Toshiyuki Aizawa/Reuter Photos

p. 135: From Psychology Today, February 1894. The Investigation © John Jonik. Reprinted with permission.

p. 143: Bettmann/CORBIS

p. 151: Illustration by Warren Gebert

p. 157: Photo by Courney Kealy/Getty Images

p. 178: Culver Pictures, Inc.

p. 191: Peter Menzel/Stock Boston.

p. 195: Patrick Dural/Sygma/CORBIS

p. 213: Sygma/CORBIS

p. 227: Illustration by Warren Gebert

p. 240: Illustration by Warren Gebert

p. 248: Chester Higgins, Jr./Photo Researchers, Inc.

p. 265: Tom McCarthy/PhotoEdit Inc.

p. 274: Illustration by Warren Gebert

p. 284: Jean Pierre Laffont/Sygma/CORBIS

p. 289: From PULP/used by permission of Louis Hellmann

p. 296: Bob Daemmrich/Stock Boston

p. 303: Spencer Grant/PhotoEdit Inc.

p. 325: Illustration by Warren Gebert

p. 332: Illustration by Warren Gebert

p. 334: Getty Images

p. 351: Courtesy of Frankel Gallery, San Francisco and copyright The Estate of Gary Winogrand

p. 354: Illustration by Warren Gebert

p. 359: Illustration by Warren Gebert

p. 374: David McNew/Newsmaker

p. 391: Matthew Pace/Getty Images

p. 399: Illustration by Warren Gebert

p. 414: Matthew Pace/Getty Images

p. 439: Alyssa Banta/Getty Images

p. 456: Illustration by Warren Gebert

p. 464: Illustration by Warren Gebert

p. 474: Stanley Milgram, 1972, by permission of Alexandra Milgram

p. 494: Illustration by Warren Gebert

p. 498: Michael Newman/PhotoEdit Inc.

p. 1-2: NY skyline: Alan Schein Photography/CORBIS

p. 1-2: NY Hotel: Jan Butchofsky-Houser/CORBIS

p. 1-3: Pamela Anderson: Photos by PETA/Getty Images

p. 1-4: Fear Factor: Photofest

p. 1-4: Fear Factor: Photofest

p. 1-4: Fear Factor: Photofest

p. 1-4: Fear Factor: Photofest

p. 1-5: Firefighter: John Labriola/AP Photo

p. 1-6: Woodstock: Bill Eppridge/Time Life Pictures/Getty Images

p. 1-7: Kids linking arms: Digital Vision/Getty Images

p. 1-8: Jackson (young): Henry Diltz/CORBIS

p. 1-8: Jackson (performing): Wally McNamee/CORBIS

p. 1-8: Jackson (older): Mitchell Gerber/CORBIS

p. 2-2: Bush: Stephen Jaffe/AFP/Getty Images

p. 2-3: Coffins: Terri Rorke/AP Photos

p. 2-6: Same sex marriage: Doublas McFadd/Getty Images

p. 2-7: Traditional wedding: Curtis © 1953 SEPS: Licensed by Curtis Publishing Col, Indianapolis, IN. All right reserved. www.curtispublishing.com

INDEX